CEDU쎄듀는 A **C**omprehensive **E**nglish e**DU**cation(**종합적 영어교육**)**의 약자입니다.**

펴낸이 김기훈 I 김진희
펴낸곳 (주)쎄듀 I 서울특별시 강남구 논현로 305 (역삼동)
발행일 2020년 9월 14일 1쇄
내용문의 www.cedubook.com
구입문의 콘텐츠 마케팅 사업본부
Tel. 02-6241-2007
Fax. 02-2058-0209
등록번호 제 22-2472호
ISBN 978-89-6806-196-7

어법끝
실전 모의고사

Grammar & Usage

저자

김기훈 現 ㈜쎄듀 대표이사
現 메가스터디 영어영역 대표강사
前 서울특별시 교육청 외국어 교육정책자문위원회 위원
저서 천일문 〈입문편·기본편·핵심편·완성편〉 / 천일문 GRAMMAR
첫단추 BASIC / 어휘끝 / 어법끝 / Grammar Q
쎄듀 본영어 / 절대평가 PLAN A / Reading Relay
독해가 된다 시리즈 / The 리딩플레이어 / 빈칸백서 / 오답백서
첫단추 Button Up / 파워업 Power Up / ALL 씀 서술형 시리즈
수능영어 절대유형 / 수능실감 등

쎄듀 영어교육연구센터
쎄듀 영어교육센터는 영어 콘텐츠에 대한 전문지식과 경험을 바탕으로
최고의 교육 콘텐츠를 만들고자 최선의 노력을 다하는 전문가 집단입니다.
인지영 선임연구원

검토위원
허경원 서울대 영어영문학과 졸업
저서 능률교육 리딩튜터 / 신사고 리스닝엔탑 / 신사고 Writing Salad

마케팅	콘텐츠 마케팅 사업본부
제작	정승호
영업	문병구
인디자인 편집	올댓에디팅
디자인	이연수·윤혜영
영문교열	Eric Scheusner·Janna Christie

Preface 이 책을 펴내며

본 교재는 2016년 발간된 Power Up! 쎄듀 어법·어휘 모의고사를 토대로 한 것으로서, 어휘 부분을 제외하고 어법을 보강하여 좀 더 어법 전문서로서의 기능을 충실히 하였습니다. 그동안 새롭게 출제되어진 어법 사항, 기출 꿰뚫기 등을 보강하고 최신 기출 문제와 한층 더 품질 높은 참신한 내용의 예상문제로 구성하였습니다.

어법 문제는 탄탄한 영어 실력을 기르는 데 많은 도움이 됩니다. 어법 문제를 풀기 위해서는 길고 복잡한 문장의 구조와 내용을 이해해야 하기 때문에 정확한 독해 실력이 동시에 향상될 수 있습니다. 이를 한층 효과적으로 달성할 수 있도록 저희 저자들은 이 책을 다음과 같이 구성하였습니다.

- **선행지식 정리 및 다듬기**

  본격적인 문제 풀이에 앞서 시험에 꼭 필요한 어법만을 골라 체계적으로 정리했습니다. 지금까지 실시된 모든 수능과 모의고사를 분석해 어법 문제의 60% 이상을 차지하는 빈출 어법 5가지를 제시하였고, 더불어 방대한 문법 지식 중에서 어법 유형에 등장하는 사항만을 추려 24개의 어법 포인트로 정리했습니다. 또한, 각 포인트에는 기출 문장을 응용한 다수의 문제가 딸려 있으므로 충분한 자가 점검도 할 수 있습니다.

- **핵심 예상문제로 실전 감각 익히기**

  엄선된 60개의 핵심 예상문제로 앞에서 익힌 어법 포인트를 스스로 적용·확인하며 실전에 대한 감을 익힙니다.

- **실전 모의고사로 집중적인 실전 훈련**

  실전 33회+고난도 5회로 구성된 총 38회 228개 문항의 실전 모의고사를 통해 어법 문제를 빠르고 정확하게 풀 수 있는 집중훈련을 실시합니다. 기출 어법 분석을 통해 출제되었으며, 고난도 모의고사를 통해 최고난도의 어법 문제에도 대비할 수 있습니다.

본 교재를 통해 어법을 확실히 마무리하는 것과 동시에 빠르고 정확한 독해까지 가능하게 될 것임을 바라마지 않습니다. 여러분의 최종 목표 달성에 함께하기를 진심으로 기원합니다.

저자

How to use this book

출제 패턴 완벽 학습!

기출편

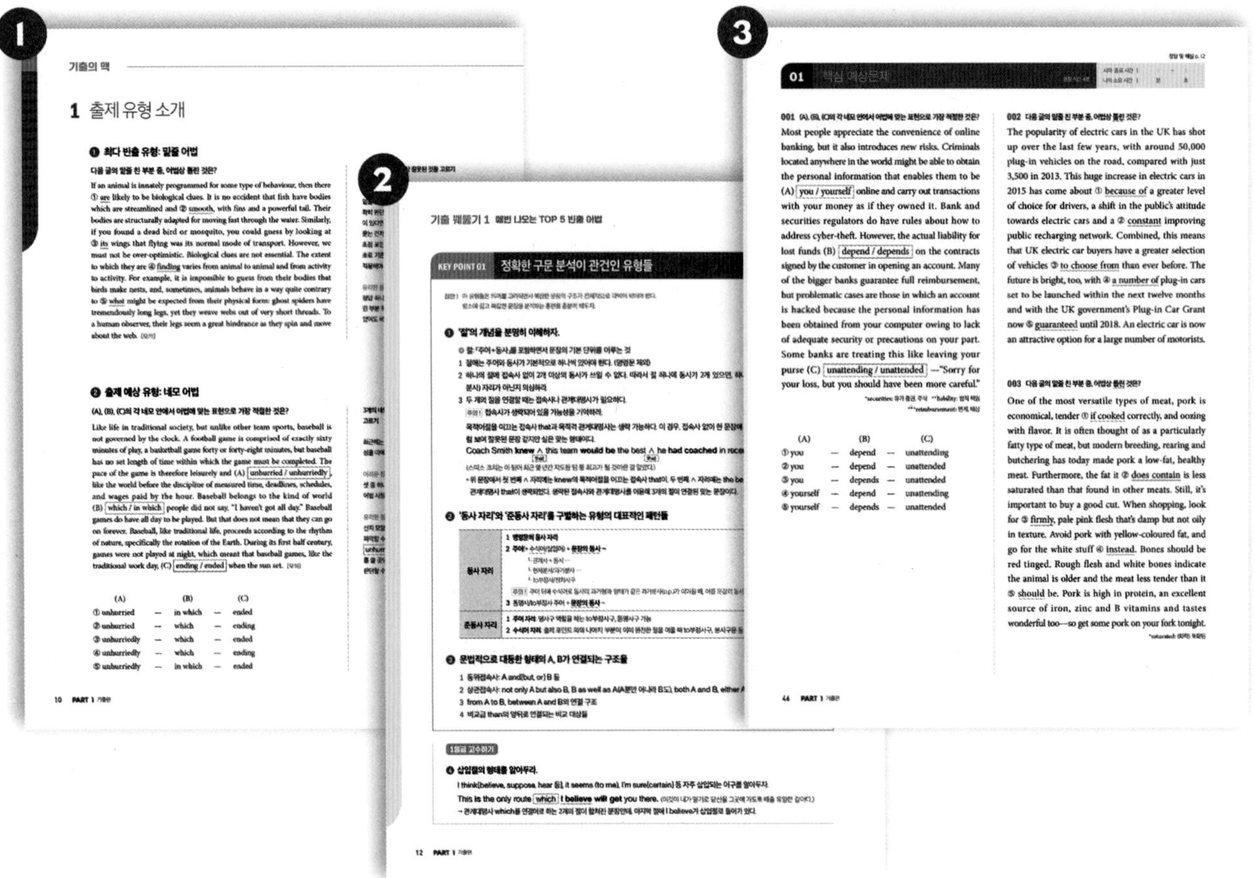

기출의 맥

어법 유형의 출제 경향을 소개하고 올바른 학습법을 제시합니다.

기출 꿰뚫기

기출 분석 결과를 토대로 시험에 꼭 나오는 어법 포인트만을 정리합니다.

핵심 예상문제 20회

총 60문항의 핵심 예상문제 20회를 통해 엄선된 출제 예상문제를 풀어봅니다.

최신 출제 경향을 완벽하게 반영한 고품격 모의고사!

실전편

실전 모의고사 33회

총 198문항의 실전 모의고사 33회가 제공됩니다. 내용, 구문, 어휘 등 모든 요소에 최신 경향을 반영한 양질의 예상문제입니다.

고난도 모의고사 5회

실전 모의고사 중간 중간 배치된 총 30문항의 고난도 모의고사 5회를 통해 가장 높은 수준의 문제까지 대비할 수 있습니다.

정답 및 해설

혼자서 학습하는 데 어려움이 없도록 자세한 정·오답 설명, 풍부한 어휘 정리, 친절한 구문해설을 수록했습니다.

Contents

PART 1
기출편

핵심 예상문제 01 – 20회

PART 2 실전편

실전 모의고사 33회 + 고난도 모의고사 5회

책속책

PART 1

기 출 편

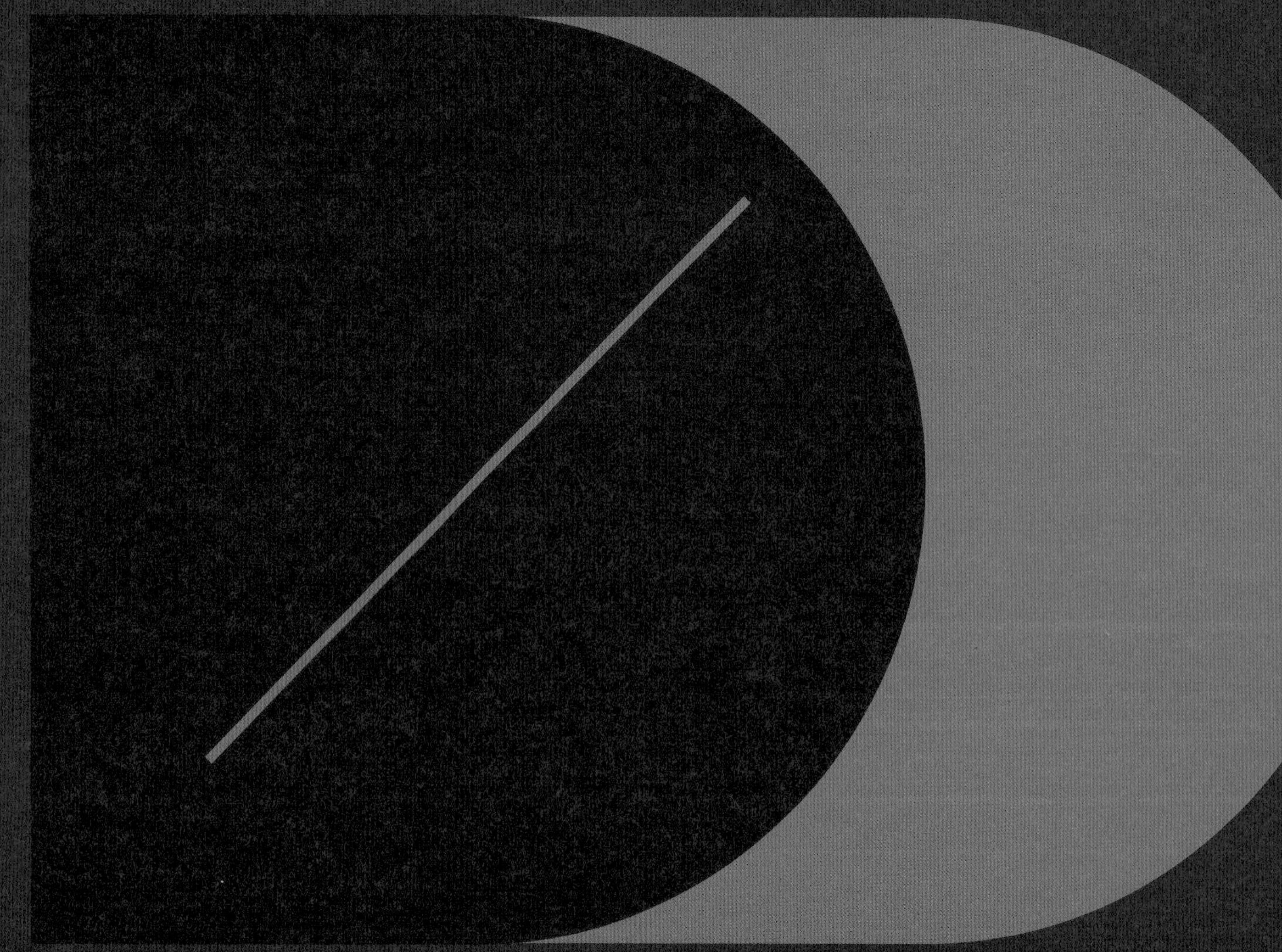

기출의 맥

출제 유형 소개

출제 경향 분석과 대처법

-

기출 꿰뚫기

매번 나오는 TOP 5 빈출 어법

시험에 나오는 것만 골라낸 24개 기출 어법

-

핵심 예상문제

01~20회

1 출제 유형 소개

❶ 최다 빈출 유형: 밑줄 어법

다음 글의 밑줄 친 부분 중, 어법상 틀린 것은?

If an animal is innately programmed for some type of behaviour, then there ① are likely to be biological clues. It is no accident that fish have bodies which are streamlined and ② smooth, with fins and a powerful tail. Their bodies are structurally adapted for moving fast through the water. Similarly, if you found a dead bird or mosquito, you could guess by looking at ③ its wings that flying was its normal mode of transport. However, we must not be over-optimistic. Biological clues are not essential. The extent to which they are ④ finding varies from animal to animal and from activity to activity. For example, it is impossible to guess from their bodies that birds make nests, and, sometimes, animals behave in a way quite contrary to ⑤ what might be expected from their physical form: ghost spiders have tremendously long legs, yet they weave webs out of very short threads. To a human observer, their legs seem a great hindrance as they spin and move about the web. [모의]

5개의 밑줄 중 어법상 잘못된 것을 고르기

어려운 점
밑줄 부분만 보고는 출제 포인트가 무엇인지 정확히 판단하기가 어렵다. 예를 들어, are에 밑줄이 있다면 시제를 묻는 건지, 주어와의 수일치를 묻는 건지, be동사를 쓰는 게 맞는 건지 등 여러 초점 포인트가 가능하다. 정확한 문장 분석을 기초로 기존에 알고 있는 어법 지식을 종합적으로 적용해야 한다.

유리한 점
정답 하나만 확실히 골라내면 되므로, 확실히 틀린 부분 한 군데가 보이면 아리송한 다른 선지가 있어도 비교적 안심하고 정답을 체크할 수 있다.

❷ 출제 예상 유형: 네모 어법

(A), (B), (C)의 각 네모 안에서 어법에 맞는 표현으로 가장 적절한 것은?

Like life in traditional society, but unlike other team sports, baseball is not governed by the clock. A football game is comprised of exactly sixty minutes of play, a basketball game forty or forty-eight minutes, but baseball has no set length of time within which the game must be completed. The pace of the game is therefore leisurely and (A) [unhurried / unhurriedly], like the world before the discipline of measured time, deadlines, schedules, and wages paid by the hour. Baseball belongs to the kind of world (B) [which / in which] people did not say, "I haven't got all day." Baseball games do have all day to be played. But that does not mean that they can go on forever. Baseball, like traditional life, proceeds according to the rhythm of nature, specifically the rotation of the Earth. During its first half century, games were not played at night, which meant that baseball games, like the traditional work day, (C) [ending / ended] when the sun set. [모의]

(A)		(B)		(C)
① unhurried	—	in which	—	ended
② unhurried	—	which	—	ending
③ unhurriedly	—	which	—	ended
④ unhurriedly	—	which	—	ending
⑤ unhurriedly	—	in which	—	ended

3개의 네모 칸에서 각각 어법상 알맞은 것을 고르기

최근에는 거의 등장하고 있지 않지만 출제 가능성을 아예 배제할 수는 없다.

어려운 점
셋 중 하나라도 잘못 맞히면 틀리게 되므로 중요 어법 사항들을 잘 숙지하고 있어야 한다.

유리한 점
선지 모양으로 무엇을 묻는 문제인지 대략 파악할 수 있다. 예를 들어, [unhurried / unhurriedly]를 보면 형용사를 쓸 곳인지 부사를 쓸 곳인지를 묻는 문제임을 판단할 수 있다.

2 출제 경향 분석과 대처법

❶ 출제 경향

글의 문맥과 구조의 통합적인 이해를 묻는다.

어법 문제는 규칙을 기계적으로 대입해서 풀 수 있는 문제가 절대 아니다. 어법은 단지 문법, 즉 규칙이라고 생각해서 암기만 잘하면 된다고 생각하는 수험자들이 있는데, 이는 큰 오산이다. **어법은 문맥 속에서 적용되는 것이므로, 글의 흐름을 정확히 파악해야 구조도 정확히 볼 수 있다.** 아무리 어법 사항을 외우고 있어도 문맥을 잘못 파악하면 구조를 잘못 보게 되고, 구조를 잘못 보면 엉뚱한 규칙을 적용하게 된다. 따라서 어법 문제도 글의 정확한 내용 파악과 함께 접근해야 한다. 또한, 현명한 학습자라면 문맥을 힌트 삼아 복잡한 문장구조 분석에 도움을 받을 것이다.

빈출되는 어법 포인트가 따로 있다.

지금까지의 모든 수능과 고1·2·3 모의고사를 통합하여 분석한 결과, **50% 이상의 어법 문제가 다섯 가지 포인트에서 출제되었다.** 즉, 모든 어법 사항이 동등하게 중요한 것이 아니라 어법 문제에서 선호되는 포인트가 따로 있다.

이는 절대 족집게 같은 접근이 아니다.

이 다섯 가지 포인트들을 살펴보면, 문장의 전체적인 구조를 제대로 파악할 수 있는지를 묻는 포괄적 성격임을 알 수 있다. 다시 말하면, 규칙을 기계적으로 암기해서 풀거나 앞뒤 일부분만 보고 답을 풀 수 있는 문제는 아니라는 뜻이다.

❷ 대처법

본 교재는 모든 기출 문제를 분석, 시험에 출제되는 어법 포인트만을 모아 <기출 꿰뚫기> 코너를 제시한다. 여기에 담긴 포인트들은 바로 위에서 설명한 출제 경향에 부합되는 것들이다.

이 <기출 꿰뚫기>는 다시

1 매번 나오는 Top 5 빈출 어법과

2 시험에 나오는 것만 골라낸 24개 기출 어법으로 나뉘는데,

위에서 말했듯 수능, 모의 어법 문제의 50% 이상이 1 에서 출제되었고 가장 최근 5개 연도에는 정답의 90% 이상이 모두 이 1 에 포진하고 있다.

따라서 1 만 확실히 공부해 놓아도 어법 문제는 90% 이상 맞힐 수 있다.

이에 속하는 어법 포인트들은 다음과 같다.

KEY POINT 1 | 정확한 구문 분석이 관건인 유형들
KEY POINT 2 | 뒤에 오는 구조가 완전한지 불완전한지를 파악하자.
KEY POINT 3 | 능동·수동 문제는 '하느냐', '되느냐'를 구별하자.
KEY POINT 4 | 형용사 자리와 부사 자리를 구별하자.
KEY POINT 5 | 문장의 주어를 제대로 찾는 게 관건이다.

여기에 2 까지 확실히 학습한다면 어법 문제는 반드시 맞추는 유형이 될 것이다.

그럼 지금부터 함께 어법을 완성해 나가도록 하자!!

KEY POINT 01 정확한 구문 분석이 관건인 유형들

문장의 구성 원리·병렬구조

잠깐! 이 유형들은 의미를 고려하면서 복잡한 문장의 구조가 전체적으로 파악이 되어야 한다.
평소에 길고 복잡한 문장을 분석하는 훈련을 충분히 해두자.

❶ '절'의 개념을 분명히 이해하자.

◎ 절: 「주어+동사」를 포함하면서 문장의 기본 단위를 이루는 것

1 절에는 주어와 동사가 기본적으로 하나씩 있어야 한다. (명령문 제외)

2 하나의 절에 접속사 없이 2개 이상의 동사가 쓰일 수 없다. 따라서 절 하나에 동사가 2개 있으면, 하나는 준동사(부정사, 동명사, 분사) 자리가 아닌지 의심하라.

3 두 개의 절을 연결할 때는 접속사나 관계대명사가 필요하다.

주의! 접속사가 생략되어 있을 가능성을 기억하라.

목적어절을 이끄는 접속사 that과 목적격 관계대명사는 생략 가능하다. 이 경우, 접속사 없이 한 문장에 여러 개의 동사가 쓰인 것처럼 보여 잘못된 문장 같지만 실은 맞는 형태이다.

Coach Smith **knew** ∧ [that] this team **would be** the best ∧ [that] he **had coached** in recent years.

(스미스 코치는 이 팀이 최근 몇 년간 지도한 팀 중 최고가 될 것이란 걸 알았다.)

• 위 문장에서 첫 번째 ∧ 자리에는 knew의 목적어절을 이끄는 접속사 that이, 두 번째 ∧ 자리에는 the best를 선행사로 취하는 목적격 관계대명사 that이 생략되었다. 생략된 접속사와 관계대명사를 이용해 3개의 절이 연결된 맞는 문장이다.

❷ '동사 자리'와 '준동사 자리'를 구별하는 유형의 대표적인 패턴들

동사 자리	**1 명령문의 동사 자리** **2 주어**(+ 수식어/삽입어) + **문장의 동사** ~ └ 관계사 + 동사 … └ 현재분사/과거분사 … └ to부정사/전치사구 **주의!** 주어 뒤에 수식어로 동사의 과거형과 형태가 같은 과거분사(p.p.)가 이어질 때, 이를 문장의 동사로 착각하지 않도록 주의하자. 3 동명사/to부정사 주어 + **문장의 동사** ~
준동사 자리	1 **주어 자리**: 명사구 역할을 하는 to부정사구, 동명사구 가능 2 **수식어 자리**: 출제 포인트 외의 나머지 부분이 이미 완전한 절을 이룰 때 to부정사구, 분사구문 등 가능

❸ 문법적으로 대등한 형태의 A, B가 연결되는 구조들

1 등위접속사: A and[but, or] B 등

2 상관접속사: not only A but also B, B as well as A(A뿐만 아니라 B도), both A and B, either A or B 등

3 from A to B, between A and B의 연결 구조

4 비교급 than의 앞뒤로 연결되는 비교 대상들

1등급 고수하기

❹ 삽입절의 형태를 알아두라.

I think[believe, suppose, hear 등], it seems (to me), I'm sure[certain] 등 자주 삽입되는 어구를 알아두자.

This **is** the only route [which] **I believe will get** you there. (이것이 내가 믿기로 당신을 그곳에 가도록 해줄 유일한 길이다.)

→ 관계대명사 which를 연결어로 하는 2개의 절이 합쳐진 문장인데, 마지막 절에 I believe가 삽입절로 들어가 있다.

※ 다음 네모 안에서 어법상 적절한 것을 고르거나, 밑줄 친 부분이 어법상 옳으면 ○표, 틀리면 ×표하고 바르게 고치시오.

정답 및 해설 p. 2

HINT

01 In many countries, amongst younger people, the habit of reading newspapers has been on the decline and some of the dollars previously [spent / were spent] on newspaper advertising have migrated to the Internet. <수능>

02 The other company proceeded with more seeming clarity and discipline, <u>dividing</u> the problem into its parts. <수능>

03 A measurement system is objective to the extent that two observers [evaluate / evaluating] the same performance arrive at the same (or very similar) measurements. <모의>

04 As you know, the costs of providing first-rate education just keep going up. We've done everything we can [contain / to contain] costs without compromising quality. <모의>

05 If you eat badly, you might resolve to start eating well. However, if you are eating burgers and ice cream to feel comforted, relaxed and happy, <u>try</u> to replace them with broccoli and carrot juice is like dealing with a leaky bathroom tap by repainting the kitchen. <모의>

06 As they get older, children will start to write in important things for themselves, <u>it</u> further helps them develop their sense of control. <모의>

07 During its first half century, games were not played at night, which meant that baseball games, like the traditional work day, [ending / ended] when the sun set. <모의>

08 [Live / Living] your life in pursuit of someone else's expectations is a difficult way to live. <모의>

09 The old maxim "I'll sleep when I'm dead" is unfortunate. [Adopt / Adopting] this mindset, and you will be dead sooner and the quality of that life will be worse. <모의>

10 The study authors figure that writing down future tasks <u>unloading</u> the thoughts so you can stop turning them over in your mind. You're telling your brain that the task will get done—just not right now. <모의>

11 An individual neuron <u>sends</u> a signal in the brain uses as much energy as a leg muscle cell running a marathon. <모의>

12 Many temples burnt down in those days. The priests were obviously not too happy about that until someone invented a clock was made of water buckets. <모의>

---

13 Tory Higgins and his colleagues had university students read a personality description of someone and then [summarize / summarized] it for someone else who was believed either to like or to dislike this person. <모의> **HINT** ❸

14 A general lack of knowledge and insufficient care being taken when fish pens were initially constructed meaning that pollution from excess feed and fish waste created huge barren underwater deserts. <수능>

15 The pace of the game is leisurely and [unhurried / unhurriedly], like the world before the discipline of measured time, deadlines, schedules, and wages paid by the hour. <모의>

16 Sometimes called brood parasites, the bees are referred to as cuckoo bees, because they are similar to cuckoo birds, which lay an egg in the nest of another bird and leaves it for that bird to raise. <모의>

*brood parasite: (알을 대신 기르도록 하는) 탁란 동물

17 The partner only has two options. He can take what's offered or refused to take anything. <모의>

18 The material they choose to publish must not only have commercial value, but being very competently written and free of editing and factual errors. <모의>

---

19 Now younger people are going digital and becoming social media journalists, making and editing their own work for the world to see, which I think is a good thing. **HINT** ❹

KEY POINT 02 뒤에 오는 구조가 완전한지 불완전한지를 파악하자.

❶ that[which] vs. what 구별이 가장 대표적인 빈출 포인트이다.

+불완전한 구조	1 **관계대명사 that, which** 선행사를 대신하면서 접속사 역할을 한다. 2 **관계대명사 what** 자체 내에 선행사를 포함한다. = the thing(s) that[which] (선행사: the thing(s))
+완전한 구조	1 **명사절 접속사 that** 주어절, 목적어절, 보어절, 동격절을 이끈다. **빈출되는 「명사+동격절」** **the fact that+완전한 절** (~이라는 사실) **the idea that+완전한 절** (~이라는 생각) **the notion that+완전한 절** (~이라는 개념[생각]) **the assumption that+완전한 절** (~이라는 가정) 2 **접속사 in that** (~이라는 점에서) in which를 잘못 쓴 in that이 아니라는 점에 주의한다.

❷ 기타 출제 패턴 정리

기본적으로, 자신이 이끄는 절 안에서 무언가를 대신하는 대명사 역할을 하면 뒤에 불완전한 구조가, 부사 역할을 하면 완전한 구조가 이어진다.

뒤에 불완전한 구조가 오는 경우	뒤에 완전한 구조가 오는 경우
관계대명사 **who, which, that, what** 의문대명사 **who, which, what** 복합관계대명사 **whoever, whichever, whatever**	관계부사 **when, where, why, how** 전치사+관계대명사 **in which, for which, from whom** 의문부사 **when, where, why, how** 복합관계부사 **whenever, wherever, however**

1등급 고수하기

❸ 관계대명사, 의문대명사, 복합관계대명사(whoever, whichever, whatever)는 '대명사'로서 문장에서 주어, 목적어, 보어 역할을 하므로 이들을 제외하면 불완전한 절이 된다.

Some of the courses **that** I took ∨ last semester have been very useful.
(내가 지난 학기에 들은 몇몇 과정은 매우 유용했다.)
• 관계대명사 that이 이끄는 절 I took last semester에서 took의 목적어가 없음.

Give me an example of **what** you said ∨. (당신이 말한 것의 예를 하나 들어주세요.)
• 관계대명사 what이 이끄는 절 you said에서 said의 목적어가 없음.

No one remembered **who** had left the message. (누가 그 메시지를 남겼는지 아무도 기억하지 못했다.)
• 의문대명사 who가 이끄는 절 had left the message에서 주어가 없음.

You can take **whatever** you want ∨ from the fridge. (냉장고에서 당신이 원하는 무엇이든 꺼내 드세요.)
• 복합관계대명사 whatever가 이끄는 절에서 want의 목적어가 없음.

Whatever ∨ happens, stay cool. (무슨 일이 일어나든지 침착해.)
• 복합관계대명사 Whatever가 이끄는 절에서 주어가 없음.

❹ 관계부사, 의문부사, 복합관계부사(whenever, wherever, however)는 '부사'이므로 제외해도 이끄는 절은 완전하다.

July and August are the months **when** most people go on holiday. (7월과 8월은 대부분의 사람이 휴가를 가는 달이다.)
• 관계사절에서 when을 제외해도 나머지 구조는 「주어(most people) + 동사(go) + 부사구(on holiday)」로서 완전함.

The head office has not made a final decision about **where** the branch office will be located.
(본사는 그 지사가 어디에 위치할지에 대해 아직 최종 결정을 내리지 않았다.)
• 의문부사 where를 제외해도 나머지는 「주어(the branch office) + 동사(will be located)」로서 완전함.

Whenever I go to that mall, I have a hard time finding a parking place.
(나는 그 쇼핑몰에 갈 때마다 주차할 장소를 찾는 데 어려움을 겪는다.)
• 복합관계부사 Whenever는 '때'를 나타내는 부사로서, 제외하더라도 나머지 부분이 「주어(I) + 동사(go) + 부사구(to that mall)」의 완전한 구조.

However you do it, the result will be the same. (네가 아무리 그것을 해도, 결과는 마찬가지일 것이다.)

주의 ! however는 「however+형용사/부사+주어+동사」의 형태로, 동사 뒤에 있어야 할 형용사나 부사를 주어 앞으로 데리고 나오는데, 주어가 추상명사일 경우 be동사는 생략 가능하다.
He agreed that drastic change was needed, however great the risk (is).
(아무리 위험이 크다고 해도, 그는 급격한 변화가 필요하다는 데 동의했다.)

❺ which, what, whichever, whatever가 형용사 역할을 하기도 한다.

Let me know ***which book*** she has ordered ∨. (그녀가 어떤 책을 주문했는지 알려줘.)
• 의문사가 명사를 만나면 의문형용사 역할을 하게 된다.
which(의문형용사)와 그의 수식을 받는 book(명사)이 함께 동사의 목적어.
cf. Let me know **which** she has ordered. (그녀가 어떤 것을 주문했는지 알려줘.)
← which는 동사 has ordered의 목적어로 명사.

Wear **whichever** shoes are the most comfortable. (어떤 신발이든 가장 편안한 것으로 신어.)
• whichever(복합관계형용사)와 그의 수식을 받는 shoes(명사)가 함께 종속절의 주어.
cf. Wear **whichever** suits you best. (어느 것이든 가장 잘 맞는 것으로 입어.)
← whichever가 목적어절의 주어로 명사.

※ 다음 네모 안에서 어법상 적절한 것을 고르거나, 밑줄 친 부분이 어법상 옳으면 ○표, 틀리면 ×표하고 바르게 고치시오.

정답 및 해설 p. 3

01 The product warranty says that you provide spare parts and materials for free, but charge for the engineer's labor. <수능>

02 Academia believes in "open architecture," meaning that the knowledge that research produces should be made public to encourage innovation. <모의>

03 When induced to give spoken or written witness to something they doubt, people will often feel bad about their deceit. Nevertheless, they begin to believe what / that they are saying. <모의>

04 Those who donate to one or two charities seek evidence about what the charity is doing and what it is really having a positive impact. If the evidence indicates that the charity is really helping others, they make a substantial donation. <수능>

05 Not all organisms are able to find sufficient food to survive, so starvation is a kind of disvalue often found in nature. What some organisms must starve in nature is deeply regrettable and sad. <모의>

06 People seeking legal advice should be assured, when discussing their rights or obligations with a lawyer, which the latter will not disclose to third parties the information provided. <모의>

07 After seven months, the first toys made landfall on beaches near Sitka, Alaska, 3,540 kilometers from what / where they were lost. <수능>

08 It is, importantly, the way in which most cultural anthropologists earn and maintain their professional standing. <모의>

09 Given that music appears to enhance physical and mental skills, are there circumstances where music is damaging to performance? One domain which this is of considerable significance is music's potentially damaging effects on the ability to drive safely. <모의>

10 In 1762, this island was taken by the English, who / where restored it the following year to the French by the Peace of Paris, and since that time it has been in the possession of the latter. <모의>

11 William H. Whyte turned video cameras on a number of spaces in New York City, watching to see how people used the spaces. <모의>

12 Many of the manufactured products made today contain so many chemicals and artificial ingredients which it is sometimes difficult to know exactly what is inside them. <모의>

13 It is no coincidence that countries where / which sleep time has declined most dramatically over the past century, such as the US, the UK, Japan, and South Korea, and several in Western Europe, are also those suffering the greatest increase in rates of physical diseases and mental disorders. <모의>

14 Similarly, how is it possible to make sense of a situation which / in which a single word "uncle" applies to the brother of one's father and to the brother of one's mother? <모의>

15 Baseball belongs to the kind of world which / in which people did not say, "I haven't got all day." Baseball games do have all day to be played. <모의>

---

16 I recently saw a news interview with an acquaintance who / whom I was certain was going to lie about a few particularly sensitive issues, and lie she did. <모의> **HINT 3**

---

17 She always tells her students they should follow their dreams, how / however hard and uncertain the path. <모의 응용> **HINT 4**

---

18 We can read the news of the day, or the latest on business, entertainment or however / whatever news on the websites of the *New York Times*, the *Guardian* or almost any other major newspaper in the world. <수능> **HINT 5**

KEY POINT 03 능동·수동 문제는 '하느냐', '되느냐'를 구별하자.

태

❶ 의미가 가장 중요하다.

1 주어가 동작을 행하면 능동, 동작을 받거나 당하면 수동을 쓴다.

2 의미상의 주체(수식받는 명사, 문장의 주어, 선행사, 목적어 등)가 동작을 행하면(수식하는 분사, 분사구문의 분사, 주격 관계대명사 뒤의 동사, 목적격보어 등) 능동, 동작을 받거나 당하면 수동을 쓴다.

주의! 분사구문의 의미상 주어는 별도로 분사 앞에 주어지지 않는 한, 문장의 주어와 같다.

❷ 동사나 준동사 뒤에 목적어(명사)가 있는지 확인한다.

◎ 능동태의 기본 형태: 「주어 + 동사 + 목적어」

◎ 수동태의 기본 형태: 「주어 + be p.p.(+ by 행위자)」

1 뒤에 목적어가 있으면 능동태, 없으면 수동태를 의심하라.

2 준동사(부정사, 동명사, 분사) 역시 동사의 성질을 가지므로 능동태일 때 뒤에 목적어가 온다.

❸ 감정을 '일으키면' 능동, 감정을 '느끼면' 수동을 쓴다.

1 -ing: 사물이나 사람이 어떤 감정을 일으킬 때 (causing a feeling)

2 -ed: 사람이 어떤 감정을 느낄 때 (having a feeling)

대표 동사 interest, excite, please, amaze, fascinate, surprise, disappoint, frustrate, depress, embarrass, shock, frighten, terrify, confuse, puzzle, touch(감동시키다) 등

1등급 고수하기

❹ SVOO 문형은 목적어가 2개이므로 수동태가 되어도 동사 뒤에 하나의 목적어(명사)가 그대로 남는다.

When a concert violinist [asked / **was asked**] **the secret of her success**, she replied, "Planned neglect." <모의>

(바이올린 연주자는 성공의 비결을 질문받자 '계획된 태만'이라고 답했다.)

• 능동태는 asked a concert violinist the secret of her success

❺ SVOC문형의 C가 명사 보어일 경우, 수동태가 되어도 동사 뒤에 목적격보어(명사)가 그대로 남는다.

Many large cities have very tall buildings [**called** / calling] **skyscrapers.** <모의>

(여러 대도시에는 마천루라고 불리는 매우 높은 빌딩들이 있다.)

• 능동태는 call very tall buildings skyscrapers

빈출 패턴 **be called + 명사** (~이라고 불리다)
be named + 명사 (~이라고 이름 지어지다)

❻ 자동사는 수동태로 쓸 수 없다.

Then it [**occurred** / was occurred] to me that my boy would never be a seven-year-old again. <모의>

(그때 내 아들이 결코 다시는 일곱 살이 될 수 없을 거란 생각이 내게 떠올랐다.)

대표적인 자동사 occur / happen / take place / appear / disappear / seem / remain / rise / exist 등

❼ 사역동사, 지각동사는 목적격보어로 원형부정사를 취하는데, 수동태 문장에서는 to부정사가 다시 살아난다.

Unlike a stream, a glacier cannot be seen move → **to move.** <모의>

(시내와 달리 빙하는 움직이는 것이 보이지 않는다.)

• 능동태 문장 we cannot see a glacier(목적어) move(목적격보어)가 수동태 문장으로 전환된 형태.

※ 다음 네모 안에서 어법상 적절한 것을 고르거나, 밑줄 친 부분이 어법상 옳으면 ○표, 틀리면 ×표하고 바르게 고치시오.

정답 및 해설 p. 4

HINT ❶

01 We are trapped deep in a paradox: deciding on the best course of action, then doing something else. <모의>

02 Aristotle explained that a stone falling through the air is due to the stone having the property of "gravity." But of course a piece of wood tossed into water floats instead of sinking. <수능>

03 High-density rearing led to outbreaks of infectious diseases that in some cases devastated not just the caged fish, but local wild fish populations too. <수능>

04 They are looking to reclaim some of the flavors of old-fashioned breads that were lost as baking became more industrialized and baked goods became more refined, standardized, and—some would say—flavorless. <모의>

05 Evidence suggests an association between loud, fast music and reckless driving, but how might music's ability to influence driving in this way be explained? <모의>

06 Having said positive things, they also then liked the person more themselves. Asked / Asking to recall what they had read, they remembered the description as being more positive than it was. <모의>

07 Many African language speakers would consider it absurd to use a single word like "cousin" to describe both male and female relatives, or not to distinguish whether the person described / describing is related by blood to the speaker's father or to his mother. <모의>

08 We must not be over-optimistic. Biological clues are not essential. The extent to which they are finding varies from animal to animal and from activity to activity. <모의>

HINT 

09 It was also found that people liked to be watched! The researcher expected lovers to be found in private, isolated spaces, but most often they sat or stood right in the center of things for everyone to see. <모의>

10 He goes on to describe his daily routine of strolling through the village observed the intimate details of family life, and as he tells it, such observations seem possible and accessible. <모의>

11 Those who are good at music are good at languages as well. That should not be [surprised / surprising], since the study of music and the study of language have a lot in common. <모의>

HINT ❸

12 If you are constantly engaged in asking yourself questions about things you are hearing, you will find that even boring lecturers become a bit more [interesting / interested], because much of the interest will be coming from what you are generating rather than what the lecturer is offering. <모의>

13 This data can often be of dubious reliability; it can be false; or it can be true but deeply humiliated. It may be increasingly difficult to have a fresh start or a second chance. <모의>

*dubious: 의심스러운

---

14 In January 1899, a German company [named / naming] Bayer trademarked "Aspirin" for this new drug. <모의>

HINT ❺

---

15 The unruly student was made staying after school to wipe down the chalkboard and clean the erasers in preparation for the next day. <모의 응용>

HINT ❼

KEY POINT 04 형용사 자리와 부사 자리를 구별하자.

형용사·부사

❶ 형용사 자리

1 명사 수식
2 보어 자리: 주격보어, 목적격보어
주로 감각동사의 보어 자리가 출제된다. look, smell, taste, sound, feel 등.

❷ 부사 자리

1 동사 수식
2 형용사 수식
3 부사 수식
4 문장 전체 수식

※ 다음 네모 안에서 어법상 적절한 것을 고르거나, 밑줄 친 부분이 어법상 옳으면 ○표, 틀리면 ×표하고 바르게 고치시오. 정답 및 해설 p. 5

01 Free radicals move uncontrollably through the body, attacking cells, rusting their proteins, piercing their membranes and corrupting their genetic code until the cells become dysfunctional and sometimes give up and die. <수능>

02 As a source of plot, character, and dialogue, the novel seemed more suitable. Many early successes of cinema were adaptations of popular novels. <수능>

03 You have to pay close attention to someone's normal pattern in order to notice a deviation from it when he or she lies. Sometimes the variation is as [subtle / subtly] as a pause. Other times it is obvious and abrupt. <모의>

04 If you push yourself to dream more expansively and to make your goals at least a step beyond what makes you [comfortable / comfortably], you will be forced to grow. <모의>

05 A well-designed technology tool—whether it's a website, video, app, simulation, or tutorial—should provide a way for students to track their progress so that they know how close they are to finishing and how much more effort it will take to achieve the learning goal.

06 We have a deep intuition that the future is open until it becomes present and that the past is fixed. Yet as naturally as this way of thinking is, you will not find it reflected in science. <모의 응용>

KEY POINT 05 문장의 주어를 제대로 찾는 게 관건이다.

주어-동사 수일치

❶ 주어를 뒤에서 수식하는 구[절] 또는 주어와 동사 사이의 삽입절을 걷어 내라.

수식어구 또는 삽입절을 묶어 내면 문장의 주어와 동사를 찾는 게 편해진다.
└ 전명구, 분사구, to부정사구, 관계사절 등
삽입절은 앞뒤에 보통 콤마가 있어 알아보기 쉽다.

❷ 주격 관계대명사절의 동사는 선행사에 수를 일치시킨다.

❸ 구나 절 주어는 단수 취급한다.

동명사구, to부정사구, 명사절 주어는 추상적인 개념이므로 단수 동사로 받는다.

❹ 도치구문은 동사 뒤에 주어가 나온다.

강조를 위해, 또는 긴 주어가 문장 앞에 오는 걸 피하기 위해 부정어, 부사(구), 보어 등이 문장 앞에 올 경우 주어와 동사가 도치된다.

1 **부정어 뒤의 도치**: 부정어에 이어 「(조)동사 + 주어」의 어순이 된다.

no, not, never, little(거의 ~ 않다), hardly(거의 ~ 않다), scarcely(거의 ~ 않다), seldom(좀처럼 ~ 않다), rarely(좀처럼 ~ 않다), nowhere(아무 데도 ~ 않다), not until(~해서야 비로소 …하다) 등

Not only **was the food** terrible, but the staff was rude. (음식이 맛이 없었을 뿐만 아니라 직원도 무례했다.)

2 **부사(구)/보어 뒤의 도치**: 부사/보어에 이어 「(조)동사 + 주어」의 어순이 된다.

Happy **is the man** who can make a living by his hobby. (취미로 생계를 꾸밀 수 있는 사람이 행복하다.)

3 **동사 + 긴 주어 도치**: 긴 주어가 균형을 맞추기 위해 「(조)동사 + 주어」의 어순이 된다.

Just as hard work contributes to success, so **does positive thinking**.
(노력이 성공에 기여하는 것과 마찬가지로 긍정적인 사고도 그렇다.)

4 **「there + 동사 + 주어」 구문**: 여기서 there는 형식적으로 문장 앞에 쓰인 것이고 주어는 동사 뒤에 나오는 것이다.

❺ 「one of ~」는 단수, 「the + 형용사」가 '~한 사람들'을 뜻할 경우에는 복수이다.

◎ one of + 복수명사 (~ 중의 하나)

◎ the + 형용사 (~한 사람들): 「형용사 + people」과 같은 표현이다.

the rich = rich people, the young = young people,
the unemployed = unemployed people (실업자들), the wounded = wounded people (부상자들),
the blind = blind people (시각장애인들), the homeless = homeless people (노숙자들),
the French = French people (프랑스인들)

참고! 부분 표현의 수일치

부분을 나타내는 명사나 분수가 주어인 경우, 뒤따르는 「of + 명사」의 '명사(N)'에 수를 일치시킨다.

all of + N (모든 ~)	the rest of + N (나머지 ~)
most of + N (대부분의 ~)	the majority of + N (대다수의 ~)
some of + N (~ 중 일부분)	분수(two thirds, one fourth, etc.) of + N
half of + N (~ 중 절반)	00 percent of + N

e.g. Nearly **a third of** the country's manufacturing **companies** (복수주어) **have** (복수동사) trouble finding sufficient numbers of skilled workers. (그 나라의 제조업체 중 거의 3분의 1이 충분한 수의 숙련된 노동자를 찾는 데 어려움을 겪는다.)

❻ 「the number of ~」는 단수, 「a number of ~」는 복수이다.

◎ the number of + 복수명사(~의 수): 이때 주어는 the number

◎ a number of[several] + 복수명사(많은[몇몇의] ~): 이때 주어는 '복수명사'

※ 다음 네모 안에서 어법상 적절한 것을 고르거나, 밑줄 친 부분이 어법상 옳으면 ○표, 틀리면 ×표하고 바르게 고치시오.

정답 및 해설 p. 5

01 At the beginning of the twenty-first century, the popularity of fine breads and pastries are growing even faster than new chefs can be trained. <모의>

02 The only difference between grapes and raisins is / are that grapes have about 6 times as much water in them. <모의>

03 This is because collisions between aircraft usually occur in the surrounding area of airports, while crashes due to aircraft malfunction tends to occur during long-haul flights. <모의>

*long-haul: 장거리 비행

04 Obviously, some of these practices, such as drinking alcohol during a marathon, are no longer recommended, but others, such as a high-carbohydrate meal the night before a competition, has stood the test of time. <모의>

05 People of Northern Burma, who think in the Jinghpaw language, has / have eighteen basic terms for describing their kin. <모의>

06 It was only in 1837, with the invention of the electric telegraph, that the traditional link between transport and the communication of messages were broken. <모의>

HINT 2

07 The great scientists are driven by an inner quest to understand the nature of the universe; the extrinsic reward that matters most to them are the recognition of their peers. <모의>

08 Malinowski, the classic anthropological fieldworker, describes the early stages of fieldwork as 'a strange, sometimes unpleasant, sometimes intensely interesting adventure which soon adopts quite a natural course.' <모의>

09 There is a deep cavern on the island, containing the bones and arms of the Indians, who, it is supposed, was / were buried there. <모의>

10 People under hypnosis come up with more information, but not necessarily more accurate information. In fact, it might actually be people's beliefs in the power of hypnosis that leads them to recall more things. <모의>

11 Adapting novels is one of the most respectable of movie projects, while a book that calls itself the novelization of a film is considered barbarous. <수능> HINT ❸

12 We want to stop watching so much TV, but demonstrably, we also want to watch lots of TV. So what we really want, it seems, is to stop wanting. <모의>

13 To make the choice to express a feeling by carving a specific form from a rock, without the use of high technology or colors, restricting the artist significantly. Such choices are not made to limit creativity, but rather to cultivate it. <모의>

---

14 Researchers studied two mobile phone companies trying to solve a technological problem. One company developed what it called a 'technology shelf,' created by a small group of engineers, on which was placed possible technical solutions that other teams might use in the future. <수능> HINT ❹

15 Not only is carbon dioxide plainly not poisonous, but changes in carbon dioxide levels don't necessarily mirror human activity. <모의>

---

16 One of the greatest ways to cultivate a possibility mind-set [is / are] to prompt yourself to dream one size bigger than you normally do. <모의> HINT ❺

---

17 A number of 'youth friendly' mental health websites have been developed. The information presented often takes the form of Frequently Asked Questions, fact sheets and suggested links. <모의> HINT ❻

시제

POINT 01 | 가장 빈출되는 시제는 완료시제다. 

❶ 현재완료의 '계속' 용법이 빈출된다.

- have[has] p.p. + since + 특정 과거 시점 (~이래로 죽 …하고 있다)
- have[has] p.p. + for + 기간 (~동안 죽 …하고 있다)

since, for 외에 over, so far 등 현재완료와 함께 쓰이는 시간 표현에 주목해야 한다.

❷ 과거보다 더 과거에 일어난 일은 과거완료(had p.p.)로 표시한다.

참고! 이를 '대과거'라고도 하며 '계속', '경험', '완료', '결과' 용법과 구분하기도 한다.

※ 다음 네모 안에서 어법상 적절한 것을 고르거나, 밑줄 친 부분이 어법상 옳으면 ○표, 틀리면 ×표하고 바르게 고치시오. 정답 및 해설 p. 6

1 Later the police realized that they [have made / had made] a terrible mistake. Their bags were full of onions, not money! <모의>

2 Today, children are more likely to think of carbon dioxide as a poison. That's because the amount of carbon dioxide in the atmosphere <u>increased</u> substantially over the past one hundred years, from about 280 parts per million to 380. <모의 응용>

POINT 02 | 시간, 조건의 부사절에서는 미래시제 대신 현재시제를 쓴다. 

- 시간을 나타내는 접속사: when, before, after, until, as soon as(~하자마자) 등
- 조건을 나타내는 접속사: if, unless(~하지 않는 한), as long as(~하는 한) 등

참고! when, if가 부사절 접속사가 아니라 명사절 접속사로 쓰일 때는 미래시제 그대로 쓴다.

We can't say exactly <u>**when** the construction ***will*** be completed.</u>
(우리는 공사가 언제 끝날지 정확히 말할 수 없다.) ← 의문사 when이 동사 say의 목적어절을 이끎

I bought a gift for my wife, but I don't know <u>**if** she ***will*** like it.</u>
(나는 아내를 위해 선물을 샀지만, 그녀가 그걸 좋아할지 모르겠다.) ← if가 동사 don't know의 목적어절을 이끎

※ 다음 네모 안에서 어법상 적절한 것을 고르시오. 정답 및 해설 p. 6

1 The famous swimmer has planned to finish the task in ten days. So, if the weather [is / will be] good, he will arrive in Dokdo on August 15. <모의>

POINT 03 | 목적격보어 자리에 올 수 있는 것은 동사가 좌우한다. ★★

❶ 동사원형을 목적격보어로 취하는 동사

- 사역동사 **make, let** + 목적어 + 동사원형
- 지각동사 **see, watch, hear, feel, notice** + 목적어 + 동사원형

참고! help는 동사원형과 to부정사 둘 다 목적격보어로 취할 수 있다.

참고! 지각동사는 진행 중인 동작에 초점을 맞출 때 현재분사(v-ing)도 목적격보어로 취할 수 있다.

❷ to부정사를 목적격보어로 취하는 동사

- **allow, enable, encourage, cause, force, expect, require, permit, persuade, advise, urge, want, tell, get, order**(명령하다), **ask**(부탁하다) 등 + 목적어 + to-v

❸ 동사원형과 현재분사를 목적격보어로 취하는 동사들의 경우, 목적어와 목적격보어가 수동 관계일 때는 동사의 종류에 관계없이 과거분사를 쓴다.

- 동사 + 목적어 + **p.p.**

※ 다음 네모 안에서 어법상 적절한 것을 고르거나, 밑줄 친 부분이 어법상 옳으면 ○표, 틀리면 ×표하고 바르게 고치시오. 정답 및 해설 p. 6

1 Because individuals of a group of fish can see, or sense, the wave <u>coming</u> toward them, they are ready to react more quickly than they would without such advance notice. <모의>

2 While he was used to making all the decisions and having them [carry / carried] out promptly, he found that the British film-making style allowed everyone to have an opinion. <모의 응용>

POINT 04 | 어떤 동사를 대신하는지 찾아서 일치시켜라. ★

❶ 앞에 나온 동사의 반복을 피하기 위해 대동사를 쓴다.

be동사는 be동사로, 일반동사는 do/does/did로, 기타 조동사 can/have[has] 등은 바로 그 조동사를 그대로 사용하여 대신한다.

❷ 대동사 주요 패턴

- 「so[neither] + 동사 + 주어」
- 비교급 문장의 than 이하
- (Just) As ~, so ...

※ 다음 네모 안에서 어법상 적절한 것을 고르거나, 밑줄 친 부분이 어법상 옳으면 ○표, 틀리면 ×표하고 바르게 고치시오. 정답 및 해설 p. 6

1 As a company's executive put it, "Many users probably spend more time on the Internet than they do / are in their cars." <모의>

2 As civilizations developed, so were / did fashions. Body decoration, however, was, and still is a most popular means of showing human vanity. <모의>

3 Productivity improvements are as important to the economy as they do to the individual business that's making them. <모의>

4 "Monumental" is a word that comes very close to expressing the basic characteristic of Egyptian art. Never before and never since has the quality of monumentality been achieved as fully as it did in Egypt. <수능>

5 Those who give small amounts to many charities are not so interested in whether what they are doing helps others. Knowing that they are giving makes them feel good, regardless of the impact of their donation. <수능>

POINT 05 | 가목적어 it을 취하는 동사를 알아두자. ★

make, think, believe, find, consider와 같은 동사들은 SVOC문형에서 목적어 자리에 to부정사나 that절이 오면, 목적어 자리에 가목적어 it을 쓰고 진목적어는 목적격보어 뒤로 보낸다.

주어 + make/think/believe/find/consider + it + 목적격보어 + to-v/that절

※ 다음 네모 안에서 어법상 적절한 것을 고르시오. 정답 및 해설 p. 7

1 They also make it a rule refund / to refund the money if purchasers return plastic or paper bags. <모의>

POINT 06 | 혼동하기 쉬운 자타동사를 외워두자.

자동사	타동사
lie(눕다; 놓여 있다)-lay-lain/lying lie(거짓말하다)-lied-lied/lying	lay(~을 놓다, ~을 두다)-laid-laid/laying
rise(오르다)-rose-risen **참고!** arise(자 생기다, 발생하다)-arose-arisen	raise(~을 올리다)-raised-raised
sit(앉다)-sat-sat	seat(~을 앉히다)-seated-seated **참고!** be seated(앉다)
wind(구불구불하다, 굽어지다)-wound-wound **참고!** '~을 감다'라는 뜻의 타동사로도 쓰인다.	wound(~에 상처를 입히다)-wounded-wounded

※ 다음 네모 안에서 어법상 적절한 것을 고르거나, 밑줄 친 부분이 어법상 옳으면 ○표, 틀리면 ×표하고 바르게 고치시오.

정답 및 해설 p. 7

1 By the time she was three, Matilda had taught herself to read by studying newspapers and magazines that [lay / laid] around the house. <모의>

2 Driving home with my family one day, I noticed smoke <u>risen</u> from the roof of an apartment building. <모의>

POINT 07 | 「조동사 + have p.p.」는 어구처럼 외워두자.

❶ **「조동사 + 동사원형」은 현재나 미래의 일을 가리키는 반면, 「조동사 + have p.p.」는 '과거'의 일을 가리킨다.**
과거 일을 뜻하느냐는 문맥상 파악해야 한다.

❷ **「조동사 + have p.p.」의 의미 정리**

추측, 가능성	후회, 유감
• must have p.p (~했음이 틀림없다) ↔ cannot[can't] have p.p. (~했을 리가 없다) • may[might] have p.p. (~했을지도 모른다)	• should[ought to] have p.p. (~했어야 하는데 (안 했다)) • shouldn't have p.p. (~하지 말았어야 하는데 (했다))

※ 다음 밑줄 친 부분이 어법상 옳으면 ○표, 틀리면 ×표하고 바르게 고치시오.

정답 및 해설 p. 7

1 If you've ever gone snorkeling, you may <u>have seen</u> an amazing sight: an entire school of fish suddenly changes direction as one unit. <모의>

2 Those victims of education <u>should receive</u> training to develop creative talents while in school. It really is a pity that they did not. <수능>

POINT 08 | 당위성을 나타내는 that절에서는 「(should+)동사원형」을 쓴다. 

주절에 '요구, 주장, 제안, 명령'을 나타내는 동사가 있고 that절에 '~해야 한다'라는 당위성의 내용이 오면 「(should+)동사원형」을 쓴다. should는 생략되고 동사원형만 남는 경우도 많다.

insist(주장하다), **suggest**(제안하다), **advise**(조언하다)
recommend(권고하다), **request**(요청하다), **order**(명령하다) 등] **+ that + 주어 + (should +)동사원형**

주의 ! that절의 내용이 당위성을 나타내지 않고 사실적인 정보를 전달하는 경우에는 위 규칙의 적용을 받지 않고 직설법으로 표현한다.

※ 다음 밑줄 친 부분이 어법상 옳으면 ○표, 틀리면 ×표하고 바르게 고치시오.

정답 및 해설 p. 7

1 The president insisted that the operation <u>had been kept</u> secret. He was afraid that worries about his health might make worse the difficult economic problems the country was facing at the time. <모의>

2 Many witnesses insisted that the accident <u>should take place</u> on the crosswalk. <수능>

POINT 09 | 가정법의 기본 패턴을 알아두자. 

현재의 사실을 가정할 때는 if절에 '과거형'을, 과거의 사실을 가정할 때는 if절에 '과거완료형'을 쓴다.

가정법 과거	1) if + 주어 + **동사의 과거형** ~, 주어 + 조동사 과거형 + 동사원형 ... (만약 ~한다면 …할 텐데) 2) I wish + 주어 + **동사의 과거형** (~하면 좋을 텐데) 3) as if[though] + 주어 + **동사의 과거형** (마치 ~인 것처럼)
가정법 과거완료	1) if + 주어 + **had p.p.** ~, 주어 + 조동사 과거형 + have p.p. ... (만약 ~했다면 …했을 텐데) 2) I wish + 주어 + **had p.p.** (~했다면 좋을 텐데) 3) as if[though] + 주어 + **had p.p.** (마치 ~였던 것처럼)

참고 ! if절에서 if가 생략되면 주어와 (조)동사가 도치된다.

***Had* she used** a microphone, more people would have heard her.
(그녀가 마이크를 사용했다면 더 많은 사람들이 그녀의 말을 들었을 텐데.)

※ 다음 네모 안에서 어법상 적절한 것을 고르시오.

정답 및 해설 p. 7

1 Even though most of the passers-by were most likely rushing to work, the scene might [be / have been] quite different if they had known that the young musician was Tony Adamson, a world famous violinist. <모의>

POINT 10 | 뒤에 부정사가 오는지 동명사가 오는지 구별하자. ★★

❶ 부정사만을 목적어로 취하는 동사 vs. 동명사만을 목적어로 취하는 동사

v+to-v	afford, refuse, manage, expect, want, decide, plan, offer 등
v+v-ing	enjoy, finish, mind, avoid, quit, give up, deny, suggest, consider 등

❷ 부정사, 동명사를 둘 다 목적어로 취할 수 있는 동사는 의미 차이에 주의한다.

보통 부정사는 '미래성', 동명사는 '과거성'이나 '현재성'을 내포한다.

1 remember/forget **to + 동사원형** ((미래에) ~할 것을 기억하다/잊다)
remember/forget **v-ing** ((과거에) ~한 것을 기억하다/잊다)

2 regret **to + 동사원형** (~하게 되어 유감이다)
regret **v-ing** ((과거에) ~한 것을 후회하다)

3 stop **to + 동사원형** (~하기 위해 멈추다): 이때의 to부정사는 '목적'을 나타내는 부사구
stop **v-ing** (~하던 것을 멈추다): 동명사를 목적어로 취하는 동사
We stopped **to ask** for directions. (우리는 길을 물어 보기 위해 멈췄다.)
Stop **asking** me questions. (나한테 질문 좀 그만해.)

❸ 부정사를 이끄는 to와 전치사 to를 구별해야 한다.

to + 동사원형	• be used to + **동사원형** (~하기 위해 사용되다) • be about to + **동사원형** (막 ~하려던 참이다) • be likely to + **동사원형** (~일 것 같다) ↔ be unlikely to + **동사원형** (~일 것 같지 않다) **참고!** 기타 뒤에 동사원형이 오는 표현 • 조동사 used to + **동사원형** (~하곤 했다)
전치사 to + v-ing	• be used to **v-ing** (~하는 데 익숙하다) • look forward to **v-ing** (~하는 것을 고대하다) • be close to + **v-ing** (~하는 것에 가깝다)

※ 다음 네모 안에서 어법상 적절한 것을 고르거나, 밑줄 친 부분이 어법상 옳으면 ○표, 틀리면 ×표하고 바르게 고치시오. 정답 및 해설 p. 7

1 Emma was very fond of singing. She had a very good voice, except that some of her high notes tended to sound like a gate which someone had forgotten [oiling / to oil]. <모의>

2 Legend has it that, during the Chinese Tang dynasty, a poor public official was so honest that he refused [taking / to take] bribes. He could not buy meat to feed his family. So, he invented tofu. <모의>

3 Initially, it made a lot of noise, and later, it stopped <u>to operate</u> entirely. <수능>

4 When the body mobilizes <u>to fight</u> off infectious agents, it generates a burst of free radicals to destroy the invaders very efficiently. <수능>

5 The boundaries among business units were deliberately ambiguous because more than technical information was needed to get a feeling for the problem. <수능>

6 "Monumental" is a word that comes very close to expressing the basic characteristic of Egyptian art. <수능>

7 In many cases the donation is so small — $10 or less — that if they stopped to think, they would realize that the cost of processing the donation is likely to exceed any benefit it brings to the charity. <수능>

POINT 11 | 동사가 전치사의 목적어로 올 때는 동명사를 쓴다. ★

❶ 전치사는 명사 상당어구를 목적어로 취하므로 전치사 뒤에 동명사(구)가 오는 패턴을 볼 수 있다.

참고! 기타 뒤에 동명사가 오는 표현

- upon[on] **v-ing** (~하자마자)
- have difficulty[trouble] **v-ing** (~하는 데 어려움을 겪다)
- spend + 목적어 + **v-ing** (~하는 데 …을 쓰다)
- end up + **v-ing** (결국 ~하게 되다)

❷ 준동사의 동사적 성질

동명사, 부정사, 분사는 동사에서 파생된 것이므로, 다음과 같은 동사적 성질을 갖는다.

1 목적어를 취할 수 있다.

2 의미상 주어가 필요하다.

참고! 의미상 주어가 문장의 주어 혹은 목적어와 일치하거나 일반인 주어인 경우 등 문맥상 알 수 있을 때는 별도로 표시하지 않는다.

3 시제와 태를 갖는다.

- 완료형: to have p.p. / having p.p. (문장의 동사보다 먼저 일어난 동작이나 상태를 나타낼 때)
- 수동형: to be p.p. / being p.p.

※ 다음 네모 안에서 어법상 적절한 것을 고르거나, 밑줄 친 부분이 어법상 옳으면 ○표, 틀리면 ×표하고 바르게 고치시오. 정답 및 해설 p. 8

1 Bakers are researching methods for producing the handmade sourdough breads of the past, and they are experimenting with specialty flours in their search for flavor. <모의>

2 Presumably four million seals could not compete with commercial fishermen for the same species without the fact [being / is] known. <모의>

3 Sleep does not appear to have evolved only in warm-blooded animals. Some studies on reptiles and amphibians indicate that they also sleep. <모의>

POINT 12 | 다양한 분사구문의 형태를 정리해두자. ★★

❶ **「v-ing ~」(~하면서<동시 동작>, ~해서<이유>, ~한다면<조건>, ~이지만<양보> 등)**
접속사, 주어, 동사를 따로 쓰지 않고 「v-ing ~」만으로 문장에 다양한 의미를 덧붙인다.

❷ **「(Being) p.p. ~」, 「(Being) 형용사 ~」**
Being이 생략되고 p.p.나 형용사로 시작될 수 있다.

❸ **「Having p.p. ~」**
완료형 분사구문으로, 주절보다 앞서 일어난 일을 나타낸다.

❹ **「접속사 + v-ing/p.p.」**
분사구문의 뜻을 명확히 하기 위해 접속사를 밝혀 써준 경우이다.

❺ **「의미상 주어 + v-ing/p.p.」**
분사구문의 의미상 주어가 주절의 주어와 다르면 분사구문 앞에 의미상 주어를 밝혀 써준다.

❻ **「with + 명사 + v-ing/p.p.」(~을 …한 채로)**
명사가 분사의 의미상 주어 역할을 한다. 둘 사이의 관계가 능동이면 v-ing, 수동이면 p.p.를 쓴다.

※ 밑줄 친 부분이 어법상 옳으면 ○표, 틀리면 ×표하고 바르게 고치시오. 정답 및 해설 p. 8

1 Adolescents have been quick to immerse themselves in technology with most <u>using</u> the Internet to communicate. <모의>

2 Picture two programmers working side by side. One is leaning back in his chair with his eyes <u>closed</u> and his feet on the desk. The other is working hard, typing code into his computer. <모의>

3 These fierce radicals, <u>built</u> into life as both protectors and avengers, are potent agents of aging. <수능>

전치사 | 접속사

POINT 13 | 전치사 뒤에는 '명사', 접속사 뒤에는 「주어 + 동사」가 온다. ★★

❶ 주요 전치사와 접속사 정리

전치사 뒤에는 '명사 상당어구'가, 접속사 뒤에는 「주어 + 동사」 형태의 절이 온다.

전치사	접속사
• because of (~ 때문에) • during (~ 동안) • despite, inspite of (~에도 불구하고) **참고!** 전치사 despite 뒤에 문장을 쓰고 싶으면 「despite the fact that + S + V」의 형태로 쓰면 된다.	• because (~ 때문에) • while (~ 동안) • though, although (비록 ~이긴 하지만)

참고! 접속사 while은 '~인 데 반해, 한편'이라는 뜻으로, <대조>를 나타내기도 한다.

People's standards of living differ greatly, and some people are well-off **while** others are not. <모의>
(사람들의 생활수준은 매우 다른데, 어떤 사람들은 부유한 데 반해 다른 사람들은 그렇지 않다.)

❷ 접속부사 vs. 접속사

접속사는 두 '절'을 연결하는 반면 접속부사는 완결된 두 '문장'을 이어주는 문장의 수식어 '부사'로서 그 뒤에 콤마(,)가 오는 게 특징이다.

주요 접속부사 besides(게다가), then, however, therefore, thus, moreover, furthermore, nevertheless, instead, likewise(마찬가지로), similarly, otherwise(그렇지 않으면), consequently, meanwhile(그동안에; 한편) 등

※ 다음 네모 안에서 어법상 적절한 것을 고르거나, 밑줄 친 부분이 어법상 옳으면 ○표, 틀리면 ×표하고 바르게 고치시오.

정답 및 해설 p. 8

1 <u>Though</u> zoological research, there are still many dark areas in our understanding about the life of this strange creature. <모의>

2 Most people dream too small. They don't think big enough. Henry Curtis advises, "Make your plans as fantastic as you like [because / because of] twenty-five years from now, they will not seem so special." <수능>

3 Dad came to football games whenever I played. I never told him how to get to a game; he just showed up. [Then / When] I left the field at the end of a period, he would call me over with his hands. <모의>

POINT 14 | 명사절 접속사 if는 '의문'을 나타내는 동사와 함께 쓰인다. 

명사절 접속사 if[whether](~인지 아닌지)와 **명사절 접속사 that**(~이라는 것)은 둘 다 명사절을 이끌므로, 구조상으로는 어느 게 맞는지 판단할 수 없다. if[whether]는 뜻 자체가 '불확실함'을 나타내므로 '의문'을 나타내는 동사 **ask, wonder, inquire** 등과 자주 쓰이나 묻는 내용을 그대로 전달하는 ask that ~ 패턴도 가능하므로 결국 문맥을 통해 파악해야 한다.

참고! whether절은 '~이든 (아니든)'의 뜻의 부사절을 이끌기도 한다.

Whether you like it or not, you have to accept the reality. (좋든 싫든 현실을 받아들여야만 한다.)

※ 다음 밑줄 친 부분이 어법상 옳으면 ○표, 틀리면 ×표하고 바르게 고치시오. 정답 및 해설 p. 8

1 He was fond of saying that the biggest problem with managing computer programmers is that you can never tell whether they are working by looking at them. <모의>

POINT 15 | 접속사 that이 오는 패턴을 정리해두자. 

❶ 「It is ~ that ...」

1 가주어-진주어 구문: It이 가주어, that절이 진주어이다. 진주어 자리에는 다양한 절(that절, whether절, wh-절)과 구(주로 to부정사구, 동명사구)가 올 수 있다.

2 강조구문: 강조하는 말이 It + be동사와 that사이에 놓인다.

참고! It is와 that을 생략할 때 완전한 문장이 성립하면 강조구문, 불완전한 문장이면 가주어-진주어 구문이다.

❷ 「so[such] ~ that ...」

so 뒤에는 형용사나 부사가 바로 이어 나오고, such 뒤에는 명사가 반드시 온다는 점에 주의하자.

- 「so + 형용사/부사 + (관사 + 명사 +) that」(매우 ~해서 …하다)
- 「such + (관사 + 형용사 +) 명사 + that」(매우 ~해서 …하다)

참고! so나 such 뒤에 늘 that절이 오는 것은 아니며 그 '정도'나 '결과'를 강조하여 서술할 때 that절이 이어진다.

❸ 「형용사 + that ...」

형용사 뒤에 수반되는 절은 크게 다음의 두 가지로 구분할 수 있다.

- **감정의 원인, 이유를 나타내는 that절:** '~해서, ~ 때문에'로 해석하는 것이 자연스럽다.

  주요 형용사 pleased, glad, happy, surprised, sad, sorry, worried 등

  She was ***pleased*** **(that)** her daughter chose a college close to home.

  (그녀는 딸이 집 근처의 대학을 선택해서 기뻤다.)

- **목적어절에 상응하는 that절**: 「be동사 + 형용사」가 하나의 타동사 역할을 한다. 절을 '~을[를]'로 해석하면 된다.

  주요 형용사 aware(알고 있는), **certain**(확신하는), **sure**, **confident**(확신하는) 등

  I'm absolutely ***certain*** **(that)** I left the keys in the kitchen.

  (나는 주방에 열쇠를 두었음을 확신한다.)

참고! that의 기타 용법

- 지시대명사: **That**'s my car, over there. (저기 있는 저게 내 차야.)
- 지시형용사: I've got **that** pain in my back again. (등에 또 그 통증이 도졌어.) ← 명사 pain 수식
- 지시부사: I know some people left before the end, but was it really **that** ***bad***?
  (끝나기 전에 몇몇 사람이 가버린 건 아는데, 그게 정말로 그렇게 안 좋았어?) ← 형용사 bad 수식

※ 다음 네모 안에서 어법상 적절한 것을 고르거나, 밑줄 친 부분이 어법상 옳으면 ○표, 틀리면 ×표하고 바르게 고치시오.

정답 및 해설 p. 9

1 As technology and the Internet are a familiar resource for young people, it is logical what they would seek assistance from this source. <모의>

2 It is also from the list of courses of each department in the catalog [while / that] a degree plan for the student can be devised. <모의>

3 Doctors have long been [aware of / aware that] women alcoholics may give birth to defective babies. <모의>

관계사

POINT 16 | 관계대명사는 「접속사 + 대명사」의 역할을 한다. ★

❶ **관계대명사는 선행사(명사)를 대신하는 '대명사' 역할 외에, 두 절을 연결하는 '접속사' 역할을 한다.**
대명사만으로는 두 절을 연결할 수 없다.

❷ **계속적 용법의 관계대명사로 연결된 문장은 「접속사 + 대명사」의 두 개 문장으로 고쳐 쓸 수 있다.**
His letter was full of regret and sadness, **which** made me forgive him. (=, and it ~)
(그의 편지는 후회와 슬픔으로 가득 차 있었고, 그것이 내가 그를 용서하게 만들었다.)

※ 다음 밑줄 친 부분이 어법상 옳으면 ○표, 틀리면 ×표하고 바르게 고치시오.

정답 및 해설 p. 9

1 In another slum area, possibly inspired by Brown's example, a culture center began to encourage the local kids to stage musical events, some of them dramatized the tragedy that they were still recovering from. <모의>

2 The violinists and pianists their names you've heard regularly earn between $30,000 and $50,000 for a single performance. <모의>

3 Application of Buddhist-style mindfulness to Western psychology came primarily from the research of Jon Kabat-Zinn at the University of Massachusetts Medical Center. He initially took on the difficult task of treating chronic-pain patients, many of them had not responded well to traditional pain-management therapy. <모의>

POINT 17 | 선행사 바로 찾기와 격 구분이 관계대명사의 기본이다. 

❶ 선행사를 바르게 찾아 관계대명사의 종류를 결정한다.

사람은 who, 동물이나 사물은 which로 받는다. that은 사람, 동물, 사물 모두 받을 수 있다.

❷ 선행사가 관계사절 내에서 어떤 역할을 하는지에 따라 관계대명사의 격이 결정된다.

주어 역할을 하면 주격, 목적어 역할을 하면 목적격, 소유를 나타내면 소유격을 쓴다.

※ 다음 밑줄 친 부분이 어법상 옳으면 ○표, 틀리면 ×표하고 바르게 고치시오.

정답 및 해설 p. 9

1 An independent artist is probably the one <u>who</u> lives closest to an unbounded creative situation. <모의>

2 In the twentieth century, advances in technology, from refrigeration to sophisticated ovens to air transportation <u>that</u> carries fresh ingredients around the world, contributed immeasurably to baking and pastry making. <모의>

3 The ultimate life force lies in tiny cellular factories of energy, called mitochondria, <u>that</u> burn nearly all the oxygen we breathe in. <수능>

POINT 18 | 이럴 땐 관계대명사 that을 쓸 수 없다. 

❶ 관계대명사 that은 계속적 용법으로 쓸 수 없다.

❷ 「전치사 + 관계대명사 that」이 함께 쓰일 수 없다.

주의! 접속사로 쓰인 in that과 구별하자.

The new system is better **in that** it provides faster access to the Internet.

(새로운 시스템은 더 빠른 인터넷 접속을 제공한다는 점에서 더 낫다.) ← 전치사 in 뒤에 명사절 접속사 that이 온 형태

※ 다음 네모 안에서 어법상 적절한 것을 고르거나, 밑줄 친 부분이 어법상 옳으면 ○표, 틀리면 ×표하고 바르게 고치시오.

정답 및 해설 p. 9

1 Like most of William Shakespeare's plays, *Romeo and Juliet* is based on earlier sources, [that / which] in this case go back to some stories popular in Italy in the late 1400s. <모의>

2 The days of the solitary inventor working on his own are gone. To oversimplify, basic ideas bubble out of universities and laboratories <u>in which</u> a group of researchers work together. <모의>

명사 | 대명사

POINT 19 | 대명사 파트에서는 명사와의 수일치가 가장 빈출된다. ★★

❶ **대명사가 지칭하는 대상을 정확하게 찾는 것이 관건이다.**

❷ **반복을 피하기 위해 앞에 나온 명사를 대신할 때는 대명사 that/those를 쓴다.**
앞에 나온 명사가 단수면 that, 복수면 those로 받는다.

※ 다음 네모 안에서 어법상 적절한 것을 고르거나, 밑줄 친 부분이 어법상 옳으면 ○표, 틀리면 ×표하고 바르게 고치시오.

정답 및 해설 p. 9

1 The company also created an open-ended conversation among its engineers in which salespeople and designers were often included. <수능>

2 By comparison, evaluation of performances such as diving, gymnastics, and figure skating is more subjective—although elaborate scoring rules help make [it / them] more objective. <모의>

3 Such choices are not made to limit creativity, but rather to cultivate it. <모의>

4 It has been proposed that sleep functions to conserve energy. This may be particularly relevant for warm-blooded animals (mammals and birds) that must expend a lot of energy to maintain a body temperature higher than that of their surroundings. <모의>

5 The Greeks' focus on the salient object and its attributes led to their failure to understand the fundamental nature of causality. <수능>

6 A scientist turned video cameras on a number of spaces in New York City, watching to see how people used the spaces. He made a number of fascinating findings, and he had the video evidence to back them up. <모의>

7 Many modern structures exceed those of Egypt in terms of purely physical size. But massiveness has nothing to do with monumentality. <수능>

POINT 20 | 재귀대명사와 소유대명사의 쓰임을 확실히 정리해두자. 

❶ 주어와 목적어가 동일한 경우, 목적어 자리에 재귀대명사를 쓴다.
동작이 동작자 본인에게 행해지는 것을 나타낸다.

❷ 소유대명사는 「소유격 + 명사」를 대신한다.

※ 다음 네모 안에서 어법상 적절한 것을 고르시오. 정답 및 해설 p. 10

1 Aging is a result of the gradual failure of the body's cells and organs to replace and repair [them / themselves]. This is because there is a limit to the number of times that each cell can divide. <모의>

2 On the way back home, we had a flat and no spare tire. We walked to a nearby farmhouse for help. The farmer who lived there took off a tire from his car and said, "Drive into town, get your tire fixed, and leave [me / mine] at the gas station." <모의>

3 Sadly, human beings are in fact the only species that will deliberately deprive [them / themselves] of sleep without legitimate gain. <모의>

POINT 21 | 명사의 수에 따라 수식어를 달리 써야 한다. 

❶

	셀 수 있는 명사 수식	셀 수 없는 명사 수식
많은	many	much
약간 있는	a few	a little
거의 없는	few	little
아주 많은	a great many of	a great deal of

참고! a lot of, lots of, plenty of는 복수명사와 셀 수 없는 명사 둘 다 수식한다.

❷

단수명사 수식	복수명사 수식
each(각각의)	both(둘 다의)
every(모든, 하나하나 다)	all(모든)
either((둘 중) 어느 하나의)	

참고! all은 셀 수 없는 명사를 수식할 수도 있다.
We gave up **all *hope*** of finding the lost tickets. (우리는 잃어버린 표를 찾겠다는 모든 희망을 포기했다.)
neither는 복수가 아닌 단수다.
Neither is happy. ((둘 중) 어느 누구도 행복하지 않다.)

※ 다음 네모 안에서 어법상 적절한 것을 고르시오.

정답 및 해설 p. 10

1 The first shops sold just [a few / a little] products such as meat and bread. <모의>

2 Investigators questioned [both / each] suspects but neither of them could speak English. <모의>

3 We know that the journalism program at our college was a source of [many / much] of these firsts for you. <모의>

POINT 22 | another, other의 쓰임을 구별하자. ★★

❶ 대명사로 쓰일 때

one, another, other 모두 불특정한 명사를 가리킨다.
another는 'an + other'의 의미로, 다른 것 '또 하나'를 가리킬 때 쓴다.
the other는 가리키는 바가 분명한 '특정한 나머지 하나'를 가리킨다.
other는 단독으로 쓰일 수 없고, 복수형 (다른 사람들, 다른 것들)의 형태로 쓰인다.
the others는 가리키는 바가 분명한 '특정한 나머지 사람들[것들]'을 가리킨다.

◉ one ● the other	둘 중 하나를 택하면 one, 나머지 하나는 the other	●●● ◉ ◉ ●●●●●● (one another)	여러 개 중 하나를 택하면 one, 또 다른 하나를 택하면 another, 그 나머지 모두는 the others (= all the rest)
some (●●●) ●●● ●●●● (●●●●) others	여러 개 중 둘 이상을 택하면 some, 또 다른 둘 이상을 택하면 others, 그 나머지 모두는 the others (= all the rest)		

❷ 형용사로 쓰일 때

• 「another + 단수명사」, 「other + 복수명사」: 불특정한 대상을 가리킴.
• 「the other + 단수/복수명사」: 특정한 대상을 가리킴.
복수명사와 함께 쓰이거나(other products) 일대일 비교에서 단수명사와 함께 쓰인다(than any other color).
My mom likes red more than any other color. (나의 엄마는 다른 색보다 빨간색을 좋아하신다.)

❸ 특정이 아닌 단수명사는 one, 특정이 아닌 복수명사는 ones로 나타낸다.

주의! 특정한 단수명사는 it, 특정한 복수명사는 them으로 받는다.
The tomatoes are all too ripe. Can I change **them** for fresher **ones**?
(토마토가 전부 너무 익었어요. 그것들을 신선한 것들로 바꿔도 될까요?)

❹ some, any(몇몇(의), 약간(의))는 문장의 종류에 따라 평서문에서는 some을, 부정문, 의문문, 조건문에서는 일반적으로 any를 쓴다. 셀 수 있는 명사로도 셀 수 없는 명사로도 쓰이며 뒤에 명사가 따라 오면 형용사로도 쓰인다.

주의! **Any** person can participate in the competition as long as he or she meets the requirements.
(자격요건을 갖추기만 하면 어떤 사람이든 시합에 참여할 수 있다.) ← any: 어떤 ~라도

※ 다음 밑줄 친 부분이 어법상 옳으면 ○표, 틀리면 ×표하고 바르게 고치시오. 정답 및 해설 p. 10

1 Being a hybrid art as well as a late one, film has always been in a dialogue with other narrative genres. <수능>

2 Basic ideas bubble out of universities and laboratories in which a group of researchers work together: both major breakthroughs, like understanding the genetic structure of life, and smaller ones, such as advances in mathematics or basic chemistry. <모의>

3 Any individual fish of the school can initiate a movement, such as a change in direction, and this sends out a "maneuver wave," which spreads through the group at an astounding speed. <모의>

형용사 | 부사

POINT 23 | 비교구문의 기출 포인트를 한꺼번에 정리하자. ★

❶ 비교급 수식 부사

much, far, even, still, a lot 등.

주의! very는 비교급을 수식할 수 없고 원급을 수식한다.

❷ 비교구문의 패턴 정리

원급, 비교급, 최상급 중 어떤 패턴으로 완성되어야 할지 판단해야 한다.

구분	패턴	의미
원급	as + 원급 + as ... / not as[so] + 원급 + as ...	…만큼 ~한 / …만큼 ~하지 않은
비교급	비교급 + than ...	…보다 ~한
	the + 비교급 ~, the + 비교급 ...	~하면 할수록 더 …한
최상급	the + 최상급 (+ in[of] ...)	(… 중에서) 가장 ~한
배수사 비교	~ times as + 원급 + as B	B의 ~배만큼 …한
	~ times + 비교급 + than B	B보다 ~배 …한
부정주어를 이용한 최상급	No ~ as + 원급 + as B	B만큼 …한 ~는 아무(것)도 없다
	No ~ 비교급 + than B	B보다 …한 ~는 아무(것)도 없다

❸ 비교급 문장은 비교하는 대상 A와 B가 무엇인지 파악하는 게 중요하다.

Nothing ruins friendships more swiftly **than** *desperate neediness and possessiveness*.

(간절한 애정 갈구와 소유욕보다 우정을 더 빠르게 망치는 것은 없다.)

→ Nothing과 desperate neediness and possessiveness가 ruins friendships swiftly하는 점을 비교

※ 다음 네모 안에서 어법상 적절한 것을 고르거나, 밑줄 친 부분이 어법상 옳으면 ○표, 틀리면 ×표하고 바르게 고치시오.

정답 및 해설 p. 10

1 Some toy animals stayed at sea [even / very] longer. They floated completely along the North Pacific currents, ending up back in Sitka. <수능>

2 Creativity is strange in that it finds its way in any kind of situation, no matter how restricted, just as the same amount of water flows faster and stronger through a narrow strait <u>than</u> across the open sea. <모의>

POINT 24 | 혼동하기 쉬운 형용사, 부사 정리 ★

❶ 뜻에 주의해야 할 형용사, 부사

-ly가 붙은 부사들의 예외적인 뜻에 주의하자. 이들은 기본 뜻에서 좀 더 확장된 의미를 갖는다.

late 형 늦은 부 늦게 lately 부 최근에	hard 부 열심히; 세게; 심하게 형 어려운; 딱딱한 hardly 부 거의 ~ 않다
near 형 가까운 부 가까이 전 ~에서 가까이 nearly 부 거의(= almost) nearby 형 가까운 부 가까이	high 형 높은 부 높게 highly 부 매우, 아주
most 형 최고의(the ~); 형 명 대부분(의) 부 가장 mostly 부 주로, 대개(= usually) almost 부 거의; 거의 ~할 뻔한	short 형 짧은; 부족한 부 짧게 shortly 부 곧
alike 형 똑같은 부 똑같이 like 형 ~와 같은 likely 형 ~할 가능성이 있는, ~함직한 부 아마	close 형 가까운 부 가까이 closely 부 긴밀히, 밀접하게; 면밀히
lively 형 생기 있는 alive 형 살아 있는 live 형 생방송의, 실시간의	

❷ enough는 수식받는 말의 품사에 따라 위치가 달라진다.

명사를 수식할 때는 다른 형용사와 마찬가지로 명사의 앞에서 수식하지만 형용사, 부사는 뒤에서 수식한다.

The father looks *strong* **enough** to lift his two kids. ← 형용사 strong을 뒤에서 수식
(그 아빠는 두 아이를 들어 올릴 만큼 힘세 보인다.)

❸ 서술형용사는 명사를 수식할 수 없다.

접두사 a-가 붙은 형용사는 서술적 용법(보어 역할)으로만 쓰인다.

asleep, alive, awake, alone, aware, afraid, ashamed 등

❹ 구체적인 특정 수치를 지칭할 때는 '단수'로, 막연히 큰 숫자를 가리킬 땐 '복수'로 쓴다.

dozen(12), score(20), hundred, thousand, million 등

e.g. **two thousand** people(이천 명의 사람들)
thousands of people(수천 명의 사람들)

※ 다음 밑줄 친 부분이 어법상 옳으면 ○표, 틀리면 ×표하고 바르게 고치시오.

정답 및 해설 p. 11

1 The negative impact on local wildlife inhabiting areas <u>close</u> to the fish farms continues to be an ongoing public relations problem for the industry. <수능>

2 Interestingly enough, many of the technological advances in bread making have sparked a reaction among bakers and consumers <u>alike</u>. <모의>

3 So are they all following the commands of a leader? Researchers have determined that there is no leader or controlling force. Rather, the individual fish or bird is reacting <u>almost</u> instantly to the movements of its neighbors in the school or flock. <모의>

PART 1

핵심 예상문제

01 - 20회

01 핵심 예상문제

권장 시간 4분

시작·종료 시간 | : ~ :
나의 소요 시간 | 분 초

001 (A), (B), (C)의 각 네모 안에서 어법에 맞는 표현으로 가장 적절한 것은?

Most people appreciate the convenience of online banking, but it also introduces new risks. Criminals located anywhere in the world might be able to obtain the personal information that enables them to be (A) [you / yourself] online and carry out transactions with your money as if they owned it. Bank and securities regulators do have rules about how to address cyber-theft. However, the actual liability for lost funds (B) [depend / depends] on the contracts signed by the customer in opening an account. Many of the bigger banks guarantee full reimbursement, but problematic cases are those in which an account is hacked because the personal information has been obtained from your computer owing to lack of adequate security or precautions on your part. Some banks are treating this like leaving your purse (C) [unattending / unattended] —"Sorry for your loss, but you should have been more careful."

*securities: 유가 증권, 주식 **liability: 법적 책임
***reimbursement: 변제, 배상

	(A)		(B)		(C)
①	you	—	depend	—	unattending
②	you	—	depend	—	unattended
③	you	—	depends	—	unattended
④	yourself	—	depend	—	unattending
⑤	yourself	—	depends	—	unattended

002 다음 글의 밑줄 친 부분 중, 어법상 틀린 것은?

The popularity of electric cars in the UK has shot up over the last few years, with around 50,000 plug-in vehicles on the road, compared with just 3,500 in 2013. This huge increase in electric cars in 2015 has come about ① <u>because of</u> a greater level of choice for drivers, a shift in the public's attitude towards electric cars and a ② <u>constant</u> improving public recharging network. Combined, this means that UK electric car buyers have a greater selection of vehicles ③ <u>to choose from</u> than ever before. The future is bright, too, with ④ <u>a number of</u> plug-in cars set to be launched within the next twelve months and with the UK government's Plug-in Car Grant now ⑤ <u>guaranteed</u> until 2018. An electric car is now an attractive option for a large number of motorists.

003 다음 글의 밑줄 친 부분 중, 어법상 틀린 것은?

One of the most versatile types of meat, pork is economical, tender ① <u>if cooked</u> correctly, and oozing with flavor. It is often thought of as a particularly fatty type of meat, but modern breeding, rearing and butchering has today made pork a low-fat, healthy meat. Furthermore, the fat it ② <u>does contain</u> is less saturated than that found in other meats. Still, it's important to buy a good cut. When shopping, look for ③ <u>firmly</u>, pale pink flesh that's damp but not oily in texture. Avoid pork with yellow-colored fat, and go for the white stuff ④ <u>instead</u>. Bones should be red tinged. Rough flesh and white bones indicate the animal is older and the meat less tender than it ⑤ <u>should</u> be. Pork is high in protein, an excellent source of iron, zinc and B vitamins and tastes wonderful too—so get some pork on your fork tonight.

*saturated: (화학) 포화된

02 핵심 예상문제

권장 시간 4분

시작·종료 시간 | : ~ :
나의 소요 시간 | 분 초

004 다음 글의 밑줄 친 부분 중, 어법상 틀린 것은?

Authoritative parenting is a style characterized by reasonable demands and high responsiveness. While authoritative parents might have high expectations for their children, these parents also give their kids the resources and support they need to succeed. Parents who ① exhibit this style listen to their kids and provide love and warmth in addition to limits and fair discipline. More often than not, authoritative parenting is linked to successful children. Maybe it's ② because authoritative parenting is associated with a package of individual practices that are more likely to produce independent, achievement-minded, socially-responsible, well-adjusted people. And maybe it depends—at least in part—on ③ which the rest of the community is doing. When schools are ④ run along authoritative principles, kids from authoritative families may have an easier time ⑤ meeting their teacher's expectations. It's also likely that a child's peer groups have an influence. Peer pressure can weaken the beneficial effects of the authoritative parenting style.

005 다음 글의 밑줄 친 부분 중, 어법상 틀린 것은?

You know better than ① to judge a book by its cover. Sizing up a person by his or her shoes, however, might at times ② be justified. A new study found that people deduce certain characteristics of strangers with better-than-chance accuracy based solely on their footwear. One group completed a personality survey and provided pictures of the shoes they wear most frequently. A second group then viewed the pictures and rated the ③ shoes' owners on various characteristics. Their guesses were accurate regarding age, gender, income and attachment anxiety. For instance, the volunteers perceived correctly that shoes with visible brand names most often belonged to men and stylish shoes ④ to women with high incomes. They also figured out that people who provided pictures of the shoes on their own feet were more emotionally stable. Shoes may help form a first impression, but avoid ⑤ to assume too much—you might end up shooting yourself in the foot.

006 다음 글의 밑줄 친 부분 중, 어법상 틀린 것은?

School districts in the U.S. spend $18 billion on teacher training each year. Most often, in terms of the total hours spent, the format for that training is collaborative professional development, a form of training ① in which teachers work together in groups to improve their teaching. These groups are often called professional learning communities (PLCs). Two-thirds of U.S. teachers now report spending time in PLCs. So far, the results of such collaboration ② have been poor. The intentions are good, but the implementation is not: teachers are even less satisfied with collaborative professional development than with the "sit and get" workshops that collaboration was intended ③ to replace. Many teachers we surveyed ④ were found programs poorly structured and the experience boring and disconnected from their day-to-day jobs. ⑤ Half as many teachers were highly satisfied with their collaborative professional development experience (11 percent) as those who were highly satisfied with workshops (22 percent), traditionally the least interactive form of teacher training.

03 핵심 예상문제

권장 시간 4분 시작·종료 시간 | : ~ : 나의 소요 시간 | 분 초

007 (A), (B), (C)의 각 네모 안에서 어법에 맞는 표현으로 가장 적절한 것은?

Materials scientists have created a small, wearable sensor that can read the molecular composition of sweat and send its results in real time to a smartphone. The flexible plastic patches—which can be incorporated into wristbands and headbands—may be able to provide early warning of changes in the body, say their creators. Users (A) [wear / wearing] the flexible sensors can run and move freely while the chemicals in their sweat are measured and analyzed. The resulting data, which is transmitted wirelessly to a mobile device, can be used (B) [to help / to helping] assess and monitor a user's state of health. "It's an impressive achievement. The sensors typically (C) [require / are required] electronics that are normally about the size of a shoebox; we miniaturized them into something that can wrap around your wrist," one of the developers says.

(A)		(B)		(C)
① wear	—	to help	—	require
② wear	—	to helping	—	are required
③ wearing	—	to help	—	require
④ wearing	—	to help	—	are required
⑤ wearing	—	to helping	—	are required

008 다음 글의 밑줄 친 부분 중, 어법상 틀린 것은?

Many people get the idea, especially from movies like Jerry Maguire, ① that sports agents are slimy, used car salesmen types who lurk in the shadows, waiting for an ② unsuspected, gullible athlete to sign on the dotted line. They do exist. And they use 'let's get you signed, and I'll make you a star' rhetoric. There's no mention of long-term plans and post-football life. Yes. Such unscrupulous agents can ruin an athlete's career before it even starts. This causes people ③ to believe they are the 'norm' in the sports agent world, but it's not so. A sports agent's ultimate dream is to have clients who value and appreciate him for ④ what he brings to the table. He desires an athlete who "thinks in the future." He craves the excitement of pursuing athletes ⑤ loaded with potential. He thrives on athletes who are willing to learn how to develop their potential on and off the field. That's a sports agent's job.

*gullible: 잘 속아 넘어가는 **unscrupulous: 양심적이지 않은, 무원칙한

009 다음 글의 밑줄 친 부분 중, 어법상 틀린 것은?

In a world where we are expected to address multiple things at one time, mindfulness ① has become a hot topic. As such, numerous scientific publications are now struggling with both offering an understandable definition of mindfulness and ② demonstrate its practical applications for modern life. Mindfulness meditation involves a willingness to simply be with ③ whatever is happening within us and around us—with a gentle and open mind. We may discover things about ourselves, others, and the way we are living that aren't working. This awareness can sometimes cause us to feel anxious at first. We may bump up against our past wounds. Mindfulness requires courage to see things as they are rather than how we wish they ④ were. We may need to engage in therapy or counseling to heal the inner conflicts and patterns that cause our suffering. The good news is that mindfulness practice helps us ⑤ have the patience and compassion necessary for positive change.

정답 및 해설 p. 15

04 핵심 예상문제

권장 시간 4분 | 시작·종료 시간 | : ~ : | 나의 소요 시간 | 분 초

010 (A), (B), (C)의 각 네모 안에서 어법에 맞는 표현으로 가장 적절한 것은?

Ancient shipwrecks might not only hold buried treasures, but also countless historical secrets. More than three million shipwrecks may be scattered across the oceans, UNESCO estimates. It is further estimated that of all the wrecks in the world, less than 10 percent (A) [have been found / has been found]. Submerged wrecks are currently detected via waterborne sonar and airborne LiDAR systems—the former searches for wrecks with sound whereas the latter (B) [uses / to use] lasers. Waterborne sonar is most effective for deep water; airborne LiDAR requires clear water. Neither method works well for cloudy, shallow waters, however. This means that near-shore waters—often both shallow and cloudy—are frequently overlooked in hunts for old shipwrecks. This is a problem because "the majority of shipwrecks (C) [lie / lay] closer to shore, just as most car accidents happen a kilometer or so away from home," an expert says.

	(A)		(B)		(C)
①	have been found	—	uses	—	lie
②	have been found	—	to use	—	lie
③	has been found	—	uses	—	lie
④	has been found	—	uses	—	lay
⑤	has been found	—	to use	—	lay

011 다음 글의 밑줄 친 부분 중, 어법상 <u>틀린</u> 것은?

Some people experience sleep paralysis, a common but somewhat ① unexplained phenomenon in which a person awakens from sleep but feels unable to move, and even sees shadowy intruders ② hovering overhead. Researchers say that sleep paralysis happens when a person awakens during a stage of sleep known as rapid eye movement (REM). We are dreaming, but our muscles are nearly paralyzed, which might be an evolutionary adaptation that ③ keeps us from acting out our dreams. One possible explanation could be that during sleep paralysis, parts of the brain are monitoring the neurons that ④ sending commands to move, but aren't detecting any actual movement in the limbs, which are temporarily paralyzed. This may lead to a disturbance ⑤ in how the brain builds a sense of body image, an expert said. The appearance of a bedroom intruder could result when the brain tries to project the person's own body image onto a hallucinated figure, he also said.

*hallucinated figure: 환각 속의 인물

012 다음 글의 밑줄 친 부분 중, 어법상 <u>틀린</u> 것은?

Everyone knows that you can sprinkle salt on an icy road or sidewalk to remove the ice. This works because ① adding salt lowers the freezing point of water. How does this melt ice? Well, it doesn't, unless there is ② little water available with the ice. The good news is you don't need a pool of water to achieve the effect. Ice typically is coated with a thin film of liquid water, which is all it ③ takes. Pure water freezes at 32°F (0°C). Water with salt (or any other substance in it) will freeze at some lower temperature. If the temperature gets down to ④ where the salt water can freeze, energy will be released when bonds form as the liquid becomes a solid. This energy may be enough to melt a small amount of the pure ice, keeping the process ⑤ going.

05 핵심 예상문제

권장 시간 4분 | 시작·종료 시간 | : ~ : | 나의 소요 시간 | 분 초

013 (A), (B), (C)의 각 네모 안에서 어법에 맞는 표현으로 가장 적절한 것은?

Women do not get credit when it is due. In a study, women who worked collaboratively with men on designing multi-year investment portfolios (A) [was / were] consistently seen as less competent than their male peers. And when their joint project was successful, women were seen as having played a less influential role in its success, while their male counterparts were assumed (B) [to take / to have taken] on leadership roles. This is bad news for working women, since most jobs today involve some measure of collaboration. Their collaborative work counts less than it does for men. And when women don't get their fair share of credit for group work, their career prospects (C) [suffer / are suffered]. One can only imagine the many undocumented career penalties that women have incurred because they go unrecognized for valuable contributions.

*incur: (좋지 않은 상황을) 초래하다

	(A)		(B)		(C)
①	was	—	to take	—	suffer
②	were	—	to have taken	—	suffer
③	were	—	to have taken	—	are suffered
④	were	—	to take	—	suffer
⑤	was	—	to have taken	—	are suffered

014 다음 글의 밑줄 친 부분 중, 어법상 틀린 것은?

Babies born vaginally are thought to have an edge over ① those born via cesarean section. They pick up bacteria from their mother's birth canal, which scientists believe ② helps protect them from asthma, obesity, and other health issues as they grow older. Mothers in labor, like the rest of us, boast a constellation of bacteria all over and in their bodies—what's called the microbiome. Babies born vaginally develop a microbial community that initially ③ is resembled that of their mother's vagina, whereas babies who enter the world via C-section have a microbial makeup similar to that of their mother's skin. These differences, in turn, ④ have been associated with increased risks of asthma, allergies, obesity, and immune deficiencies, in human and mouse studies. Now, a new study offers hints ⑤ that researchers may be able to remove these disadvantages intrinsic in C-section babies by "remaking" their microscopic community shortly after birth—"a very interesting and simple intervention" that opens up new avenues of exploration.

*vaginally: 질로, 질을 통해 **cesarean section: 제왕절개
***microbiome: 미생물군유전체

015 다음 글의 밑줄 친 부분 중, 어법상 틀린 것은?

Hibernating squirrels can drop their body temperatures to just above freezing for weeks at a time. Even bears, ① much closer to us in size, are capable of surviving up to five months on their own body fat. But lots of non-hibernating animals make it through winter in a dormant state, reducing their body temperatures and slowing their metabolisms down to a minimum. Madagascan lemurs retire to a tree hole during the winter, ② where they sit like zombies for days on end. It's lack of food, rather than cold, ③ that drives them to hibernate. Since humans evolved in the equatorial climates of Africa, our hunter-gatherer ancestors ④ may evolve a similar ability to survive long periods without food. Nowadays, we just have to survive long nights. Luckily, we can crawl under the covers, get the candles lit and the fire ⑤ roaring and hit the remote control. Feel guilty? We don't need to. After all, we are just doing what comes naturally.

*Madagascan lemur: 마다가스카르 여우원숭이

06 핵심 예상문제

권장 시간 4분

시작·종료 시간 |	:	~	:
나의 소요 시간 |	분		초

016 (A), (B), (C)의 각 네모 안에서 어법에 맞는 표현으로 가장 적절한 것은?

In most child abuse cases, children who are abused or neglected (A) [suffer / suffering] greater emotional than physical damage. Emotional and psychological abuse and neglect deny the child the tools needed to cope with stress, and to learn life's lessons. So a child who is severely mistreated may become depressed or develop suicidal, withdrawn, or violent behavior. As he gets older, he may use drugs or alcohol, try to run away, refuse discipline, or abuse others. As an adult, he may develop marital difficulties, depression, or suicidal behavior. To prevent this situation, identifying child victims is the first step. The problem here is that not all abuse victims (B) [have / has] severe reactions. Usually the younger the child, the longer the abuse continues; and the closer the child's relationship with the abuser, the more (C) [serious / seriously] the emotional damage will be.

	(A)		(B)		(C)
①	suffer	—	have	—	serious
②	suffer	—	has	—	seriously
③	suffering	—	have	—	serious
④	suffering	—	has	—	serious
⑤	suffering	—	has	—	seriously

017 다음 글의 밑줄 친 부분 중, 어법상 틀린 것은?

Your phone's alarm goes off at 6 a.m. You ① gleefully switch it off, spring out of bed, fling open the curtains and the window and take a deep, ② satisfying breath of fresh air. Here's another picture: Your phone screeching at 6 a.m., your left arm slithers under your pillow to hit the snooze button. Just an extra 30 minutes—that's all you need. Then at 6:30 a.m., the alarm goes off again, and then at 7:00 a.m., 7:30 a.m., 7:35 a.m... Most of us are certainly the latter, ③ ending up starting a day without the feeling of seizing the day. As far as I understand, the people who are best at waking up ④ energized in the morning are those who feel like they are on a mission. The mission needs to be very compelling and something that you actually want to achieve, which ⑤ is driven you out of bed rather than drags you out screaming for five more minutes.

*slither: 스르르 나아가다[기어가다]
**snooze button: 스누즈 버튼 (아침에 잠이 깬 뒤 조금 더 자기 위해 누르는 타이머 버튼)

018 다음 글의 밑줄 친 부분 중, 어법상 틀린 것은?

Graduation is only a few weeks away, and I am getting excited. I will finally graduate with my degree. It ① has been a long road at times, and was rather difficult. Yet, here I am. I have made it through college. I survived all those late-night study sessions and final exams. The most significant thing that graduation means to me is ② that I learned a lot about myself. When I immigrated to the U.S., I went through an ③ extreme identity change. I was separated from my old way of life, my family, my friends, and my city. I lost my social status, personal identity, and ability to operate ④ effectively in the environment. The transition was painful, but throughout my educational journey I discovered that I was forming a new identity, new values and new attitudes. I was able to overcome painful obstacles of transition, find peace with ⑤ me and resettle comfortably in my new country.

07 핵심 예상문제

권장 시간 4분

시작·종료 시간 | : ~ :
나의 소요 시간 | 분 초

019 다음 글의 밑줄 친 부분 중, 어법상 틀린 것은?

In 2010, a study explored how gratitude motivated pro-social behavior. After ① being thanked for their personal contributions, participants in the study experienced increased feelings of value and worth, ② which in turn more than doubled their likelihood of repeating that helpful behavior. For everyone, this study unveils an easy way to support the self-esteem of your colleagues. For people at the management level, it also suggests just how much support and ③ productivity you could be losing by not expressing gratitude. To make sure you're taking advantage of the benefits of appreciation and acknowledgment, try building intentional and genuine thanking into your team meetings or one-on-ones. While it's ④ much easier to high-five a leader in your organization for her or his team's accomplishments, ⑤ acknowledge the whole team with a warm email will highlight the critical support of each individual, and boost the happiness of an entire group of individuals instead of just one.

020 다음 글의 밑줄 친 부분 중, 어법상 틀린 것은?

Don't wait to go shopping until you have to. This doesn't apply to grocery shopping, but it ① does to clothes shopping. There are some times when we suddenly feel that we need a new version of everything in our wardrobe: black pants, jeans with a flawless fit, boots, a blouse, a blazer, and so on. Or maybe you have a family wedding this weekend and need ② that perfect modest-but-cool-but-also-elegant dress in two days. ③ Whatever the case, if you're looking for something specific, chances are, you're not going to find ④ it. The key is to shop often and not in bulk, so when you happen to stumble across a denim vest that you can literally wear with everything in your closet, you buy it ... even if that wasn't ⑤ which you had in mind for the day. Eventually, you'll find that you've secured a very balanced wardrobe over time. Slow and steady wins the race—that's what they say, right?

*blazer: 블레이저(운동선수들이 입는 밝은색의 윗도리) **denim vest: 청조끼

021 다음 글의 밑줄 친 부분 중, 어법상 틀린 것은?

Actors and actresses are generally creative individuals who work well as part of a team. They develop strong critical thinking skills necessary for interpreting all of the different characters they ① are called on to portray. A good memory is also essential for actors because they must learn lines quickly. They need to accept constructive criticism on a regular basis and ② be able to adjust to changing sets of expectations. Throughout their career, it is critical for actors and actresses to continue ③ to work on developing these qualities. Most actors and actresses accomplish this by performing for free in local theater groups and ④ attending regular acting classes and workshops. For many, this is where their real professional training begins. They also provide one of the most effective networking opportunities available. And a good reputation ⑤ is spread by word-of-mouth is possibly the best tool an aspiring actor or actress can hope for.

08 핵심 예상문제

권장 시간 4분

시작·종료 시간 | : ~ :
나의 소요 시간 | 분 초

022 (A), (B), (C)의 각 네모 안에서 어법에 맞는 표현으로 가장 적절한 것은?

All sophomore and junior transfer students (A) [require / are required] to live on campus unless they meet one of the exemption requirements. Transfer students are assigned to housing throughout campus, typically with other students of similar age and class year. Transfer students are not housed with freshmen. Our office does not accommodate requests for specific residential areas or rooms. Students with medical needs for specific housing must contact the Academic Resource Center, at 202-687-8354. Single rooms are only available for juniors and seniors. Junior transfer students may request (B) [to add / to be added] to the wait-list for single rooms by contacting the Office of Residential Living for more information. Only juniors and seniors are permitted to live in university-owned townhouses. You should fill out a Living Preference Questionnaire (LPQ), which will be used to (C) [match / matching] you with other students who have similar preferences.

*exemption: 면제, 감면

	(A)		(B)		(C)
①	require	—	to add	—	match
②	require	—	to be added	—	matching
③	are required	—	to add	—	match
④	are required	—	to be added	—	match
⑤	are required	—	to be added	—	matching

023 다음 글의 밑줄 친 부분 중, 어법상 틀린 것은?

Tuberculosis (TB) is an ancient disease that ① has affected mankind for more than 4,000 years. It is a chronic disease caused by the bacillus Mycobacterium tuberculosis and ② spreads from person to person through air. The association between poverty and TB is well-recognized, and the highest rates of TB are found in the poorest sections of a community. TB ③ occurs more frequently among low-income people living in overcrowded areas and persons with ④ little schooling. Poverty may result in poor nutrition, which may be associated with alterations in immune function. At the same time, poverty resulting in overcrowded living conditions, poor ventilation, and poor hygiene habits ⑤ are likely to increase the risk of transmission of TB. The knowledge, attitudes, and practices regarding tuberculosis also play a critical role in the prevalence of the disease among the poor.

*bacillus: 대장균
**Mycobacterium tuberculosis: 마이코 박테리아 결핵균

024 다음 글의 밑줄 친 부분 중, 어법상 틀린 것은?

Mentors provide the knowledge we are missing, open doors to new connections, and impart philosophies we otherwise ① would have had to wait years to learn. Companies don't invest in that model anymore, which is why almost every job listing these days ② is required the applicant to "take initiative." It really means, "I don't want to have to hold your hand," which in itself means, "I don't have the time/energy available to teach you." While this can put new hires in a sink-or-swim situation, the new generation ③ has been built to handle it. Millennials are more self-sufficient than their bosses might assume; after all, we ④ did grow up with Internet search engines and Google tools at our fingertips. Just as most of us would balk at the idea of an arranged marriage, there are no arranged mentorships waiting ⑤ patiently for you. In the modern world, mentors aren't given; they're made.

*balk at: ~을 꺼리다, ~을 망설이다

09 핵심 예상문제

권장 시간 4분 | 시작·종료 시간 | : ~ : | 나의 소요 시간 | 분 초

025 (A), (B), (C)의 각 네모 안에서 어법에 맞는 표현으로 가장 적절한 것은?

Our flight landed at midnight. We called for a shuttle and were told it would be a 20-minute wait. At 1 a.m., the shuttle still hadn't arrived. We were traveling as a group of ten, including some young children. We called the hotel again, but no one answered. I had to let it (A) [ring / to ring] 32 times. Wow! We were then told that the shuttle had looked for us but had been unable to find us, and that the driver was now off shift and no shuttle was available. That's weird because we stood for an hour at the designated spot that they (B) [had chosen / had been chosen]. So we were told, very impolitely, to take a cab. Seriously! So, we grabbed a couple of cabs. The hotel was (C) [close / closely], but it was still $12 for each cab—not a big deal. The hotel reception was obviously not designed for customer service.

	(A)		(B)		(C)
①	ring	—	had chosen	—	close
②	ring	—	had been chosen	—	close
③	to ring	—	had chosen	—	close
④	to ring	—	had chosen	—	closely
⑤	to ring	—	had been chosen	—	closely

026 다음 글의 밑줄 친 부분 중, 어법상 틀린 것은?

We tend to associate trolling—online harassment—with celebrities, journalists, and anyone who dares to share strong views online. But trolling doesn't just affect people in the public eye—some of ① its victims haven't even left school yet. "Trolling can take a variety of different forms," explains an expert. "It can be ② sending threatening messages, creating and sharing images, or hacking people's accounts and using their names to embarrass them." Trolling can occur on platforms where teens feel comfortable such as Facebook and Instagram, where they can receive nasty comments on photographs they've posted. The problem is ingrained in social media use itself. Children are so used to ③ see celebrities and high-profile people ④ being trolled online that they're simply mimicking what they've come to view as normal. "Children are following the celebrities and seeing the messages they're getting, while also falling victim to the 'bystander effect,' ⑤ where people post comments and 'likes' on hateful content without really thinking about what they're doing."

*trolling: 인터넷에서 화를 부추기는 메시지; 돌림 노래 부르기
**ingrained: 뿌리 깊은, 몸에 밴

027 다음 글의 밑줄 친 부분 중, 어법상 틀린 것은?

All flying objects, from rockets to airplanes to birds, have something in common—they need to remain ① stable when they fly. You may have noticed that rockets and missiles usually have triangular fins at their bases. What purpose do these fins ② serve? Let's say you made a rocket with no fins at the base. It flew straight at first but quickly spiraled out of control. It might have tumbled through the air and fluttered to the ground, almost like a leaf ③ falling from a tree. If it started turning just a little bit, then it would start turning even more rapidly until it completely lost control. In contrast, your second rocket that had fins should have flown straight, and traveled much ④ far as a result. This is because the fins help ⑤ keep the rocket stable, or pointed in the same direction. If the rocket turns a little bit, the fins help turn it back in the original direction.

028 다음 글의 밑줄 친 부분 중, 어법상 틀린 것은?

A new analysis found various factors that ① put older adults at risk of developing serious memory problems in old age. The participants were given regular memory tests, ② as well as mental health assessments, over a period of about five years. The researchers looked for signs of mild cognitive impairment, or MCI, a form of memory loss that can precede the onset of Alzheimer's and other forms of dementia. The researchers also combed the participants' medical charts for ③ other factors that may heighten dementia risk. After analyzing the data, the researchers identified a list of factors that increase the risk of developing mild cognitive impairment, and ④ were assigned each of the factors a score based on how much they contributed to the risk of developing thinking problems. This risk scale is expected to be an inexpensive and easy way ⑤ for doctors to identify people who should undergo more advanced testing for memory issues.

*cognitive impairment: 인지력 손상
**Alzheimer: 노인성 치매
***dementia: 치매

029 다음 글의 밑줄 친 부분 중, 어법상 틀린 것은?

Life is all a bit of a gamble. It's like deciding whether or not to buy 'collision insurance' on a rental car. In many cases, you probably won't need it; but you never know what ① will happen. Once I took a trip to Spain and Morocco with a girlfriend. Spain felt ② safe, but what about Morocco? We knew nothing about medical practices there or of crime and this 'lack of knowing', in our minds, ③ equating a bit of danger. Getting travel insurance seemed smart and my intuition agreed. I didn't regret it. On our first day in Morocco, our luggage didn't arrive with us. We didn't know when or where our bags would arrive and we'd even get 'false alarm' notifications ④ to show up at the airport and find ... no bags. Finally, two days before we left, we got our belongings back. My bag was intact, but my girlfriend's jewelry was stolen. ⑤ Thankfully, we were insured.

*intact: 손상이 안 된, 그대로의

030 다음 글의 밑줄 친 부분 중, 어법상 틀린 것은?

A *fallacy* is an error in ① reasoning, usually based on mistaken assumptions. Researchers are very familiar with all the ② ways they could go wrong —with the fallacies they are susceptible to. Two of the most common are the *ecological fallacy* and the *exception fallacy*. The *ecological fallacy* occurs when you make conclusions about individuals based only on analyses of group data. For instance, ③ assuming that you measured the math scores of a particular classroom and found that they had the highest average score in the district. Later (probably at the mall) you run into one of the kids from that class and you think to yourself, "She ④ must be a math whiz." The *exception fallacy* is sort of the reverse of the *ecological fallacy*. It occurs when you reach a group conclusion on the basis of exceptional cases. The stereotype is of the guy who sees a woman make a driving error and ⑤ concludes that "women are terrible drivers."

11 핵심 예상문제

권장 시간 4분 | 시작·종료 시간 | : ~ : | 나의 소요 시간 | 분 초

031 (A), (B), (C)의 각 네모 안에서 어법에 맞는 표현으로 가장 적절한 것은?

A new study showed that artificial sweeteners (A) [alter / altering] the microbiome, the population of bacteria that is in the digestive system. In a set of experiments, the scientists added saccharin, an artificial sweetener, to the drinking water of 10-week-old mice. Other mice drank plain water or water supplemented with glucose or with ordinary table sugar. After a week, there was little change in the mice that drank water or sugar water, but the group getting artificial sweeteners developed marked intolerance to glucose. (B) [That / What] is scary about this is that glucose intolerance, in which the body is less able to cope with large amounts of sugar, can lead to more serious illnesses like metabolic syndrome and diabetes. Nothing is as (C) [sweet / sweetly] as a healthy child, so let's all lay off the artificial sweeteners.

*microbiome: 미생물 군집, 미생물군 유전체
**saccharin: 사카린(설탕 대체재로 알려진 인공 감미료)
***glucose: 포도당

	(A)		(B)		(C)
①	alter	—	That	—	sweet
②	alter	—	That	—	sweetly
③	alter	—	What	—	sweet
④	altering	—	That	—	sweet
⑤	altering	—	What	—	sweetly

032 다음 글의 밑줄 친 부분 중, 어법상 틀린 것은?

An armed prisoner was on the run early Tuesday after escaping from a hospital in northern Virginia close to the city of Washington, ① where a shot was fired during a struggle with a guard, police said. The prisoner, identified as Wossen Assaye by the Fairfax County Police Department, broke ② freely from a private security guard at the hospital, and fled with the guard's weapon, the department said via Twitter. Police said he was thought ③ to be driving a stolen car identified as a 2002 Toyota Camry with damage to the front and the license plate number XZP-8153. They also said Assaye might be with his girlfriend, whose photo was posted on Twitter but who was not named. Assaye ④ had been held by the nearby city of Alexandria on charges of armed bank robbery and ⑤ was taken to a local hospital after he tried to harm himself, according to police.

033 다음 글의 밑줄 친 부분 중, 어법상 틀린 것은?

When I was a teenager, I was never able to relate to the kinds of heroes that were completely pure of heart. They always know ① what the right thing to do is. And it is so easy for them to do it. I was not attracted to them because, as a young adult, I had to struggle with the idea of right versus wrong. In fact, I was able to relate ② better to heroes who had flaws and who had a more difficult time making the right choices. It seems that I thought, "There's a guy that's similar to me." They are exactly ③ who I would be. I like the fact that my favorite anti-hero characters, while flawed, ④ is able to achieve glory and greatness for themselves and for others around them. The hero that is pure of heart, on the other hand, sends the message ⑤ that only those who are perfect can achieve greatness.

12 핵심 예상문제

권장 시간 4분

시작·종료 시간 | : ~ :
나의 소요 시간 | 분 초

034 (A), (B), (C)의 각 네모 안에서 어법에 맞는 표현으로 가장 적절한 것은?

Rap is a complex mix of influences, including elements of speech, prose, poetry, and song. In order to be a great rapper, you need to understand "rhythm." Rapping is about more than saying something that (A) [rhyme / rhymes]. If you want to rap, you'll have to get a feel for the music in your bones. If your brain and body are not (B) [conscious / consciously] in tune with the beat, your rap will feel stiff and unnatural. To improve in this area, try to ignore the words when listening to some rap that you like. Just listen to the instrumental, and how the flow of the words seems to fit into the beat. You can also consider beatboxing as a tool for learning rhythm—not only (C) [this will / will this] help you understand rhythm, but it will be a useful technique once you start rapping yourself.

(A)		(B)		(C)
① rhyme	—	conscious	—	this will
② rhyme	—	consciously	—	this will
③ rhyme	—	consciously	—	will this
④ rhymes	—	conscious	—	will this
⑤ rhymes	—	consciously	—	will this

035 다음 글의 밑줄 친 부분 중, 어법상 틀린 것은?

One day Toad loses a button while out walking and ① leading his friend Frog through a fruitless, frustrating search—retracing the steps of an earlier journey—before discovering that the button was at home. Embarrassed, he makes a special jacket for Frog ② decorated with all the buttons they gathered along the way. This is a story I told my four-year-old students in Sunday school. I remember many of them carried that story with them through the days after hearing it. The story is far from simple in ③ its meaning, even though the words are simple. For the students, it ④ may have raised significant questions about what it means to be a loyal and caring friend, even if these questions were too difficult for their young minds to clearly formulate. Even at that age, they had the ⑤ thirst as well as the capacity to reach for illumination and insight. That's how deep reading begins.

036 다음 글의 밑줄 친 부분 중, 어법상 틀린 것은?

① Imagining you're sitting in a boat on a rolling ocean. As the waves pass under you, the boat gently lifts up and down in the water. Now, suppose that the boat is speeding across the water. Are the waves travelling ② any faster? No, not really. But you will notice a change. As you travel through the water you will ride over more waves more often. This is to say that (from your new perspective) the wave's "frequency" ③ has increased. Light is also a wave. So when you run towards a "light wave," its frequency will also increase. Running away from a "light wave" will decrease its frequency. At everyday speeds, you won't notice ④ anything, but (since your eyes interpret the frequency of light as color) running actually changes the color of the objects around you (though the change is too small ⑤ to be detected). Astronomers observe this phenomenon all the time; stars traveling towards us appear more blue (higher frequency) while stars traveling away from us appear more red (lower frequency).

13 핵심 예상문제

권장 시간 4분 | 시작·종료 시간 | : ~ : | 나의 소요 시간 | 분 초

037 (A), (B), (C)의 각 네모 안에서 어법에 맞는 표현으로 가장 적절한 것은?

Writing Center tutoring sessions are an opportunity for you to receive feedback and guidance from an experienced writer. Your tutor will be a graduate or undergraduate student who has experience (A) [help / helping] students from a range of disciplines. You can expect your session to be collaborative: consider your tutor a writing coach who can offer insight into the specific project you are (B) [working / working on], as well as strategies to help you develop your writing skills overall. To make an appointment, you will need to register for an account. After you have an account, you can just log in. You will be able to schedule appointments online by clicking on one of the white squares in the schedule. Please remember (C) [to bring / bringing] a copy of the assignment, the instructor's grading criteria, and a draft of your paper to the tutoring session.

	(A)		(B)		(C)
①	help	—	working	—	to bring
②	help	—	working on	—	bringing
③	helping	—	working	—	to bring
④	helping	—	working on	—	to bring
⑤	helping	—	working on	—	bringing

038 다음 글의 밑줄 친 부분 중, 어법상 틀린 것은?

In a research study, one group of students was told that each time they ① faced with a temptation, they would tell themselves, "I can't do X," while the second group were told to say, "I don't do X." For example, ② when tempted with ice cream, they would say, "I can't eat ice cream," and "I don't eat ice cream," respectively. After repeating these phrases, each student answered a set of questions unrelated to the study. As each student walked out of the room and handed in their answer sheet, they were offered a complimentary treat. The student could choose ③ between a chocolate candy bar and a granola health bar. Their snack choices showed a striking gap, with the first group ④ choosing the chocolate candy bar 61% of the time, and the second group only 36% of the time. Indeed, your words help ⑤ to frame your sense of empowerment and control.

*granola health bar: 그래놀라 바 (볶은 곡물, 견과류 등을 넣어 만든 바 모양의 아침 식사용 건강식품)

039 다음 글의 밑줄 친 부분 중, 어법상 틀린 것은?

Fog may make everything look ① a little prettier and more autumnal, but it can be a hazard if you're driving or cycling. According to the Highway Code, you have to use headlights when visibility is 'seriously reduced'—generally defined as less than 100 meters. The general guidance for driving in fog is common sense—take your time, keep a generous distance ② between yourself and the car in front, and keep your front and rear fog lights on. You should be aware of how to operate your fog lights, and take care ③ not to rely too much on automatic lighting—if you have this feature in your car, your lights might not come on during the day, ④ putting you and other drivers at risk. Staying as ⑤ visibly as possible and taking it easy should help keep you safe.

14 핵심 예상문제

권장 시간 4분 시작·종료 시간 | : ~ : 나의 소요 시간 | 분 초

040 (A), (B), (C)의 각 네모 안에서 어법에 맞는 표현으로 가장 적절한 것은?

Tim Berners-Lee is not extremely rich or famous like Bill Gates. He could (A) [be / have been], but he didn't want to be. He is a quiet man who does not like the spotlight. He is the man who invented the World Wide Web and revolutionized the Internet. Berners-Lee's invention permits anyone with a computer to (B) [easy / easily] access a vast amount of information on any subject. This is a great contribution to the use of computers and to society. Some people believe it is no less (C) [important / importantly] than Gutenberg's printing press.

	(A)		(B)		(C)
①	be	—	easy	—	importantly
②	have been	—	easily	—	important
③	have been	—	easy	—	importantly
④	have been	—	easy	—	important
⑤	be	—	easily	—	important

041 다음 글의 밑줄 친 부분 중, 어법상 틀린 것은?

Good news for supermarkets: ① Despite the boom in online grocery shopping options, brick-and-mortar stores are not going to disappear. A new survey from Nielsen found that while a quarter of global respondents are using online grocery ordering and 55% are willing to use it down the road, 61% reported that they still find grocery shopping at the store to be an "enjoyable and ② engaging experience." Nearly ③ as much—57%—said that retail grocery shopping is a "fun day out for the family." While online grocery shopping is positioned to grow, actual stores still serve an important purpose. Besides ④ providing a "fun day out for the family," some foods are just better suited for buying in-person, like fresh and frozen foods, beverages, and other immediate-use items, the study found. As anyone who has ordered produce online has likely experienced, it's rare that someone else ⑤ can be trusted to pick your fruit.

042 다음 글의 밑줄 친 부분 중, 어법상 틀린 것은?

Businesses that sell food will be affected by a new law. "The new food act aims to modernize and simplify food safety procedures. It will also help businesses keep costs down. For example, those who manage food safety ① well will need less-frequent checks," says Helen Jones, Wellington City Council's public health manager. Under the new law, business owners will face a change in inspection regimes and will be required to keep their own records on how they are producing ② safely and suitable food and show ③ these to inspectors when they visit. Changes will be implemented by way of a food control plan (higher-risk foods—*e.g.* restaurants, cafes, caterers, hotels) or compliance with national program requirements (lower-risk—for example, home-made biscuits at a coffee cart). She says the new law is designed to help businesses and consumers by ④ moving from a one-size-fits-all approach, to ⑤ one that regulates businesses according to risk.

*caterer: 음식 공급업자, 출장 뷔페 업자

15 핵심 예상문제

권장 시간 4분

시작·종료 시간 | : ~ :
나의 소요 시간 | 분 초

043 다음 글의 밑줄 친 부분 중, 어법상 틀린 것은?

Most writers are world-class procrastinators. Writing is hard, so we ① put it off. But not all procrastination is to avoid writing. Some is to let the ideas soak in. Sometimes we need to literally sleep on it. I, of course, am a master at letting ideas marinate. I've been known ② to wait ten years or more before ③ putting pen to paper on an idea. Still, I do have a secret trick for getting started. First, write a single sentence on a card or slip of paper—"He called me this morning."—and then carry it with you for at least one day. Put it in your pocket. Let your mind ④ return to your sentence throughout the day. Take it out and look at it a few times. And as ideas come to you, write them down. And then, the following day, or later in the week, sit down with your sentence and your thoughts and write about what ⑤ you've been thought.

*marinate: 무언가를 오래 생각하다; 양념에 재워두다

044 다음 글의 밑줄 친 부분 중, 어법상 틀린 것은?

Smartphones, tablets and other devices can be very ① handy at school. Curious about something the teacher said? A quick Internet search can turn up more facts. Want to prepare charts and present top-notch class reports? As the saying goes, "There's an app for that." But this can also undermine your attention ② significantly. The problem is ③ that's just too easy to open the texting screen or some app. Whenever they let their guard down, students quickly—and without thinking—log onto Facebook to check their notifications. What can be done about this? "Try to avoid ④ splitting your attention between what's going on in class and ⑤ whatever you might feel a need to do with your mobile device," advises an expert. "A good way to avoid this is to turn your cellphone or tablet off, or at least put it in airplane mode. Then you won't wind up checking texts or using social media sites without thinking."

*top-notch: 최고의, 아주 뛰어난

045 다음 글의 밑줄 친 부분 중, 어법상 틀린 것은?

Teenagers get stuck deciding what course to study at university, ① scared they'll make the wrong choice. "Try not to stress too much about what you study," says a counselor. "Steve Jobs studied calligraphy, and ended up building Apple." The lesson? Your choice of degree now ② doesn't have to define your future. As he notes, "③ Much of the jobs that will be available to a person when they are 23 are not even invented when they are 18." Often the skills you develop through your degree—be that critical thinking or public speaking—will become almost as ④ important as the subject itself. So whatever you decide to study, delight in it. You are unlikely to ever have the opportunity again to spend so much time exploring the knowledge available to the human race. It's a wonderful time to sculpt who you are as a person—your worldview, values and purpose. Study ⑤ to do that and the rest of your career will work itself out just fine.

*calligraphy: 서예

16 핵심 예상문제

권장 시간 4분

시작·종료 시간 | : ~ :
나의 소요 시간 | 분 초

046 (A), (B), (C)의 각 네모 안에서 어법에 맞는 표현으로 가장 적절한 것은?

Why is it better to wash dishes in hot water rather than cold? There are two reasons. First, hot water softens any bits of food stuck to the dishes and melts any fat, which makes (A) [it / them] easier for the surfactants in the dishwashing detergent to do their job. Surfactants are chemicals that attach solids and fat molecules to water molecules, so they can be easily rinsed off the dish. It's very hard, if not impossible, to properly clean a greasy or oily plate without using detergent and hot water. Without detergent, you're going to (B) [leave / be left] with a still-greasy dish. Second, rinsing dishes with very hot water (C) [get / gets] rid of the film of soapy dishwater that is left behind after washing. Hot water eliminates soapy residue that creates puddles on dishes. These puddles cause unattractive spots when the water evaporates.

*surfactant: 계면 활성제

	(A)		(B)		(C)
①	it	—	leave	—	get
②	it	—	be left	—	get
③	it	—	be left	—	gets
④	them	—	leave	—	get
⑤	them	—	be left	—	gets

047 다음 글의 밑줄 친 부분 중, 어법상 틀린 것은?

A study has found that the stick is ① far more effective than the carrot when it comes to motivation. A marketing professor gave his two consumer behavior classes optional quizzes: if they did ② well, they scored a point. But if they did badly, they lost ③ one. He then proceeded by ④ divide the classes into two groups: In the first class, the students were told that the final exam was required but that they could earn the right not to take it with five points from the quizzes. In the second class, however, they were told that the final exam was optional, but that they could lose the right if they did not get five points from the quizzes. The result? The second class was far more engaged with the idea of "giving up" their right not to sit the exam. This finding supports the idea ⑤ that our dislike of losing something is stronger than our pleasure at gaining something.

048 다음 글의 밑줄 친 부분 중, 어법상 틀린 것은?

Being infected with a parasite is usually not good news. When an animal has to deal with ① both a parasite and pollutants such as toxic heavy metals, the stressors may add up. But that isn't true for Artemia brine shrimp in Spain, a new study finds. A research team collected shrimp from an area ② which is tainted with arsenic and other heavy metals, separated the parasite-infected and uninfected brine shrimp and then ran tests to see how ③ well they survived in arsenic-laced waters. As the concentration of arsenic in the water increased, so ④ was the number of brine shrimp that died. But more brine shrimp that were infected survived than uninfected ones. It may not be obvious, but causing a quick death is not a good strategy for a parasite. That's because a parasite needs its host to stay alive long enough for the parasite to reproduce, leave and find a new host. This results in the parasite ⑤ providing assistance when conditions become harsh enough.

*parasite: 기생충
**Artemia brine shrimp: 아르테미아 브라인 슈림프 (사육하는 바닷물고기의 먹이로 이용하는 작은 새우)
***arsenic: 비소(중금속의 일종)

17 핵심 예상문제

권장 시간 4분

시작·종료 시간 | : ~ :
나의 소요 시간 | 분 초

049 (A), (B), (C)의 각 네모 안에서 어법에 맞는 표현으로 가장 적절한 것은?

It requires a huge amount of force (A) [launched / to launch] a spacecraft out of the atmosphere and into orbit around Earth. It requires even more energy to leave Earth's orbit and go out into space. The Saturn V rocket (B) [used / was used] in the Apollo missions to the moon had to create a huge push, or thrust, to put itself into orbit and beyond. The rocket needed so much energy (C) [that / which] fuel alone made up 90% of the weight of the rocket at liftoff. Orbiting Earth required Apollo 11 to travel at more than 25,000 feet per second. To break out of orbit and get to the moon, the craft had to accelerate to more than 35,000 feet per second.

	(A)		(B)		(C)
①	launched	—	used	—	which
②	launched	—	was used	—	that
③	to launch	—	used	—	which
④	to launch	—	was used	—	that
⑤	to launch	—	used	—	that

050 다음 글의 밑줄 친 부분 중, 어법상 틀린 것은?

Did Harvard University student Mark Zuckerberg set out to build a billion-dollar company with more than six hundred million active users? Not hardly. As shown in the 2010 movie *The Social Network*, Zuckerberg's original concept in 2003 had a dark nature. After being dumped by his girlfriend, a bitter Zuckerberg created a website called "FaceMash" ① where the attractiveness of young women could be voted on. This evolved first into an online social network called Thefacebook that was for Harvard students only. When the network became ② surprisingly popular, it then morphed into Facebook, a website open to everyone. Facebook is so pervasive today ③ that it has changed the way we speak, such as the word "friend" ④ being used as a verb. Ironically, Facebook's emphasis on connecting with existing and new friends is about as ⑤ differently as it could be from Zuckerberg's original mean-spirited concept. Certainly, Zuckerberg's later strategies turned out to be far nobler than the intended strategy that began his adventure in entrepreneurship.

*morph: 모핑되다(컴퓨터 동영상을 이용하여 이미지가 자연스럽게 변하다)

051 다음 글의 밑줄 친 부분 중, 어법상 틀린 것은?

Students ① entering college shouldn't bet on today's job market. They should bet on the job market five to ten years from now. And what the job market is going to require ② are skill—not a degree. Fortunately, learning a skill has never been so easy. There are plenty of places to learn skills online for free or cheap. This is true whether it's learning how to program, trade stocks, use Excel, design—the list goes on. The best way to prep for a career is not to sit in a lecture hall for three hours ③ listening to something you're not truly passionate about. It's ④ to do it on your own. In this economy, businesses don't have the time or capital to train you to become employable. To differentiate ⑤ yourself, you have to learn in-demand skills—a framed degree doesn't get you very far anymore.

18 핵심 예상문제

권장 시간 4분

시작·종료 시간 | : ~ :
나의 소요 시간 | 분 초

052 (A), (B), (C)의 각 네모 안에서 어법에 맞는 표현으로 가장 적절한 것은?

Since ancient times, people have known that certain plants can treat disease or stop pain. They discovered these treatments through trial and error. This valuable information was passed down from generation to generation. Even today, companies that make drugs (A) [both / either] raise the traditional plants to extract the healing substances or study the plants and copy the chemical substances in laboratories. At least 25% of all the drugs prescribed by doctors today still (B) [use / uses] extracts that come from plants. For instance, the common drug, digitalin, (C) [made / is made] from the leaves of the foxglove plant and continues to help people with heart problems. New plants with healing properties are still being discovered in unexplored places like rainforests.

*digitalin: 디기탈린(심장질환약의 일종)
*foxglove: ((식물)) 디기탈리스

	(A)		(B)		(C)
①	both	—	use	—	made
②	both	—	use	—	is made
③	either	—	uses	—	is made
④	both	—	uses	—	made
⑤	either	—	use	—	is made

053 다음 글의 밑줄 친 부분 중, 어법상 틀린 것은?

This was an excellent hotel. I ① could not have asked more for my dollar. I got this hotel on an "early purchase" deal, ② where I got a king suite at a discounted rate. The mattress was comfortable, the room cooled down quickly, the shower water warmed up fast and it had plenty of sleeping room. It felt ③ safely, clean and well managed. They didn't charge my card until I showed up (just in case we couldn't make the reservation) and they still gave us the discounted rate. The free hotel shuttle picked us up within minutes of our call and the continental breakfast was ④ of great quality. It was more than just cold cereal, coffee, and a bag of fruit to choose from. Overall, I was very impressed with this hotel. This was well worth more than ⑤ what I paid, and it exceeded my expectations.

*continental breakfast: 유럽식 아침 식사(격식을 중요시하는 영국인의 아침 식사와 대비하여 빵과 뜨거운 차 한 잔의 간단한 아침 식사를 뜻함)

054 다음 글의 밑줄 친 부분 중, 어법상 틀린 것은?

It is the year 2023, and for the first time, a self-driving car navigating city streets ① is struck and kills a pedestrian. A lawsuit is sure to follow. But exactly what laws will apply? Nobody knows. Today, the law is struggling to keep up with the technology, ② which is moving forward at a breakneck pace, thanks to efforts by Apple, Audi, BMW, Google, etc. The law now assumes that a human being is in the driver's seat, which makes the vehicles street legal for now, but it doesn't help ③ speed the launch of fully autonomous vehicles. We can't put off ④ changing the laws until the advent of robotic driving, because today's laws leave a lot of room for uncertainty, and uncertainty discourages progress. A car company can't be expected ⑤ to invest in putting out a new fleet of autonomous cars when it could be forced to pull them all off the road after the first accident.

19 핵심 예상문제

권장 시간 4분

시작·종료 시간 | : ~ :
나의 소요 시간 | 분 초

055 다음 글의 밑줄 친 부분 중, 어법상 틀린 것은?

When I was a kid, I knew what the worst parts of me ① were. My hair was nappy. My lips were big. Nearly every kid around me knew something similar of ② themselves—dark skin, nappy hair, broad nose, full lips—③ that opened them up to ridicule from others. So did we want to be white? I don't think so. We didn't want to look like Madonna. We hated and mocked Michael Jackson's aesthetic changes as ④ vicious as we mocked each other. What we wanted was to be on the "right" end of the paper bag tests. We wanted hazel eyes. We wanted wavy hair. I had neither hazel eyes nor wavy hair. Still I didn't suffer in the same way that I saw other kids around me ⑤ suffer. It's because I was not dark-skinned. And, more importantly, I was not a girl. Boys had some ways of climbing the social ladder—humor, or a reputation for violence—that were unavailable to girls.

*nappy: (머리털이) 곱슬곱슬한, 보풀이 인
**paper bag tests: 흑인을 파티 등 사람들이 모이는 장소에 출입을 허용할 것인지를 정하는 데 사용된 갈색 종이가방(이 종이가방 색보다 피부가 짙으면 출입을 금하였다 함)

056 다음 글의 밑줄 친 부분 중, 어법상 틀린 것은?

There's no doubt about it: I'm a chocoholic. Some days, it's the only thing that will really get me through ① that mid-afternoon slump. I bet I'm not the only one that benefits from that dark magic stuff. A little chocolate treat can instantly make you feel more energized, ② more happily, and now, even healthier. Yes, there's good news for people like me. Chocolatiers are now combining heart-healthy dark chocolate with superfoods, herbal extracts and other mind/body-boosting ingredients ③ using artisanal precision. The result is a delicious guilt-free treat that not only ④ satisfies your sweet tooth, but can also help lift you out of a slump, boost your immune system, fire up your antioxidant levels, reduce the day's stress load and put a smile on your face. Why not stock up on ⑤ a few today?

*superfood: 슈퍼푸드(활성산소들을 제거하고 체내에서 필요로 하는 영양소를 많이 함유하고 있는 웰빙 식품)
**antioxidant: 항산화(제), 산화 방지(제)

057 다음 글의 밑줄 친 부분 중, 어법상 틀린 것은?

The idea that children are ① inherently better language learners than adults is turning out to be a myth. New research cannot find a direct link between age and the ability to learn. The key to ② learning as quickly as a child may be to simply take on certain childlike attitudes: for instance, lack of self-consciousness, a desire to play in the language and willingness to make mistakes. As kids, we are expected to make mistakes, but as adults mistakes become taboo. Think ③ how an adult is more likely to say, "I can't," rather than, "I haven't learned that yet" (I can't swim, I can't drive, I can't speak Spanish). To be seen ④ failing (or merely struggling) is a social taboo that doesn't burden children. When it comes to learning a language, ⑤ admit that you don't know everything (and being okay with that) is the key to growth and freedom. Let go of your grown-up inhibitions!

*inhibition: 억제, 억압, 금지

20 핵심 예상문제

권장 시간 4분

시작·종료 시간	: ~ :
나의 소요 시간	분 초

058 (A), (B), (C)의 각 네모 안에서 어법에 맞는 표현으로 가장 적절한 것은?

People have adapted to living at high altitudes where there is less than two-thirds the oxygen available at sea level. So far scientists have discovered several groups of people with different responses to (A) [live / living] at these heights. For instance, native Andeans in South America have relatively large lungs with more surface area. This means that they can take in oxygen more quickly (B) [to / than] get it into their blood. Tibetans in the Himalayas don't have larger lungs, but they tend to breathe more quickly. They can live with less oxygen in their blood. They have a (C) [normal / normally] red blood cell count, but have not yet been tested to see if they have a higher flow of blood.

*red blood cell: 적혈구

	(A)		(B)		(C)
①	live	—	to	—	normal
②	live	—	than	—	normally
③	living	—	to	—	normally
④	living	—	than	—	normally
⑤	living	—	to	—	normal

059 다음 글의 밑줄 친 부분 중, 어법상 틀린 것은?

The compact car is back and better than ever. First ① released in the U.S. in 1950, these vehicles with 100+ inch wheelbases now have all the technological advances, comforts, safety features, performance enhancements, and style of much ② larger and more expensive vehicles. Two reasons many people choose compact cars are a low price and great gas mileage. The Nissan Sentra—one of the compact cars that is making a splash—offers ③ either of these. It gets an average of almost 30 miles per gallon in the city and as ④ many as 40 miles per gallon on the highway. Plus, it costs under $20,000. Add a 1.8 liter, 4-cylinder engine that delivers 130 horsepower, a 6-speed manual transmission, and seating for 5, and the Sentra compares quite ⑤ nicely with other vehicles in its class.

*make a splash: 큰 인기를 끌다, 대 성공을 거두다

060 다음 글의 밑줄 친 부분 중, 어법상 틀린 것은?

It's a busy morning. You drop by a ① nearby dry cleaner's and hand over your clothes, believing that you'll get new fresh garments again. "Dry cleaners are not mind readers, and they're not perfect," a man who ran a high-end dry-cleaning company for 16 years ② cautions. Every dry cleaner will treat your garment a little differently. Some will inspect it thoroughly, others won't. Some read labels, some ③ are not. To get the best care, read your labels beforehand, make sure the dry cleaner ④ is aware of the fabrication, and point out any issues (especially stains) you need him to focus on. There's also the issue of how to interpret the label itself. "Dry clean" and "dry clean only" are quite different. For the label "dry clean," consider: Is it valuable? Could it fade or shrink? Does it have oily stains? If you answer yes to ⑤ any of these, take it to a dry cleaner.

PART 2

실 전 편

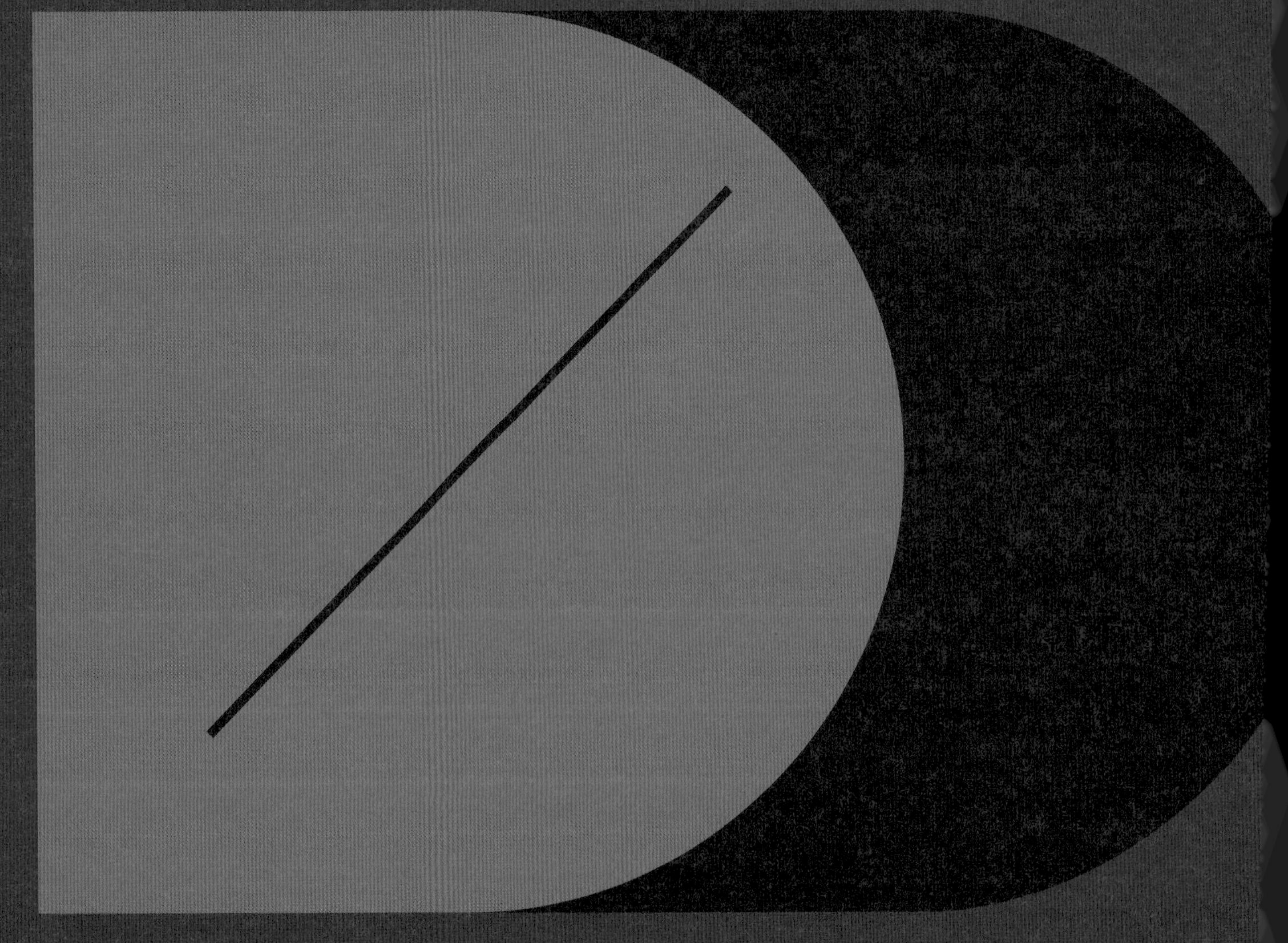

실전 모의고사 33회
고난도 모의고사 5회

061 다음 글의 밑줄 친 부분 중, 어법상 틀린 것은?

German researchers ① have identified a previously unknown source of methane, a potent greenhouse gas. The culprit: ordinary plants. The European Space Agency's ENVISAT satellite detected huge clouds of methane over forested areas, and scientists were confused. They thought methane ② was produced only in oxygen-poor environments like swamps where decomposition occurs. In experiments, scientists were amazed ③ to see chemical sensors detecting methane when a variety of plants were placed in a room originally filled with methane-free air. Higher heat seems to increase the rate at ④ that plants produce methane, which could explain why levels of methane were high hundreds of thousands of years ago ⑤ when global temperatures were warmer.

062 다음 글의 밑줄 친 부분 중, 어법상 틀린 것은?

Westward movement marked the early centuries of America's history. To the west ① lay freedom and the opportunity for a better life for diverse groups in diverse times: the Pilgrims and Puritans in the seventeenth century; the frontiersmen in the eighteenth century; and the pioneers, prospectors, and politicians in the nineteenth century. The Pilgrims moved west across the Atlantic Ocean in a dangerous voyage on the Mayflower. ② Their Mayflower Compact, which established a "Civil Body Politic," was the first self-government in the New World. Closely behind them came the Puritans, ③ that also sought religious freedom. The discovery of gold at John Sutter's mill in 1848 unleashed an epidemic of gold fever and a rush westward to California. In the first three centuries of America's history, the land seemed limitless, as ④ did the opportunities for freedom and a better life for ⑤ anyone who had the courage, conviction, and strength to move westward.

*Mayflower Compact: 메이플라워 맹약(1620년 11월 11일 메이플라워호 위에서 청교도들에 의해 맺어진 정부 수립의 맹약)

063 다음 글의 밑줄 친 부분 중, 어법상 틀린 것은?

My family frequently takes weekend trips, and my son Jesse, six, especially likes to go to places ① where he can learn about history and nature. Like most children, he always asks for something from the souvenir shops at the places we visit. At first, I would give in, thinking the souvenir could be something he would keep ② remembering the trip, but Jesse would lose interest in the item soon after we returned home. Then, I started to notice that almost every museum store, national park, and tourist attraction ③ sold emblem patches for a few dollars. Now Jesse collects patches, ④ which I attach to his travel vest. The vest makes ⑤ frequent show-and-tell appearances at school. By having the patches, Jesse remembers the place, not just the toy, and he is now popular at school for his detailed stories about his travel adventures.

*show-and-tell: 각자 물건을 가져와서 발표하기

064 다음 글의 밑줄 친 부분 중, 어법상 틀린 것은?

If there are no community mediation programs or professional mediators available to settle a dispute, one option is to ask an outsider—a friend or acquaintance. This kind of informal mediation is typically the most ① immediately available option when discussions break down. During conflict, people can become frustrated, feel that they are constantly being interrupted, feel that they have repeated ② themselves again and again without being heard, and so on. A third party can assist in guiding people out of this situation by facilitating the conversation, establishing some neutral ground, ensuring that everyone involved ③ having a turn to speak, and reframing what each person says in order to help everyone feel understood. The third party could also meet with each person separately, to try to understand any unspoken feelings that may be ④ affecting the dispute. If a third party is able to understand and empathize with both sides, the dispute is ⑤ much more likely to be resolved.

권장 시간 8분 | 시작·종료 시간 | : ~ : | 나의 소요 시간 | 분 초

065 (A), (B), (C)의 각 네모 안에서 어법에 맞는 표현으로 가장 적절한 것은?

One of the common questions about love is whether it is staccato or legato. That is, when one feels romantic love, does he or she feel it in breaks, with interruptions or changes (staccato), or does one feel it (A) [continuous / continuously], without interruption or change (legato)? Poetry and song seduce one into thinking that love is legato. 'True love' and 'I Love You Truly' are two of the best-known popular songs describing (B) [what / how] love goes on. In reality, however, love is closer to staccato. It is difficult to suppose that one can experience anything without interruption. Sleep interrupts wakefulness, and sleep itself is punctuated by dreams and nightmares. The feeling one has for a lover during wakefulness may be blotted out or intensified by sleep. In (C) [either / both] case, the feeling changes.

*staccato: 스타카토(음을 끊어서 연주)
**legato: 레가토(끊지 않고 이어서 연주)

	(A)		(B)		(C)
①	continuous	—	what	—	either
②	continuous	—	how	—	both
③	continuously	—	how	—	either
④	continuously	—	how	—	both
⑤	continuously	—	what	—	both

066 다음 글의 밑줄 친 부분 중, 어법상 틀린 것은?

Several years ago, my friends instituted a rather unique rule: For thirty minutes after the children get home, they are not allowed in any room in which their parents happen to be. They can play in their rooms or, weather ① permitting, go outside. The parents take this time to unwind and talk as they prepare the evening meal. Until they created the thirty-minute rule, my friends ② had felt obligated to devote themselves to their children throughout the entire evening. The more attention they gave the children, however, the more demanding, self-centered, and disobedient the children became. Now the children have changed so dramatically that few people believe ③ what they were like before. They are independent, secure, happy, mature, and polite. Their parents stopped ④ to give in, which cured the children of their addiction to attention. ⑤ Sticking to this rule, they defied a whole set of "shoulds" that exist in many, if not most, dual-career families.

067 다음 글의 밑줄 친 부분 중, 어법상 틀린 것은?

Scientific studies have shown that plants grow better if they ① are talked to. Since plants don't have sound receptors or nervous systems, it is clear ② that they aren't responding to specific words. The obvious answer is that when you talk, you breathe out carbon dioxide and water vapor which all plants need to grow. Sound waves from your voice also cause plant cells ③ to vibrate. More experiments showed that certain types of sound make plants ④ grow better or worse than normal. Plants exposed to classical music or jazz, for example, ⑤ growing thick, healthy leaves. But plants tested with rock music did very poorly. In fact, the plants began to die because their root development was so terrible.

*receptor: 감각기관

068 다음 글의 밑줄 친 부분 중, 어법상 틀린 것은?

My mom and I were sitting on a bench in Central Park, gently rocking Amelia in the stroller and ① talking about having to gear up to go back to work. On the lawn in front of us, there was a big group of babysitters, with all the kids who were in their care ② were running around. The babysitters were great—running after those who strayed from the group, encouraging them ③ to play different games, helping resolve disputes, feeding them lunch and cradling those who just wanted to snuggle. My mom said, "Go and ask them ④ if they know of any babysitters looking for work." It was a great idea—as the saying goes, birds of the same feather flock together. So that's how I met Sharon, my babysitter. Sharon has been caring for my children now for 10 years. I can't believe that much time has passed, but I ⑤ wouldn't have been able to continue to work and maintain my sanity without her.

*snuggle: (사람에게) 바싹 파고들다, 달라붙다

069 다음 글의 밑줄 친 부분 중, 어법상 틀린 것은?

What is the appropriate response to "You're so pretty"? "Thank you" certainly seems to fall short. "So ① are you" sounds weird if it's a man and somewhat insincere regardless, but no response doesn't feel right, ② too. In other words, how should you accept a compliment about your looks? For starters, "Thank you" might not be as bad as it initially seems if it's said with genuine appreciation. The thing to remember is that this person is most likely ③ complimenting you because he or she wants to get to know you better. Anything you say, so long as it's not rude, will be received ④ favorably. So, while a return compliment certainly isn't required, feel free to offer ⑤ one if you genuinely mean it. Just say whatever you want with earnestness and enjoy the moment. That will be more than enough to eliminate any awkwardness that might follow silence on your part.

070 다음 글의 밑줄 친 부분 중, 어법상 틀린 것은?

Diabetes is reaching epidemic levels in Britain with 235,000 people diagnosed with the condition in the last year, according to a leading charity. The yearly amount spent on diabetes treatment ① being currently equal to 10 percent of the nation's total budget. Experts say around 90 percent of sufferers have type 2, with their weight being the most potent risk factor. This ② devastating illness can lead to heart attacks, stroke, blindness and kidney failure. Yet widespread warnings ③ that people should be eating less and exercising more have failed to stop the shocking escalation of cases. Diabetes UK is now calling on the government to act by restricting food advertisements aimed at children and ④ forcing manufacturers to cut salt, sugar and fat in products. "The majority of sufferers have type 2, which is linked to lifestyle, meaning there are steps that ⑤ can be taken to reduce the number of patients," it says.

권장 시간 8분 | 시작·종료 시간 | : ~ : | 나의 소요 시간 | 분 초

071 (A), (B), (C)의 각 네모 안에서 어법에 맞는 표현으로 가장 적절한 것은?

Today, most people smile when their picture is taken, but look at some of the earliest photographs. You'll see a batch of serious, even frowning faces staring back at you. There are several reasons why early photographic subjects never smiled. For one thing, photography was a serious business back then. Not everyone was (A) [enough lucky / lucky enough] to be in a picture. People expected their photos (B) [to pass / to be passed] on from generation to generation. They wanted to be remembered as serious and dignified. Second, photography was hard work. People had to stay (C) [perfect / perfectly] still for ten or twenty minutes while the camera took the photo. No one can smile that long without moving, which would make the picture come out blurry.

	(A)		(B)		(C)
①	enough lucky	—	to be passed	—	perfect
②	enough lucky	—	to pass	—	perfect
③	lucky enough	—	to be passed	—	perfect
④	lucky enough	—	to pass	—	perfectly
⑤	lucky enough	—	to be passed	—	perfectly

072 (A), (B), (C)의 각 네모 안에서 어법에 맞는 표현으로 가장 적절한 것은?

Do you ever get the feeling that you're being watched? Well, you probably are. Surveillance systems are becoming more sophisticated and wider reaching. One city council in England hired a spy plane to fly over the city to discover (A) [that / which] homes were losing the most heat. The resulting map was posted online, so that residents could see how their homes rated for energy efficiency. And in the United States, a futuristic urban map project to chart the movements of its inhabitants (B) [has / have] been developed by the Massachusetts Institute of Technology. By collecting data from mobile phones and global positioning systems, a map can (C) [produce / be produced] that shows the changing locations of a city's people, buses, taxis, trains, and cars.

	(A)		(B)		(C)
①	that	—	has	—	produce
②	that	—	have	—	be produced
③	which	—	has	—	be produced
④	which	—	has	—	produce
⑤	which	—	have	—	be produced

073 다음 글의 밑줄 친 부분 중, 어법상 틀린 것은?

Because of the way we treat information, not only ① do we occasionally accept inaccurate information, we actually need it. Specifically, inaccurate information can sometimes be an important part of news reporting. While the news media should aim to produce truthful information, it is as important ② that they get the information out quickly. Accurate information too late is of little value in news terms. For example, a journalist covering a train crash ③ is told by the police chief that there are 60 people dead, but the ambulance chief says 58, while the hospital says the number is 59. What should the journalist report? Should he or she say that a number of people were killed, or choose one of the numbers and try to confirm ④ which is right later on? Of course it might be weeks before the final death toll is determined. Most consumers, I suspect, would prefer to know the approximate number rather than wonder ⑤ that range 'a number of deaths' came into.

074 다음 글의 밑줄 친 부분 중, 어법상 틀린 것은?

Why does high humidity make a day feel warmer? Humidity is the moisture in the air, and it affects ① how we feel temperature. When the air is full of moisture, it slows down the evaporation of perspiration (or sweat), ② that our bodies produce to help us cool off. If you ③ compare two days with the same temperature but different levels of humidity, the day with the higher humidity will feel warmer. A chart called the heat index ④ was developed to show how different levels of humidity make various temperatures feel to us. This is important ⑤ because of our body's reaction. Hot, humid days can cause serious health problems, like heat exhaustion and heat stroke, if care is not taken.

075 다음 글의 밑줄 친 부분 중, 어법상 틀린 것은?

One symptom of a coming nervous breakdown is the belief that one's job is so important that ① to take a holiday would bring a disaster. If I were a doctor, I would prescribe a holiday to any person who considered himself or his work this important. The nervous breakdown which appears ② to be produced by one's work is usually produced by some emotional problem ③ which the person is attempting to escape from by means of his job. This occurs because of a long period of stress which ④ has not adequately dealt with, resulting in further difficulty in fulfilling obligations. He doesn't want to give up this work because, if he does so, he will no longer have ⑤ anything to distract his mind from his possible misfortunes.

076 다음 글의 밑줄 친 부분 중, 어법상 틀린 것은?

Wouldn't it be wonderful if all teachers ① were as great as Socrates? Of course, it's unrealistic to expect every teacher to live up to this standard, and it's obvious that not every teacher will send children home every day ② thrilled about going to school. However, it's frequently the case that inexperienced teachers who aren't up to the challenge ③ are in charge of classrooms. Even when young teachers are outstanding, they're often so discouraged after a couple of years ④ that they quit teaching, and this leads to a cycle of inexperience. Parents need to offer support to their child's teacher. Even the best young teachers can feel isolated, and encouragement and appreciation from parents can make the difference between a young instructor developing and ⑤ remain on the job for many years and one of the countless teachers who walk away before achieving their potential.

077 (A), (B), (C)의 각 네모 안에서 어법에 맞는 표현으로 가장 적절한 것은?

Once (A) [regarding / regarded] as a minor art form, what has made Korean musicals so popular in the past couple of years? Many suggest that it is due to the five-day workweek which (B) [give / gives] people more spare time and, of course, the improved standard of living. An unusual reason is Korea's high Internet usage. Young people build online communities and share reviews on various musicals and even (C) [organize /organizing] group attendance at discounted prices. If ticket sales begin to fall for a good musical, lovers of that musical will organize campaigns and promotions over cyberspace to sell hundreds more tickets and revive the musical.

	(A)		(B)		(C)
①	regarding	—	gives	—	organize
②	regarding	—	give	—	organizing
③	regarded	—	gives	—	organizing
④	regarded	—	give	—	organizing
⑤	regarded	—	gives	—	organize

078 다음 글의 밑줄 친 부분 중, 어법상 틀린 것은?

Herbs are being embraced on a scale ① unmatched for two centuries—not only in cosmetics, foods and teas, but in domestic products, alternative medicines, and even veterinary remedies. Just ② what proportion of the original plant ingredients find their way into some of these products may be open to question. The advertising world in particular has not been slow to play on worries about the increasing quantities of man-made chemicals in the environment, and the images and virtues associated with herbs ③ having often been merged into a vague green wholesomeness that may have little to do with a specific plant or product. But ④ collectively their message is clear and the Western world has seen an unprecedented resurgence of interest in herbalism and useful plants in the last two decades. Even their images are ubiquitous—on fabrics, furniture, and street decorations. So as fossil fuels and the chemicals that depend on ⑤ them run out, it may not be fanciful to see the Chemical Age replaced by the Age of Plants.

*unprecedented: 선례가 없는
**herbalism: (의학적인) 약초 이용

079 (A), (B), (C)의 각 네모 안에서 어법에 맞는 표현으로 가장 적절한 것은?

In recent years, postcards (A) [used / are used] in a wide variety of activist and educational campaigns have deliberately challenged our norms. In 1993, the Canadian Parks and Wilderness Society (CPAWS), hoping to halt the development taking place in Banff National Park, (B) [launched / has launched] a postcard campaign. Subscribers to Borealis, the official publication of CPAWS, received postcards featuring photographs of recent construction projects in Banff as well as facts about the rate of commercial development inside the park. Such imagery utilizes the well-known format of the picture postcard but challenges the messages usually associated with the popular souvenir postcard. The blend of the familiar and the unexpected (C) [make / makes] this an effective tool for environmental activism. The link between environmental education and tourism promotion has been further established by a recent postcard campaign aimed at encouraging more sustainable relationships between tourists and wildlife in the region.

(A)		(B)		(C)
① used	—	launched	—	make
② used	—	has launched	—	make
③ used	—	launched	—	makes
④ are used	—	has launched	—	makes
⑤ are used	—	launched	—	makes

080 다음 글의 밑줄 친 부분 중, 어법상 틀린 것은?

For true sticking power, chewing gum really holds its ground. Unfortunately, holding its ground all too often means clinging to the bottom of your shoe, or ① adheres to your seat on the bus, or even worse, getting stuck in your hair. Cleaning up the ② unsightly and dirty blobs of gum that people spit out ③ costs British taxpayers about £150 million a year. But there could be an end in sight to the mess, with the recent invention of the world's first nonstick gum. The gum, called "Rev 7" by ④ its Bristol University inventors, is not attracted to clothing or hair, is ⑤ easily removed from concrete, and will simply dissolve in just a few minutes of rain. City of London officials have welcomed the invention as a means of reducing their budgets for cleaning.

081 다음 글의 밑줄 친 부분 중, 어법상 틀린 것은?

Managing your time isn't about squeezing as ① many tasks into your day as possible. It's about simplifying how you work, doing things faster, and relieving stress. It's about clearing away space in your life to make time for people, play, and rest. We get so caught up in busyness ② that we forget to enjoy what we're doing. Even when we focus on working smarter, not just working harder, we're still often too focused on getting things ③ to do. This should never be the point. Always ask yourself: 'What can I do to spend more time ④ enjoying what I'm doing?' The goal should be to arrange your commitments in a way ⑤ that you're happy living out the details of your daily life even while you're working. This may sound like a pipe dream, but it's more possible than ever in today's world. Be curious. Be open to opportunity. Know yourself. Embrace your passions.

권장 시간 8분 | 시작·종료 시간 | : ~ : | 나의 소요 시간 | 분 초

082 다음 글의 밑줄 친 부분 중, 어법상 틀린 것은?

How do restaurant chefs manage to serve multiple dishes to different people at a table at the same time, ① when it is clear that the preparation time is different for all of them? First, when it looks like the right time, the waiter will "fire" the dishes, which is the cue ② for the kitchen to start. Then there is someone who stands around in the kitchen like a conductor ③ makes sure everything is getting cooked in the right sequence. For example, the dishes that will take 10 minutes get started 4 minutes earlier than ④ those that will take 6 minutes. Depending on the restaurant, ⑤ that may be the job of the head chef or a deputy, or a specialist. In this way, chefs are juggling many different tables' dishes all at the same time. This might all sound quite confusing, but you don't need to worry. They are professionals. they've done it every day for years and years.

083 (A), (B), (C)의 각 네모 안에서 어법에 맞는 표현으로 가장 적절한 것은?

An attitude of interest and curiosity is good to have, and can (A) [cultivate / be cultivated] if you care to try. Make an effort to be surprised every day by at least one thing. Stop (B) [taking / to take] a good look at the car parked outside, or the tree on the sidewalk, or the building across the road, and ask yourself, how is it different from other cars, trees, or buildings? Don't just assume that you already know the essence of the thing, or that it doesn't really matter if you don't know. Be open to what the thing is telling you, and try to find the freshest, truest words (C) [describe / to describe] the thing and how it makes you feel. Life is a river of experiences, and the deeper you dive in and the farther you swim, the richer your life will be.

	(A)		(B)		(C)
①	cultivate	—	taking	—	describe
②	cultivate	—	to take	—	to describe
③	be cultivated	—	taking	—	to describe
④	be cultivated	—	to take	—	to describe
⑤	be cultivated	—	taking	—	describe

084 다음 글의 밑줄 친 부분 중, 어법상 틀린 것은?

In 1832, after his death in a duel at the age of 20, the French mathematician Galois was found ① to have left a body of mathematical writings that were examined and pronounced to be valueless despite the fact that he had frantically worked on them almost to his final moments. The mathematical propositions were novel, certainly, but were judged to have no basis in mathematical knowledge and ② to lead nowhere. It was only after the passage of several years during which mathematics advanced enough for the relevance and effectiveness of Galois's work ③ became apparent that its creativity was recognized. Other creative scientists such as Galileo have also suffered extreme social disapproval because they introduced what was in effect a new paradigm ④ whose relevance and effectiveness were beyond the ability of a particular age to appreciate. In Galileo's case, this was the now commonplace idea ⑤ that the earth revolves around the sun.

*duel: 결투
**proposition: 명제

085 다음 글의 밑줄 친 부분 중, 어법상 틀린 것은?

The walls of the Sistine Chapel were decorated by ① the number of Renaissance painters who were among the most highly-regarded artists of the late 15th-century Italy. The chapel's restoration process was started in 1980. For the restoration of the Sistine Chapel, one of the most useful materials was a mild cleanser ② made of baking soda and other ingredients mixed with water to form a drip-free gel. Several applications of the cleanser ③ were often needed to remove the grime completely from sections of the ceiling and walls. This cleaning agent, ④ which has been available to art restorers for only about 20 years, was particularly suited to the Sistine Chapel job. Its drip-free formula allowed exact quantities to be applied where they were needed without spreading any dirt around the area ⑤ being cleaned.

086 다음 글의 밑줄 친 부분 중, 어법상 틀린 것은?

The Framingham Osteoporosis Study, released last October, showed that carbonated drinks, like cola, ① are associated with lower bone mineral density in older women. There is a clear association between drinking these drinks more than three times a week and ② having weaker bones. In fact, the more cola a woman drank, ③ the lower her bone mineral density. Although these studies did not look at teeth, it makes sense that the results would be similar. So far, carbonated water has not been studied, but it's generally ④ considered neutral in relation to bone health. But the best choice is mineral water containing calcium and magnesium, which, when ⑤ consuming daily, has been shown to protect the bones of adults.

*osteoporosis: 골다공증
**bone (mineral) density: 골밀도

087 다음 글의 밑줄 친 부분 중, 어법상 틀린 것은?

Writing gives me such enormous pleasure, and I'm a much happier (and therefore nicer) person when I'm doing it. There's a place in my head that I ① go to when I write, and it's so rich and unexpected—and scary sometimes—but never ever dull. I first went there when I was seven, and I wrote a poem which ② was startled me a bit because it felt like someone else ③ had written it. The adrenaline rush that it gave me was incredible and I wanted more. These days, maybe because I can now access that place quite easily, writing feels like something I simply could not live ④ without. It is a joyous thing. I feel very lucky to be paid to do it, but even if I'd never been published, I think I'd still be writing. I love ⑤ being read, but the person I'm really always writing for is me.

088 다음 글의 밑줄 친 부분 중, 어법상 틀린 것은?

Most schools are structured around performance goals, ① which focus on the importance of avoiding mistakes, outperforming other students, and meeting extrinsic objectives such as high grades, standards, and awards. A focus on mastery goals, on the other hand, ② tends to build intrinsic motivation and creativity, along with positive feelings about learning, and more perseverance and curiosity, as well as higher academic engagement. A classroom with a mastery focus is also more student-centered and individualized, and its students attribute success to effort rather than just ③ ability. Mastery goal focused classrooms encourage the growth mindset among learners, which is characterized by knowing that abilities can develop over time with effort and practice. Many teachers and school districts say they value the very things that a mastery focus ④ develops, yet schools are typically performance oriented, with data-driven goals for higher math and reading scores, in particular, which contributes to ⑤ discourage love of learning in students.

089 (A), (B), (C)의 각 네모 안에서 어법에 맞는 표현으로 가장 적절한 것은?

Skill in sports such as basketball, golf, or horseshoe pitching improves with practice, but not because repetition has any value in itself. If it (A) [did / had done], we would learn from our mistakes instead of our successes. For example, when someone is learning to pitch horseshoes, he will miss many more times than he hits the stake. If improved skill came from repetition, he would become an expert at missing, since that's (B) [how / what] he has practiced most. His misses will outnumber his hits 10 to 1. However, with time, the misses become fewer and the hits more frequent. This is (C) [why / because] our brain remembers the successes and forgets the misses.

	(A)		(B)		(C)
①	did	—	what	—	why
②	had done	—	how	—	because
③	did	—	how	—	because
④	had done	—	how	—	why
⑤	did	—	what	—	because

090 (A), (B), (C)의 각 네모 안에서 어법에 맞는 표현으로 가장 적절한 것은?

The notion (A) [that / which] individual pieces of popular music may be distinguishable by their own identity or character is common across popular music genres. However, this notion is not necessarily established by virtue of the composed elements alone. The performance, whether live or recorded, and technical production in the recording studio (B) [is / are] major sites of the elements that enable identity distinctions to be drawn between pieces. Indeed, identity can sometimes be seen to reside in the activity of performance *tout court*, without particular concern for the end product. Yet, at the same time, it would be wrong to ignore the powerful influence that the recording, as the end result of a combination of activities, (C) [exerts / exerting] over the notion of identity.

*tout court: 간단히 말해

	(A)		(B)		(C)
①	that	—	is	—	exerts
②	that	—	are	—	exerts
③	that	—	are	—	exerting
④	which	—	is	—	exerts
⑤	which	—	are	—	exerting

091 다음 글의 밑줄 친 부분 중, 어법상 틀린 것은?

Given the dominance of economics in public life, it is no surprise that so many university students, if ① given the chance, opt to study a little as part of their education. Every year, around five million college students in the United States alone ② graduate with at least one economics course under their belts. A standard introductory course that originated in the United States—and is widely known as Econ 101—is now taught throughout the world, with students from China to Chile ③ learning from translations of the very same textbooks used in Chicago and Cambridge, Massachusetts. For all of these students, Econ 101 has become a staple part of a broad education, whether they then head off ④ becomes an entrepreneur or doctor, journalist or political activist. Even for those who never study economics, the language and mindset of Econ 101 so pervades public debate ⑤ that it shapes the way that we all think about the economy: what it is, how it works, and what it is for.

092 다음 글의 밑줄 친 부분 중, 어법상 틀린 것은?

Paying pocket money for household chores is a win-win situation: your child learns that money is earned and you have less housework to do. Various chores that my children have been responsible for ① include making their bed, keeping their rooms tidy and putting their belongings away. As they got older, it progressed to mowing the lawn, putting the clothes on the line to dry and ② to do the dishes. Pocket money for chores can definitely help children appreciate the value of money. However, care must be taken to ensure that it doesn't create a mindset in your child that they should be paid for ③ anything helpful they do around the house. Where else does pocket money work? For example, if pocket money were given ④ regularly as a reward for good behavior? In some cases, tying pocket money to some polite and respectful behavior can indeed be a good way to help young children ⑤ to practice their social skills.

093 다음 글의 밑줄 친 부분 중, 어법상 틀린 것은?

By spring 1775, armed conflict ① had already begun in the New England colonies; the city of Boston was under attack. The Second Continental Congress, assembled in Philadelphia, sent George Washington to New England to organize a military force, but the colonial resolve ② stopped there. The representatives had to decide what to do and quickly if the infant army were to survive. The problem ③ laid in the colonists themselves: the shopkeepers, artisans, and farmers of the various regions had no ④ unified opinion on how to respond to the mother country. In January 1776, Thomas Paine, sensing the wavering public opinion, printed a pamphlet called Common Sense, America's first political blockbuster, selling 150,000 copies in its first printing. Common Sense argued in language, metaphors, and analogies that everyone could understand a complete separation from England, and ⑤ provided a vision for a new government.

*Continental Congress: 대륙회의(미국 독립전쟁 때의 기구로서 나중에 '미국(United States of America)'으로 발전한 여러 식민지의 대표기구)

**Common Sense: Thomas Paine이 쓴 정치적 문제를 다룬 소책자로 미국 독립전쟁에 중요한 영향을 끼침.

094 다음 글의 밑줄 친 부분 중, 어법상 틀린 것은?

A chimpanzee that escaped from a Sendai zoo was caught Thursday afternoon in a ① nearby residential area after being shot with a tranquilizer gun and falling from power lines. The male chimpanzee, Chacha, was one of the five chimpanzees ② were kept at the Yagiyama Zoological Park in the Miyagi Prefecture capital. No one ③ was reported injured in the incident. Zoo staff noticed one of the chimpanzees was missing from a cage around 1:20 p.m. and the park was subsequently closed as a precaution, according to zoo officials. The chimpanzee was spotted ④ moving along power lines in the residential area and was shot with a tranquilizer and caught around 3:10 p.m. A local elementary school, which had some 400 pupils inside at the time, ordered the students not to leave the school for home ⑤ until the chimpanzee was caught.

095 (A), (B), (C)의 각 네모 안에서 어법에 맞는 표현으로 가장 적절한 것은?

When the first colonists arrived in North America from Europe, the native people already living there greeted them as friends. Agreements were drawn up and boundaries (A) [were laid / were lain] down between the new settlers and the people they called 'Indians.' But, as time passed, more and more Indian lands were taken over by the settlers. Confused and angry, the Indians were pushed farther west, away from the land that was rightfully theirs. The greatest of the Indian leaders understood that the only chance for their people (B) [was / were] for all the tribes to unite against the common enemy. But centuries of warfare between the various tribes (C) [made / were made] this impossible. Fighting each other had become a way of life.

	(A)		(B)		(C)
①	were laid	—	was	—	made
②	were laid	—	were	—	made
③	were laid	—	was	—	were made
④	were lain	—	were	—	were made
⑤	were lain	—	was	—	made

096 다음 글의 밑줄 친 부분 중, 어법상 틀린 것은?

Throughout the 20th century, science was seen as the solution to the problems of land degradation and pollution resulting from agricultural and industrial activities. As a result, there is now an increasing focus on funding for science being linked to ① providing practical solutions to environmental problems. This creates a dilemma, for while excellent science can be conducted, science ② alone will not create widespread change, mainly because the channels to use this information and create change are poorly developed. In order to create changes in behavior and beliefs of the general public, more effective communication of the new scientific insights being gained ③ are required. Even ④ where the solutions to environmental problems are clear, management, political, and ultimately public support are needed to implement the (usually) expensive solutions. Therefore, utilizing our current research effectively will require new tools ⑤ to facilitate effective communication, not only to scientists, but also to managers, governments, and ultimately, the general public.

*land degradation: 토지 황폐화

097 (A), (B), (C)의 각 네모 안에서 어법에 맞는 표현으로 가장 적절한 것은?

People with red hair usually have light eyes, pale skin, and freckles. Their skin burns easily in the sun, and their skin cancer risk is high. Researchers believe that changes triggered by the sun in melanin, the pigment which darkens skin in the sun, (A) [cause / causes] DNA damage and eventually cancer. This is more likely to occur in redheads than in black-haired people. The researchers compared the reaction of melanin in red hair with (B) [that / those] in black hair to various wavelengths of ultraviolet light. It was found that the pigment isolated from red hair requires less energy to start the chemical reaction that produces the damaging free radicals linked to cancer. Melanin in black hair needs more energy to produce free radicals, (C) [reduces / reducing] the risk of cancer.

*pigment: 색소 **free radical: 활성 산소

	(A)		(B)		(C)
①	causes	—	that	—	reduces
②	causes	—	those	—	reduces
③	causes	—	that	—	reducing
④	cause	—	those	—	reducing
⑤	cause	—	that	—	reducing

098 다음 글의 밑줄 친 부분 중, 어법상 틀린 것은?

Having salespeople 'on the road' is less convenient than keeping them ① working in the office. Much of the salesperson's time is spent unproductively ② traveling. Selling over the phone or having a face-to-face meeting in the office may be better and less expensive. Export trade companies often ③ have a separate export sales force. Its travel and accommodation expenses can be very high. As a result, servicing overseas customers ④ are frequently done by phone, fax, or letter, and personal visits may be less often. Another option is for a business to appoint an overseas agent or distributor ⑤ whose own sales force can take over the responsibility for selling the product in that country.

099 다음 글의 밑줄 친 부분 중, 어법상 틀린 것은?

Many South Korean corporations contribute to the world economy by producing goods of high quality and ① hiring foreign employees. However, South Korean companies ② have preferred to establish their own research and development operations rather than enter into arrangements with universities, a common phenomenon in Europe and the United States. For South Korea ③ being even more widely recognized as a knowledge-based society led by higher educational institutions, there should be stronger connections ④ between companies and higher educational institutions, especially on the research and development side. Also, higher educational institutions should have greater autonomy and should be ⑤ highly flexible in order to adapt to a changing society.

100 다음 글의 밑줄 친 부분 중, 어법상 틀린 것은?

It's impossible ① for kids to reach the top in a single bound. 'Scaffolding' can give them a framework to go upward step by step. If, for example, the child ② asks, "Where's Thailand?" a scaffold-building parent might say, "Let's look it up together." The parent seizes the opportunity ③ to be taught how to use reference materials, equipping the child with a tool for moving higher on his own. Also, don't do your kid's homework yourself: homework is the kid's responsibility. A child generally benefits when his or her parents become ④ involved in the homework process. However, too much parental involvement can prevent the positive effects of homework. If you solve your son's arithmetic problems or ⑤ do the research for his report on Einstein, he doesn't learn to stand on his own two feet.

*scaffolding: ((교육)) 스스로 학습할 수 있도록 지원해주는 교육방식

101 (A), (B), (C)의 각 네모 안에서 어법에 맞는 표현으로 가장 적절한 것은?

Change is the very nature of family life. Your baby's needs are different from (A) [that / those] of your teenager preparing for university. The arrival of siblings shifts focus and brings new dynamics and new relationships. More families are undergoing a radical change in structure, too. In Australia, for example, a third of marriages (B) [involve / involves] at least one person who has been married before—and who often already has children. Another form of family unit on the rise is one headed by a single parent. This parent is likely to be under more stress than someone in a two-parent family and is also less likely to be satisfied with life. One study showed that 29 percent of single parents were satisfied with life (C) [comparing / compared] to between 53 and 71 percent of married parents.

	(A)		(B)		(C)
①	that	—	involve	—	comparing
②	that	—	involves	—	compared
③	those	—	involve	—	comparing
④	those	—	involves	—	comparing
⑤	those	—	involve	—	compared

102 다음 글의 밑줄 친 부분 중, 어법상 틀린 것은?

Given all the drawbacks and disadvantages of electronic documents, why not just stick with paper? The best way of answering that question is ① to look back on the one other occasion in human history when a writing medium was replaced. To societies accustomed to writing on stone or clay, paper ② must have seemed terribly short-lived stuff, vulnerable to fire and water, with inscribed marks that all too easily smudged or faded away. And yet paper prevailed. Moses' tablets were stone, but the story of Moses ③ was told on paper. The economic incentives were just too powerful to be ignored: with paper, information became ④ very cheaper to record, to store and to transport. Exactly the same considerations argue ⑤ that a transition to paperless, electronic writing is now inevitable.

*smudge: 번지다

103 다음 글의 밑줄 친 부분 중, 어법상 틀린 것은?

Some parents have daily battles with their kids over routine tasks like getting dressed and brushing teeth. The problem arises partly from childish stubbornness and partly from parental inflexibility regarding the order ① in which tasks are done. A child may simply want to mix things up a bit to make his or her tasks ② seem less burdensome. The parents might benefit from ③ a little variety in their routine, too, but it can be hard for them to let go of their need for total control and consistency, especially if their own parents were strict. One way to train children in the culture of time management ④ is to use a device called a "time tracker." It combines a timer with bright lights ⑤ intending to visually condition a child to adhere to a strict schedule. Actually, thousands of them have been sold, giving help to many parents.

104 다음 글의 밑줄 친 부분 중, 어법상 틀린 것은?

Why does the sound of running water make me want to pee? Most of you are familiar with the name Pavlov and know that he had something to do with dogs. ① That something is an experiment where the Russian doctor showed that autonomic responses could be triggered by outside stimuli. Pavlov thought that a lot of this unconscious learning ② happens all the time to people, and you can probably think of a few cases from your own life ③ where you reflexively react a certain way to a seemingly unrelated stimulus. Having to pee at the sound of running water appears to be the same sort of conditioned response. The sound of running water not only mimics the sound of urination ④ itself to create a Pavlovian association, but flushing and washing one's hands also produce that same sound and are closely associated with urinating and further ⑤ strengthens the connection.

*urination: 배뇨

105 다음 글의 밑줄 친 부분 중, 어법상 틀린 것은?

As terrorist attacks of all kinds continue to be carried out worldwide, organizations specifically designed to address terrorism are working harder than ever, but they face a number of challenges in ① coordinating their efforts. First, it is difficult to obtain accurate information about the intentions and activities of secretive and sometimes ② highly organized terrorist groups. Many are based in inaccessible areas overseas, and some are under the protection of governments whose interest they ③ are served. There are also limits to what can be done to prevent attacks planned and launched abroad. The techniques of these agencies, and the way ④ in which they cooperate with other agencies (at home and overseas), have to keep pace with the terrorists' methods and capabilities. Fortunately, across the intelligence community, resources ⑤ have been re-prioritized to reflect the increased threat from international terrorism. All these agencies aim to erode the terrorists' capability to initiate and sustain campaigns against a specific nation and/or its allies.

106 다음 글의 밑줄 친 부분 중, 어법상 틀린 것은?

As the danger of digital infrastructure ① being attacked continues to increase, so does the emphasis on protecting and defending it. The problem is, however, that the defensive mindset of Internet security today very much mimics that of the Dark Ages. "We're simply building taller castle walls and digging deeper moats. Many organizations are still locked into the concept ② that the castle walls will protect the bad guys from getting in," a security and risk manager said. "Most are not thinking about those who climbed over or tunneled under those walls. The challenge for defenders is that the bad guys ③ only have to succeed once, while defending data has to succeed 100% of the time," he added. "And the battle moves ④ much quickly and is even more multi-dimensional than it used to ⑤ be."

*Dark Ages: (중세) 암흑시대 **moat: (성 둘레의) 해자, 도랑

107 다음 글의 밑줄 친 부분 중, 어법상 틀린 것은?

Self-awareness is observed in chimpanzees and the other apes. When chimps are placed in front of a mirror, it takes just a few minutes for them ① to figure out that they are seeing themselves. They then spend a while examining inside their mouths, the top of their head, and everywhere else they couldn't see before. Monkeys never figure out that they are seeing their own image—or they just don't behave as a human would ② do as the image is recognized. One can put a red dot on the forehead of an animal and then place that animal in front of a mirror. We then watch to see ③ whether the animal touches the dot in the mirror or the dot on its own head. ④ Touching the dot on its own forehead shows that the animal understands that it is seeing its own image in the mirror. A chimp will touch the dot on its own forehead. All of the ape species ⑤ have found to touch their own forehead, while every monkey species touches the dot in the mirror.

108 다음 글의 밑줄 친 부분 중, 어법상 틀린 것은?

The human compulsion towards the community and communal life is revealed in institutions whose forms we do not need to understand fully; for example in religion, ① where group worship creates a bond between members of the congregation. Just as the conditions of our lives are determined in the first place by the facts of the universe, further conditions arise through the social and communal life of human beings and the laws and regulations ② spring from it. The needs of the community ③ govern all human relationships. Communal life predates the individual life of humanity. In the history of human civilization no way of life has emerged of which the foundations were not laid communally; human beings developed not ④ singly but in communities. This is very easily explained. The whole animal kingdom demonstrates the fundamental law that species ⑤ whose members are individually incapable of facing the battle for self-preservation gain additional strength through herd life.

109 다음 글의 밑줄 친 부분 중, 어법상 <u>틀린</u> 것은?

For almost 50 years, governments ① <u>have been launching</u> objects into space, creating an orbiting junkyard. The United States is tracking more than 10,000 pieces of debris four inches or larger, but tens of millions of smaller fragments ② <u>are</u> also whizzing through space at speeds of up to 17,000 mph. At this speed, a collision with even tiny objects could destroy a spacecraft. Space agencies continue ③ <u>to monitor</u> the debris as new objects are added and old junk falls back through the atmosphere, ④ <u>which</u> happens about once a day. Usually these pieces burn up on re-entry, but several 1000-pound-plus fragments have crashed to Earth. Fortunately, only one person is known ⑤ <u>to have hit</u>.

110 (A), (B), (C)의 각 네모 안에서 어법에 맞는 표현으로 가장 적절한 것은?

There might be several different reasons why faces seem naturally interesting and eye-catching to humans. The generally accepted theory is (A) [that / what] an infant's attraction to faces develops as an adaptive mechanism to stimulate parent-child attachment. Being able to recognize and engage the primary caregiver increases the likelihood that an infant will become emotionally attached to that individual and receive proper nurturance. The need to recognize, engage, and extract information from faces (B) [continues / to continue], of course, through childhood and into adulthood. Having the ability to read the minds of others in a social setting is also important for survival and reproductive success. Humans can't read minds, but the next best thing is being able to understand the emotional mind-set of your peers. No other body part even comes close to providing such rich emotional information about the bearer (C) [as / which] is the case with the face.

*nurturance: (애정 어린) 양육

	(A)		(B)		(C)
①	that	—	continues	—	as
②	that	—	to continue	—	which
③	that	—	continues	—	which
④	what	—	to continue	—	as
⑤	what	—	continues	—	which

111 다음 글의 밑줄 친 부분 중, 어법상 <u>틀린</u> 것은?

Most people understand the limits of their bodies and live their lives ① <u>accordingly</u>, but some don't recognize those limits, and they are the subjects of the two-hour special "Sekai Chojintai Mystery" (*The World's Human Body Mysteries*; TBS, Tues., 8:57 p.m.). The program travels the world looking for people ② <u>who</u> physical abilities are not just out of the ordinary but downright unexplainable. One of the subjects ③ <u>is</u> an American stuntman whose main gig is ④ <u>to set</u> himself on fire, usually for uncomfortably long periods of time. Then there is a tribe of people in the South Pacific who live in houses on stilts in the middle of the sea. They subsist on fish that they catch after diving 40 meters underwater and walking on the seabed for very long stretches. Finally, another American man can control his body ⑤ <u>so as to</u> feel no pain, even when needles are thrust through his arms.

*gig: (주로 하는) 공연, 일
**stilt: (건물을 지면·수면 위로 떠받치는) 기둥[지주]
***subsist on: ~으로 연명하다

112 다음 글의 밑줄 친 부분 중, 어법상 틀린 것은?

There are two main strategies you can ① use to improve your quality of life. The first is to change external factors to match your needs, and the second is to try to change the way you experience those factors. For instance, feeling secure is necessary for happiness, and you can strengthen your sense of security in many ways, such as moving to a safer apartment or neighborhood, or ② taking classes in self-defense. Such proactive steps bring conditions in the environment more in line with your needs. The other method ③ by which you can feel more secure involves modifying your perception of what it means to be secure. You can accept the idea ④ which a certain amount of danger and risk is inevitable in life. And then, if you can still enjoy this less than ⑤ perfectly predictable world, you'll have an inner strength to shield you from insecurity.

113 (A), (B), (C)의 각 네모 안에서 어법에 맞는 표현으로 가장 적절한 것은?

Northern California offers the same cool climate and scenic beauty that is afforded by Oregon and Washington. On the coast, near the Oregon line, is the Del Norte Coast Redwoods State Park with (A) [its / their] fern-carpeted forest of rugged redwood trees. Tourists can drive or hike through the dense forest to the ocean (B) [which / where] the giant redwoods, found only on the Pacific coast, grow almost to the shore. Also to be enjoyed from April to July are outstanding displays of rhododendrons and azaleas. Inland in the north are many other beautiful parks, including Mount Shasta. Besides an abundance of skiing terrain, this park (C) [is contained / contains] white water in deep canyons, exquisite lakes, thick forests, and open valleys.

*fern: 양치류 **rhododendron: 철쭉 ***azalea: 진달래

	(A)		(B)		(C)
①	its	—	where	—	is contained
②	its	—	which	—	contains
③	its	—	where	—	contains
④	their	—	which	—	contains
⑤	their	—	where	—	is contained

114 다음 글의 밑줄 친 부분 중, 어법상 틀린 것은?

When people maintain patterns of caring, ① whether for a house, a garden, pets, or other people, they are protecting themselves against despair, against giving up. They are rewarded by feeling ② needed. The word "care" has many meanings, however, and one of them is "worry," as when someone is burdened with care. You do worry about the things you care for. Unfortunately, the association of care with effort and worry leads us to conceive of old age as a period ③ in which one should live a "carefree existence." After retirement, people are urged to give up their cares. It can be a dangerous trade-off. The person who stops ④ to care for something may have taken the first steps to the hopelessness/helplessness syndrome. And those who cope best with old age are those who continue the daily acts of caring, especially the most satisfying ⑤ ones—care provided to living things, such as pets and gardens.

115 다음 글의 밑줄 친 부분 중, 어법상 틀린 것은?

One of the most potentially explosive international problems is ① that of mass tourism. Of the nearly seven billion people in the world, an increasing number of them ② are determined to travel. By the end of the century, there ③ is expected to be more than 500 million travel-hungry tourists ④ wandering around the world. Already ⑤ thousands of perfect beaches, quaint villages, historic cities, and regions of exquisite natural beauty have fallen under developers' building schemes. Attempts to accommodate tourists have led to the destruction of the very attractions that they have come to enjoy and have made daily living almost impossible for the local residents.

116 다음 글의 밑줄 친 부분 중, 어법상 틀린 것은?

Millions of children around the world miss out on their childhood as a result of poverty. Poverty deprives ① them of the capabilities needed to survive, develop and thrive. It prevents them from enjoying equal opportunities. It makes children more vulnerable to exploitation, abuse, violence, discrimination and stigmatization. The statistical evidence on children living in poverty ② confronts us with a stark reality: millions of children are poor; they lack access to safe drinking water, essential vaccines, education and nutrition; they are at risk of being exploited and ③ abused. This reality calls into question the commitment of governments, the private sector and the international community to act upon the Millennium Development Goals and "A World Fit for Children" agenda. We know what needs ④ to do; what is needed is the will to turn words into concrete action. When governments, civil society and the international community ⑤ work toward a common goal, great feats can be achieved.

*stigmatization: 오명 씌우기, 낙인찍기
**Millennium Development Goals: 새천년 개발 목표(2000년 UN에서 채택된 의제로, 2015년까지 빈곤을 반으로 감소시키자는 범세계인 약속)

117 (A), (B), (C)의 각 네모 안에서 어법에 맞는 표현으로 가장 적절한 것은?

General psychology deals with the general principles underlying the study of man's perception, sensation, thinking, memory, attention, learning and other mental activities, nervous system, etc. Child psychology studies all these things but (A) [its / their] subject is the child. It is an independent field of study, because, as has been demonstrated by modern researchers, the child is not a miniature of an adult. Hence, it is impossible to say that the principles of general psychology can be applied to the study of a child after making necessary adaptation. Neither (B) [does / is] child psychology a branch of general psychology, because it has been found by continuous research that the child's thinking, understanding, learning, perception, emotion and other activities differ from those of an adult not only in quantity but also in quality. That's (C) [why / what] child psychology carries out its own research rather than adopting the conclusions of general psychology.

	(A)		(B)		(C)
①	its	—	does	—	why
②	its	—	is	—	why
③	its	—	is	—	what
④	their	—	does	—	why
⑤	their	—	is	—	what

118 다음 글의 밑줄 친 부분 중, 어법상 틀린 것은?

"Restrictions will set you free." There is no other area ① where this statement resonates more than in the realm of music. One could even argue that without form there is no such thing as music at all. This is also relevant to why composers are instantly recognizable—their "audio fingerprint," their unique sound, ② is a result of their individual choice of musical restrictions. The art is in choosing the restrictions that suit your style and then ③ honing your technique within this framework. All great composers created rules, explored them, and became masters of their own universe. However, to create rules, shifts and paradigms in music, you must be prepared to sound ④ radical different to anything that has gone before. This is something many musicians talk about but never have the guts to go through with because they want to sound ⑤ like their favorite composer or band. Limitations have the potential to set them free, but familiarity ends up grounding them like a ball and chain.

*paradigm: 전형적인 예[양식]
**ball and chain: 사슬에 쇠뭉치가 달린 족쇄; 속박, 구속

119 다음 글의 밑줄 친 부분 중, 어법상 틀린 것은?

Glands are so complex and are affected by so many different things that it would be very difficult to ① simply list what is harmful and what is beneficial to them. Yet, there is one main thing that is vital for all glandular functions. All the glands of the body ② requiring minerals to produce hormones and to perform their specific jobs. When there are not enough minerals in the diet, the digestive juices receive the supply that is available. This means that the nerves, tissues, teeth and bones will be mineral deficient and ③ that their functions will be greatly hampered. If this state of mineral deficiency is not remedied, eventually the glands will become ④ affected. This will in turn cause abnormal body conditions that can only result in disease. Because the body obtains minerals through the food that is eaten, it is essential that a variety of fresh, raw food ⑤ be eaten so the body will receive the necessary minerals.

*gland: ((생물)) (분비)샘

120 (A), (B), (C)의 각 네모 안에서 어법에 맞는 표현으로 가장 적절한 것은?

The rise of computer technologies and networking is due to collective action similar to (A) [one / that] of other social movements, such as the environmental movement, the anti-tobacco movement, the movement against drinking and driving, or the women's movement, to name a few. While each has its own specific goals, for instance, clean air, elimination of smoking in public places, reduced traffic accidents and deaths from drunk driving, or equality of opportunity, they all focus on correcting some situation to which they object or (B) [change / changing] the circumstances for a group that is harmed by some kind of social disadvantage. Likewise, advocates of computerization focus on the development of a new world order (C) [where / which] people and organizations use state-of-the-art computing equipment and the physical limitations of time and space are conquered.

*state-of-the-art: 최첨단의

	(A)		(B)		(C)
①	one	—	changing	—	where
②	one	—	change	—	which
③	that	—	changing	—	which
④	that	—	change	—	where
⑤	that	—	changing	—	where

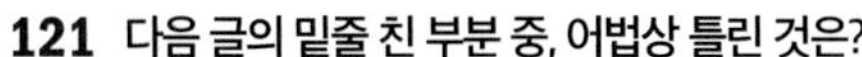

121 다음 글의 밑줄 친 부분 중, 어법상 틀린 것은?

Nothing ruins a friendship as ① swiftly as desperate neediness or possessiveness. Friends can spend heaps of time together only as long as it's a mutually agreed-upon arrangement. As soon as one starts demanding too much of another, the relationship is in big trouble. Feeling ② suffocated by a friend makes you want to run and hide. That's why not putting all your eggs in one basket ③ are so important. ④ Having diverse interests and friendships helps to shrink the desperation that so often troubles those who have ⑤ few. Think of it this way: your life is like a cake. The richer your life, the more excellent your cake. A friend can be icing on the cake, but never the cake itself. That's too much to ask of anyone.

122 다음 글의 밑줄 친 부분 중, 어법상 틀린 것은?

We're thrilled to announce that Silvia Killingsworth will be joining us here in April. Silvia is currently the managing editor of *The New Yorker*, where she has spent the last seven years ① managing the workflow of the magazine. Silvia's breadth of experience and wealth of ideas and genuine enthusiasm about things make her the clear and obvious choice ② to head *The Hairpin* as it evolves into its next stage of life. In fact, we're so impressed by her vision for the site ③ that we have also tasked her to take the reins at *The Awl*. It's an enormous undertaking, but we ④ would not have assigned it to any one person unless we were completely convinced that she was eager and able to do it. We hope you're as excited as we ⑤ do to watch this new phase unfold, and we ask you to join us in welcoming Silvia aboard.

123 다음 글의 밑줄 친 부분 중, 어법상 틀린 것은?

Displaying strong negative emotions, such as jealousy or rage, directly ① affects people around you, arousing negative feelings in them towards you. If you often have emotional outbursts, it's probably because you have poor self-control or because you care less about the trouble you're causing ② than you care about your "right" to show how you feel. Teenagers' emotions are somewhat at the mercy of the huge changes ③ happened to their bodies and hormones. But if a teen doesn't learn to handle bad feelings well, he or she is likely to become an overemotional adult who uses violent emotions ④ to control others and get attention. To help overemotional people, show them the effect they are having on themselves and others, and get them to understand that when they feel ⑤ emotional, they have the power not to act overemotionally.

124 다음 글의 밑줄 친 부분 중, 어법상 틀린 것은?

The first Christmas gift I ever bought, at the age of eight, was five doll-size bottles of pastel-colored perfume. I just knew they'd ① be thrilled my sister Joyce, who was four. They were expensive enough to have cleaned out my piggy bank. Of course Joyce quickly forgot ② those little bottles. Yet I still look back on that gift as the ③ one that taught me the joy of giving. When I counted out my change to buy her present, I discovered what it meant to put someone else's happiness front and center. Now my shopping for a gift is a project so complex ④ that it can feel like the "job" of giving. Is the necklace too edgy, the sweater too predictable? In my relentless quest for objects that will prove how much I care, I completely exhaust myself. At eight I knew ⑤ better. I just wanted to make my sister happy.

*relentless: 가차없는, 무자비한 **quest: 추구, 탐색

125 (A), (B), (C)의 각 네모 안에서 어법에 맞는 표현으로 가장 적절한 것은?

Whereas characters' names are rarely changed in the translation of adult fiction, translators writing for children often adapt (A) [it / them], for example by using equivalents in the target language such as Hans/John/Jean, William/Guillermo/Guillaume, Alice/Alicia. This issue causes a lot of disagreement, however, since names are a powerful signal of social and cultural context. If (B) [leaving / left] untranslated, names constantly remind young readers that they are reading a story set in another country, whereas the use of an equivalent name or an alternative in the target language may lead to an incongruous relationship between names and setting. Nonetheless, editors and translators fear that children might struggle with foreign names, thus giving rise to a dilemma that Anthea Bell cites in her *Translator's Notebook*: "The idea behind all this is (C) [avoided / to avoid] putting young readers off by presenting them with an impenetrable-looking set of foreign names the moment they open a book. It's the kind of problem that constantly challenges a translator of children's literature."

*incongruous: 어울리지 않는
**impenetrable-looking: 이해할 수 없을 것처럼 보이는

	(A)		(B)		(C)
①	it	—	leaving	—	to avoid
②	it	—	left	—	to avoid
③	them	—	leaving	—	avoided
④	them	—	left	—	to avoid
⑤	them	—	left	—	avoided

126 다음 글의 밑줄 친 부분 중, 어법상 틀린 것은?

The paradox of modern life is that ① while technological acceleration—in transportation, communication, and production—should provide *more* free time, those same inventions increase our options at an exponential rate. Email was ② far faster than snail mail, but the Internet also brought Twitter, YouTube, and so on. As the German sociologist Hartmut Rosa described it, "no matter how ③ much we increase the 'pace of life,'" we cannot keep up with the flood of information. The result is that "our share of the world" feels continually ④ squeezed, even as we gain more efficient access to it. Estimates are that 90 percent of the world's data has been created in the last five years. We're all drowning in information, a reality that makes even the simplest decisions—where to eat, which health plan to sign up for, which coffee maker to buy—more ⑤ complicatedly.

*exponential: 기하급수적인

127 다음 글의 밑줄 친 부분 중, 어법상 틀린 것은?

Some of my fondest memories of growing up ① are of tiptoeing into my mother's kitchen to sneak a slice of her delicious apple pie. Where cinnamon came from or its nutritional benefits ② might have been a mystery to me, but its special taste kept me coming back. People have been using spices to add special flavor to food for thousands of years. And they ③ have been used for their medicinal qualities too. For example, garlic was fed to laborers ④ building the Egyptian pyramids to keep disease away. And ginger has the ability to help calm an upset stomach. Dioscorides, who ⑤ was referred to the surgeon general for both emperors Claudius and Nero, wrote in the famous *De Materia Medica* in 77 A.D. that ginger "warms and softens the stomach."

128 (A), (B), (C)의 각 네모 안에서 어법에 맞는 표현으로 가장 적절한 것은?

Past behavior is the strongest predictor of current self-efficacy judgments. So by observing themselves executing successful moves, learners pay greater attention to and are provided with the information on how to best perform skills to continue progressing. Although limited in number, the sport studies that have examined the effect of self-modeling on psychosocial variables such as self-efficacy and performance (A) [have yielded / has yielded] encouraging results. For example, Halliwell found improvements in performance and confidence of professional hockey players coming back from injury or after experiencing slumps when he developed music videos (B) [showing / shown] only the successful highlights of their games. Likewise, Singleton and Feltz examined the effect of self-modeling on college hockey players' performance and found (C) [that / what] the players exposed to self-modeling experienced greater shooting accuracy and self-efficacy for shooting performance compared with controls.

*self-efficacy: 자기 효능감
(자신이 어떤 일을 성공적으로 수행할 수 있다고 믿는 기대와 신념)

	(A)		(B)		(C)
①	have yielded	—	showing	—	that
②	have yielded	—	shown	—	that
③	have yielded	—	shown	—	what
④	has yielded	—	showing	—	that
⑤	has yielded	—	shown	—	what

129 다음 글의 밑줄 친 부분 중, 어법상 틀린 것은?

I've always tried to make a distinction ① between "writer" and "author." The first implies a desire to pursue an activity. The second implies a desire to have others approve of that activity by consuming one's work. There's nothing wrong with thinking of ② oneself as an author, of course. But it's often useful to revert to the former mindset in order to gain perspective and overcome self-doubt. Write for yourself. Write because it's fun. Write because it's an area of your life you can control ③ completely. Don't judge your writing, and don't ask others ④ to judge it for you. Don't worry about whether anyone else will ever see what you write. Just be a writer. And then, when writing becomes a simple and joyful part of your everyday existence, you can start thinking about being an author. Or not—it's your choice. But as long as you feel ⑤ fulfilling by what you've written, the opinions of others should ultimately mean little.

130 다음 글의 밑줄 친 부분 중, 어법상 틀린 것은?

As an online business owner, you may be under pressure ① to be available to your customers around the clock. That means you need a payment system you can rely on. You may also want to give customers the choice of ② how they pay you, such as payments over the phone or by direct debit. In contacting your future provider, you have to take three factors—speed, reliability, security—into account. Speed matters because it reduces the chance ③ that a customer will become frustrated and abandon their transaction, resulting in lost business. Reliability is also important when you're choosing an e-commerce platform, because every minute that you can't take payments is a minute you aren't making money. However, protecting your customer data and the reputation of your business is the key to customer loyalty. When you're choosing an e-commerce facility, ④ that's important to choose a provider that encrypts credit card numbers ⑤ so cyber criminals will never be able to access the real card data.

*encrypt: 암호화하다

131 (A), (B), (C)의 각 네모 안에서 어법에 맞는 표현으로 가장 적절한 것은?

When a magician fools you, it is not your vision (A) [that / what] is to blame. Rather it is the parietal cortex, a small region of the brain behind your ear that aids in concentration. Psychologist Nilli Lavie discovered that this part of the brain holds the key to the phenomenon known as change blindness, (B) [which / where] people overlook the obvious when their attention is challenged. A classic example is the face test. A test subject is (C) [showing / shown] pictures of two faces in quick succession. Normally, the subject notices that the two are different, but if the subjects are diverted by a task, such as counting, or distracted by a flicker on the screen, they will usually not notice the difference.

*parietal cortex: ((해부)) 두정피질 **change blindness: 변화 맹시

	(A)		(B)		(C)
①	that	—	which	—	showing
②	that	—	where	—	showing
③	that	—	where	—	shown
④	what	—	where	—	shown
⑤	what	—	which	—	shown

132 다음 글의 밑줄 친 부분 중, 어법상 틀린 것은?

One of the goals of sociology courses ① is to help students develop a "sociological imagination," an ability to view human behavior and beliefs in terms of cultural forces. Understanding how culture shapes human lives is essential to ② acquiring a sociological imagination. But while it's fairly easy to detect culture's pervasive influence when you're in a foreign land, it's quite another matter ③ to recognize how your culture shapes you. We take it for granted ④ what our beliefs and our way of doing things are perfectly natural, and if we're asked why we believe or do the things we do, we may find ⑤ it very hard to answer. Someone once said that the last thing a fish would ever notice is water, and so it is with us: we rarely perceive our own culture's power over us.

133 다음 글의 밑줄 친 부분 중, 어법상 틀린 것은?

The most ① pressing task may lie in the issue of climate change. Long before fossil fuels run out, we'll have to face up to the consequences of using these fuels. Global warming will be a much greater threat in 20 years than it is today. Changes in the atmosphere have never ② occurred as rapidly as they do now. Our current tools and social structures are not ③ sufficiently effective for us to manage the climate or to prosper in hostile surroundings. We must either learn how to change the climate in our favor or ④ develop technologies that will enable us to survive in different environments. Both are clearly lacking today. The development of science and technology in these areas should therefore ⑤ give the highest priority. If we manage to solve these problems in the decades ahead, we have grounds for hoping that our descendants will also survive into the distant future.

134 다음 글의 밑줄 친 부분 중, 어법상 틀린 것은?

West Side Story is a 1961 film directed by Robert Wise and Jerome Robbins. It is an adaptation of the Broadway musical of the same name, which was itself ① adapted from William Shakespeare's *Romeo and Juliet*. The film was released on October 18, 1961 through United Artists. The film won 10 Academy Awards in its 11 nominated categories, and the soundtrack album made more money than any other album before ② it. Elvis Presley was originally approached for the role of Tony in the film. However, his manager strongly believed the role to be wrong for Elvis and made him ③ decline in favor of other movie musicals. When the movie became a hit and earned 10 Oscars, Elvis deeply regretted ④ to give up the part. He was only one of many young stars that ⑤ were under consideration for the role of Tony.

135 다음 글의 밑줄 친 부분 중, 어법상 틀린 것은?

Mental illness is one of the last societal ① taboos. Although we've made progress in talking about mental health issues from depression and ② anxious to addiction, the stigma of mental illness remains. For some people, it could even be seen as a result of laziness, attention-seeking, or weakness. However, it certainly has neurobiological origins. To tell a depressed person to just 'snap out of it' or 'shake it off' ③ is just like saying this to someone who lives with diabetes. The problem is even if someone wants to help, it's not uncommon for them to back away when the real, damaging symptoms appear. Depression is ④ depressing, even to those who want to give help. "I can't have this conversation anymore. It just cycles," one sufferer's friend says. And she was right; cycling thoughts—the inability to roll an idea around in your head ⑤ until you come to a logical conclusion—is a hallmark of depression.

*stigma: 낙인, 오명 *hallmark (전형적인): 특징, 품질 증명

136 다음 글의 밑줄 친 부분 중, 어법상 틀린 것은?

Scientists still do not agree on ① how the first musical instruments looked and when they were developed. Some scientists believe that the first true musical instruments were a fairly recent development, dating back to around 60,000 years ago. ② Others believe that early humans were using some form of instrument as long as they had been using simple tools. If this is the case, music may date as far back as 2 million years ago! It is hard to pinpoint a time because many instruments may not have ③ been preserved. Also, many of the first musical instruments probably also had other uses. This would make ④ it hard to recognize as musical instruments. Scientists working on an ancient archaeological site today would have a difficult time figuring out ⑤ if certain objects were used for their sound or were used only as tools.

*pinpoint: (위치·시간을) 정확히 찾아내다

권장 시간 8분 | 시작·종료 시간 | : ~ : | 나의 소요 시간 | 분 초

137 다음 글의 밑줄 친 부분 중, 어법상 틀린 것은?

Often students work multiple part-time jobs while studying to make ends meet. When tax season comes around, they are confused since they are ignorant of how their ① keeping multiple jobs affects their tax. What you should know is, if you are an Australian resident, for example, you do not pay tax on the first $18,200 you earn each financial year. This is called the tax-free threshold and can be tricky to determine when you are holding down multiple jobs. If you have multiple jobs, an important concept to understand is ② that this tax-free threshold is strictly on the first $18,200 you earn in total, not per employer. To avoid ③ getting caught out, it's recommended that you only claim the tax-free threshold from the employer you expect to earn the highest income ④ from. While this will mean that you'll pay a higher tax rate on your other jobs now, come tax return time you'll more than ⑤ likely to get some of this back.

138 (A), (B), (C)의 각 네모 안에서 어법에 맞는 표현으로 가장 적절한 것은?

Single-person households and "empty nesters" have different lifestyles and preferences than larger families. Singles, especially, spend heavily on foodservice, both for convenience and for social occasions. The increasing domination of these smaller all-adult households and single-person households (A) [have / has] implications for restaurant patronage patterns. For instance, the use of takeout has grown among both families with children and adult-only households (singles and couples). But these different types of households tend (B) [to interest / to be interested] in different types of takeout, and for different reasons. While the family with kids may order a crowd-pleasing, inexpensive meal such as a large pizza or a bucket of chicken, the single adult might be more likely to stop on the way home after work for a sophisticated green salad that's "too much trouble" to make for just one person. Adults who live alone or with one other person are more likely to rely on takeout as a routine pattern of sourcing food, (C) [whether / that] they are in an older age group or a younger one.

*empty nester: (장성한 자녀가 집을 떠난 뒤) 남게 된 부부
**patronage: (특정 식당 등에 대한 고객의) 애용

	(A)		(B)		(C)
①	have	—	to interest	—	whether
②	have	—	to be interested	—	that
③	has	—	to interest	—	whether
④	has	—	to be interested	—	whether
⑤	has	—	to be interested	—	that

139 다음 글의 밑줄 친 부분 중, 어법상 틀린 것은?

Making your home ① safe for toddlers requires careful planning. Every home ② contains many things that are tempting to small children. Experts have proposed many useful ideas that can cheaply and easily protect them. Most importantly, all medicines and cleaning products should ③ be stored in locked boxes. Kitchen appliances, like stoves, should have safety locks so they can't be turned on by a child, and drawers in the bathroom and kitchen should have special devices that make ④ them impossible for kids to open them. Also, electrical outlets should be covered with a mechanism ⑤ that shuts automatically when not in use. Finally, it is a good idea to buy tables and other furniture with round edges to avoid injuries if a toddler falls into them.

140 다음 글의 밑줄 친 부분 중, 어법상 틀린 것은?

I remember how ① pleased I was when I first climbed a cliff. My forearms were so cramped from exertion that I ② could not barely pull the rope up as my climbing partner, Leonard Coyne, followed the route. After ③ reaching the top, Leonard mentioned that he knew the descent route was fairly hard, though the previous climbers had taken it lightly. ④ Filled with overconfidence, I simply tossed the rope to the ground below. We had just done the tough ascent, so surely we did not need a rope now. Then I started down the nearly ⑤ vertical face. Suddenly Leonard yelled, "Your handhold is loose! Grab my leg!" There I was—unroped, 150 feet above the ground, holding a couple of loose flakes of rock—when my foothold broke.

141 다음 글의 밑줄 친 부분 중, 어법상 틀린 것은?

Why do we love roller coasters, even though they can make our stomachs ① feel like they've dropped entirely out of our bodies? Why do we insist upon ② watching horror movies that leave us huddling beneath the covers on the couch? In short: because it's fun. "Fear has a bad reputation, but it's not all bad," an expert says. Our bodies respond to fear with the basic physiological reaction of fight or flight and release chemicals that help ③ protect us by boosting energy, protecting us from feeling pain, and shutting down non-essential systems, like pesky critical thought. When we're in real danger, these physiological responses are necessary for our survival. But when we're not in any danger, like when we are merely riding a roller coaster for the fifth time in a row, our bodies are free to stop ④ to focus on survival and start focusing on a little thing that can only be described as "the natural high of ⑤ being scared."

142 다음 글의 밑줄 친 부분 중, 어법상 틀린 것은?

People love to shop around holidays and seasonal events—in fact, our retail spending jumps ① by around one-third in December as we gear up for the festive season. It isn't just about gifts: at Christmas, we double our turkey consumption and buy 60% more alcohol. While Christmas clearly gives retailers ② cause to celebrate—there are plenty of other seasonal events and occasions throughout the year that can help give businesses a major sales boost. For instance, in February, Australians spend almost $800 m ③ on Valentine's Day shopping, with florists generating 10% of their total annual sales on a single day. The Easter Bunny's arrival in March or April brings around $3 bn in spending, and 50% more chocolate sales than any other ④ weeks of the year. With this in mind, there's opportunity to take advantage of ⑤ these seasonal events to benefit sales.

권장 시간 8분 | 시작·종료 시간 | : ~ : | 나의 소요 시간 | 분 초

143 (A), (B), (C)의 각 네모 안에서 어법에 맞는 표현으로 가장 적절한 것은?

Our modern equivalent to the use of music in coordinating agricultural labor is the provision of music in factories. Opinion is divided as to its effects. Judging from its use in agriculture, one might expect (A) [that / what] music would improve the performance of the routine operations which are common in factory work. Repetitive movements are less tedious when synchronized with musical rhythms. The provision of music is certainly popular amongst factory workers. However, the heightening of morale is not (B) [necessary / necessarily] accompanied by increase in output. Whilst music probably enhances the performance of routine tasks, especially those in which repetitive physical actions prevail, it tends to interfere with the performance of non-repetitive actions which need (C) [thinking / to think] about. For example, there is evidence suggesting that music increases the number of errors in typing.

*synchronize: 동시에 일어나게 하다

(A)		(B)		(C)
① that	—	necessarily	—	thinking
② that	—	necessarily	—	to think
③ what	—	necessarily	—	thinking
④ what	—	necessary	—	thinking
⑤ what	—	necessary	—	to think

144 다음 글의 밑줄 친 부분 중, 어법상 틀린 것은?

Genocide, the willful killing of specific groups of people—as occurred in the Nazi extermination camps during World War II—is ① universally considered wrong even if it is sanctioned by a government or an entire society. The Nuremberg trials that were conducted after World War II ② supported this point. Even though most of the accused individuals tried to claim they were merely following orders when they murdered or arranged for the murder of large numbers of Jews and other groups, many ③ were found guilty. The reasoning was that there is a higher moral order ④ under which certain human actions are wrong regardless of who endorses them. Thus, despite their desire to view events from a culturally relative standpoint, most sociologists find certain actions wrong, no matter ⑤ how the context.

*sanction: 승인하다
**endorse: (공개적으로) 승인하다

145 (A), (B), (C)의 각 네모 안에서 어법에 맞는 표현으로 가장 적절한 것은?

Responding to powerful timber interests, a controversial bill that permitted salvage logging in national forests (A) [were / was] signed into law in 1995. The law allowed loggers to cut down dead trees and trees weakened by insects, disease, or fire, as well as healthy trees (B) [considered / are considered] to be in danger of catching a disease. The law, which expired at the end of 1996, allowed loggers access to parts of the forest that (C) [have / had] been declared off-limits by the Northwest Forest Plan as well as other national forest areas not normally open to logging. It also excused timber companies from complying with provisions of the Clean Water Act and Endangered Species Act.

*salvage: 폐품 이용; 재난 구조

	(A)		(B)		(C)
①	were	—	considered	—	had
②	were	—	are considered	—	have
③	was	—	are considered	—	had
④	was	—	considered	—	had
⑤	was	—	considered	—	have

146 다음 글의 밑줄 친 부분 중, 어법상 <u>틀린</u> 것은?

Students must leave campus 24 hours after their last exam or by 12 p.m. (noon) on Sunday, May 15, 2016. Vacating requires that you move out, remove all your belongings from your residence and lounge, and ① return your key. Students are responsible for the following: remove all personal items from your residence; items left in rooms after closing will be donated or ② disposed. The university assumes no liability for items left behind. All furniture within a residence at the move-in inspection must be ③ present and in good condition during the move-out inspection, or you will be charged for replacement. Please remember to lock doors and close windows when you leave ④ to avoid damage to your room after your departure. If you neglect ⑤ to lock your doors and windows, you are responsible if damages are found or any furniture is missing during the final inspection.

*liability: (법적) 책임

147 다음 글의 밑줄 친 부분 중, 어법상 <u>틀린</u> 것은?

Considerations about print size may eventually become outmoded ① because of the rise in availability of talking books or the talking text option found in some e-books. For example, Bouchard Ryan and her colleagues observed that older adults with visual problems were more likely to change from reading newspapers and magazines (which typically have small print and poor contrast) ② to listen to talking books. They also noted that about a quarter of their sample used computer technology to enlarge print. However, ③ although talking books offer a solution to people with sight difficulties, they are not, as is commonly supposed, a direct substitute for reading. Two reasons can be cited. First, the narrator will almost certainly place emphases upon what is being read out that may not match what the listener would emphasize ④ were he or she reading for themselves. Second, in reading it is easy to move back over a passage of print just read, or to skim through a section of prose. This is either very difficult or impossible to do when ⑤ using a talking book.

148 다음 글의 밑줄 친 부분 중, 어법상 틀린 것은?

"Mother, I will be an actress." "But what if you don't succeed, and will not be able to play the wonderful parts you are so ① excited about?" "It doesn't matter. I will be an actress ② even if they only let me walk across the stage and wave a handkerchief." Years later, after dozens of important and less important acting parts, after many disappointments and calamities in the realm of the theater, I always returned to the same truism: I must be in the theater and ③ belong to it, even if I can only walk across the stage and wave a handkerchief. I believe an actress is born an actress; she does not learn to be ④ one. My earliest memory is the wish to express a persona, whether in song or in text. I didn't think about the audience, it didn't exist for me. Being an actor, indeed, ⑤ have nothing to do with success.

*calamity: 불행, 재난 **persona: 극 중 인물

149 (A), (B), (C)의 각 네모 안에서 어법에 맞는 표현으로 가장 적절한 것은?

Science fiction stories are full of people disappearing through walls, riding in starships that move faster than light, and (A) [travel / traveling] instantly to distant places in space and time. While these ideas seem like creative fantasies, they actually come from theoretical physics, in particular the work of Albert Einstein, (B) [who / whose] theories include how the universe curves back on itself in the three dimensions of space plus the fourth invisible dimension of time. If Einstein is correct (and experiments done over the last hundred years suggest that he is) then those sci-fi stories might be possible. This idea has become so appealing that serious physicists regularly (C) [comment / to comment] on these technologies in respected professional journals.

(A)		(B)		(C)
① travel	—	who	—	to comment
② travel	—	whose	—	to comment
③ traveling	—	who	—	to comment
④ traveling	—	whose	—	comment
⑤ traveling	—	who	—	comment

150 다음 글의 밑줄 친 부분 중, 어법상 틀린 것은?

It might be surprising that one byproduct of polar ice melt ① is the release of microbes that have been frozen for more than 750,000 years. The real surprise, however, is that the microbes are still alive and capable of ② being reanimated once thawed. As reported by *Daily Climate*, scientists aren't too worried about a sudden spread of ancient diseases, but rather the hard-to-predict impact of an enormous amount of organic matter that will begin decomposing. Scientists estimate that the entire biomass ③ held within the ice sheet could amount to more than 1,000 times that of the humans on earth. The amount of carbon dioxide and methane emitted would constitute a major source of greenhouse gases ④ that climate researchers haven't considered. The concerns ⑤ worsening when scientists start thinking about how these ancient microbes might impact the delicate chemistry of the ocean and its existing microbial populations.

*thaw: 녹다

151 다음 글의 밑줄 친 부분 중, 어법상 틀린 것은?

'Open source' is a development method for software ① that utilizes the power of distributed user review and transparency of process. This permits users ② to change and improve the software and to redistribute it in modified or unmodified form. The promise of open source is better quality, higher reliability, more flexibility, and lower cost. Software developed through open source even ③ including computer operating systems. ④ They are downloadable from the Internet or available with a support contract for a few dollars. Since these operating systems are a significant part of the cost of a new computer system, ⑤ not having to buy one with your machine can save you good money.

*open source: 오픈 소스(무상으로 공개된 소프트웨어의 소스코드)

152 다음 글의 밑줄 친 부분 중, 어법상 틀린 것은?

When people began to plant stored seed stock intentionally, they also began protecting their plants. This changed the evolutionary pressure ① that these food plants experienced, as they no longer had to survive in a natural environment. Instead, humans created a new environment for ② themselves, and selected for other characteristics than nature previously had. Seeds ③ recovered at archaeological sites clearly show that early farmers selected for larger seeds and thinner seed coats. Thick, hardy seed coats are often necessary for seeds to survive in a natural environment, because the seeds of many wild plants remain ④ dormant for months until winter has passed and rain sets in. But under human management, thick seed coats are unnecessary, as farmers take over responsibility for storing seeds away from moisture and predators. In fact, seeds with thinner coats were preferred as they are easier to eat or process (into flour), and they allow seedlings to sprout more quickly when ⑤ sown.

153 다음 글의 밑줄 친 부분 중, 어법상 틀린 것은?

The house chores kids grow up ① accepting, albeit unwillingly at times, as part and parcel of family life make them emotionally and mentally stronger. And in making them do so, it's definitely nurturing to pay your children for their efforts. The satisfaction our daughter gains from contributing to the running of our home, the life skills she's learning as a result, and the hard cash ② which she's rewarded give her a sense of responsibility, value and purpose. Some might argue that giving rewards for good behavior in this way is wrong, but isn't that ③ what adult working life—something she'll eventually enter into—is all about? Naturally, there are times when I think I could get a job ④ done in half the time and perhaps to a higher standard than she might offer. But ⑤ how else will my daughter learn to look after herself if she spends her earliest years living in fully serviced accommodation?

154 다음 글의 밑줄 친 부분 중, 어법상 틀린 것은?

For a child to one day become free from his parents' control, the child must be secure in his parents' power as represented by their loving authority. The more ① effective they communicate that authority, the more secure the child feels, and the better able he will be to eventually establish a life of his own. During this journey toward independence, ② whenever he feels threatened, he turns back toward the safety of his parents' love and authority. In other words, it is impossible for a child to become independent unless he knows exactly ③ where his parents stand, both literally and figuratively. That requires, of course, ④ that his parents know where they themselves stand. If the parents are unsure of ⑤ themselves—if, in other words, they are insecure in their authority—they cannot communicate security to their child, and the child cannot move successfully away from them. In such cases, the child will become clinging, or disobedient, or both.

155 다음 글의 밑줄 친 부분 중, 어법상 틀린 것은?

When Columbus discovered America, European culture ① hadn't yet grasped the concept of discovery. Various languages had verbs that could be translated as "discover," but only in the sense of discovering things like a worm under a rock. Scholars operated within a worldview ② that all knowledge had been described by the ancients, such as Ptolemy, the astronomer who compiled the mathematical details of the Earth-centered universe. As well as being an astronomer, Ptolemy was also the greatest of ancient geographers. So when Columbus showed that Ptolemy's grasp on geography was ③ flawed, it opened the way for Copernicus to challenge Ptolemy on his picture of the cosmos as well. Deep thinkers who were paying attention then realized that nature possessed secrets ④ for humankind to "discover." "The existence of the idea of discovery is necessary for science," writes historian David Wootton. "The discovery of America in 1492 created a new activity ⑤ where intellectuals could engage in: the discovery of new knowledge."

156 다음 글의 밑줄 친 부분 중, 어법상 틀린 것은?

It is a common presumption that all fields of science—or even all intellectual disciplines—are ① essentially the same sort of thing: the pursuit of truth, albeit about different topics. In point of fact, this is quite wrong. Each intellectual discipline carries with it peculiar beliefs about what "truth" even means, about what is valuable and what is trivial, about how much or little objectivity is possible, about how certain the knowledge that can be obtained ② is, and much more. There is good reason to think of the academic disciplines as cultures, ③ their members have not only a common intellectual task but also many values and many characteristics of behavior in common. Each discipline develops a distinct culture specifically ④ suited to its particular intellectual task—for example, differences between pure mathematics and mathematical physics. One consequence is that disparate answers may be offered by various disciplines on any given questions, say as to ⑤ how science works: each discipline looks in its own manner for the answer, and each seeks its own sort of answer.

*disparate: 상이한

157 다음 글의 밑줄 친 부분 중, 어법상 틀린 것은?

About two years ago my friend and I were on a cruise through the western Mediterranean aboard a Princess Liner. At dinner we noticed an elderly lady ① sitting alone in the main dining room. I also noticed that all the staff—the ship's officers, waiters, etc.—all of them seemed very ② familiar with this lady. I asked our waiter who the lady was, expecting to be told she owned the line. But he said he only knew that she ③ had been on board for the last four cruises back to back. One evening I caught her eye and stopped ④ saying hello. We chatted and I said, "I understand you ⑤ have been on this ship for the last four cruises." She replied, "Yes, that's true." I stated, "I don't understand." And she replied, "It's cheaper than a nursing home."

158 다음 글의 밑줄 친 부분 중, 어법상 틀린 것은?

Rapid changes in modern society ① are affecting education. Due to changes in information technology, neither teachers nor students are able to prepare for ② working in these times. Teachers must adjust to the fact ③ which they can't know everything, but must support learning. The Internet is one way to create new learning environments for teachers and students. Teachers today are unable to use the same methods and materials ④ that they have developed during a lifetime of teaching. It is important ⑤ for teachers to keep up with changes and practice lifelong learning. Without an environment that allows teachers to grow within the profession, they will be unable to give their students all the necessary tools to succeed in modern life.

159 다음 글의 밑줄 친 부분 중, 어법상 틀린 것은?

Grocery shopping is sometimes a hard thing to do. Ingredients are costly and prices can fluctuate due to weather or plant shortages or animal illnesses. But most of us tend to buy the same ingredients all the time, so with ① a little added attention, we can monitor what our most-bought foods ② cost. If you're not already making a weekly shopping list, start doing so now. I start a new shopping list early in the week and begin to make notes of what needs ③ to purchase and ideas for the next week's meals. This makes ④ creating a list no big deal. Since I shop in more than one place, I can keep track of prices for things I buy regularly by making notes on my shopping list. Knowing this information can have a huge budget impact. Clearly ⑤ keeping track helps you know where and when to buy the core items you constantly require.

160 다음 글의 밑줄 친 부분 중, 어법상 틀린 것은?

Most child abuse ① occurs within the family. Risk factors include parental depression, a parental history of childhood abuse, and domestic violence. Child neglect and mistreatment is also more common in families ② live in poverty and among parents who are drug or alcohol abusers. Most often, child abuse is done by a caregiver or someone the child knows, not a stranger. Children who have been mistreated are often afraid to tell anyone, thinking they will be blamed or ③ that no one will believe them. Sometimes they remain quiet because the person who abused them is someone they love very much, or ④ because of fear, or both. Parents also tend to overlook signs and symptoms of abuse, because they don't want to face the truth. This is a serious mistake. The longer a child continues to be abused or ⑤ is left to deal with the situation on his own, the less likely he is to make a full recovery.

161 (A), (B), (C)의 각 네모 안에서 어법에 맞는 표현으로 가장 적절한 것은?

Our necks work hard every day (A) [support / supporting] the weight of our heads, whether we're in motion or sitting quietly. We usually ignore this vital body part until we wake up one morning in pain. This discomfort can be made worse by carrying a heavy shoulder bag or (B) [sleep / sleeping] in the wrong position. But a painful neck is also a part of growing older, because the disks that act as cushions between each bone of the neck gradually (C) [lose / loses] their thickness. Eventually the bones actually squish the disks. Your body compensates when this happens by shifting the weight of your head from your neck to your joints, which can cause shoulder or arm pain.

*squish: ((구어)) ~을 찌그러뜨리다

	(A)		(B)		(C)
①	support	—	sleep	—	loses
②	support	—	sleeping	—	lose
③	supporting	—	sleep	—	lose
④	supporting	—	sleeping	—	loses
⑤	supporting	—	sleeping	—	lose

162 (A), (B), (C)의 각 네모 안에서 어법에 맞는 표현으로 가장 적절한 것은?

One explanation for why the world (A) [maintained / has maintained] a nuclear cease-fire since 1945 is that it was understood that war between the United States and the former Soviet Union would have meant almost total destruction of life on Earth. Now, if nuclear proliferation (B) [continues / will continue], the danger of a nuclear weapon being used by a smaller country against another will increase. In the future, such an event may be more likely to occur than nuclear war between the superpowers was, (C) [because / because of] the continued existence of conditions that have helped to maintain nuclear peace—such as powerful second-strike forces and strong, stable governments in nuclear states—cannot be guaranteed.

	(A)		(B)		(C)
①	maintained	—	continues	—	because
②	maintained	—	continues	—	because of
③	maintained	—	will continue	—	because of
④	has maintained	—	continues	—	because
⑤	has maintained	—	will continue	—	because of

163 다음 글의 밑줄 친 부분 중, 어법상 틀린 것은?

Most of us ① have experienced enough buffet meals to know that we must walk up and down the two hundred foot long table of dishes to "graze" and "browse" the contents before ② loading up our plates. Still, our plates are usually loaded up before we make it past the first twenty feet. We do the same thing with information. We search the Web, find twenty thousand hits and light up with joy. ③ Confused quantity with success, we ④ greedily scoop up everything within our reach, saving it for later. We must beware of a "buffet mentality" when we step up to the information feast. Perhaps we need to replace that "more is better" mindset with "less is more." Wisdom has ⑤ more to do with distillation and reduction than volume. While we may want to search widely, we must harvest sparingly and wisely.

*distillation: 증류

164 다음 글의 밑줄 친 부분 중, 어법상 틀린 것은?

Do you go shopping in your sweats with no makeup on? It's not a good idea. Think about it this way: If you're trying on a pretty dress with a nest of ① unwashed hair on your head and a shiny T-zone, you're sort of setting yourself up for failure. That's when you get yourself into "nothing looks good on me" thinking, which we all know is never fun. Another important tip is that you have to TRY ON ② whatever attracts you while shopping. You really don't know ③ how something is going to look on you until you try it on. Sometimes a piece is ④ stunned on the hanger but just doesn't look right on your frame, and sometimes it's the other way around. It's also important to try on a variety of silhouettes ⑤ so you have an idea of which styles tend to work best for your body.

*T-zone: 티존(얼굴에서 이마와 코 부위를 이르는 말)

165 다음 글의 밑줄 친 부분 중, 어법상 틀린 것은?

Willingness to make mistakes means being ready to put yourself in potentially ① embarrassing situations. This can be scary, but it's the only way to develop and improve. No matter ② how much you learn, you won't ever speak a language without putting yourself out there: talk to strangers in the language, ask for directions, order food, try to tell a joke. The more often you do this, the bigger your comfort zone becomes and the more at ease you can ③ be in new situations. "At the beginning you're going to encounter difficulties: maybe the pronunciation, maybe the grammar, the syntax, or the sayings. But I think the most important thing is to develop a feeling for the language. Every native speaker has a feel for his or her own language, and that's basically ④ which makes a native speaker— ⑤ whether you can make the language your own," an expert says.

*syntax: 구문론, 통사론

166 다음 글의 밑줄 친 부분 중, 어법상 틀린 것은?

Buying groceries—for most of us it's a chore. Still, I actually rather like it, except when I have to shop in Fairway's west-side store a few days ① before a holiday. No one likes that. Usually, I practice my own grocery manifesto: you can't be a great cook ② unless you're first a good food shopper. That's because most of the work and key decisions about our home cooking get ③ done when we shop, not when we're back in the kitchen. You'd never know this if you've drawn your understanding of cooking from the Food Network or Instagram—there's not much to see there when it comes to going shopping. Similarly, if you refer to cookbooks and food blogs, you'd think ④ what matters the most is the recipe. It's not. It's the shopping. ⑤ Shopping well and you'll eat well. It's a small idea. But it has a big impact.

*manifesto: 선언서, 실천 강령

167 (A), (B), (C)의 각 네모 안에서 어법에 맞는 표현으로 가장 적절한 것은?

How does a seed know which way is up? No matter which way a seed is planted, it sends its stem growing upwards and the root downwards. One answer was found in experiments (A) [where / which] seeds were planted in zero gravity. It was found that this made the seeds grow in all directions. This result suggests that a seed (B) [respond / responds] to gravity. The roots grow towards it and the stem grows away. Scientists do not fully understand the process where heavy starch grain found in plant cells shifts if a plant falls over, which produces growth hormones in certain areas in a plant. These hormones cause the cells on the bottom of the stem (C) [to grow / growing] faster and push the stem upward.

*starch grain: 녹말 입자

	(A)		(B)		(C)
①	where	—	respond	—	to grow
②	where	—	responds	—	to grow
③	where	—	respond	—	growing
④	which	—	responds	—	growing
⑤	which	—	respond	—	growing

168 (A), (B), (C)의 각 네모 안에서 어법에 맞는 표현으로 가장 적절한 것은?

Transport is an exciting and rapidly evolving field. The main drivers of change are technological progress and societal evolution. In recent years, new technologies of information and communication have emerged (A) [that / what] are leading to major innovations in applications such as traveler information services and pricing of infrastructure usage. These technologies have also profoundly transformed logistics for firms, and they are (B) [beginning / begun] to have noticeable impacts on the daily activity and travel patterns of households. The volume of travel is affected by two opposing forces: economic growth which tends to boost mobility and concerns about the environment and energy supply which tend to restrain (C) [it / them].

*logistics: 물류 업무

	(A)		(B)		(C)
①	that	—	beginning	—	it
②	that	—	begun	—	them
③	that	—	beginning	—	them
④	what	—	begun	—	them
⑤	what	—	beginning	—	it

169 다음 글의 밑줄 친 부분 중, 어법상 <u>틀린</u> 것은?

Continental land masses are usually covered by a layer of topsoil ① <u>in which</u> plants can grow. This topsoil can be from a few inches to several feet deep. It consists of tiny pieces of rock, ② <u>mixed</u> with air and water. But the most important ingredient of topsoil, called humus, is made of decomposed plant remains. Because humus contains nutrients and absorbs water, the more humus soil contains, ③ <u>the better</u> it is for growing new plants. The different types of rock that make up soils ④ <u>is</u> usually the remains of 'parent rock' that is now farther below the surface. These rocks are made of minerals and ⑤ <u>formed</u> in various ways, such as by volcanoes. Erosion from wind and water has turned them into fine particles.

*humus: 거름흙

170 다음 글의 밑줄 친 부분 중, 어법상 <u>틀린</u> 것은?

We've all had the experience of being stuck trying to decide ① <u>whether</u> to buy some new piece of clothing or just pass on it. When this happens, try to picture the item in your wardrobe. Some people say you should be able to think of at least three items you can pair it with in order to make it worth ② <u>getting</u>, but I say as long as you can think of one, you're all set. The reason? You love it, and that's the most important thing. From there, you really just need one thing to wear it with and you're good to go. This will encourage you ③ <u>shopping</u> outside of your comfort zone, and chances are, you'll start finding more things that will go with ④ <u>that</u> new piece. Styles evolve—don't hold ⑤ <u>yourself</u> back by choosing the same things over and over again.

171 다음 글의 밑줄 친 부분 중, 어법상 <u>틀린</u> 것은?

In the past, the highest number of what are called 'repetitive motion injuries' ① <u>were occurred</u> among workers in meat factories who chopped meat all day. But, now with computers being used constantly, office workers are suffering from the same symptoms. An aching back or neck and eye strain ② <u>are</u> among the most common complaints. Carpal Tunnel Syndrome results in numb fingers and wrist pain and ③ <u>it</u> often requires surgery to bring relief. Pain is now the unpleasant result of holding our arms over the keyboard, a position ④ <u>that</u>, according to doctors, the human arm wasn't designed to be in for hours on end. If it ⑤ <u>is held</u> like that, pain will be the result.

*Carpal Tunnel Syndrome: 손목터널증후군

172 다음 글의 밑줄 친 부분 중, 어법상 <u>틀린</u> 것은?

An increasing number of people now ① <u>prefer</u> to beat the seasonal crowds by doing all their shopping from the comfort of their home. In December, there is a surge in online sales—with seven out of ten major retailers ② <u>recording</u> major increases in the number of unique visitors to their websites. The display of your business plays an important part in shaping the customer experience. You can create a positive environment by decorating your store with a seasonal theme. ③ <u>To stand out</u> from your competitors online and create a more enjoyable shopping experience for your customers there ④ <u>are</u> a number of things you can do: put some festive cheer on your website; add a blog with season-themed content; highlight relevant sales and gift ideas; offer last-minute shipping options and a wider variety of shipping times. With upcoming festivals and events this year, plan ahead and prepare your business to maximize the opportunity to boost sales during ⑤ <u>this</u> periods.

권장 시간 8분 | 시작·종료 시간 | : ~ : | 나의 소요 시간 | 분 초

173 (A), (B), (C)의 각 네모 안에서 어법에 맞는 표현으로 가장 적절한 것은?

In India, Hindu women have traditionally applied a spot of ground vermilion powder to their forehead. The decorative spot is called a "bindi." It was a sign (A) [that / which] a woman was married, like wearing a wedding ring. Red, an important color in the Hindu religion, was always (B) [using / used] for bindis. But in modern India, bindis have become a fashion statement. Whereas in the past, only round red bindis were worn by married women, now both married and unmarried women have started wearing different sizes and shapes on their foreheads. They now are like fashion stickers to match the color of the outfit (C) [that / what] they are wearing and many are even decorated with beads, crystals, or glitter.

*vermilion: 주홍색의
*bindi: 빈디(인도 여성이 양미간에 붙이는 점)

	(A)		(B)		(C)
①	that	—	using	—	that
②	that	—	used	—	that
③	that	—	using	—	what
④	which	—	used	—	what
⑤	which	—	using	—	that

174 (A), (B), (C)의 각 네모 안에서 어법에 맞는 표현으로 가장 적절한 것은?

A messy desk can actually be an effective system. On messy desks, in general, the most important work tends to stay nearest to hand, while work that's safe to ignore (A) [tending / tends] to get pushed to the back or the bottom. Of course, having a messy desk means spending at least some of your time (B) [to root / rooting] through the mess to find things. This is where you can waste anywhere from an hour a week to an hour a day of your precious time. But as long as you keep the disorder to a reasonable level, you may even manage your work better. According to a survey, people who say they keep a very neat desk spend an average 36 percent more time looking for things at work than people who say they keep their desks fairly (C) [messy / messily].

	(A)		(B)		(C)
①	tends	—	rooting	—	messily
②	tends	—	to root	—	messily
③	tends	—	rooting	—	messy
④	tending	—	to root	—	messy
⑤	tending	—	rooting	—	messy

175 다음 글의 밑줄 친 부분 중, 어법상 틀린 것은?

Modern life makes it impossible to escape from nervous fatigue. All through the working hours and even more so in the time spent traveling between work and home, an urban worker is surrounded by noise, most of ① which he or she learns to ignore. ② Other thing which causes fatigue without our being aware of it is the constant nearness of strangers. The natural instinct of every animal, including man, is to investigate every stranger to decide ③ if he or she is a friend or a foe. This natural response has to be inhibited by ④ those who travel on the subway during rush hour. The result of this constant inhibition is a general rage against the crowd of strangers ⑤ with whom they are forced to have close contact.

176 다음 글의 밑줄 친 부분 중, 어법상 틀린 것은?

Terrorism, it is often noted, is the weapon of the weak against the strong. Terror is utilized to overcome ① seemingly insurmountable odds facing terrorists. Terrorists will typically strike out against targets that will have an impact on the group they wish ② to be influenced. An expert on terrorism states that "the relatively high efficiency of terrorism derives from its symbolic nature. If the terrorist comprehends that he is seeking a demonstration effect, he will attack targets with a maximum symbolic value so that he may gain publicity and elicit support for a cause." If these symbolic targets are destroyed, then the terrorist has succeeded in isolating individuals from the society in which they formerly felt secure and ③ protected. In the information age, some of the structures that constitute the "supporting framework" of society ④ are likely to be the high technology networks that allow individuals to communicate, access their money, and ⑤ be employed. Thus, it's inevitable that they become primary targets for terrorists.

*insurmountable: 대처할 수 없는, 수행 불가능한

177 (A), (B), (C)의 각 네모 안에서 어법에 맞는 표현으로 가장 적절한 것은?

The World Health Organization (WHO) said a family in Pakistan showed a high probability of human-to-human infection in a bird flu case last year. In that case, an animal doctor was infected with the bird flu virus (A) [which / when] he helped destroy diseased birds in Peshawar. His three brothers became infected later (B) [although / since] they had no contact with diseased birds. A professor says experts can not be 100 percent certain that human-to-human infection with the virus has occurred. But he says there seems (C) [to be / to have been] at least six cases, including those in Pakistan and China in 2007. Scientists worry that the virus might change over time into a form that passes easily among humans.

	(A)		(B)		(C)
①	which	—	although	—	to be
②	which	—	since	—	to have been
③	when	—	although	—	to have been
④	when	—	since	—	to have been
⑤	when	—	although	—	to be

권장 시간 8분 | 시작·종료 시간 | : ~ : | 나의 소요 시간 | 분 초

178 다음 글의 밑줄 친 부분 중, 어법상 틀린 것은?

Because of the increased circulation of media gossip and publicity, stars ① are required more than they were in the past to be performers in their personal lives. They are now expected to create and recreate ② themselves as "characters in the drama of their own biographies." Because of the global market for celebrity gossip and the increased competition within the acting profession, stars must constantly reaffirm their star status by ③ heightening the sensationalism of their image. A sociologist proposes that stars must prove over and over again ④ that they are sensational (both) on screen and in their personal lives in order to create the illusion of unending success. The ubiquity of contemporary star images, however, also creates what is called a "weakening of star persona" as stars become almost ⑤ constant on display.

*ubiquity: 도처에 있음
**persona: (무대 속에서의) 모습, 인물

179 다음 글의 밑줄 친 부분 중, 어법상 틀린 것은?

I'll never forget the day I took my daughter Julia for her first day at nursery school. When I tried to leave her, she clung so tightly to my knees that she had to be ① gently pulled off by a pair of young teachers. As I made my escape, and scurried off to the station, her screams and wails ② followed me down the street, as she rolled around in a frenzy on the floor, ③ furiously at this act of parental abandonment, deaf to all assurances ④ that I would collect her in a couple of hours. Fast-forward 18 years, to her graduation ceremony at Newcastle University, and this time the tears are coming down parental faces, as my wife and I watch our grown-up girl ⑤ take her first steps into the great, wide adult world of work.

180 (A), (B), (C)의 각 네모 안에서 어법에 맞는 표현으로 가장 적절한 것은?

"Identity theft" may sound like something from a futuristic fantasy, but it's very real and it's happening all over the world. Identity thieves gain access to your personal information, usually via the Internet or email, and pass themselves off as you, invariably (A) [makes / to make] purchases or bank transactions. Signs that your identity has been stolen (B) [include / includes] letters or phone calls approving or rejecting an application for credit that you didn't make; charges on your credit card statement for things you didn't buy; failing to receive credit card statements in the mail; and receiving calls or visits from debt collection agencies (C) [concerned / concerning] bank accounts that you didn't open.

	(A)		(B)		(C)
①	makes	—	include	—	concerned
②	makes	—	include	—	concerning
③	makes	—	includes	—	concerning
④	to make	—	include	—	concerning
⑤	to make	—	includes	—	concerned

181 다음 글의 밑줄 친 부분 중, 어법상 틀린 것은?

When we plant a rose seed in the earth, we notice ① that it is small, but we do not criticize it as "rootless and stemless." We treat it as a seed, giving it the water and nourishment ② required of a seed. When it first shoots up out of the earth, we don't condemn it as immature and underdeveloped; nor ③ do we criticize the buds for not being open when they appear. We stand in wonder at the process taking place and ④ giving the plant the care it needs at each stage of its development. The rose is a rose from the time it is a seed to the time it dies. Within it, at all times, it contains its whole potential. It seems to be ⑤ constantly in the process of change; yet at each state, at each moment, it is perfectly all right as it is.

*nourishment: 영양(분)

182 다음 글의 밑줄 친 부분 중, 어법상 틀린 것은?

The Bettmann Archive is a picture library that ① was founded in the 1930s by German immigrant Otto Bettmann. He arrived in New York City with two suitcases of photographs and opened a picture library, which he built into the biggest commercial operation of ② its kind in the world. Among the millions of photographs the archive ③ contains are some of the most memorable images of the 20th century: Marilyn Monroe standing over a street grate ④ ventilating her skirt, and Einstein sticking out his tongue. According to Bettmann, the archive's success was due to its unique filing system, ⑤ that he designed to suit journalistic needs. For example, the *Mona Lisa* was not filed under 'Paintings' or 'Leonardo da Vinci.' It was filed under 'Smiling.'

183 다음 글의 밑줄 친 부분 중, 어법상 틀린 것은?

Chefs love reservations. They love ① advance orders even more. That means they'll be able to predict the order volume without having to use their crystal ball, prepare the dining area without much fuss, and devote their efforts to ② cook the dishes well. So if you want a pleasant dining experience, pre-order your food. A good host or hostess will space out the reservations and walk-ins ③ to ensure the kitchen doesn't get swamped. Ever wonder why some restaurant hostesses say they're full even though you can clearly see empty tables around? Take a good look at the tables ④ currently seated. If you see a lot of people waiting for their food, that's because the kitchen is overwhelmed. ⑤ To prevent things from getting even worse, the hostess will put a halt on the walk-ins until things get back under control.

*crystal ball: (점칠 때 쓰는) 수정 구슬

184 다음 글의 밑줄 친 부분 중, 어법상 틀린 것은?

The emergent literacy perspective has provided ample evidence ① that children use their oral language as a foundation for developing early literacy. Although written language is an extension of oral language, there are many important differences between the two. One difference between oral and written language ② lies in their conventions. Some language learners require explicit instruction to make sentences and paragraphs connect to each other, to spell words, and to organize ideas in writing for an imagined or a real audience. Unlike writing, oral language offers more opportunities for the listener to ask questions for clarification and ③ to apply both verbal and nonverbal context cues. However, writers must learn to express their ideas clearly ④ used precise and accurate language, without the benefit of elaboration to the prospective reader. This is often a major struggle for many second language writers in ⑤ their early development of writing in English.

권장 시간 8분 | 시작·종료 시간 | : ~ : | 나의 소요 시간 | 분 초

185 (A), (B), (C)의 각 네모 안에서 어법에 맞는 표현으로 가장 적절한 것은?

Krebs and Davies identified ways in which predators can improve their odds of catching prey. Predators may develop more effective ways of searching through improved eyesight. Alternatively, they may find prey (A) [easier / more easily] by forming a search image, which involves learning about the visual features of their prey. Forming a search image may also relate to improved attentional processes. Evidence for the development of a search image in chicks (B) [was / were] reported by Dawkins. The prey consisted of colored rice grains on a background that was either the same or a very different color to the grains. The chicks initially found it hard to detect the prey when it was the same color as the background. After a few minutes, however, they started to detect the prey more quickly, which suggests that the chicks (C) [have formed / had formed] a suitable search image.

	(A)		(B)		(C)
①	easier	—	was	—	have formed
②	easier	—	were	—	had formed
③	more easily	—	was	—	have formed
④	more easily	—	were	—	had formed
⑤	more easily	—	was	—	had formed

186 (A), (B), (C)의 각 네모 안에서 어법에 맞는 표현으로 가장 적절한 것은?

Painting a room is often a refreshing experience, especially when the weather is changing. If your room has furnishings in it, your preliminary step to getting ready is to protect the furnishings. First, (A) [move / moving] all the furniture away from the walls and into the center of the room, stacking wherever possible to use as little floor space as you can. If the carpet is not fastened down, roll it up from each end toward the middle of the room. The next step is to cover the furniture with drop sheets. The cheap, lightweight, disposable plastic sheets are best. Use as (B) [many / much] of the 9 by 12 foot sheets as you need, to protect the furniture and carpet. Use masking tape to fasten loose plastic so as not to trip over it and (C) [to keep out / keeping out] stray paint spatters.

	(A)		(B)		(C)
①	move	—	many	—	to keep out
②	move	—	many	—	keeping out
③	move	—	much	—	keeping out
④	moving	—	much	—	keeping out
⑤	moving	—	many	—	to keep out

187 다음 글의 밑줄 친 부분 중, 어법상 틀린 것은?

It took a long while ① for scientists to figure out that counting sheep doesn't help you get to sleep. To prove it, researchers at Oxford University asked 50 insomniacs to try different focusing techniques over a series of nights. On average those ② imagining relaxing scenes—such as taking a holiday—fell asleep 20 minutes earlier, and those who counted sheep or were left to their own devices took ③ a little longer than normal. Then, there's the Swiss research that suggests wearing bed socks and hugging a hot-water bottle may help more than a sleeping pill. Apparently, as we drift off to sleep, the body redistributes heat from ④ its core to the hands and feet. At the same time, it releases hormones such as melatonin. Poor blood flow to the feet and hands ⑤ hinder this mechanism. Warming your fingers and toes should help the process along.

188 (A), (B), (C)의 각 네모 안에서 어법에 맞는 표현으로 가장 적절한 것은?

Pots, bags, and baskets—and eventually bottles—were central to early preservation technologies. Innovation in this realm was a long and drawn-out process extending across millennia, and one that does not easily give up all of its clues. Early containers were no doubt made from perishable materials such as leaves or grass or leather, (A) [leaving / left] little or no trace in the archaeological record. Later technologies of ceramics and glass radically expanded human capacity to preserve nature and made (B) [possible / possibly] the great ancient civilizations of China, India, Sumer, and Mesoamerica. Changes along these lines accelerated after the Industrial Revolution, especially in the generation around 1900. Industrial containerization made it possible to distribute foods throughout the globe; think only of (C) [what / whether] it would be like to live in a world without tin cans, cardboard cartons, and bottled drinks.

*Mesoamerica: 중앙아메리카
**containerization: 컨테이너에 의한 화물 수송

	(A)		(B)		(C)
①	leaving	—	possible	—	what
②	leaving	—	possible	—	whether
③	leaving	—	possibly	—	what
④	left	—	possible	—	what
⑤	left	—	possibly	—	whether

189 다음 글의 밑줄 친 부분 중, 어법상 틀린 것은?

Several years ago, using text-analysis software, researchers ① compared 156 poems by nine poets who committed suicide to 135 poems by nine poets who ② did not. Poets in both groups were matched as ③ close as possible by nationality, education, era, and gender. The study, published in 2001 in the *Journal of Psychosomatic Medicine*, showed that poets who committed suicide were more likely to ④ have used first person singular references (I, me, my) and fewer first person plural forms (we, us, our) in their poems than did non-suicidal poets. They also found that, over time, suicidal poets used fewer terms like talk, share, and listen, while non-suicidal poets ⑤ commonly increased their use of these words.

권장 시간 8분 | 시작·종료 시간 | : ~ : | 나의 소요 시간 | 분 초

190 다음 글의 밑줄 친 부분 중, 어법상 틀린 것은?

At times, coaches are so focused on helping athletes ① improve that they take good performance efforts for granted. Nonreinforcement means ② failing to acknowledge athletes' effort, skill execution, and performance improvements. Have you ever failed to point out the positives because you were so focused on identifying ③ that athletes needed to do to improve? It's an easy trap to fall into. Coaches who fail to provide reinforcement when it is warranted ④ assume that athletes know their work is noticed and appreciated. In reality, when you fail to acknowledge strong effort and performance, this communicates a negative message to athletes, ⑤ leaving them to question whether their effort and improvement are recognized and valued.

*warrant: 정당하게 만들다

191 (A), (B), (C)의 각 네모 안에서 어법에 맞는 표현으로 가장 적절한 것은?

If it is true that there are always many ways of seeing things, then the hard part is finding other points of view to choose from. One's own perspective is bound to feel most (A) [convincing / convinced], especially in the heat of the moment. Try to step back from your viewpoint and look at the facts objectively, to give yourself a choice of perspectives. As you change your perspective, you will find that your mood also shifts. Looking for new, and wider, perspectives prevents you from becoming trapped in a one-sided view and (B) [gives / giving] you more control over how you feel. The spectacles through which you view life are so familiar that you hardly notice that you are wearing them. By taking them off and experimenting with others, you can discover which things were out of focus and (C) [what / whether] you have been looking through distorted or colored glass.

	(A)		(B)		(C)
①	convincing	—	gives	—	what
②	convincing	—	giving	—	what
③	convinced	—	gives	—	whether
④	convinced	—	giving	—	what
⑤	convincing	—	gives	—	whether

192 다음 글의 밑줄 친 부분 중, 어법상 틀린 것은?

When you answer questions in class or take oral exams, present yourself in a credible way. Even when a person has successfully recalled something in a social context, he or she may still have a problem convincing others that what has been recalled ① is correct. There are five ways you can increase the likelihood ② that others will believe in what you recall. Express your recall with an appropriate degree of confidence. ③ Striving to make the contents of your recall include the most essential details. Claim an honest level of confidence in the accuracy of what you say you know. Express your certitude or doubt ④ prudently. Avoid overstatement or understatement in your confidence in ⑤ what you have recalled. Alternatively, do not be shy; sit up and speak confidently if you are sure of what you know.

*certitude: 확신

193 다음 글의 밑줄 친 부분 중, 어법상 틀린 것은?

It was a day when, upon opening my eyes at dawn, I had no desire to do anything but ① take a good rest. It was my third day in Melbourne, Australia. The day's schedule—a trip to the Dandenong Ranges National Park—didn't hold much appeal at ② that early hour. Interestingly enough, however, it was the time I spent in the Dandenong Ranges ③ that was still hovering in my memory on the day I flew back home. The Dandenong Ranges are densely forested hills ④ located to the east of Melbourne, where sky-high eucalyptus trees create a majestic atmosphere. The area is also home to Puffing Billy, a century-old steam locomotive ⑤ whom engineers, with long white beards, transport tourists from all over the world.

194 다음 글의 밑줄 친 부분 중, 어법상 틀린 것은?

Many voters distrust rich or well-educated political candidates. They feel that these candidates, if ① elected, will be unable to understand the problems of average working people like themselves. Therefore, some candidates use the 'plain folks' technique, presenting ② themselves as ordinary, average citizens. They try to show that they are 'plain folks' by referring to hard times in their lives in their speeches or ③ to pose for photographs while wearing a hard hat and mingling with everyday people. They will even change their speech ④ so that they don't sound too educated. In a similar way, the president of a giant corporation might appear in a company advertisement, as if the company is just a family business ⑤ run by ordinary folk.

195 (A), (B), (C)의 각 네모 안에서 어법에 맞는 표현으로 가장 적절한 것은?

In 1990, researchers moved to Vietnam to set up a program to fight child malnutrition in poor rural villages. While conducting surveys to understand the scope of the issue, they grew (A) [curious / curiously] about the handful of children who, despite coming from families as poor as all the others, were perfectly healthy—the positive deviants. What were these families doing differently? If they could discover behaviors that enabled even the most materially deprived parents (B) [to raise / raising] healthy children, the implications would be tremendous. They found that all the parents of the positive deviants for some reason collected tiny pieces of shell from crabs and shrimp from rice fields and added them to their children's diet, along with the greens from sweet potato tops. None of the other families (C) [did / were]. Both these ingredients, though free and available to anyone for the taking, were commonly considered to be inappropriate if not dangerous for children, and so were generally excluded from their diets.

*deviant: 사회의 상식[습관]에서 벗어난 사람, 괴짜

	(A)		(B)		(C)
①	curious	—	to raise	—	were
②	curious	—	raising	—	did
③	curious	—	to raise	—	did
④	curiously	—	raising	—	were
⑤	curiously	—	to raise	—	did

196 다음 글의 밑줄 친 부분 중, 어법상 틀린 것은?

With Uber, if you want to pay for someone else's ride, you have to use some clever tricks, like entering your friend's location and having them pretend to be ① yourself, which is awkward. Soon, there will be a better way. ② Using "Family Profile," a pilot program created by Uber, you can give any other Uber user you know a free ride, as long as they accept your invitation via email to join your "Family." While the feature is designed for people who want to ③ regularly pay for other riders, you can also use the new feature as a single-serve gift, if you invite someone to your "Family Profile," ④ give them a ride, and then delete them. But keep in mind that ⑤ allowing someone to join your "Family" also means they'll be able to see where you go on rides you pay for.

197 (A), (B), (C)의 각 네모 안에서 어법에 맞는 표현으로 가장 적절한 것은?

You know (A) [how / however] tough the current market is and that we recently had a difficult situation. It has become a question of survival of the fittest, and we must make ourselves fit. Our only choice is to cut costs and that means slimming down the workforce. Hopefully, these lay-offs will allow us to keep most of our workers. In the present business climate, only companies (B) [which / where] are prepared to take quick action to cut their employee costs will survive. Failure or bankruptcy is the only other option. We can inform you (C) [what / that] the proposed job cuts will apply to everyone, including management, office staff, and factory workers alike.

*survival of the fittest: 적자생존

	(A)		(B)		(C)
①	how	—	which	—	what
②	how	—	which	—	that
③	how	—	where	—	that
④	however	—	which	—	that
⑤	however	—	where	—	what

198 다음 글의 밑줄 친 부분 중, 어법상 틀린 것은?

Suppose one devotes a great deal of time and energy to making a decision, and then, ① because some combination of regret, missed opportunities, and high expectations, one ends up disappointed with the results. The questions this person might ask ② are, "Why?" or "What went wrong?" or "Whose fault is it?" And what is the likely answer to these questions? When the choice set is small, it seems natural and straightforward ③ to blame the world for disappointing results. "They only had three styles of jeans. What could I do? I did the best I could." However, when the choice set is large, ④ blaming the world is a much less plausible option. "With so many options available, success was out there to be had. I have only myself to blame for a disappointing result." In other words, self-blame for disappointing results becomes more likely ⑤ as the choice set grows larger.

*plausible: 그럴듯한, 이치에 맞는

199 다음 글의 밑줄 친 부분 중, 어법상 틀린 것은?

It is worth remembering that the idea of classical music widely ① accepted today did not exist until about 300 years ago. Performing music in concert halls to a ② paying audience, as something inherently pleasurable and significant, was pretty much unheard of until the eighteenth century and not widely established until the nineteenth. The concert hall, the audience, and the idea of 'masterpieces' of classical music were all effectively invented during the course of the eighteenth century in European cities. Much of the music that is now performed in public concerts ③ were not composed for that purpose. The cantatas of J. S. Bach, for example, were written ④ to be sung in religious services at the Church of St. Thomas in Leipzig where Bach was cantor. These pieces were part of weekly worship, and included chorales for the congregation to join in with the singing. ⑤ Sing along during a modern concert hall performance of one of these works today and you're likely to be told to shut up.

*cantor: 성가대 합창 지휘자 **chorale: 합창곡 찬송가 ***congregation: 신자들

200 다음 글의 밑줄 친 부분 중, 어법상 틀린 것은?

A few years ago, a consultant posed a question to executives: "Is your industry ① facing overcapacity and fierce price competition?" All but one said "yes." The only "no" came from the manager of a unique operation—the Panama Canal! This manager was fortunate to be in charge of a venture ② whose services are desperately needed by shipping companies and that offers the only simple route ③ links the Atlantic and Pacific Oceans. The canal's success could only be threatened if transoceanic shipping were to cease or if a new canal were built. ④ Both of these possibilities are extremely remote. When an organization's environment is stable and predictable, the executives can simply create a plan and execute it, and they can be confident that their plan will not be undermined by changes over time. But as the consultant's experience shows, only a few executives enjoy a stable and predictable situation, because change affects the strategies of ⑤ almost all organizations.

*the Panama Canal: 파나마 운하

201 다음 글의 밑줄 친 부분 중, 어법상 틀린 것은?

The phrase "Walking is man's best medicine," allegedly spoken by Hippocrates two millennia ago, is ① even more timely today. This fact is particularly true in industrialized societies where new technologies have not only changed the way we work but, even more ② profoundly, have also affected our lifestyles by reducing the physical effort of most of our daily activities. If you're now convinced you need walking, then it's time to buy a good pair of walking shoes. The main thing to be ③ aware is not to choose shoes or boots that have rigid arch supports. They can, over time, degrade the natural flexibility of the foot. This is because ④ the very muscles that make the arch resilient will eventually weaken owing to the unyielding rigidity of the footwear. Furthermore, no matter how great the shoe, occasionally ⑤ going barefoot is beneficial, because being barefoot can partly restore the natural flexibility of your feet.

202 다음 글의 밑줄 친 부분 중, 어법상 틀린 것은?

A group of scientists succeeded in recreating a dinosaur, Dreadnoughtus schrani, which is estimated ① to have been the same size and weight as a Boeing 737. To figure out how it walked, the scientists 3D scanned its leg bones. But first, they needed to fix the damage caused by 77 million years of ② being part of a rock, and then reduce the bones to a manageable size. By 3D printing cartilage and then ③ attach everything together with some motors, the physical model could be brought to life and then analyzed with more accuracy than would be possible using a computer simulation. Using a physical model like this ④ enables you to advance quickly. You can try different arrangements of ligaments, muscles, and tendons, and if they don't work, you rebuild the robot and maybe next time, it works better. After enough steps, you might end up with a robotic dinosaur leg that is a likely model of ⑤ what the real dinosaur leg actually looked like.

*Dreadnoughtus schrani: 드레드노투스 슈라니
(남미 아르헨티나에서 발견된 지구 역사상 가장 큰 육상 생물)
**cartilage: 연골 ***ligament: (관절의) 인대 ****tendon: 힘줄

203 다음 글의 밑줄 친 부분 중, 어법상 틀린 것은?

Lillian Bauer was ① extremely talented and driven, but she took giving so far that it took away from her reputation and her productivity. "She never said no to anything," described one consulting colleague. "She was so generous and giving with her time ② that she fell into the trap of becoming a pushover. It really delayed her promotion to partner." In a performance review, Bauer ③ was told that she wasn't meeting expectations: she lacked the assertive edge that was required of a consulting partner. She spent too much time developing those around her, and she was so committed to ④ helping clients that she bent over backward to meet their requests. It was known that Bauer "wasn't as forceful in pushing clients as people felt she needed to ⑤ do, in those crucial situations where clients needed to hear a harsh truth, or clients had been pushing an agenda in the wrong direction." For Bauer, being a giver turned out to be a career-limiting move.

*pushover: 만만한 사람

204 다음 글의 밑줄 친 부분 중, 어법상 틀린 것은?

Children have a range of attachment behaviors that signal to the parents ① that they need comfort —for example, a child might cry, follow or cling to the parent. The child is letting the parent ② know that at this moment he needs attention and nurture. Similarly, the child has a range of exploratory behaviors that signal that he is ready to investigate the world around him. These behaviors are characterized by moving away from the parent and ③ take an interest in events and objects in the world. The sensitive caregiver is able to read these signals and support the child on a moment-to-moment basis. A secure attachment forms between them. ④ Beginning early in life, children use this experience to understand how relationships work. An internal working model—a template or memory of the relationship—is formed; this will be a guide for the children both in the present and with future relationships. Children learn ⑤ what to expect from other people as a result of this early experience.

*template: 원형, 형판

205 다음 글의 밑줄 친 부분 중, 어법상 틀린 것은?

One of the best environments in which to examine cultural imperialism ① lies not in Western Europe or in developing countries but in Miami, Florida. Whites and blacks in that city frequently object to ② what they call Hispanic cultural imperialism. More than 40 percent of the city's population ③ is Hispanic (Spanish speaking, usually from Mexico, Cuba, Puerto Rico, Central America or South America) so non-Hispanics can feel ④ strangers in their own country. They point to Miami's Spanish-language newspapers, television stations, radio stations, and to the political predominance of Hispanics. Some whites and blacks say they are especially incensed that they increasingly need to know two languages, and ⑤ that if they don't, their job opportunities are seriously hampered.

206 다음 글의 밑줄 친 부분 중, 어법상 틀린 것은?

There is a book written by Daniel Goleman entitled *Emotional Intelligence* that I recommend people ① read if they are ready to make significant changes in their lives. In it Goleman quotes the 16th-century humanist Erasmus of Rotterdam, ② who states that emotional thinking can be 24 times more powerful than rational thinking. Frequently, people are unsuccessful at something ③ not because they lack knowledge, but because they are afraid to fail. For example, I know many smart people with good grades ④ which are less successful than they could be simply because they live in terror of making a mistake or failing. Many people do not make money simply because they fear ⑤ that they might lose money.

207 다음 글의 밑줄 친 부분 중, 어법상 틀린 것은?

When I smile, my friends playfully yell at me. I often hear, "Stop ① smiling!" or "You smile too much!" However, these same friends fail to keep me from smiling. I think that I and other smilers really make a difference in this cold world. If you smile at people, they usually smile back. They ② must have felt good that someone smiled at them. Since they feel better, their actions toward ③ others may be nicer. Even if your smiling face shines on just one person, ④ think of how it will brighten that person's day! And your smile also does good things for you. For instance, it's almost impossible to feel sad or to think bad thoughts when you have a genuine smile on your face. Therefore, next time you leave your house, don't forget ⑤ smiling. As the song goes, "You're never fully dressed without a smile."

권장 시간 8분 | 시작·종료 시간 | : ~ : | 나의 소요 시간 | 분 초

208 다음 글의 밑줄 친 부분 중, 어법상 틀린 것은?

"Noma My Perfect Storm," a documentary that profiles chef Rene Redzepi and explores ingredients ① seen as exotic in the West—such as insects, tree bark and animal blood—offers insight into the mind of one of today's most exciting ② chefs and his outrageous creations. His dishes seem less like food and more like a series of art installations. He strives ③ to be surprised, and like an artist he wants the whole world to come around to his vision of dining—whether it's through a swirl of cream topped with ants, or fermented blood (one of Redzepi's favorite sauces) ④ surrounding a single wildflower. It's no doubt he's crossing into new territory when it comes to our perception of food and ⑤ what it means to "fine dine," and it's no wonder many restaurateurs agree that Redzepi is the most influential chef of his time.

*Noma: 'nordisk(북유럽의)'와 'mad(음식)'의 덴마크어 합성어

209 (A), (B), (C)의 각 네모 안에서 어법에 맞는 표현으로 가장 적절한 것은?

The demilitarized zone (DMZ) between North and South Korea is a narrow no-man's-land about 150 miles long and two and a half miles wide. No settlements or permanent structures are allowed there, and for the past 50 years, only a few soldiers, observers, and the 225 residents of Daeseong-dong, a small village on the southern border, have been allowed in. (A) [Because of / Because] this forced isolation, the politically tense zone has accidentally become a sanctuary for wildlife. Areas like this, which (B) [was / were] once war zones, can sometimes become places where animals and plants flourish, free from human interference. Even in countries with no recent conflicts, conservationists are exploring how unpopulated border zones could be used to (C) [preserving / preserve] wildlife.

	(A)		(B)		(C)
①	Because of	—	was	—	preserving
②	Because of	—	were	—	preserve
③	Because	—	was	—	preserving
④	Because	—	were	—	preserve
⑤	Because	—	were	—	preserving

210 (A), (B), (C)의 각 네모 안에서 어법에 맞는 표현으로 가장 적절한 것은?

In a traditional tale from the mystical Sufi branch of Islam, a boy named Nasreddin wished to have a beautiful flower garden. He planted some seeds, but as the flowers came up so (A) [did / were] a great many dandelion weeds among them. Nasreddin asked some gardeners (B) [nearby / nearly] what he could do to get rid of the weeds. Not one of their suggestions worked. Finally, Nasreddin went to the palace seeking the advice of the royal gardener himself. The kind old man recommended a few methods (C) [eradicate / for eradicating] the weeds but, sadly, Nasreddin had already tried them. The pair sat in silence for a long while. At last, the old man looked at Nasreddin and said, "Dear boy, there is just one thing left that you can do. You must learn to love them."

*Sufi: (이슬람교의 한 종파인) 수피교(의)

	(A)		(B)		(C)
①	did	—	nearby	—	eradicate
②	did	—	nearby	—	for eradicating
③	did	—	nearly	—	eradicate
④	were	—	nearby	—	for eradicating
⑤	were	—	nearly	—	eradicate

211 다음 글의 밑줄 친 부분 중, 어법상 틀린 것은?

The hot hand belief is that if a player is in a hot streak, the chance that that player will *continue* to score is higher than his or her personal average, and that this is true even if the game is ① purely random. It says that the mere fact of success in the past alters the probability of success in the future. There's a very strong belief in this phenomenon —even to the extent ② that it influences play. In basketball, teammates will often pass the ball to players ③ believing to be in a hot hand streak, believing that their sequence of successful shots makes them more likely to score next time. This shows that the belief in the hot hand phenomenon changes ④ how the players are behaving, and that very change might alter the chance of scoring. It will certainly give the player who receives the ball more opportunities to score, even if it doesn't alter the chance of scoring at each attempt. And if those increased opportunities to score ⑤ translate into more points, it could well reinforce the impression of a hot hand streak.

*hot streak: 연속적인 호조

212 다음 글의 밑줄 친 부분 중, 어법상 틀린 것은?

Sleep is somehow tied to our ability ① to remember. The reigning theory has been that brain activity during sleep reactivates neurons that were active during the day, strengthening neuronal connections and cementing ② it into memories. Now, Guilio Tononi, a neuroscientist, says sleep scientists have it all wrong: we don't sleep to remember, we sleep to forget. As we sleep, he says, the brain isn't developing, but rather ③ relaxing. "Going up and down, basically all the neurons fire and then all are silent—it's a wonderful way for the brain to tell the synapses ④ to soften," Tononi explains. So, when we wake up, our synapses are not as strong, and some ⑤ have vanished. With them, our smallest memories may be lost forever.

*synapse: ((해부)) 시냅스(신경 세포의 연결 부위)

213 (A), (B), (C)의 각 네모 안에서 어법에 맞는 표현으로 가장 적절한 것은?

If whales have rights, then they must be treated with respect. Their value and dignity do not rest on their place in our plans, purposes, and projects. From this perspective our exploitation of whales for recreational purposes (A) [is / are] not morally acceptable. They are creatures of inherent value with lives of their own and the capacity to lead them in their own ways. To confine them in aquatic parks and to make them perform tricks that people find (B) [amused / amusing] is to try to remake them into our own creations. This attempt to appropriate such marvelous and magnificent creatures for such trivial purposes, which denies them their liberty in the bargain, is (C) [moral / morally] to be condemned.

*confine: 가두다 **appropriate: 부당하게 이용하다

	(A)		(B)		(C)
①	is	—	amused	—	moral
②	is	—	amusing	—	morally
③	is	—	amusing	—	moral
④	are	—	amusing	—	morally
⑤	are	—	amused	—	moral

권장 시간 8분 시작·종료 시간 | : ~ : 나의 소요 시간 | 분 초

214 다음 글의 밑줄 친 부분 중, 어법상 틀린 것은?

We live in an age of expertise, ① when earnings and knowledge are closely linked. For each worker, an extra year of schooling ② typically leads to about 8 percent higher earnings. On average, an extra year of schooling for a country's entire population ③ is associated with a more than 30 percent increase in gross domestic product per person. The striking correlation between education and a country's GDP may reflect what economists call human capital externalities, a term for the idea ④ that people become more productive when they work around other skilled people. When a country gets more educated, people experience both the direct effect of their own extra learning plus the benefits that come from everyone around them ⑤ are more skilled.

215 (A), (B), (C)의 각 네모 안에서 어법에 맞는 표현으로 가장 적절한 것은?

Convicts (A) [has / had] never been sent to Western Australia, but in the middle of the 19th century, the colony there suddenly asked for them. There was a shortage of labor in the region, and the colony could not progress without convict labor. Britain provided the colony with convicts from 1850 to 1868, and the convicts helped (B) [building / build] it up by constructing roads, bridges, jails, and other public buildings. A total of 162,000 men and women came as convicts to Australia. By the time the British policy of convict transportation ended, the population of Australia had increased to over a million. Without the convicts' hard work, first as servants and later as settlers, it wouldn't (C) [be / have been] possible for the government and the free settlers to create a nation.

	(A)		(B)		(C)
①	has	—	building	—	be
②	has	—	build	—	have been
③	had	—	build	—	have been
④	has	—	building	—	have been
⑤	had	—	build	—	be

216 다음 글의 밑줄 친 부분 중, 어법상 틀린 것은?

Life is so familiar and ubiquitous that it is easy to forget how ① astonishing it is, and how sharply living things differ from those that are not alive. Living things draw matter and energy to ② themselves, maintain their identity, reproduce their own kind and evolve over time. Nothing else in the known universe has this capacity. Living things are made up of lifeless chemicals; their composition, and everything they ③ do, is consistent with the laws of physics and chemistry. And yet there is nothing in those laws that would lead one to expect a universe that harbors life. At the heart of the mystery ④ lies cells, the elementary units of life and the smallest entities that display all its characteristics. Every living thing is made up of cells, either one cell or many, and every cell is itself a ⑤ highly integrated ensemble of millions of molecules structured in space.

*ensemble: (조화된) 총체

217 다음 글의 밑줄 친 부분 중, 어법상 틀린 것은?

I got the chance to find out ① how it actually feels in the zero-g simulator—a Russian IL-76 MDK aircraft better known as the Flying Laboratory. This plane goes up and makes a series of maneuvers in the sky to simulate zero gravity for ② its occupants. I go up with 11 ③ others. "Get ready," says a voice on the loudspeaker, and suddenly invisible forces press us all to the floor. For a few seconds we feel twice as ④ heavily as normal and then we all rise from the floor majestically, totally weightless. We float all over the airplane, ⑤ bouncing into each other, the walls and the ceiling. "Time's up. Get down!" Abruptly, the zero-g ends and we all tumble to the floor.

*zero-g (zero gravity): 무중력

218 다음 글의 밑줄 친 부분 중, 어법상 틀린 것은?

In New England, summers are short—they start on the first of June and end on the last day of August but for the whole of those three months, the weather is agreeably warm and ① nearly always sunny. Best of all, the temperature stays at a generally congenial level, ② unlike in Iowa, where I grew up and where the temperature and humidity climb steadily with every passing day of summer. By mid-August, in Iowa, it is so hot and airless that even the flies can be seen lying down on their backs and just quietly ③ to gasp. It even gets department store mannequins ④ to sweat. If you try to get some important work done, ⑤ it's almost impossible to concentrate.

*congenial: 알맞은

219 (A), (B), (C)의 각 네모 안에서 어법에 맞는 표현으로 가장 적절한 것은?

A restaurant is a destination in itself as a place to eat, rather than a place of local gathering (like an inn) or traveller's shelter that also offers food. Within the restricted opening hours of the establishment, a restaurant offers a variety of dishes, more so than (A) [is / does] the case with an inn. Thus most restaurants do not open for breakfast, and those that do serve breakfast (outside of hotels or modern-day inns) specialize to some extent in it, which means that the meals these breakfast restaurants serve (B) [have / having] more options than a traditional inn could provide. At a restaurant one eats what one desires from an often extensive menu. During most of its history, the restaurant has offered meals served by a waiter (C) [his / whose] job is limited to this. Rather than gathering with the other lodgers at an inn or guesthouse, the customers of a restaurant come with their friends, sit apart from others, and pay for a specific meal when they are finished.

	(A)		(B)		(C)
①	is	—	have	—	his
②	is	—	having	—	whose
③	is	—	have	—	whose
④	does	—	having	—	his
⑤	does	—	having	—	whose

권장 시간 8분 | 시작·종료 시간 | : ~ : | 나의 소요 시간 | 분 초

220 다음 글의 밑줄 친 부분 중, 어법상 틀린 것은?

Many people drift aimlessly through life struggling against things without a clear-cut goal. Choosing a goal may not be easy, but it is worth the effort, ① because the advantages that it brings. If you know what you want, it gets you moving in the right direction. The more you think about your goal, the more ② enthusiastic you become. Enthusiasm can build into a ③ burning desire. It will help you to become alert to opportunities as they present ④ themselves in your everyday life. It can even make up for your lack of experience and talent. Thus, when you have finally settled on your dream, do not give up on it easily. Instead, hold on to your enthusiasm, because it will be the force that drives you ⑤ to succeed.

221 (A), (B), (C)의 각 네모 안에서 어법에 맞는 표현으로 가장 적절한 것은?

The worst Amazon drought since record keeping began about a century ago began in 2005, bringing many problems to the Amazon basin. In western Brazil, there were three times as many fires in September 2005 as during September 2004. In some areas water levels have dropped so low (A) [which / that] some communities that depend on streams for transportation are completely isolated. Crops rot because they cannot (B) [transport / be transported] to market, and children cannot get to school. Fish die in the shallow water, forcing people to depend on government food packages. Streams do not flow enough to remove human waste, and the backup of sewage raises fears of an epidemic of cholera and other waterborne illnesses. Stagnant pools allow mosquitoes to breed, which has the potential to increase the number of cases of malaria. The Amazon drought is being blamed on high ocean temperatures in the Caribbean Sea and the Atlantic Ocean, which (C) [is / are] likely the result of global warming.

*basin: (큰 강의) 유역 **epidemic: (병 등의) 확산 ***stagnant: 고여 있는

	(A)		(B)		(C)
①	which	—	transport	—	is
②	which	—	be transported	—	are
③	that	—	transport	—	is
④	that	—	be transported	—	is
⑤	that	—	be transported	—	are

222 다음 글의 밑줄 친 부분 중, 어법상 틀린 것은?

The importance of selecting ingredients for use in home canning cannot be stressed too ① strongly. The old saying that you only get back out ② what you put in is absolutely true when it comes to home canned foods. Quality ingredients are the most important factor in creating preserved foods that you will be proud ③ to serve to your family and friends. You can follow every canning procedure to the letter, use every technique ④ known to produce the best-preserved food you possibly can, but if you use inferior ingredients, the final product will be a disappointment. The outstanding flavor found in superior preserved foods ⑤ coming directly from using the very best fruits and vegetables available and by not cutting down on the quality of any ingredient.

223 다음 글의 밑줄 친 부분 중, 어법상 틀린 것은?

It was my very first teaching job, and I was anxious to make an excellent first impression. I had been hired ① to lead a vibrant group of four-year-olds. As the parents escorted their children into the room, I ② attempted to deal with crying kids, teary-eyed moms and tense dads. Finally, I managed ③ to be seated the kids on the carpet, and we were ready to start our 'morning circle time.' We were in the middle of a rousing performance of 'Old MacDonald' when the door opened and the principal of the kindergarten ④ entered the room. She stood next to the door, quietly ⑤ observing the children and me. My voice and smile never stumbled, but frankly speaking, I was very nervous.

224 다음 글의 밑줄 친 부분 중, 어법상 틀린 것은?

Teeth grinding is often a way of dealing with tension. It may be an attempt to indirectly release aggression ① that you couldn't show directly. For example, you might resent ② having to submit to someone at work or in a relationship. First ask yourself ③ if any of your relationships might be a source of tension. Are any unresolved issues in your life causing stress? In psychotherapy, we ask people questions like this to get them ④ open up about their problems. Even just ⑤ writing down the answers to these questions might help you to understand your feelings without the help of a therapist. To help release any stress or tension, activities such as yoga, breathing exercises, and meditation can help.

225 (A), (B), (C)의 각 네모 안에서 어법에 맞는 표현으로 가장 적절한 것은?

If leadership ability is inherited, the selection and recruitment of managers as potential leaders would only focus on the candidate's parents and ancestors —evidence of work experience would not be valued. Moreover, if leaders are born and not developed, then (A) [high / highly]-performing people would always emerge regardless of the business context, their management ability, or the company's willingness to recruit and select well, or coach, mentor, train, develop, and evaluate employees. Furthermore, attempts to improve performance would be a wasteful exercise. Such an idea should not be taken too (B) [serious / seriously], so why, then, have I mentioned it? Simply because, in my experience, some managers manage their people based on this idea, and it prevents them from applying the person-management skills and techniques that lead to improved performance. I feel that it is far better to accept that the work environment, (C) [includes / including] management action, shapes people's behavior and abilities and that every manager can improve the way they manage people regardless of innate characteristics.

	(A)		(B)		(C)
①	high	—	serious	—	includes
②	high	—	serious	—	including
③	high	—	seriously	—	including
④	highly	—	seriously	—	includes
⑤	highly	—	seriously	—	including

권장 시간 8분 | 시작·종료 시간 | : ~ : | 나의 소요 시간 | 분 초

226 다음 글의 밑줄 친 부분 중, 어법상 틀린 것은?

Firstborn children often get more discipline from their parents than ① later children, but the parents also give them ② more attention. Researchers feel that this gives firstborns a stronger drive for success, which is ③ why they are more likely to earn higher grades, attend college, and go further in college than their siblings. You are more likely to see a firstborn on the cover of a magazine or as CEO of a large corporation. By contrast, younger children are less anxious about being successful and are more ④ relaxed in their relationships. Firstborns are inclined to dislike change, and support conservative ideas, while their younger sisters and brothers ⑤ tending to be more rebellious and support liberal ideas.

227 (A), (B), (C)의 각 네모 안에서 어법에 맞는 표현으로 가장 적절한 것은?

Imagine if you could only see the front of your home and the back side always remained hidden. That's (A) [when / how] astronomers feel a lot of the time, because we can observe only one side of some of the most interesting places in the universe. The most familiar example is the moon. Because it always keeps one hemisphere (B) [faced / facing] Earth, every month we see the same 'man-in-the-moon' pattern. Astronomers had long assumed that the far side was just like the near side. Wrong. Pictures taken in 1959 by the Soviet spacecraft Luna 3 (C) [show / showing] a very different landscape. Now we know that the moon is unevenly round because Earth's gravity has pulled the moon's mass slightly off-center toward us.

	(A)		(B)		(C)
①	when	—	faced	—	show
②	when	—	faced	—	showing
③	how	—	faced	—	show
④	how	—	facing	—	showing
⑤	how	—	facing	—	show

228 다음 글의 밑줄 친 부분 중, 어법상 틀린 것은?

Successful prediction is usually considered stronger support for a hypothesis than the explanation of an equal quantity of observation ① known to the creator of the hypothesis at the time of its creation. This is not hard to justify on purely logical grounds and ② appears valid as a result of experience. Perhaps an additional explanation is as follows: A hypothesis not only should fit the facts ③ which brought about its creation but should also be compatible with the rest of the body of science. This is a very hard condition to satisfy because of the scope and complexity of modern science. It is laborious to ascertain ④ whether a given hypothesis is in fact compatible with everything already known. But if the investigator knows that his hypothesis is going to ⑤ test in the near future by experiments based on its predicted consequences, he will probably be much more careful to see if it does fit the known facts than will be the case if he does not expect an immediate test of this sort.

*ascertain: 확인하다

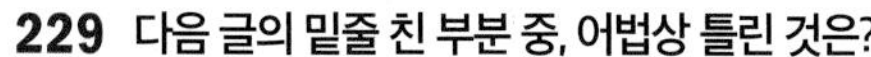

229 다음 글의 밑줄 친 부분 중, 어법상 틀린 것은?

My friend Martin always ① used to complain about the city of Los Angeles, where he lived for three years while getting his doctorate. He complained incessantly about the smog, the traffic, and the expensive lifestyle. Martin was convinced life would be far rosier if he ② were able to move to another city. Within a few weeks of finishing his program and ③ earning his degree, Martin packed his belongings and moved to Boulder. Within months of his arrival there, he began to complain about the cold weather, the slow pace, and how much difficulty he was having ④ to find a house that was up to his standards. Suddenly, he regretted not ⑤ appreciating the sunny weather and the exciting lifestyle of Los Angeles.

230 다음 글의 밑줄 친 부분 중, 어법상 틀린 것은?

Most people believe that watching television isn't very good for you. So it may be surprising to learn that television can actually be quite beneficial for those who ① chooses carefully the programs they watch. Anything that makes you ② laugh is beneficial, so it's good to watch comedy shows and entertaining dramas on TV. And there are many excellent educational programs and documentaries that can help you ③ to understand important fields such as science, medicine, history, and art. Television is very helpful for people ④ who can't often leave the house because of old age or illness, and especially for patients in hospitals. For students of English, TV offers opportunities for daily language practice; students can build their vocabulary and ⑤ practice listening as they watch a foreign-language show.

231 (A), (B), (C)의 각 네모 안에서 어법에 맞는 표현으로 가장 적절한 것은?

There are often good reasons for coining new terms. "Prosumption (production+consumption)" and "produsage (production+usage)," for example, cause us to think anew on what production and consumption entail. However, in our view these two concepts are problematic in (A) [what / that] they confuse the increasingly connected nature of two separate practices—production and consumption—with the conflation of these two practices. Beer and Burrows write that "participation in acts that blur the line between production and consumption (B) [is / are] now an established part of the everyday lives of millions of people." It is this blurring of distinctions we would like to question. It is definitely true that people spend more free time than ever before consuming and (C) [produce / producing] media, but that does not mean that the practices are blurred. Instead, they continue to exist as two distinct practices.

*conflation: 융합, 합성

	(A)		(B)		(C)
①	that	—	is	—	produce
②	that	—	are	—	produce
③	that	—	is	—	producing
④	what	—	is	—	produce
⑤	what	—	are	—	producing

권장 시간 8분 | 시작·종료 시간 | : ~ : | 나의 소요 시간 | 분 초

232 다음 글의 밑줄 친 부분 중, 어법상 틀린 것은?

Many of us think that we can tell someone's personality by simply looking at them. However, researchers believe that most of us use stereotypes when ① judged character in others. That is, we expect a certain type of person to have a certain personality, so we see certain traits ② whether they are there or not. For example, muscular people are strong, so they ③ must be good leaders. But often they are actually shy and timid. Fat people are thought to be jolly, optimistic, and warmhearted, but they are just ④ as likely to be depressed. Many times people will even act the way ⑤ that they think people expect them to act. They will try to become the stereotype.

233 (A), (B), (C)의 각 네모 안에서 어법에 맞는 표현으로 가장 적절한 것은?

The primary goal of good writers is to present their thoughts clearly so that a reader can understand. If they don't, they fail no matter (A) [what / how] kind of creativity or insight they might show. It is important to choose the correct word to avoid misunderstandings. But, many people are afraid of appearing too (B) [committing / committed] to a particular point of view and want to appear as reasonable and fair-minded as possible. They use qualifiers such as 'rather,' 'fairly,' and 'somewhat.' Using words such as these (C) [weaken / weakens] the impact of an argument or position by making it seem uncertain. So, if you want to give your thoughts increased power, eliminate unnecessary qualifiers and write with confidence in your opinions.

	(A)		(B)		(C)
①	what	—	committing	—	weaken
②	what	—	committed	—	weakens
③	what	—	committing	—	weakens
④	how	—	committed	—	weakens
⑤	how	—	committing	—	weaken

234 다음 글의 밑줄 친 부분 중, 어법상 틀린 것은?

Eight of the 10 largest cities in the United States have inner city areas ① where were developed in the 19th century. These cities were all settled ② before automobiles and buses became widespread, and businesses and houses had to be close together to permit people ③ to travel on foot between them. The rivers on which they are located often divided the cities and ④ created barriers to land transportation. Newer cities, such as Dallas, Los Angeles, and Phoenix, were designed with automobile transportation uppermost in mind and have fewer water barriers, although they still have traffic jams due to population growth beyond ⑤ what was expected when the road systems were designed.

235 다음 글의 밑줄 친 부분 중, 어법상 <u>틀린</u> 것은?

According to new genetic evidence, evolution has continued to shape the human species, ① <u>making</u> changes even within the past 100,000 years. Researchers have found that as much as 10 percent of the human genome may ② <u>be linked</u> to recent mutations or adaptive genetic changes. Population geneticists analyzed over a million genetic variations in DNA samples from 24 individuals, ③ <u>including</u> African Americans, European Americans, and Chinese. They were looking for areas in the genome ④ <u>which</u> a beneficial mutation is carried by everyone in a population. They were able to figure out how long ago the mutation began to spread throughout the population, by ⑤ <u>looking</u> at the variability in the DNA surrounding the mutation.

*genome: ((생물)) 게놈(염색체 한 세트) **mutation: ((생물)) 돌연변이

236 다음 글의 밑줄 친 부분 중, 어법상 <u>틀린</u> 것은?

Some cats may fear water ① <u>because of</u> how we use it around them: Many a noisy tomcat has had a bucket of water thrown its way, and naughty kids often tease kittens with a garden hose. Forcing a bath on a cat is a sure way to get it ② <u>to hate</u> water. Aside from these examples, there's actually a lot of evidence that cats love water. Many cats don't hesitate to jump into a filled sink or running shower and some actually seem ③ <u>amusing</u> as water from a faucet drips over their heads. One reason for these positive reactions is ④ <u>that</u> cats are attracted to the motion and sound of water. Cats are creatures of habit, so a pet that has been exposed to water since it was young will tolerate a bath much better than one ⑤ <u>whose</u> human companion shielded it from water out of fear for its safety.

237 (A), (B), (C)의 각 네모 안에서 어법에 맞는 표현으로 가장 적절한 것은?

If you go into a store looking for a new computer and the first salesperson you meet immediately points to a row of computers and says, "Any of those are good," and then leaves, there is a good chance you will leave, too, and with good reason. Why? You were never asked what you were seeking, what you could afford to spend, or (A) [that / if] the computer would be used for business or pleasure or your child's homework assignments. In brief, the salesperson never considered or asked about your needs and preferences. Just as it wouldn't be a shock to learn the salesperson who was indifferent to a potential customer's needs (B) [was / were] soon out of a job, the same holds true for writers who ignore their readers. The reader is the writer's "customer" and one (C) [what / whose] business or approval you need to earn. The more you know about your reader, the greater the chances you will meet his or her needs and expectations.

	(A)		(B)		(C)
①	that	—	was	—	whose
②	that	—	were	—	whose
③	if	—	was	—	what
④	if	—	were	—	what
⑤	if	—	was	—	whose

권장 시간 8분 | 시작·종료 시간 | : ~ : | 나의 소요 시간 | 분 초

238 다음 글의 밑줄 친 부분 중, 어법상 틀린 것은?

Many of us have observed public speakers and thought to ourselves, "Wow, I could never be that smart, ① calmly, witty, and polished." But you don't have to be perfect to succeed in public speaking. That is not ② what public speaking is about. It all depends on what you, and your audience, expect from your speech. Your audience ③ doesn't expect perfection. Before I discovered this, I used to ④ put incredible pressure on myself to deliver a perfect performance. The essence of public speaking is this: give your audience something of value. As long as they get something of value, they will be thankful. If you criticize people, or if you stir them up to ultimately benefit them, they might still appreciate you, even though you don't make them ⑤ feel good at the time.

239 (A), (B), (C)의 각 네모 안에서 어법에 맞는 표현으로 가장 적절한 것은?

Keeping a journal can do wonders for your soul. It can comfort you and let you express yourself, (A) [whatever / however] angry, happy, or scared you feel. You can pour your heart out: your journal won't complain or give you unneeded advice and, as long as you keep it well hidden, you can trust that nobody else will be told about your secrets. (B) [Then / When] you put down in writing all that's on your mind, without editing, your thoughts become clearer and you can find yourself. And journals are great records of your personal history: you can see, for example, how childish or grown-up you once were or how much has changed. You don't have to limit yourself to words, either: notes from friends, photos, movie tickets, and anything that (C) [preserve / preserves] a memory can be pasted or taped in there, too.

	(A)		(B)		(C)
①	whatever	—	Then	—	preserve
②	whatever	—	When	—	preserves
③	whatever	—	Then	—	preserves
④	however	—	When	—	preserves
⑤	however	—	Then	—	preserve

240 다음 글의 밑줄 친 부분 중, 어법상 틀린 것은?

Do you buckle up while driving? Of course you do—most of the time. But what is the reason ① if you don't? In a survey of 3,000 people in Singapore, Kuala Lumpur, and Manila, two-thirds of respondents admitted to ② not wearing a seat belt sometimes, usually on short trips. Research has proven that the proper use of seat belts ③ has saved hundreds of thousands of lives. It's obvious: non seat belt wearers are at far greater risk of serious injury than ④ those wearing seat belts. Some people buckle up for the freeway, but not for a neighborhood trip. It's a bad mistake. Statistics show that most car accidents happen within 5km of home. Make ⑤ them a habit to buckle up as soon as you get in the car.

241 다음 글의 밑줄 친 부분 중, 어법상 틀린 것은?

At the beginning of the universe, there ① were only the three lightest elements: hydrogen, helium, and a little lithium. But life needs heavier elements—such as oxygen, which we breathe, and iron, which is in our blood. During their lives, massive stars like Antares cause helium nuclei to join ② to make oxygen. ③ When exploding, their oxygen is cast into space, while the explosions themselves produce iron. Astronomers think that supernova explosions made most of the iron and cast ④ it and oxygen into space. These elements became part of a cloud of gas and dust ⑤ that also contained other elements and gave birth to our solar system.

*Antares: 안타레스(전갈자리의 주성(主星)) **supernova: 초신성

242 다음 글의 밑줄 친 부분 중, 어법상 틀린 것은?

The more scientists study genetic code, the more surprises they find. Areas of DNA often called 'junk DNA' are not junk, but ① have a powerful regulatory role. And a new study has found that DNA ② can be invaded by genes from another species. The fruit fly was found to have the entire genome of a bacteria on its DNA, ③ where it will be passed on. The baby fruit flies will be born with this DNA. For decades, ④ they were thought that this bacterial DNA found during genome mapping was from accidental contamination. Do we humans have invaders who are doing the same thing? So far, none have been found, but it is possible ⑤ that bacteria are using our DNA to transfer their DNA, too.

*junk DNA: DNA 내에서 아무런 유전정보도 갖고 있지 않은 부분
**genome: 유전자 또는 염색체군

243 다음 글의 밑줄 친 부분 중, 어법상 틀린 것은?

"Deep reading" has its historical roots in the times before the printing press ① when there were very few books owned by very few people. The book was most likely something like a Bible which would be read over and over, with certain passages ② being "revisited" repeatedly in the search for understanding. The more metaphorical and poetic the language, the more ③ satisfying and challenging the return visits. The arrival of the printing press, however, resulted in the production of far more books on many topics for far more people, a change which ④ made it possible what is called "horizontal reading"—a broader form of information gathering which has generally replaced the deep-reading tradition. With the right balance, the information gathered by horizontal reading ⑤ fuels the thinking done in deep reading. But the problem is it's not easy to find a healthy balance between both types of reading.

244 다음 글의 밑줄 친 부분 중, 어법상 틀린 것은?

To people like me, who ① have written for most of their adult lives, it's likely that writing is a conscious variant of an unconscious activity, like dreaming. Why do we dream? No one seems to really know, just as no one seems to really know why we crave stories, especially stories we know ② to be fiction. My experience of writing is invariably a blend of the initial inspiration and the more difficult, or plodding, execution of inspiration. Most writers find first drafts ③ painfully difficult, like climbing a steep set of stairs, the end of ④ it isn't in sight. We can only persevere! Eventually, you will get where you are going, or ⑤ so you hope. And when you get there, you will not ask "why?"—the relief you feel is but a brief breathing spell, before beginning again with another inspiration, another draft, another steep climb.

245 다음 글의 밑줄 친 부분 중, 어법상 틀린 것은?

Humans breathe automatically every few seconds, whereas dolphins breathe voluntarily and can hold their breath for over thirty minutes. How do they sleep without ① drowning? To control their breathing while sleeping, dolphins let one half of their brain ② to sleep at a time. Electroencephalograms, measuring the activity in their brains, show that in the sleep cycle, half of the brain does indeed "shut down" while ③ the other half maintains basic life functions. Researchers have observed that dolphins are in this state for approximately eight hours a day. Dolphins get their eight hours of sleep while maintaining the ability to swim and surface ④ to breathe. This strange sleep habit might explain a behavior known as "logging," ⑤ swimming slowly along the surface, with very little movement.

*Electroencephalogram: ((의학)) 뇌전도, 뇌파도

246 다음 글의 밑줄 친 부분 중, 어법상 틀린 것은?

Foods are refined to ① such an extent that their value is lost, even if they become more pleasing to the taste buds and the eye. In the process of preparing food, we tend to lose many of the vitamins. An example is the boiling of vegetables, most of ② which tend to lose their value if over-boiled. The polishing of rice and the refining of sugar are other examples ③ where the preference for a nicer look leads to the destruction of their essential value as foods. As is known to everybody, there are certain trace elements in our body which ④ require to keep us in good health. Any ⑤ lowering of their small amounts in the system will give rise to many disorders; for example, the lack of iron in the blood will give rise to anaemia and weakness. Sodium deficiency similarly leads to many disorders.

*anaemia: 빈혈 **sodium: 나트륨

247 다음 글의 밑줄 친 부분 중, 어법상 틀린 것은?

① During the Spanish Civil War in the late 1930s, farmer Dan West was serving as a volunteer relief worker. Deciding how to distribute the limited food aid ② was very frustrating for him. Once he returned home, he founded an unusual organization now ③ known as Heifer International, whose aim was to provide permanent hunger relief by giving families their own cow. A unique feature of the program is ④ what families must pass on at least one of their animal's female offspring to a neighbor, who in turn passes on one of its offspring, and so on. Although originally the program shipped cows abroad, now the organization buys locally and gives many animals, such as chickens, goats, ducks, camels, honeybees, and also ⑤ gives trees.

248 다음 글의 밑줄 친 부분 중, 어법상 틀린 것은?

Evan Green always worried that the places where animals lived were being destroyed when forests were cleared. When he was little, he told his mother, "I want to buy all the land in the world ① so no one can build on it." He had learned about how animals depend on ② one another and that the rainforest trees help clean the air for everyone. Evan talked to everyone about protecting the land and ③ wrote to businesses and schools. He went door-to-door ④ explaining why he was raising money to save wild places. Finally, he formed the Red Dragon Conservation Team, and with the money they collected, they helped ⑤ saving more than 16 acres in Rincon Rainforest in Costa Rica.

249 (A), (B), (C)의 각 네모 안에서 어법에 맞는 표현으로 가장 적절한 것은?

Having a strong mindset as an athlete is indispensable because many big games come down to inches and split seconds. A significant majority of the most celebrated highlights in sports history (A) [come / comes] down to fractions. Another fourth of a second on the clock or two inches to the left and an entirely different set of players are having their names (B) [engrave / engraved] on that iconic trophy and wind up wearing the most coveted jewelry in sports. So what differentiates the breathtaking players from the average athletes? Many fans attribute turning points in games to a bad bounce or poor call by a referee. In their minds, some players are just luckier than others. Their attitude is weak and the reason they are dissatisfied has everything to do with the excuses they use (C) [justify / to justify] their shortcomings.

	(A)		(B)		(C)
①	come	—	engrave	—	justify
②	come	—	engraved	—	justify
③	come	—	engraved	—	to justify
④	comes	—	engrave	—	to justify
⑤	comes	—	engraved	—	to justify

권장 시간 8분 | 시작·종료 시간 | : ~ : | 나의 소요 시간 | 분 초

250 다음 글의 밑줄 친 부분 중, 어법상 틀린 것은?

According to the National Snow and Ice Data Center (NSIDC), only 4.3 million square km of Arctic sea ice ① survived the summer of 2007. That's the least left over at the end of any September on record. The NSIDC also estimates that the total amount of Arctic ice is now half the amount that it ② was in the 1950s. Worse, the rate of the Arctic ice melt is accelerating. All ice in the Arctic may be gone by 2030, far ③ earlier than previous predictions. Melting sea ice doesn't cause sea levels to rise, but it adds to global warming by ④ being exposed larger amounts of water to the sun. How the Arctic climate is changing isn't fully understood, but this much we do know: what ⑤ happens there will eventually affect us all.

251 (A), (B), (C)의 각 네모 안에서 어법에 맞는 표현으로 가장 적절한 것은?

Education can make a fundamental difference in your life because it changes your outlook and thinking patterns. In order to make the best educational choices after high school, ask friends and family members (A) [what / how] they think your strengths and weaknesses are. Get their suggestions for ideal courses of study for you. You will be (B) [amazing / amazed] at how they know things about you that you have never realized. Remember not (C) [to limit / limiting] yourself. There are so many opportunities nowadays and you don't have to be a lawyer or a nurse. Perhaps that is what you want to be, but open your mind to other possibilities. The goal is to find something you love to do, not something you have to do.

	(A)		(B)		(C)
①	what	—	amazing	—	to limit
②	what	—	amazed	—	to limit
③	what	—	amazing	—	limiting
④	how	—	amazed	—	limiting
⑤	how	—	amazing	—	to limit

252 다음 글의 밑줄 친 부분 중, 어법상 틀린 것은?

The vast library of data about you is being supplemented all the time. This advance was made ① possible by computers that can capture and store all of this data, and especially by the sudden drop in the price of data storage capacity through the early 2000s. But computers have also allowed other changes that ② increases your vulnerability and the value of information about you. Not only ③ is new data stored electronically but it also resides in searchable databases. They allow collectors to make useful lists of the types of data that interest ④ them. It is easy to see a list of all advance ticket purchasers for the concert next Saturday, or who checked into the gym on Saturday, and then to further process this list by gender, age, income level, or zip code ⑤ to find exactly the class of person you seek.

*vulnerability: 취약성

253 다음 글의 밑줄 친 부분 중, 어법상 틀린 것은?

Drivers in Maine must follow a new rule when they hit the road. A law took effect statewide on April 10, making ① it illegal to smoke in a car carrying a passenger younger than 16 years old. Health experts say ② that harmful secondhand smoke is more concentrated in closed environments such as cars. "Especially at risk ③ is our youngest citizens, who don't have the choice of whether or not to be exposed to dangerous secondhand smoke." says Maine Governor John Baldacci. "This bill is important because it will protect children's health." Arkansas, California, and Louisiana ④ have passed similar laws. Supporters see ⑤ them as an important step. Previously, most anti-tobacco laws banned smoking only in public spaces.

254 다음 글의 밑줄 친 부분 중, 어법상 틀린 것은?

The International Astronomical Union has adopted new rules and the solar system now contains planets as well as a ① puzzled new category called a dwarf planet. A real planet gravitationally dominates ② its region of the solar system, while a dwarf is any object that orbits the sun, is not a satellite, and is nearly round. This unclear definition has left astronomers ③ confused. How round is 'nearly round'? This all but guarantees future conflicts between scientists about whether a new object is a dwarf planet or just a 'small solar system body.' By ④ coining the new term 'dwarf planet,' the IAU acknowledges that Pluto belongs to a different category while allowing millions of schoolchildren ⑤ to continue to call it a planet.

*dwarf planet: 왜소행성

255 (A), (B), (C)의 각 네모 안에서 어법에 맞는 표현으로 가장 적절한 것은?

Have you ever been in such a hurry to get somewhere (A) [that / what] your memory of the journey is faint? The same can be true if you are searching for that specific someone to move your career forward or provide that perfect connection—you will miss some people that could have been very influential in your life. By all means (B) [set / setting] yourself a goal of contacting a whole group of people that fall into a specific category or job title if that is what you have decided will further your ambitions, but make sure you enjoy the journey, too. You just don't know how some people will influence your life over time. You may determine that the shop owner will be of no benefit to your aspirations of being a DJ on the radio, only (C) [find / to find] that his sister is the star presenter on the local station. You can count the number of seeds in the apple, but not the number of apples in the seed.

	(A)		(B)		(C)
①	that	—	set	—	find
②	that	—	setting	—	to find
③	that	—	set	—	to find
④	what	—	setting	—	find
⑤	what	—	set	—	to find

권장 시간 8분 | 시작·종료 시간 | : ~ : | 나의 소요 시간 | 분 초

256 다음 글의 밑줄 친 부분 중, 어법상 틀린 것은?

Most people think that puppies and kittens are cute. When ① asked to explain why they think a kitten or a puppy is cute, however, most people would probably have difficulty ② giving a clear explanation. It turns out, however, that there is a clear scientific reason why we find these animals ③ adorable. Cuteness apparently depends on a few factors, some of which are physical and some of which have to do with how these animals act. First, cuteness is most often associated with animals or people that have small bodies when compared to the size of ④ its head and eyes, as is true with human babies and many other baby animals. ⑤ Looking at actions, playfulness is seen as being cute. This is again another characteristic of babies.

257 (A), (B), (C)의 각 네모 안에서 어법에 맞는 표현으로 가장 적절한 것은?

Population growth may have had a negative effect on development in many countries, but the magnitude of this effect is difficult to assess. And in some cases, population growth probably has stimulated development. For instance, the fact that children consume goods and services and thus lower the ability of a nation to save (A) [ignore / ignores] the fact that the children grow up and become productive adults. Furthermore, any diversion of investment from infrastructure to education and health care is not necessarily a loss, as education and health care will build up the productivity of the labor force. The harmful effect of population growth should be most pronounced in countries (B) [which / where] usable land and water are relatively scarce. Although generalizations about acceptable levels of population growth do not fit all circumstances, the World Bank has stated that population growth rates above 2 percent a year (C) [act / acting] as a brake on economic development.

	(A)		(B)		(C)
①	ignore	—	which	—	act
②	ignore	—	which	—	acting
③	ignore	—	where	—	acting
④	ignores	—	where	—	act
⑤	ignores	—	which	—	acting

258 다음 글의 밑줄 친 부분 중, 어법상 틀린 것은?

All parents should have received a copy of information about the Bakersfield High School Wildfire Action Plan ① sent home with students at the start of the year. It is vital that all students and staff know what to do ② should we face a wildfire. The seriousness of this plan has been carefully explained to all students. The weather conditions for the start of this year ③ have been quite mild, but the risk of fire has still been extreme, making ④ them critical that all students and staff know what to do. The whole school rehearsed our evacuation to the Yontville Sports Center, the designated "wildfire refuge" in a wildfire situation, and emergency lockdown procedures ⑤ during the first week of school. The students were impressive with a mature and serious approach to the drills and should be praised for this.

*lockdown: (행동에 대한) 통제, 제재

259 다음 글의 밑줄 친 부분 중, 어법상 틀린 것은?

Studies have shown that compared with single men, married men are healthier. Men whose wives visited them often after their surgery ① recovering more quickly. "We can't say definitively why," says John L. Gore, MD, "but one theory is that being married or partnered ② means you've got someone in your corner, looking out for your welfare and helping to ease a lot of life's pressures." Everything from paying bills to ③ attending social functions feels less stressful when we feel that we are not having to do everything alone. A spouse is often a ④ motivating factor when it comes to making healthy lifestyle choices. Married men are less likely to smoke or ⑤ engage in risky activities.

260 다음 글의 밑줄 친 부분 중, 어법상 틀린 것은?

The process of separating the components of liquid mixtures based on ① their separate boiling points is called distillation. Distillation can also be used to purify water by separating the pure water from any foreign matter ② dissolved in it. The process is relatively simple: the impure water is heated in a glass flask over a burner until the water ③ reaches boiling point. At boiling point, the water vaporizes into steam, which rises and is directed into the tube called the condenser. In the condenser, the steam cools, ④ returning to its original liquid form. The condensing tube is angled downward and connected to another flask, ⑤ which the now purified water is collected. Any particles and foreign matter remain behind in the boiled flask.

*distillation: 증류(법)

261 (A), (B), (C)의 각 네모 안에서 어법에 맞는 표현으로 가장 적절한 것은?

According to a study, forgiveness reduces your level of stress, (A) [it / which] is a major risk factor for heart disease and other illnesses. When asked to imagine forgiving a person who has done them wrong, people showed immediate improvements in blood pressure, muscle tension, and immune response. Even people who have suffered devastating harm (B) [report / to report] feeling better after forgiving their attackers. On the other hand, refusing to forgive seems to increase your risk of developing illnesses such as heart disease and cancer. When people were asked to imagine not forgiving someone who has wronged (C) [him / them], their blood pressure, muscle tension, and immune response all worsened.

(A)		(B)		(C)
① it	—	report	—	him
② it	—	to report	—	them
③ which	—	report	—	him
④ which	—	report	—	them
⑤ which	—	to report	—	him

262 다음 글의 밑줄 친 부분 중, 어법상 틀린 것은?

Animals typically join groups in order to avoid predators, to obtain adequate amounts of food, or to protect ① themselves against other members of their own species. Groups protect against predators because scanning for predators ② is shared among group members. Animals in a group may obtain more food ③ because of being in a group makes it easier to find or to catch prey, or to defend prey that has been caught. Nevertheless, there can be costs to being in a group, such as competition among group members for any food ④ that is obtained, and there are increased dangers from parasites and disease. The ideal size of a group of animals ⑤ is usually neither small (because too much time is spent scanning for predators) nor large (too much time is spent fighting).

263 (A), (B), (C)의 각 네모 안에서 어법에 맞는 표현으로 가장 적절한 것은?

Why do we yawn? Yawning is a natural process of the body caused by not breathing deeply enough. Oxygen, the gas that the body needs to function, and carbon dioxide, the waste gas produced by our body processes, (A) [travel / travels] in your bloodstream, entering and exiting your body through your lungs. If you don't breathe deeply enough, carbon dioxide builds up in the body. Your brain gets a message (B) [telling / tells] you to breathe deeply to remove it. Often you require a series of yawns. A bigger mystery is that if you see someone yawn, you often start yawning too. Even scientists don't understand (C) [that / why] yawning seems to be contagious.

	(A)		(B)		(C)
①	travel	—	telling	—	why
②	travel	—	tells	—	why
③	travel	—	telling	—	that
④	travels	—	tells	—	that
⑤	travels	—	telling	—	that

264 다음 글의 밑줄 친 부분 중, 어법상 틀린 것은?

The more important a sporting event is, the more ① stressful we are likely to find it. It is probably true to say, for example, that most footballers would find themselves more anxious competing in the World Cup than in a friendly game. However, we must remember that it is the importance of the event to the individual ② that counts. This does not necessarily depend on the status of the competition. For example, athletes who know they are ③ being watched by talent scouts, or perhaps by their family for the first time, may feel particularly anxious. Marchant and his colleagues carried out an experiment ④ in which event importance was artificially set up. Pairs of golfers competed for either three new balls (low importance) or a new pair of golfing shoes (high importance). As expected, those competing for the new shoes experienced more anxiety than ⑤ them competing for golf balls.

265 다음 글의 밑줄 친 부분 중, 어법상 틀린 것은?

When Eliza Rader was 17 months old, she tasted peanut butter. Immediately afterward, she broke out in hives and had trouble ① breathing. Later, tests confirmed that Eliza had a severe peanut allergy and was also allergic to sesame seeds and to tree nuts, ② which include almonds, hazelnuts and walnuts. Now, Eliza is 12 years old. She says, "I want to make kids feel more comfortable and safe." But, as Eliza has discovered, kids who have food allergies like her are ③ hardly alone anymore. A study found that peanut allergies in children doubled over the last five years. Kids commonly outgrow allergies to milk and eggs. But experts say that today it is taking longer for ④ them to do so. Some doctors say that the increase in the number of kids with food allergies ⑤ are nothing to sneeze at.

*hives: 두드러기

266 다음 글의 밑줄 친 부분 중, 어법상 틀린 것은?

Forget bonuses and incentives—① what would really pump up the pulse of worker productivity is a nice afternoon nap. The way people sleep does not prepare ② themselves properly for the demands of the traditional nine-to-five working day. The majority of people ③ regard themselves as working best either in the evening or in the morning. By showing a preference for morning or evening work, the implication is ④ that the majority are not fully alert in the middle of the day—the traditional time for a siesta in hot countries. In other words, the traditional nine-to-five working day does not suit the majority. Allowing workers to follow their natural sleeping habits and ⑤ extend their working hours would be more productive.

*siesta: (주로 더운 나라에서) 낮잠

267 다음 글의 밑줄 친 부분 중, 어법상 틀린 것은?

Long before the establishment of the evidence-based scientific method, people were coming up with explanations for ① what fossils are and how they got to where they were found. Not surprisingly, many of these explanations ② fit the fossils into myths and legends or existing beliefs. In ancient China, farmers would occasionally dig up what looked to be the bones of giant lizards; some people ground the "dragon bones" into powder and swallowed ③ it, thinking it would be a good medicine. In Europe, the fossils of sea shells and fish found on mountains were taken by many as evidence ④ which the great Biblical flood really happened. Then, from around the 18th century onwards, the modern scientific movement began to formulate the explanation we trust today: fossils are the remains of plants and animals that ⑤ lived as many as millions of years ago.

권장 시간 8분 | 시작·종료 시간 | : ~ : | 나의 소요 시간 | 분 초

268 (A), (B), (C)의 각 네모 안에서 어법에 맞는 표현으로 가장 적절한 것은?

We believe things that fit quickly and easily with what we already know. This is not surprising since coherence is precisely (A) [how / what] we learn and expand our understanding of the world. What is surprising is the ferocity with which we both welcome beliefs that fit and reject beliefs that (B) [are / do] not. It is not just that we test possible interpretations for the degree to which they cohere with existing knowledge; it is also that we unthinkingly and uncritically accept ideas that cohere. As we rush toward certainty, the first explanation that coheres with our web of previously accepted beliefs (C) [invoke / invokes] the feeling of knowing, generating cognitive confidence.

*ferocity: 격렬함, 사나움 **invoke: 불러일으키다

	(A)		(B)		(C)
①	how	—	are	—	invoke
②	how	—	do	—	invokes
③	how	—	do	—	invoke
④	what	—	do	—	invokes
⑤	what	—	are	—	invoke

269 (A), (B), (C)의 각 네모 안에서 어법에 맞는 표현으로 가장 적절한 것은?

Twice each year, millions of birds leave their homes to travel hundreds and thousands of miles. These (A) [migrating / migrated] birds travel back and forth to the same places year after year. How do they find their way? Scientists have many theories, but we are not sure. They (B) [might use / might have used] the stars or the moon to guide their way, but wouldn't they be lost on cloudy nights? Perhaps they have a sort of internal compass that shows them which direction is north. They may also be able to detect low level sounds which provide clues about direction, like (C) [them / those] made by ocean waves. It is likely that many birds use a combination of more than one navigational technique.

	(A)		(B)		(C)
①	migrating	—	might use	—	those
②	migrating	—	might use	—	them
③	migrating	—	might have used	—	those
④	migrated	—	might have used	—	them
⑤	migrated	—	might use	—	those

270 다음 글의 밑줄 친 부분 중, 어법상 틀린 것은?

Some anxious teens feel as if they rely too much on friends and family to help them cope with anxiety. But these teens do not rely on friends and family ① enough! They are unwilling to ask for help because they worry ② that they will put others off or upset them if they request their help. Teens who do not want to bother other people may think that asking parents or friends for help will burden them with their problems or that their anxiety is so extreme that ③ it will overwhelm them. However, nothing could be farther from the truth. Most parents and friends often feel honored when ④ asking to help a teen learn and apply tools to manage anxiety. Parents and friends much prefer helping in this way rather than providing a lot of reassurance to calm the anxious teen or ⑤ doing all the things he is unable to do because of his anxiety.

271 다음 글의 밑줄 친 부분 중, 어법상 틀린 것은?

Because the symptoms of some genetic diseases are so nonspecific, it can take years for a child ① to be diagnosed. University College London is developing a computer program ② to spot facial characteristics that are found in a variety of genetic disorders. A photographer projects a pattern of thousands of dots onto the patient's face and then ③ take photos with a digital camera from different angles. The software takes the data and converts it into a three-dimensional 'map' of the face which can be compared to the different face 'maps' ④ linked to various genetic diseases. The technique has produced diagnoses of greater than 90% accuracy among children ⑤ whose genetic disorder has been compiled in the face-shape models.

272 (A), (B), (C)의 각 네모 안에서 어법에 맞는 표현으로 가장 적절한 것은?

Speech is one of the few things that (A) [set / sets] us apart from other animals and is closely connected with our ability to think abstractly. Nevertheless, it's fair to think that writing is a more important means of communication than speech. This is because the written word and the output of printing presses appear to be more efficient and durable ways of transmitting information. Yet, no matter how many books and newspapers are printed, and how much written matter is produced online, the amount of information (B) [exchanged / is exchanged] by speech is still greater. The exchange of information via the Internet, books, and other print media has expanded greatly, but (C) [so / neither] has spoken communication via telephone, radio, and television.

	(A)		(B)		(C)
①	set	—	is exchanged	—	so
②	set	—	exchanged	—	so
③	set	—	is exchanged	—	neither
④	sets	—	is exchanged	—	neither
⑤	sets	—	exchanged	—	so

273 다음 글의 밑줄 친 부분 중, 어법상 틀린 것은?

As I was walking down a path, a pair of birds were chirping ① excitedly in a nearby bush. Because I paid no attention to their warning, I came ② close to disaster. Suddenly, I was standing directly in front of a puff adder, which is the snake ③ that is responsible for more deaths in Africa than any other. There I was standing barefoot, a young boy ④ was filled with terror. Somehow I managed to jump up and land on the side of the path. I saw the snake lift its diamond shaped head ⑤ high and strike blindly in my direction. Although the strike fell short, I was unable to take the opening to escape. I was rooted to the spot.

*puff adder: (아프리카 산) 큰 독사

274 다음 글의 밑줄 친 부분 중, 어법상 틀린 것은?

Having your doctor ① tell you that you're in good shape, and your blood pressure and cholesterol are good, is no reason to sit back and get self-satisfied. This ② continuing to be good news will depend on whether you adopt healthy habits or bad ones. Exercise is very important for the heart. It helps to lower blood pressure and reduces inflammation in the arteries and veins, ③ preventing plaque from sticking to the blood vessel walls. "I'd always put exercise first," says Dr. Mehmet Oz. Studies have shown ④ what exercise is more important than diet. A study showed that women who were fat and fit ⑤ were less likely to have a stroke or heart attack than their peers who were thin, but out of shape.

*plaque: 혈소판

275 (A), (B), (C)의 각 네모 안에서 어법에 맞는 표현으로 가장 적절한 것은?

Some critics of the Olympic Games argue that the events foster aggression, glorify commercialism, and support the dangerous view that nations are either superior or inferior but never equal to one another. On the other hand are those who praise the Games for promoting excellence, encouraging understanding, and (A) [create / creating] goodwill around the globe. Both sides have their supporters, but ever since Hitler hosted the 1936 Berlin Olympics, little has been done to discredit the former argument. Not only (B) [there have / have there] been fatal incidents of terrorism and violence at the Games, but the events have also caused countless diplomatic conflicts. In the search for a solution to the problems, the suggestion (C) [that / which] athletes should compete as individuals instead of as citizens of separate nations offers some hope.

	(A)		(B)		(C)
①	create	—	there have	—	that
②	create	—	have there	—	which
③	creating	—	there have	—	that
④	creating	—	have there	—	which
⑤	creating	—	have there	—	that

276 다음 글의 밑줄 친 부분 중, 어법상 틀린 것은?

Like product quality, once an organization develops a reputation for poor service, it is hard to lose it. This is certainly the case with bus users, ① many of whom have defected to other means of transport, particularly cars, over the last ten to fifteen years. Despite the high operating costs of cars, the congested roads, and the difficulty of parking them in cities, customers were fed up with waiting at bus stops for buses that never arrived, or arrived so late ② that two came together. They were tired of sitting on dirty seats and ③ having to wipe a hole in the condensation to see out the window. They were unimpressed by the unfriendly drivers and the noise, smells, and vibration from vehicles which were long past their retirement dates. Huge numbers of one-time bus riders still believe it to be like this ④ although the investment bus companies have made in new vehicles which are cleaner, faster, quieter, and more comfortable. Old opinions die hard, and ⑤ it will take a major shift in opinion (or legislation) to bring people back to buses.

*congested: 혼잡한 **condensation: 응결

277 다음 글의 밑줄 친 부분 중, 어법상 틀린 것은?

It is not surprising, ① given their evolutionary history, that dogs and cats are opposites in almost everything. For example, dogs like repetition, and ② petting them the same way for a long time will make them very happy. Cats, on the other hand, are easily overstimulated by repetition, which explains ③ what, in the middle of what you think is a perfectly nice petting session with your cat, she will suddenly bite or scratch you. Your cat doesn't hate you. You ④ have just overstimulated her. The way to keep your cat happy is ⑤ not to pet any one part for long. Move the love around—to her head, ears, chin, back—and then repeat and keep moving to her favorite spots.

278 다음 글의 밑줄 친 부분 중, 어법상 틀린 것은?

For anyone who is struggling to 'make it,' a look at a list of people who were failures before they finally succeeded is inspiring. The number of people who became successes in their first ventures ① are small. Humphrey Bogart was ② such a misfit in college that he got expelled for throwing a professor into a fountain. He failed as a Wall Street stockbroker and even as a tugboat inspector. ③ Trying show business as a stage manager, he got fired. He turned to ④ acting and in his first stage appearance he played a houseboy. ⑤ During the opening night performance, he accidentally dropped a tray of dishes. But, eventually he scored as an actor and became a film legend.

*misfit: 부적응자

279 다음 글의 밑줄 친 부분 중, 어법상 틀린 것은?

Have you ever looked in the sky and seen the white trails ① following an airplane? These are called condensation trails and are formed by the hot exhaust. They not only reflect sunlight, but also prevent heat from escaping into space. During the day, the effect of the blocked incoming radiation outweighs ② that of trapped heat, thereby cooling the atmosphere. When all flights stopped ③ to fly for three days in the USA after the attacks of 9/11, daytime temperatures across the country rose slightly, whereas nighttime temperatures dropped. This evidence supported the hypothesis ④ that condensation trails reduce the temperature range by cooling during the day and heating the atmosphere at night. Thus, overnight flights contribute more ⑤ to atmospheric warming.

*condensation trail: 비행운(雲)

280 다음 글의 밑줄 친 부분 중, 어법상 틀린 것은?

Thank you for your patience ① while the tenure committee considered your possible promotion to Associate Professor. We all agree that you have made significant contributions to the Biology Department with your teaching, and we congratulate you on ② being voted "Teacher of the Year." After reviewing the list of your publications, however, we have decided to withhold the promotion to Associate Professor ③ by a later date. While you have several ④ promising research projects in progress, the committee would like to see more publications before granting Associate Professor status. We will be happy to reconsider your request for advancement next year if the number and quality of your publications increase. Again, we salute your contributions to our department and wish ⑤ you continued success in your professional and academic career.

*tenure: (대학 교수의) 종신 재직권

권장 시간 8분 | 시작·종료 시간 | : ~ : | 나의 소요 시간 | 분 초

281 (A), (B), (C)의 각 네모 안에서 어법에 맞는 표현으로 가장 적절한 것은?

Madonna Louise Veronica Ciccone Ritchie was 20 when she left the University of Michigan and went to New York with just $35 in her pocket to pursue her dreams of fame. Her first album was a huge hit and she soon became a world famous star, (A) [redefined / redefining] herself and her music with each new album. Always outspoken, often shocking, she is known as a woman who does whatever she wants, no matter (B) [how / what] the public reaction is. A few years ago, she spoke out against music piracy and illegal downloading from peer-to-peer(P2P) filesharing sites. This led to a major campaign (C) [which / in which] many artists united to condemn illegal downloading and piracy of music and movies.

	(A)		(B)		(C)
①	redefined	—	what	—	in which
②	redefined	—	how	—	which
③	redefining	—	what	—	which
④	redefining	—	what	—	in which
⑤	redefining	—	how	—	which

282 (A), (B), (C)의 각 네모 안에서 어법에 맞는 표현으로 가장 적절한 것은?

Despite the (A) [common / commonly] held notion that dampness makes joint pain worse, medical research has found no relationship between arthritis pain and the weather. Dampness, meaning moisture on the surface of things, and high humidity, meaning a large amount of moisture in the air, (B) [is / are] characteristics that many people think cause their arthritis to worsen. But these same patients do not experience an increase in their symptoms when bathing or swimming, which would be considered a similar environmental situation. High barometric pressure may not be the cause either. Patients easily handle the same increase in pressure during a plane flight as would occur during a storm. Common beliefs reveal more about the workings of the mind than (C) [that / those] of the body.

*arthritis: 관절염
**barometric pressure: 기압

	(A)		(B)		(C)
①	common	—	is	—	that
②	common	—	are	—	those
③	commonly	—	is	—	those
④	commonly	—	are	—	those
⑤	commonly	—	is	—	that

283 다음 글의 밑줄 친 부분 중, 어법상 틀린 것은?

There are ① a few obvious ways that we learn about the experiences of others. Experiences are communicated to us, ② either by natural signs in the form of gestures, tears, laughter, and so forth, or by the use of language. A very good way ③ to find out what another person is thinking or feeling is to ask. They may not answer, or if they do answer they may not answer truthfully, but very often they will. However, we do not depend on words alone; it may be, indeed, that the inferences which we draw from people's nonverbal behavior are more dependable than ④ those that we base upon what they say about themselves, and ⑤ what actions speak more honestly than words.

284 다음 글의 밑줄 친 부분 중, 어법상 틀린 것은?

The quality of the graphics output on a computer printer is measured in dpi (dots per inch). Simply by changing the density of dots that ① make up each part of an image, the printer can produce images that look almost photographic. To understand how this works, ② consider how a black-and-white photograph shows the shades which, in real life, are colors. Each color is a different shade of gray. For graphics to be produced on the computer printer, a piece of software ③ is called a printer driver decides upon a dot pattern which will represent each color shade. These different patterns or textures each ④ create an individual effect which your eye translates into gray shades. The closer you look at the image, however, ⑤ the less lifelike it looks.

285 다음 글의 밑줄 친 부분 중, 어법상 틀린 것은?

Meditation treats humans from a holistic perspective—the body, emotions, mind, and spirit ① are viewed as a whole, with the Chi (life energy) connecting them. Injury or stress in any one component will affect all ② the others. Worry, tension, or excessive thinking will upset the balance of Chi and inhibit ③ their flow. This can cause physical and emotional problems over time. The ancients discovered that the best cure for an overworked mind ④ was meditation. It aims to calm the mind enough that the body, emotions, Chi, and spirit have a chance to get back in balance. Learn ⑤ how to calm your racing mind and relax your body the healthy way.

286 다음 글의 밑줄 친 부분 중, 어법상 틀린 것은?

Sometimes, it seems that people simply like to try new things—they are interested in variety seeking, ① in which the priority is to vary one's product experiences, perhaps as a form of stimulation or to avoid being bored. Variety seeking is especially likely ② to occur when people are in a good mood, or when there is relatively little stimulation elsewhere in their environment. In the case of foods and beverages, variety seeking can occur due to a phenomenon ③ known as sensory-specific satiety. Put simply, this means the pleasantness of a food item just eaten drops, ④ despite the pleasantness of uneaten foods remains unchanged. So even though we have favorites, we still like to sample ⑤ other possibilities. Ironically, consumers may actually switch to less preferred options for variety's sake even though they enjoy the more familiar option more.

*satiety: 포만(감)

287 다음 글의 밑줄 친 부분 중, 어법상 틀린 것은?

Supermarkets are the most powerful actors along tropical fruit supply chains. With their buying power, they can achieve substantial profits by squeezing suppliers and paying ① unsustainably low prices for fruit. Other abusive practices can include demanding special discounts, delaying payments and threatening suppliers. As the grocery market sector becomes concentrated in the hands of fewer retailers, suppliers have ② little option but to accept such conditions. This behavior is driving the continued exploitation of workers and destruction of the natural environment in exporting communities. Research demonstrates that in many instances there is simply not enough money passing down the supply chain ③ for workers to earn a 'living' wage that covers basic household needs. Less money encourages suppliers to take ④ however means necessary to reduce costs: for example, taking less responsibility for how agrochemicals are stored and applied, polluting air and water in the ⑤ surrounding environment.

288 다음 글의 밑줄 친 부분 중, 어법상 틀린 것은?

Very recently, scientists have been able to add a level of complexity to the classification of organisms. Researchers now use genetic or molecular techniques ① to complement taxonomic techniques. Specifically, they look at organisms' DNA in order to classify them according to their degree of relatedness. This capability is important because animals frequently seem to belong in the same category based on a similar appearance when, in fact, these distant relatives have come to take on a similar appearance because ② it became advantageous for one reason or another. As an example of such misleading similarities in appearance, many flies look like bumblebees. Though they look superficially like bumblebees, genetic and taxonomic techniques confirm ③ what they are as related as dogs are to cats. Genetic studies can also help with the problem of having only dead specimens to study; wasps and bees can look ④ extraordinarily similar to each other when their behavior can't be observed. Molecular studies, which can be conducted ⑤ using dead specimens, can confirm that they are truly distant cousins.

*taxonomic: 분류학상의 **specimen: 견본, 표본 ***wasp: 말벌

Answer

PART 1 기출편

핵심 예상문제

01회	001 ③	002 ②	003 ③
02회	004 ③	005 ⑤	006 ④
03회	007 ③	008 ②	009 ②
04회	010 ①	011 ④	012 ②
05회	013 ②	014 ③	015 ④
06회	016 ①	017 ⑤	018 ⑤
07회	019 ⑤	020 ⑤	021 ⑤
08회	022 ④	023 ⑤	024 ②
09회	025 ①	026 ③	027 ④
10회	028 ④	029 ③	030 ③
11회	031 ③	032 ②	033 ④
12회	034 ⑤	035 ①	036 ①
13회	037 ④	038 ①	039 ⑤
14회	040 ②	041 ③	042 ②
15회	043 ⑤	044 ③	045 ③
16회	046 ③	047 ④	048 ④
17회	049 ⑤	050 ⑤	051 ②
18회	052 ⑤	053 ③	054 ①
19회	055 ④	056 ②	057 ⑤
20회	058 ⑤	059 ③	060 ③

PART 2 실전편

실전 모의고사

01회	061 ④	062 ③	063 ②	064 ③	065 ③	066 ④
02회	067 ⑤	068 ②	069 ②	070 ①	071 ⑤	072 ③
03회	073 ⑤	074 ②	075 ④	076 ⑤	077 ⑤	078 ③
04회	079 ③	080 ①	081 ③	082 ③	083 ④	084 ③
05회	085 ①	086 ⑤	087 ②	088 ⑤	089 ⑤	090 ②
06회	091 ④	092 ②	093 ③	094 ②	095 ①	096 ③
07회	097 ⑤	098 ④	099 ③	100 ③	101 ⑤	102 ④

고난도 모의고사

01회	103 ⑤	104 ⑤	105 ③	106 ④	107 ⑤	108 ②

실전 모의고사

08회	109 ⑤	110 ①	111 ②	112 ④	113 ③	114 ④
09회	115 ③	116 ④	117 ②	118 ④	119 ②	120 ⑤
10회	121 ③	122 ⑤	123 ③	124 ①	125 ④	126 ⑤
11회	127 ⑤	128 ①	129 ⑤	130 ④	131 ③	132 ④

12회	133 ⑤	134 ④	135 ②	136 ④	137 ⑤	138 ④
13회	139 ④	140 ②	141 ④	142 ④	143 ①	144 ⑤
14회	145 ④	146 ②	147 ②	148 ⑤	149 ④	150 ⑤

고난도 모의고사

02회	151 ③	152 ②	153 ②	154 ①	155 ⑤	156 ③

실전 모의고사

15회	157 ④	158 ③	159 ③	160 ②	161 ⑤	162 ④
16회	163 ③	164 ④	165 ④	166 ⑤	167 ②	168 ①
17회	169 ④	170 ③	171 ①	172 ⑤	173 ②	174 ③
18회	175 ②	176 ②	177 ③	178 ⑤	179 ③	180 ④
19회	181 ④	182 ⑤	183 ②	184 ④	185 ⑤	186 ①
20회	187 ⑤	188 ①	189 ③	190 ③	191 ⑤	192 ③
21회	193 ⑤	194 ③	195 ③	196 ①	197 ②	198 ①

고난도 모의고사

03회	199 ③	200 ③	201 ③	202 ③	203 ⑤	204 ③

실전 모의고사

22회	205 ④	206 ④	207 ⑤	208 ③	209 ②	210 ②
23회	211 ③	212 ②	213 ②	214 ⑤	215 ③	216 ④
24회	217 ④	218 ③	219 ③	220 ①	221 ⑤	222 ⑤
25회	223 ③	224 ④	225 ③	226 ⑤	227 ⑤	228 ⑤
26회	229 ④	230 ①	231 ③	232 ①	233 ②	234 ①
27회	235 ④	236 ③	237 ⑤	238 ①	239 ④	240 ⑤

고난도 모의고사

04회	241 ③	242 ④	243 ④	244 ④	245 ②	246 ④

실전 모의고사

28회	247 ④	248 ⑤	249 ③	250 ④	251 ②	252 ②
29회	253 ③	254 ①	255 ③	256 ④	257 ④	258 ④
30회	259 ①	260 ⑤	261 ④	262 ③	263 ①	264 ⑤
31회	265 ⑤	266 ②	267 ④	268 ②	269 ①	270 ④
32회	271 ③	272 ②	273 ④	274 ④	275 ⑤	276 ④
33회	277 ③	278 ①	279 ③	280 ③	281 ④	282 ④

고난도 모의고사

05회	283 ⑤	284 ③	285 ③	286 ④	287 ④	288 ③

Memo

Memo

어법끝

실전 모의고사

Grammar & Usage

정답 및 해설

PART 1 기출 정리 & 핵심 예상문제

기출 꿰뚫기 1 매번 나오는 TOP 5 빈출 어법

KEY POINT 01 정확한 구문 분석이 관건인 유형들

정답 & 해설 1 **spent** | and 이하의 절을 보면 주어(some of the dollars) 이하에 have migrated라는 동사가 명백히 있으므로 이곳은 동사 자리가 아님을 알 수 있다. 둘 중 수식어로 쓰일 수 있는 과거분사 spent가 정답.

2 ○ | 두 개의 절을 접속사 없이 분사가 자연스럽게 이어주고 있는 분사구문이 적절히 쓰였다.

3 **evaluating** | 조건을 제한하는 to the extent that ~(~하는 한에서)을 보면, 주어(two observers)에 이어 곧 동사(arrive)가 나오므로 이곳은 동사가 올 수 없는 자리. 주어를 수식하는 후치 수식 구조의 일부가 될 수 있는 현재분사 evaluating이 알맞다.

4 **to contain** | <주어(We)+동사(have done)+목적어(everything [we can])>의 완전한 구조이므로 수식어가 올 수 있는 자리. 문맥상 <목적(~하기 위하여)>을 나타내는 to부정사가 적절하다. contain이 '~을 포함하다, ~이 들어 있다'의 뜻이 아니라 문맥상 '억제하다'의 뜻임을 짐작할 수 있어야 동사가 필요한지 to부정사가 필요한지 판단할 수 있다.

5 ×, **try → trying** | 종속절 if절에 이어 주절이 시작되는 부분이다. 주절이 명령문일 수도 있지만 뒤에 동사(is)가 나오므로 이곳은 주어가 되어야 할 자리이다. 즉, 동명사 trying으로 고쳐 써야 한다.

6 ×, **it → and it[which]** | 세 개의 절을 연결하는데 접속사 As밖에 없으므로 it은 접속사나 관계대명사 자리이다. 의미적으로 and it을 쓰거나 관계대명사 which가 필요하다.

7 **ended** | meant의 목적어절인 that절의 동사 자리이다.

8 **Living** | 하나의 절이 문장을 구성한 경우이므로 is의 주어가 될 수 있는 동명사 Living이 알맞다.

9 **Adopt** | 세 개의 절을 연결하는데 이미 두 개의 and가 있고 첫 번째 절에 동사가 없으므로 동사 자리이다. <명령문+and>는 '~하라 그러면 ...'의 의미가 되어 문맥도 자연스럽다.

10 ×, **unloading → unloads** | 동사 figure의 목적어절인 that절의 동명사 주어 writing down의 동사 자리이다. 앞의 tasks는 명사로서 동사가 아님에 주의한다.

11 ×, **sends → sending** | 앞의 명사 An individual neuron을 수식하는 준동사 자리. 문장의 동사는 uses이다. use가 명사로도 잘 쓰이지만 여기서는 동사로 쓰였다.

12 ×, **was made → made** | until이 이끄는 절이 <주어(someone)+동사(invented)+목적어(a clock)>의 완전한 구조이므로 밑줄 친 곳은 수식어 자리이다. 수식받는 명사 a clock과 make는 수동 관계이므로 made가 되어야 한다.

13 **summarize** | <had+O(university students)+OC(read ~)> 구조에서 목적격보어가 병렬구조를 이루고 있으므로 read와 마찬가지로 원형부정사 summarize가 정답.

14 ×, **meaning → meant** | and로 이어진 두 개의 주어(a general lack of knowledge와 insufficient care being taken)의 동사가 올 자리이다.

A general lack of knowledge [and] insufficient care (being taken) [**when** fish pens were initially constructed] (S) meant (V) **that** pollution [*from* excess feed and fish waste] created *huge barren underwater deserts*. (O)

15 **unhurried** | 형용사인 leisurely와 and로 연결된 것이므로 형용사형이 되어야 한다.

16 ×, **leaves → leave** | A and B에서 A는 관계대명사절의 동사인 lay이므로 leave가 되어야 한다.

17 ×, **refused → refuse** | A or B에서 A는 take이므로 refuse가 되어야 한다. 바로 앞의 offered를 A로 착각하지 말아야 한다. 병렬관계는 반드시 의미를 같이 생각하여 의미적으로 연결되고 있는 대상이 무엇인지를 정확히 찾고 확인해야 한다.

18 ×, **being → be** | <조동사(must)+not only+A(원형동사), but+B(원형동사)>로 이어지는 병렬구조이다.

19 ○ | 관계대명사 which 뒤에 I think가 삽입된 것이므로 동사 자리가 맞다.

해석 1 많은 나라에서 더 젊은 사람들 사이에서 신문 읽는 습관이 감소해 오고 있으며 전에 신문광고에 쓰였던 돈의 일부가 인터넷으로 이동해 오고 있다.

2 다른 회사는 문제를 각 부문으로 나누면서 겉으로 보기에는 보다 명료하고 질서 있게 일을 진행했다.

3 측정 시스템은 같은 동작을 평가하는 두 명의 관찰자가 같은 (혹은 매우 비슷한) 측정치를 얻게 되는 한 객관적이다.

4 아시다시피, 최고 수준의 교육을 제공하기 위한 비용은 계속 오르고 있습니다. 우리는 교육의 질을 손상시키지 않으면서 비용을 억제하기 위해 우리가 할 수 있는 모든 일을 다 했습니다.

5 만일 당신이 나쁘게 먹고 있다면, 당신은 잘 먹기 시작하기로 결심을 할 수도 있다. 하지만, 만약 당신이 편안하고, 느긋하고, 행복하게 느끼기 위해 햄버거와 아이스크림을 먹고 있다면, 그것들을 브로콜리와 당근 주스로 대체하려고 노력하는 것은 부엌에 다시 페인트를 칠함으로써 물이 새는 목욕탕의 수도꼭지에 대처하려고 하는 것과 비슷하다.

6 아이들은 나이가 더 들어감에 따라 스스로 중요한 일들을 적기 시작할 것이며 그것은 나아가 그들이 자신의 통제감을 발달시키는 데 도움을 준다.

7 (야구의) 첫 반세기 동안에는 경기가 밤에 열리지 않았는데, 그것은 야구 경기가 전통적인 근무일처럼 해가 지면 끝난다는 것을 의미했다.

8 다른 사람의 기대를 좇아 당신의 삶을 사는 것은 살기 어려운 방식이다.

9 '잠은 죽어서야 자겠다.'라는 오래된 금언은 불행한 결과를 가져온다. 이런 사고방식을 가지면 더 빨리 죽게 될 것이고 삶의 질은 악화될 것이다.

10 연구 저자들은 미래 과업을 적으면 생각을 내려놓게 되어 깊게 생각하는 것을 멈출 수 있다고 판단한다. 자신의 뇌에게 그 과업이 처리될 것이며, 지금 당장이 아닐 뿐이라고 말하고 있는 것이다.

11 뇌에 신호를 보내는 개개의 신경세포는 마라톤을 뛰는 다리 근육 세포만큼의 에너지를 이용한다.

12 그 당시는 많은 사원들이 화재로 전소되었다. 확실히 승려들은 누군가 물 바구니로 만들어진 시계를 발명할 때까지 그것(사원들이 화재로 전소되는 것)을 썩 내키지 않아 했다.

13 Tory Higgins와 그의 동료들은 대학생들에게 어떤 사람의 성격을 기술한 것을 읽게 한 다음 이 사람을 좋아하거나 싫어하는 것으로 여겨지고 있는 어떤 다른 이가 읽도록 그것을 요약해보게 시켰다.

14 어류 양식용 가두리가 처음에 만들어졌을 때 전반적인 지식의 부족과 불충분하게 행해지던 관리는 초과량의 사료와 어류 폐기물로부터 발생하는 오염이 거대하고도 황폐한 해저 사막을 만들어냈다는 것을 의미했다.

15 측정된 시간, 마감 시간, 일정, 그리고 시간 단위로 지급되는 임금의 규율 이전의 세상과 마찬가지로, 그 경기의 속도는 여유롭고 서둘지 않는다.

16 때로 탁란 동물이라 일컫는 벌들은 뻐꾸기 벌이라고도 하는데, 뻐꾸기 새와 유사하기 때문이며, 뻐꾸기 새들은 다른 새의 둥지에 알을 낳아 그것을 그 새가 기르도록 내버려 둔다.

17 동업자는 오직 두 가지 선택 사항만이 있다. 그는 제안된 것을 받아들이거나 어떤 것도 취하기를 거절할 수 있다.

18 그들이 발행하기로 선택하는 자료는 상업적 가치가 있어야 할 뿐 아니라 매우 능숙하게 쓰여 편집과 사실 오류가 없어야 한다.

19 이제 젊은이들은 디지털화되어 소셜 미디어 기자가 되고 있고 자신들의 작품을 세계가 보도록 만들고 편집하는데, 나는 이것이 좋은 일이라고 생각한다.

KEY POINT 02 뒤에 오는 구조가 완전한지 불완전한지를 파악하자.

정답 & 해설 1 ○ | 동사(says)의 목적어가 시작되는 부분으로 목적어절을 이끄는 접속사 that이 맞게 쓰였다. that 종속절은 동사구 두 개(provide ~, but charge ~)가 접속사 but을 가운데 두고 대등하게 연결된 구조.

2 ○ | "open architecture"라는 개념을 수식하는 수식어구 meaning ~에서 동사 mean의 목적어가 시작되는 곳으로, 목적어절을 이끄는 접속사 that이 맞게 쓰였다. 이어 나오는 that은 명사절 that절의 주어인 선행사 the knowledge를 수식하는 목적격 관계대명사.

3 **what** | 접속사 that을 쓰게 되면 that절이 완전한 구조여야 하는데 동사(say)의 성격상 목적어 없이 쓰이는 게 어색하다. 선행사를 포함하는 관계대명사절 what절이 동사 believe의 목적어로 쓰이는 구조.

4 **×, what → whether** | A and B로 이어지는 구조로서 A와 B는 모두 전치사 about의 목적어가 되는 절이므로 명사절을 이끄는 접속사가 필요하다. 밑줄 친 부분 뒤에 완전한 절이 왔고 의미적으로 '~인지(에 대한 증거)'를 뜻하는 접속사가 필요하므로 what은 whether로 고쳐야 한다.

5 **×, What → That** | is 앞은 주어가 되는 절이 와야 할 자리인데 절의 동사인 starve는 자동사로서 뒤에 목적어 없이 완전한 구조를 이룬다. 그러므로 What은 That으로 고쳐야 한다.

6 **×, which → that** | 우선 삽입절인 콤마 사이의 when discussing ~ with a lawyer는 생각하지 말고 밑줄 뒤가 완전한지와 문장의 동사인 should be assured부터 살펴보자. 밑줄 뒤는 <주어(the latter)+동사(will not disclose)+부사구(to third parties)+목적어(the information provided)>의 완전한 구조가 왔다. 또한 assure는 <assure+A+that~>의 형태로 'A에게 that ~을 장담하다, 확언하다'를 뜻한다. 목적어인 A를 주어로 수동태가 되어도 that절은 그대로 남는다.

7 **where** | what은 관계대명사이든 의문사이든 본질이 명사이기 때문에 완전한 구조를 갖춘 이어지는 절(they were lost) 앞에 쓸 수 없다. 장소를 나타내는 관계부사 where는 구조상 의미상 가능하다. where they were lost가 전치사 from의 목적어 역할을 하는 명사절.

8 ○ | 이어지는 절의 구성을 보면 <주어(most cultural anthropologists)+동사(earn and maintain)+목적어(their professional standing)>로 완벽하고 수식어구는 더해질 수 있으므로, 전치사 수식어구 in which가 맞게 쓰였다.

9 **×, which → in which[where]** | 선행사(One domain)를 수식하는 관계사절의 구조를 살펴보면 <주어(this)+동사(is)+보어(of considerable significance)>로 완전한 구조를 이루고 있으므로 명사인 which가 들어갈 곳이 없다. 부사어구 in which(= in this domain) 또는 관계부사 where가 구조상 문맥상 자연스럽다.

10 **who** | 관계사 다음에 바로 동사가 이어지는, 주어가 없는 불완전한 구조이므로 주어가 될 수 있는 관계대명사의 주격 who가 올 자리.

11 ○ | 의문부사인 how(어떻게)가 문장에 적절한가 물어보고 있다. 주어, 동사에 이어 목적어(the spaces)까지 있는 구조이므로 명사인 what은 쓰이지 못하고 <방법>을 얘기하는 수식어인 부사의 쓰임은 적절하다.

12 **×, which → that** | it is 이하는 완전한 구조이고 문맥상 '너무나 ~하여 ...하다'를 나타낼 수 있는 so ~ that의 that이 와야 한다.

13 **where** | decline은 자동사로서 sleep time has declined는 완전한 구조이다. 그러므로 관계부사인 where가 적절하다.

14 **in which** | a single word 이하가 완전한 구조이므로 <전치사+관계대명사>가 와야 한다. 동사 apply는 to와 함께 쓰여 '~에 적용되다[해당되다]'의 의미로 쓰인다.

15 **in which** | 뒤의 구조는 <주어(people)+동사(did not say)+목적어(I haven't got all day.)>로서 완전하므로 <전치사+관계대명사>가 적절하다.

16 **who** | 관계대명사 뒤에 삽입절인 I was certain이 나오고 뒤에 동사 was going to lie가 이어지므로 주어가 없는 불완전한 절이다. 그러므로 주격 관계대명사가 필요한 자리임을 알 수 있다. 관계대명사 뒤에 <주어+동사>가 이어 나온다고 해서 섣불리 주격 관계대명사는 못 온다고 판단해서는 안 된다.

17 **however** | 문맥상 '아무리 ~할지라도'를 의미하는 <however+형용사/부사+주어+동사> 구문이 적절한데, be동사인 is가 생략된 형태이다. 주절 뒤에 콤마로 연결된 부사절 자리이므로 명사절을 이끄는 의문부사 how는 올 수 없다.

18 **whatever** | 명사와 같이 쓸 수 있는 것은 whatever(어떤 ~든). however는 형용사 또는 부사와 함께 쓰인다. (however expensive, however hard ...)

해석 1 제품 보증서에는 귀사에서 여분의 부품과 재료들은 무료로 제공하지만, 기사의 노동에 대해서는 비용을 부과한다고 되어 있습니다.

2 학계는 '공개된 구조'에 믿음을 두고 있는데, 이는 연구가 산출한 지식은 기술 혁신을 장려하도록 공개되어야 한다는 것을 의미한다.

3 사람들은 그들이 의심스러워하는 무엇인가에 대해 말이나 글로 증언을 해달라고 권유를 받을 때, 종종 그들이 한 기만에 대해 안 좋게 느껴지는 경우가 많다. 그럼에도 불구하고, 그들은 그들이 말하고 있는 것을 믿기 시작한다.

4 한두 군데의 자선단체에 기부하는 사람들은 그 자선단체가 무슨 일을 하고 있는지 그리고 정말로 긍정적인 영향을 끼치고 있는지에 대한 증거를 구한다. 만약 그 증거가 그 자선단체가 정말로 다른 사람들을 돕고 있다는 것을 가리키면 그들은 막대한 기부를 한다.

5 모든 유기체가 생존하기에 충분한 먹이를 구할 수는 없으므로, 기아는 자연에서 자주 발견되는 일종의 부정적 가치이다. 일부 유기체들이 자연에서 굶어 죽어야 한다는 것은 매우 유감스럽고 슬프다.

6 법률 자문을 구하는 사람들은 변호사에게 자신들의 권리와 의무를 상의할 때 제공된 정보를 제3자에게 그 변호사가 누설하지 않을 것이라는 것을 확약받아야 한다.

7 7개월 후에 잃어버린 장소에서 3,540킬로미터 떨어진 알래스카의 Sitka 근처 해변 육지에 첫 번째 장난감들이 도달했다.

8 그리고 중요하게도 그것은 대부분의 문화 인류학자들이 자신들의 입장을 획득하고 유지하는 방식이다.

9 음악이 신체적, 정신적 기술을 향상시키는 듯하다는 점을 감안할 때, 음악이 작업 수행에 해로운 상황이 있는가? 이것이 상당히 중요한 의미를 갖는 한 영역은 잠재적으로 음악이 안전하게 운전하는 능력에 미치는 해로운 영향이다.

10 1762년에 이 섬은 영국인들에 의해 점령되는데, 그들은 이듬해에 파리 조약에 의해 그것을 프랑스인들에게 돌려주었으며, 그 이후로 그것은 후자의 소유 상태가 되었다.

11 William H. Whyte는 뉴욕시의 많은 장소에 사람들이 어떻게 공간을 활용하는지 알아보기 위해 비디오카메라를 켜 두었다.

12 오늘날 만들어지는 많은 제조품들은 그 속에 정확히 무엇이 들어있는지를 때로 알기 어려운 너무나 많은 화학물과 인공 첨가물을 함유한다.

13 미국, 영국, 일본, 대한민국, 그리고 서구의 여러 나라와 같이, 지난 세기에 걸쳐 수면 시간이 가장 극적으로 감소한 나라들이 또한 신체적 그리고 정신적 질병률이 가장 크게 증가한 나라들이라는 것은 우연이 아니다.

14 마찬가지로, 단 하나의 단어인 "삼촌"이 아버지의 남자 형제와 어머니의 남자 형제에 적용되는 상황을 이해하는 것이 어떻게 가능한가?

15 야구는 사람들이 "나는 시간이 없어요."라고 말하지 않았던 종류의 세계에 속해 있다. 야구 경기는 정말로 온종일 경기를 한다.

16 나는 최근에 몇 가지 특별히 민감한 이슈에 대해 거짓말을 할 것으로 내가 확신하고 있던, 아는 사람을 인터뷰한 뉴스를 봤는데 그녀는 정말로 거짓말을 했다.

17 그녀는 언제나 학생들에게 그 길이 아무리 힘들고 불확실해도 꿈을 좇아야 한다고 말한다.

18 우리는 <New York Times>, <Guardian> 혹은 세상의 거의 모든 주요 신문의 웹사이트에서 그날의 뉴스나 비즈니스, 연예 또는 어떤 뉴스든지 그 최신 내용을 읽을 수 있다.

KEY POINT 03 능동·수동 문제는 '하느냐', '되느냐'를 구별하자.

정답 & 해설 1 ○ | trap(~을 덫에 가두다)은 목적어를 취하는 타동사. 우리가 덫에 '갇힌' 것이므로 수동태를 쓴 것이 맞다.

2 ○ | 수식을 받는 명사와 수식하는 분사 간에 능동·수동 관계를 따져보는 문제. a piece of wood가 toss(~을 가볍게 던지다) 당하는 입장이므로 수동태에 쓰이는 과거분사 tossed로 쓴 것이 맞다.

3 ○ | 주격 관계대명사에 이어지는 동사이므로 선행사와의 능동·수동 관계를 따져 보면, 주어 outbreaks (of infectious diseases)가 목적어(the caged fish와 local wild fish populations)를 황폐화시키는(devastate) 주체이므로 능동형으로 쓴 것이 맞다.

4 ○ | 선행사가 some (of the flavors of old-fashioned breads)으로 이것이 lose의 주체가 아니라 객체이므로 수동태 were lost가 맞게 쓰였다. 이때 복수 명사 flavors의 수식을 받는 some은 복수. 따라서 were lost로 쓰였다.

5 ○ | how로 시작하는 의문문의 주어가 music's ability (to influence driving in this way)로, 설명되어야 할 대상이므로 수동태로 맞게 쓰였다. 조동사(might)에 이어지므로 원형인 be를 써서 be explained로 쓰였다.

6 **Asked** | 이어지는 콤마 이하를 보면 they가 질문을 받는 입장이므로 Asked가 정답. (Being) asked에서 Being이 생략된 형태. 한편 Having said는 이어지는 liked보다 앞서 일어난 일이므로 완료형 분사 having p.p.형으로 표현되었다.

7 **described** | whether절은 distinguish의 목적어절로서 주어는 the person, 동사는 is related이다. 그러므로 describe는 주어를 수식하는 수식어구 자리인데 the person과 수동관계이므로 described가 되어야 한다.

8 **×, finding → found** | they는 biological clues를 의미하고 find와는 수동관계이므로 found가 되어야 한다. 전체 문장은 <주어(the extent)+수식어절(to which they are found)+동사(varies)~>의 구조이다.

9 ○ | 5형식 <expect+O+OC>의 구조에서 목적어와 목적격보어는 의미상 주어 동사 관계. find하는 것은 관찰자, lovers는 그 대상이므로 to부정사가 수동형으로 맞게 쓰였다.

10 **×, observed → observing** | observe 뒤에 목적어가 이어 나오고 있고 observe의 주체가 전체 문장의 주어 He이므로 능동의 현재분사 observing으로 써야 한다.

11 **surprising** | That은 앞 문장 전체를 받는다. '음악을 잘하는 사람이 언어도 잘한다'는 사실이 '놀라움을 일으키지' 않는다는 문맥이므로 능동의 현재분사가 정답.

12 **interesting** | boring lecturers가 나의 흥미를 불러일으키는 것이므로 interesting이 되어야 한다.

13 **×, humiliated → humiliating** | it은 this data를 받는 것으로서 그 데이터가 우리에게 굴욕감을 주는 것이므로 humiliating이 되어야 한다.

14 **named** | 독일 회사가 Bayer(바이엘)이라고 '이름 지어진' 것이므로 수동을 나타내는 과거분사 수식어가 오는 게 맞다. name은 뒤에 목적어와 명사 목적보어를 취할 수 있는 동사로서 수동형 과거분사 수식어로 바뀌어도 명사 목적보어(Bayer)는 뒤에 그대로 남아 있다.

15 **×, staying → to stay** | 사역동사 make는 능동태일 때 목적격보어로 원형부정사를 취하지만, 수동태가 되면 원형부정사가 to부정사로 전환된다. 능동태 The teacher made the unruly student stay after ~가 수동태로 전환된 구조.

해석 1 우리는 역설에 깊이 갇혀 있는데, 최상의 행동 방식을 따르기로 결정하고 나서 다른 것을 하는 것이다.

2 아리스토텔레스는 돌이 공중에서 떨어지는 것은 돌이 '중력'이라는 성질을 가지고 있기 때문이라고 설명했다. 하지만 물론 물에 던져진 나무 조각은 가라앉는 대신 뜬다.

3 고밀도의 사육은 몇몇 경우에 가두리에 있는 어류뿐만 아니라 지역의 야생 어류 개체군 또한 황폐화시키는 전염병의 발생을 초래했다.

4 그들은 제빵이 더 산업화되고, 제빵 제품이 더 세련되고, 표준화되고, (어떤 사람들이 말하기를) 맛이 없어지면서 사라진 옛날 빵의 몇 가지 맛을 되찾기를 원하고 있다.

5 시끄럽고 빠른 음악과 난폭한 운전 사이의 연관성을 제시하는 증거가 있는데, 이런 식으로 운전에 미치는 음악의 영향력이 어떻게 설명될 수 있을까?

6 긍정적인 것을 말하고 난 다음, 그들 자신도 그 사람을 좋아하게 되었다. 그들이 읽은 것을 회상해 보라는 요청을 받았을 때, 그들은 성격 기술을 원래 그랬던 것보다 더 긍정적인 것으로 기억했다.

7 많은 아프리카어 화자들은 '사촌'과 같은 단 하나의 단어가 남자와 여자 친척 모두를 묘사한다거나, 또는 묘사되는 사람이 화자의 아버지나 어머니와 혈연관계인지를 구분하지 않고 사용되는 것을 터무니없다고 여길 것이다.

8 우리는 과도하게 낙관해서는 안 된다. 생물학적 단서들은 필수적인 것은 아니다. 그것들이 발견되는 정도는 동물마다 다르고 활동마다 다르다.

9 사람들은 다른 사람들에게 주목받는 것도 좋아하는 것으로 또한 밝혀졌다! 조사자는 연인들이 사적이고 외진 공간에서 발견될 것이라 예상했으나, 대부분 그들은 모든 사람들이 볼 수 있는 한가운데에 앉거나 서 있었다.

10 그는 계속해서 가정생활의 사소한 세부 사항들을 관찰하면서 마을 구석구석을 이리저리 돌아다니는 일상의 일과에 대해서 기술하고 있는데, 그가 말하듯이, 그러한 관찰들은 가능하고 (누구나) 해볼 수 있는 것처럼 보인다.

11 음악을 잘하는 사람들은 언어에도 또한 능숙하다. 그것은 놀라운 일이 아닌데, 왜냐하면 음악 공부와 언어 공부는 많은 공통점을 가지고 있기 때문이다.

12 듣고 있는 것에 대해 계속해서 자문하는 것에 매진한다면 지루한 강의자라도 약간은 흥미로워지는 것을 발견하게 될 것이다. 그 이유는 흥미의 많은 부분이 강의자가 제공하는 것이라기보다는 당신이 불러일으키는 것에서 올 것이기 때문이다.

13 이 데이터는 흔히 신뢰성이 의심스러울 수 있다. 거짓일 수도 있으며 또한 사실일지라도 깊은 굴욕감을 줄 수 있다. 새로 출발하거나 두 번째의 기회를 갖기 점점 어려울지도 모른다.

14 1899년 1월에 '바이엘'이라는 이름의 독일 회사가 이 신약을 '아스피린'으로 상표 등록했다.

15 그 버릇없는 학생은 수업 후에 남아 다음 날 (수업의) 준비를 위해 칠판을 닦고 지우개를 청소하게 시켜졌다.

KEY POINT 04 형용사 자리와 부사 자리를 구별하자.

정답 & 해설 1 ○ | 동사(move)를 꾸며주는 요소로 형용사 아닌 부사가 맞게 쓰였다.

2 ○ | <S+seem+SC>의 구조에서 주어인 명사의 상태를 설명하는 주격보어 자리에 형용사가 맞게 왔다.

3 **subtle** | 비교급 패턴(as ~ as)을 제거하고 보면 The variation is subtle.이므로 주격보어로 형용사가 정답.

4 **comfortable** | what makes you comfortable이 전치사 beyond의 목적어. <make+O+OC>의 구조에서 명사인 목적어를 표현할 수 있는 것은 부사가 아닌 형용사 comfortable. <목적어-목적격보어>에서 흔히 볼 수 있는 <명사-형용사> 구조.

5 ○ | be동사 are의 보어 자리이므로 close가 맞다. know의 목적어절인 명사절을 이끄는 의문부사 how는 뒤에 「형용사/부사+주어+동사」의 형식을 취할 수 있다.

6 ×, **naturally → natural** | be동사 is의 보어 자리이므로 natural이 되어야 한다.

해석 1 활성 산소는 통제할 수 없을 정도로 신체를 돌아다니면서 세포를 공격하고, 세포의 단백질을 부식시키고, 세포막을 뚫으며 세포의 유전 암호를 변질시키는 것을 그 세포들이 제대로 기능을 하지 못하게 되고 때로는 포기하고 죽어버릴 때까지 한다.

2 줄거리, 등장인물, 대화의 공급원으로서 소설이 (연극보다 영화에) 더 적합해 보였다. 영화의 초기 성공작의 다수가 유명 소설을 각색한 것이었다.

3 누군가가 거짓말을 할 때, 그의 통상적인 패턴에서 벗어나는 것을 알아채기 위해 당신은 그의 통상적인 패턴에 주의를 면밀히 기울여야 한다. 때때로 그 변화는 아무 일도 없는 것처럼 감지하기 힘들다. 어떤 때는 그것은 명백하고 갑작스럽다.

4 당신이 더 광대하게 꿈을 꾸고 당신을 편안하게 해주는 것보다 적어도 한 단계 위로 목표를 정하도록 당신을 밀고 나가게 하면, 당신은 성장할 수밖에 없을 것이다.

5 잘 고안된 기술 도구는, 그것이 웹사이트든, 비디오든, 앱이든, 시뮬레이션이든 또는 개별지도든, 학생들이 종료 지점에 얼마나 가까운지를 알고 학습 목표를 달성하는 데 얼마나 더 많은 노력을 기울여야 할지를 알도록 자신들의 발전을 추적하는 방법을 제공해야 한다.

6 우리는 미래가 그것이 현재가 될 때까지 열려 있고 과거는 고정되어 있다는 직관을 깊이 가지고 있다. 그러나 이런 사고방식이 자연스러울지라도 그것이 과학에 반영된 것은 발견하지 못할 것이다.

KEY POINT 05 문장의 주어를 제대로 찾는 게 관건이다.

정답 & 해설 1 ×, **are → is** | 성장하고 있는 것은 fine breads and pastries가 아니라 popularity이므로 단수형 is (growing)가 되어야 한다.

2 **is** | 전명구(between grapes and raisins)의 후치 수식을 받는 주어(The only difference)는 단수이므로 is가 맞다.

3 ×, **tends → tend** | while이 이끄는 부사절에서 복수 명사 crashes가 주어이다. 따라서 동사 tends를 tend로 바꿔야 한다. 주어와 동사 사이의 due to aircraft malfunction은 <전치사구(due to)+명사(aircraft malfunction)>으로 이루어진 전명구로서 주어를 수식하고 있다.

4 ×, **has → have** | but이 이끄는 절의 주어인 others와 동사 사이에 삽입구가 콤마로 연결되어 들어간 구조이므로 복수명사 주어 others에 대한 동사는 복수인 have가 되어야 한다.

5 **have** | 주어인 People ~와 동사 사이에 삽입절인 who think ~ language가 콤마로 연결되어 들어간 구조이므로 복수명사 주어 People ~에 대한 동사는 복수인 have가 되어야 한다.

6 ×, **were → was** | that절의 주어 the traditional link 뒤에 수식어구인 between transport ~ messages가 이어지고 그 뒤에 동사 자리이다. 단수주어를 받으므로 단수동사인 was가 되어야 한다.

7 ×, **are → is** | 관계사절 수식어(that matters most to them)의 수식을 받는 주어(the extrinsic reward)는 단수, 따라서 is로 써야 한다.

8 ○ | 주격 관계대명사는 선행사의 수에 일치하므로 선행사를 찾아보면 되는데, 많은 형용사 수식어 끝에 나타난 선행사 adventure가 단수이므로 adopts가 맞게 쓰였다.

9 **were** | 여러 개의 콤마로 쪼개어진 문장에서 who의 선행사를 찾아보면, bury된 것은 the Indians로 복수, 따라서 were가 맞다.

10 ×, **leads → lead** | it ~ that 강조구문으로서 원래 문장은 People's beliefs (in the power of hypnosis) lead them to recall more things.이다. 복수명사 주어이므로 동사도 복수인 lead가 되어야 한다.

11 ○ | 주어가 동명사구로 추상적인 개념이므로 단수형 is가 맞게 쓰였다.

12 ○ | 주어는 what we really want로 추상적인 개념의 명사절이므로 단수 is가 맞게 쓰였다.

13 ×, **restricting → restricts** | To make ~ from a rock이 긴 주어를 만들고 있고 삽입구인 without the use ~ or colors 뒤에 동사가 나올 자리이다.

to부정사는 단수 취급하므로 동사도 단수동사인 restricts가 되어야 한다.

14 ╳, **was placed → were placed** | 선행사 'technology shelf'에 이어지는 관계대명사절(계속적 용법)에서 긴 주어로 인해 도치가 일어난 경우. 주어의 핵심 명사가 solutions로 복수이므로 were placed가 되어야 한다.

15 ○ | not only로 인해 주어와 동사가 도치된 절. 주어는 이어 나오는 carbon dioxide로 단수이므로 is가 맞게 쓰였다.

16 **is** | of 이하의 긴 수식어의 수식을 받는 주어는 One. 따라서 is가 맞다.

17 ○ | 셀 수 있는 복수에 쓰이는 수량형용사 A number of(많은 ~)로 시작한 복수 주어(websites) 뒤에 복수형 have been developed가 맞게 왔다.

해석 1 21세기 초에 고급 빵과 페이스트리의 인기는 새로운 요리사가 훈련될 수 있는 것보다 훨씬 더 빠르게 상승하고 있다.

2 포도와 건포도의 유일한 차이는 포도가 약 여섯 배 더 많은 수분을 함유하고 있다는 것이다.

3 이는 항공기 간의 충돌은 대개 공항 주변 지역에서 발생하는 반면 항공기 오작동으로 인한 추락은 장거리 비행 중에 발생하는 경향이 있기 때문이다.

4 명백히, 마라톤 도중에 음주를 하는 것과 같은, 이러한 관습 중 일부는 더 이상 추천되지 않는다. 그러나 경쟁 전날 밤의 고탄수화물 식사와 같은 다른 것들은 오랜 세월에도 건재해 왔다.

5 북부 버마의 사람들은 Jinghpaw 언어로 사고하는데, 친척을 묘사하는 열여덟 개의 기본 용어를 가지고 있다.

6 운송과 메시지 전달 사이의 전통적인 관계가 깨진 것은 바로 1837년이 되어서야 전기 전신의 발명으로 인해서였다.

7 위대한 과학자들은 우주의 본질을 이해하려는 내적인 탐구에 의해 동기를 부여받는다. 그들에게 가장 중요시되는 외재적 보상은 동료들의 인정이다.

8 전형적인 인류학 현지 탐험가인 Malinowski는 현지 조사의 초기 단계들을 '이내 자연스러운 과정을 채택하게 되는 낯설고, 때로는 불쾌하기도 하며, 때로는 강렬하게 흥미를 유발하는 모험'이라고 기술하고 있다.

9 섬에는 인디언들의 뼈와 무기가 들어 있는 깊은 동굴이 있는데, 인디언들이 그곳에 매장되었다고 추정된다.

10 최면에 걸린 사람들은 좀 더 많은 정보를 기억해내지만 반드시 더 정확한 정보인 것은 아니다. 사실, 사람들이 더 많은 것을 기억해 내도록 하는 것은 실제로는 최면의 힘에 대한 사람들의 믿음일지도 모른다.

11 소설을 각색하는 것은 가장 훌륭한 영화 프로젝트들 중 하나인 반면, 영화를 소설화했다고 하는 책은 상스럽게 여겨진다.

12 우리는 텔레비전을 너무 많이 보는 것을 중단하고 싶어 하지만, 명백히 우리는 또한 텔레비전을 많이 보기를 원한다. 그래서 우리가 진정으로 원하는 것은 원하기를 그만하는 것처럼 보인다.

13 첨단 기술이나 색상을 사용하지 않고 돌을 특정한 형태로 조각하여 감정을 표현하는 선택을 하는 것은 조각가에게 상당한 제약을 가한다. 그러한 선택은 창의성을 제한하기 위한 것이 아니라 오히려 그것을 기르기 위해서 이루어진다.

14 연구원들이 기술적인 문제를 해결하려고 애쓰는 두 개의 휴대 전화 회사를 연구했다. 한 회사는 '기술 선반'이라고 부르는 것을 개발했는데, 그것은 소집단의 기술자들에 의해 만들어졌고, 그 위에는 장차 다른 팀이 사용할 수도 있는 가능한 기술적인 해결책들이 올려져 있었다.

15 이산화탄소가 명백히 독성을 가지고 있지 않을 뿐만 아니라 이산화탄소 수치의 변화가 꼭 인간 활동을 반영하는 것도 아니다.

16 실현 가능하다는 사고방식을 계발하는 가장 좋은 방법 중 하나는 평소에 꾸는 것보다 조금 더 큰 꿈을 꾸도록 당신 자신을 자극하는 것이다.

17 많은 수의 '젊은이 친화적인' 정신 건강 웹 사이트들이 개발되어 왔다. 제공되는 정보는 '자주 묻는 질문', 자료표, 추천 링크의 형태를 띠는 경우가 많다.

기출 꿰뚫기 2 시험에 나오는 것만 골라낸 24개 기출 어법

POINT 01 가장 빈출되는 시제는 완료시제다.

정답 & 해설 1 **had made** | 경찰이 실수를 저지른 것은 그 사실을 깨달은 것보다 앞서 일어난 일이다. 과거보다 더 과거를 나타내야 하므로 과거완료 형태가 정답.

2 ╳, **increased → has increased** | 과거에 일어난 일이 아니라 지난 백 년에 걸쳐 일어난(over ~), 즉 현재까지 일어난 일을 말하므로 과거시제가 아닌 현재완료로 써야 한다. 주어가 the amount ~로 단수이므로 has increased.

해석 1 나중에 경찰은 심각한 실수를 저질렀다는 것을 깨달았다. 그들의 가방은 돈이 아니라 양파로 가득 차 있었다!

2 오늘날 아이들은 이산화탄소를 독소라고 생각하기가 더 쉽다. 왜냐하면 대기 중의 이산화탄소의 양이 지난 백 년에 걸쳐서 입자 백만 개당 약 280개에서 380개로 크게 상승했기 때문이다.

POINT 02 시간, 조건의 부사절에서는 미래시제 대신 현재시제를 쓴다.

정답 & 해설 1 **is** | if가 이끄는 조건의 부사절이므로 현재시제 is가 정답.

해석 1 그 유명한 수영 선수는 열흘 만에 그 과업을 끝내기로 계획했다. 그래서 만약 날씨가 좋다면, 그는 8월 15일에 독도에 도착할 것이다.

POINT 03 목적격보어 자리에 올 수 있는 것은 동사가 좌우한다.

정답 & 해설 1 ○ | <지각동사(see/sense)+목적어(the wave)+목적격보어(coming ~)> 구조이다. 진행의 의미를 나타내기 위해 현재분사가 적절히 쓰였다.

2 **carried** | <have+O+OC> 구조에서 목적어 them이 all the decisions로 carry out의 대상이므로 수동의 과거분사 carried out이 맞다.

해석 1 물고기 떼의 (각) 개체들이 자신들에게 다가오는 파장을 보거나, 혹은 느낄 수 있기 때문에, 그것들은 그러한 사전 감지 없이 반응하는 것보다 더 빨리 반응할 준비가 되어 있다.

2 그는 모든 결정을 하고 그것들을 신속히 수행되도록 하는 데 익숙했지만, 영국의 영화 제작 방식은 모두가 의견을 개진하도록 허용한다는 것을 알게 되었다.

POINT 04 어떤 동사를 대신하는지 찾아서 일치시켜라.

정답 & 해설 1 **do** | 일반동사 spend를 대신하므로 do가 정답.

2 **did** | <As ~, so ...(~하듯이 …하다)>의 주절 부분. 부사 so로 시작하여 <so+동사+주어>의 도치 어순을 취한다. 일반동사 developed를 대신하므로 did가 정답.

3 **×, do → are** | 앞에 나온 be 동사 are를 대신하는 자리. Productivity improvements are important to the economy.와 They are important to the individual business that's making them.의 두 문장을 as important as ~구문으로 연결한 것이다.

4 **×, did → was** | 앞에 나온 일반동사 achieve의 수동태 자리인데 be동사인 was만 남기고 achieved는 생략하고 쓸 수 있다.

5 **○** | 앞에 나온 일반동사 give를 현재진행형으로 바꾼 자리이므로 doing이 적절하다.

해석 1 어떤 회사의 간부가 말했듯이, "많은 사용자가 그들이 차에서 보내는 것보다 더 많은 시간을 아마 인터넷에서 보낼 것이다."

2 문명이 발달하면서 패션도 발달했다. 하지만, 몸치장은 과거에도 그랬고 지금도 여전히 인간의 허영심을 보여주는 가장 보편적인 수단이다.

3 생산성 향상은 그것을 만들어내고 있는 각 기업에 중요한 만큼 경제에 똑같이 중요하다.

4 "장대함"은 이집트 예술의 기본적인 성격을 표현하는 것에 매우 가깝게 접근하는 단어이다. 그 장대함의 특질은 이집트에서 완전하게 달성되었던 것만큼 달성된 적은 그 이전이나 그 이후에도 결코 없어 왔다.

5 많은 자선기관에 소액을 기부하는 사람들은 자신들이 기부하고 있는 것이 남을 돕는지에 대해서는 그렇게 관심이 없다. 기부금의 영향과 상관없이 자신들이 기부를 하고 있다는 것을 아는 것이 그들을 기분 좋게 만든다.

POINT 05 가목적어 it을 취하는 동사를 알아두자.

정답 & 해설 1 **to refund** | 문맥상 '돈을 환불해주는 것을 원칙으로 만들다'란 뜻으로, <동사(make)+가목적어(it)+목적격보어(a rule)+진목적어>의 구조이다. 명사구를 이끌어 목적어 역할을 할 수 있는 to refund가 정답. <make it a rule to-v (v하는 것을 원칙으로 하다)>를 어구로 알아두자.

해석 1 그들은 또한 구매자들이 비닐봉지나 종이봉투를 돌려주면 돈을 환불해주는 것을 원칙으로 하고 있다.

POINT 06 혼동하기 쉬운 자타동사를 외워두자.

정답 & 해설 1 **lay** | '신문과 잡지가 놓여 있다'라는 문맥이므로, 자동사 lie의 과거형인 lay가 적절하다.

2 **×, risen → rising** | 지각동사 notice의 목적격보어 자리에 과거분사 risen이 쓰였다. 목적격보어 자리에 과거분사가 쓰이면 수동이나 완료를 나타내는데, 동사 rise(오르다, 올라가다)는 자동사로서 수동태로 쓰일 수 없다. 또한, 바로 눈앞에서 연기가 피어오르는 것을 목격하는 문맥이므로 완료도 부적절. 따라서 능동, 진행을 나타내는 현재분사 rising으로 고쳐야 맞다.

해석 1 마틸다가 세 살이 되었을 무렵, 그녀는 집안에 널려 있는 신문과 잡지를 공부함으로써 스스로 읽는 법을 배웠다.

2 어느 날 가족과 함께 차를 타고 집으로 오는 길에 나는 아파트 건물 지붕에서 연기가 올라오는 것을 보았다.

POINT 07 「조동사 + have p.p.」는 어구처럼 외워두자.

정답 & 해설 1 **○** | If절이 지금까지의 경험(have ever gone)을 전제로 하고 있으므로 과거 일에 대한 추측을 얘기하는 <may have p.p.(~했을지도 모른다)> 형태가 맞게 쓰였다.

2 **×, should receive → should have received** | 과거에 학교에 다니는 동안 창의력을 기르는 교육을 받았어야 하는데 그러지 못해 유감이라는 내용. 과거에 대한 후회나 유감을 나타낼 때는 <should have p.p.>를 쓴다.

해석 1 스노클링을 가 본 적이 있다면, 여러분은 전체 물고기 떼가 하나의 단일체로 갑자기 방향을 바꾸는 놀라운 장면을 본 적이 있을지 모른다.

2 그런 교육의 희생자들은 학교에 다니는 동안 창의적인 재능을 계발하는 훈련을 받았어야 한다. 그들이 그러지 못했던 건 정말로 유감스럽다.

POINT 08 당위성을 나타내는 that절에서는 「(should+)동사원형」을 쓴다.

정답 & 해설 1 **×, had been kept → (should) be kept** | 주장을 나타내는 동사 insisted 뒤에 '~해야 한다'라는 내용의 that절이 오므로 <(should+)동사원형>으로 고쳐야 맞다.

2 **×, should take place → had taken place** | insisted 뒤 that절의 내용이 '~해야 한다'라는 당위성을 나타내지 않고 사실적인 정보를 전달하고 있으므로 <(should+)동사원형>을 쓰지 않는다. 사고가 일어난 것은 목격자들이 주장하는 것보다 더 과거의 일이므로 과거완료를 써야 한다.

해석 1 대통령은 수술이 비밀에 부쳐져야 한다고 주장했다. 그는 자신의 건강에 대한 우려가 당시 나라가 직면하고 있던 어려운 경제 문제들을 악화시킬지도 모른다고 염려했다.

2 많은 목격자가 그 사고는 횡단보도에서 발생했다고 주장했다.

POINT 09 가정법의 기본 패턴을 알아두자.

정답 & 해설 1 **have been** | if절의 동사가 had p.p. 형태이며 문맥상 과거의 사실을 가정하고 있으므로 가정법 과거완료 구문. 따라서 조동사 might 뒤에 have been이 와야 적절하다.

해석 1 행인 대부분은 일터로 서둘러 가고 있었겠지만, 만일 그 젊은 음악가가 세계적으로 유명한 바이올린 연주자인 토니 애덤슨이라는 것을 알았다면 상황은 매우 달랐을 것이다.

POINT 10 뒤에 부정사가 오는지 동명사가 오는지 구별하자.

정답 & 해설 1 **to oil** | 고음이 기름칠 '해야 하는 것을 깜박한' 문처럼 들린다는 내용. 따라서 '미래성'을 나타내는 to부정사가 정답.

2 **to take** | refuse는 to부정사만을 목적어로 취하는 동사.

3 **×, to operate → operating** | 문맥상 '~하기를 멈추다[중단하다]'로 stop이 동명사 목적어를 취해야 자연스럽다. stop to-v는 '~ 하기 위해 (가던 길을) 멈춰 서다'의 의미이다.

4 ○ | mobilize(전시 체제를 갖추다, 동원되다) 다음에 그것의 목적(~하기 위하여)을 나타내는 to부정사가 맞게 왔다. 수식어로 쓰인 to부정사.

5 ○ | 주어(more (than technical information)), 동사 (was needed)로서 완전한 구조를 이루는 절에 더해질 수 있는 수식어로서의 to부정사. 목적(~하기 위해, ~하려면)을 나타낸다.

6 ○ | be close to v-ing는 '~하는 것에 가깝다'를 의미한다.

7 ○ | '생각하기 위해 멈추다'란 문맥이므로 stopped to think가 적절히 쓰였다.

해석 1 엠마는 노래 부르기를 매우 좋아했다. 그녀는 매우 좋은 목소리를 가지고 있었다. 일부 고음에서 기름칠하는 것을 잊은 문과 같은 소리가 나는 경향이 있다는 것만 제외하면 말이다.

2 전설에 따르면 중국 당나라 왕조 때 한 가난한 관리가 매우 정직해서 뇌물을 받기를 거절했다고 한다. 그는 가족을 먹일 고기를 살 수 없었다. 그래서 그는 두부를 발명했다.

3 처음에는 그것이 많은 소음을 내더니, 나중에 가서는 완전히 작동을 멈추었다.

4 감염원과 싸워 물리치기 위해 신체가 동원될 때, 그것(신체)은 침입자들을 매우 효율적으로 파괴하기 위해 한바탕 활성 산소를 생성한다.

5 사업 단위 간의 경계는 일부러 불명확하게 했는데, 왜냐하면 문제에 대한 감을 얻기 위해서는 기술적인 정보 이상의 것이 필요했기 때문이다.

6 "장대함"은 이집트 예술의 기본적인 성격을 표현하는 것에 매우 가깝게 접근하는 단어이다.

7 많은 경우에 있어서 기부액은 10달러나 그 미만의 소액이어서 만약 그들이 멈추고 생각을 한다면 기부금을 처리하는 비용이 그것이 자선단체에 가져올 이득보다 초과할 가능성이 크다는 것을 깨달을 것이다.

POINT 11 동사가 전치사의 목적어로 올 때는 동명사를 쓴다.

정답 & 해설 1 ○ | 전치사 for 뒤에 produce가 명사 개념을 나타내는 동명사형으로 맞게 쓰였다.

2 **being** | 동명사를 쓸 곳인지 동사를 쓸 곳인지 묻는 문제. without 이하가 절이 아니므로 <주어+동사> 구조는 될 수 없다. without -ing의 <전치사+동명사>에 의미상의 주어 the fact가 동명사 앞에 더해진 구조. the fact가 know의 객체이므로 knowing이 아닌 being known.

3 ○ | evolve(서서히 발전하다, 진화하다)의 행위가 appear보다 먼저 진행된 것이므로 이전 시점의 일임을 말해주는 to부정사의 완료형으로 맞게 표현하였다.

해석 1 제빵사들은 과거의 시큼한 맛이 나는 수제 반죽으로 만든 빵을 생산하는 방법을 연구하고 있으며, 그들은 맛을 찾기 위한 자신들의 연구에서 특별한 밀가루로 실험하고 있다.

2 추측건대, 4백만 마리의 물개들이 같은 종을 놓고 상업을 목적으로 하는 어부들과 경쟁을 한다면 그 사실이 알려지지 않을 수는 없을 것이다.

3 수면은 온혈동물들에게서만 진화되어 온 것 같지 않다. 파충류나 양서류에 관한 몇몇 연구들은 그것들 또한 잠을 잔다는 것을 보여준다.

POINT 12 다양한 분사구문의 형태를 정리해두자.

정답 & 해설 1 ○ | <with+O+OC> 구조에서 목적어 most가 most adolescents를 가리키므로 use의 주체. 따라서 능동의 -ing를 쓴 것이 알맞다.

2 ○ | '~가 …한 채로'로 상태를 나타내는 <with+O+OC> 구조에서 목적어(his eyes)와 목적격보어(close)는 수동 관계, 그러므로 과거분사가 맞게 쓰였다. with his eyes closed and (with) his feet on the desk의 병렬구조. 한편 is working ~에 이어 나오는, typing ~은 <동시동작>을 나타내는 분사구문.

3 ○ | These fierce radicals가 build의 주체가 아닌 객체. life라는 구조의 일부로 build되어 들어가는 존재. (being) built ~로 앞서 나온 개념을 부연 설명하는 분사구문을 이끌고 있다.

해석 1 청소년들은 대부분이 소통을 목적으로 인터넷을 사용하면서 빠르게 과학기술에 빠져들었다.

2 나란히 앉아 일하고 있는 두 명의 프로그래머를 상상해 보라. 한 명은 눈을 감고 책상 위에 발을 올린 채로 뒤로 기대어 의자에 앉아 있다. 다른 한 명은 컴퓨터에 코드를 타이핑해서 넣으며 열심히 일하고 있다.

3 보호자인 동시에 보복자로 생명체의 일부가 되어 있는 이런 사나운 활성 산소가 노화의 강력한 동인(動因)이다.

POINT 13 전치사 뒤에는 '명사', 접속사 뒤에는 「주어+동사」가 온다.

정답 & 해설 1 ×, **Though → Despite[In spite of]** | 명사구 zoological research를 이끌므로 접속사가 아닌 전치사가 와야 한다.

2 **because** | 바로 뒤에 오는 twenty-five years from now는 시간을 나타내는 부사적 수식어에 불과하다. 그 뒤에 주어(they), 동사(will not seem)를 갖춘 절이 오므로 접속사 because를 써야 맞다.

3 **When** | 두 절을 연결해주는 말이 필요하므로 접속사 When이 정답. 접속부사 Then은 부사이므로 문장의 일부는 될 수 있으나 두 절을 연결해 하나의 문장을 만들 수 없다.

해석 1 동물학적인 연구에도 불구하고 이 신기한 생명체의 삶에 대한 우리의 이해에는 아직 미지의 영역이 많다.

2 대부분의 사람들은 꿈을 너무 작게 꾼다. 그들은 충분히 크게 생각하지 않는다. Henry Curtis는 "지금부터 25년이 지나면 당신의 계획은 아주 특별하게 보이지 않을 것이므로, 당신의 계획을 원하는 만큼 환상적으로 만들어라."라고 조언한다.

3 아버지는 내가 미식축구 시합을 할 때마다 경기에 오셨다. 나는 경기장에 오는 법을 아버지께 말씀드린 적이 없는데, 아버지는 어쨌든 나타나셨다. 한 피리어드가 끝나고 내가 운동장에서 나올 때 아버지는 손짓으로 나를 부르시곤 했다.

POINT 14 명사절 접속사 if는 '의문'을 나타내는 동사와 함께 쓰인다.

정답 & 해설 1 ○ | tell that ~에서 that절에는 전달하는 내용이 담기고, tell whether[if] ~에서 tell은 단순히 '말하다'가 아닌 '구분하다(distinguish)'의 의미이다. 문맥상 whether ~ (or not)이 어울린다.

해석 1 그는 컴퓨터 프로그래머를 관리하는 데 있어 가장 큰 문제점은 겉으로 보아서는 그들이 일을 하고 있는지를 결코 알 수 없다는 것이라고 말하는 것을 좋아했다.

POINT 15 접속사 that이 오는 패턴을 정리해두자.

정답 & 해설 1 ×, **what → that** | what은 의문사이든 관계대명사이든 명사이므로 이어지는 절에 주어 또는 목적어 등 중요한 요소가 빠져 있을 때만 올 수 있다. 주어(they)와 목적어(assistance)를 모두 갖춘 완전한 구조이므로 what이 올 수 없고, it이 가리키는 내용이 they would seek ~이므로 it은 가주어, 밑줄 이하는 진주어 자리이다. 명사절을 이끄는 접속사 that이 올 자리이다.

2 **that** | from the list of courses of each department in the catalog를 It is와 that 사이에 두어 강조한 구문이다. 강조구문은 It is와 that을 생략해도 완전한 문장이 되는 특징이 있다.(A degree plan for the student can also be devised from the list of courses of each department in the catalog.)

3 **aware that** | 뒤에 주어(women alcoholics)와 동사(may give)를 갖춘 절이 나오므로 aware 뒤에 접속사 that이 와야 한다. aware of는 명사구를 이끈다.

해석 1 과학기술과 인터넷이 젊은이들에게 친숙한 수단이기에, 그들이 이 정보원에서 도움을 구하리라는 것은 논리적이다.

2 학생을 위한 학위 계획이 세워질 수 있는 것도 바로 편람에 있는 각 학과의 교육과정 목록으로부터이다.

3 의사들은 여성 알코올 중독자가 장애 아동을 출산할 가능성이 있다는 사실을 오랫동안 알고 있었다.

POINT 16 관계대명사는 「접속사+대명사」의 역할을 한다.

정답 & 해설 1 ×, **them → which** | 의미상 아무 문제 없어 보이는 연결이지만 두 개의 절을 접속사 없이 연결할 수는 없다. 대명사 them이 아닌, 앞 문장의 명사와 연결고리가 있음을 나타내는, 즉 접속사 역할까지 하는 관계대명사를 써서 some of which로 써야 정확하다. 접속사를 쓰면 ~ and some of them(=musical events) dramatized ~라고 하면 된다.

2 ×, **their → whose** | The violinists and pianists와 their names가 연결어 없이 이어지고 있는 것이 부자연스럽다. 또한 접속사 없이 두 개의 동사(have heard, earn)가 이어지는 것도 어색하다. 문맥상 대명사 their는 The violinists and pianists를 가리키는 것이 분명하므로 대명사인 their를 '두 개 절을 이어주는' 접속사와 '명사를 대신하는' 대명사 역할을 동시에 하는 관계대명사 소유격 whose로 바꿔보면 의아했던 두 의문점이 모두 해결된다.

The violinists and pianists [whose names you've heard ∨] regularly earn between $30,000 and $50,000 for a single performance.

(The violinists and pianists: S / whose names: O′ / you: S′ / 've heard: V′ / earn: V)

3 ×, **them → whom** | 두 개의 절을 접속사 없이 연결할 수는 없다. 대명사 them이 아닌, 앞 문장의 명사인 chronic-pain patients와 연결고리가 있음을 나타내는, 즉 접속사 역할까지 하는 관계대명사를 써서 many of whom으로 써야 정확하다.

해석 1 Brown의 본보기에 영감을 받았을지도 모르는 또 다른 빈민가 지역에서, 문화센터가 그 지역 아이들로 하여금 뮤지컬 공연을 무대에 올리도록 권장하기 시작했으며, 이 중 몇몇은 아이들이 아직 회복 중이던 비극적인 일을 극화한 것이었다.

2 여러분이 자주 이름을 들어 본 바이올린 연주자와 피아노 연주자들은 한 번의 공연으로 3만 달러에서 5만 달러를 주기적으로 번다.

3 불교식 명상을 서구 심리학에 적용하는 것은 주로 매사추세츠 대학교 의료센터의 Jon Kabat-Zinn 교수의 연구에서 나왔다. 그는 처음에 만성통증 환자들을 치료하는 어려운 과업을 떠맡았는데, 그들 중 많은 수는 전통적인 통증관리 요법에 잘 반응하지 않았었다.

POINT 17 선행사 바로 찾기와 격 구분이 관계대명사의 기본이다.

정답 & 해설 1 ○ | 주어가 artist로 사람이므로 보어 the one도 사람. 따라서 선행사가 사람일 때 쓰는 주격 관계대명사 who가 맞게 쓰였다.

2 ○ | 이어지는 동사부 carries fresh ingredients의 주체는 바로 앞에 있는 명사 air transportation이다. 주격 관계대명사 that은 선행사가 사람이든 사물이든 추상적인 개념이든 모두 받을 수 있으므로 맞게 쓰였다.

3 ○ | that은 콤마 삽입구(called mitochondria) 앞에 나오는 (tiny cellular) factories (of energy)를 가리키는 주격 관계대명사. 선행사가 복수이므로 이어지는 동사의 형태도 burn으로 맞게 쓰였다.

해석 1 독립 예술가는 아마도 무한한 창조적인 상황과 가장 가까이에서 살아가는 사람일 것이다.

2 20세기에 냉장에서부터 고성능 오븐, 신선한 재료를 전 세계에 실어 나르는 항공 수송에 이르기까지 기술의 진보는 제빵과 페이스트리 만드는 것에 헤아릴 수 없을 정도로 기여했다.

3 궁극적인 생명력은 우리가 들이쉬는 거의 모든 산소를 태우는, 미토콘드리아라고 불리는 아주 작은 에너지 세포 공장에 있다.

POINT 18 이럴 땐 관계대명사 that을 쓸 수 없다.

정답 & 해설 1 **which** | earlier sources에 대해 부수적으로 정보를 덧붙이는 계속적 용법으로 쓰이고 있으므로, that은 쓸 수 없다. which가 정답.

2 ○ | 이어지는 절 <주어(a group of researchers)+동사(work)+수식어1(together)+수식어2(in universities and laboratories)>에서 수식어2(장소 개념)에 해당하는 부분으로서, 선행사(universities and laboratories)와의 연결고리가 드러나게 in which로 맞게 썼다.

해석 1 윌리엄 셰익스피어의 대부분의 희곡처럼 <로미오와 줄리엣>도 이전의 자료들에 바탕을 두고 있는데, 이 경우에는 그 자료들이 1400년대 후반 이탈리아에서 유행한 일부 이야기들로 거슬러 올라간다.

2 혼자서 작업하는 고독한 발명가의 시대는 지나갔다. 지나치게 단순화시켜 말하자면, 기본적 아이디어들은 한 집단의 발명가들이 함께 일하는 대학과 실험실에서 부글거리며 넘쳐 나온다.

POINT 19 대명사 파트에서는 명사와의 수일치가 가장 빈출된다.

정답 & 해설 1 ○ | it이 가리키는 내용이 The company이므로 단수인 사물의 소유격 its가 맞게 쓰였다.

2 **it** | 가리키는 내용이 performances가 아닌 evaluation으로 단수이므로 it이 정답. '평가'가 객관적이거나 주관적이거나 한 주체.

3 ○ | 대명사의 수일치 문제는 지시하는 바가 무엇인지를 찾는 것이 관건. 앞에 언급된 두 개의 명사(Such choices, creativity) 중 cultivate(기르다, 갈고 닦다)할 수 있는 것은 creativity이므로 단수 it이 맞게 쓰였다.

4 ○ | a body temperature와 the temperature of their surroundings가 비교되고 있는 구조. 앞서 나온 명사 temperature의 반복을 피하기 위해 단수 대명사 that이 맞게 쓰였다.

5 ○ | 이해하지 못한(failure to understand) 주체는 문장의 주어 The Greeks(그리스인들)이므로 복수 대명사의 소유격 their가 맞게 쓰였다.

6 ○ | them이 가리키는 것이 a number of fascinating findings로 복수이므로, it이 아닌 them으로 수일치에 맞게 잘 쓰였다.

7 ○ | 앞에 나온 structures를 대신하므로 those가 적절히 쓰였다.

해석 1 그 회사는 또한 판매원들과 디자이너들이 자주 포함되는, 기술자들 간의 제한 없는 대화의 자리를 마련하였다.

2 그에 비해, 정교한 점수 규정이 평가를 더 객관적인 것으로 만드는 데 도움을 주기는 하지만, 다이빙, 체조, 피겨스케이팅과 같은 동작에 대한 평가는 더 주관적이다.

3 그러한 선택은 창의성을 제한하기 위해서가 아니라 오히려 창의성을 기르기 위해서 이루어진다.

4 수면은 에너지를 보존하는 기능을 한다고 주장되어 왔다. 이는 주변 온도보다 체온을 더 높게 유지하기 위해 많은 에너지를 소비해야 하는 온혈동물(포유류와 조류)과 특히 관련 있을 수 있다.

5 그리스인은 두드러진 물체와 그것의 속성에 초점을 맞추느라 인과 관계의 근본적인 성질을 이해하지 못했다.

6 한 과학자가 뉴욕시의 많은 장소에 사람들이 어떻게 공간을 활용하는지 알아보기 위해 비디오카메라를 켜 두었다. 그는 많은 놀라운 사실들을 발견하였고, 그것들을 뒷받침해주는 비디오 증거를 갖게 되었다.

7 많은 현대 건축물들이 순전히 물리적 규모 면에서 이집트 건축물들을 앞선다. 그러나 거대함은 장대함과는 전혀 관계가 없다.

POINT 20 재귀대명사와 소유대명사의 쓰임을 확실히 정리해두자.

정답 & 해설 1 **themselves** | '신체의 세포와 기관(the body's cells and organs)이 자신을 대체하고 재생하지(to replace and repair) 못한다'는 내용. to 부정사구의 의미상 주어와 목적어가 동일하므로 재귀대명사가 정답.

2 **mine** | '내 타이어'를 주유소에 놔두라는 내용이므로, my tire를 대신할 수 있는 소유대명사 mine이 정답.

3 **themselves** | 주격 관계대명사인 that의 선행사가 the only species이고 네모 안은 목적어 자리로, 의미상 주어와 동일하므로 재귀대명사가 정답.

해석 1 노화는 신체의 세포와 기관이 자신을 대체하고 재생하는 것이 점진적으로 쇠퇴해 나타나는 결과이다. 이는 각 세포가 분열할 수 있는 횟수에 한계가 있기 때문이다.

2 집에 돌아오는 길에, 타이어에 구멍이 났는데 여분의 타이어가 없었다. 우리는 도움을 청하려고 근처의 농가로 걸어갔다. 그곳에 살고 있던 농부가 자신의 차에서 타이어를 뗀 뒤 말했다. "시내로 차를 몰고 가서 타이어를 고치고 주유소에 제 것을 놔두고 가세요."

3 안타깝게도, 인간은 사실 합당한 이득 없이 의도적으로 자신들에게서 잠을 빼앗는 유일한 종이다.

POINT 21 명사의 수에 따라 수식어를 달리 써야 한다.

정답 & 해설 1 **a few** | 셀 수 있는 개념의 복수명사 products를 수식하므로 a few가 정답. a little은 셀 수 없는 명사를 수식한다.

2 **both** | 뒤에 복수명사 suspects가 오므로 both가 정답. each는 단수명사를 수식. 이어지는 neither of them에서 질문의 대상이 둘임을 짐작할 수 있다.

3 **many** | of 뒤의 명사가 these firsts로 셀 수 있는 개념의 복수이므로 셀 수 있는 개념에 쓰이는 many가 정답.

해석 1 초기의 상점들은 고기와 빵 같은 소수의 상품만 팔았다.

2 수사관들은 두 용의자를 심문했지만, 둘 다 영어를 하지 못했다.

3 우리 대학의 언론학 프로그램이 당신에게 이런 많은 첫 경험들의 원천이었다는 것을 우리는 알고 있습니다.

POINT 22 another, other의 쓰임을 구별하자.

정답 & 해설 1 ○ | film과 기타 장르들과의 관계를 언급하고 있다. other가 narrative와 마찬가지로 명사(genres)를 수식하는 형용사로 맞게 쓰였다. 명사 others(다른 사람들, 다른 것들)는 쓰일 수 없는 자리이다.

2 ○ | 전후 구조를 살펴보면, both A and B(major breakthroughs와 smaller breakthroughs)의 구조임을 파악할 수 있다. 복수명사를 대신하는 ones가 맞게 쓰였다.

3 ○ | '약간의, 몇몇의'의 뜻으로 문장의 종류에 따라 쓰임에 제약이 있는 some, any가 아닌, '어떤 ~라도'라는 뜻의 any이다. 문맥에 맞게 잘 쓰였다.

해석 1 후발 예술이면서 동시에 혼합 예술이기도 한 영화는 다른 서사 장르와 항상 대화를 해왔다.

2 기본적 아이디어들은 한 그룹의 연구자들이 함께 일하는 대학과 실험실에서 부글거리며 넘쳐 나온다. 생명체의 유전자 구조의 이해와 같은 중대한 발견과 수학이나 기초 화학에서의 진보와 같은 보다 작은 발견 두 경우 모두 다 그렇다.

3 물고기 무리 중 어떤 개체라도 방향 전환과 같은 움직임을 시작할 수 있고, 이것은 '움직임 파장'을 내보내는데, 이것은 놀라운 속도로 집단 속으로 퍼져 나간다.

POINT 23 비교구문의 기출 포인트를 한꺼번에 정리하자.

정답 & 해설 1 **even** | 비교급(longer)을 수식할 수 있는 강조어로는 even(훨씬 더 ~)이 적절. 이 외에도 a lot, still, far, much 등이 비교급을 수식한다.

2 ○ | just as 이하의 절을 보면 비교급 표현(faster and stronger)이 있으므로 비교하는 대상을 이끄는 than으로 이어진 게 자연스럽다. through a narrow strait와 across the open sea가 비교되고 있는 대상들. <비교급 + than ...>의 비교급 문장의 틀이 잘 완성되었다.

해석 1 어떤 장난감 동물들은 바다에 훨씬 더 오래 있었다. 그것들은 완전히 북태평양 해류를 따라 떠다녔고, 결국에는 Sitka로 되돌아갔다.

2 창의성이 이상한 점은 아무리 제약을 받을지라도 어떤 종류의 상황에서든 자기의 갈 길을 찾아내기 때문인데, 이는 똑같은 양의 물이 탁 트인 바다를 가로지를 때보다 좁은 해협을 통과할 때 더 빠르고 더 세게 흐르는 것과 같다.

POINT 24 혼동하기 쉬운 형용사, 부사 정리

정답 & 해설 1 ○ | 문맥상 거리상으로 '가까운'의 뜻이므로 closely(긴밀히, 밀접하게)가 아닌 close가 맞게 쓰였다. close to the fish farms가 local wildlife inhabiting areas를 후치 수식하는 구조.

2 ○ | 독립적으로 쓰일 수 있는 부사 alike(A and B alike(A와 B 똑같이))가 어울리는 자리. 비슷한 모양의 like는 전치사로, 혼자 쓰일 수 없다.

3 ○ | instantly(즉각적으로)를 almost(거의 ~)가 꾸미는 구조. 비슷한 모양의 most(대부분의 ~)는 쓸 수 없는 자리이다. almost는 almost always, almost all 등 주로 '완전함'을 나타내는 말 앞에 수식어로 잘 쓰인다.

해석 1 양식장에서 가까운 지역에 서식하는 그 지역 야생 생물에 미치는 부정적 영향이 계속 그 산업의 지속적인 홍보 문제가 되고 있다.

2 아주 흥미롭게도 제빵에서의 많은 기술적 발전은 제빵사와 소비자들 사이에 똑같이 하나의 반응을 촉발했다.

3 그렇다면 그것들은 모두 한 지도자의 명령을 따르고 있는 것인가? 연구자들은 지도자나 통제 세력은 없다는 것을 밝혀냈다. 그보다는 (어떤가 하면), 개개의 물고기나 새가 (물고기) 떼나 (새) 무리에서 자신의 옆에 있는 동료들의 움직임에 거의 즉각적으로 반응하고 있는 것이다.

001 ③

해설 (A) 동사 enables의 주어가 the personal information이므로 재귀대명사가 올 자리가 아니다.
(B) depend on(~에 달려 있다)의 주어는 바로 앞 lost funds가 아니라 the actual liability이므로 단수형 depends가 알맞다.
(C) <leave + O + OC> 구조에서 목적어가 사람이 아닌 your purse이므로 -ing형이 아닌 수동형 unattended가 알맞다.

해석 대부분의 사람들이 온라인 뱅킹의 편리함을 고마워하지만, 그것은 새로운 위험들을 들여오기도 한다. 세계 어디에든 포진해 있는 범죄자들이, 그들을 온라인상에서 당신이 되어 마치 돈의 주인이기라도 한 듯 당신 돈으로 거래하는 것을 가능하게 하는 개인정보를 손에 넣을 수도 있는 것이다. 은행 및 증권 감독원들은 사이버 절도에 어떻게 대처해야 할지에 관한 규칙을 갖추고 있다. 그러나 잃은 금액에 대한 실제 책임은 계좌를 만들 때 고객이 서명한 계약서 내용에 좌우된다. 큰 은행 중 많은 곳이 전액 배상을 보장하지만, 문제의 소지가 많은 경우는 당신[고객] 쪽에서의 적절한 보안 및 경계 부족으로 인해 당신(이 사용하는) 컴퓨터에서 개인 정보가 입수되어 계좌가 해킹당한 경우들이다. 몇몇 은행들은 이를 자기 지갑을 주의 않고 내버려 둔 것과 같이—"고객님의 손실은 유감스럽시만 좀 더 소심하셨어야죠."— 취급한다.

어휘 **appreciate** 고마워하다; 진가를 알다 **obtain** 손에 넣다, 입수하다 **carry out** 수행하다, 완수하다 **transaction** 거래, 매매 **regulator** 단속[규제] 기관 **address** (문제를) 다루다, 대처하다 **contract** 계약, 약정 **guarantee** 보증하다 **adequate** 적절한 **precaution** 예방책

구문 02~06행 Criminals (located anywhere in the world) might be able to obtain the personal information [**that** enables them to *be* you online and *carry out* transactions with your money as if they owned *it*].
(Criminals: S, them: O′, to be you online: A, carry out ... they: B, it = your money)

→ <enable+O+OC> 구조에서 A와 B가 OC로 병렬구조를 이루고 있음.

002 ② | constant → constantly

해설 ② 분사 형용사(improving)를 수식하고 있으므로 형용사가 아닌 부사(constantly)가 되어야 한다.

① 이어지는 내용이 절이 아닌 구이므로 접속사 because가 아닌 because of가 온 경우.
③ to부정사가 명사(selection)를 수식하여 형용사로 쓰인 경우. choose from a selection이므로 from을 쓴 것.
④ 문맥상 '수많은' 차가 출시 준비 상태이다. 셀 수 있는 개념에 쓰이는 수량형용사 a number of(많은 ~)의 쓰임이 자연스럽다.
⑤ 의미상의 주체가 Grant이므로 수동형 guaranteed로 쓰인 경우.

해석 영국에서 전기 차의 인기가 2013년 3천 5백 대에 불과했던 것에 비해 약 5만 대의 전기 차가 도로에 나오면서 지난 몇 해 동안 급속히 치솟았다. 2015년의 전기 차의 이 엄청난 증가는 운전자에게 더 커진 선택의 폭, 전기 차에 대한 대중의 태도 변화, 부단히 개선되고 있는 공공 충전 네트워크 때문에 일어났다. (이 모두가) 결합되었을 때, 이는 영국 전기 차 구매자가 일찍이 그 어느 때보다 차량 선택의 폭이 커졌음을 뜻한다. 수많은 전기 차가 다음 12개월 이내에 출시될 준비를 갖추고 있고, 영국 정부의 전기 차 보조금이 이제 2018년까지는 보장될 가운데 미래 또한 밝다. 전기 차가 이제는 많은 운전자에게 매력적인 선택사항이다.

어휘 **shoot up** 급등[급증]하다 **plug-in** 플러그로 연결되는, 전기를 사용하는 **come about** 발생하다, 일어나다 **shift** 전환, 변화 **recharge** 충전하다 **launch** (상품을) 출시하다 **grant** 장려금, 보조금 **guarantee** 보장하다 **motorist** 운전자

구문 10~14행 The future is bright, too, **with** a number of plug-in cars *set* to be launched within the next twelve months and **with** the UK government's Plug-in Car Grant now *guaranteed* until 2018.
(a number of plug-in cars: O, set to be launched: OC, the UK government's Plug-in Car Grant: O, guaranteed: OC)

→ <with+O+OC>의 병렬구조. O와 OC가 수동 관계여서 목적격보어로 p.p.가 쓰인 경우.

003 ③ | firmly → firm

해설 ③ pale pink와 함께 명사 flesh를 수식하고 있으므로 형용사로 써야 한다.

① if (it is) cooked에서 주어 it(=pork)과 be동사 is가 생략되어 수동태의 과거분사만 남은 형태.
② the fat it contains에서 동사가 강조되어 does contain으로 쓰인 경우.
④ yellow-colored fat 말고 '대신에' the white stuff를 권하고 있다. 뒤에 목적어(instead of A) 없이 instead 단독으로 쓰일 수 있다.
⑤ 원래 '그래야 하는' 보통의 정도를 말하고 있는 should.

해석 가장 다양한 방면으로 쓰이는 육류 중 하나인 돼지고기는 경제적이고, 제대로 요리되면 부드럽고 향이 스며 나온다. 그것은 특히 지방이 많은 육류로 여겨지는 일이 많은데 현대적 번식, 사육, 도살 방식으로 인해 요즘에는 돼지고기가 저지방의, 몸에 좋은 육류가 되었다. 게다가 돼지고기가 함유하고 있는 지방은 다른 육류에서 발견되는 것에 비해 포화지방이 덜하다. 그래도 좋은 덩어리를 사는 것은 중요하다. 쇼핑하러 가면 살이 단단하고 연분홍빛에 촉촉하지만 육질이 기름지지는 않는 것을 찾아라. 기름이 노란빛을 띠는 돼지고기는 피하고, 대신 흰빛 나는 걸로 택하라. 뼈는 붉은빛을 띠어야 한다. 거친 살과 흰 뼈는 돼지가 늙었고 고기가 보통보다 덜 연하다는 걸 뜻한다. 돼지고기는 단백질이 많고 철분, 아연, 비타민 B의 훌륭한 공급원이며 맛도 또한 훌륭하다. 그러니까 오늘 밤 당신의 포크에 돼지고기를 좀 찔러라[돼지고기를 좀 먹으라].

어휘 **versatile** 다용도의, 쓰임새가 많은 **economical** 경제적인, 돈이 덜 드는 **tender** 부드러운, 연한 **oozing** 줄줄 흘리는 **think of A as B** A를 B로 여기다 **breed** 번식시키다 **rear** 사육하다, 기르다 **butcher** 도살하다, (동물을) 잡다 **firm** 단단한 **flesh** 살, 고기 **damp** 축축한, 눅눅한 **texture** 결, 조직, 감촉 **tinged** ~의 빛을 띠는

구문 01~03행 **One** (of the most versatile types of meat), **pork** is economical, tender [if (*it is*) cooked correctly], and oozing (with flavor).
(동격의 콤마(,); economical: A, tender [if (it is) cooked correctly]: B, oozing (with flavor): C)

→ <A, B, and C>의 구조로 돼지고기에 대해 설명하고 있다.

004 ③ | which → what

해설 ❸ depend on의 목적어로는 명사절이 와야 하므로 선행사를 포함한 관계대명사 what절이 와야 한다.

① 복수인 선행사에 맞게 복수형으로 쓰였고, parents가 이런 스타일을 드러내 보이는 것이므로 능동형으로 맞게 쓰였다.
② 뒤이어 절이 오므로 접속사 because가 맞게 쓰였다. 권위적인 부모 슬하에서 큰 아이들이 잘된 경우가 많은 이유를 설명하고 있으므로 that's why가 아닌 it's because로 시작한 게 자연스럽다.
④ 주어가 schools이므로 학교는 운영하는 입장이 아닌 운영되는, 즉 수동태로 쓰인 게 맞다. *cf.* run: 경영하다, 운영하다
⑤ have an easier time -ing: ~하기가 더 쉽다 meet: ~을 만족시키다(=satisfy), ~에 맞추다

해석 권위적인 양육은 합리적인 요구와 높은 반응성을 특징으로 하는 (양육) 스타일이다. 권위적인 부모는 자녀에 대한 기대치가 높을 수 있으나 또한 성공하기 위해 필요한 자원과 뒷받침을 자녀에게 해준다. 이런 스타일을 보이는 부모는 자녀의 말에 귀 기울이고, (행동의) 제한과 공정한 규율을 부과하는 외에 사랑과 온화함을 제공한다. 자주 권위적인 양육은 성공적인 아동과 결부된다. 아마도 이는 권위적인 양육이 독립적이며 성취 지향적인 마음 자세의, 사회적으로 책임감이 있으며 잘 적응하는 사람을 만들어 내기 쉬운 일련의 개개인의 습관과 결부되기 때문이다. 그리고 아마도 그것은 — 적어도 부분적으로는 — 사회의 다른 부분이 하고 있는 바에도 좌우된다. 학교가 권위적인 원칙에 따라 운영될 때 권위적인 가정의 아이들은 선생님의 기대치를 맞추기가 보다 쉬울 수 있다. 아이의 동년배 집단이 영향을 미칠 가능성도 있다. 동년배로부터의 압박이 권위적인 양육 스타일의 좋은 점을 약화시킬 수 있다.

어휘 **authoritative** 권위적인, 고압적인, 신뢰가 가는 **parenting** 육아, 양육 **characterized by** ~가 특징인, ~로 특징지어지는 **responsiveness** 반응성, 대응성 **expectation** 기대, 예상 **resource** 자원, 물자 **exhibit** 보이다, 드러내다 **discipline** 훈육, 규율 **more often than not** 자주 **a package of** 일괄의, 일련의 **socially-responsible** 사회적 책임감이 있는 **well-adjusted** 잘 적응하는 **peer pressure** 또래[동년배]로부터 받는 압박 **weaken** 약화시키다

005 ⑤ | to assume → assuming

해설 ❺ avoid는 동명사를 목적어로 취하는 동사이므로 avoid assuming이 맞다.

① 명사로 쓰인 to부정사.
② 우리의 '태도', '행위'가 주어이므로 수동태로 쓴 것이 적절.
③ -s로 끝나는 복수명사의 소유격은 아포스트로피(')만 붙이는 것이 맞다.
④ stylish shoes (belonged) to women with high incomes에서 belonged가 생략된 형태.

해석 여러분은 표지로 책을 판단할 만큼 어리석지는 않다. 그러나 어떤 사람을 신고 있는 신발로 평가하는 것이 때로는 타당할 수도 있다. 한 새 연구가 사람들이 처음 보는 사람의 어떤 성격 특징들을 발에 신은 것만 토대로 하여 우연 이상으로 정확하게 추론해 낸다는 사실을 발견했다. 한 그룹이 성격 조사를 끝내고 가장 자주 신는 신발 사진을 제공했다. 두 번째 그룹이 다음으로 그 사진을 보고 신발 주인을 다양한 성격 특성 면에서 평가했다. 그들의 추측은 연령, 성별, 소득, 애착불안 면에서 정확했다. 예를 들어, 지원자들은 눈에 띄는 브랜드의 신발은 남자, 모양이 돋보이는 신발은 고소득의 여자 것인 경우가 많음을 정확히 감지했다. 그들은 또한 자기 발에 신은 신발 사진을 제공한 사람들이 정서적으로 더 안정적임을 알아냈다. 신발이 (사람의) 첫인상을 형성하는 데 도움이 될 수 있지만 너무 많이 지레짐작하지는 말라. 결국 자기 발등 찧는 꼴이 될 수도 있으니까.

어휘 **know better than** ~보다는 더 안다, ~할 정도로 바보는 아니다 **justify** 정당화하다, 옳음을 보여주다 **deduce** 추론하다, 연역하다 **accuracy** 정확성 **footwear** 발에 신는 것(신발이나 양말류) **rate** 등급을 매기다 **regarding** ~에 관하여 **gender** 성별 **attachment anxiety** 애착 불안 **perceive** 감지하다, 느끼다 **visible** 눈에 띄는 **stable** 안정적인 **assume** ~라고 추정하다 **end up v-ing** 결국 v하게 되다 **shoot yourself in the foot** 자기 발등을 찧다, 자기 무덤을 파다

구문 12~15행 For instance, the volunteers perceived correctly that shoes (with visible brand names)[A] most often **belonged to** men and stylish shoes[B] ∨ **to** women (with high incomes).

→ ∨는 belonged가 중복을 피하기 위해 생략된 곳.

006 ④ | were found → found

해설 ❹ 동사 다음에 <목적어(programs)-목적격보어(poorly structured)> 구조가 이어지므로 수동태가 아닌 능동태 구조(find+O+OC: ~가 …하다고 느끼다)가 알맞다.

① 선행사 a form of training 다음에 그 자세한 내용이 소개되고 있으므로 in which(=in this form of training)로 시작하는 게 적절.
② So far(지금까지)라는 시간 표현이 있으므로 현재완료가 적절. 주어가 the results로 복수이므로 has가 아닌 have도 적절.
③ to replace의 대상이 the "sit and get" workshops이므로 능동형으로 쓴 것이 적절.
⑤ **Half as many** teachers were ~ **as** were ...의 비교급 문장. teachers는 셀 수 있는 명사이므로 many가 적절.

해석 미국의 학군들에서 해마다 교사 훈련에 180억 달러를 쓴다. 소요되는 총 시간 면에서 볼 때, 그 훈련의 구성 방식은 주로 협력적 전문성 신장으로, 교사가 교수 지도를 향상시키기 위해 그룹으로 모여 함께 작업하는 훈련의 한 형태이다. 이 그룹들은 흔히 전문 학습 공동체[교사 학습 공동체(PLC)]로 불린다. 미국 교사의 2/3가 현재 PLC에서 시간을 보낸다고 보고한다. 지금까지 그러한 협업의 결과물은 형편없었다. 의도는 좋으나 실행은 그렇지 않아서, 협업이 대체하고자 했던 '앉아서 (그냥) 받는' 워크숍에 대해서보다 교사 만족도가 훨씬 떨어진다. 우리가 조사한 많은 교사들이 프로그램이 구성이 엉성하고, 그 경험이 따분하고 그들의 일상 업무와 동떨어져 있다고 느꼈다. 전통적으로 쌍방향성이 가장 적은 교사 훈련의 형태인 워크숍에 매우 만족한 그룹(22%)의 절반의 교사(11%)가 협업 전문성 신장 경험에 매우 만족해했다.

어휘 **district** 구역, 지구 **in terms of** ~의 면에서, ~의 점에서 **format** 구성 방식, 포맷 **collaborative** 협업의, 공동작업의 **implementation** 실행, 이행, 구현 **replace** 대체하다, 교체하다 **disconnected** 동떨어진, 단절된 **interactive** 상호적인, 쌍방향의

구문 14~17행 Many teachers [we surveyed] **found** programs[O_1] poorly structured[OC_1] and the experience[O_2] boring and disconnected from their day-to-day jobs[OC_2].

→ <find+O+OC(~가 …하다고 느끼다)>의 병렬구조.

007 ③

해설 (A) 동사가 뒤에 있으므로(can run ~) 주어 Users를 수식하는 분사구가 오는 것이 알맞다.

(B) <목적>을 나타내는 to부정사가 문맥에 알맞다. *cf.* be used to v-ing: v하는데 익숙하다.

(C) 뒤에 목적어(electronics)가 이어 나오므로 능동태형으로 쓰는 것이 알맞다.

해석 재료과학자들이 땀의 분자구성을 읽어 그 결과를 실시간으로 스마트폰에 보낼 수 있는 작고 착용 가능한 감지기를 만들어냈다. 신축성 있는 플라스틱 패치— 손목밴드와 머리띠 모양으로 만들어질 수 있는—가 몸의 변화를 초기에 경고할 수 있을지 모른다고 만든 이들이 말한다. 그 신축성 있는 감지기를 착용한 사용자들이 뛰고 자유롭게 움직이는 동안 한편에서는 그들의 땀에 있는 화학성분이 측정되고 분석된다. 결과로 나온 데이터들이—이것이 무선으로 이동기기에 전송되는데—사용자의 건강 상태를 평가하고 점검하는 데 보조 역할을 할 수 있다. "그것은 인상적인 성취입니다. 감지기들은 보통 신발 상자 크기만 한 전자기기가 필요한데, 우리는 손목에 둘러찰 수 있는 어떤 것으로 소형화했죠."라고 개발자 중 하나가 말한다.

어휘 **material** 재료, 소재 **sensor** 센서, 감지기 **composition** 구성, 구성요소 **sweat** 땀 **patch** 패치; 조각 **incorporate** 결합하다 **transmit** 전송하다, 전달하다 **assess** 평가하다, 산정하다 **miniaturize** 소형화하다, 축소하다

008 ② | unsuspected → unsuspecting

해설 ❷ athlete가 의심을 하고 안 하는 주체이므로 능동의 의미가 있는 unsuspecting이 알맞다.

① the idea that ~으로 이어지는 동격의 that.
③ <cause+O+OC>의 구조에서 목적격보어로 to-v가 온 경우.
④ 명사절 what he brings to the table이 전치사 for의 목적어로 온 경우.
⑤ athletes를 분사 수식어 loaded with potential이 후치 수식하고 있는 구조. 한편 현재분사 수식어 pursuing도 athletes를 앞에서 수식하고 있다.

해석 많은 사람들이 특히 Jerry Maguire 같은 영화를 보고는 스포츠 에이전트가 비열하고, 그늘진 곳에 몸을 숨기고는 의심을 품지 않고 잘 속아 넘어가는 프로선수가 서명란에 서명하길 기다리는 중고차 영업사원 타입의 인물이라는 생각을 갖고 있다. 그런 이들이 존재하긴 한다. 그리고 그들은 '사인하면[계약 체결되면] 내가 스타로 만들어주겠어' 식의 수사법을 사용한다. 장기적인 계획이나 축구선수 생활 이후에 대한 언급은 전혀 없다. 맞다. 이러한 양심적이지 않은 에이전트가 한 선수의 경력을 그것이 채 시작되기도 전에 망쳐버릴 수 있다. 이 때문에 사람들이 그들을 스포츠 에이전트 세계에서 '표본'인 것으로 믿게 되지만 실은 그렇지 않다. 스포츠 에이전트의 궁극적인 꿈은, 에이전트가 협상 테이블에 가져오는 것에 대해 그를 소중히 여기고 고마워하는 고객을 갖는 것이다. 그는 '미래의 관점에서 생각하는' 운동선수를 열망한다. 그는 잠재력으로 가득한, 추구하는 바가 있는 운동선수의 열정을 갈망한다. 그는 자기의 잠재력을 운동장 안팎에서 기꺼이 키워나가는 법을 아는 선수를 발판으로 번성한다. 그것이 스포츠 에이전트의 할 일이다.

어휘 **agent** (연예·스포츠 부문의) 에이전트 **slimy** 비열한, 끈적끈적한 **lurk** 숨어 있다, 도사리다 **unsuspecting** 의심하지 않는, 이상한 낌새를 못 차리고 있는 **rhetoric** 미사여구, 수사 **post-** ((접두사)) ~ 후의, ~ 다음의 **ruin** 망치다, 파멸시키다 **ultimate** 궁극적인, 최후의 **crave** 갈망하다 **pursue** 추구하다 **loaded** 가득한 **thrive on** ~을 토대로 번성하다, ~로 잘해 가다

009 ② | demonstrate → demonstrating

해설 ❷ 전치사 with의 목적어가 <both A and B> 구조로 두 개 제시되고 있다. A가 동명사구(offering ~ mindfulness)이므로 B도 동명사 형태인 demonstrating으로 시작되어야 한다.

① 유념이 '현재' 주목받는 주제가 '되었음'을 현재완료로 얘기하고 있다.
③ 명사절 whatever is happening within us and around us가 전치사 with의 목적어로 쓰이고 있다. *cf.* whatever: ~은 무엇이든지
④ 가정이나 바람을 나타내는 we wish가 앞에 있으므로 가정법 과거(were) 형태로 쓴 것이 자연스럽다.
⑤ help는 목적격보어로 원형부정사가 올 수 있다.

해석 한 번에 수많은 것들을 다루도록 기대되는 세상에서 유념은 뜨거운 주제가 되었다. 그러한바 무수한 과학 출판물이 유념의 이해 가능한 정의를 제시하고 현대 생활에 그것이 어떻게 실질적으로 적용되는지 보여주려 애쓰고 있다. 마음을 기울이는 명상은 우리 안팎에 일어나고 있는 무엇이든지 온화하고 열린 마음으로 함께하겠다는 기꺼운 마음을 포함한다. 우리는 우리 자신과 타인, 그리고 우리의 사는 방식 중에서 제대로 안 돌아가고 있는 부분이 있음을 발견할 수 있다. 이 깨달음이 처음에는 가끔 우리를 불안한 마음이 들게 할 수도 있다. 우리는 과거의 상처에 우연히 맞닥뜨릴 수 있다. 일어나는 일을 우리가 그렇게 되었으면 하고 바라는 식으로 보다는 있는 그대로 보기 위해서 유념은 용기를 필요로 한다. 우리는 내적 갈등과 우리의 고통을 유발하는 (반복되는) 패턴을 치유하기 위해 치료 요법이나 상담이 필요할 수도 있다. 다행스러운 소식은 유념 연습이 긍정적인 변화에 필요한 인내심과 연민을 우리가 갖추는 데 도움이 된다는 것이다.

어휘 **address** (문제를) 다루다, 대처하다 **mindfulness** 유념함, 마음 기울임 **numerous** 무수한, 수많은 **publication** 출판물, 출판 **meditation** 명상 **willingness** 기꺼이 하는 마음, 자발성 **awareness** 깨달음, 각성 **anxious** 불안해하는, 염려하는 **wound** 상처; 상처를 입히다 **therapy** 치료, 요법 **inner** 내적인 **compassion** 연민, 동정심

구문 13~15행 Mindfulness requires courage to see things as they are(A) **rather than** how (we wish) *they*(= things) were(B).

→ <A rather than B> 구조. 현재와 반대되는, 바라는 바를 나타내고 있으므로 가정법 과거 were를 썼다.

010 ①

해설 (A) of 뒤의 명사가 복수형이므로 동사도 have been found가 알맞다. 지금까지 파악된 수치를 말하므로 현재완료로 쓰였다.
(B) 접속사 whereas를 가운데 두고 the former와 the latter가 각각 문장의 주어로 쓰인 <주절 whereas 종속절> 구조이다. 동사 uses가 맞다.
(C) 해안 가까이 '있는', '놓여 있는' 것이므로 lie가 맞다. 과거시제로 쓰인다면 lay(lie의 과거)도 가능하겠지만 현재 발굴 안 된 채로 있는 것이므로 현재가 자연스럽다.

해석 고대의 난파선은 매장된 보물뿐만 아니라 무수한 역사적 비밀도 품고 있을지 모른다. 3백만이 넘는 난파선이 대양 곳곳에 산재해 있다고 UNESCO는 추정한다. 나아가 전 세계의 모든 난파선 중 10% 이하가 (지금까지) 발견된 것으로 추정된다. 물속에 가라앉은 난파선들이 현재 수중 음파 탐지기와 공중 광속 시스템을 통해 감지되는데, 전자는 소리로 난파선을 수색하는 반면 후자는 레이저를 사용한다. 수중 음파 탐지기는 깊은 바다에서 가장 효과적이고 공중 광속 탐지기는 맑은 물이 필요하다. 그러나 두 가지 다 흐릿하고 얕은 물에서는 작동이 잘 안 된다. 이는 해안 가까운 바다 — 얕고도 탁한 경우가 많은데 — 는 난파선을 찾아 나서는 탐색에서 소홀히 취급되기 쉽다는 걸 뜻한다. 이것이 문제인데, 그 이유는 전문가가 말하듯 "대부분의 교통사고가 집에서 1km 가량 떨어진 곳에서 일어나는 것처럼 난파선의 대다수가 해안 가까이에 있기" 때문이다.

어휘 **shipwreck** 난파선 **scatter** 흩뿌리다 **estimate** 추정하다 **submerge** 가라앉다 **currently** 현재, 지금 **detect** 감지하다, 탐지하다 **via** ~을 통해서, ~을 경유하여 **waterborne** 물에 떠 있는, 수상 운송의 **airborne** 하늘에 떠 있는, 바람에 의해 운반되는 **the former ~ the latter** ... 전자는 ~ 후자는 … **shallow** 얕은 **shore** 해안 **overlook** 간과하다, 빠뜨리고 안 보다 **majority** 대다수, 다수

구문 04~06행 **It**(가주어) is further estimated **that**(진주어) (of all the wrecks in the world,) less than 10 percent(S′) have been found(V′).
→ 또 한 가지 추정치를 that절로 소개하고 있다.

011 ④ | sending → are sending[send]

해설 ❹ 주격 관계대명사가 앞에 있으므로 be동사와 함께 that are sending으로 쓰거나 send로 써야 한다. that이 없다면 the neurons sending ~으로 쓸 수 있다.

① phenomenon은 왜 이런 일이 일어나는지 설명'되거나 안 되거나' 하는 수동의 입장. 이에 맞게 과거분사 형용사가 잘 쓰였다.
② <see+O+OC> 구조에서 목적격보어로 -ing가 온 경우.
③ 선행사가 an evolutionary adaptation으로 단수이므로 keeps가 적절.
⑤ how the brain builds ~가 전치사 in의 목적어로 쓰인 경우.

해석 어떤 이들은 잠에서는 깨었는데 움직일 수 없다고 느껴지는, 어슴푸레한 침입자가 머리 위를 맴돌고 있는 게 보이는 상태인, 흔하지만 왠지 설명이 잘 안 되는 현상인 수면 마비를 경험한다. 연구자들은 수면 마비는 급속 안구 운동(REM)으로 알려져 있는 수면 단계에 잠이 깰 때 일어난다고 한다. 꿈을 꾸고 있는데 근육은 거의 마비 상태로, 이것은 우리가 꿈에서 일어나는 일을 실제로 옮기지 못 하도록 해주는 진화적 적응의 하나로 볼 수 있다. 한 가지 가능한 설명은, 수면 마비 중에 두뇌의 일부가 움직임 명령을 보내고 있는 신경세포를 지켜보고 있는데, 팔다리에 실제 움직임은 탐지되지 않는 것이, 그것들이 일시적으로 마비되어 있기 때문이라는 것이다. 이것이 뇌가 몸을 어떤 이미지로 느끼는가에 혼란을 초래할 수 있다고 전문가는 말했다. 뇌가 자기 몸의 이미지를 환각 이미지에 투영하려고 할 때 침대 옆 침입자가 나타나는 일이 일어날 수 있다고 그는 말했다.

어휘 **paralysis** 마비 ***cf.*** **paralyze** 마비시키다 **shadowy** 그늘진, 어슴푸레한 **intruder** 침입자 **hover** (공중에서) 맴돌다 **evolutionary** 진화의, 점진적인 **adaptation** 적응, 순응 **act out** 실연하다, 행동을 취하다 **command** 명령 **limb** 팔다리, 사지 **temporarily** 일시적으로 **disturbance** 방해, 장애 **project** 투영하다

012 ② | little → a little

해설 ❷ 물이 약간 있을 때 어떤 일이 일어나는지 설명하고 있으므로 a little이라고 해야 한다.

① because 이하의 절에서 주어부를 이끌므로 동명사 adding이 적절.
③ 주어가 it이므로 takes가 적절. *cf.* take: ~를 필요로 하다, (…하는 데) ~가 들다
④ 명사절 where the salt water can freeze가 전치사 to의 목적어로 쓰이고 있는 경우.
⑤ <keep+O+OC> 구조에서 목적격보어로 진행형이 쓰인 구조.

해석 얼음이 덮인 도로나 보도에 얼음을 없애기 위해서는 소금을 뿌리면 된다는 걸 다들 알고 있다. 이 방법이 듣는 것은 소금을 더하면 물의 어는점이 낮아지기 때문이다. 이것이 어떻게 얼음을 녹이는가? 그게, 얼음과 함께 쓸 수 있는 물이 약간 있지 않으면 그러지 못한다. 다행인 것은 그 효과를 거두기 위해서 엄청난 양의 물이 필요하지는 않다는 것이다. 얼음은 보통 액체인 물의 얇은 막이 입혀져 있는데, 그거면 충분하다. 순수한 물은 화씨 32도(섭씨 0도)에서 언다. 소금이 든(또는 다른 어떤 성분이든 들어 있는) 물은 (그보다) 더 낮은 온도에서 얼 것이다. 기온이 소금물이 얼 수 있는 지점까지 내려가면 그 액체가 고체가 되면서 결합이 형성되면서 에너지가 방출될 것이다. 이 에너지면 아무것도 안 섞인 소량의 물을 녹이기에 충분할 수 있고, 그 과정이 계속되도록 해 준다.

어휘 **sprinkle** 뿌리다 **freezing point** 어는점 **effect** 효과, 영향 **be coated with** ~로 입혀져 있다 **film** (얇은) 막 **liquid** 액체(의) **pure** 순수한, 불순물이 섞이지 않은 **substance** 물질 **bond** 결합, 결속 **solid** 고체(의)

013 ②

해설 (A) 관계사절의 수식을 받는 주어 women은 복수이므로 were로 써야 한다.
(B) 끝난 joint project에 대해 얘기하고 있으므로 assume보다 시점이 앞섬을 나타내는 완료형 to have taken으로 써야 한다.
(C) suffer(피해를 입다)는 수동태로 쓰이지 않는 동사이다.

해석 여자는 당연히 받아야 할 때 공로를 인정받지 못한다. 한 연구에서 수년에 걸친 투자 계획을 잡는 일에 있어 남자와 협업했던 여자들이 남성 동료보다 덜 유능한 것으로 지속적으로 여겨진 걸로 나왔다. 그리고 함께 작업한 일이 성공적이었을 때 여자는 그 성공에 덜 중요한 역할을 한 것으로 비친 반면 같은 일을 한 남자는 주도적인 역할을 한 것으로 여겨졌다. 이는 일하는 여성에게는 나쁜 소식인 것이, 오늘날 대부분의 일은 어느 정도의 협업으로 이루어지기 때문이다. 양성의 협업은 남자에게 보다 여자에게 덜 인정된다. 그리고 여자가 함께하는 일에 대해 공정한 몫의 인정을 받지 못할 때 그들의 직업 전망은 피해를 본다. 여자가 값진 공헌을 한 데 대해 인정받지 못하고 지나갔을 때 초래된, 기록에 남지 않은 수많은 직업적 불이익은 상상만 할 수 있을 정도[실제로는 얼마나 많은지 이루 말할 수 없을 정도]일 것이다.

어휘 **credit** 공로, 칭찬 **due** 당연한, 받아야 할 **collaboratively** 협업으로 (**collaboration** 공동작업) **portfolio** 포트폴리오[작품집, 자산구성] **consistently** 지속적으로, 항상 **competent** 유능한 **peer** 동료 **influential** 영향력 있는 **counterpart** 대응되는 인물, 기능 등이 비슷한 것 **assume** 지레짐작하다 **take on** (일, 업무 등을) 맡다 **prospect** 전망, 가망 **suffer** 피해를 입다, 시달리다 **undocumented** 기록되지 않은 **penalty** 불이익; 처벌 **unrecognized** 인정받지 못하는, 의식되지 않는

구문 11~12행 Their collaborative work counts **less** (*for women*) **than** it does for men.
(does =counts)
→ 비교하는 대상이 숨어 있는 경우.

014 ③ | is resembled → resembles

해설 ③ 선행사가 a microbial community이므로 능동으로 쓰여야 (resembles) 맞다. resemble은 수동태로 쓰이지 않는 동사이기도 하다.

① 복수명사 babies를 대신해서 쓰인 지시대명사.
② 주격 관계대명사 which에 이어지는 동사로, which가 앞의 내용 전체를 받는 단수 개념이므로 helps로 받은 경우. scientists believe는 삽입절.
④ differences와 risks 사이의 연관성이 그간의 연구에서 죽 드러났다는 얘기이므로 현재완료 수동태로 쓰인 것이 적절.
⑤ hints(암시, 힌트)의 내용을 설명하는 동격의 that절.

해석 질로 분만된 아기는 제왕절개로 난 아이보다 유리한 점이 있는 것으로 여겨진다. 그들은 엄마의 산도에서 박테리아를 끌어모으는데, 이것이 성장하면서 천식, 비만, 기타 건강 문제들에서 그들을 보호하는 데 도움이 된다고 과학자들은 믿고 있다. 분만 중인 산모는 나머지 우리들과 마찬가지로, 무수한 박테리아 — 미생물세균 유전체로 불리는 — 를 온몸 여기저기 안팎으로 갖고 있다. 질로 분만된 아기에게는 초기에 엄마의 질의 그것을 닮은 미생물 군집이 발달하는 반면, 제왕절개를 통해 세상에 나온 아기는 엄마 피부의 그것을 닮은 미생물 조합을 갖는다. 이 차이점들이 결국 인간과 쥐를 대상으로 하는 연구에서 천식, 알레르기, 비만, 면역 결핍의 증가된 위험과 관련되어 왔다. 이제 새 연구가 연구자들이 탄생 직후 미생물군 조합을 '개조' — 새로운 탐사의 길을 여는 '아주 흥미롭고도 간단한 개입' — 함으로써 제왕절개술 아기에게 타고난 불리한 점을 없애 줄 수 있을지도 모른다는 암시를 준다.

어휘 **edge** 유리한 점, 이점 **via** ~을 통하여 **birth canal** 산도(産道) **asthma** 천식 **obesity** 비만 **labor** 분만, 노동 **boast** 보유하다; 뽐내다 **a constellation of** 일단의 ~, 기라성 같은 ~ ***cf.*** **constellation** 성좌 **initially** 처음에는, 최초에는 **immune deficiency** 면역 결핍 **disadvantage** 불리한 점, 단점 **intrinsic** 내재된, 원래 있는 **intervention** 개입, 간섭

015 ④ | may evolve → may have evolved

해설 ④ 과거의 일(our hunter-gatherer ancestors ~)에 대해 추측하고 있으므로 may have p.p.(~했을지도 모른다) 형태로 쓰여야 자연스럽다.

① 비교급을 강조하는 much.
② 선행사 a tree hole이 장소이므로 관계부사 where가 쓰인 경우. '이곳에서' 뭘 하는지의 내용이 이어 나온다.
③ <It is ~ that...> 강조구문으로 쓰인 that.
⑤ <get+O+OC> 구조(get the fire roaring)에서 the fire가 사자처럼 포효하고 있는(roaring) 것이므로 진행형을 쓴 것이 자연스럽다.

해석 동면 중인 다람쥐는 체온을 한 번에 여러 주씩 얼기 살짝 위의 온도까지 떨어뜨릴 수 있다. 크기 면에서 우리와 훨씬 가까운 곰도 갖고 있는 체지방으로 최고 다섯 달까지 버틸 수 있다. 그러나 동면하지 않는 많은 동물들은 체온을 낮추고 신진대사를 최소한으로 늦춤으로써 휴면 상태로 겨울을 난다. 마다가스카르 여우원숭이는 겨울 동안 나무 구멍 속으로 물러나 있는데, 이곳에서 몇 날 며칠이고 좀비처럼 앉아 있는다. 그것들을 동면하게 만드는 것은 추위라기보다는 먹을 게 없어서이다. 인간은 아프리카의 적도 기후에서 진화했으므로, 사냥꾼·수렵꾼의 삶을 산 우리 선조는 아마도 먹을 것 없이 긴 시간을 살아남는 유사한 능력을 서서히 발달시켰을 것이다. 요즘은 긴긴밤들을 넘기기만 하면 된다. 다행히 우리는 이불 밑으로 기어들어갈 수도 있고, 초를 밝힐 수도, 난로가 이글거리며 타게도, 리모컨을 누를 수도 있다. 죄책감이 든다고? 그럴 필요는 없다. 어쨌거나 우리는 우리에게 자연스러운 일을 하고 있을 뿐이니까.

어휘 **hibernate** 동면하다 **at a time** 한 번에 **be capable of** ~을 할 수 있다 **survive on** ~로 목숨을 유지하다 **up to** (수, 정도 등) ~까지 **dormant** 휴면의, 활동을 중단하는 **metabolism** 신진대사 **retire** ~로 물러나다[후퇴하다] **for days on end** 날이면 날마다 **equatorial** 적도의 **crawl** 기다 **light** (lit-lit, lighted-lighted) 불 밝히다 **roaring** 맹렬히 타오르는

구문 10~11행 **It's** lack of food (A), *rather than* cold (B), **that** drives them to hibernate.

→ <It is ~ that ...>의 강조구문에서, 강조하는 부분에 A rather than B(B이기보다는 A) 구문이 사용되어 A가 다시 강조되고 있다.

16~18행 Luckily, we can crawl under the covers (A), get **the candles** *lit* and **the fire** *roaring* (B) and hit the remote control (C).

→ A, B and C의 열거 구조. B는 get the candles lit and (get) the fire roaring의 병렬구조를 이루고 있으며 각각 과거분사 lit(수동)과 현재분사 roaring(진행)을 목적격보어로 쓰고 있다.

016 ①

해설 (A) 앞에 오는 who are abused or neglected는 주어 children을 꾸며주는 수식어. 동사 자리이므로 suffer가 올바른 형태이다.
(B) <all+복수명사>이므로 동사도 복수형 have가 맞다.
(C) the emotional damage will be ∨ 자리에 올 것은 부사가 아니라 형용사 serious이다.

해석 대부분의 아동 학대 사건에서 학대당하거나 방치된 아동은 육체적인 손상보다 정서적인 손상으로 더 고통받는다. 정서적, 심리적 학대와 방치는 아이가 스트레스에 대처하고 인생의 교훈을 배워나가는 데 필요한 도구를 갖추지 못 하게 한다. 그래서 심하게 학대받는 아이는 우울한 성격이 되거나 자살 충동적이고 움츠러들며 폭력적인 행동을 보이게 된다. 성장하면서는 마약이나 술을 할 수 있고, 가출하거나 규율을 거부하거나 타인을 학대할 수 있다. 성인이 되어서는 결혼생활에 어려움을 겪고 우울증이나 자살 행동을 보인다. 이런 상황을 예방하기 위해서는 아동 희생자를 알아보는 것이 첫 단계이다. 여기에서의 문제점은 학대 희생자 전부가 심각한 반응을 보이지는 않는다는 점이다. 보통 아이가 어릴수록 학대는 더 오래 지속되고, 아이의 학대자와의 관계가 가까울수록 정서적 폐해는 더 심각하다.

어휘 **abuse** 학대, 유린 ***cf.* abuser** 학대자 **neglect** 방치하다, 소홀히 하다; 방치, 소홀 **suffer** 고통 받다 **deny A B** A에게 B를 주지 않다 **cope with** ~을 다루다[대처하다] **severely** 몹시, 심하게 **mistreat** 학대하다 **depressed** 우울한, 의기소침한 **suicidal** 자살의, 자멸적인 **withdrawn** 움츠러드는 **discipline** 훈육, 규율 **marital** 결혼의, 결혼 생활의 **identify** 알아보다, 파악하다 **victim** 희생자

구문 03~05행 Emotional and psychological abuse and neglect deny(V) the child(IO) **the tools** (needed *to cope with stress*, [and] *to learn life's lessons*)(DO).

→ to cope with ~와 to learn ~은 둘 다 needed에 연결되는 어구로 병렬구조를 이루고 있다.

15~18행 Usually **the younger** the child (is), **the longer** the abuse continues; and **the closer** the child's relationship with the abuser (is), **the more serious** the emotional damage will be.

→ <the 비교급+S+V, the 비교급+S+V>의 구조가 세미콜론(;) 좌우로 두 개 쓰인 구조. 동사의 성격에 따라 형용사 또는 부사가 비교급으로 쓰이고 있다.

017 ⑤ | is driven → drives

해설 ⑤ something이 당신을 침대에서 내모는 주체이므로 능동태 drives(내몰다, ~하게 만들다)가 알맞다.

① 동사 switch off를 꾸며주는 수식어로 부사가 쓰인 경우.
② breath가 나를 '만족시키는' 경우이므로 능동의 현재분사(satisfying)가 적절.
③ 분사구문으로, 앞 문장에 이어 접속사 없이 뒤 내용을 자연스럽게 이어주고 있다.
④ energize(활력을 띠게 하다)는 타동사. 문맥상 '활력을 띤 채로'의 의미로 쓰일 곳으로 주격보어가 과거분사 형태로 맞게 쓰였다.

해석 전화기의 알람이 오전 6시에 울린다. 기분 좋게 끄고, 침대에서 용수철처럼 튀어나와 커튼과 창을 활짝 열어젖히고는 신선한 공기를 깊고 만족스럽게 들이마신다. 여기 또 다른 그림이 있다. 전화기가 오전 6시에 삑 하고 울린다. 왼팔이 알람 버튼을 누르려고 베개 밑으로 미끄러져 들어간다. 딱 30분만 더—그거면 돼. 그러다가 오전 6시 30분, 알람이 다시 울리고, 그러고 나서 7시, 7시 30분, 7시 35분 … 우리들 대부분은 분명 후자로, 움켜쥔다는 느낌 없이 결국 하루를 시작한다. 내가 이해하는 바로는 아침에 활기찬 상태로 깨는 걸 제일 잘하는 사람은 임무를 띠고 있다고 느끼는 사람이다. 그 할 일은 마음을 몹시 끄는 것이어야 하고 실제로 이루고 싶은 어떤 것이어야 하는데, 그것이 5분만 더 하고 비명 지르며 시간을 끌게 하기보다는 침대에서 나오도록 만들어 준다.

어휘 **go off** 울리다 **gleefully** 신이 나서, 유쾌하게 **fling open** 열어젖히다 **screech** (귀에 거슬리는) 삑 하는 소리를 내다 **extra** 추가의, 과외의 **the latter** 후자 **seize** 움켜잡다, 붙잡다 **energize** 활기를 띠게 하다, 열정을 돋우다 **compelling** 마음이 안 갈 수 없는, 주목하지 않을 수 없는

018 ⑤ | me → myself

해설 ⑤ 정체성 변화에 시달리던 내가 드디어 '나 자신'과의 평화를 찾게 된 것이므로 재귀대명사 myself로 고쳐 써야 한다.

① 지난 시간이 어땠는지 죽 돌이켜보는 관점이므로 be동사의 현재완료가 자연스럽다.
② 주어(The most significant thing)를 설명하는 주격보어가 시작되는 곳에 종속절을 이끄는 that이 맞게 왔다.
③ 명사(identity change)를 형용사(extreme)가 수식하는 구조.
④ 동사(operate)를 부사(effectively)가 수식하는 구조.

해석 졸업이 몇 주밖에 안 남았고, 나는 점점 맘이 설렌다. 드디어 학위를 갖고 졸업을 할 것이다. 때로는 긴 길이었고, 다소 힘들었다. 하지만 여기 내가 있다. 대학 생활을 잘 해냈다. 밤늦게 하는 그 모든 공부 모임과 기말시험들을 무사히 해냈다. 졸업이 내게 뜻하는 가장 큰 의미는 내가 나 자신에 대해 많이 알게 됐다는 것이다. 미국에 이민 왔을 때 나는 극도의 정체성 변화를 겪었다. 이전의 삶의 방식, 내 가족, 친구들, 내가 살던 도시로부터 분리되었다. 내 사회적 신분과 정체성, 주변 환경 속에서 효과적으로 돌아가는 능력을 상실했다. 그 변화는 고통스러웠으나, 배움의 여정 내내 나는 내가 새 정체성과 가치관, 그리고 태도를 형성해가고 있음을 발견했다. 나는 과도기의 고통스러운 장애물들을 극복하고, 나 자신과의 평화를 찾고 내 새 나라에 편안하게 정착할 수 있었다.

어휘 **degree** 학위 **session** (특정 활동을 위한) 시간, 기간 **significant** 중요한, 의미심장한 **immigrate** 이민 오다, 이주해오다 **extreme** 극도의, 극단의 **identity** 정체성 **separate A from B** A를 B에게서 분리하다 **status** 신분, 지위 **transition** 변화, 이행, 과도기 **throughout** ~의 내내 **values** 가치관 **overcome** 극복하다 **resettle** 재정착하다

구문 06~08행 *The most significant thing*(S) [**that** graduation means ∨ to me] is **that** I learned a lot about myself(C).

→ that은 각각 관계대명사와 접속사로 주어를 수식하고, 보어절을 이끌고 있다.

019 ⑤ | acknowledge → acknowledging

해설 ⑤ <While+S′+V′~, S+V~>의 복문 구조에서 주절의 주어가 시작되는 부분이므로 명사 개념(acknowledging the whole team ~)이 와야 한다.

① 문장의 주어가 participants in the study이고 그들의 개인적 기여에 대해 (for their personal contributions) thank를 받는 입장이다. 전치사(After) 뒤에 동명사가 수동형으로 온 구조.
② 앞 문장 전체(participants in the study experienced increased feelings of value and worth)를 받는 계속적 용법의 관계대명사.
③ lose의 목적어로 명사(how much support and productivity)가 오는 것이 알맞다.
④ 비교급(easier)을 강조하는 부사 much.

해석 2010년에 한 연구가 감사의 마음이 어떻게 친사회 행동을 유발하는지를 탐구했다. 개인적으로 기여를 해준 것에 대해 감사의 말을 들은 뒤에 연구의 참가자들은 (스스로의) 가치와 진가가 증가되는 감정을 경험했는데, 그 점이 그들이 (타인에게) 도움이 되는 그 행동을 반복할 가능성을 2배 이상 끌어올렸다. 누구에게나 이 연구는 당신의 동료의 자아 존중감을 지지해주는 손쉬운 방법을 드러내 보여준다. 관리직에 있는 사람에게 그것은 또한 감사함을 표현하지 않음으로써 얼마나 많은 지지와 생산성을 잃게 될지도 시사해 준다. 감사하고 (다른 이의 공을) 인정하는 것의 이점을 확실히 이용하도록 일부러 하는 진정한 감사를 팀 회의나 일대일 미팅에 포함시켜 보라. 맡은 팀의 성과에 대해 조직의 리더에게 축하하는 것은 훨씬 쉽지만 따뜻한 한 통의 이메일로 팀 전체의 (공로를) 인정하는 것은 각 개인의 (조직에 끼치는) 결정적인 뒷받침을 강조하고, 그저 한 사람이 아닌, 한 사람 한 사람이 모여 이뤄진 전체 그룹의 행복감을 끌어올릴 것이다.

어휘 **gratitude** 감사, 고마움 **motivate** 동기를 유발하다, ~하게 자극하다 **pro-** ((접두사)) 찬성하는, 지지하는, 친- **thank A for B** A에게 B에 대해 감사하다 **likelihood** 가능성, 공산 **unveil** 덮개를 벗기다, 진상을 밝히다 **self-esteem** 자아 존중감, 자긍심 **productivity** 생산성 **take advantage of** ~을 이용하다 **appreciation** 고마움, 감사 **acknowledgment** 인정, 승인 ***cf.* acknowledge** 인정하다 **intentional** 의도적인 **genuine** 진정한, 진짜의 **accomplishment** 업적, 공적 **boost** 신장시키다, 북돋우다

구문 15~19행 While **it**'s much easier **to high-five** ~, acknowledging the whole team (with a warm email) will highlight ~, and boost ~.
(it: 가주어, to high-five: 진주어, acknowledging the whole team (with a warm email): S, will highlight: V_1, boost: V_2)

020 ⑤ | which → what

해설 ⑤ 보어 자리에 오는 절이므로 명사절이어야 한다. which로 시작하는 관계대명사절은 형용사절로서 보어 자리에 올 수 없다. '여러분이 그날 (사려고) 마음에 두고 있던 것'이라는 의미가 되어야 하므로 선행사를 포함한 관계대명사 what을 써야 한다.

① applies 대신에 쓰인 대동사.
② that이 perfect, modest-but-cool-but-also-elegant와 함께 형용사로 쓰여 dress를 꾸미는 구조. 지시형용사 that.
③ Whatever the case (is)에서 Whatever는 명사로, the case를 설명하는 주격보어로 쓰였다. *cf.* whatever: ~은 …이든 간에
④ something specific을 가리키는 대명사 it.

해석 해야만 할 때까지 기다렸다가 쇼핑하지 마라. 이는 장 보는 것에는 해당 안 되는 말이지만 옷 사는 것에는 해당된다. 검정 바지, 흠잡을 데 없는 피트감의 청바지, 부츠, 블라우스, 블레이저 등등 옷장에 있는 모든 것들을 새로 쫙 갖춰야 할 것 같은 느낌이 갑자기 드는 때가 있다. 아니면 주말에 가족 결혼식이 있어서 그 조신해 보이지만 멋있고 뿐만 아니라 우아하기도 한 완벽한 드레스가 이틀 후 필요할 수도 있다. 어떤 경우이든 간에 구체적인 뭔가를 찾아 나설 때 그것을 발견 못 하게 될 가능성이 크다. 핵심은 자주 쇼핑하고 한 뭉치씩 사지 않는 것이다. 따라서 말 그대로 옷장에 있는 어떤 것 하고도 같이 입을 수 있는 뭔가를 우연히 봤을 땐 그것을 사는 것이다. 그것이 그날 (사려고) 마음에 두고 있던 것이 아니더라도 말이다. (그러다 보면) 결국 시간이 지나서는 아주 균형 있는 옷가지를 갖추었음을 깨닫게 될 것이다. 천천히 그리고 꾸준한 것이 경기에서 이긴다. 그것이 사람들이 하는 말인 거, 아닌가?

어휘 **apply to** ~에 해당되다, ~에 적용되다 **version** ~판, 버전 **wardrobe** 옷장, (갖추고 있는) 의상 (전부) **flawless** 무결점의, 완벽한 **modest** 얌전한, 조신한 **elegant** 우아한, 고상한 **specific** 구체적인, 특정한 **chances are (that)** ~의 가능성이 크다 **in bulk** 대량으로 **happen to** 우연히 ~하다 **stumble across** 우연히 마주치다 **literally** 글자 그대로, 말 그대로 **secure** 확보하다, ~을 획득하다 **steady** 꾸준한

구문 09~11행 **Whatever** the case (*is*), [**if** you're looking for something specific], chances are, ***(that)*** you're not going to find it.
(종속절 / 주절)

→ <종속절+주절> 구조에서 주절은 다시 <종속절(if 부사절)+주절> 구조로, 다시 주절은 <주절+종속절(that 명사절(보어절))> 구조로 나눠지는 복합구조이다.

021 ⑤ | is spread → spread

해설 ⑤ 진짜 동사(is)가 바로 이어 나오므로 이 부분은 동사가 아닌 수식어 자리이다. good reputation이 동사 spread의 동작의 대상이 되므로 수동을 나타내는 과거 분사 spread로 고쳐 써야 알맞다.

① call on(요청하다, 시키다)하는 것은 제작자나 감독일 것이고 그들(배우들)은 그려내라고 요구 받을 것이므로 수동태 표현 are called on은 맞게 쓰였다.
② accept ~와 be able to adjust ~ 모두 조동사 need에 이어지는 병렬구조. 동사원형이 맞게 쓰였다.
③ continue는 to부정사(to-v)와 동명사(v-ing) 둘 다를 목적어로 취하는 동사.
④ by performing ~ and (by) attending ~의 병렬구조.

해석 배우는 일반적으로 팀의 일원으로서 일을 잘 해내는 창의적인 개인들이다. 그들은 그려내라고 요구받는 갖가지의 그 모든 인물을 해석해내는 데 필수적인 강한 비판적 사고 능력을 키워나간다. 좋은 기억력 또한 대사를 빨리 숙지해야 하므로 배우에게는 꼭 필요하다. 그들은 정기적으로 (주어지는) 건설적 비판을 수용하고 달라지는 일련의 기대 사항들에 맞출 필요가 있다. 배우 생활 내내 배우가 이 자질들을 키우는 데 계속 힘을 쏟는 것은 매우 중요하다. 대부분의 배우가 지방 극단에서 공짜로 연기하고 정기적으로 열리는 연기 수업과 세미나에 참석함으로써 이를 달성한다. 많은 이들에게 이곳이 그들의 직업 훈련이 시작되는 곳이다. 그것들은 또한 이용할 수 있는 가장 효과적인 네트워크 기회 중 하나를 제공한다. 또한 입소문을 통해 퍼지는 좋은 평판은 (배우를) 열망하는 배우가 소망해 볼 수 있는 아마도 가장 좋은 도구일 것이다.

어휘 **individual** 개인 **critical** 비판적인 **interpret** 해석하다, 이해하다 **call on** 요청하다, 시키다 **portray** (그림, 글로) 묘사하다, (인물을) 연기하다 **line** 대사 **constructive** 건설적인, 도움이 되는 **on a regular basis** 규칙적으로, 정기적으로 **adjust to** ~에 맞추다, ~에 적응하다 **expectation** 기대, 예상 **quality** 자질, 특성 **reputation** 평판 **aspire** 열망하다

구문 17~20행 And **a good reputation** (spread by word-of-mouth) is possibly **the best tool** [an aspiring actor or actress can hope for].
(a good reputation (spread by word-of-mouth): S, the best tool [...]: C)

022 ④

해설 (A) 2, 3학년 전학생들의 의무사항을 얘기하고 있는 문장으로 요구하는(require) 주체는 학교 당국이고, 학생들은 '~하도록 요구받는(are required to)' 입장이므로 수동태가 맞다.

(B) 3학년 전학생은 대기 명단에 '더해지는' 입장이므로 to부정사를 수동형으로 쓴 to be added가 알맞다.

(C) LPQ 작성의 목적(~하기 위하여)을 설명하는 부분이므로 to부정사로 쓰는 것이 맞다. *cf.* be used to v-ing: v하는 데 익숙하다.

해석 2, 3학년 전학생은 면제 조건 중 하나를 충족시키지 못하면 전원 캠퍼스 내에 살아야 한다. 전학생은 보통 비슷한 연령과 학년의 다른 학생과 함께 캠퍼스 곳곳에 있는 숙소에 배당된다. 전학생은 신입생과는 함께 묵지 않는다. 우리 사무소는 특정 주거지나 특정 방에 대한 요청을 수용하지 않는다. 의료적 필요로 인해 특정한 숙소가 필요한 학생은 학사 자원 센터(202-687-8354)로 연락해야 한다. 1인실은 3, 4학년만 이용할 수 있다. 3학년 전학생은 주거생활소에 더 자세한 내용을 알아보아 1인실 대기 명단에 추가로 넣어지도록 요청할 수 있다. 3, 4학년 학생만 대학 소유의 타운하우스에 사는 것이 허용된다. 주거 선호도 설문지를 작성해야 하는데, 이것은 작성자와 선호도가 비슷한 학생을 짝 맞출 용도로 사용될 것이다.

어휘 **sophomore** 2학년 **transfer student** 전학생 **require** 요구하다 ***cf.* requirements** 필요한 것, 필요조건 **assign** 배당하다 **house** 묵게 하다, 집에 들이다 **accommodate** ~을 수용하다 **request** 요청(하다) **residential** 거주의, 거주에 관한 **resource** 자원 **permit** 허락하다 **preference** 선호 **questionnaire** 설문지

023 ⑤ | are → is

해설 ⑤ 주어가 poverty로 단수이므로 is로 써야 한다. resulting in A, B, and C의 수식어구가 뒤에서 꾸며주고 있는 구조.

① '계속'의 의미로 쓰이고 있는 현재완료. 지난 4천 년 이상 '죽' 영향을 끼쳐 왔다.
② 주어가 It이므로((It) spreads ~) 단수형으로 맞게 쓰였다.
③ occur(일어나다, 발생하다)는 수동태로 쓰이지 않는 자동사. 단수주어에 맞게 쓰였다. TB에 관한 일반적인 사실이므로 현재시제로 쓰였다.
④ 학교 교육을 받았다면 병의 전염성 등 병에 대해 잘 알고 병에 걸리지 않게 대처했을 것이다. '거의 ~ 않는'의 의미인 little이 맞게 쓰였다.

해석 결핵은 인류에게 4천 년 이상 영향을 끼쳐 온 오래된 질병이다. 그것은 마이코 박테리아 결핵균이라는 대장균으로 인해 발생하는 만성 질병으로 공기를 통해 이 사람 저 사람 전파된다. 가난과 결핵의 관계는 잘 알려져 있고, 높은 결핵 발병률은 사회의 가장 빈곤한 구역에서 발견된다. 결핵은 인구 밀집 지역에 사는 저소득층과 교육을 거의 못 받는 사람들에게서 흔히 발병한다. 가난은 나쁜 섭생을 초래할 수 있는데, 그것이 면역 기능 변화와 연관될 수 있다. 이와 동시에 밀집 주거 환경과 나쁜 환기 상태, 비위생적인 습관을 초래하는 가난이 결핵의 전파 위험을 더 높이기 쉽다. 결핵 관련한 지식, 태도, 습관 또한 빈민들 사이에 그 병이 널리 퍼지게 되는 데 결정적인 역할을 한다.

어휘 **mankind** 인류 **chronic** 만성의, 옛날부터 내려오는 **association** 연관, 결합 **section** 부문, 구획 **nutrition** 영양, 섭생 **alteration** 변화, 변경 **immune function** 면역 기능 **ventilation** 환기, 통풍 **hygiene** 위생 **transmission** 전파 **regarding** ~에 관한, ~ 관련한 **prevalence** 널리 퍼짐, 만연

024 ② | is required → requires

해설 ② 동사 require 다음에 목적어와 목적격보어가 이어 나오는 <require +O+to-v> 구조가 알맞다. 주어(almost every job)가 단수이므로 requires로 써야 한다.

① 지금 멘토가 우리에게 전하는 철학을 '그러지 않았다면(otherwise: 멘토가 주지 않았다면)'으로 가정해 보는 내용. otherwise가 가정법의 if절, 이어지는 내용이 귀결절에 해당한다. 이 모두가 관계대명사절로, 선행사 philosophies를 수식하는 구조이다. would have had to wait(기다렸어야 했을: 과거 일을 반대로 가정), 또는 would have to(기다려야 할지도 모를: 현재 일을 반대로 가정)로 쓸 수 있다.
③ 집짓기에 비유하여 the new generation이 그 상황에 대처할 수 있도록 '만들어진' 것이므로 현재완료 수동태형이 적절.
④ grew up에서 그렇게 컸다는 '과거'를 강조하여 쓴 강조의 조동사.
⑤ 동사 wait를 꾸며주므로 부사 patiently가 맞게 쓰였다.

해석 멘토는 우리가 놓치고 있는 지식을 제공하고 새로운 연결성으로 통하는 문을 열어주고 그러지 않았다면 몇 년씩 걸려서야 알게 됐을 철학을 우리에게 전한다. 기업들이 이제 더 이상 그 모델에 투자하지 않는데, 그것이 요즘 거의 모든 구인목록이 지원자가 '주도적으로 일할' 것을 요구하는 이유이다. 그것이 진정으로 의미하는 것은 "나는 네 손을 잡아줘야 하는 걸 원치 않는다."로 그것 자체가 의미하는 바는 "난 네게 가르칠 시간이나 에너지가 없어."이다. 이것이 신규 채용자들을 죽느냐 사느냐의 상황에 처하게 하기도 하지만, 한편 새 세대는 이를 다루도록 만들어졌다. 새천년 세대는 그들의 상관이 짐작하는 것보다 더 자족적인데, 어쨌든 우리는 인터넷 검색엔진과 구글 툴을 손가락 끝으로 다루며 성장했다. 우리들 대부분이 주선된 결혼이라는 것을 꺼릴 것과 꼭 마찬가지로 너를 위해 참을성 있게 기다리고 있는 주선된 멘토링이라는 것은 없다. 현대 세계에서 멘토는 주어지는 게 아니라 만들어지는 것이다.

어휘 **mentor** 멘토(경험 없는 사람에게 오랜 기간에 걸쳐 조언과 도움을 베풀어 주는 유경험자) **impart** (지식 등을) 전하다, 주다 **invest** 투자하다 **applicant** 지원자, 후보자 **initiative** 주도, 적극성 **in itself** 그 자체 **new hire** 신규 채용자 **millenial** 새천년 세대 (2000년 출간된 <Millennials Rising: The Next Great Generation>에 등장하는 개념으로 새천년을 앞두고 태어나고 성장한 세대를 가리킴.) **self-sufficient** 자급자족하는 **assume** 지레짐작하다, 추정하다 **arranged** 주선된, 마련된

025 ①

해설 (A) let이 사역동사이므로 목적격보어로 원형부정사 ring이 알맞다.
(B) they가 호텔 측을 말하고 호텔이 지정한 장소이므로 능동의 had chosen이 맞다. 기다리고 서 있었던 게 과거(stood)이고 장소 지정은 그 이전이었을 것이므로 과거완료로 쓰였다.
(C) 형용사가 올 자리이므로 '(거리가) 가까운'의 뜻인 close가 알맞다. closely(아주, 유심히)는 부사로 주로 일반동사와 함께 쓰인다(*e.g.* look closely(자세히 관찰하다), closely related(밀접하게 관련되다))

해석 우리 비행기는 자정에 착륙했다. 우리는 셔틀을 불렀고, 20분 기다리면 도착할 거라는 얘기를 들었다. 밤 한 시, 셔틀이 아직 도착하지 않았다. 우리는 어린 아이들 몇을 포함해서 모두 10명이 무리를 이뤄 여행 중이었다. 우리는 호텔에 다시 전화했지만 아무도 전화를 받지 않았다. 나는 그것(전화벨)이 32번까지 울리게 둬야 했다. 와우[대단하지 않은가]! 그러고는 들은 말이 셔틀이 우리를 찾아 헤맸으나 찾을 수 없었고, 운전자가 이제 근무가 끝나서 셔틀을 이용할 수 없다는 것이었다. 그것이 이상한 이유는, 우리는 그쪽에서 정한 장소에 한 시간 동안이나 서 있었기 때문이다. 그래서 우리는, 아주 무례하게도, 택시를 타라는 말을 들었다. 진담으로 말이다! 그래서 우리는 택시를 두 대 잡아 탔다. 호텔은 가까웠으나 택시 한 대당 12달러나 나왔다 — 물론 별 건 아니었다[실은 엄청난 일이었다]. 호텔 접수대는 명백히 고객 서비스를 위해 만들어진 게 아니었다.

어휘 **flight** 비행편 **land** 착륙하다 **be unable to** ~할 수 없다 **shift** 교대근무 **available** 이용 가능한 **weird** 이상한, 기괴한 **designated spot** 지정된 장소 **seriously** 진심으로, 진지하게 **grab** 움켜잡다 **Not a big deal.** 별것도 아니다. **reception** (호텔 등의) 접수처, 프런트 **design** 고안되다, 의도되다

026 ③ | see → seeing

해설 ③ '~하는 데 익숙해져 있다'이므로 are (so) used to 다음에 동명사 형태(seeing)가 되어야 한다.

① trolling을 가리키는 소유격 its.
② 주어 It(Trolling)의 구체적인 양상을 설명하는 주격보어 부분으로 동명사 sending이 맞게 쓰였다. 이어지는 creating and sharing ~, hacking ~ and using ~ 모두 병렬구조로 같은 동명사형이다.
④ 목적어(celebrities and high-profile people)가 troll 당하고 있는 걸 보는(see) 것이므로 목적격보어 자리에 v-ing 아닌 수동형 being trolled가 쓰였다.
⑤ 전문 용어인 선행사 bystander effect를 구체적으로 설명하는 부분으로, 관계부사 where가 맞게 쓰였다. where가 추상적인 의미의 장소 개념으로 쓰인 경우이다.

해석 우리는 트롤 — 온라인상의 희롱 — 하면 유명인, 기자, 그리고 강한 의견을 온라인상에서 겁 없이 나누고자 하는 어떤 사람을 떠올린다. 그러나 트롤은 대중의 눈에 들어오는 사람들만 영향을 끼치는 게 아니고, 그 희생자들 가운데 몇몇은 아직 학교를 떠나지도 않았다. "트롤은 다양한 형태를 띨 수 있는데, 그것은 위협적인 메시지를 보내는 것일 수도, 영상을 만들고 공유하는 것일 수도, 사람들의 계정을 해킹하고 곤란하게 할 목적으로 그들의 이름을 사용하는 것일 수도 있다." 라고 전문가는 말한다. 트롤은 페이스북과 인스타그램과 같은, 십 대들이 편하게 느끼는 플랫폼에서 발생하는데, 이곳에서 그들은 그들이 올린 사진에 대해 고약한 논평을 받을 수 있다. 문제는 소셜 미디어의 사용 그 자체에 뿌리 박혀 있다. 아이들은 유명인이나 세간의 이목을 끄는 이들이 트롤 당하는 걸 보는 데 너무 익숙해져 있어서 그들이 통상적인 것으로 여기게 된 것을 그냥 흉내 내고 있는 것이다. "아이들이 유명인을 쫓다가 유명인들이 받는 메시지들을 보게 되고, 한편으로는 (자기들도) 또한 '방관자 효과'의 희생자가 되는데, 이 효과에서 사람들은 자기들이 무슨 짓을 하고 있는지 별생각도 없이 한마디 올리거나 혐오스러운 내용에 '좋아요'를 누르는 것이다."

어휘 **associate A with B** A를 B와 연관 짓다 **harassment** 괴롭힘, 희롱 **celebrity** 유명인사 **journalist** 저널리스트, 기자 **dare to-v** 감히 ~하다 **view** 견해, 관점 **victim** 희생자 ***cf.* fall victim to** ~의 희생양이 되다 **account** 계정 **nasty** 불쾌한, 못된 **high-profile** 세간의 눈에 띄는 **mimic** 흉내 내다, 모방하다 ***cf.*** 현재분사형: **mimicking** **bystander effect** 방관자 효과 (주변에 사람이 많을수록 책임이 분산되어 오히려 위험에 처한 사람을 덜 돕게 되는 현상) **hateful** 혐오스러운

구문 14~17행 Children are **so** used to *seeing* celebrities and high-profile people (O′) *being trolled* online (OC′) **that** they're simply mimicking what they've come to view as normal.

→ <so ~ that ...(너무 ~하여 …하다)> 구조. <see+O+OC>에서 목적어가 trolling의 '대상'이 되는 걸 보는 것이므로 v-ing가 수동형 being p.p.로 쓰였다.

027 ④ | far → farther[further]

해설 ④ 비교급을 강조하는 much가 앞에 쓰이고 있으므로 원급(far)이 아닌 비교급을 쓴 much farther가 되어야 한다. 아래에 삼각형의 수직판이 없는 경우와 비교하고 있다.

① they(=flying objects)의 상태를 설명하는 보어로 형용사(stable)가 맞게 쓰였다.
② serve(수행하다)의 목적어가 문두의 what purpose로, 목적어가 있는 문장이므로 능동태로 쓴 것은 어법상 적절하다.
③ 나무에서 '떨어지고 있는' 나뭇잎에 비유하고 있으므로 진행을 나타내는 현재분사가 맞게 쓰였다.
⑤ help는 사역동사로 to 없는 원형부정사를 목적어로 취할 수 있다.

해석 로켓에서 비행기, 새에 이르기까지 모든 나는 물체는 뭔가 공통점이 있는데, 날 때 안정적인 자세를 취해야 한다는 것이다. 로켓과 미사일이 보통 바닥에 삼각형의 수직판이 있는 것을 눈여겨봤을지도 모르겠다. 이 수직판들이 하는 일이 뭘까? 바닥에 수직판이 없는 로켓을 만들었다 치자. 처음에는 곧장 앞으로 날겠지만 금방 제어가 안 된 채 나선형으로 돈다. 그것은 나무에서 떨어지는 나뭇잎과 거의 비슷하게 공기 중에서 비틀비틀하다가 땅으로 퍼덕거리며 떨어졌을지도 모른다. 처음에 아주 살짝 돌기 시작해서는 (처음보다) 훨씬 더 빨리 돌기 시작하다가 결국은 완전히 제어가 안 된다. 대조적으로, 수직판이 있는 두 번째 로켓은 곧장 날아서 그 결과 훨씬 더 많이 갔을 것이다. 수직판들이 로켓이 균형을 유지하도록 해주거나 같은 방향으로 계속 향하도록 해주기 때문이다. 로켓이 살짝 돌면 수직판이 원래 방향으로 다시 돌아오도록 도와주는 것이다.

어휘 **object** 물체, 사물 **have ~ in common** ~을 공통점으로 갖고 있다 **stable** 안정적인 **triangular** 삼각의 **fin** 지느러미; 수직판 **base** 바닥, 기저 **serve** 일하다; ~에 쓸모가 있다 **spiral** 나선형으로 돌다 **tumble** 구르다시피 넘어지다 **flutter** 퍼덕거리다, 팔랑거리다 **point** 가리키다 **direction** 방향

구문 10~12행 If it started turning just *a little bit* (A), **then** it would start turning *even more rapidly* (B) **until** it *completely* lost control (C).

→ 단계별로 변하는 양상을 잘 묘사하고 있다.

028 ④ | were assigned → assigned

해설 ④ 주어가 the researchers이고, 동사 뒤에 간접목적어(each of the factors)와 직접목적어(a score based on ~)가 이어 나오므로 능동태(assigned)로 써야 한다.

① put A at risk(A를 위험에 처하게 하다)에서 선행사 various factors가 위험을 유발하는 요소, 즉 동사 put의 주체이므로 능동형으로 쓴 것이 맞다.
② A as well as B(B는 물론 A도)의 구조.
③ other+복수명사.
⑤ an inexpensive and easy way to identify ~에서 identify하는 주체 doctors가 <for+목적격>의 형태로 to 부정사 앞에 쓰인 경우.

해석 새 분석이 노인들을 노년에 심각한 기억 문제에 처하게 하는 다양한 요인들을 알아냈다. 참가자들에게 정신 건강 평가는 물론 정기적인 기억력 테스트가 약 5년에 걸쳐 실시됐다. 연구자들은 알츠하이머의 시작 및 다른 형태의 치매에 앞서 나타나는 기억 손상의 한 형태인 경미한 인지력 손상(MCI)이 있나 살펴보았다. 연구자들은 또한 치매에 걸릴 위험을 높일 수 있는 기타 요인들이 있나 참가자의 의료 차트를 샅샅이 찾아보았다. 데이터를 분석한 후에 연구자들은 경미한 인지 손상을 가져올 수 있는 위험을 높이는 요인들의 목록을 규명하고 각각의 요인들에 사고 문제를 일으킬 위험에 얼마나 기여하는가를 토대로 점수를 부여하였다. 이 위험표가 누가 기억 문제용 심화 진단을 받아야 하는지를 의사가 알아낼 수 있는 저가의 편리한 방법이 될 것으로 기대된다.

어휘 **analysis** 분석 ***cf.*** **analyze** 분석하다 **assessment** 평가 **mild** 경미한, 가벼운 **precede** ~보다 우선하다, 선행하다 **onset** 개시, 공격 **comb** 꼼꼼히 훑다, 구석구석 수색하다 **heighten** 높이다, 강화하다 **identify** 정체를 파악하다, 알아내다 **assign** 부여하다, 배정하다 **scale** 등급, 눈금, 자, 저울 **undergo** ~을 받다, 경험하다

029 ③ | equating → equated (to)

해설 ③ 문장 구조상 동사가 와야 할 자리이고 지나간 일을 얘기하고 있으므로 equated (to)가 되어야 한다. this 'lack of knowing'이 주어.

① what will happen이 동사 know의 목적어절. 앞으로 일어날 일에 대한 얘기이므로 미래시제가 맞게 쓰였다.
② Spain을 설명하는 보어로 형용사 safe가 맞게 쓰였다.
④ 앞에 나온 명사 notifications를 꾸며주는 형용사적 용법으로 쓰인 to부정사.
⑤ 문장 전체를 꾸며주는 부사가 문장의 맨 앞에 적절히 쓰인 경우.

해석 인생은 전부 약간의 도박이다. 그것은 차를 렌트하는 데 '충돌 보험'을 들 것인가 말 것인가를 정하는 것과 같다. 많은 경우에 아마도 그게 필요 없을지 모르지만 무슨 일이 생길지는 전혀 알 수 없다. 한번은 내가 스페인과 모로코로 여자 친구와 여행을 갔다. 스페인은 안전하게 느껴졌지만 모로코는 어떤가? 그곳의 의료 관행에 대해서나 범죄에 대해 우리는 전혀 몰랐고, 이 '앎의 부족'이 우리 마음에는 약간의 위험과 같은 걸로 여겨졌다. 여행자 보험을 드는 것이 잘하는 일 같아 보였고, 나의 직관이 그러라고 했다. 나는 그것을 후회하지 않았다. 모로코에서의 첫날, 수하물이 우리와 함께 도착하지 않았다. 우리는 짐이 언제 어디로 도착할지 알지 못했고, 공항에 와서 찾아가라는 엉터리 통보도 받았지만... 짐은 없었다. 떠나기 이틀 전 마침내 우리는 짐을 돌려받았다. 내 가방은 그대로였지만 여자 친구의 보석은 도난당했다. 다행히도 우리는 보험에 들어 있었다.

어휘 **gamble** 도박 **collision** 충돌 **insurance** 보험 ***cf.*** **insure** 보험을 들다 **medical practice** 의료 관행 **equate** 동일시하다, 같은 것으로 보다 **intuition** 직관 **regret** 후회하다 **luggage** 수하물, 여행 가방 **notification** 통보, 알림, 고지 **show up** 나타나다, 출두하다 **belongings** 소지품, (내 소유의) 물건

구문 06~09행 We knew nothing *about* medical practices there (A) or of crime (B) and this 'lack of knowing' (S), (in our minds), equated (V) a bit of danger (O).

030 ③ | assuming → assume

해설 ③ assuming으로 시작한다면 주어가 끝나는 곳에 동사가 나와야 하는데 목적절 that으로 이어질 뿐 따로 동사가 나오지 않으므로 assume이 동사가 되어야 한다. 명령문 구조의 문장이다.

① 전치사 뒤에 동명사가 온 구조.
② 온갖 방식으로 잘못 판단할 수 있는 점, 즉 빠져들 수 있는 다양한 논리적 오류들을 얘기하고 있으므로 복수명사로 맞게 쓰였다.
④ 추측을 나타내는 must(~임에 틀림없다)로 assume, reasoning한 사례로 알맞다.
⑤ the guy who sees ~ and concludes ~로 이어지는 병렬구조로, 선행사가 단수(the guy)인 주격 관계대명사 뒤의 동사형으로 맞게 표현되었다.

해석 '오류'는 논리적인 추론 (과정)에서 나는 실수로, 대개 잘못된 가정에 입각했을 때 발생한다. 연구자들은 잘못 (사고해) 나갈 수 있는 온갖 방식—그들이 취약한 오류들—에 아주 친숙하다. 가장 흔한 것들 중 두 가지가 '생태적 오류(ecological fallacy)'와 '예외 오류(exception fallacy)'이다. '생태적 오류'는 개개인에 대한 결론을 그룹 데이터 분석에만 근거하여 낼 때 일어난다. 예를 들어 특정 학급의 수학 점수를 측정하고는 그들이 그 지구에서 가장 평균 점수가 높다는 걸 알게 됐다고 가정해 보라. 나중에(아마도 쇼핑몰에서) 그 반 아이 하나를 우연히 보게 되고는 속으로 "걔는 수학 신동임이 틀림없어."라고 생각하는 것이다. '예외 오류'는 생태적 오류의 일종의 반대 경우이다. 그것은 예외적인 경우에 입각해서 한 그룹에 대한 결론을 내릴 때 일어난다. 전형적인 예는 여자가 운전 실수를 하는 것을 보고는 "여자들은 형편없는 운전자들이야."라고 결론짓는 남자의 경우이다.

어휘 **fallacy** 오류, 틀린 생각 **reason** 논리적으로 생각하다, 추론하다 **based on** ~에 기반하여 **assumption** 가정, 추정 **be susceptible to** ~의 영향을 받기 쉬운, ~에 취약한 **ecological** 생태학적인 **exception** 예외 ***cf.*** **exceptional** 예외적인, 이례적인 **analysis** 분석 **(*pl.* analyses)** **assume** 가정하다, 추측하다 **district** 지구, 구역 **run into** 우연히 마주치다 **whiz** 신동 **reverse** 역(의), 반대(의)

구문 08~11행 For instance, assume that *you* **measured** the math scores of a particular classroom and **found** that they had the highest average score in the district.

→ assume의 목적절이 두 개의 동사부로 이뤄져 있고, found가 다시 목적어절을 취한 구조.

17~19행 The stereotype is of *the guy* [who **sees** (V') a woman (O') make a driving error (OC') and **concludes** (V') that "women are terrible drivers] (O')."

031 ③

해설 (A) that절의 콤마(,) 이하는 microbiome에 대한 부수적인 설명에 지나지 않으므로 that절의 주어(artificial sweeteners)에 이어 동사(alter)가 올 자리이다.
(B) 지시대명사 That은 문장의 주어가 되어 버리므로 이어지는 두 번째 is와 문맥상으로도 구조상으로도 자연스럽게 연결되지 않는다. 선행사를 포함하는 관계대명사 What 주어절에 이어 이를 설명하는 보어절이 이어지는 것이(What is scary about this / is / that ~) 자연스럽다.
(C) Nothing과 healthy child의 sweet한 정도를 비교하는 비교 문장. be동사와 함께 형용사가 쓰이는 게 자연스럽다.

해석 새 연구가 인공 감미료가 소화기 계통에 사는 박테리아군인 미생물 군집을 변형시킨다는 점을 보여줬다. 일련의 실험에서 과학자들이 인공감미료인 사카린을 10주 된 쥐들의 마실 물에 섞었다. 다른 쥐들은 아무것도 안 들어간 물이나 포도당 또는 그냥 보통 설탕을 보충한 물을 마셨다. 일주일 후 그냥 물이나 설탕물을 마신 쥐들에게는 변화가 거의 없었으나 인공 감미료를 섭취한 그룹은 포도당에 눈에 띄게 과민 반응을 보였다. 이 사실에 관해 무서운 점은 신체가 다량의 설탕 처리 능력이 떨어지는 상태인 포도당 과민이 신진대사 장애와 당뇨와 같은 보다 심각한 질병으로 이어질 수 있다는 것이다. 건강한 아이만큼 달콤한[사랑스러운] 것은 없으니, 우리 모두 인공 감미료를 그만 먹자.

어휘 **artificial sweetener** 인공 감미료 **alter** 변경하다, 바꾸다 **digestive system** 소화기 계통 **plain** 아무것도 들어 있지 않은 **supplemented with** ~로 보충된 **ordinary** 평범한 **intolerance** 참지 못함, 과민함 **cope with** ~에 대처하다 **metabolic syndrome** 신진대사 장애 **diabetes** 당뇨병 **lay off** ~을 그만 먹다

구문 11~15행 **What** is scary about this (S) is (V) [that (C) *glucose intolerance*, (S′) [in which the body is less able to cope with large amounts of sugar], can lead (V′) to more serious illnesses like metabolic syndrome and diabetes].

→ 주어절에 이어 보어절(that절)이 이어지고 있다. 보어절의 주어를 부연 설명하는 관계사절(in which ~)이 앞뒤 콤마로 삽입된 구조이다.

032 ② | freely → free

해설 ② 주어(The prisoner)가 탈출해 '자유의 몸이 된' 것이므로 명사인 주어를 보충해 주는 형용사 free로 표현되어야 한다.

① a hospital(선행사)에서 구체적으로 무슨 일이 벌어졌는지 설명하는 내용이 이어 나온다. where가 at the hospital을 대신하므로 장소의 관계부사 where가 맞게 쓰였다.
③ 경찰이 추정하는 '현재'의 그의 행적이 나오는 부분으로, to부정사를 단순형, 진행형으로 쓴 것이 적절하다.
④ 병원으로 호송된 것이 과거(was taken to a local hospital)로 표현되었으므로 그 이전의 감금 상태는 과거완료 (had been held by ~)로 표현된 게 적절하다.
⑤ 데려간 것은 경찰, 범인은 호송'된' 것이므로 수동태로 맞게 표현되었다. take A to B: A를 B로 데려가다

해석 무장한 죄수가 화요일 오전 Washington시 근방 Virginia 북쪽 소재 병원에서 탈출 후 도주 중이고, 이곳에서 경호원과 몸싸움을 벌이던 중 총알 한 방이 발사됐다고 경찰이 전했다. Fairfax 카운티 경찰서가 Wossen Assaye라고 신원을 밝힌 죄수는 그 병원에서 사설 경호원에게서 탈출해 경호원의 무기를 갖고 달아났다고 트위터를 통해 경찰서는 밝혔다. 경찰은 앞부분에 손상이 있고 차량 번호가 XZP-8153인 2002 Toyota Camry로 파악된 도난 차를 탈주범이 운전 중인 것으로 여겨진다고 말했다. 또한 여자 친구와 동행일 수도 있다고 경찰은 밝혔는데, 그녀의 사진은 트위터에 올라와 있으나 이름은 언급되지 않았다. 경찰에 따르면, Assaye는 무장 은행 강도의 죄목으로 근처 Alexandria시에 감금되어 있다가 자해 시도 후 지방병원에 후송됐다.

어휘 **armed** 무장한, 무기를 사용하는 **on the run** 도주 중인 **fire** 발사하다 **guard** 경호원, 보안요원 **identified as** 정체가 ~로 밝혀진 **security** 보안, 안전 **flee** (**fled-fled**) 도주하다 **via** ~을 통해서, ~을 경유하여 **license plate** 차량 번호판 **nearby** 근처의, 가까운 곳의 **on charges of** ~의 죄목으로 **robbery** 강도(사건), 강도질

구문 09~12행 Police said he was thought to be driving *a stolen car* (identified as a 2002 Toyota Camry) (**with** damage (A) (to the front) (B) [and] the license plate number XZP-8153 (B′)).

→ a stolen car가 차종(A), 차 상태(B) 및 차량번호(B′)의 수식어들로 수식되고 있는 구조.

033 ④ | is → are

해설 ④ my favorite anti-hero characters가 주어로 복수이므로 are로 써야 한다.

① <what+주어(the right thing to do)+동사(is)>의 간접의문문 어순이 맞게 쓰였다.
② 비교급 대상이 나와 있지 않지만 (결점이 없고 결정이 어렵지 않은 인물들보다) 결점이 있고 결정을 힘들어하는 인물들에 '더' 공감한다는 비교급 표현이다.
③ who I would be가 전체 문장의 보어로 쓰이는 명사절.
⑤ that 이하는 message의 내용을 구체적으로 보여주는 동격의 that.

해석 십 대 때 나는 마음이 너무나 순수한 영웅들에게는 전혀 공감할 수가 없었다. 그들은 늘 무엇이 해야 할 옳은 일인지 알고 있다. 그리고 그들이 그것을 하기란 너무 쉽다. 청년으로서 무엇이 옳고 그른지 하는 생각으로 늘 고심해야 했기 때문에 나는 그들에게 끌리지 않았다. 실은 나는 결점이 있고 옳은 선택을 하는 데 더 어려움을 겪는 영웅들에게 더 공감할 수 있었다. 나는 "나랑 비슷한 녀석이 하나 있네."라고 생각했던 것 같다. 그들은 내가 될 수 있는 바로 그런 존재였다. 나는 내가 좋아하는 반영웅 인물들이 결함은 있지만 자기 자신과 주변 사람들에게 영광과 위대함을 이뤄낼 수 있다는 사실이 좋다. 순수한 마음의 영웅은 반면, 완벽한 이들만이 위대함을 이뤄낼 수 있다는 메시지를 전달한다.

어휘 **relate to** 자기 얘기처럼 느끼다, ~을 이해하다 **pure** 순수한, 흠 없는 **struggle with** ~하느라 애쓰다, 고군분투하다 **versus** ~대 …, ~와 대비해서 **flaw** 결점, 결함, 흠; 결점[흠집]을 내다 **glory** 영광

구문 11~14행 I like the fact **that** (동격의 that) my favorite anti-hero characters, (S′) [while (*they are*) flawed] (종속절), are able to achieve (V′) glory and greatness **for** themselves [and] **for** others around them.

→ 동격의 that절이 다시 주절과 종속절로 나뉜 구조. 종속절이 주절 사이에 삽입된 경우.

핵심 예상문제 12

034 ⑤ 035 ① 036 ① | 본문 57p

034 ⑤

해설 (A) 선행사가 something으로 단수이므로 주격 관계대명사 뒤 동사의 모양으로는 rhymes가 맞다.
(B) be in tune with(~와 조화를 이루다)에 부사 수식어(consciously(의식적으로))가 어울린다.
(C) 부사어구 not only가 문장의 앞에 나와 있으므로 주어와 동사가 도치되는 것이 자연스럽다.

해석 랩은 말, 산문, 시, 노래의 요소를 포함한 (곡에) 영향을 미치는 요소들이 복잡하게 섞인 것이다. 훌륭한 래퍼가 되기 위해서는 '리듬'을 이해할 필요가 있다. 랩을 한다는 것은 운이 맞는 뭔가를 그냥 말하는 것 그 이상이다. 랩을 하고 싶으면 뼛속 깊이 그 음악에 대한 느낌을 가져야 할 것이다. 당신의 머리와 몸이 의식적으로 비트를 맞추지 못하면 당신이 하는 랩은 딱딱하고 부자연스럽게 느껴질 것이다. 이 분야에서 나아지기 위해서는 좋아하는 랩을 들을 때 말의 내용은 무시하려고 애쓰라. 기악곡만 들으면서 말의 흐름이 그 비트에 어떻게 어울려 들어가는지 들으라. 비트박스를 리듬을 익히는 수단으로 고려해 볼 수도 있다. 이는 리듬을 이해하는 데에도 도움이 될 뿐 아니라 일단 직접 랩핑을 시작하면 유용한 기술이 될 수도 있다.

어휘 **rap** 랩(음악의 한 종류); 톡톡 두드림 **complex** 복잡한 **mix** 조합, 섞인 것 **element** 요소, 성분 **prose** 산문 **rhyme** 운(음조가 비슷한 글자); 운이 맞다 **in tune with** ~와 장단을 맞춘, ~와 조화되어 **stiff** 뻣뻣한, 경직된 **instrumental** 기악곡 **fit into** ~에 꼭 들어맞다, ~에 어울리다 **beatboxing** 비트박스(입으로 드럼 소리를 내기)

035 ① | leading → leads

해설 ❶ 내용상 walking과 leading의 병렬구조가 아니라 loses ~와 leads ~의 병렬 구조이다. and가 없다면 leading ~이 가능하다(loses ~, leading ~).

② jacket이 장식되는 것이므로 수동형 분사로 맞게 수식되고 있다. decorate A with B(A를 B로 장식하다)에서 A가 jacket.
③ 내가 일요학교에서 네 살짜리 학생들에게 들려준 '그 이야기가 지니고 있는' 의미로, 대명사 소유격이 잘 쓰였다.
④ 얘기를 들은 후 두고두고 그 이야기를 하고 다닌 '과거의 일'에 대해 그 이유를 '추측'해 보고 있으므로 may have p.p. 형태로 쓰였다.
⑤ as well as를 전후로 비교되고 있는 것이 the thirst와 the capacity로, 명사가 같은 형태로 잘 쓰인 경우이다.

해석 하루는 두꺼비가 밖에서 걸어 다니다가 단추를 하나 잃어버려서 친구인 개구리와 함께 성과도 없는, 좌절감만 주는 수색—앞서 다녔던 길을 한 발짝 한 발짝 되돌아가 보는—을 내내 같이하게 하고서야 단추가 집에 있었음을 알게 된다. 당황스러워서 그는 길을 죽 따라가며 주워 모은 단추 전부로 장식된 특별한 재킷을 개구리에게 만들어준다. 이것은 내가 일요학교의 네 살짜리 학생들에게 해준 이야기이다. 그중 많은 아이들이 그것을 듣고 나서 날이면 날마다 얘기하고 다닌 게 생각난다. 그 이야기는 그 표현들은 단순하지만 그 의미에 있어서는 전혀 단순하지 않다. 학생들에게 그것은 신의 있고 배려하는 친구란 어떤 것인가에 관한 의미심장한 질문을 제기했을지도 모른다. 물론 이 질문들은 그들의 어린 마음들이 명확히 표현해 내기에는 너무 난해했겠지만 말이다. 그 나이에도 그들에게 이해와 통찰력에 도달하는 능력과 갈증이 있었던 것이다. 그렇게 해서 바로 깊이 읽기가 시작되는 것이다.

어휘 **toad** 두꺼비 **fruitless** 성과 없는, 헛된 **retrace** (왔던 길을) 되짚어가다 **far from** ~와는 거리가 멀다, ~는 전혀 아니다 **significant** 중대한, 의미심장한 **loyal** 충실한, 신의 있는 **caring** 배려심이 있는 **formulate** 공식화하다, 명확하게 나타내다 **thirst** 갈증 **A as well as B** B는 물론 A도 **capacity** 역량, 능력 **illumination** 이해, 계몽 **insight** 통찰력

구문 11~15행 For the students, it may have raised significant questions about what **it**(가주어) means ∨ **to be** a loyal and caring friend(진주어), even if these questions were **too** difficult **for** *their young minds* **to** clearly formulate.

→ <too ~ to ...(…하기에는 너무 ~한)> 구조에 의미상의 주어 <for+목적격>이 to부정사 앞에 쓰인 경우.

036 ① | Imagining → Imagine

해설 ❶ Imagining ~에 이어 동사가 나오지 않으므로 문장의 시작이 동사인 명령문 (Imagine (that) ~) 형태가 되어야 한다.

② any가 부사(faster)를 수식하는 부사로 쓰인 경우. '조금[약간]이라도'의 의미.
③ 주어(the wave's "frequency")에 맞게 단수동사형으로 쓰였다.
④ 부정문이므로 something이 아닌 anything이 쓰인 경우.
⑤ the change가 detect의 대상이므로 to be detected로 맞게 쓰였다. the change is too small to detect로도 쓰인다.

해석 넘실거리는 대양 위 보트에 앉아 있다고 상상해 보라. 아래로 파도가 지나가면서 보트는 물속에서 부드럽게 아래위로 오르락내리락한다. 이제, 그 보트가 물살을 가르고 속도를 내고 있다. 물결이 조금이라도 더 빨리 지나가는가? 아니다, 실제로는 그렇지 않다. 그러나 당신은 변화를 알아챌 것이다. 물살을 뚫고 지나가면서 더 많은 물결 위를 더 자주 타고 지나가게 될 것이다. 이것이 (당신의 새 관점에서) 물결의 '빈도'가 증가했다고 말하는 것이다. 빛도 하나의 물결이다. 따라서 '빛의 물결'을 향해 달려갈 때 그 빈도도 증가한다. '빛의 물결'에서 벗어나는 쪽으로 달려가는 것은 그 빈도를 줄일 것이다. 일상적인 것들의 속도로는 아무것도 눈치채지 못하겠지만 달리게 되면 (눈은 빛의 빈도[주파수]를 색상으로 인식하기 때문에) 사실상 주변 사물의 색상이 변한다(물론 그 변화가 감지되기에는 너무 작긴 하지만). 천문학자들은 이 현상을 줄곧 관찰하는데, 우리 쪽으로 오는 별들은 보다 푸른색(고주파수)처럼 보이는 데 반해 우리에게서 멀어지는 별들은 보다 붉은색(저주파수)으로 보인다.

어휘 **waves** 파도, 물결 **up and down** 아래위로 **perspective** 관점, 시각 **frequency** 빈도, 주파수 **interpret** 해석하다, 풀이하다 **object** 물체, 사물 **detect** 감지하다, 탐지하다 **astronomer** 천문학자 **observe** 관찰하다 **phenomenon** 현상

037 ④

해설 (A) have experience (in) v-ing: v하는 데 경험이 있다
(B) work는 목적어를 바로 취하지 않는 동사. work on(~에 노력을 들이다, ~을 착수하다)의 대상이 the specific project이다.
(C) remember가 앞으로 할 일을 표현할 때(~하는 것을 잊지 않다, ~할 것을 기억하다)는 동명사가 아닌 to부정사 목적어(remember to bring)를 취한다.

해석 글쓰기 센터 개인 교습은 경험 있는 작가에게서 피드백과 지도를 받을 수 있는 기회이다. 지도해 줄 개인 교사는 다양한 학과 학생들을 도운 경험이 있는 대학원 또는 학부 학생이 될 것이다. 수업은 협력적인 것이 될 걸로 예상하면 된다. 개인 교사를 글쓰기 기술을 전반적으로 개발하는 데 도움이 될 전략뿐만 아니라 지금 진행하고 있는 구체적인 프로젝트에 통찰력을 제공해 줄 수 있는 글쓰기 코치라고 생각하라. 시간 약속을 잡으려면 계정 등록이 필요할 것이다. 계정이 생긴 다음에는 로그인만 하면 된다. 일정표에 있는 흰색 네모 칸 중 하나에 클릭하여 온라인상에서 시간 약속을 잡을 수 있을 것이다. 과제 복사본 한 부와, 강사의 채점 기준, 논문 초안을 개인교습에 가져와야 하는 걸 잊지 마라.

어휘 **tutoring session** 개인교습 (시간) **graduate** 석사 과정의 (학생) **undergraduate** 학부 과정의 (학생) **a range of** 다양한 ~ **discipline** 학과, 학문 분야 **collaborative** 협력적인, 합작의 **insight** 통찰력 **overall** 전반적으로 **register** 등록하다 **account** 계정 **square** 네모, 정사각형 **assignment** 과제 **instructor** 강사 **criteria** 기준, 표준, 준거 **draft** 초안

구문 06~10행 You can expect your session(O) to be collaborative(OC): consider your tutor(O) *a writing coach*(OC) [**who** can offer insight(A) (into *the specific project*) [(***that***) you are working on]], **as well as** strategies(B) (to help you develop your writing skills overall).

→ <A as well as B(B는 물론 A도)>에서 A가 강조된 패턴이다.

038 ① | faced with → faced[were faced with]

해설 ❶ face(~와 마주하다)는 전치사 없이 목적어를 취하므로 faced로 써야 한다. 수동태 형태인 were faced with로 쓸 수도 있다.

② 유혹하는 것은 아이스크림, 실험집단의 사람들은 유혹되는 것이므로 수동태로 쓰인 것이 맞다. when (they were) tempted에서 they were가 생략된 형태.
③ 둘 중에서 고르는 것이므로 between이 알맞다.
④ a striking gap의 구체적인 수치를 알려주는 부분으로 <with + 명사 + v-ing>의 구조를 보이고 있다. 의미상 주어인 명사와 분사의 관계가 능동이므로 현재분사(-ing)가 알맞게 쓰였다.
⑤ help는 to부정사를 목적어로 취할 수 있는 사역동사이다. to를 생략하고 help frame ~으로도 쓰인다.

해석 한 조사 연구에서 학생들 한 그룹은 유혹이 부딪칠 때마다 마음속으로 "나는 X를 할 수 없어."라고, 두 번째 그룹은 "나는 X를 하지 않아."라고 말하라고 시켰다. 예를 들어 아이스크림으로 유혹받을 때는 각각, "나는 아이스크림을 먹을 수가 없어."와 "나는 아이스크림을 먹지 않아."라고 말하는 것이다. 이 표현들을 반복한 후에 학생들은 각자 연구와 무관한 일련의 질문들에 대답했다. 한 명 한 명 방에서 나가며 답지를 제출할 때 그들은 무료로 맛있는 것을 제공받았다. 학생은 초콜릿 캔디 바와 그래놀라 건강 바 중에서 하나를 고를 수 있었다. 그들의 간식 선택은 첫 번째 그룹은 61%가, 두 번째 그룹은 36%만이 초콜릿 바를 선택하여 눈에 띄는 차이를 보였다. 참으로 우리가 하는 말이 우리가 힘을 발휘하고 스스로를 통제하는지 틀을 정하는 데 도움이 된다.

어휘 **face** ~에 직면하다 ***cf.*** **be faced with** ~와 직면하다 **temptation** 유혹 **respectively** 각각 **unrelated to** ~와 무관한 **hand in** 제출하다 **complimentary** 무료의; 칭찬하는 **striking** 현저한, 두드러진 **frame** 틀을 짜다, 마음의 상태를 정하다 **empowerment** 힘을 실어주기, 힘을 북돋우기

구문 13~16행 Their snack choices showed a striking gap, **with** the first group *choosing* the chocolate candy bar 61% of the time, and the second group ∨ only 36% of the time.

→ <with+명사+v-ing>의 병렬구조. ∨에 choosing the chocolate candy bar가 중복을 피하기 위해 생략되어 있는 구조이다.

039 ⑤ | visibly → visible

해설 ❺ 눈에 띄는 상태로 계속 있기(stay visible)를 권하므로 stay 다음에는 주격보어로 쓰일 수 있는 형용사가 와야 한다. stay[keep, remain] + 형용사: ~한 채로 있다, 계속 ~하다

① '정도'를 나타내는 부사로 쓰인 a little.
② yourself와 the car in front '둘' 사이를 말하므로 between이 적절.
③ to부정사의 부정은 <not + to-v>로 표현한다.
④ 앞 문장에 이어지는 분사구문으로 접속사 없이 잘 표현되었다. 자동 조명 장치 작동 시 낮에 불이 안 들어올 경우 위험으로 이어질 수 있다는 결과의 내용을 담고 있다.

해석 안개는 모든 것을 약간 더 예쁘고 가을 느낌이 나 보이게 할 수 있지만, 운전 중이거나 자전거를 타고 있다면 위험 요소가 될 수 있다. 고속도로 법규에 따르면 가시성이 '심각하게 줄어든' 경우 — 보통 1백 미터 이하로 규정된다 — 전조등을 켜야 한다. 안개 속 운전에 대한 일반 지침은 천천히 운전하기, 앞차와의 사이에 넉넉한 거리 유지하기, 앞뒤 안개등을 켜 놓기 등 상식적이다. 안개등을 어떻게 조작하는지 알고 있어야 하고 자동 조명 장치를 너무 신뢰하지 않도록 주의해야 하는 것이, 차에 이 특징[장치]이 있다면 낮에 혹 불이 안 들어오면 당신과 다른 운전자들을 위험에 빠뜨릴 수 있는 것이다. 최대한 눈에 띄게 있고[가시거리를 유지하고] 쉬엄쉬엄 가는 것이 안전에 도움이 될 것이다.

어휘 **autumnal** 가을의 **hazard** 위험, 위험 요소 **visibility** 가시성, 시계(視界) ***cf.*** **visible** 눈에 보이는, 알아볼 수 있는 **define** 규정하다, 정의하다 **common sense** 상식 **generous** 넉넉한; 관대한 **operate** 작동하다, 운전하다 **rely on** ~에 의존하다 **feature** 특징, 특색 **put A at risk** A를 위험에 빠뜨리다

구문 14~16행 **Staying** as visible as possible and **taking** it easy(S) should help(V) (to) keep you safe(O).

→ 두 개의 동명사가 주어부를 이루고 있고, 목적어부가 <keep+O+OC>의 구조를 취하고 있다. help는 to부정사(to-v), 원형부정사 둘 다를 목적어로 취할 수 있다.

040 ②

해설 (A) 문맥상 '과거'에 그가 원했으면 유명해질 수도 있었다는 내용이므로 '~할 수 있었는데 (안 했다)'는 의미의 could have p.p.가 적절. if절의 의미가 함축된 가정법 과거 완료 구문.

(B) <permit+O+to-v>에서 to부정사를 꾸며주는 게 형용사인지 부사인지 물어보는 문제. 동사를 꾸며주는 건 부사 easily. access는 access to(~로의 접근)의 형태로 명사로도 쓰이나 이 문장에서는 목적어(a vast amount of information ~)를 갖는 동사로 쓰였다.

(C) 동사 is에 이어지는 주격보어 자리이므로 형용사 important가 알맞음. <no less A than B> B 못지않게 A한

해석 팀 버너스리는 빌 게이츠처럼 엄청나게 부자이거나 유명하지는 않다. 그는 그렇게 될 수도 있었지만, 그렇게 되길 원하지 않았다. 그는 주목받는 것을 좋아하지 않는 조용한 사람이다. 그는 월드와이드웹(WWW)을 발명하여 인터넷에 혁명을 일으킨 사람이다. 버너스리의 발명으로 컴퓨터를 가진 사람이면 누구나 쉽게 어떤 주제에 대해서건 엄청난 양의 정보에 접근할 수 있게 되었다. 이것은 컴퓨터의 사용과 사회에 대한 대단한 공헌이다. 어떤 사람들은 그것이 구텐베르크의 인쇄기 못지않게 중요하다고 믿고 있다.

어휘 **extremely** 극도로 **spotlight** 주목, 스포트라이트 **revolutionize** ~에 혁신을 일으키다 **permit** ~을 가능하게 하다, 허락하다 **access** ~에 접근하다 **vast** 엄청난, 광대한 **contribution** 공헌, 기여 **printing press** 인쇄기

041 ③ | as much → as many

해설 ❸ 앞서 언급된 55%, 61%의 수치들이 respondents의 수치로 모두 복수동사로 표현되었으므로 57%도 셀 수 있는 명사의 수치이다. 따라서 as many로 표현되어야 한다.

① 뒤에 문장이 아닌 명사구(the boom ~)가 왔으므로 전치사의 쓰임이 맞다.
② experience가 우리를 engage((주의, 관심을) 끌다, 사로잡다)'시키는' 개념이므로 능동의 -ing형 분사형용사가 쓰인 것이 자연스럽다.
④ 전치사 Besides(~외에도) 뒤에 동명사 명사구가 온 경우.
⑤ (당신 아닌) 누군가 다른 사람(판매자)이 당신의 과일을 (잘) 골라줄 것으로 신뢰'받기'란 드문 일이다. 신뢰하는 것은 구매자, 신뢰받는 것은 판매자(someone else)이므로 수동태로 맞게 표현되었다.

해석 슈퍼마켓에 좋은 뉴스가 있다. 온라인 장보기 선택권에 찾아온 호황에도 불구하고 재래식 가게들이 사라지지는 않을 것 같다. Nielsen에서 나온 새 조사 결과를 보면, 전 세계 응답자의 4분이 1이 온라인으로 식품 주문 방식을 이용하고 있고 55%가 언젠가는 그것(온라인 쇼핑)을 기꺼이 이용하겠다고 답한 반면, 61%는 가게에서 장을 보는 것이 여전히 '즐겁고 흥미로운 경험'이라고 보고했다. 거의 비슷한 수 — 57% — 가 소매점에서 장 보는 것이 '가족들에게 밖에서 보내는 즐거운 하루'라고 답했다. 온라인 장보기가 (시장에서) 성장할 위치에 있긴 하지만 실재하는 가게도 여전히 중요한 기능을 하고 있다. '가족에게 즐거운 하루'를 제공하는 외에도 신선식품과 냉동식품, 음료, 그 밖의 바로 사용하는 것들 같은 몇몇 식품은 그냥 직접 사는 것이 더 적합하다. 온라인으로 천연 산물을 주문해본 사람은 아마 다 경험했듯이 (사는 사람 말고) 누군가 다른 사람이 당신의 과일을 골라줄 것으로 믿고 맡길 수 있는 일은 드물다.

어휘 **brick-and-mortar** 재래식의; 오프라인 거래의 **respondent** 응답자 **engaging** (마음을) 끄는, 매력적인 **retail** 소매의 **in-person** 직접, 몸소 **beverage** 음료 **immediate-use** 바로 사용하는 **produce** (농산물, 수산물 등) 천연 산물 **rare** 드문, 희귀한 **trust** 신뢰하다

구문 07~09행 ~ 61% reported that they still **find** grocery shopping (O) at the store to be an "enjoyable and engaging experience." (OC)

→ <find+O+OC>의 구조로 이때 find는 '~하다고 느끼다, ~을 알다[깨닫다]'의 뜻.

042 ② | safely → safe

해설 ❷ 동사 produce를 produce safely처럼 부사로 수식할 수 있겠으나 이어지는 구조를 보면 safe와 suitable 모두 명사 food를 수식하는 형용사로 쓰인 경우이다.

① manage ~ well의 <동사-부사> 구조.
③ their own records on ~을 가리키는 대명사로, records가 복수이므로 these로 쓰였다.
④ <by -ing> 구조. 전치사의 목적어로 동명사가 쓰인 경우.
⑤ <from A to B>의 구조에서 명사 an approach의 중복을 피해 쓰인 부정대명사 one. one 뒤에 이를 수식하는 관계대명사절이 이어지고 있다.

해석 음식을 파는 업체들이 새 법에 영향을 받게 될 것이다. "새 식품 법안은 식품 안전 절차를 현대화하고 단순화하는 것을 목표로 합니다. 그것은 또한 업체들이 비용을 절감하는 데도 도움이 될 것입니다. 예를 들어, 식품 안전을 잘 관리하는 곳은 덜 빈번한 점검을 받게 될 겁니다."라고 Wellington 시의회 공중보건 관리자인 Helen Jones가 말한다. 새 법안 하에서는 업체 소유주들은 검사 제도에 있어 변화를 겪게 될 것이며 안전하고 적절한 식품을 생산하는 과정을 직접 기록하고 이것을 검사관이 방문했을 때 보여줘야 한다. 변화는 식품 통제안(고위험 식품 — 식당, 카페, 연회 뷔페 업체, 호텔 등) 또는 전국 프로그램 요건들에 맞추느냐(저위험 식품 — 이동 카페에서 판매하는 수제 비스킷 등)를 통해 이행될 것이다. 새 법안은 한 가지로 통일됐던 접근법에서 위험 수준에 따라 업체별로 규제하는 방법으로 나아감으로써 업체와 소비자에게 도움이 되기 위해 만들어진 것이라고 그녀는 말한다.

어휘 **act** 법안, 법령, 조례 **modernize** 현대화하다 **simplify** 단순화하다 **procedure** 절차, 과정 **frequent** 빈번한 **inspection** 검사, 시찰 ***cf.* inspector** 조사관, 검사관 **regime** 체제, 제도 **implement** 시행하다, 행동에 옮기다 **by way of** ~을 거쳐, ~을 통하여 **compliance with** ~을 지켜서, ~을 준수해서 **one-size-fits-all** 두루 적용되는 **regulate** 규제하다, 단속하다

구문 07~11행 Under the new law, business owners will face (A) ~ and will be required (B) *to keep* (a) *their own records on how they are producing* safe (ⓐ) *and* suitable (ⓑ) *food* and *(to) show* (b) *these to inspectors when they visit.*

→ and 좌우로 A와 B(동사부)가 주어 business owners에, a와 b(to부정사구)가 동사 will be required에, ⓐ와 ⓑ(형용사)가 명사 food에 공통으로 걸리는 병렬 구조를 이루고 있다.

16~19행 She says (that) the new law (S′) is designed (V′) (to help businesses and consumers) (by moving **from** a one-size-fits-all approach, **to** one (=an approach) [that regulates businesses according to risk]).

→ 종속절의 주어, 동사 뒤에 새 법안 제정의 '목적, 취지'와 '방법'의 두 개의 수식어구가 이어지고 있다. from A to B: A에서 B로

핵심 예상문제 15

043 ⑤ 044 ③ 045 ③ | 본문 60p

043 ⑤ | you've been thought → you've been thinking

해설 ⑤ have been thought는 수동태로서 문맥상 주어 you와 어울리지 않는다. 계속 마음을 떠나지 않았던, 즉 당신이 계속 '생각하고 있었던' 것이므로 현재완료 진행형 have been thinking으로 써야 자연스럽다.

① 동사구 put off의 대명사 목적어를 동사와 부사 사이에 쓴 경우. put off it이라고는 하지 않는다.
② 늘 하는 습성이므로 to부정사의 단순형으로 쓴 것이 맞다.
③ 전치사 뒤에 오는 동사는 동명사형으로 쓰는 것이 맞다.
④ <let+O+OC(원형부정사)> 구조.

해석 대부분의 작가들은 세계적 수준의 미루기 선수들이다. 글쓰기는 어려워서 우리는 그것을 미룬다. 하지만 모든 미루기 경우가 글 쓰는 걸 피하는 행태는 아니다. 어떤 것들은 아이디어가 푹 스며들도록 놔두는 거다. 때로 우리는 글자 그대로 하룻밤 곰곰이 그것에 대해 생각할 필요가 있다. 물론 나는 아이디어가 양념이 잘 배도록 놔두는 데에 대가이다. 나는 10여 년을 기다린 후에야 펜을 들어 그 아이디어에 대해 종이에 쓰는 것으로 죽 알려져 왔다. 그러나 내게도 시작하는 비밀 요령이 한 가지 있다. 첫째, 카드나 종이쪽지에 딱 한 문장 — "그는 오늘 아침 내게 전화했다." — 을 쓴 다음 그것을 최소한 하루 동안 몸에 지니고 다녀라. 그것을 호주머니에 넣어라. 그날 하루 내내 마음이 그 문장에 (자꾸) 돌아가도록 놔두라. 그것을 꺼내어 몇 번 보라. 그리고는 아이디어가 떠오르는 대로 그것을 적어두라. 그런 다음 그다음 날 또는 그 주 후반부에 당신이 만든 문장과 당신의 생각을 갖고 (제대로) 앉아서 (본격적으로) 지금까지 생각하고 있던 것을 써라.

어휘 **procrastinator** 미루는 사람 ***cf.*** **procrastination** 질질 끌기, 미루기 **put off** 미루다, 연기하다 **soak in** 푹 담그다, 스며들게 하다 **literally** 글자 그대로 **sleep on** ~을 하룻밤 자며 신중히 생각하다 **master** 대가, 전문가 **trick** 요령, 속임수 **slip** (가늘고 긴) 종이 조각

구문 06~07행 I've *been known* to wait ten years or more(A) **before** putting pen to paper on an idea(B).

→ 현재완료가 수동태로 쓰인 경우. A하고 나서야 B하는 것으로 (지금까지 사람들에게) '알려져 온' 경우로 현재완료의 '계속'을 나타낸다.

044 ③ | that's → it's

해설 ③ The problem is that ~(문제는 ~이다)의 접속사 that이 아니라 생략된 that절의 주어가 올 자리이다. just too easy는 이어지는 to부정사(to open the texting screen or some app)에 대한 평가. 긴 to부정사구를 대신하는 가주어 it이 와야 할 자리이다. The problem is (that) it is ~.의 형태로 써야 어법에 맞다.

① 스마트폰, 태블릿, 그리고 다른 기기들에 대한 평가로 형용사 handy(편리한, 간편한)가 잘 쓰였다.
② undermine ~ significantly로 이어지는 <동사-부사> 구조.
④ avoid의 목적어로 동명사(splitting)가 맞게 쓰였다.
⑤ <between A and B>의 B 자리에 whatever절이 왔다. do의 목적어 역할을 하는 '~하는 것은 무엇이든'의 의미를 가진 whatever는 어법상 알맞다.

해석 스마트폰, 태블릿, 그리고 다른 기기들이 학교에서 아주 편리할 수 있다. 선생님이 말씀하신 어떤 게 궁금한가? 인터넷을 바로 검색하면 더 많은 사실이 나온다. 차트를 준비하고 아주 뛰어난 수업 리포트를 발표하고 싶은가? 속담에 있듯이 "그것에는 앱이 있다"(Where there is a will, there is a way.(뜻이 있는 곳에 길이 있다.)를 염두에 두고 한 말). 그러나 이것이 또한 당신의 집중을 상당히 훼손할 수도 있다. 문제는 텍스트 화면이나 앱을 열기가 너무 쉽다는 것이다. 경계를 늦출 때마다 학생들은 바로 — 그리고 저도 모르게 — 페이스북에 로그인해 새로 떠 있는 내용을 살피게 된다. 이걸 어떻게 하면 좋은가? "수업 시간에 진행되는 것과 모바일 기기로 하고 싶어질지도 모를 뭐든 그 둘 간에 주의가 쪼개지는 것을 피하려 애쓰라"라고 전문가가 충고한다. "이를 피할 수 있는 한 가지 좋은 방법은 핸드폰이나 태블릿을 꺼두거나, 아니면 최소한 비행 모드로 설정해 놓는 것이다. 그렇게 되면 자신도 모르게 문자 메시지를 확인하거나 소셜 미디어 사이트를 이용하고 있고 하지는 않을 것이다.

어휘 **handy** 유용한, 편리한 **turn up** 찾게 되다; 나타나다 **undermine** 훼손하다, 해치다 **significantly** 상당히, 크게 **notification** 알림, 통지 **split** 쪼개다 **expert** 전문가 **wind up v-ing** v하는 것으로 끝나다

구문 12~15행 "Try to avoid splitting your attention **between** what's going on in class(A) **and** *whatever* [you might feel a need to do ∨ with your mobile device](B)," advises an expert.

→ <between A and B> 구조에서 A와 B에 명사절 목적어가 왔다. 복합관계대명사 whatever는 anything that으로 바꿔 쓸 수 있다.

045 ③ | Much → Many

해설 ③ of 뒤의 명사가 셀 수 있는 명사의 복수(jobs)이므로 이것의 수식을 받는 부분도 셀 수 있는 개념에 쓰이는 Many로 써야 한다.

① (being) scared ~의 분사구문. as they are scared ~의 의미.
② 단수주어에 맞게 doesn't have to(~할 필요가 없다)로 썼다.
④ 동등 비교(as ~ as)의 틀을 뺀 나머지를 보면 the skills(주어)-will become(동사)-important(보어)로 보어 자리에 형용사가 맞게 쓰였다.
⑤ <목적(~하기 위해)>을 나타내는 to부정사의 부사적 용법으로 맞게 쓰였다. 전체 문장은 '~하라, 그러면 …할 것이다'라는 의미의 <명령문+and ~> 구조.

해석 십 대들이 잘못된 선택을 하게 될까 봐 두려워 대학에서 어떤 공부를 해야 할지 결정을 못 하고 막혀 있다. "무엇을 공부할지에 관해 너무 스트레스 안 받도록 하세요. 스티브 잡스는 서예를 공부해서 결국 애플을 창립했습니다."라고 한 카운슬러가 말한다. 교훈이 뭐냐고? 당신이 지금 선택하는 학위가 당신의 미래를 꼭 규정하는 것은 아니라는 것이다. 그가 특히 얘기하듯이 "어떤 사람이 23살이 되었을 때 선택 가능한 직업 중 많은 것이 18살일 때는 생겨나지도 않는다." 학위를 하면서 쌓게 되는 기술—비판적 사고력이나 사람들 앞에서 말하기 등—이 배우는 과목 거의 그 자체만큼이나 중요해지는 경우가 많다. 그러니 무엇을 공부하기로 하든 그 안에서 기쁨을 누려라. 인간 종족에게 허용된 지식을 탐구하느라 그토록 많은 시간을 쓸 수 있는 기회를 결코 다시 갖게 될 일은 없을 것이다. 한 개인으로서 당신 자신을—당신의 세계관, 가치관, 삶의 목표—조각하는 멋진 시간이다. 그것을 하기 위해 (지금) 공부하라, 그러면 당신의 나머지 진로는 그저 알아서 잘되어 나갈 것이다.

어휘 **degree** 학위 **define** 정의하다, 규정하다 **delight** 기뻐하다 **be unlikely to** ~할 가능성이 없다 **explore** 탐구하다 **race** 인종, 민족 **sculpt** 조각하다

046 ③

해설 (A) 문맥상 '계면 활성제의 작용을 더 쉽게 만든다'라는 뜻으로, 동사 makes의 진목적어는 to do their job이고 easier는 목적격보어다. 따라서 가목적어로 쓰일 수 있는 it이 적절. for the surfactants ~ detergent는 to부정사구의 의미상 주어.
(B) 기름투성이의 그릇과 함께 '남겨지는' 것이므로 be left가 적절. 뒤에 목적어가 없는 것으로도 수동태임을 확인할 수 있다.
(C) rinsing이 이끄는 동명사구가 주어이므로 단수동사 gets가 적절.

해석 왜 설거지를 찬물보다 뜨거운 물로 하는 게 더 나을까? 두 가지 이유가 있다. 첫째로, 뜨거운 물은 그릇에 붙어 있는 음식 부스러기들을 부드럽게 하고 기름기를 녹이는데, 이는 주방용 세제의 계면 활성제가 그 역할을 더 쉽게 하도록 한다. 계면 활성제는 고체와 기름 분자를 물 분자에 붙게 하는 화학 물질이어서 그것들이 쉽게 그릇에서 씻겨나갈 수 있다. 세제와 뜨거운 물 없이는 기름투성이의 그릇을 제대로 닦는 것이 불가능하지는 않더라도 매우 어렵다. 세제가 없다면, 당신에게는 여전히 기름투성이인 그릇이 남아 있을 것이다. 둘째로, 매우 뜨거운 물로 그릇을 헹구면 설거지 후에 남아 있는 비눗물의 얇은 막을 없앨 수 있다. 뜨거운 물은 그릇 위에 물웅덩이들을 만드는 비누투성이의 잔여물을 제거한다. 이 물웅덩이들은 물이 증발할 때 보기 싫은 얼룩을 만든다.

어휘 **soften** ~을 부드럽게 하다 **a bit of** 한 조각의 **detergent** 세제 **chemical** 화학 물질; 화학의 **attach** ~을 붙이다 **molecule** ((화학)) 분자 **rinse** ~을 헹구다; 헹구기 **greasy** 기름투성이의 **oily** 기름기가 있는 **get rid of** ~을 없애다 **film** (표면을 덮은) 얇은 막; 영화 **soapy** 비누투성이의 **residue** 잔여물 **puddle** 물웅덩이 **unattractive** 보기 안 좋은 **evaporate** 증발하다

구문 08~10행 **It**'s very hard, / ***if*** not impossible, / **to** properly **clean** a greasy or oily plate without using detergent and hot water.

→ It은 가주어, to부정사 이하가 진주어이다. 여기서 if는 '~이긴 하지만, ~더라도'라는 뜻의 양보를 나타내는 접속사로 쓰였다.

047 ④ | divide → dividing

해설 ④ 전치사 뒤이므로 동사를 동명사 형태로 써야 한다. <by v-ing>: v함으로써

① 비교급(more effective)을 더 강조하는 형태.
② 동사(did)를 수식하는 부사(well)가 맞게 쓰였다.
③ a point 대신에 쓰인 부정대명사.
⑤ the idea에 이어 나오는 동격의 that이 맞게 쓰였다.

해석 한 연구가 동기 부여에 관한 한 매(회초리)가 당근보다 훨씬 효과적이라는 것을 알아냈다. 마케팅 교수가 두 개의 소비자 행동 반에게 잘하면 한 점 얻지만 잘못하면 한 점을 잃는 선택형 퀴즈를 냈다. 그리고는 그 반들을 두 개 그룹으로 나누는 것으로 계속 진행했다. 첫 번째 반에서는 학생들이 기말시험이 필수지만 퀴즈에서 5점을 받으면 기말시험을 안 봐도 되는 권리가 생길 수 있다고 얘기를 들었다. 그러나 두 번째 반에서는 기말시험은 선택적이나 퀴즈 시험에서 5점을 못 올리면 그 권리를 잃을 수도 있다고 얘기를 듣는다. 그 결과는 (어떻게 되었을까)? 두 번째 그룹이 시험을 안 봐도 되는 권리를 '포기한다'는 생각에 훨씬 더 몰두했다. 이 발견은 뭔가를 잃기를 싫어하는 마음이 뭔가를 얻어서 기쁜 것보다 훨씬 강하다는 생각을 뒷받침해준다.

어휘 **stick** 막대기, 회초리 **when it comes to** ~에 관한 한, ~의 점에서는 **motivation** 동기 부여, 의욕 **optional** 선택적인 **score** 점수를 거두다 **proceed** 진행하다 **divide** 나누다, 분할하다 **required** 필수의, 꼭 해야 하는 **earn** 획득하다, (노력으로) 얻다 **engaged** 열심인, 몰두하는 **dislike** 싫어함, 혐오

구문 10~13행 In the second class, however, they *were told* **that** the final exam was optional, [but] **that** they could lose the right [if they did not get five points from the quizzes].
(A: that the final exam was optional / B: that they could lose the right [if they did not get five points from the quizzes])

→ 실험대상 그룹이 들은 내용 A와 B가 접속사 but을 전후로 연결된 구조. 둘 다 전달 내용이므로 that절로 표현되었다.

048 ④ | was → did

해설 ④ <As ~, so ...(~하듯이, …하다)>에서 비교하는 As절의 동사가 increased이므로 so로 시작되는 주절의 동사도 과거시제의 일반동사를 대신하는 대동사 did로 써야 한다.

① a parasite, pollutants 두 가지가 언급되었으므로 <both A and B>로 쓴 것이 맞다.
② 이어 나오는 것이 동사(is tainted with)이고 선행사(an area)가 사람이 아니므로 주격 관계대명사 which가 알맞다.
③ survived well로 동사를 수식하는 부사가 맞게 쓰였다.
⑤ 전치사 in에 이어 동명사 providing이 맞게 왔다. the parasite는 동명사의 의미상의 주어이다.

해석 기생충에 감염되는 것은 보통 좋은 소식이 아니다. 동물이 기생충과 독성 중금속과 같은 오염물질 둘 다에 대처해야 할 때 스트레스 요인이 더 쌓인다. 하지만 이 사실은 스페인의 아르테미아 브라인 슈림프에게는 해당하지 않는다고 새 연구가 밝힌다. 한 조사팀이 비소와 기타 중금속으로 오염된 지역에서 새우를 수집하여 기생충에 감염된 것들과 감염되지 않은 것들을 분리한 다음 비소가 섞인 물에서는 얼마나 잘 살아남는지 보려고 테스트를 실시했다. 물속 비소 농도가 올라가자 죽는 브라인 슈림프의 수도 증가했다. 그러나 기생충에 감염된 것들이 감염되지 않은 것들보다 더 많이 살아남았다. 분명하진 않을 수도 있지만 빠른 죽음을 초래하는 것이 기생충에게는 좋은 전략이 아니다. 그것은 기생충이 번식하고 떠나서 새 숙주를 찾기에 충분히 오래 살려면 숙주가 필요하기 때문이다. 이것이 기생충이 상황이 충분히 냉혹해졌을 때 (숙주에게) 도움을 제공하는 결과를 가져온다.

어휘 **be infected with** ~에 감염되다, ~에 걸리다 **pollutant** 오염 물질 **toxic** 독성의 **stressor** 스트레스 유발 인자 **be tainted with** ~로 더럽혀지다 **separate** 분리하다 **-laced** ~가 섞인, ~을 탄 **concentration** 농도, 결집 **host** 집주인; 숙주 **reproduce** 번식하다, 복제하다

구문 11~13행 **As** the concentration of arsenic in the water (S′) increased (V′), **so** did (V(=increased)) the number of *brine shrimp* (S) [that died].

→ <As ~, so ...(~하듯이, …하다)> 구조. 부사인 so 뒤에 주어, 동사가 도치되어 쓰였다.

16~18행 That's because a parasite needs its host to stay alive *long* **enough** [**for** the parasite] **to** *reproduce* (A), *leave* (B) [and] *find a new host* (C).

→ <A enough to-v(v하기에 충분히 A하는)> 구조에서 to부정사 앞에 의미상의 주어 for the parasite가 쓰였다.

049 ⑤

해설 (A) '우주선을 발사하는 것'이 엄청난 양의 힘을 필요로 한다는 문맥이므로 가주어 It의 진주어 역할을 하는 to launch가 적절하다.
(B) had to create ~라는 동사가 뒤에 나오므로 이곳은 수식어가 올 자리. The Saturn V rocket과 동사 use가 수동의 관계이므로 과거분사 used가 적절.
(C) 뒤에 완전한 구조의 절이 오므로 불완전한 구조를 이끄는 관계대명사 which는 올 수 없다. '매우 ~해서 …하다'라는 의미의 <so ~ that ...> 구조.

해석 우주선을 대기권 바깥으로 발사하여 지구를 도는 궤도에 진입시키는 데는 엄청난 양의 힘이 필요하다. 지구 궤도를 벗어나 우주로 나가는 것은 훨씬 더 많은 에너지를 필요로 한다. 아폴로의 달 착륙 임무에서 사용된 새턴 V 로켓은 궤도에 진입하고 또 벗어나기 위해 엄청난 추진력을 만들어야 했다. 그 로켓은 너무 많은 에너지를 필요로 하여 이륙 시 연료만 로켓 무게의 90%를 차지했다. 지구 둘레를 회전하기 위해서 아폴로 11호는 초속 2만 5천 피트 이상의 속도로 운행해야 했다. 궤도를 벗어나 달에 착륙하기 위해서 그 우주선은 초속 3만 5천 피트 이상의 속도까지 가속해야 했다.

어휘 **launch** ~을 발사하다; ~에 착수하다 **orbit** 궤도; ~의 궤도를 돌다 **thrust** 추진력; ~을 밀어 넣다 **liftoff** (로켓 등의) 수직 이륙 순간 **accelerate** 가속하다

구문 04~07행 The Saturn V rocket (used in the Apollo missions to the moon) had to create a huge push, or thrust, / to put itself into orbit and beyond.
(S: The Saturn V rocket / V: had to create / O: a huge push, or thrust)

→ a huge push와 thrust는 동격. or는 '즉[곧]'의 의미로 동격어구를 연결함.

050 ⑤ | differently → different

해설 ⑤ 비교급의 틀(as ~ as it could be)을 뺀 나머지를 보면, 페이스북의 현재 강조점은 Zuckerberg의 원래 의도와는 다르다는, 즉 '명사(emphasis)-형용사(different)'로 표현되어야 할 부분이다.

① 선행사가 a website. where 이하에서 '이곳에서' 무슨 일이 이뤄지는지 설명하므로 장소 개념의 where가 오는 것이 알맞다.
② 형용사(popular)를 부사 (surprisingly)가 수식하는 구조.
③ <so ~ that ...(너무 ~해서 …하다)>으로 이어지는 부분이다.
④ 'friend'라는 어휘가 사용'되는' 것이므로 수동형의 being used가 맞게 쓰였다.

해석 하버드 대학 학생인 Mark Zuckerberg가 6억이 넘는 사용자를 갖춘 십억 달러 가치의 기업 설립에 착수했던가? 그렇지 않다. 2010년에 나온 영화 <소셜 네트워크(The Social Network)>에서 보듯이 2003년 당시 Zuckerberg의 원래 착상은 어두운 속성을 띠고 있었다. 여자 친구에게 차인 후 비통했던 Zuckerberg는 젊은 여성의 매력도에 투표해 볼 수 있는 'FaceMash'라는 웹사이트를 만들어냈다. 이것이 처음에 하버드대 학생들만 대상으로 하는 Thefacebook이라는 온라인 소셜 네트워크로 발전했다. 그 네트워크가 놀랄 정도로 인기 있어지자 누구나 이용할 수 있는 웹사이트인 Facebook으로 모습이 바뀌었다. 페이스북은 요즘에는 쫙 퍼져서 '친구'라는 말이 동사로 쓰이는 것과 같이 우리의 말하는 방식을 바꿔놓을 정도이다. 아이러니하게도 지금 있는 친구나 새 친구와 연결되는 것에 초점을 두는 페이스북의 강조점은 Zuckerberg가 처음에 품었던 옹졸한 발상과는 지극히 다르다. 확실히, Zuckerberg가 후에 쓴 전략들이 그의 사업적 모험을 촉발시킨 그 의도된 전략보다 훨씬 고귀한 것으로 드러났다.

어휘 **set out** 착수하다, 시작하다 **nature** 속성, 본성 **dump** 버리다, (쓰레기처럼) 차버리다 **bitter** 쓰라린; 비통한 **vote** 투표하다 **evolve** 진화하다, 서서히 발전하다 **pervasive** 곳곳에 스며드는, 만연한 **ironically** 역설적이게도, 얄궂게도 **mean-spirited** 비열한, 옹졸한 **noble** 고귀한, 숭고한 **entrepreneurship** 기업가 정신

구문 16~19행 Ironically, Facebook's emphasis [**on** connecting with existing and new friends] *is* about **as** *different* **as** it **could be** ∨ *from* Zuckerberg's original mean-spirited concept.
(it = Facebook's (current) emphasis)

→ as ~ as A can[could] be: 더할 나위 없이 ~한. 페이스북이 만들어진 원래 의도와 현재의 강조점은 판이하다는 점을 원급 비교 표현을 통해 강조하고 있다.
be different from: ~와는 다른

051 ② | are → is

해설 ② what절은 추상적인 의미로 단수 개념이다. 따라서 동사도 is가 되어야 한다.

① Students를 수식하는 분사 형용사구로 맞는 표현이다.
③ '~하면서'라는 의미의 동시동작을 나타내는 분사구문.
④ 두 문장에 걸쳐 표현된 not A but B(A가 아니라 B) 패턴의 B에 해당하는 부분으로, to부정사로 표현된(not to sit ~) A처럼 B도 to부정사로(to do it on your own) 맞게 표현되었다.
⑤ 문장의 주어가 하는 행위(differentiate)의 대상이 you이므로 재귀대명사를 써야 할 곳이 맞다.

해석 대학에 들어가는 학생이 지금의 직업 시장에 운을 걸어서는 안 된다. 그들은 지금으로부터 5~10년 후의 직업 시장에 운을 걸어야 한다. 그리고 직업 시장이 요구하게 될 것은 기술이지 학위가 아니다. 다행히도 기술을 익히는 것이 일찍이 이토록 쉬운 적이 없었다. 무료로 또는 싸게 온라인으로 기술을 배울 수 있는 곳이 많다. 이는 프로그래밍을 배우는 것이든, 주식 거래, 엑셀 사용, 디자인 어느 것이든 — 그 리스트는 끝도 없다 — 해당된다. 직업생활을 준비하는 가장 좋은 방법은 진정으로 열정을 느끼지 못하는 뭔가를 듣느라 세 시간씩 강의실에 앉아 있는 게 아니라 그것을 직접 해보는 것이다. 이 경제에서 기업은 당신을 고용할 만한 인력이 되도록 훈련시킬 시간이나 자본이 없다. 스스로를 구별되게 하기 위해서는 수요가 많은 기술을 익혀야지, 액자에 담긴 학위는 이제 더 이상 당신을 그다지 멀리 가게 해주지 못한다.

어휘 **bet on** ~에 내기 걸다 **trade** 거래하다, 교역하다 **stock** 주식 **passionate** 열정을 느끼는 **capital** 자본 **employable** 고용할 만한, 고용 자격을 갖춘 **differentiate** 구별하다, 식별하다 **in-demand** 수요가 많은 **framed degree** 액자에 담긴 학위, 졸업장

구문 09~12행 The best *way* (to prep for a career) is **not** *to sit* (in a lecture hall) (for three hours) (listening to something [(that) you're not truly passionate about]). It's *to do* it on your own.
(A: not to sit ~ / B: to do it on your own)

→ not A but B가 <not A. (But) B>로 두 문장에 걸쳐 표현되었다.

052 ⑤

해설 (A) 뒤이어 or가 나오므로 or와 호응하는 either가 올 자리이다. <either A or B>: A 하거나 B하다, A나 B 둘 중 하나
(B) of 이하의 명사가 복수명사(all the drugs ~)이므로 그것의 25%도 복수, 따라서 use가 맞다.
(C) 접속사 and 앞 절에 달리 동사가 없으므로 이곳이 동사 자리. 만드는 재료를 얘기하는 is made from(~로 만들어지다)이다.

해석 고대부터 사람들은 특정 식물이 질병을 치료하거나 통증을 멈추게 할 수 있다는 것을 알았다. 사람들은 시행착오를 거치면서 이러한 치료법들을 발견했다. 이 귀중한 정보는 세대에서 세대로 전해져 왔다. 오늘날에도 약을 만드는 회사들은 치유 물질을 추출하기 위해 전통 식물을 재배하거나 실험실에서 식물들을 연구하여 화학 물질을 모방하기도 한다. 오늘날 의사들에 의해 처방되는 모든 약품의 적어도 25퍼센트가 식물에서 나온 추출물을 여전히 이용하고 있다. 예를 들어, '디기탈린'이라는 흔히 쓰이는 약은 디기탈리스 식물의 잎으로 만들어지며 심장에 문제가 있는 사람들을 지속적으로 돕고 있다. 치유 성질이 있는 새로운 식물들은 열대우림과 같은 미개척 지역에서 여전히 발견되고 있다.

어휘 **trial and error** 시행착오 **extract** ~을 추출하다, ~을 뽑다; 추출물 **healing** 치유, 치료 **substance** 물질 **laboratory** 실험실 **prescribe** ~을 처방하다 **property** 속성, 특성; 재산, 부동산

053 ③ | safely → safe

해설 ❸ It(=The hotel)이 '어떻게' 느껴졌는지 그 소감을 형용사 A, B and C로 표현하고 있는 구조. (대)명사를 설명하는 부분이므로 A, C와 마찬가지로 형용사 safe로 써야 한다.

① 묵었던 호텔에 대한 소감, 즉 과거 일에 대해 <조동사+have p.p.>로 알맞게 썼다. '(이보다 더) 요구할 수는 없었을 것이다'로 간접적으로 '최상'으로 만족했음을 드러내고 있다.
② 선행사 deal의 내용을 구체적으로 소개하고 있는 부분이다. 장소의 관계부사 where(=in this deal)가 추상적인 개념으로 쓰였다.
④ of+추상명사 = 형용사. excellent의 의미.
⑤ more와 what I paid가 명사, 명사절로 비교되고 있는 구조. worth(~의 가치가 있는)는 드물게 명사를 목적어로 취하는 형용사이다.

해석 이곳은 아주 훌륭한 호텔이었다. 나는 내가 (낸) 돈에 대해 더 많은 것을 요구할 수는 없었을 것이다. 나는 이 호텔을 '조기 구매' 건으로 확보했는데, 이것에서 스위트룸을 할인 가격에 구했다. 매트리스는 안락했고 방은 빨리 시원해졌으며, 샤워 물이 빨리 데워지고 잘 공간이 아주 널찍했다. 그곳은 안전하고 깨끗하며 잘 관리되는 것처럼 느껴졌다. 그들은 내가 나타나기 전까지 (예약을 이행 못 하는 경우를 대비해) 카드에 요금을 물리지 않으면서도 할인요율을 적용해 주었다. 무임 호텔 셔틀이 전화한 지 몇 분 안에 우리를 태워 가고 유럽식 조식은 아주 수준이 높았다. 그것은 골라먹을 것이라고는 그저 차가운 시리얼에 커피, 과일 약간이 다인 것 그 이상이었다. 전반적으로 나는 이 호텔이 아주 인상적이었다. 이곳은 내가 낸 요금보다 훨씬 값어치 있었고, 나의 기대치를 능가했다.

어휘 **purchase** 구매(하다) **deal** 거래 **suite** (호텔의) 특실, 스위트룸 **discounted** 할인된 **plenty of** 많은 ~ **well managed** 관리가 잘 된 **charge** (요금을) 매기다, 부과하다 **show up** (모습을) 나타내다 **make reservations** 예약하다 **rate** 요금, 비율 **overall** 전반적으로 **worth** ~의 가치가 있는 **exceed** ~을 넘다, 초과하다 **expectation** 기대, 기대치

054 ① | is struck → strikes

해설 ❶ car가 뭔가에 부딪힐 수도(is struck by ~) 있으나 이어지는 부분을 보면 kills와 함께 목적어 a pedestrian을 공유하고 있는 구조이다. 따라서 *strikes* and *kills* a pedestrian으로 고쳐 써야 알맞다.

② the technology를 선행사로 가지는 계속적 용법의 관계대명사 which.
③ help의 목적어로 쓰인 원형부정사. help (to) speed로도 쓰일 수 있다.
④ 이어동사 put off의 목적어로 동명사가 맞게 쓰였다.
⑤ 자동차 회사가 투자를 하는 입장이므로 능동형 to부정사 to invest를 쓴 것이 문맥에 맞다.

해석 해는 2023년, 그리고 처음으로, 도시의 거리를 누비며 자동 운전해 가던 차가 행인을 치어 죽이게 된다. 소송이 당연히 잇따를 것이다. 그러나 정확히 무슨 법이 적용될까? 아무도 모른다. 오늘날 법률이 과학기술에 발맞추려고 안간힘을 쓰고 있는데, 이 과학기술이 애플, 아우디, BMW, 구글 등의 노력 덕분에 위험할 정도로 빠른 속도로 앞으로 나아가고 있다. 지금의 법은 인간이 운전석에 앉아 있는 걸 가정하는데, 그것이 지금은 그 차량들이 거리에 나오는 걸 합법적이게 하고 있지만, 완전히 자동화된 차량의 시장 진입을 가속화하는 데는 도움이 되지 않는다. 우리는 법 개정을 로봇을 이용한 운전의 도래까지 미룰 수가 없는 것이다. 왜냐하면, 지금의 법들은 불확실한 소지가 많고, 불확실함은 전진을 막기 때문이다. 자동차 회사가 최초의 사고 이후 모든 차량을 길에서 끌어낼 수밖에 없는 상황에 처할 수도 있는데 자동화된 차 군단을 출시하는 데 투자할 것으로 예상할 수는 없다.

어휘 **navigate** 운전[조종]하다; 길을 찾다 **strike** ~에 부딪히다[충돌하다]; ~을 치다 **pedestrian** 행인, 보행자 **lawsuit** 소송 사건 **apply** 적용되다 **keep up with** ~에 발맞추다, ~와 보폭을 맞추다 **assume** 추정하다, ~일 거라 여기다 **legal** 합법적인 **launch** 개시, 착수 **autonomous** 자율적인, 자치의 **advent** 도래, 출현 **uncertainty** 불확실성 **discourage** 단념케 하다, 용기를 꺾어 놓다 **put out** 생산하다; 출항하다 **a fleet of** ~의 한 군단 ***cf.*** **fleet** 함대

구문 15~18행 A car company can't **be expected to** invest in putting out a new fleet of autonomous cars (주절) *when* it could **be forced to** pull them all off the road after the first accident. (종속절)

→ 주절, 종속절 모두 수동태로 쓰였다. (=We can't expect a car company to invest ~ when we could force it to pull them all off the road ~.)

055 ④ | vicious → viciously

해설 ④ 동사(mocked)를 꾸며주는 부분이므로 형용사가 아닌 부사로 써야 한다.

① 주어가 복수(the worst parts)이므로 복수동사 were는 맞게 쓰였다.
② 주어 (every kid around me)가 '스스로'에 대해 유사점이 있음을 안(knew) 것이므로 재귀대명사가 맞게 쓰였다.
③ something similar를 선행사로 하는 주격 관계대명사 that.
⑤ 지각동사 see의 목적격보어로 쓰인 부분으로 원형부정사(suffer)가 맞게 쓰였다.

해석 어렸을 때 나는 나의 가장 나쁜 부분이 뭔지 알고 있었다. 내 머리털은 곱슬거리고, 내 입술은 큼지막했다. 내 주위의 거의 모든 아이들이 다른 사람에게서 조롱받을 만한 뭔가 유사한 것—검은 피부, 곱슬거리는 머리털, 펑퍼짐한 코, 두터운 입술—이 있음을 알고 있었다. 그래서 우리가 백인이 되고 싶어 했던가? 나는 그렇게 생각하지 않는다. 우리는 마돈나처럼 보이고 싶어 하지 않았다. 우리는 우리가 서로를 조롱했던 것과 같이 마이클 잭슨의 미적 변화를 증오하고 악의적으로 조롱했다. 우리가 원했던 것은 종이가방 검문의 '유리한' 쪽에 있는 것이었다. 우리는 옅은 갈색 눈을 원했고 곱슬거리는 머리털을 원했다. 나는 갈색 눈도 머릿결이 웨이브도 아니었다. 그럼에도 불구하고 나는 내 주위 아이들이 당하는 것과 같은 식으로 괴로움을 당하지는 않았다. 그건 내가 검은 피부는 아니었기 때문이다. 그리고, 더 중요한 것이, 난 여자애가 아니었던 것이다. 남자애들에게는 유머나 싸움을 잘한다는 평판 같은, 여자에게는 소용이 없는, 사회적 계단을 올라가는 몇 가지 방법이 있었다.

어휘 **ridicule** 조롱(하다) **mock** (흉내 내며) 놀리다, 조소하다 **aesthetic** 심미적인, 미적인 **viciously** 잔혹하게, 몹시 **hazel** 개암(나무); 담갈색(의) **suffer** 고통받다, 시달리다 **social ladder** 사회적 위계[구조, 계층] **reputation** 평판, 명성 **unavailable** 이용할 수 없는, 도움이 안 되는

056 ② | more happily → happier

해설 ② 보어 자리이므로 형용사 happy의 비교급 happier로 써야 한다. feel energized, happy, and healthy의 <감각동사+형용사>의 병렬구조.

① (누구나 다 경험했을 법한) 오후 중반 무렵에 찾아오는 '그' 슬럼프를 뜻하는 지시형용사 that.
③ 수단, 방법을 나타내는 능동형 분사 using으로 맞게 쓰였다.
④ 선행사가 A delicious guilt-free treat로 단수이므로 주격 관계대명사(that)에 이어 나오는 동사도 단수(satisfies)로 맞게 쓰였다.
⑤ 초콜릿은 원래 셀 수 없는 개념인데, 여기서는 초콜릿 바 등 구체적인 사물로 언급하고 있으므로 '두어 개, 약간'이라는 셀 수 있는 개념의 a few로도 쓸 수 있다.

해석 내가 초콜릿 중독자라는 것에 대해서는 의심의 여지가 없다. 어떤 날에는 그것이 오후 중반에 찾아오는 그 슬럼프를 정말이지 이겨낼 수 있게 해줄 유일한 것이다. 장담하건대 내가 그 검은 마법 같은 것의 혜택을 받는 유일한 사람은 아닐 것이다. 자그마한 초콜릿 하나면 바로 기운이 더 나고, 더 행복해지고, 그리고 이제는 훨씬 더 건강해질 수도 있다. 맞다, 나와 같은 사람들에게 좋은 소식이 있다. 초콜릿 아티스트들이 이제 심장에 좋은 다크초콜릿을 숙련된 정밀함을 발휘해 슈퍼푸드, 허브 추출물, 그 밖의 심신을 북돋워 주는 재료들과 결합하고 있다. 결과는 달콤해진 이만 만족시키는 것이 아니라 슬럼프에서 당신을 들어 올려 주고 면역력을 높여주고 항산화 물질을 증가시켜 주며, 그날의 스트레스 부담을 줄여주고 얼굴에 미소를 띠게 하는 죄의식 없이 즐길 수 있는 맛있는 것이다. (그러니) 오늘 약간 사두는 게 어떤가?

어휘 **chocoholic** 초콜릿 중독자 **get through** ~을 끝내다 **slump** 부진, 침체 **instantly** 즉각, 즉시 **combine A with B** A와 B를 결합하다 **heart-healthy** 심장에 좋은 **extract** 추출물 **boost** 북돋우다, 진작시키다 **artisanal** 장인의; 숙련된 **precision** 정밀함, 정확성 **immune system** 면역체계 **load** 짐, 부담 **stock up** ~을 많이 사다, ~을 사서 비축하다

057 ⑤ | admit → admitting

해설 ⑤ 뒤에 동사(is)가 나오므로 명령문의 동사가 아닌 주어가 와야 할 자리이다. 따라서 주어 역할을 하는 동명사 admitting으로 고쳐 써야 알맞다.

① better(형용사 good의 비교급)를 부사 inherently가 수식하고 있는 구조.
② the key to A(A로 통하는 열쇠[핵심])에서 전치사 to의 목적어가 될 수 있는 동명사형으로 맞게 쓰였다. learning as quickly as a child에 이르는 핵심 방법을 소개하고 있다.
③ how는 more likely를 꾸며주는 것으로, 부사가 부사어구를 수식하는 것은 자연스럽다. 실제로 의미하는 바는 far more likely('훨씬' 더 가능성이 높은)이다.
④ 거듭 실패'하고 있는 것'이 (사람들 눈에) 보이는 것이므로 진행형을 나타내는 현재분사로 쓴 것이 자연스럽다. 일회성으로 To be seen to fail이라고 할 수도 있다.

해석 아이들이 어른보다 원래 언어를 더 잘 습득한다는 생각이 잘못된 생각이라는 게 밝혀지고 있다. 새 연구가 나이와 배우는 능력 사이에 직접적인 연관을 찾지 못한다. 아이처럼 빨리 배우는 핵심 비결은 그저 어떤 아이다운 태도—예를 들어 자의식의 결핍, 언어 속에서 놀고자 하는 욕망, 실수를 기꺼이 하겠다는 마음가짐—를 띠기만 하면 되는 것일지 모른다. 아이 때는 실수를 할 것으로 기대되지만 어른이 되면 실수는 하면 안 되는 어떤 것이 되어 버린다. 어른이 "난 아직 그건 안 배웠어."라고 하기보다는 "나는 못 해.(난 수영 못 해. 난 운전 못 해. 난 스페인어 못 해)"라고 얘기할 확률이 얼마나 높을지 생각해 보라. 실패를 계속하는 것(또는 (성공은 못하고) 그냥 애쓰고만 있는 것)으로 보여지는 것은 아이에게는 부담이 되지 않는 사회적인 한 가지 터부이다. 언어를 배우는 일에 있어서는 당신이 모든 걸 알지는 못한다는 (그리고 그 점에 대해 괜찮다는) 점을 인정하는 것이 성장과 자유에 이르는 비결이다. 당신이 가지고 있는 어른으로서의 거리낌을 놓아버려라.

어휘 **inherently** 선천적으로, 타고나서 **turn out** ~임이 판명되다 **take on** (색채, 태도 등을) 띠다, ~의 어조이다 **self-consciousness** 자의식, 남의 시선을 의식함 **willingness** 기꺼이 하기, ~하려는 의지 **taboo** 금기(사항), 터부시하는 것 **merely** 단지, 그저 **burden** 부담(을 지우다) **when it comes to** ~에 관한 한 **let go of** (쥐고 있던 것을) 놓다

구문 15~17행 [When it comes to learning a language], **admitting**(S) that you don't know everything (and **being** okay with that) is(V) the key (to growth and freedom)(C).

→ admitting ~과 being ~ 두 개의 동명사구가 주어부를 이루고 있다. admit은 다시 접속사 that이 이끄는 목적어절을 취하고 있다.

058 ⑤

해설 (A) 앞에 있는 to가 전치사이므로 living이 적절. *cf.* responses to: ~에 대한 반응
(B) 문맥상 '목적'을 나타내는 to부정사가 와야 자연스럽다.
(C) 명사구 red blood cell count(적혈구 수)를 수식하므로 형용사인 normal이 적절.

해석 사람들은 산소가 해수면의 3분의 2 이하로 존재하는 높은 고도에서 사는 데 적응해왔다. 지금까지 과학자들은 이 높이에서 사는 데 서로 다른 대응을 보이는 몇몇 그룹의 사람들을 발견했다. 예를 들어, 남아메리카 안데스 산맥 원주민들은 표면적이 넓은 비교적 큰 폐를 가지고 있다. 이것은 그들이 혈액으로 공급하기 위해 산소를 더 빨리 받아들인다는 것을 의미한다. 히말라야 산맥의 티베트 사람들은 더 큰 폐를 가지고 있지는 않지만 더 빠르게 숨을 쉬는 경향이 있다. 그들은 혈액 속에 산소를 더 적게 가지고도 살아갈 수 있다. 그들은 정상적인 적혈구 수를 가지고 있지만 혈액 순환이 더 원활한지를 알아보는 실험은 아직 시행되지 않았다.

어휘 **adapt to** ~에 적응[순응]하다 **altitude** 고도 **oxygen** 산소 **available** 이용할 수 있는 **relatively** 상대적으로 **lung** 폐 **count** 수, 수치; ~을 세다

059 ③ | either → both

해설 ❸ low price와 great gas mileage라는 장점 '둘 다'를 가리키므로 both가 되어야 한다.

① these vehicles의 첫 출시 연도를 알리는 분사구문. Having first been released ~에서 Having been이 생략된 구조.
② 비교급의 형용사 두 개(larger and more expensive)가 나란히 온 구조. 비교급을 강조하는 much(훨씬 더 ~)가 비교급이 올 자리임을 확인해 준다.
④ 40마일이나 달릴 수 있음을 강조하여 쓴 as many as ~ 구문. miles가 셀 수 있는 개념의 복수명사이므로 many가 쓰였다.
⑤ compare nicely로 이어지는 <동사-부사> 구조이다. 부사 quite(상당히, 꽤)가 nicely를 앞에서 수식해 주고 있다.

해석 소형차가 다시 돌아왔고 이전 어느 때보다 좋아졌다. 1950년 미국에서 처음 출시되었던 이 차량은 바퀴 간 거리가 약 100인치로 이제 앞선 기술, 안락함, 안전 특징, 성능 향상, 대형의 고가 차의 외관을 갖추었다. 많은 이들이 소형차를 선택하는 두 가지 이유는 낮은 가격과 높은 연비이다. Nissan Sentra — 히트 중인 소형차들 중 하나 — 는 이 두 가지를 다 제공한다. 그것은 도심에서는 갤런당 평균 약 30마일을, 고속도로에서는 40마일이나 낸다. 거기다가 2만 달러가 안 든다. 130마력을 내는 1.8리터의 4기통 엔진에 수동기어 6단, 5인용 좌석의 Sentra는 동급의 다른 차량과 제법 근사하게 견줄 만하다.

어휘 **compact** 소형의 **release** 출시하다, (시장에) 내놓다 **vehicle** 차량, 탈것 **wheelbase** (차의) 바퀴 간 거리 **feature** 특징, 특질 **enhancement** 향상, 증대 **mileage** (단위 연료당) 주행거리, 연비 **average** 평균 **cylinder** (엔진의) 실린더[기통] **deliver** 내놓다 **manual** 수동의 **transmission** 변속기, 변속장치

060 ③ | are → do

해설 ❸ 앞 문장(Some read labels)에서 일반동사의 현재형을 썼으니 do가 알맞다. some은 '어떤 사람들'의 의미로 복수형이다.

① 명사 laundry house를 꾸미는 형용사 nearby(근처의, 가까운 곳의)가 맞게 쓰였다. *cf.* near: ~ 가까이에(전치사)
② 긴 주어(a man ~ 16 years) 끝에 쓰인 동사로, 주어가 a man으로 단수이므로 단수 동사로 맞게 쓰였다.
④ <make sure (that)+S+V(틀림없이 ~되도록 하다)> 패턴에서 주어(the dry cleaner)에 맞게 동사가 단수형으로 쓰였다.
⑤ any가 '어떤 ~이라도'의 의미로 쓰인 경우. 위에 언급된 것 중 '어느 하나에라도' 해당되는 경우 전문가의 손에 맡겨야 한다는 경고성 얘기이다.

해석 바쁜 아침이다. 가까운 세탁소에 들러 다시 보송보송 새 옷이 될 거라고 믿으면서 옷가지를 넘긴다. "드라이클리닝 업자들은 독심술사가 아니며 완벽하지 않습니다."라고 고급 드라이클리닝 회사를 16년간 운영한 사람이 주의를 준다. 드라이클리닝 업자마다 당신의 옷을 약간씩 다르게 취급할 것이다. 어떤 사람은 철저히 살펴볼 것이고 어떤 사람은 안 그럴 것이다. 어떤 이는 제품 라벨을 읽고 어떤 사람은 안 읽는다. 최고로 주의를 기울여 다루게 하려면 상품 라벨을 (직접) 먼저 읽고 드라이클리닝 하는 사람이 그 천 조직을 잘 알고 있도록 하고 그가 특히 주의를 기울일 필요가 있겠다고 생각되는 문제점(특히 얼룩 같은)은 뭐든 지적해두라. 또한 라벨 내용 자체를 어떻게 해석할 것인가 하는 문제가 있다. '드라이클리닝 할 것'과 '드라이클리닝만 가능'은 상당히 다르다. '드라이클리닝 할 것'이라는 라벨을 보면 '귀중한 옷인가?', '빛바래거나 줄어들 수 있나?' '기름때가 있나?'를 고려해 보라. 이 중 어떤 것 하나라도 그렇다고 생각되면 드라이클리닝 하는 곳에 가져가라.

어휘 **drop by** 잠깐 들르다 **dry cleaner's** 세탁소 **hand over** 넘기다, 양도하다 **garment** 의상, 의류 한 점 **high-end** 고급의, 고가의 **caution** 주의(를 주다), 조심(시키다) **inspect** 점검하다, 검사하다 **thoroughly** 철저히 **beforehand** 사전에, 미리 **be aware of** ~을 알고 있다, ~을 의식하다 **fabrication** (섬유의) 구성, 조직 **point out** (주의를 기울이도록) 지적하다 **issue** 문제점, (중요) 사안 **stain** 얼룩, 더러움 **interpret** 해석하다, 이해하다 **fade** 빛바래다, 희미해지다 **shrink** 줄어들다, 수축하다 **oily** 기름기가 있는

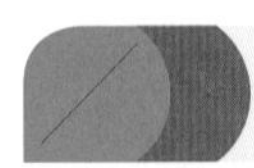

실전 모의고사 01회

061 ④ 062 ③ 063 ② 064 ③ 065 ③ 066 ④ | 본문 68p

061 ④ | that → which

해설 ④ 관계대명사 that은 전치사 바로 뒤에 쓸 수 없다. the rate를 선행사로 받으며, 전치사 at의 목적어 역할을 할 수 있는 which가 적절. 원래의 두 문장은 Higher heat seems to increase the rate. + Plants produce methane at the rate.

① 전체 문맥상 과거 어느 시점에서 연구를 시작해서 '강력한 온실가스인 메탄의 원인이 현재 밝혀진 것'이므로 현재완료 시제는 적절.
② 동사 produce와 주어 methane의 관계가 수동이므로 수동형 적절.
③ 놀라게 된 이유를 나타내는 to 부정사의 부사적 용법으로 적절히 쓰임.
⑤ hundreds of thousands of years ago를 선행사로 하는 관계부사인 when 적절.

해석 독일 연구자들이 예전에는 알려지지 않았던, 강력한 온실가스인 메탄의 원인을 규명했다. 범인은 바로 평범한 식물이었다. 유럽우주국의 ENVISAT 인공위성이 숲 지대 상공의 거대한 메탄 구름을 탐지하자 과학자들은 혼란스러웠다. 그들은 분해 작용이 일어나는 늪지대처럼 산소가 부족한 환경에서만 메탄이 생긴다고 생각했다. 실험에서, 다양한 식물들을 원래 메탄이 없는 공기로 채워져 있던 방에 두었더니 화학 감지기가 메탄을 감지하는 것을 보고 과학자들은 놀랐다. 더 높은 열은 식물이 메탄을 만들어내는 속도를 높이는 것으로 보이며, 이는 수십만 년 전 지구 온도가 더 따뜻했을 때 왜 메탄의 농도가 높았는지 설명할 수 있다.

어휘 **identify** ~을 밝히다, 확인하다 **methane** 메탄(가스) **potent** 강력한, 세력 있는 **culprit** 범인 **satellite** 인공위성 **swamp** 늪, 습지 **decomposition** 분해; 부패

062 ③ | that → who

해설 ③ 계속적 용법으로 쓰인 주격 관계대명사 자리. that은 계속적 용법의 관계대명사로 사용될 수 없으므로 who가 알맞다.

① 문장의 주어와 동사가 도치된 형태. 주어(freedom and ~)가 To the west에 '있었다'는 얘기이므로 자동사 lie의 과거형 lay가 맞게 쓰였다.
② The Pilgrims의 소유격 Their.
④ seemed limitless 대신 쓰인 대동사이므로 과거형 did로 맞게 쓰였다.
⑤ '~하는 누구든'의 뜻으로 쓰인 anyone who ~(=whoever ~).

해석 서부로의 이동은 미국 역사의 초기 몇 세기를 특징짓는다. 자유와 (역사상) 다양한 시기의 다양한 집단—17세기에는 순례자와 청교도들, 18세기에는 국경 개척자들, 19세기에는 개척자, 금광을 쫓는 이들, 정치인들—에게 더 나은 삶을 위한 기회가 서쪽에 놓여 있었다. 청교도들은 메이플라워호에 몸을 싣고 위험한 항해 속 대서양을 횡단하여 서쪽을 향했다. 그들의 메이플라워호 맹약이—이것이 '시민 주체의 정치'의 토대가 됐다—신세계에서의 최초의 자치 정부였다. 그들을 바짝 뒤쫓아 청교도들이 왔는데, 그들 또한 종교적 자유를 추구했다. 1848년 John Sutter의 방앗간에서 금이 발견된 것이 금광 찾기 열기가 전염병처럼 번지고 캘리포니아를 향해 서쪽으로 서둘러 몰려가는 일을 부추겼다. 미국의 첫 3세기 동안 땅은 서쪽으로 가려는 용기와 신념, 힘을 가진 자에게 자유와 더 나은 삶을 위한 기회가 그랬듯이 무한한 듯 보였다.

어휘 **diverse** 다양한, 가지각색의 **frontiersman** 개척자 **prospector** (금, 광물 등을) 찾는 탐사자 **voyage** (뱃길로 하는) 항해 **civil body** 시민 단체 **mill** 방앗간, 제분소 **unleash** (고삐를 풀어) 놓아주다, (강력한 반응을) 촉발시키다 **epidemic** 전염병 **limitless** 무한의 **conviction** 신념, 확신

063 ② | remembering → to remember

해설 ② 문맥상 '여행을 기억하기 위해'라는 의미가 되어야 자연스러우므로 '목적'을 나타내는 to부정사인 to remember로 고쳐야 한다. <keep v-ing(계속해서 v하다)>로 생각하지 않도록 주의한다. 아울러 <keep from v-ing (v를 하지 않다, v를 참다)>도 구분해서 알아 두자.

① 완전한 구조를 이끌며 장소를 나타내는 선행사 places를 선행사로 하는 관계부사 where가 적절하게 쓰였다.
③ that절 내의 주어 almost every ~ tourist attraction에 호응하는 동사 자리로 알맞게 쓰였다.
④ 선행사 patches를 보충 설명하며, 뒤에 불완전한 구조를 이끌고 있으므로 관계대명사 which가 적절.
⑤ 명사구 show-and-tell appearances를 수식하므로 형용사가 적절.

해석 우리 가족은 주말여행을 자주 하고, 여섯 살 난 내 아들 제시는 역사와 자연에 대해 배울 수 있는 장소로 가는 것을 특히 좋아한다. 대부분의 아이처럼 그는 우리가 방문하는 곳에 있는 기념품 가게에서 무엇인가를 항상 사고 싶어 한다. 처음에는 기념품이 그가 여행을 기억하기 위해 간직할 무엇인가가 될 수 있다는 생각으로 마지못해 받아들였으나, 제시는 우리가 집으로 돌아오자마자 기념품에 대한 흥미를 잃어버리곤 했다. 그런 뒤에 나는 거의 모든 박물관의 상점, 국립공원, 그리고 관광 명소에서 상징 패치들을 몇 달러에 판매한다는 것을 알아채기 시작했다. 이제 제시는 패치들을 수집하는데, 나는 그것들을 그의 여행 조끼에 붙여준다. 그 조끼는 학교에서 각자의 물건을 가져와 발표하는 시간에 자주 등장한다. 패치를 가짐으로써, 제시는 단지 장난감이 아닌 장소를 기억하고, 여행에서의 모험에 관한 자세한 이야기로 이제 학교에서 유명하다.

어휘 **souvenir** (휴가지 등에서 사는) 기념품 **give in** 항복하다; (마지못해) 받아들이다 **tourist attraction** 관광 명소 **emblem** 상징, 표상 **patch** (작은) 부분; 조각; ~을 덧대다[때우다]

구문 06~08행 I would give in, **thinking** the souvenir could be *something* [**(that)** he would keep ∨ / to remember the trip],

→ thinking이 이끄는 분사구문이 삽입된 구조. he 앞에는 목적격 관계대명사 that이 생략되었다.

064 ③ | having → has

해설 ③ ensuring 다음에 나온 that은 목적어절을 이끄는 접속사 that으로 주어는 everyone이고 involved는 과거동사가 아닌 과거분사로 주어를 수식하고 있다. 동사가 필요하므로 having을 has로 바꾸어 써야 한다.

① immediately는 부사로 뒤에 나온 형용사 available을 수식하고 있어 적절하다.
② 목적어가 주어(they)와 같으므로 재귀대명사 themselves가 적절하다.
④ 관계사절의 주어 역할을 하는 선행사 any unspoken feelings와의 관계가 능동이므로 affecting이 적절하다.
⑤ 비교급 more를 강조하는 부사로 much가 적절하다.

해석 갈등을 조정하는 지역사회 분쟁조정 프로그램이나 전문 중재자를 이용할 수 없다면 선택할 수 있는 한 가지는 (갈등의) 외부인, 즉 친구나 지인에게 요청하는 것이다. 이런 종류의 비공식적인 중재는 보통 협의가 결렬될 때 가장 즉각적으로 이용 가능한 선택사항이다. 갈등하는 동안 사람들은 좌절하게 될 수 있고, 끊임없이 방해받고 있다고 느낄 수 있으며, 그들이 받아들여지지 않고 되풀이하여 같은 말을 반복하고 있다는 것 등등을 느낄 수 있다. 제삼자는 대화를 촉진하고, 중립적 입장을 만들어내며, 관련된 모든 사람이 말할 순서를 반드시 가지도록 하고, 모든 사람이 이해받는다고 느끼도록 돕기 위해서 각 사람이 말한 것을 재구성함으로써 사람들이 이 상황에서 벗어나도록 이끄는 것을 도울 수 있다. 제삼자는 또한 논쟁에 영향을 줄 수도 있는 어떤 말 하지 못한 감정들을 이해하려 하기 위해 각 사람과 개별적으로 만날 수도 있다. 만약 제삼자가 양측 모두를 이해하고 공감할 수 있다면, 논쟁은 훨씬 더 해결되기 쉽다.

어휘 **community mediation** 지역사회 분쟁조정 **dispute** 분쟁, 분규; 논란, 논쟁; ~을 반박하다 **acquaintance** 아는 사람, 지인 **break down** 고장 나다; 실패하다, 결렬되다 **interrupt** ~을 가로막다, 방해하다; ~을 중단시키다 **repeat oneself** 반복해서 일어나다; 같은 말[일]을 되풀이하다 **third party** 제삼자 **facilitate** ~을 가능하게[용이하게] 하다 **empathize with** ~와 공감하다 **resolve** ~을 풀다, 해결하다; 결심하다

구문 10~15행 A third party can assist in guiding people out of this situation by **facilitating** the conversation, **establishing** some neutral ground, **ensuring** that everyone involved has a turn to speak, and **reframing** what each person says in order to help everyone feel understood.
→ 전치사 by의 목적어 역할을 하는 4개의 동명사 facilitating, establishing, ensuring, reframing이 병렬구조를 이루고 있다.

065 ③

해설 (A) 문맥상 '사랑이란 감정을 지속적으로 느끼는지'를 묻는 것이므로 동사 feel을 수식하는 부사 continuously가 적절.
(B) 문맥상 '어떻게'를 뜻하며 완전한 형태의 절을 이끌므로 의문사 how가 적절. '방법'으로 해석하여 관계부사로 볼 수도 있다. go on은 '(어떤 상황이) 계속되다'라는 뜻의 자동사. how love goes on은 현재분사 describing의 목적어가 되는 절이다.
(C) both는 복수명사를 수식하고 either는 단수명사를 수식하는데, 수식을 받는 명사 case가 단수이므로 either가 적절.

해석 사랑에 관해 흔히 하는 질문들 가운데 하나가 그것이 스타카토인가 레가토인가 하는 것이다. 즉, 어떤 사람이 낭만적인 사랑의 감정을 느낄 때 그 사람이 그것을 방해받거나 변화되어 짧게 느끼느냐 (스타카토), 아니면 그가 그것을 방해받지 않고 혹은 변화되는 일 없이 지속적으로 느끼느냐 (레가토) 하는 것이다. 시와 노래는 사랑이 레가토라고 생각하게 한다. 'True Love'와 'I Love You Truly'는 사랑이 어떻게 지속되는지를 이야기하는 아주 유명한 두 곡의 팝송이다. 그러나 현실에서 사랑은 스타카토에 더 가깝다. 어떤 사람이 방해받지 않고 무언가를 경험할 수 있으리라 여기기는 어려운 일이다. 수면은 깨어 있는 상태를 방해하고, 수면 그 자체도 꿈과 악몽에 의해 중단된다. 어떤 이가 깨어 있는 동안 연인에게 느끼는 감정은 수면으로 말미암아 망각되거나 강화될 수 있다. 두 경우 모두에서 그 감정은 변화한다.

어휘 **interruption** 방해; 중단 ***cf.* interrupt** ~을 방해하다; ~을 중단하다 **seduce** ~을 부추기다; ~을 유혹하다 **go on** (어떤 상황이) 계속되다 **wakefulness** 잠들지 않음 **punctuate** ~을 중단시키다, ~에 구두점을 찍다 **blot** ~을 더럽히다, 오점을 남기다 ***cf.* blot out** ~을 지우다 **intensify** ~을 강렬하게 하다, 세게 하다

066 ④ | to give in → giving in

해설 ④ 부모가 아이들의 요구를 받아주는 것을 멈춘 것이므로, stop v-ing(v하는 것을 멈추다)로 표현해야 적절하다. 참고로 stop to-v는 '~하기 위해 멈추다'라는 뜻.

① weather permitting은 '날씨가 좋으면(if the weather permits)'이란 뜻의 독립분사구문.
② 30분 규칙을 만든 것(created)보다 아이들에게 전념해야 한다는 의무감을 느낀 것이 시간상 먼저이므로 과거완료 시제(had felt)가 알맞게 쓰였다.
③ <what S be like>는 'S가 무엇 같은지(= 어떤지)'라는 뜻으로, what은 전치사 like의 목적어가 되는 의문대명사로서 바르게 쓰였다.
⑤ 분사구문의 의미상 주어가 문장 주어와 동일하고, 문장 주어인 they와 stick to가 능동 관계이므로 적절한 형태이다.

해석 몇 년 전, 내 친구들은 다소 독특한 규칙을 도입했는데, 그것은 아이들이 귀가 후 30분 동안은 부모가 있을 법한 어떤 공간에도 들어오지 못 하게 하는 것이다. 아이들은 자신들의 방에서 놀거나, 날씨가 좋으면 밖으로 나갈 수 있다. 부모들은 저녁 식사를 준비하면서 이 시간을 긴장을 풀고 이야기를 나누는 시간으로 활용한다. 30분 규칙을 만들어내기 전까지, 그들은 저녁 시간 내내 자녀들에게 헌신해야 한다는 의무감을 느꼈다. 하지만, 그들이 아이들에게 주의를 기울일수록, 아이들은 더욱더 요구사항이 많아지고, 자기중심적이고, 말을 듣지 않게 되었다. 이제 그 아이들은 너무나 급격히 달라져서 그들이 전에는 어땠는지에 대해 믿는 사람은 거의 없다. 아이들은 독립적이고, 안정되고, 행복하며, 성숙하고, 예의 바르다. 그들의 부모는 (아이들의 요구를) 받아주는 것을 멈추었고, 이것은 자녀들의 관심 중독을 고쳤다. 이 규칙을 고수했기 때문에 (이 규칙을 고수하면서), 대부분은 아닐지라도, 많은 맞벌이 가정에 존재하는 모든 '해야 할 의무들'을 그들은 거부했다.

어휘 **institute** (교육) 기관; (제도 등을) 도입하다 **happen to-v** 우연히[마침] ~하다 **unwind (unwound-unwound)** (감긴 것을) 풀다; 긴장을 풀다 ***cf.* wind** 구불구불하다; (실 등을) 감다 **feel obligated to-v** ~할 의무를 느끼다 **devote oneself to** ~에 헌신하다, (노력, 시간 등을) 쏟다 **demanding** 부담이 큰; 요구사항이 많은 **self-centered** 자기중심의, 이기적인 **disobedient** 반항하는, 거역하는 (↔ **obedient** 말을 잘 듣는, 순종적인) **give in** 항복하다; (마지못해) 받아들이다 **defy** ~에 저항하다, 거역하다 **dual-career family** 맞벌이 가정

구문 16~18행 | *Their parents stopped giving in*, / **which** cured the children of their addiction to attention.
→ 관계대명사의 계속적 용법으로 쓰인 which는 앞 내용 전체를 가리킨다.

18~20행 | **Sticking to this rule**, / they(S) defied(V) a whole set of "*shoulds*"(O) [**that** exist in many, **if not most**, dual-career families].
(= As they stuck to this rule,)
→ Sticking to this rule은 '원인' 또는 '부대상황'을 나타내는 분사구문. 분사구문의 의미상 주어는 문장의 주어와 동일한 they. if not most는 '대부분은 아닐지라도'라는 뜻의 삽입어구.

067 ⑤ | growing → grew

해설 ⑤ 주어가 Plants이고 이에 해당하는 적절한 동사가 없으므로 동사 자리에 있는 growing을 grew로 표현하는 것이 적절. exposed는 후치 수식 분사이며 문맥상으로도 전체 문장의 동사가 되는 것은 적절치 않음. 또한, 타동사이므로 능동태 동사로 쓰일 때 뒤에 목적어가 필요함. Plants [exposed to ~ jazz], for example, grew thick, ~.

① if people talk to them(=plants) 문장이 수동태로 바뀌어 if they are talked to가 된 것.
② 진주어인 명사절을 이끄는 that.
③ 동사 cause는 목적격보어로 to부정사를 취한다. <cause A to-v>는 'A로 하여금 v하게 하다'라는 뜻.
④ <make+O+OC(원형부정사)> 구조.

해석 과학 연구는 식물에 말을 걸면 더 잘 자란다는 것을 보여주었다. 식물은 소리를 느낄 수 있는 감각기관이나 신경계가 없으므로 그들이 특정 단어에 반응하지 않는 것은 분명하다. 명백한 해답은 당신이 말을 할 때, 모든 식물이 성장하는 데 필요한 이산화탄소와 수증기를 당신이 내뿜는다는 것이다. 당신의 목소리에서 나오는 소리의 파동 또한 식물 세포가 진동하도록 한다. 더 많은 실험이 특정 유형의 소리가 일반적인 것보다 식물이 더 잘 자라게 하거나 혹은 더 못 자라게 한다는 것을 보여주었다. 예를 들어, 클래식 음악이나 재즈에 노출된 식물들은 두껍고 건강한 잎을 자라게 했다. 그러나 록 음악으로 실험한 식물은 매우 좋지 않았다. 사실 그 식물들은 뿌리 발달이 매우 좋지 않아서 죽기 시작했다.

어휘 **nervous** 신경의; 불안해하는 **specific** 특정한 **obvious** 명백한, 분명한 **breathe out** ~을 내뿜다 **carbon dioxide** 이산화탄소 **vapor** 증기 ***cf.* water vapor** 수증기 **wave** 파동 **vibrate** 진동하다, 울려 퍼지다 **expose** ~을 노출시키다, 드러내다 **classical** 클래식의, 고전의

068 ② | were running → running

해설 ② 문장이 아니므로 동사처럼 were running으로 쓸 수 없다. <with+명사+분사 (~가 …하는 가운데)> 구조로 kids가 run하고 있는 것이므로 능동, 진행의 의미를 나타내는 running으로 고쳐 쓰는 것이 알맞다.

① '동시동작'의 분사구문 두 개(gently rocking ~, and talking ~)가 and를 가운데 두고 나란히 쓰인 구조.
③ <encourage+O+OC> 구조에서 목적격보어로 to부정사가 맞게 쓰였다.
④ <ask+IO+DO>의 4형식 구조에서 직접목적어로 if절 (~인지 아닌지(=whether))이 온 구조.
⑤ 그녀가 없었더라면(without her) ~가 가능하지 못했을 거라는 '과거 (또는 현재완료)'의 일을 반대로 가정하는 문맥이므로 wouldn't 뒤에 be able to의 완료형 have been able to가 맞게 쓰였다. 과거의 일을 반대로 가정하는 가정법 과거완료는 <if+주어+had+p.p. ~, 주어+조동사의 과거형+have p.p. ~>의 형태로 쓰는데, 여기서는 without her가 if절 대신 사용되었다.

해석 엄마와 내가 Central Park의 한 벤치에 앉아 유모차에 탄 Amelia를 부드럽게 흔들며 다시 직장으로 돌아가기 위해 준비해야 하는 점에 대해 얘기 나누고 있었다. 우리 앞 잔디밭에는 많은 수의 베이비시터들이 그들이 돌보는 아이들이 온통 주변을 이리저리 뛰어다니는 가운데 무리를 지어 있었다. 그 베이비시터들은 훌륭했다. 무리에서 떨어져 나온 아이들을 쫓아다니고, 갖가지 다른 게임을 해보도록 북돋우고, 분쟁의 해결을 돕고, 점심을 먹이고, 그냥 따뜻하게 파고들고 싶어 하는 아이들을 흔들어 재우고 있었다. 엄마가 "가서 일자리를 찾고 있는 누구 아는 베이비시터 있는지 물어봐."라고 하셨다. 그건 훌륭한 생각이었던 게 속담에도 그러듯이 깃털이 같은 새들끼리 모여 다니는 법이니까. 그러니까 그렇게 해서 내가 나의 베이비 시터인 Sharon을 만나게 되었던 거다. Sharon은 이제 10년째 우리 아이들을 돌보고 있다. 그렇게 많은 시간이 흘렀다니 믿기지 않는다. 하지만 그녀가 없었더라면 난 일을 계속할 수도 온전한 정신을 유지할 수도 없었을 것이다.

어휘 **rock** (살살) 흔들다 **stroller** 유모차 **gear up** 준비를 갖추다 **stray** ~을 [제 위치를] 벗어나다, (길을) 잃다 **resolve** 해결하다 **cradle** 흔들어 재우다; 요람 **flock** 떼 지어 다니다 **sanity** 온전한 정신 (상태)

069 ② | too → either

해설 ② 부정문이므로 '~도 또한[역시] …하다'라고 할 때 too 대신 either를 써야 한다.

① 상대방이 하는 말에 맞장구를 치는 <So+V+S>에서 동사는 "You're so pretty."의 동사 be동사(are)로 쓴 것이 맞다.
③ is complimenting으로 이어지는 현재진행형.
④ 동사(will be received)를 수식하는 부사.
⑤ a return compliment의 중복을 피하기 위해 쓰인 대명사 one. 불특정의 칭찬 한마디이므로 it이 아닌 one으로 쓰였다.

해석 "당신 정말 예뻐요."라는 말에 적절한 응답은 무엇인가? "감사합니다."는 분명 뭔가 부족해 보인다. "당신도요."는 상대가 남자면 이상하게 들리고, (실제로 그런지에 상관없이) 다소 마음에도 없이 하는 말인 것처럼 들린다. 하지만 아무 말도 안 하는 것도 왠지 적절한 것 같지 않다. 다시 말해, 당신의 외모에 대한 칭찬의 말을 어떻게 받아들여야 하는가? 처음 해보는 사람에게는 "감사합니다."가 진심을 담아 말해지는 거라면 처음에 여겨진 것만큼 그렇게 나쁘지 않을 수도 있다. 기억해야 할 점은 이 사람이 당신을 더 잘 알고 싶어서 당신에게 칭찬의 말을 하고 있을 공산[가능성]이 크다는 것이다. 당신이 뭐라고 하든 무례하지만 않다면 호의적으로 받아들여질 것이다. 그러니 답례 칭찬이 꼭 해야 하는 것은 물론 아니지만 진심이 실린 거라면 부담 없이 한마디 하라. 하고 싶은 말은 뭐든 진정을 담아서 하고 그 순간을 즐겨라. 그 편이 당신이 아무 말도 안 했을 때 잇따를지도 모를 어색함을 없애기에 충분하고도 남는다.

어휘 **fall short** 부족하다, 모자라다 **insincere** 진실 되지 못한, 마음에도 없는 **regardless** 어떻든지 간에 **compliment** 칭찬(의 말), 찬사; 찬사를 보내다 **initially** 처음에는, 초기에 **genuine** 진짜의, 진정한 **appreciation** 감사 **favorably** 호의적으로 **earnestness** 진심, 진정함 **eliminate** 제거하다, 없애다 **awkwardness** 어색함, 거북함

070 ① | being → is

해설 ① 주어(The yearly amount (spent on diabetes treatment))가 끝나고 동사가 와야 할 자리이므로 being이 아닌 is (equal to ~)가 되어야 한다.

② illness가 (환자를) devastate(완전히 파괴하다)시키는 주체이므로 능동을 나타내는 현재분사 devastating이 맞게 쓰였다.
③ warnings의 내용이 이어 나오는 동격의 that.
④ by v-ing and v-ing(by restricting ~ and (by) forcing ~)의 병렬구조.
⑤ 선행사 steps에 맞게 주격 관계대명사절이 수동태로 시작되었다. take steps: 조치를 취하다

해석 어느 선도적인 자선단체에 따르면, 당뇨병이 영국에서 지난해 23만 5천 명이 이 병으로 진단받으면서 전염병 수준에 도달하고 있다. 당뇨병 치료에 연간 쓰이는 금액은 현재 국가 전체 예산의 10%에 맞먹는다. 전문가들은 고통받는 사람의 약 90%가 체중이 가장 강력한 위험 요인인 2유형이라고 말한다. 이 파괴적인 질병은 심장마비, 뇌졸중, 실명, 신장 기능 장애로 이어질 수 있다. 그럼에도 불구하고 적게 먹고 운동을 더 해야 한다는 널리 알려진 경고가 이 병의 놀랄 만한 증가를 멈추게 하지 못하였다. 당뇨병 영국 단체가 이제 정부에 아이들을 겨냥한 음식 광고를 제한하고, 제조업자들을 제품에 소금, 설탕, 지방 사용을 줄이도록 강제함으로써 조치를 취해달라고 촉구하고 있다. "환자 대다수가 2유형으로, 이는 생활방식과 관련되고, 즉 환자 수를 줄이기 위해 취해질 수 있는 조치가 있음을 뜻한다."고 그 단체는 얘기한다.

어휘 **diabetes** 당뇨병 **epidemic** 전염성의; 전염병 **diagnose** 진단하다 **charity** 자선단체 **yearly** 연간, 한 해의 **equal to** ~와 같은, ~와 맞먹는 **budget** 예산 **sufferer** 고통받는 자, 시달리는 사람 **potent** 강한, 강력한 **devastating** 초토화시키는, 대단히 파괴적인 **stroke** (병의) 발작, 뇌졸중 **kidney** 신장 **widespread** 보편화된, 널리 퍼진 **escalation** 상승 **call on** ~에게 촉구하다[요청하다] **restrict** 제한하다 **majority** 다수

구문 12~15행 Diabetes UK is now calling on the government to act **by** *restricting* food advertisements (aimed at children) [A] and *forcing* manufacturers to cut salt, sugar and fat in products. [B]

→ by -ing(~함으로써)의 병렬구조. <call on+O+to-v>와 <force+O+to-v>의 SVOC 구조에 주목할 것.

071 ⑤

해설 (A) enough가 형용사, 동사, 부사를 수식할 때는 수식받는 말 뒤에 위치함. <형용사+enough+to-v> *cf.* 명사를 수식할 때는 명사의 앞, 뒤 어디에도 올 수 있다.
(B) 사진들이 대대로 '전해지는' 것이므로 의미상 주어(their photos)와 to부정사는 수동관계이다. 따라서 to be p.p. 형태가 적절.
(C) stay는 형용사를 보어로 취하는 동사로서 여기서 보어는 형용사인 still이다. 형용사를 수식하는 것은 부사이므로 perfectly가 적절.

해석 오늘날 대부분의 사람은 사진을 찍을 때 미소를 짓는다. 그러나 초창기의 몇몇 사진들을 보라. 당신은 당신을 노려보며 심각하고 심지어 찡그린 표정을 지은 한 무리의 사람들을 보게 될 것이다. 초창기에 사진 찍은 사람들이 절대 미소를 짓지 않은 몇 가지 이유가 있다. 우선, 사진 촬영은 당시 진지한 사업이었다. 모든 사람이 사진을 찍을 만큼 운이 좋았던 것은 아니었다. 사람들은 그들의 사진이 대대로 전해지리라 기대했다. 그들은 진지하고 위엄 있게 기억되고 싶었다. 둘째, 사진 촬영은 매우 힘든 작업이었다. 사람들은 카메라가 사진을 찍는 동안 10분 또는 20분을 완전히 꼼짝하지 않고 있어야 했다. 움직이지 않고 그렇게 오랫동안 미소를 지을 수 있는 사람은 없는데, 움직이면 사진이 흐릿하게 나올 것이다.

어휘 **batch** 무리, 묶음 **frown** 얼굴을 찡그리다 **stare** 응시하다 **photographic** 사진(술)의 **subject** 대상; 주제 **from generation to generation** 대대로 **dignified** 위엄 있는 **still** 정지한 **blurry** 흐릿한

072 ③

해설 (A) 문맥상 '어떤 집'이라는 의미가 되어야 하고, discover의 목적어절을 이끌면서 homes를 수식해 주는 자리이므로 의문형용사 which가 적절.
(B) 주어가 3인칭 단수인 a futuristic urban map project이므로 단수동사 has가 적절.
(C) a map이 만드는 것이 아니라 '만들어지는' 것이므로 수동형인 be produced가 적절.

해석 감시를 받고 있다는 느낌을 받아 본 적이 있는가? 아마 그럴지도 모른다. 감시 시스템이 점점 더 정교해지고 더 넓은 구역에까지 미치고 있다. 영국의 한 시의회는 정찰 비행기를 고용하여 도시 상공을 날아다니며 어떤 집이 열 손실이 가장 큰지 알아내도록 했다. 그 결과를 보여주는 도표가 온라인상에 게시되어 주민들은 에너지 효율성 측면에서 자기의 집이 어떤 평가를 받았는지 알 수 있었다. 또한, 미국에서는 도시 주민들의 움직임을 기록하는 미래형 도시 지도 프로젝트가 MIT(매사추세츠 공과 대학)에서 개발되고 있다. 휴대전화와 위치 파악 시스템에서 모은 자료로 시민, 버스, 택시, 기차, 자동차의 변화하는 위치를 보여주는 지도를 만들어 낼 수 있다.

어휘 **surveillance** 감시 **sophisticated** 정교한, 고도화된 **council** 의회 **post** ~을 게시하다, 공표하다 **rate** ~을 평가하다, 어림잡다 **efficiency** 효율(성) **futuristic** 미래의, 미래형의 **urban** 도시의 **chart** ~을 기록하다; ~을 도표로 만들다 **inhabitant** 주민, 거주자 **global positioning system(GPS)** 위치 파악 시스템

구문 06~09행 I The resulting map was posted online, **so that** residents could see how their homes rated for energy efficiency.
→ 이 문장에서 so that은 '그 결과, 그러므로'란 의미로 '결과'를 나타내는 부사절을 이끈다.

073 ⑤ | that → what

해설 ❺ 동사 wonder의 목적어절을 이끄는 자리이므로 접속사 that 다음에는 완전한 절이 위치해야 하는데, range 'a number of deaths' came into에서 into 뒤의 목적어에 해당하는 것이 없고 range 앞에 있어야 할 관사 the도 없다. 그러므로 의문사 what을 써야 하며, what range는 전치사 into의 목적어이다.

① not only가 문두에 위치하면 <조동사+주어+동사>의 어순으로 도치가 일어나므로 do we occasionally accept의 어순이 잘 사용되었다.
② 진주어절을 이끄는 that이 적절히 쓰였다.
③ '60명이 죽었다'고 경찰이 하는 말을 기자가 '듣는' 상황이므로 수동태 형태로 잘 사용했다.
④ 'which is right'은 confirm의 목적어 역할을 하는 간접의문문으로, <의문사주어(which)+동사(is)>의 어순이 잘 사용되었다.

해석 우리가 정보를 다루는 방식으로 인해 우리는 때때로 부정확한 정보를 받아들일 뿐만 아니라 실제 부정확한 정보가 필요하기도 하다. 분명히, 부정확한 정보는 때때로 뉴스 보도의 중요한 한 부분이 될 수 있다. 뉴스매체는 진실한 정보를 생산하는 것을 목표로 해야 하지만 뉴스 매체가 정보를 신속하게 내보내는 것 역시 똑같이 중요하다. 너무 늦어버린 정확한 정보는 뉴스 면에서 거의 가치가 없다. 예를 들어, 기차 충돌을 다루는 한 기자가 경찰 서장으로부터는 사망자가 60명이라는 말을 듣지만 구급차 대장은 58명이라는 말을 하고, 반면 병원은 그 수가 59명이라고 말한다. 그 기자는 무엇을 보도해야 할까? 그는 많은 사람들이 죽었다고 말해야 할까, 아니면 그 숫자 중 하나를 골라서 어떤 것이 옳은지를 나중에 확인하도록 노력해야 할까? 물론 최종 사망자 수가 결정되기까지 여러 주가 걸릴 수 있을 것이다. 나는 대부분의 소비자들이 '수많은 사망자'가 어느 정도를 포함하는지 궁금해하기보다는 대강의 숫자를 더 알고 싶어 하지 않을까 하고 생각한다.

어휘 **occasionally** 때때로 **inaccurate** 부정확한 **specifically** 명확하게, 구체적으로 말하면 **truthful** 진실한 **of little value** 거의 가치 없는 **term** 용어, 조건 **cover** 보도하다 **police chief** 경찰서장 **confirm** 확인하다 **death toll** 사망자 수 **suspect** 의심하다 **approximate** 대략의 **range** 범위, 영역; (범위가) ~에 이르다

구문 05~07행 **While** the news media should aim to produce truthful information, *it* is as important ***that*** they get the information out *quickly*.
→ 접속사 While은 '~이지만, ~하는 반면에'의 뜻이다. it은 가주어이고 that 이하가 진주어다. quickly 다음에는 as that they produce truthful information이 의미상 생략된 것으로 볼 수 있다.

074 ② | that → which

해설 ❷ perspiration(or sweat)을 선행사로 취하면서 뒤에 나오는 produce의 목적어 역할을 하는 계속적 용법의 관계대명사 자리이다. 관계대명사 that은 계속적 용법으로 쓰이지 못하므로 which가 되어야 한다.

① affects의 목적어가 되는 절을 이끄는 의문부사이면서 '우리가 어떻게 온도를 느끼는가'라는 의미에 부합하는 how는 적절.
③ 조건 부사절에서는 현재시제가 미래시제를 대신한다.
④ 도표(chart)가 '개발된' 것이므로 develop과 수동관계를 이룸. 따라서 수동태 형태가 적절.
⑤ 명사구 our body's reaction을 이끌므로 because of가 적절. 접속사 because는 절을 이끈다.

해석 습도가 높으면 왜 날이 더 덥게 느껴질까? 습도는 공기 중의 수분인데 이것은 우리가 온도를 어떻게 느끼는지에 영향을 미친다. 공기가 수분으로 가득 차 있으면, 그것은 발한(發汗) 작용, 즉 땀의 증발을 지연시키는데, 땀은 우리 신체가 열을 식히는 것을 돕기 위해 만들어내는 것이다. 만약 당신이 온도는 같지만 습도의 수준이 다른 두 날을 비교하면, 습도가 더 높은 날이 더 덥게 느껴질 것이다. 열지수라고 불리는 도표는 서로 다른 수준의 습도가 어떻게 우리에게 다양한 온도가 느껴지게 하는지를 보여주기 위해 개발되었다. 이것은 우리의 신체 반응 때문에 중요하다. 덥고 습한 날은 조심하지 않으면 열사병이나 일사병과 같은 심각한 건강 문제를 일으킬 수 있다.

어휘 **humidity** 습도, 습기 **moisture** 수분, 습기, 수증기 **evaporation** 증발, 발산 **perspiration** 발한, 땀 **index** 지수, 지표; 색인 **heat exhaustion [stroke]** 열사병, 일사병

075 ④ | has not adequately dealt with → has not been adequately dealt with

해설 ❹ 선행사가 a long period of stress로 deal with의 객체이므로 능동이 아닌 수동태로 써야 한다. 현재완료시제에 수식어인 부사 not과 adequately가 끼어들어 동사의 모양이 능동인지 수동인지 한눈에 판단하기 어려운 경우이다.

① 동격의 that(the belief that ~)절이 <so ~ that ...(너무 ~해서 …하다)> 패턴을 이루고 있고, that절의 주어로 to부정사구가 온 경우.
② produce의 대상이 문장의 주어 The nervous breakdown이므로 to부정사가 수동형 to be p.p. 형태로 맞게 표현되었다. one's work이 nervous breakdown을 produce한 주체.
③ 이어지는 절은 원래 the person is attempting to escape from some emotional problem이므로 전치사 없이 관계대명사만 쓰인 게 맞다. 전치사와 관계대명사를 함께 써서 from which the person is attempting to escape로도 쓸 수 있다.
⑤ 부정문이므로(no longer ~) something이 아닌 anything을 쓴 경우. 부정어 no가 이미 나왔으므로 nothing으로도 쓸 수 없다.

해석 신경쇠약의 전조는 자기 일이 너무 중요해 하루만 휴식을 취해도 큰 재앙을 불러올 것이라는 믿음이다. 내가 만약 의사라면 자신 혹은 자기 일을 이처럼 중요하게 생각하는 사람 모두에게 휴일을 하루 처방할 것이다. 일에 의해 생기는 것처럼 보이는 신경쇠약은 보통 그 사람이 일이라는 수단을 통해 벗어나려고 시도하는 어떤 정서적인 문제 때문에 생긴다. 이는 제대로 해결되지 못한 오랜 기간의 스트레스 때문에 발생하며, 의무를 이행하는 데 있어서 더 어려움을 겪는 결과를 가져온다. 그는 이 일을 포기하길 원하지 않는다. 왜냐하면, 만약 그가 포기하게 되면 혹 있을지 모르는 불행으로부터 그의 마음을 다른 데로 돌릴 어떤 것도 더 이상 없기 때문이다.

어휘 **symptom** 전조, 징후; 증상 **nervous** 신경의 **breakdown** 쇠약; 붕괴, 파손 **prescribe** ~을 처방하다 **attempt** ~을 시도하다 **adequately** 적절하게, 제대로 **fulfill** ~을 이행하다; ~을 성취하다 **obligation** 의무 **distract** (마음, 주의를) 딴 데로 돌리다 **misfortune** 불행

076 ⑤ | remain → remaining

해설 ❺ '교직에 남다'라는 문맥이므로 a young instructor를 수식하는 분사 developing과 and로 연결된 병렬구조로 보는 것이 적절. 따라서 remaining으로

고쳐야 한다.

① 주절의 동사로 <조동사 과거형+동사원형(wouldn't be)>이 쓰였고, 문맥상 현재 사실을 반대로 가정하고 있다. if절도 '~라면'이라는 의미이므로 가정법 과거 구문. 따라서 if절에는 were가 적절하다.
② 의미상 주어인 children이 신이 나는 감정을 '느끼게 되는' 것이므로 과거분사가 적절.
③ that절 내의 주어 inexperienced teachers에 호응하는 동사이므로 복수동사가 적절.
④ 앞의 so discouraged와 함께 쓰여 문맥상 '매우 낙담해서 교직을 그만둔다'는 의미가 되어야 하므로 <so ~ that ... (매우 ~해서 …하다)> 구문이 적절하게 쓰였다.

해석 모든 교사가 소크라테스만큼 훌륭하다면 좋지 않을까? 물론 모든 교사가 이 기준에 부응하리라고 예상하는 것은 비현실적이고, 모든 교사가 아이들이 학교에 가는 것을 매일 신이 나게 한 채로 집에 돌려보내지 않는다는 것은 명백하다. 하지만 문제를 감당하지 못하는 미숙한 교사가 교실을 관리하는 경우는 빈번하다. 젊은 교사가 뛰어날 때조차도, 2~3년 후에는 종종 매우 낙담해서 교직을 그만두는데, 이것이 미숙함의 순환으로 이어지고 있다. 부모들은 자녀의 교사를 지지할 필요가 있다. 가장 훌륭한 젊은 교사조차도 소외감을 느낄 수 있는데, 학부모들로부터의 격려와 감사는 발전하며 수년 동안 교직에 남는 젊은 교사와 자신의 잠재력을 달성하기 전에 떠나 버리는 수많은 교사 중 한 명 사이의 차이를 만들 수 있다.

어휘 **live up to** ~에 부응하다[합당하다] **thrilled** 아주 흥분한[신이 난] **inexperienced** 경험이 부족한, 미숙한 (↔ **experienced** 경험이 풍부한, 능숙한) **outstanding** 뛰어난; 두드러진; (문제·보수 등이) 미해결된, 미지급된 **discouraged** 낙담한, 낙심한 **isolated** 외떨어진, 고립된; 단 한 번의

구문 15~18행 ~*the difference* [**between** *a young instructor* [developing and remaining on the job for many years]$_A$ **and** one of *the countless teachers* [**who** walk away before achieving their potential]$_B$].

→ <between A and B> 구조에서 A와 B가 각각 분사구와 관계사절의 수식을 받아 길어졌다.

077 ⑤

해설 (A) 전체 문장은 <접속사+분사구문, 주절>의 구조이다. 분사구문의 의미상 주어는 Korean musicals이며 regard와의 관계가 수동이므로 regarded가 적절.
(B) 주격 관계대명사 which의 선행사가 the five-day workweek이므로 단수동사 gives가 적절.
(C) build ~ and share ~ and even organize ~로 이어지는 병렬관계이다.

해석 한때 비주류 예술 형식으로 간주되던 한국의 뮤지컬이 과거 몇 년 사이에 매우 인기를 얻은 이유는 무엇일까? 이는 사람들에게 더 많은 여가 시간을 허용한 주 5일 근무와 당연히 향상된 생활 수준 때문이라고 말하는 이들이 많다. 특별난 이유로는 한국의 높은 인터넷 사용을 들 수 있다. 젊은이들은 온라인 모임을 만들어 다양한 뮤지컬에 대한 논평을 공유하고 심지어 할인된 가격으로 단체 관람을 조직하기도 한다. 만약 좋은 뮤지컬에 대한 티켓 판매량이 감소하기 시작하면 그 뮤지컬을 좋아하는 사람들은 수백 장의 입장권을 더 팔고 그 뮤지컬을 되살리기 위해 사이버 공간에서 캠페인과 홍보 활동을 할 것이다.

어휘 **regard A as B** A를 B라고 간주하다, 여기다 **minor** 중요치 않은 **spare** 여분의 **usage** 사용(법) **promotion** 홍보, 판촉; 승진 **revive** ~을 소생시키다, 되살리다

078 ③ | having → have

해설 ③ having이 어법상 적절하다면 앞에 나온 명사 herbs를 수식하게 되어 and 이하 절에 동사가 없다. associated는 앞에 주어로 나온 명사구 the images and virtues를 수식하므로 having을 have로 고쳐 동사가 되어야 어법상 적절하다.

① 형용사 unmatched가 뒤에서 명사 a scale을 수식하고 있는 것으로 적절히 쓰였다.
② 이 문장의 주어는 의문사 what이 이끄는 명사절 what proportion ~ these products로서 적절히 쓰였다.
④ 부사가 문장 앞에 나와 문장 전체를 수식하는 경우로서 쓰임이 적절하다.
⑤ 앞에 나온 fossil fuels를 가리키는 것이므로 복수형의 대명사 them이 나오는 것이 문맥상 적절하다.

해석 약초는 2세기 동안 화장품, 식품, 그리고 차에서뿐만 아니라 가정용 제품, 대체 의약품, 심지어 동물 치료 약 분야에서도 필적할 수 없는 규모로 받아들여지고 있다. 정확히 얼마만큼의 비율로 식물의 원재료가 이런 제품들 일부에 포함되는지에 대해서는 의문의 여지가 있을 수 있다. 특히 광고계는 환경 내에 증가하는 인공 화학 물질의 양에 관한 우려를 늦지 않게 이용하였고, 약초와 연관된 이미지와 장점은 특정한 식물이나 제품과 거의 관련이 없을 것 같은 모호한 친환경적인 유익함으로 흔히 섞여 들어가 버렸다. 그렇지만 전체적으로 그들의 메시지는 분명하며 서양은 지난 20년 동안 약초 이용과 유용한 식물에 대한 관심의, 선례 없는 부활을 경험해 왔다. 심지어 그들의 이미지도 옷감, 가구와 거리 장식과 같이 곳곳에 나타난다. 그래서 화석 연료와 그것에 의존하는 화학물질이 고갈되면서, '화학의 시대'가 '식물의 시대'로 대체될 것이라고 보는 것이 비현실적이 아닐 수 있다.

어휘 **embrace** 받아들이다, 채택하다 **unmatched** 필적할 수 없는 **alternative medicine** 대체 의학 **veterinary** 수의학의 **remedy** 치료 약 **proportion** 비율 **play on** ~을 이용하다 **quantity** 양 **man-made** 인공의 **virtue** 장점, 미덕 **associated with** ~와 연관된 **be merged into** ~와 섞이다, 통합되다 **vague** 애매한 **wholesomeness** 유익함 **collectively** 전체적으로, 포괄적으로 **decade** 십 년 **fabric** 옷감, 천 **fossil fuel** 화석 연료 **run out** 고갈되다 **fanciful** 비현실적인 **replace** 교체하다

구문 18~21행 I So **as** *fossil fuels and the chemicals* [that depend on them] run out, // ***it*** may not be fanciful *to see the Chemical Age replaced by the Age of Plants*.
→ 접속사 as가 이끄는 절에서 주어는 fossil fuels and the chemicals이고, [ ] 부분은 관계대명사절로 앞에 나온 the chemicals를 수식하고 있다. 주절에서 it은 가주어이고 to see 이하가 진주어이다.

079 ③

해설 (A): 문장의 주어는 postcards, 동사는 have challenged이므로 또 다른 동사가 올 수 없다. 따라서 주어 postcards를 수식하는 과거분사 used가 쓰여야 한다.
(B): 문장 첫머리에 과거를 나타내는 부사구(In 1993)가 나왔으므로 과거 시제의 동사 launched가 쓰여야 한다. 현재완료는 명백한 과거를 나타내는 부사구와 같이 쓸 수 없다.
(C): 주어가 The blend이므로 단수동사 makes가 적절하다. 수식어구의 일부인 the familiar and the unexpected를 복수주어로 착각하지 않도록 주의한다.

해석 최근 몇 년간 매우 다양한 활동가의 캠페인 및 교육적 캠페인에 의해 사용된 엽서들은 의도적으로 우리의 일반적 기준에 이의를 제기해왔다. 1993년에 Banff 국립공원에서 진행되는 개발을 중단하기 바라던 캐나다 공원 야생 협회(CPAWS)는 한 엽서 캠페인을 시작했다. CPAWS의 공식 출판물인 Borealis의 구독자들은 공원의 상업적 개발 비율에 관한 정보뿐 아니라 최근의 Banff의 건설 프로젝트의 사진이 담긴 우편엽서를 받았다. 그러한 사진은 그림엽서의 잘 알려진 구성 방식을 활용하지만, 대개 대중적 기념엽서와 연결되는 메시지에 도전한다. 익숙한 것과 예기치 못한 것을 혼합하면 이것을 환경 활동에 효과적인 도구로 만들어준다. 환경 교육과 관광 홍보 사이의 연결은 관광객과 지역 야생 생물 사이에 좀 더 지속 가능한 관계를 장려하는 것을 목표로 한 최근의 우편엽서 캠페인에 의해 보다 더 확고해졌다.

어휘 **activist** 활동가 ***cf.* activism** (정치적 목적을 위한) 행동주의 **deliberately** 고의로, 의도적으로; 신중하게 **norm** 표준, 일반적인 것; 규범; 기준 **halt** ~을 멈추다, 중단시키다 **launch** ~을 시작하다; ~을 출시하다 **subscriber** 구독자 **feature** 특징, 특색; ~을 특별히 포함하다, 특징으로 삼다 **imagery** 형상화, 사진 **sustainable** 지속 가능한

구문 01~03행 In recent years, postcards(S) (used in a wide variety of activist (campaigns) and educational campaigns) have deliberately challenged(V) our norms(O).

080 ① | adheres → adhering

해설 ❶ means clinging ~, or adhering ~, or even worse, getting stuck ~의 병렬구조의 일부이므로 동사 means의 목적어인 동명사 adhering이 되어야 한다.

② and로 연결된 dirty와 마찬가지로 형용사가 와야 할 자리이다. un+sight(명사) + ly → unsightly(보기 흉한, 볼품없는)로 명사에 -ly가 붙어 형용사가 된 경우.
③ cost(비용이 들다)의 주체는 동명사 주어 Cleaning up ~이므로 단수형 costs가 맞게 쓰였다.
④ The gum을 가리키는 소유격 its.
⑤ 동사 is removed의 수식어로 부사 easily가 맞게 쓰였다.

해석 껌은 접착력이 좋아 끈질기게 자기 자리를 지킨다. 불행히도, 자기 자리를 지킨다는 것은 흔히 신발 밑창에 들러붙거나 버스 좌석에 붙거나 심지어는 머리카락에까지 붙는 것을 의미한다. 사람들이 내뱉는 보기 싫고 지저분한 껌 자국을 청소하는 데 영국의 납세자들은 연간 약 1억 5천만 파운드의 비용을 낸다. 그러나 최근 세계 최초의 달라붙지 않는 껌 발명으로 이런 엉망인 상황의 끝이 보일 듯하다. 브리스톨 대학의 개발자들이 'Rev 7'이라고 이름 붙인 이 껌은 옷이나 머리카락에 붙지 않고, 콘크리트에서 쉽게 제거되며, 몇 분 동안 내린 비에도 그냥 녹아 없어질 것이다. 런던 시 공무원들은 이 발명품을 청소비용을 줄이는 수단으로써 환영해왔다.

어휘 **adhere to** ~에 들러붙다 **unsightly** 보기 흉한 **blob** 얼룩, 방울 **spit out** ~을 내뱉다 **in sight** 눈에 보이는 **mess** 엉망인 상태 **nonstick** 들러붙지 않는 **dissolve** 녹다, 용해되다 **official** 공무원; 공식적인 **budget** 예산

구문 10~14행 The gum(S), **called** *"Rev 7" by its Bristol University inventors*, is not attracted(V_1) to clothing or hair, is easily removed(V_2) from concrete, and will simply dissolve(V_3) in just a few minutes of rain.

→ 삽입된 과거분사구(called ~ inventors)는 주어 The gum에 대한 부가 정보를 제공한다.

081 ③ | to do → done

해설 ❸ <get+O+OC> 구조에서 목적어와 목적격보어의 관계가 능동이 아닌 수동이므로 과거분사 done으로 써야 한다.

① task가 셀 수 있는 개념의 복수로 쓰였으므로 many가 알맞다. as many ~ as possible: 가능한 한 많은 ~
② <so ~ that ...(너무 ~해서 …하다)>의 '결과'를 나타내는 접속사 that.
④ spend+O(시간/돈) + v-ing: O를 v하는 데 쓰다
⑤ a way 뒤에 '방식, 양태'를 나타내는 관계부사절을 이끄는 관계부사 that이 왔다. a way how ~로는 쓰지 않음에 유의한다.

해석 시간 관리라는 것이 당신의 하루에 될 수 있으면 많은 할 일을 쑤셔 넣는 것은 아니다. 그것은 당신이 일을 하는 방식을 단순화하고, 일을 보다 빨리하며 스트레스를 더는 그런 것이다. 그것은 사람과 놀이, 휴식을 위한 시간을 만들기 위해 당신의 삶에서 (일정) 공간을 치워 놓는 일이다. 우리는 바쁨에 사로잡힌 나머지 우리가 하고 있는 일을 즐기는 법을 까먹는다. 그저 단순히 더 열심히 하는 것이 아니라 더 지혜롭게 일하는 것에 초점을 맞추고 있을 때조차도, 우리는 일을 완료하는 데에 너무 자주 집중한다. 이것이 중점이 되어서는 안 된다. '내가 하고 있는 일을 더 즐기며 하려면 어떻게 해야 하지?' 하고 늘 자신에게 물어보라. 목표는 당신이 하기로 한 것들을, 일하는 중이더라도 일상의 소소한 것들을 행하면서 행복감을 느끼는 식으로 엮어나가는 것이 되어야 한다. 이는 헛된 생각처럼 들릴지 모르나 오늘날의 세계에서는 그 어느 때보다 더 가능하다. 호기심을 가져라. 기회에 늘 열린 마음을 갖춰라. 자신을 알라. 당신의 열정을 끌어안아라.

어휘 **manage** 관리하다, 경영하다 **squeeze** (좁은 곳에) 밀어 넣다 **simplify** 단순화하다 **relieve** (근심 등을) 덜다 **busyness** 바쁨, 다망, 무의미한 활동 **arrange** 배열하다, (일을) 처리[조정]하다 **commitment** 약속, 전념 **live out** (생각만 하던 것을) 실행하다, 실현하다 **pipe dream** 몽상, (속이 텅 비어 있는) 헛된 꿈 **embrace** 끌어안다, 수용하다 **passion** 열정

구문 07~09행 Even when we focus on working smarter, **not** just working harder,(종속절) we're still often too focused on **getting** things done.(주절)

→ <A, not B(B가 아니라 A)>의 구조로 A를 강조하고 있다. not이 부정하는 B는

working harder가 아니라 just working harder인 데 주의한다.
→ 목적어와 목적격보어가 수동관계일 때는 <get+O+p.p.> 패턴으로 쓴다.

082 ③ | makes → making[to make]

해설 ③ 문장의 주어와 동사는 이미 나왔으므로(there is someone ~), 밑줄 부분은 주어인 someone을 꾸며주는 수식어 부분이다. 능동형 분사인 현재분사 making이나 to부정사의 형용사적 용법 to make로 고쳐 써야 한다.

① while(~인 반면, ~인데도)의 뜻에 가까운 when.
② to부정사의 주체를 밝히는 의미상의 주어 <for+목적격>이 그 앞에 온 경우.
④ 앞에 나온 복수명사 the dishes 대신 쓰인 지시대명사 those.
⑤ 앞 문장 일부(making sure ~ sequence)를 가리키는 지시대명사 that.

해석 식사 준비 시간이 요리마다 다 다른 게 명백한데 레스토랑 요리사들은 어떻게 많은 요리를 테이블마다 다 다른 사람들에게 동시에 용케 내는 것인가? 우선, 이때다 싶어 보일 때 웨이터가 요리에 '발사 신호를 내릴' 거고 이것이 주방이 가동되는 신호탄이 된다. 그리고는 모든 것이 올바른 순서대로 틀림없이 요리되도록 하는, 지휘자처럼 주방 이곳저곳 돌아다니며 서 있는 사람이 있다. 예를 들어, 10분 걸리는 요리는 6분 걸릴 요리보다 4분 일찍 시작된다. 레스토랑에 따라 그것은 주방장이나 부주방장, 또는 (이 일을 위한) 전문가의 일이 될 수 있다. 이런 식으로 해서 요리사들은 서로 다른 많은 테이블의 요리를 전부 동시에 해내는 묘기를 부리는 것이다. 이렇게 하는 게 몹시 헷갈릴 것으로 들릴지 모르지만 걱정할 필요는 없다. 그들은 전문가들이고 여러 해 동안 매일 그 일을 해왔으니까 말이다.

어휘 **chef** 주방장, 요리사 **manage to** 어렵사리[가까스로] ~해내다 **serve** 음식을 (손님에게) 내다 **at the same time** 동시에 **cue** 신호 **conductor** 지휘자 **sequence** 순서, 수순 **deputy** 부-; 대리의 **juggle** 저글링 하다, 묘기를 부리다 **professional** 전문가

구문 06~09행 Then there is *someone* [**who** stands around in the kitchen like a conductor] [**making** sure *(that)* everything is getting cooked in the right sequence]]].

→ make sure (that~): 틀림없이 ~되도록 하다

083 ④

해설 (A) 주어는 An attitude of interest and curiosity. 태도는 '길러지는' 것이므로 수동태 be cultivated가 적절.
(B) 문맥상 '사물을 관찰하기 위해 멈추다'라는 내용이 자연스러우므로, '~하기 위해 멈추다'란 뜻의 stop to-v가 알맞다. *cf.* stop v-ing: v하던 것을 멈추다
(C) and 이하의 절에서 동사는 try이므로 또다시 동사형 describe가 올 수 없다. 문맥상 the freshest, truest words를 수식하는 형용사적 용법의 to describe가 적절.

해석 관심과 호기심을 갖는 자세는 유익하며, 이는 당신이 노력한다면 길러질 수 있다. 매일 적어도 한 가지 사물에 놀라워하려고 노력해라. 바깥에 주차된 차나 보도의 나무, 또는 길 건너편의 빌딩을 자세히 보기 위해 멈춰 서서 자신에게 물어보라. 그것은 다른 차들이나 나무들, 빌딩들과 어떻게 다른가? 당신이 이미 그 사물의 본질을 알고 있다거나 당신이 모른다고 해도 그리 중요하지는 않다고 넘겨짚지 마라. 사물이 당신에게 말하는 것에 마음을 열고, 그 사물과 그에 대한 느낌이 어떤지를 묘사하는 가장 참신하고 가장 정확한 낱말들을 찾으려고 노력해라. 삶이란 경험의 강이어서, 당신이 더 깊이 잠수하고 더 멀리 헤엄칠수록 당신의 삶은 더욱 풍요로워질 것이다.

어휘 **curiosity** 호기심 **cultivate** (말, 행동 방식 등을) 기르다; ~을 경작하다 **make an effort to-v** v하려고 노력하다 **take a (good) look at** ~을 (자세히) 보다 **assume** ~라고 추정하다 **essence** 본질

구문 10~13행 **Be** open to what the thing is telling you, and **try** to find *the freshest, truest words* (**to describe** the thing and how it makes you feel).
(it =the thing)

→ 두 개의 명령문으로 이루어진 문장. to describe 이하는 the freshest, truest words를 수식한다.

084 ③ | became → to become

해설 ③ during which ~ apparent가 관계사절인데, 이 절 속의 동사는 advanced이므로 became을 쓰면 동사를 두 번 쓴 격이 되어 옳지 않다. to become의 형태로 고쳐서 <enough to-v (v할 정도로 충분히)>와 같이 써야 하며, 이때 바로 앞의 for the ~ Galois's work는 to become의 의미상 주어이다.

① Galois는 많은 수학 저작을 남겼다고 밝혀졌는데, 수학 저작을 남긴 것이 그 사실이 밝혀졌을 때보다 더 과거의 일이므로 to have p.p.의 형태는 적절하다.
② were judged 다음에 to have와 to lead가 and로 연결되어 병렬구조를 이룬다.
④ whose는 의미상 the new paradigm's가 되며, 바로 뒤에 나오는 명사 relevance and effectiveness와도 잘 연결된다.
⑤ that 이하는 the now commonplace idea에 대한 동격절이다.

해석 1832년에, 20세의 나이에 결투에서 사망한 뒤, 프랑스 수학자 Galois는 자신의 거의 마지막 순간까지도 광적으로 작업했었음에도 불구하고 검토된 뒤 무가치하다고 선언된 많은 양의 수학적 저술을 남긴 것으로 밝혀졌다. 그 수학적 명제는 분명 참신했으나, 수학적 지식에 아무런 기반을 두지 않았으며 어떠한 결과도 끌어내지 못한다고 판단되었다. Galois의 업적의 타당성과 유효성이 명백해질 만큼 충분히 수학이 발전하게 된 수년의 세월이 흐른 뒤에야 비로소 그것의 창의성이 인정받게 되었다. Galileo 같은 다른 창의적인 과학자들도 또한 타당성과 유효성이 특정한 시대가 이해할 수 있는 능력을 넘어선 사실상 새로운 패러다임을 도입했기 때문에 극심한 사회적 불인정을 받았다. Galileo의 경우 이것은 지구가 태양 주변을 돈다는, 지금은 평범한 개념이었다.

어휘 **a body of** 많은 양의 ~ **pronounce** 선언하다 **frantically** 광적으로, 열성적으로 **novel** 참신한 **passage** (시간의) 흐름, 경과 **relevance** 타당성 **effectiveness** 유효성 **apparent** 명백한 **in effect** 사실상 **appreciate** 이해하다 **commonplace** 평범한, 흔한 **revolve** 돌다, 회전하다

구문 09~13행 **It was** *only after the passage of several years during which mathematics advanced enough for the relevance and effectiveness of Galois's work to become apparent* that its creativity was recognized.
→ <It was ~ that ...> 강조구문으로서, 이 문장에서는 only after ~ to become apparent가 강조되고 있다. which는 앞에 나온 명사구 the passage of several years를 받는다.

085 ① | the number of → a number of

해설 ❶ '다수의 르네상스 화가들'이 문맥상 자연스러우므로, '다수의'라는 뜻으로 명사를 수식하는 a number of가 적절. *cf.* the number of: ~의 수

② 베이킹 소다와 다른 재료들로 '만들어진' 것이므로 a mild cleanser를 꾸며주는 과거분사형이 적절.

③ 주어가 Several applications이므로 복수형 were가 적절.

④ 선행사가 This cleaning agent이고, 계속적 용법의 관계대명사 자리이므로 which 적절.

⑤ 앞선 명사 the area를 수식하는 분사구인데, the area가 '청소되고 있는' 것이므로 being p.p. 형태가 적절.

해석 시스티나 성당의 벽들은 15세기 후반 이탈리아에서 가장 높이 평가받는 예술가들에 속했던 다수의 르네상스 화가들에 의해 장식되었다. 성당의 복원 작업은 1980년에 시작되었다. 시스티나 성당의 복원에서 가장 유용한 재료 중 하나는, 흘러내리지 않는 젤을 만들기 위해서 물과 섞은 베이킹 소다와 다른 원료들로 만들어진 부드러운 세척제였다. 천장과 벽의 구역들에서 때를 완전히 제거하기 위해 세척제를 여러 번 사용해야 할 필요가 종종 있었다. 이 세척물질은 예술품 복원가들에게 이용된 지 약 20년밖에 되지 않았는데, 시스티나 성당을 복원하는 일에 특히 적합했다. 흘러내리지 않는 방식 덕분에 청소되는 지역 주변에 어떤 먼지도 퍼뜨리지 않고 필요한 곳에 정확한 양이 사용되었다.

어휘 **chapel** 예배당, 교회당 **restoration** 복원 ***cf.* restorer** 복원가 **mild** 순한; 온화한 **cleanser** 세척제 **ingredient** 원료, 성분, 재료 **drip** (액체가) 뚝뚝 떨어짐; 뚝뚝 떨어지다 **application** 적용, 응용; 신청 **grime** 때, 먼지 **suit** ~에 적합하게 하다 **formula** 제조법; 공식

086 ⑤ | consuming → consumed

해설 ❺ 광천수(mineral water)는 사람들이 '마시는' 대상이므로 consume과 수동관계이다. 과거분사 형태가 적절.

① that절 내 주어 carbonated drinks에 호응하는 동사이므로 복수동사 are가 적절.

② drinking과 <between A and B>로 연결된 병렬관계이므로 동명사인 having이 맞다.

③ <the+비교급 ~, the+비교급 ...>: ~할수록 점점 더 …하다

④ it은 앞의 carbonated water를 가리키며 뼈 건강과 관련이 없다고 '여겨지는' 것이므로 consider와 수동관계를 이룬다.

해석 지난 10월 발표된 프레이밍햄 골다공증 연구는 콜라와 같은 탄산음료가 노년 여성들의 낮은 골밀도와 관련이 있다는 것을 보여주었다. 일주일에 세 번 이상 이런 음료를 마시는 것과 더 약한 뼈를 갖는 것 사이에는 뚜렷한 관련성이 있다. 사실 여성이 콜라를 더 많이 마실수록 그 여성의 골밀도는 더 낮아졌다. 이 연구들에 치아는 다뤄지지 않았지만 그 결과는 비슷할 것이라 할 수 있다. 지금까지 탄산수는 연구되지 않았지만 뼈 건강에 특별한 영향을 미치지 않는다는 것이 일반적인 생각이다. 그러나 최상의 선택은 칼슘과 마그네슘을 함유한 광천수인데 매일 마셨을 때 성인의 뼈를 보호하는 것으로 나타났다.

어휘 **carbonated** 탄산가스로 된 **be associated with** ~와 관련되다 ***cf.* association** 관련; 연합 **neutral** 관련이 없는, 중립의 **consume** ~을 마시다; ~을 소비하다

구문 12~15행 But the best choice is mineral water (**containing** calcium and magnesium), **which**, when consumed daily, has been shown to protect the bones of adults.

(when consumed daily: 삽입구)

→ which 이하는 보어 mineral water를 부연 설명한다.

087 ② | was startled → startled

해설 ❷ a poem이 나를 놀라게 한 것이므로 수동태가 아니라 능동태의 과거시제인 startled로 고쳐 써야 알맞다.

① go to a place이므로 전치사 to가 필요하다.

③ 시를 쓴 시점은 과거(wrote a poem)이고, 누군가 다른 사람이 '그 전에 이미 썼던' 것처럼 느껴졌다고 했으니 과거 이전을 나타내는 과거완료(had written)가 알맞다. 첫 작품을 아마추어 같지 않게 잘 썼다는 느낌을 표현한 것.

④ 그것 '없이는' 살 수 없을 어떤 것처럼 느껴진다 했으므로 without이 적절하다.

⑤ I는 작가로 읽히는 존재이므로 동명사의 수동형(being read)으로 맞게 쓰였다.

해석 글쓰기는 내게 너무나 큰 즐거움을 주며 나는 그것을 할 때 훨씬 행복한 (그래서 더 괜찮은) 사람이 된다. 내 머릿속에 글을 쓸 때 가는 곳이 있는데 그곳은 너무나 풍요롭고 뜻밖이고—그리고 가끔은 무섭기도 한—하지만 결코 따분하지 않은 곳이다. 나는 일곱 살 때 그곳에 처음 갔고, 나 자신을 약간 놀라게 한 시 한 편을 썼는데, 그 이유는 다른 누군가가 그것을 쓴 것 같은 느낌이 들었기 때문이었다. 그것이 나에게 준 아드레날린 방출은 엄청났고 나는 더 많은 걸[더 큰 짜릿함을] 원했다. 요즘은 아마도 그곳에 꽤 쉽게 다가갈 수 있기 때문에 글쓰기가 그것 없이는 도저히 살 수 없는 어떤 것으로 느껴진다. 그것은 기쁨을 주는 것이다. 나는 그것을 해서 돈을 벌 수 있어 아주 운이 좋다고 생각하지만 (내 글이) 한 번도 출판되지 않았더라도 글을 계속 쓰고 있을 것 같다. 나는 (내 글이) 읽히는 것을 사랑하지만 내가 진짜로 염두에 두고 글을 쓰는 대상은 나이다.

어휘 **enormous** 막대한, 크나큰 **unexpected** 예상치 못한, 기대하지 않은 **startle** 깜짝 놀라게 하다 **rush** 돌진, 쇄도 **access** ~에 접근하다 **joyous** 아주 기뻐하는, 기쁨을 주는 **publish** 출판하다

088 ⑤ | discourage → discouraging

해설 ❺ contribute to(~에 기여하다)에서 to는 전치사로, 뒤에는 명사 개념이 와야 한다. 따라서 동명사인 discouraging으로 고쳐야 알맞다.

① 앞에 나온 performance goals를 가리키는 계속적 용법의 관계대명사. 다소 생소한 개념에 대한 설명을 덧붙일 때 쓰인다.

② 단수주어 A focus에 맞게 단수형 동사가 쓰였다.

③ <A rather than B(B라기보다는 A)>의 구조에서 A, B 모두 나란히 명사로 쓰였다.

④ 주어(a mastery focus)에 맞게 단수형 동사를 썼고, the very things를 목적어로 갖는 능동형으로 맞게 쓰였다.

해석 대부분의 학교는 수행 목표를 중심으로 틀이 짜지는데, 이는 실수를 피하고 다른 학생보다 잘하며 높은 점수, 기준, 상과 같은 외적인 목표에 부응하는 것의 중요성에 초점을 둔다. 반면 숙달 목표 초점은 배움에 대한 긍정적인 느낌과 함께 내적 동기와 창의성을 키우고 보다 높은 학업 열의는 물론 보다 강한 인내심 및 호기심을 키우는 경향이

있다. 숙달 초점식의 교실은 또한 보다 학생 중심적이고 개별화되어 있으며 학생들이 성공을 단순히 능력 때문이 아닌 노력 덕이라고 생각한다. 숙달 목표에 초점을 둔 교실에서는 학습자들 사이에 성장 마인드를 북돋우는데, 이는 능력이라는 것이 시간이 흐를수록 노력과 연습으로 개발된다는 사실을 알고 있다는 특징이 있다. 많은 교사와 학교 지구들이 숙달 초점식이 발달시키는 바로 그것들을 가치 있게 본다고 말하지만 정작 학교들은 대개 수행 지향적인데, 특히 수학과 읽기에서 보다 높은 점수를 거두는 것을 목표로 하는 데이터 기반의 목표를 갖고 있어 이 점이 학생들에게서 배움에 대한 사랑을 꺾어 놓는 데 기여한다.

어휘 **performance goal** 수행 목표 **outperform** 더 나은 결과를 내다, 능가하다 **extrinsic** 외적인 **objective** 목표 **mastery goal** 숙달 목표 **intrinsic** 내적인, 내재된 **along with** ~와 나란히, ~와 함께 **perseverance** 끈기, 인내심 **academic engagement** 수업 참여, 수업에 열중함 **attribute A to B** A를 B 탓으로 돌리다[덕으로 보다] **mindset** 마음가짐, 태도 **be characterized by** ~을 특징으로 하다 **district** 구역, 지구 **oriented** ~ 지향적인, ~에 중점을 둔 **data-driven** 자료 중심의, 데이터 기반의 **discourage** 말리다, 단념시키다

구문 16~22행 Many teachers and school districts(S) say(V) *(that)*(O) they value *the very things* [**that** a mastery focus develops], yet schools(S) are(V) typically performance oriented(C), (with data-driven goals for higher math and reading scores, in particular), **which** contributes(V′) to *discouraging love of learning in students*(O′(전치사 to의 목적어)).

→ 접속부사 yet을 중심으로 두 개의 문장이 연결된 구조.

→ 두 개의 that은 각각 목적어절을 이끄는 생략된 접속사(say (that))와 목적격 관계대명사(the very things that)로 쓰임.

→ 관계자들이 겉으로 표명하는 것과는 달리 실제 학교는 performance oriented로, 이것이 학생들에게 어떤 영향을 끼치는지 부연 설명해주는 계속적 용법의 which로 이어지고 있다.

089 ⑤

해설 (A) 현재 사실을 반대로 가정하는 것이므로 가정법 과거를 써야 한다.

(B) that's의 보어절을 이끌면서 has practiced의 목적어 역할을 할 수 있는 관계대명사 what이 적절.

(C) our brain 이하가 앞 내용에 대한 이유를 설명하고 있으므로 because가 적절. because는 <결과+because+원인>, why는 <원인+why 결과>의 형태로 쓰인다.

해석 농구, 골프, 편자 던지기 같은 스포츠에서 기술은 연습하면서 향상되지만 반복이 그 자체로 어떤 가치를 갖기 때문에 그런 것은 아니다. 만약 그렇다면 우리는 성공 대신 실수에서 배울 것이다. 예를 들어, 누군가가 편자를 던지는 것을 배운다면 그는 말뚝을 맞히는 것보다 빗맞히는 횟수가 더 많을 것이다. 만약 반복을 통해 기술 향상이 일어난다면, 그는 빗맞히는 데 전문가가 될 것이다. 왜냐하면 그것이 그가 가장 많이 연습한 것이기 때문이다. 그가 빗맞히는 횟수는 맞히는 것보다 열 배는 많을 것이다. 그러나 시간이 흐르면서 빗맞히는 경우는 점점 적어지고 맞히는 경우는 더 잦아진다. 이는 우리의 뇌가, 성공은 기억하고 실수는 잊어버리기 때문이다.

어휘 **horseshoe** 편자(말굽에 대어 붙이는 U자 모양의 쇳조각) **pitch** ~을 던지다 **repetition** 반복 **in itself** 그 자체로서 **miss** 빗맞히다; ~을 그리워하다; 실수 **stake** 막대기, 말뚝 **outnumber** ~보다 수가 많다, ~보다 우세하다

090 ②

해설 (A) the notion과 뒤에 이어지는 individual pieces ~ character가 동격이므로 동격절을 이끄는 접속사 that이 적절하다.

(B) and로 연결된 The performance와 technical production이 주어이므로 복수동사 are를 써야 한다. 삽입된 whether절과 수식하는 전명구(in ~studio)가 각각의 뒤를 따르는 구조이다.

(C) 콤마로 삽입된 구문 as the end result ~ activities 앞의 the recording이 that 관계절의 주어이고, 해당 위치는 관계절의 동사 자리이므로 단수동사 exerts를 써야 한다.

해석 각각의 대중음악 곡들이 그것들만의 고유성과 특징으로 구별될 수 있을 것이라는 생각은 대중음악 장르 전반에 걸쳐 흔하다. 그러나 이 생각은 반드시 작곡된 요소에 의해서만 확립되는 것은 아니다. 실황이든 녹음이든 간에 연주와 녹음실에서의 기술적 제작은 곡들 간에 고유성이 구별되게 해주는 요소들의 주요 현장이다(요소들이 생겨나는 곳이다). 사실, 고유성이 때때로 최종 결과물에 대한 특별한 관심 없이, '간단히 말해' 연주라는 활동에 들어 있음을 볼 수 있다. 하지만, 동시에, 여러 활동들이 조합된 최종 결과로서 녹음된 음반이 고유성의 개념에 행사하는 강력한 영향을 무시하는 것은 잘못일 것이다.

어휘 **notion** 생각, 개념 **distinguishable** 구별할 수 있는; 분간할 수 있는 **identity** 독자성; 고유성 **by virtue of** ~에 의해 **site** (사건 등의) 현장; (특정 용도용) 장소 **distinction** 구별 **reside** 존재하다; 살다 **exert** (권력·영향력을) 행사하다, 가하다

구문 01~04행 **The notion** [that individual pieces of popular music may be distinguishable by their own identity or character] / **is** common across popular music genres.

→ [ ] 부분은 주어 The notion의 동격절이며, 문장의 동사는 is이다.

12~16행 Yet, at the same time, **it** would be wrong **to ignore** *the powerful influence* [**that** the recording, as the end result of a combination of activities, exerts over the notion of identity].

→ it은 가주어이며 to ignore ~ the notion of identity가 진주어이다. [ ] 부분은 the powerful influence를 수식하는 관계절이다.

091 ④ | becomes → to become

해설 ④ 부사절 접속사 whether가 이끄는 절 내에서 주어는 they이고 동사는 head off이다. 접속사 없이 동사가 다시 나올 수 없고, 문맥상 목적을 나타내야 하므로 becomes는 to become으로 바꾸어 써야 한다.

① if 다음에 <주어+be동사(so many university students are)>가 생략되어 있다. 학생들은 기회를 '받는' 것이므로 과거분사 형태 given을 쓰는 것이 적절하다.
② 주어는 around five million college students로 복수이므로 복수형 동사 graduate는 적절하다.
③ <with+O+v-ing> 분사구문은 'O가 v한 채로'의 뜻이다. students from China to Chile가 '학습하는' 것이므로 능동의 의미의 현재분사 learning을 쓴다.
⑤ <so ~ that ...(너무 ~해서 …하다)> 구문에 나오는 접속사 that으로 쓰임이 적절하다.

해석 공적 삶에서의 경제학의 우세함을 고려하면, 그토록 많은 대학생들이 기회가 주어진다면 자신들의 교육의 일부로 약간 공부하기로 선택한다는 것이 놀랍지 않다. 매년 미국에서만 약 5백만 명의 대학생들이 적어도 하나의 경제학 강좌를 경험하고 졸업한다. 미국에서 시작된, 그리고 Econ 101로 널리 알려진 표준 개론 강좌가 이제 전 세계에서 교육되고 있으며, 중국에서 칠레에 이르는 학생들이 시카고와 매사추세츠 주의 케임브리지에서 사용되는 것과 동일한 바로 그 교재의 번역서로 공부하고 있다. 이 모든 학생들에게, 그들이 후에 사업가가 혹은 의사가 되기 위해서 떠나건, 기자 혹은 정치 활동가가 되기 위해서 떠나건, Econ 101은 폭넓은 교육의 주된 부분이 되었다. 심지어 경제학을 결코 공부하지 않은 사람들에게도, Econ 101의 언어와 사고방식이 대중 토론에 너무 퍼져서 그것이 우리 모두가 경제에 대해 생각하는 방식(경제가 무엇인지, 경제가 어떻게 돌아가는지, 그리고 경제는 무엇을 위한 것인지)을 형성한다.

어휘 **dominance** 우세; 지배 **opt** 선택하다, 채택하다 **course** 강좌; 과목; 진행 **under one's belt** 경험의 일부로 **introductory** 입문의; 서두의 **originate** 시작되다, 생기다 **translation** 번역(본); 통역 **staple** 주요한; 주요 산물 **head off** 떠나다 **entrepreneur** 기업가 **mindset** 사고방식 **pervade** ~에 퍼지다, 전체에 보급되다

구문 01~04행 **Given** the dominance of economics in public life, it is no surprise **that so many university students**, *if given the chance*, **opt to** study a little as part of their education.
→ given은 독립분사구문을 이끌어 '~라고 가정하면, 생각하면'이라는 의미이다. 밑줄 친 it은 가주어, that이 이끄는 절이 진주어이다. that절 내의 주어와 동사 사이에 접속사 if를 포함한 분사구문이 삽입되었다.

16~20행 Even for *those* [who never study economics], the language and mindset of Econ 101 **so** pervades public debate **that** it shapes *the way* [that we all think about the economy]: what **it** is, how **it** works, and what **it** is for.
→ 두 개의 [ ] 부분은 관계사절로 각각 those와 the way를 수식한다. '너무 ~해서 …하다'의 뜻인 <so ~ that ...> 구문이 사용되었다. 밑줄 친 세 개의 대명사 it이 가리키는 것은 the economy이다.

092 ② | to do → doing

해설 ② do the dishes는 바로 앞의 to dry가 아닌 mowing the lawn, putting the clothes ~와 병렬구조를 이루고 있으므로(A, B and C) 동명사구인 doing the dishes로 표현되어야 한다. to dry는 옷을 빨랫줄에 너는 '목적'을 나타내는 부사구로 B의 일부.

① 주어가 Various chores로 복수이고, 이 chores의 구체적인 내용을 목적어로 소개하고 있으므로 능동태(include)로 쓴 것이 알맞다.
③ -thing으로 끝나는 명사이므로 형용사가 뒤에서 수식하고 있다.
④ were given - regularly의 <동사-부사> 구조.
⑤ help는 목적격보어로 to부정사와 원형부정사 둘 다 취할 수 있는 준사역동사.

해석 집안일 하는 것에 대해 용돈을 지불하는 것은 서로서로 좋은 상황이다. 즉, 아이는 돈이라는 것이 힘들게 벌어야 하는 것이라는 걸 배우고 당신은 해야 할 집안일이 줄어든다. 우리 아이들이 책임지고 해왔던 다양한 집안일에는 잠자리 정리하기, 자기 방 늘 깔끔히 하기, 쓰고 난 물건 치워 놓기 등이 있다. 나이가 들면서는 그 일은 잔디 깎기, 옷가지를 말리기 위해 빨랫줄에 널기, 그리고 설거지 등으로 발전해 갔다. 집안일에 대한 대가로 주는 용돈은 분명 아이들이 돈의 가치를 제대로 이해하는 데 도움이 될 수 있다. 그러나 그것이 집안 곳곳에서 그들이 하는 도움이 되는 일은 무엇이든 다 대가를 받아야 한다는 마음가짐을 아이들에게 조장하는 일이 없도록 주의를 기울여야 한다. 그 밖에 용돈이 어디에 또 쓰이는가? 예를 들어, 용돈이 착한 행동에 대한 보상으로 규칙적으로 주어지는 거라면? 어떤 경우에는 용돈을 어떤 예의 바르고 공손한 행동과 결부시키는 것이 실제로 어린아이들의 사회적 기술 연마에 보탬이 되는 좋은 방법이 될 수 있다.

어휘 **household chore** 집안일 **earn** (노력해서) 얻다, 획득하다 **be responsible for** ~을 책임지고 있다, 책임지고 ~하다 **tidy** 말끔한, 단정한 **put ~ away** ~을 치우다 **belongings** 소유물, 재산 **progress** 진전되다, 발전하다 **mow** (잔디를) 깎다, (풀 등을) 베다 **appreciate** 진가를 제대로 알다 **ensure** 확실히 하다, 반드시 ~이게 하다 **mindset** 마음가짐, 태도 **tie A to B** A를 B와 묶다[연관 짓다] **respectful** 존경심을 보이는, 공손한

구문 10~13행 However, care must be taken to ensure **that** it doesn't create *a mindset* (in your child) **that** they should be paid for *anything* (helpful) [(**that**) they do ∨ around the house].
(동격의 that / 선행사 / 관계대명사)
→ 동사의 목적어인 명사절을 이끄는 접속사 that, a mindset의 내용을 소개하는 동격의 that이 사용되었고, 선행사인 anything을 수식하는 목적격 관계대명사 that은 생략되어 있다.

093 ③ | laid → lay

해설 ③ 동사 다음에 목적어가 바로 오지 않고 전명구 in ~으로 이어지므로 타동사 lay(~을 두다)는 아니다. 자동사 lie(~에 눕다)가 lie in의 형태로 '~에 있다'의 뜻으로 쓰인 경우이므로 lie의 과거형 lay로 써야 맞다. (lie-lay-lain)

① spring 1775가 과거이므로 그즈음에는 이미 시작되어 있었다는 '완료'를 나타내는 과거완료가 맞게 쓰였다.
② resolve가 동사(해결하다)가 아닌 명사(결의, 의결) 뜻의 주어로 쓰였다. stop이 목적어 없이 '중지되다, 중단되다'의 자동사로 맞게 쓰인 경우.
④ unify가 '통합하다'라는 의미이므로 opinion 입장에서는 'unified', 즉 수동을 나타내는 과거분사로 맞게 쓰였다.
⑤ argued ~ and provided ~의 병렬구조.

해석 1775년 봄 무렵에 무장 갈등이 뉴잉글랜드 식민지 지방에 이미 발생해 보스턴시가 공격을 당하고 있었다. 필라델피아에 소집된 제2차 대륙회의에서 군대를 조직하라고 조지 워싱턴을 뉴잉글랜드에 보냈지만 식민지의 결의안은 거기에서 중단되었다. 대표들은 무엇을 할지 그리고 유아기의 군대가 그대로 존속되도록 할지를 신속히 결정해야 했다. 문제는 식민지 시민들 자체에 있었던 것이, 다양한 지역의 가게 운영자, 기능공, 농부들은 모국에 어떻게 대응해야 할지에 대해 단합된 의견을 갖지 못했다. 1776년 1월에 토머스 페인이 흔들리는 민심을 느끼고는 <상식(Common Sense)>이라고 불리는

소책자인, 초판 시 십오만 부가 팔린 미국 최초의 정치적 대인기작을 찍어냈다. <상식>은 누구나가 이해할 수 있는 언어와 비유, 유추로 영국으로부터의 완전한 분리를 주장하였으며 새 정부의 청사진을 제공하였다.

어휘 **armed** 무장한, 무기를 사용하는 **colony** 식민지 *cf.* **colonial** 식민지의 **colonist** 식민지 주민 **assemble** 모으다 **military force** 군대 **resolve** 결의 **representative** 대표자 **lie in** ~에 있다 **artisan** 장인, 기능공 **unified** 단합된 **sense** 느끼다, 감지하다 **wavering** 흔들리는, 요동치는 **blockbuster** 블록버스터(크게 성공한 책이나 영화) **copy** 복사본 **metaphor** 은유, 비유 **analogy** 비유, 유추 **vision** 비전, 미래상

094 ② | were kept → kept

해설 ② 문장의 동사(was)가 앞에 이미 나왔으므로 이 부분은 the five chimpanzees를 수식하는 수식어부(the five chimpanzees (kept at the ~))가 되어야 한다.

① 명사(residential area) 앞에 형용사인 nearby(근처의)가 맞게 쓰였다.
cf. near: ~ 가까이(전치사)
③ report(보고하는)하는 것은 경찰이므로 수동태로 맞게 쓰였다.
④ 움직이고 있는 것이, 즉 동작을 '진행 중'인 것이 포착되었으므로 진행을 나타내는 현재분사로 쓴 것이 자연스럽다. 능동태로 고치면 People spotted the chimpanzee moving ~.이 된다.
⑤ 침팬지가 잡힐 때까지 not to leave the school의 행위가 '지속'되는 것이므로 완료를 나타내는 by가 아닌 계속을 나타내는 until을 쓴 것이 맞다.

해석 센다이의 한 동물원에서 탈출한 침팬지 한 마리가 목요일 오후 근처 주거 지역에서 마취 총에 맞아 송전선에서 떨어진 후 잡혔다. 수컷 침팬지인 차차는 미야기 현 수도에 있는 야기야마 동물원에 있는 다섯 마리 침팬지 중 하나였다. 이 사건으로 다친 사람은 아무도 없는 것으로 보고되었다. 동물원 직원이 오후 1시 20분경 침팬지 중 한 마리가 우리에 안 보이는 걸 알아챘고, 잇달아 공원이 예방조치로 폐쇄됐다고 동물원 측이 말했다. 그 침팬지는 주거 지역의 송전선을 따라 이동하는 게 포착됐고 마취 총을 맞고 오후 3시 10분경 잡혔다. 이 지방의 한 초등학교는, 당시 교내에 약 4백 명의 학생이 있었는데 침팬지가 잡힐 때까지 귀가를 위해 학교를 떠나지 않도록 지시했다.

어휘 **residential** 주거의, 주거 용도의 **tranquilizer** 마취제 **subsequently** 그 뒤에, 이어서 **precaution** 예방책, 예방 조치 **spot** (보고) 알다, 발견하다 **power line** 전깃줄 **pupil** 학생

구문 04~07행 The male chimpanzee (S), Chacha, (동격의 콤마(,)) was (V) *one of the five chimpanzees* (C) [(*which were*) kept at the Yagiyama Zoological Park in the Miyagi Prefecture capital].

095 ①

해설 (A) 주어인 boundaries가 '놓여진' 것이므로 타동사 lay(~을 놓다)의 수동태 were laid가 쓰여야 한다. 참고로 lie(눕다)는 자동사로서 수동태로 쓸 수 없다. (lie-lay-lain)
(B) that절의 동사 자리인데 주어가 the only chance이므로 단수동사인 was가 적절.
(C) 수백 년에 걸친 전쟁(centuries of warfare)이 연합을 불가능하게 '만든' 것이므로 make와 능동관계이다. made가 적절. <make+O+OC>: O를 …한 상태로 만들다

해석 최초의 식민지 개척자들이 유럽에서 북미에 도착했을 때 이미 그곳에 살고 있던 원주민들은 그들을 친구로서 환영했다. 새로운 정착민들과 그들이 '인디언'이라고 부르는 사람들 사이에 협정서가 작성되고 경계선이 그어졌다. 그러나 시간이 지나면서 점점 더 많은 인디언의 땅이 정착민들에게 넘어갔다. 혼란과 분노에 휩싸인 채 인디언들은 정당하게 그들의 것이었던 땅으로부터 점점 더 멀리 서쪽으로 밀려났다. 위대한 인디언 지도자들은 그들의 종족을 위한 유일한 기회는 모든 종족이 공동의 적에 대항하여 뭉치는 것이라 생각했다. 그러나 여러 종족 간의 수백 년에 걸친 전쟁은 이를 불가능하게 했다. 서로 싸우는 것이 삶의 방식이 되어 있었다.

어휘 **colonist** 식민지 개척자 **greet** ~을 환영하다, ~에게 인사하다 **agreement** 협정, 협약 **draw up** (문서를) 작성하다 **boundary** 경계선, 경계 **settler** 정착민, 개척자 **rightfully** 정의롭게, 합법적으로 **tribe** 종족, 부족 **warfare** 전쟁, 전투

구문 10~12행 ~ that the only chance (for their people) (S′) was (V′) *for all the tribes* **to unite** against the common enemy.

→ for all the tribes는 이어지는 to부정사구의 의미상 주어.

096 ③ | are → is

해설 ③ 문장의 주어가 단수형의 어구 more effective communication이므로 동사도 단수형인 is로 일치시켜야 한다.

① be linked to ~는 '~과 연관되다'라는 뜻이고, to가 전치사이므로 명사나 동명사가 목적어로 나와야 하므로 여기서 동명사 providing의 쓰임은 적절하다.
② 형용사 alone은 '~하나만으로도'의 뜻으로 명사나 대명사 뒤에 쓰여 특정한 그것 하나만을 가리킴을 강조한다. 여기서는 science를 수식하여 쓰임이 적절하다.
④ 접속사 where는 '~하는 경우에'라는 의미로 부사절을 이끌 수 있다.
⑤ 부정사 to facilitate는 앞에 나온 명사 new tools를 수식하는 형용사 역할을 하고 있고, 쓰임이 적절하다.

해석 20세기 내내 과학은 농업과 산업 활동에서 생겨난 토지 황폐화와 오염이라는 문제의 해결책으로 간주되었다. 그 결과 이제 환경 문제에 실질적인 해결책을 제공하는 것과 연관된 과학에 대한 재정 지원에 점점 더 많은 중점을 두고 있다. 이것은 난관을 만들어 내는데, 왜냐하면 우수한 과학이 실행될 수 있지만, 과학만으로는 광범위한 변화를 만들어 내지 못할 것이기 때문이며, 주로 이는 이 정보를 이용해서 변화를 만들어 낼 의사소통 수단의 개발이 부족하기 때문이다. 일반 대중의 행동과 신념에 변화를 이루어 내기 위해서는 (우리가) 얻고 있는 새로운 과학적 통찰력의 더 효과적인 소통이 요구된다. 심지어 환경 문제에 대한 해결책이 분명한 경우조차도 (보통) 비용이 많이 드는 해결책을 실행하기 위해서는 (기업체의) 경영진, 정치권, 그리고 궁극적으로는 일반 대중의 지지가 필요하다. 따라서 우리의 현재의 연구를 효과적으로 이용하는 것은 과학자들뿐만 아니라 경영자들, 정부와 그리고 궁극적으로는 일반 대중에게로도 효과적인 전달을 쉽게 해주는 새로운 수단을 필요로 할 것이다.

어휘 **pollution** 오염 **agricultural** 농업의 **industrial** 산업의 **funding** 재정지원 **be linked to** ~와 연관되다 **dilemma** 난관, 진퇴양난 **conduct** 실행하다, 실시하다 **channel** (의사소통의) 수단[경로] **insight** 식견, 통찰(력) **management** (회사의) 경영진 **ultimately** 궁극적으로 **support** 지지, 지원 **implement** 실행하다 **utilize** 이용[활용]하다 **facilitate** 가능하게 하다, 용이하게 하다 **general public** 일반 대중

구문 01~04행 ~, science was seen as the solution to the problems of *land degradation and pollution* (**resulting** from ~).
→ 분사 resulting은 앞의 명사구 land degradation and pollution을 수식한다.

07~11행 This creates a dilemma, **for** *while excellent science can be conducted*, science alone will not create widespread change, mainly ***because*** the channels (to use this information and create change) / are poorly developed.
→ for는 '~ 때문에'란 뜻의 접속사로 쓰였다. while ~ conducted는 부사절이므로 for가 이끄는 내용은 science alone will not create widespread change가 된다. because 이하에서 주어는 the channels이고 동사는 are developed이다.

097 ⑤

해설 (A) 명사절 that절 내의 주어는 복수명사 changes이므로 복수동사 cause가 적절.

Researchers believe that ***changes*** [triggered ~ in melanin, *the pigment* [which darkens ~ the sun]], **cause** ~.
(S′: changes / (=동격삽입구) / V′: cause)

(B) 앞에 나온 the reaction of melanin의 반복을 피하기 위한 대명사 자리이므로 단수형 that이 적절.

(C) 완전한 형태의 절이 앞에 나왔고, 접속사 없이 동사가 올 수 없으므로 <접속사+주어+동사>의 역할을 할 수 있는 분사구문이 와야 한다. '결과'를 나타내는 부대상황의 분사구문이다.

해석 붉은색 머리카락을 가진 사람은 대개 옅은 색 눈동자, 창백한 피부와 주근깨를 가지고 있다. 그들의 피부는 햇빛에서 쉽게 타서, 피부암 위험성이 높다. 연구자들은 햇빛을 받으면 피부를 검게 만드는 색소인 멜라닌에서 햇빛 때문에 변화가 생기면 DNA 손상을 일으켜 결국 암에 걸리게 된다고 믿는다. 이는 검은색 머리카락을 가진 사람보다 붉은색 머리카락을 가진 사람에게 일어날 확률이 더 높다. 연구자들은 자외선의 다양한 파장에 대한 붉은색 머리카락의 멜라닌 반응을 검은색 머리카락의 그것(멜라닌 반응)과 비교해 보았다. 붉은색 머리카락으로부터 분리된 색소는 암과 관련된 해로운 활성 산소를 발생시키는 화학 반응을 시작하는 데 더 적은 에너지를 필요로 한다는 것이 밝혀졌다. 검은색 머리카락의 멜라닌은 활성 산소를 발생시키려면 더 많은 에너지가 있어야 하므로 암 위험도를 낮춘다.

어휘 **freckle** 주근깨, 기미 **trigger** (반응을) 일으키다; (장치를) 작동시키다 **eventually** 결국 **wavelength** 파장 **ultraviolet** 자외선의 **isolate** ~을 분리하다; ~을 고립시키다

구문 11~14행 **It** was found **that** the pigment (isolated from red hair) requires less energy to start *the chemical reaction* [**that** produces *the damaging free radicals* (linked to cancer)].
(It: 가주어 / that: 진주어 / the pigment: S′ / requires: V′ / less energy: O′)

→ 가주어 It이 진주어 that절 전체를 대신한다. 진주어 that절 내에 여러 수식구조가 쓰여 길어졌다.

098 ④ | are → is

해설 ④ 동명사구 servicing ~ customers가 주어이므로 단수동사인 is가 적절.

① keeping의 목적어 them이 salespeople을 가리키고 문맥상 이들이 '일하게' 하는 것이므로 현재분사 working은 적절.
② <spend A v-ing>의 수동태 형태인 <A is spent v-ing>가 쓰였다. unproductively는 traveling을 수식하는 부사.
③ 주어가 Export trade companies이므로 복수동사 have는 적절.
⑤ 앞의 an overseas agent or distributor를 선행사로 하면서 뒤에 나오는 own sales force와 함께 관계사절의 주어를 이루어야 하므로 소유격 관계대명사가 적절.

해석 세일즈맨을 '외부에 나가도록' 하는 것은 그들이 사무실에서 일하도록 하는 것보다 불편하다. 세일즈맨의 많은 시간이 이동하는 데 비생산적으로 소모된다. 전화 판매나 사무실에서 직접 대면하는 회의가 더 낫고 비용도 더 적게 들지 모른다. 수출 무역 기업은 종종 별도의 수출 판매 인력을 두고 있다. 이들 인력의 이동이나 숙박경비는 매우 비쌀 수 있다. 그 결과, 국외 고객에게 서비스하는 것은 주로 전화나 팩스 혹은 편지로 이루어지며, 그에 따라 직접적인 방문은 더 줄어들 것이다. 또 하나의 선택은, 한 사업체가 외국 대리인 혹은 판매 대리점을 지정하여 그들의 자체적인 판매 인력이 해당 국가에서의 제품 판매에 대한 책임을 대신하도록 하는 것이다.

어휘 **unproductively** 비생산적으로 **export** 수출(의) **trade** 무역 **separate** 개별적인, 독립된 **sales force** 판매 인력[조직] **accommodation** 숙박 **expense** 경비, 비용 **appoint** ~을 지정하다; ~을 임명하다 **distributor** 판매자, 배급업자 **take over** ~을 인계받다, 대신하다 **responsibility** 책임

099 ③ | being → to be

해설 ③ For South Korea의 for는 to부정사의 의미상의 주어 for. 주어 자리가 아니므로 동명사가 아닌, '목적(~하도록)'을 나타내는 부사 수식어 to부정사가 와야 할 곳이다. 의미상의 주어 South Korea가 recognize의 대상이므로 수동형 to부정사 to be (even more widely) recognized로 쓰는 것이 알맞다.

① by producing ~ and (by) hiring ~의 병렬구조이므로 전치사 뒤에 동명사가 맞게 쓰였다.
② 주어인 South Korean companies가 독자적 연구개발 활동을 '더 선호해 온' 것이므로 능동형인 have preferred는 적절.
④ companies와 higher educational institutions의 두 주체 간의 connections이므로 둘 사이에 쓰는 between을 쓴 것이 적절하다.
⑤ 형용사를 꾸며주는 부사 highly(매우, 대단히)가 맞게 쓰였다. high(높게; 높이)는 형용사를 수식하지 못한다.

해석 많은 한국 기업들이 고품질의 제품을 생산하고 외국인 직원들을 고용함으로써 세계 경제에 기여한다. 그러나 한국 기업들은 유럽과 미국에서 일반적인 형태인 대학과 협정을 체결하는 것보다는 독자적인 연구 개발 활동을 수행하는 것을 더 선호해왔다. 한국이 고등교육 기관들에 의해 선도되는 지식 기반 사회로 더욱 널리 인정받기 위해서는, 특히 연구 개발의 측면에서 기업과 고등교육기관 사이에 좀 더 강력한 관계가 있어야 한다. 또한, 고등교육 기관들은 변화하는 사회에 적응할 수 있도록, 자율성을 더 많이 확보하여 고도로 유연한 조직이 되어야 한다.

어휘 **corporation** 회사, 법인 **contribute to** ~에 기여하다 **enter into** ~을 체결하다, 계약하다 **arrangement** 협정; 조정 **phenomenon** 현상 **institution** 기관 **connection** 연결, 관계 **autonomy** 자율, 자치

구문 03~08행 However, South Korean companies have preferred **to establish** their own research and development operations rather than ***(to)* enter into** arrangements with universities, / a common phenomenon in Europe and the United States.
(South Korean companies: S / have preferred: V)

→ a common phenomenon 이하는 앞의 명사구 (to) enter into ~ universities를 부연 설명하는 동격어구.

100 ③ | to be taught → to teach

해설 ❸ the opportunity를 수식하는 형용사적 용법의 to부정사 자리. 문맥상 '참고 자료를 사용하는 법을 가르칠' 기회라는 뜻이므로, 명사구 how to ~ materials를 목적어로 취하는 능동형 to부정사가 적절.

① 진주어 to reach의 의미상 주어로 <for+목적격>이 바르게 쓰였다.
② If가 이끄는 조건의 부사절이고, 주어가 단수 the child이므로 현재시제의 동사 asks가 적절.
④ involve는 '~을 관여시키다'라는 뜻의 타동사. 부모가 숙제에 '관여되는' 것이므로, become의 보어로 과거분사 involved가 적절하다.
⑤ 앞의 동사 solve와 or로 연결된 병렬구조이므로 현재형 do가 알맞음.

해석 단 한 번의 도약으로 정상까지 오르는 것은 아이들에게 불가능하다. '스캐폴딩'은 그들이 한 걸음 한 걸음 위로 올라가는 틀을 제공해 줄 수 있다. 예를 들어, 아이가 "태국은 어디 있어요?"라고 물으면, 스스로 학습을 할 수 있도록 발판을 만들어 주는 부모는 "우리 함께 알아보기로 하자."라고 말할 것이다. 부모는 참고 자료들을 사용하는 법을 가르칠 기회를 얻게 되는데, 이는 아이에게 스스로 더 높이 움직일 수 있게 하는 도구를 갖춰주는 것이다. 또한, 아이의 숙제를 당신이 해서는 안 된다. 숙제는 아이의 책임이다. 아이의 부모가 숙제 과정에 관여될 때 아이는 일반적으로 혜택을 받는다. 그러나 부모의 지나친 관여는 숙제의 긍정적인 효과를 방해할 수 있다. 만약 당신이 아들의 산수 문제를 풀어주거나 아인슈타인에 대한 보고서를 위한 조사를 해주면 그는 스스로 하는 법을 배우지 못하게 된다.

어휘 **bound** 뛰기, 도약; 반동 **framework** 틀, 구조 **seize** ~을 붙잡다, 꽉 쥐다 **reference** 참조; 언급; 관련 **equip** (~에게 필요한 것을) 갖추어 주다 **involve** ~을 참여[관여]시키다; ~을 포함하다 ***cf.* involvement** 참여, 관여 **process** 과정; ~을 처리하다 **arithmetic** 산수, 셈 **stand on one's own (two) feet** 독립하다, 자급자족하다

구문 05~08행 The parent(S) seizes(V) the opportunity(O) (**to teach** how to use reference materials) [to부정사의 형용사적 용법], **equipping** the child with a tool for moving higher on his own. [=and it equips]

101 ⑤

해설 (A) 대명사가 지칭하는 것은 복수명사인 needs이므로 대명사도 복수형인 those가 되어야 함.
(B) <분수 등의 부분 표현+of+명사>가 주어일 때는 명사의 수에 따라 동사가 결정된다. 즉, marriages에 수를 일치시킨 복수동사 involve가 와야 함.
(C) compared to[with]는 '~와 비교해서'라는 의미를 가지는 어구임.

해석 변화는 정말로 가정생활의 본질이다. 당신의 아기가 필요로 하는 것들은 대학을 준비하는 당신의 십 대 자녀가 필요로 하는 것들과는 다르다. 형제·자매가 태어나는 것은 관심의 초점을 바꾸고 새로운 원동력과 새로운 관계를 가져온다. 또한 더 많은 가족이 구조에 있어서 급격한 변화를 겪고 있다. 예를 들어, 호주에서는 결혼의 3분의 1이 전에 결혼한 적이 있고 종종 이미 아이들이 있는 사람을 적어도 한 명 포함한다. 증가하고 있는 또 다른 형태의 가족 단위는 한쪽 부모만 있는 것이다. 이들은 양쪽 부모가 다 있는 가족의 부모보다 스트레스를 더 많이 받기 쉽고 또한 삶에 덜 만족스러워하는 것 같다. 한 연구에 따르면, 53%에서 71% 사이의 기혼 부부가 삶에 만족한 것과 비교했을 때 한 부모는 29%가 만족했다.

어휘 **very** 진짜의, 정말의; 바로 그 **sibling** 형제, 자매 **dynamic** 원동력; 동적인 **undergo** ~을 겪다, 경험하다 **radical** 급격한

102 ④ | very → much, far, still, even, a lot

해설 ❹ very는 비교급을 강조할 수 없으므로, 뒤에 있는 비교급 cheaper를 강조하기 위해서는 much, far 등을 사용해야 한다.

① be동사의 보어로 쓰이면서 '~하는 것'의 의미를 나타내기 위해서 to부정사가 쓰였으므로 어법상 적절하다.
② <must have+p.p.>는 '~했음이 틀림없다'는 과거의 일에 대한 확신을 나타내는 표현이므로 어법상 적절하다.
③ 주어인 the story of Moses는 단수이며, 문맥상 '말해지는' 것이므로 수동태 was told는 적절하다.
⑤ 동사 argue의 목적어인 명사절을 이끌고, a transition ~ inevitable이라는 완전한 문장을 이끌며 '~라는 것'이라는 의미로 쓰이므로 접속사 that은 적절하다.

해석 전자 문서의 모든 단점과 불이익을 고려할 때 왜 그냥 종이를 계속 고수하지 않을까? 이 질문에 대답하는 가장 좋은 방법은 인류의 역사에서 글을 쓰기 위한 매체가 교체되었던 또 다른 경우를 되돌아보는 것이다. 돌이나 점토에 쓰는 것이 익숙했던 사회에게, 종이는 불과 물에 취약하고 쓰인 자국이 너무 쉽게 번지거나 흐려져 없어지는 끔찍이도 수명이 짧은 재료처럼 보였음이 틀림없다. 그렇지만 종이는 보편화되었다. 모세의 십계명 판은 돌이었지만 모세의 이야기는 종이로 말해진다. 경제적인 동기는 너무 강력해서 무시할 수 없었는데, 종이를 사용하면 정보는 기록하고 보관하고 옮기는 데 비용이 훨씬 적게 들게 되었다. 바로 그와 동일한 고려가 종이 없는 전자적 필기로의 전환이 이제 피할 수 없다는 것을 입증한다.

어휘 **given** ~을 고려하여 **drawback** 단점 **stick with** ~를 고수하다 **medium** 매개물, 도구 **stuff** 재료; 물건 **vulnerable** 취약한, 연약한 **inscribe** 새기다 **fade away** 흐려져 없어지다 **prevail** 보편화되다 **tablet** (금속·돌 등의) 명판 **incentive** 유인, 동기 **consideration** 고려, 사려 **inevitable** 피할 수 없는, 불가피한

구문 01~02행 **Given** all the drawbacks and disadvantages of electronic documents, ~?
→ <Given+명사>는 '~를 고려할 때'라는 의미의 분사구문이다. 명사 자리에 that절이 올 수도 있다.

03~05행 The best way of answering that question / is (to look back on *the one other occasion in human history* [when a writing medium was replaced]).
→ ( )로 표시된 to부정사구는 is의 보어이다. ( ) 내에서 [ ]로 표시된 부분은 the one other occasion in human history를 수식하는 관계절이다.

05~09행 To *societies* (accustomed to writing on stone or clay), paper must have seemed *terribly short-lived stuff*, {vulnerable to fire and water}, {with *inscribed marks* [that all too easily smudged or faded away]}.
→ 두 개의 { } 부분은 terribly short-lived stuff를 부가 설명한다.

103 ⑤ | intending → intended

해설 ⑤ '밝은 불빛'이 아이들의 시각적 훈련을 위해 '의도된' 것이므로 bright lights와 intend는 수동관계. 따라서 과거분사인 intended가 되어야 한다.

① 전치사 in의 목적어로 관계대명사 which가 온 형태. the order를 선행사로 받는다. ~ regarding the order. + Tasks are done in the order. → ~ regarding the order + in which tasks are done.
② 사역동사 make는 목적격보어로 원형부정사를 취한다.
③ '약간의'라는 뜻의 a little은 셀 수 없는 명사를 수식하므로 적절.
④ 주어가 One way이므로 단수동사 is가 적절. to train ~ management는 주어를 수식하는 to부정사구이다.

해석 어떤 부모들은 옷 입기와 이 닦기 같은 일상적인 일들 때문에 아이들과 매일 전쟁을 벌인다. 문제는 어느 정도는 아이들 특유의 고집 때문에, 또 어느 정도는 일이 행해지는 순서와 관련된 부모들의 경직성 때문에 발생한다. 어린이는 단순히 자신의 일이 덜 부담스러워 보이게 하려고 일들을 약간 뒤섞어보기를 원하는 것일 수 있다. 부모들 역시 자신의 일상에서 약간의 변화를 통해 혜택을 얻을 수도 있지만, 그들에게 전반적인 통제와 일관성에 대한 욕구를 포기하는 것은 어려울 수 있고, 특히 그들 자신의 부모가 엄격했을 때 그렇다. 어린이를 시간 관리 문화의 측면에서 훈련하는 한 방법은 '타임 트래커'라고 불리는 기구를 사용하는 것이다. 그것은 어린이가 엄격한 일정을 따르게끔 시각적으로 훈련하도록 의도된, 밝은 불빛들과 타이머를 결합한 것이다. 실제로, 그것은 수천 개가 판매되어 많은 부모에게 도움을 주고 있다.

어휘 **routine** 일상적인; 일상의 일 **arise from** ~ 때문에 발생하다 **stubbornness** 완고함 **inflexibility** 융통성 없음 **burdensome** 부담스러운, 힘든 **let go of** ~에서 손을 놓다 **consistency** 일관성 **device** 기구, 장치 **combine A with B** A와 B를 결합하다 **intend to-v** v할 의도[생각]이다 **visually** 시각적으로 **condition** ~을 (특정 조건에 반응하도록) 훈련시키다 **adhere to** (규칙이나 법을) 따르다; (의견을) 고수하다

104 ⑤ | strengthens → strengthen

해설 ⑤ strengthen의 주어는 flushing and washing one's hands로 복수이므로 strengthens가 아닌 strengthen이 되어야 한다.

① 바로 앞 something을 가리키는 지시형용사 that.
② a lot of this unconscious learning이 주어, happens가 동사로 수의 일치가 자연스럽다.
③ a few cases를 선행사로 하는 관계부사. 추상적인 개념의 where로, 어떤 경우인지 설명하는 내용이 이어지고 있다.
④ the sound of urination을 강조하기 위해 쓰인 강조 용법의 itself.

해석 흐르는 물소리가 왜 우리를 소변보고 싶게 하는가? 여러분 대부분은 파블로프라는 이름이 친숙할 것이며 그가 개와 뭔가 관련이 있다는 걸 알고 있을 것이다. 그 뭔가가 그 러시아인 의사가 외적 자극 요인에 의해 자동적인 반응이 일어날 수 있음을 보여준 실험이다. 파블로프는 이러한 많은 무의식적인 학습이 사람들에게 늘 일어난다고 생각했는데, 여러분도 겉으로 무관해 보이는 자극에 어떤 특정한 방식으로 반사적으로 반응하는 몇몇 경우를 각자 삶에서 아마도 생각해 낼 수 있을 것이다. 흐르는 물소리를 듣고 소변을 봐야 할 것 같은 느낌이 드는 것이 같은 종류의 조건 반응처럼 보인다. 흐르는 물소리가 소변보는 소리를 닮아 파블로프 연상을 일으킬 뿐 아니라, 물 내리고 손 씻는 소리도 같은 소리를 내어 소변보기와 밀접하게 관련되어 그 연결고리를 더 강화하게 된다.

어휘 **pee** 소변을 보다(= **urinate**) **autonomic** (신경이) 자율적인, 자율 신경계의 **trigger** 야기하다, 방아쇠를 당기다 **stimuli** stimulus의 복수 ***cf.* stimulus** 자극제, 자극이 되는 것 **unconscious** 무의식적인 **reflexively** 반사적으로 **seemingly** 겉으로 보기에는 **mimic** 흉내 내다 **association** 연상, 연관 ***cf.* be associated with** ~와 연관 있다 **strengthen** 강화하다, 더 튼튼하게 하다

구문 13~18행 The sound of running water **not only** mimics the sound of urination itself to create a Pavlovian association, **but** flushing and washing one's hands **also** *produce that same sound* (A =the sound of urination) and *are closely associated with urinating* and further strengthen the connection. (B)

→ <not only ~ but also ...(~는 물론 …도)> 구조.

105 ③ | are served → serve

해설 ③ governments whose interest they serve로 고쳐야 적절. 선행사가 governments, 그들의 이익(whose interest)을 they(highly organized terrorist groups)가 serve 하는 것이므로 능동태로 쓰는 것이 알맞다.

① 전치사 in 뒤에 동명사구(coordinating their efforts)가 온 구조.
② <부사+형용사+명사>의 수식 구조. *cf.* highly: 고도의, 매우
④ the way 뒤에 <전치사+관계대명사(in which)>가 와서 관계절(← they cooperate with other agencies in the way)을 이끌고 있는 경우.
⑤ resources의 우선순위가 새로이 자리매김 '되었으므로' 현재완료의 수동태(have been re-prioritized)로 쓴 것이 적절.

해석 온갖 종류의 테러 공격이 세계 도처에서 계속 감행되면서 테러 대처 목적으로 특히 조직된 기관들이 그 어느 때보다 열심히 일을 하고 있으나 그들의 노력을 조직화하는 데 수많은 어려움에 직면하고 있다. 우선 비밀스럽고 때로는 고도로 조직화된 테러 집단의 의도와 활동에 관한 정확한 정보를 입수하기가 어렵다. 많은 집단이 해외의 접근 불가능한 지역에 본거지를 두고 있으며 일부는 그 집단이 그 이해관계를 받드는 정부의 보호 하에 있다. 또한 해외에서 계획되고 감행되는 공격을 예방하는 데 취할 수 있는 조치에 한계가 있다. 이 기관들의 기술과 이들이 (국내외의) 다른 기관과 협력하는 방식은 테러리스트들의 방법과 역량에 보폭을 맞춰야 한다. 다행히 정보기관들 간에 국제적인 테러로 인한 증가된 위협을 반영하기 위해 자원들이 우선순위가 새로 매겨졌다. 이 모든 기관이 특정 국가 그리고[또는] 그 동맹국에 대한 테러 작전을 개시하고 지속하는 테러리스트들의 역량을 서서히 약화시키는 것을 목적으로 한다.

어휘 **carry out** 수행하다 **specifically** 구체적으로, 명확하게 **address** (문제를) 다루다, 대처하다 **coordinate** 조정하다, 조직화하다 **obtain** 입수하다, 확보하다 **secretive** 비밀스러운 **inaccessible** 접근 불가능한 **interest** 이익, 이해관계 **serve** 받들다, 수행하다 **launch** 착수하다 **agency** 기관, 대행사 **capability** 능력, 역량 **intelligence community** 정보기관 **resource** 자원 **re-prioritize** 우선순위를 재매김하다 **erode** 침식시키다, 약화시키다 **initiate** 개시하다 **sustain** 지속하다, 지탱하다 **ally** 동맹국

106 ④ | much quickly → much more quickly

해설 ④ 과거에 비해 요즘은 어떤가를 얘기하고 있으므로 비교급(more quickly)으로 쓰는 것이 자연스럽다. 이어지는 형용사도 비교급(more multi-dimensional)으로 쓰여 even(훨씬)으로 강조되고 있으므로 같은 패턴의 much more quickly라고 써야 자연스럽다.

① 전치사 of 뒤에 동명사가 온 구조. 의미상의 주어(digital infrastructure)가 그 사이에 있고, 이것이 공격 '받는' 입장이므로 동명사의 수동형 being attacked로 쓰인 것이 적절.
② the concept의 내용을 이어 소개하는 동격의 that.
③ have to를 only가 강조하여 '~하기만 하면 된다'의 뜻으로 쓰였다.
⑤ 앞부분이 the battle is multi-dimensional로 be동사가 쓰이고 있으므로 비교하는 곳도 be로 쓰인 게(than it used to be) 맞다. *cf.* used to: 이전에는 ~였다

해석 디지털 기간 구조가 공격받을 위험이 계속 증가하면서 이를 보호하고 방어하는 데 대한 강조점도 마찬가지로 증가하고 있다. 그러나 문제는 오늘날의 인터넷 보안의 방어적 태도가 (중세기) 암흑시대의 그것을 몹시 흉내 내고 있다는 점이다. "우리는 그저 더 높은 성벽을 짓고 더 깊은 해자를 파고 있을 뿐이다. 많은 기관들이 여전히 성벽이 나쁜 놈이 안으로 못 들어오게 막아줄 거라는 생각에 갇혀 있다."라고 보안 전문가가 말했다. "대부분이 성벽 위로 기어 올라오거나 아래로 굴을 파고들어 오는 자들에 대해서는 생각을 못 하고 있다. 방어자들에게 어려운 점은, 나쁜 놈은 한 번만 성공하면 되지만 방어 데이터는 상시 성공해야 한다는 점이다. 또한 전투는 (과거보다) 훨씬 빨리 전개되고 이전보다 훨씬 더 다각적으로 진행된다."고 그는 덧붙였다.

어휘 **infrastructure** (사회의) 기반시설, 기간 구조 **defensive** 방어적인, 수호적인 *cf.* **defender** 방어자, 수호자 **mindset** 사고방식, 심적 태도 **security** 보안, 안전 **mimic** 흉내 내다, 모방하다 **concept** 개념, 의견 **multi-dimensional** 다차원적인, 다면적인

구문 01~03행 **As** the danger (S′) (*of* digital infrastructure *being attacked*) (동격의 of) continues (V′) to increase, **so** does (V) the emphasis (S) (on protecting and defending it).

→ <As ~ so ...(~하면서 …하게 되다)>의 구조에서 so 이하는 <so+V+S>의 도치 구조를 이루고 있다. continues to increase 대신 대동사 does가 쓰였다.

107 ⑤ | have found → have been found

해설 ⑤ 모든 유인원 종들이 자신의 이마를 만진다고 스스로 찾아낸(have found) 것이 아니라 판명된 상황이므로 have found를 수동태인 have been found로 바꿔써야 한다.

① <it takes 시간 for … to-v>는 '…가 v하는 데 (시간)이 걸리다'라는 의미의 구문으로 의미상 주어인 for them(침팬지들)이 알아내는 것이므로 to figure out은 적절하다.
② do는 대동사로서 앞에 나온 behave를 대신하여 쓰였다.
③ whether는 명사절을 이끄는 접속사로 to see의 목적어절을 이끈다.
④ 문장의 주어로써 쓰인 동명사는 적절하다.

해석 자기 인식은 침팬지와 다른 유인원에서 관찰된다. 침팬지 들이 거울 앞에 배치될 때 그것들이 자기 자신을 보고 있음을 알아내는 데는 단 몇 분밖에 안 걸린다. 그것들은 그러고 나서 자기들의 입속, 자기들의 머리 꼭대기와 전에는 볼 수 없었던 그 밖에 모든 곳을 검토하는 데 한동안 시간을 보낸다. 원숭이들은 자기들이 자기 자신의 이미지를 보고 있음을 결코 알아내지 못한다. 그것들은 그저 이미지가 인식될 때 인간이 할 것처럼 행동하지도 않는다. 동물의 이마에 빨간 점을 찍고서 그 동물을 거울 앞에 둘 수 있다. 우리는 그러고 나서 그 동물이 거울에서 점을 만지는지 아니면 자기 자신의 머리에 있는 점을 만지는지를 알아보려고 관찰한다. 자기 자신의 이마에 있는 점을 만지는 것은 그 동물이 자기가 자기 자신의 이미지를 거울 속에서 보고 있음을 이해한다는 것을 보여준다. 침팬지는 자신의 이마에 있는 점을 만질 것이다. 모든 유인원 종들은 자기 자신의 이마를 만진다고 판명된 반면 모든 원숭이 종들은 거울의 점을 만진다.

어휘 **self-awareness** 자기 인식 **ape** 유인원 **figure out** ~을 알아내다[이해하다] **recognize** 인식하다 **forehead** 이마 **species** (분류상의) 종

구문 05~07행 They then spend a while **examining** inside their mouths, the top of their head, and *everywhere else* [(that) they couldn't see before].

→ examining의 목적어로 밑줄 친 세 부분이 병렬 연결된다. [ ] 부분은 목적격 관계대명사 that이 생략된 관계사절로 everywhere else를 수식한다.

14~16행 *Touching the dot on its own forehead* shows that the animal **understands** that *it* is seeing its own image in the mirror.

→ Touching ~ forehead는 동명사구로 문장의 주어 역할을 한다. understands의 목적어로 밑줄 친 that이 이끄는 명사절이 쓰였고, that절의 주어인 it은 the animal을 지칭한다.

108 ② | spring → springing

해설 ② 문장의 주어(further conditions)에 대한 동사는 arise이고, ②는 앞에 있는 the laws and regulations를 수식하는 말이므로, 동사 형태의 spring이 아닌 springing이 와야 한다.

① 선행사 religion을 대신해 '종교에서(는)'라는 부사구의 의미가 되어야 한다. 또한, 뒤에 완전한 문장이 나오므로 관계부사 where은 어법상 적절하다.
③ 수일치를 묻는 문제로 of the community의 수식을 받는 주어 The needs가 복수명사이므로 동사로 쓰인 govern은 어법상 적절하다.
④ 동사 developed를 수식하는 말이므로 부사 singly는 어법상 적절하다.
⑤ 선행사 species를 대신하고, 절 속에 있는 명사 members를 수식해서 their members라는 의미가 되어야 하므로, 소유격의 의미를 나타내는 whose는 어법상 적절하다.

해석 공동체와 공동생활을 향한 인간의 누르기 힘든 욕망은 우리가 완전히 이해할 필요가 없는 형식들을 가진 제도들에서 드러난다. 집단 예배가 집회의 구성원들 사이에 유대를 만들어내는 종교를 예로 들 수 있다. 우리의 삶의 조건들이 우선적으로 우주의 사실들에 의해 결정되듯이, 그 이상의 조건들도 인간의 사회생활과 공동생활, 그리고 거기에서 생겨나는 법률과 규정을 통해서 생겨난다. 공동체에 대한 욕구는 모든 인간관계를 지배한다. 공동생활은 인류의 개인적 삶을 앞선다. 인류 문명의 역사에서 기초가 공동으로 마련되지 않은 그 어떤 생활 방식도 출현하지 않았다. 왜냐하면, 인간은 혼자서가 아니라 공동체에서 발전했기 때문이다. 이것은 매우 쉽게 설명된다. 그 구성원들이 개별적으로는 자기 보호를 위해 전투에 맞설 수 없는 종들은 무리 생활을 통해서 부가적인 힘을 얻는다는 근본적인 법칙을 동물의 세계 전체가 보여준다.

어휘 **compulsion** 누르기 힘든 (강한) 욕망; 강요 **community** 공동체; 지역 사회; 주민 **communal** 공동[단체]의 **institution** 제도, 관습; 기관, 단체; 보호 시설; 시행, 도입 **worship** 예배(하다), 숭배(하다) **bond** 유대, 결속 **congregation** 집회; (예배를 보기 위해 모인) 신자[신도]들 **further** 그 이상의, 추가의 **predate** 앞서다, 먼저 일어나다 **humanity** 인류 **civilization** 문명 **emerge** 출현하다, 나오다 **foundation** 기초; 설립; 재단 **demonstrate** 보여주다; 증명하다 **fundamental** 근본적인, 본질적인; 핵심적인, 필수적인 **species** 종 **incapable of** ~할 수 없는 **self-preservation** 자기 보호 **herd** 무리

구문 07~10행 further conditions arise / **through** the social and communal life of human beings and the laws and regulations **(springing from it)**.
→ 밑줄 친 부분은 through의 목적어들로서, and로 연결되어 병렬구조를 이룬다.
→ ( ) 부분은 형용사구로 앞의 명사 the laws and regulations를 수식하고 있다.
→ ( ) 안의 it은 the social ~ beings를 가리킨다.

12~15행 In the history of human civilization no way of life has emerged **[of which the foundations were not laid communally]** ~.
→ [ ] 부분에서 which는 (the) way of life를 선행사로 한다. 관계대명사가 자신이 이끄는 절 속에서 전치사의 목적어로 쓰일 때, 그 전치사는 관계대명사 바로 앞에 위치할 수 있다. 이 문장에서 전치사 of가 그 목적어인 관계대명사 바로 앞에 왔다.

17~21행 The whole animal kingdom demonstrates / **the fundamental law** / **that** *species* [**whose** members are individually incapable of facing the battle for self-preservation] / gain additional strength through herd life.
동물의 세계 전체는 (~을) 보여준다 / 근본적인 법칙을 / 종들은 [그 구성원들이 개별적으로는 자기 보호를 위해 전투에 맞설 수 없는] / 무리 생활을 통해서 부가적인 힘을 얻는다는.
→ the fundamental law는 명사절 접속사 that이 이끄는 that ~ life와 동격 관계이다.
→ [ ] 부분 내의 소유격 관계대명사 whose는 species를 선행사로 하며, 형용사절을 이끌어 species를 수식하고 있다.

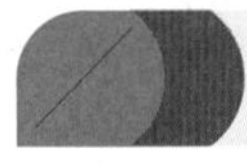

실전 모의고사 08회

109 ⑤ 110 ① 111 ② 112 ④ 113 ③ 114 ④ | 본문 84p

109 ⑤ | to have hit → to have been hit

해설 ⑤ to부정사의 의미상 주어는 one person이며, 파편에 의해 '맞는' 대상이기 때문에 수동 형태가 되어야 한다. 또한, 문장의 동사(is known)가 나타내는 때보다 '이전' 시점의 일을 말하고 있으므로 완료수동형인 to have been hit이 적절.

① For almost 50 years가 '과거부터 지금까지 거의 50년 동안'이라는 의미이므로 현재완료 진행시제는 적절.
② 주어(tens of ~ fragments)가 복수이므로 복수 동사 are 적절.
③ 동사 continue는 목적어로 동명사와 to부정사를 모두 취할 수 있다.
④ 앞 절 new objects ~ through the atmosphere를 대신하는 관계대명사인 which가 적절히 쓰임. 여기서 which는 앞 절을 보충 설명하는 관계사절을 이끈다.

해석 거의 50년 동안 각국 정부는 여러 물체를 우주로 쏘아 올려 궤도를 선회하는 쓰레기장을 만들어버렸다. 미국은 4인치 혹은 약간 더 큰 파편 1만여 개 이상을 추적하고 있지만 더 작은 파편 수천만 개도 시속 1만 7천 마일에 육박하는 속력으로 우주를 떠다니고 있다. 이 속도라면 아주 작은 물체와 충돌하는 것만으로 우주선 한 대를 파괴할 수 있다. 새로운 물체가 첨가되고 오래된 쓰레기가 대기로 떨어져 나감에 따라, 우주국은 파편을 지속적으로 감시하는데, 이런 일들은 대략 하루에 한 번씩 발생한다. 이 조각들은 보통 (대기에) 재진입할 때 불타버리지만 1천 파운드 이상의 몇몇 파편들은 지구에 충돌하기도 했다. 다행히 한 사람만이 (파편에) 맞은 것으로 알려졌다.

어휘 **launch** ~을 쏘아 올리다, 발사하다 **orbit** (~의) 궤도를 돌다 **track** ~을 추적하다 **debris** 잔해, 파편 **fragment** 파편, 단편 **whiz** 윙하며 움직이다 **collision** 충돌 **monitor** ~을 감시하다 **re-entry** 재진입 **crash** 충돌하다

110 ①

해설 (A) 뒤의 an infant's attraction ~ parent-child attachment 부분이 완전한 절이므로 관계대명사가 아닌 접속사 that을 써야 한다. that은 동사 is의 보어가 되는 절을 이끈다.
(B) 문장의 동사 자리이므로 준동사가 아닌 동사가 와야 한다. 주어는 단수명사인 The need이므로 continues가 맞다.
(C) <A so[such] ~ as B> 구문은 'A가 B만큼 ~하다'의 뜻으로서 문장 앞에 부정어인 No와 합쳐져서 전체적으로는 'A가 B만큼 ~하는 …는 없다'란 의미를 형성한다. such 다음에는 <such+(a)+형용사+명사>의 어순을 따른다.

해석 얼굴이 인간에게 당연히 흥미롭고 눈길을 사로잡는 것처럼 보이는 몇 가지 다른 이유들이 있을지도 모른다. 일반적으로 받아들여지는 이론은 유아가 얼굴에 이끌리는 것이 부모-자녀의 애착을 자극하기 위한 적응 기제로 발달했다는 것이다. 주로 돌봐주는 사람을 알아보고 끌어들일 수 있다는 것은 유아가 그 사람에게 감정적으로 애착을 갖게 되고 애정 어린 적절한 양육을 받게 될 가능성을 증가시킨다. 얼굴을 알아보고 끌어들이고 얼굴로부터 정보를 추출할 필요는 물론 유년기 동안 그리고 성인기에도 계속된다. 사회적 상황에서 타인의 마음을 읽을 수 있는 능력을 가진다는 것은 생존과 번식의 성공을 위해서도 또한 중요하다. 인간은 마음을 읽을 수 없지만, 다음으로 좋은 것은 또래 사람들의 정서적 경향을 이해할 수 있다는 것이다. (메시지) 전달자에 대하여 얼굴의 경우만큼 풍부한 감정 정보를 제공해주는 것에 근접한 다른 신체 부위는 없다.

어휘 **eye-catching** 눈길을 끄는 **adaptive** 적응의 **mechanism** 기제 **stimulate** 자극하다 **attachment** 애착 **engage** (주의를) 사로잡다, 끌다 **caregiver** 돌봐주는 사람 **likelihood** 가능성 **extract** 추출하다 **reproductive** 번식의 **mind-set** 심적 경향, 사고방식; 태도 **bearer** 운반인; (메시지 등의) 전달자

구문 01~03행 There might be *several different reasons* [**why** faces seem naturally interesting and eye-catching to humans].
→ [ ] 부분은 이유를 나타내는 관계부사절로 앞의 several different reasons를 수식한다.

06~09행 **Being** able to recognize and engage the primary caregiver / increases *the likelihood* / *that* an infant will **become** emotionally attached to that individual and **receive** proper nurturance.
→ 동명사 Being이 이끄는 구가 주어이며 Being able to 뒤의 동사원형 recognize와 engage가 병렬구조를 이룬다. that 이하는 the likelihood에 대한 동격절이다. 동격절에서 동사원형 become과 receive는 병렬구조를 이룬다.

111 ② | who → whose

해설 ❷ who 다음에 바로 동사가 이어 나오지 않고 명사 개념(physical abilities)이 이어 나오는 점이 어색하다. 동사(are) 앞까지가 주어가 되려면 physical abilities를 수식할 수 있는 소유격 관계대명사가 오는 것이 자연스럽다. 선행사 people의 조건을 제한하고 한정하고 있다.

① 동사(live)에 어울리게 부사로 맞게 쓰였다. according to the limits of their bodies의 의미.
③ 주어가 One (of the subjects)이므로 단수형 is가 알맞다.
④ whose main gig을 설명하는 주격보어 부분에 to부정사가 명사 개념(자기 몸에 불 지르는 것)으로 맞게 쓰였다.
⑤ '목적(~할 수 있도록)'을 나타내는 so as to로 to부정사를 이끈다. 그냥 to feel no pain이라고 바꿔 써도 된다.

해석 대부분의 사람은 자기 신체의 한계를 잘 알고 그에 맞게 살아가지만 어떤 이들은 그 한계를 인식하지 못하는데, 그들이 2시간짜리 특별 프로그램 <Sekai Chojintai Mystery(전 세계 인체 미스터리들(화요일 저녁 8시 57분, TBS)>의 소재들이다. 이 프로그램은 그 신체 능력이 단순히 비범할 뿐 아니라 한마디로 전혀 설명 불가능한 사람들을 찾아 전 세계를 누비고 다닌다. 그 대상 중 하나가 주로 하는 공연이 자기 몸에 불을 지르고 대개 불편할 정도로 오랫동안 있는 일인 미국인 스턴트맨이다. 또 바다 한가운데에 기둥을 박아 만든 집에 사는, 남태평양의 한 부족들이 있다. 그들은 물속 40미터를 다이빙해 들어가 바다 밑 먼 거리를 걸은 후 잡는 물고기로 연명하며 산다. 끝으로 또 한 사람의 미국인은 바늘을 팔에 찔러 넣어도 고통을 느끼지 않도록 자기 몸을 통제할 수 있다.

어휘 **accordingly** 그에 맞게 **subject** (실험 등의) 대상, 소재 **ordinary** 평범한 **downright** 순전한, 노골적인 **unexplainable** 설명될 수 없는, 수수께끼의 **set ~ on fire** ~에 불붙이다 **uncomfortably** 불편하게 **tribe** 부족 **seabed** 해저, 바다 밑 **stretch** (시간, 거리) 죽 뻗어 있는 긴 시간[길이] **thrust** 밀치다, 찔러 넣다

112 ④ | which → that

해설 ❹ the idea에 대한 동격 내용의 절이 뒤에 이어지므로, which를 that으로 바꿔야 한다.

① use 다음의 to improve는 '~하기 위하여'라는 뜻의 부사적 용법 to부정사이므로 적절하다.
② such as 뒤의 동명사 moving과 병렬구조를 이루는 동명사 형태가 적절하게 쓰였다.
③ 선행사 The other method를 수식하는 관계사절의 범위는 you can feel more secure로 문장 요소가 온전하다. 따라서 관계대명사 which 앞에 선행사와 연결시키는 by가 필요하다.
⑤ perfectly는 뒤의 형용사 predictable을 수식하는 부사이므로 적절하게 쓰였다.

해석 당신의 삶의 질을 향상시키기 위해 쓸 수 있는 두 가지의 주요 전략이 있다. 첫째는 당신의 필요에 맞게 외부적 요인을 바꾸는 것이고, 두 번째는 당신이 그 요인들을 경험하는 방식을 바꾸려고 하는 것이다. 예를 들어, 안전함을 느끼는 것은 행복에 필수적이므로, 당신은 더 안전한 아파트나 동네로 이사하거나 호신술 수업을 듣는 것과 같은 많은 방법으로 안전감을 강화할 수 있다. 이러한 사전 대책 조치들은 생활환경을 좀 더 당신의 요구사항에 맞게 가져올 것이다. 당신이 더 안전함을 느끼게 하는 다른 방법은 안전함이 무엇을 의미하는지에 대한 당신의 인식을 바꾸는 것을 포함한다. 당신은 삶에서 어느 정도의 위험은 불가피하다는 생각을 받아들일 수 있다. 그런 다음, 당신이 이렇게 완벽하게 예측하기는 어려운 세상을 여전히 즐길 수 있다면 당신은 불안감으로부터 당신을 보호할 내면의 힘을 갖게 될 것이다.

어휘 **external** 외부의 **factor** 요인 **secure** 안전한 ***cf.*** **insecurity** 불안(감) **strengthen** ~을 강화하다 **self-defense** 호신술 **proactive** 사전 대책을 강구하는 **in line with** ~에 따라, ~와 함께 **modify** ~을 수정[변경]하다 **perception** 인식 **inevitable** 불가피한 **shield** ~을 보호하다; 방패, 보호막

113 ③

해설 (A) 대명사는 앞의 단수명사인 the Del Norte Coast Redwoods State Park를 가리키고 있으므로 단수형 its가 와야 한다.
(B) 뒤에는 완전한 형태의 절이 왔고, 선행사가 the ocean이라는 '장소'이므로 관계부사 where가 적절.
Tourists ~ hike through the dense forest to *the ocean* [**where** the giant redwoods, / found ~ coast, / grow ~].
(선행사 *the ocean* ← 관계사절; S′ giant redwoods / 삽입구 found ~ coast / V′ grow)
(C) 문맥상 주어 this park가 '포함하는' 것이며, white water ~ open valleys를 목적어로 취하고 있으므로 능동형 contains가 적절.

해석 북부 캘리포니아는 오리건 주와 워싱턴 주에서 보이는 것과 같은 서늘한 기후와 아름다운 경치를 제공한다. 오리건 주 경계선 근처의 해안가에는 양치류가 바닥을 뒤덮은 울퉁불퉁한 삼나무 숲이 있는 델 노르트 코스트 레드우즈 주립공원이 있다. 여행자들은 빽빽한 숲을 지나서, 태평양 연안에서만 볼 수 있는 거대한 삼나무들이 거의 해안까지 자라있는 바다로 차를 타거나 도보로 여행할 수 있다. 4월부터 7월까지 또한 즐길 수 있는 것은 철쭉과 진달래의 멋진 풍경이다. 북부 내륙에는 샤스타 산을 비롯해서 그 밖에도 아름다운 공원이 많이 있다. 스키를 탈 수 있는 많은 지역 외에도, 이 공원에는 깊은 협곡을 흐르는 하얀 물살, 매우 아름다운 호수, 울창한 삼림, 탁 트인 계곡이 있다.

어휘 **scenic** 경치의; 무대의 **afford** ~을 제공하다; ~할 여유가 되다 **rugged** 울퉁불퉁한; 주름진 **redwood** 미국삼나무 **dense** 빽빽한, 밀집한 **outstanding** 아주 멋진, 눈에 띄는 **inland** 내륙(의); 국내(의) **abundance** 풍부, 대량 **terrain** 지역, 지형 **canyon** 협곡 **exquisite** 아주 아름다운, 훌륭한

114 ④ | to care → caring

해설 ❹ 문맥상 '보살피는 것을 멈추다'라는 의미가 되어야 하므로 <stop v-ing (v하는 것을 멈추다)>를 써야 한다. 따라서 v-ing 형태인 caring이 어법상 적절하다. <stop to-v>는 'v하기 위해 멈추다'라는 의미이다.

① whether they care for a house, ~에서 they care가 생략된 형태로, 부사절로 쓰이고 있다. 또한, '~이든지 아니든지 간에'로 해석되므로 whether가 적절하다.
② 주어 They는 보살핌을 주는 사람이고, 그들이 누군가에 의해 필요로 되는 것이므로 수동형인 needed는 어법상 적절하다.
③ 의미상 in the period의 의미이면서, 뒤에 완전한 절을 이끌고 접속사 역할을 해야 하므로, in which는 어법상 적절하다.
⑤ 앞에 있는 복수 명사 daily acts를 대신하고 있으므로 one의 복수형인 ones가 어법상 적절하다.

해석 사람들이 집이든, 정원이든, 애완동물이든, 또는 다른 사람이든 간에, 보살핌의 방식을 유지할 때, 그들은 자기 자신을 절망으로부터, 그리고 포기로부터 보호하고 있는 것이다. 그들은 (누군가가) 자신을 필요로 한다는 것을 느낌으로써 보상을 받는다. 하지만, '보살핌'이라는 단어는 많은 의미를 가지고 있고 그중 하나는 어떤 사람이 보살핌의 부담을 질 때와 같은 '걱정'이라는 의미이다. 당신은 보살피고 있는 것들에 대해 정말로 걱정한다. 불행하게도, 보살핌을 노력 그리고 걱정과 연관시키는 것은 우리가 노년을 '근심 없는 존재'로 살아야 하는 시기로 생각하도록 이끈다. 은퇴 후에 사람들은 자신들

이 (무엇인가를) 보살피는 일을 그만두라고 재촉을 받는다. 그것은 위험한 거래일 수 있다. 무엇인가를 보살피는 일을 그만두는 사람은 희망 없음 또는 무력감이라는 증후군을 향해 첫발을 내디딘 것일지도 모른다. 그리고 노년을 가장 잘 대처하는 사람들은 매일 보살핌의 행위, 특히 애완동물과 정원처럼 살아 있는 것에 제공되는 보살핌 같은 가장 만족감을 주는 것(행위)을 계속하는 사람들이다.

어휘 **maintain** 유지하다; 지속하다; 주장하다 **care** 보살피다; 보살핌, 돌봄 ***cf.*** **carefree** 근심 없는 **despair** 절망; 절망[체념]하다 **burden** 부담 지우다; 부담, 짐 **association** 연관, 관련; 협회 **conceive** 생각하다; 상상하다 **existence** 존재, 실재; 생존 **retirement** 은퇴 **urge** 권고[촉구]하다; 충고하다; 재촉하다 **trade-off** 거래, 교환 **hopelessness** 희망 없음, 절망 (상태) **helplessness** 무력감; 난감함 **syndrome** 증후군 **cope with** ~에 대처[대응]하다; ~에 대항하다

구문 08~11행 Unfortunately, the association of care with effort and worry leads us to **conceive of** old age **as** *a period* **[in which one should live a "carefree existence"]**.

→ conceive of A as B는 'A를 B로 인식하다'라는 의미이다.
→ <전치사+관계대명사> 형태인 in which가 이끄는 절이 앞에 있는 명사 a period를 수식하고 있다.

15~19행 And *those* **[who cope best with old age]** / are *those* **[who continue the daily acts of caring]**, / **especially the most satisfying ones**—*care* **(provided to living things, such as pets and gardens)**.
그리고 사람들은 [노년을 가장 잘 대처하는] / 사람들이다 [매일 보살핌의 행위를 계속하는], / 특히 가장 만족감을 주는 것을 / 보살핌 같은 [애완동물과 정원처럼 살아 있는 것에 제공되는].

→ 첫 번째, 두 번째 관계대명사 who가 이끄는 절이 바로 앞의 those를 각각 수식한다.
→ 대시(—) 이하는 especially the most satisfying ones를 구체적으로 풀어 쓴 설명에 해당한다.
→ provided ~ gardens는 과거분사 provided가 이끄는 형용사구로, care를 수식한다.

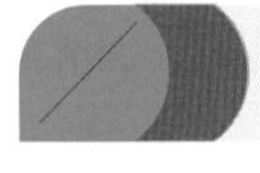

실전 모의고사 09회

115 ③ 116 ④ 117 ② 118 ④ 119 ② 120 ⑤ | 본문 86p

115 ③ | is → are

해설 ③ <There is/are ~> 구문의 주어가 more than 500 million travel-hungry tourists, 즉 복수이므로 are로 써야 한다.

① 국제 문제 중 하나, 즉 a problem의 반복을 피하기 위해 쓰인 것이므로 단수형인 that이 적절.
② <a number of(다수의 ~)>가 셀 수 있는 명사의 복수와 함께 쓰이므로 그 변형인 an increasing number of ~도 복수. 따라서 are가 적절.
④ 분사의 의미상 주어인 more than 500 million travel-hungry tourists가 '돌아다니는' 주체이므로 능동을 나타내는 현재분사가 적절.
⑤ hundred, thousand, million 등의 수를 나타내는 표현이 '막연한 수'를 나타낼 때는 복수형이 된다.

해석 가장 잠재적으로 문제를 일으키기 쉬운 국제 문제 중의 하나는 대규모 관광이다. 거의 70억에 달하는 세계 인구 중에서 여행을 결심하는 사람들이 증가하고 있다. 금세기 말까지, 세계 방방곡곡을 돌아다니는 여행을 갈구하는 5억 명 이상의 관광객들이 예상된다. 이미 수천 군데의 멋진 해변, 흥미로운 마을, 역사적 도시들, 아름다운 자연미를 가진 지역들이 개발업자들의 건설 계획에 포함되었다. 관광객들을 수용하려는 시도 때문에 사람들이 와서 즐기려 한 바로 그 명소들이 파괴되었고 현지 거주민들의 일상생활은 불가능해지게 되었다.

어휘 **explosive** 폭발적인; 폭발물 **quaint** 흥미를 끄는; 기이한 **exquisite** 아주 아름다운, 절묘한 **accommodate** ~을 수용하다, 숙박시키다 **resident** 거주자, 거주인

구문 10~13행 *Attempts* (to accommodate tourists) **have led** to the destruction of *the very attractions* [that they have come to enjoy] and **have made** daily living ~.
(S: Attempts ~ tourists, V_1: have led, V_2: have made)

116 ④ | to do → to be done

해설 ④ 주어인 what이 우리가 해야 할 어떤 '일'로, '일'이 do의 주체가 아니라 객체이므로 수동형(what needs to be done)으로 써야 한다. 주어가 we라면 what we need to do처럼 능동형으로 쓸 수 있다.

① 가난으로 인해 어린 시절을 제대로 경험하지 못하는 전 세계 수백만 명의 어린이를 가리키는 대명사 them.
② statistical evidence가 우리를 a stark reality와 대면시키는 주체이므로 능동태로 쓴 것이 맞다. we가 주어라면 we are confronted with ~로 쓸 수 있다.
③ risk of being exploited and (being) abused의 병렬구조.
⑤ 주체가 모두 셋으로 복수이므로 복수주어에 맞게 work로 쓰였다.

해석 전 세계 수백만 어린이들이 가난으로 인해 어린 시절을 누리지 못한다. 빈곤이 그들에게서 생존과 발전, 번성하는 데 필요한 능력을 앗아간다. 그것은 그들이 평등한 기회를 누리지 못 하도록 한다. 그것은 아이들을 착취, 학대, 폭력, 차별, 낙인찍기에 더 취약하도록 만든다. 빈곤 상태로 사는 아동들에 관한 통계적 증거는 우리를 냉혹한 현실

— 수백만의 어린이들이 가난하다는 것, 안전한 식수와 꼭 필요한 백신도 잘 구할 수 없으며 교육과 섭생의 기회도 별로 없다는 것, 착취당하고 학대당할 위험이 있다는 것 — 에 직면하게 한다. 이러한 현실은 정부와 민간 부문, 그리고 국제사회가 새천년 개발 목표와 '어린이들에게 꼭 맞는 세상'이라는 의제에 따라 행동해 나가고 있는지 의문을 제기한다. 우리는 무엇이 이뤄져야 하는지 알고 있다. 필요한 것은 말을 구체적인 행동으로 옮기는 의지이다. 정부와 시민사회, 국제사회가 공통의 목표를 향해 일해 나가면 놀라운 일이 달성될 수 있다.

어휘 **miss out on** ~을 놓치다 **deprive A of B** A에게서 B를 박탈하다[빼앗다] **capability** 능력 **thrive** 번창하다, 잘 자라다 **vulnerable** 취약한, 상처받기 쉬운 **exploitation** 착취 *cf.* **exploit** 착취하다 **abuse** 학대(하다), 남용(하다) **discrimination** 차별 **statistical** 통계적인 **confront A with B** A에게 B를 직면하게 하다[대면시키다] **stark** 냉엄한, 황량한 **access to** ~에의 접근, ~을 구할 수 있음 **nutrition** 영양, 섭생 **commitment** 헌신, 전념 **sector** (사회, 경제 등의) 부문, 활동 분야 **act upon** ~에 의거하여 행동하다 **agenda** (회의의) 의제, 안건 **concrete** 구체적인 **feat** 위업, 놀라운 일

구문 07~09행 The statistical evidence (on *children* (living in poverty)) **confronts** us **with** a stark reality: ~.
(S: The statistical evidence ... poverty)), V: confronts)

→ 주어부가 층층이 수식 구조를 이루고 있어 길어진 경우. confront A with B: A를 B와 대면시키다(= A is confronted with B by ~)

117 ②

해설 (A): 바로 뒤에 subject가 나오므로 문맥상 의미가 '아동 심리학의 대상'이 되도록 주어 Child psychology의 소유격 its가 적절하다.
(B): 도치구문으로 주어는 child psychology이고 보어는 a branch of general psychology이다. 따라서 be동사인 is가 적절하다.
(C): 뒤에 주어는 child psychology, 동사는 carries out, 목적어는 its own research로 문장의 구성 요소를 모두 갖춘 완전한 문장이 오므로 what이 들어갈 수 없고, 문맥상으로도 why가 적절하다. That's why를 For that reason으로 바꾸어 생각하면 이해하기 쉽다.

해석 일반 심리학은 인간의 지각, 감각, 사고, 기억, 주의, 학습과 기타 정신 활동들, 신경계 등에 관한 연구의 기저에 있는 일반 원리를 다룬다. 아동 심리학은 이 모든 것들을 연구하지만, 그 대상은 아동이다. 그것은 독립적인 연구 분야인데, 왜냐하면 현대 연구자들에 의해 증명되어 왔듯이 아동은 성인의 축소형이 아니기 때문이다. 따라서 일반 심리학의 원리에 필요한 개조를 한 후에는 그 원리가 아동에 대한 연구에 적용될 수 있다고 말하는 것은 불가능하다. 아동 심리학은 일반 심리학의 한 갈래 또한 아닌데, 왜냐하면 아동의 사고, 이해, 학습, 지각, 감정과 기타 행동들이 성인의 그것들과는 양적으로뿐만 아니라 질적으로도 다르다는 것이 지속적인 연구에 의해 발견되었기 때문이다. 그것이 아동 심리학이 일반 심리학의 결론을 채택하기보다는 자체적인 연구를 수행하는 이유이다.

어휘 **underlie** ~의 기초가 되다, ~의 기저에 있다 **perception** 지각, 인식 **sensation** 감각 **nervous system** 신경계 **subject** 주제; 과목; 연구 대상 **miniature** 모형, 축소형 **continuous** 계속되는, 지속적인

118 ④ | radical → radically

해설 ④ <sound+주격보어(radical)>의 형태가 아니라 <sound+(radically) different>의 구조. 형용사를 수식할 수 있는 것은 부사이므로 radically different가 되어야 한다.

① where 이하의 문장이 완벽하므로 문장 내에서 수식어인 관계부사가 온 것이 자연스럽다. 추상적인 의미에서의 장소 개념을 가리키는 where.
② their audio fingerprint가 곧 their unique sound로 동격이므로 단수동사로 쓴 것이 맞다.
③ The art is in A and then (in) B의 병렬구조이므로 A, B 모두 동명사로 쓰이고 있다.
⑤ 전치사(like)가 명사(their favorite composer or band)를 목적어로 취하고 있다. <sound like+명사>: ~처럼 들리다

해석 "제약이 너를 자유롭게 해 줄 것이다." 이 말이 음악 분야에서보다 더 울림이 있는 곳은 없을 것이다. 형식이 없이는 음악과 같은 것은 아예 존재할 수 없다고까지 주장할 수 있을 것이다. 이는 왜 작곡가들이 바로 (누군지) 쉽게 알아 맞혀지는지와도 상관있는 얘기일 것이다. 그들의 '청각적인 지문', 즉 그들의 독특한 소리가 그들이 제각각 선택한 음악적 제약의 결과물인 셈이다. 예술은 너의 스타일에 맞는 제약을 선택하고, 그런 다음 이 틀 안에서 너의 기술을 갈고 닦는 데 있다. 모든 위대한 작곡가들이 규칙을 만들어 냈고 그것들을 탐구했으며 자기가 만들어낸 우주의 거장이 되었다. 그러나 음악에서 규칙과 변화, 전형적인 양식을 만들어 내기 위해서는 이전에 지나갔던 그 어떤 것과도 근본적으로 다르게 들리기 위해 준비되어 있어야 한다. 이것은 많은 음악가가 얘기하는 주제이기는 하지만 그럴 배짱은 결코 갖지 못하는 어떤 것인데, 자기가 좋아하는 작곡가나 밴드처럼 들리기를 원하기 때문이다. 제약은 그들을 자유롭게 해줄 잠재력이 있으나 친숙함이 결국 그들을 쇠사슬 달린 족쇄처럼 아무것도 못 하게 하는 것으로 끝난다.

어휘 **restriction** 제한 **statement** 진술, 말 **resonate** 울려 퍼지다, 공명하다 **realm** (활동, 지식 등의) 영역, 범위 **form** 형식, 틀 **relevant** 적절한, 관련 있는 **composer** 작곡가 **instantly** 바로, 즉시 **recognizable** 쉽게 알아볼 수 있는 **hone** (칼 등을) 갈다, (기술을) 연마하다 **framework** 뼈대, 골조 **master** 장인, 거장 **radically** 근본적으로, 철저히 **guts** 용기, 배짱 **go through with** ~을 거치다 **limitation** 제한, 한도 **ground** 좌초시키다, 비행을 허락하지 않다, 외출을 금지시키다

구문 01~03행 There is **no other** area where this statement resonates **more than** *in the realm of music*.

→ 부정 주어를 사용한 최상급 구문. <No other + 단수명사 + more ~ than A>: A보다 더 ~한 것은 아무것도 없다(= A가 가장 ~하다)

08~10행 The art is **in** choosing *the restrictions* [that suit your style], and then honing your technique within this framework.
(A: choosing the restrictions [that suit your style], B: honing your technique within this framework)

119 ② | requiring → require

해설 ② 문장 전체의 동사가 없으므로 준동사 requiring 대신 문장의 동사가 필요한 자리이다. of the body의 수식을 받는 주어 All the glands가 복수이므로 동사도 복수형인 require로 수일치시켜야 한다.

① to부정사구 to list ~them을 수식하는 부사 자리이므로 simply가 적절하다.
③ 앞에 나온 목적어절을 이끄는 접속사 that과 and로 연결된 병렬구조로 접속사 that이 적절하다.
④ become은 뒤에 보어를 취하는 SVC 구조의 동사로 형용사 affected가 적절하다.
⑤ 당위성을 나타내는 표현 <it is essential that ~> 구문에서 that절의 should가 생략된 형태이므로 동사원형 be가 적절하다.

해석 분비샘은 너무 복잡하고 너무 많은 다른 것들에 의해 영향을 받기 때문에 그것에 해로운 것과 이로운 것을 단순하게 목록으로 작성하는 것은 매우 어려울 것이다. 하지만 모든 분비샘의 기능에 필수적인 중요한 한 가지가 있다. 몸의 모든 분비샘은 호르몬을 생산하고 자신들의 특정한 기능을 수행하기 위해 미네랄을 필요로 한다. 음식에 미네

랄이 충분하지 않을 때, 소화액은 이용 가능한 공급량을 받는다. 이것은 신경, 조직, 치아, 그리고 뼈가 미네랄이 부족하게 되리라는 것과 그것들의 기능이 대단히 방해받으리라는 것을 의미한다. 이러한 미네랄 부족 상태가 개선되지 않는다면 결국 분비샘이 영향을 받게 될 것이다. 이것은 결과적으로 질병을 가져올 수밖에 없는 비정상적인 몸 상태를 야기할 것이다. 몸은 섭취되는 음식을 통해 미네랄을 얻기 때문에 신선하고 익히지 않은 다양한 음식이 섭취되어서 몸이 필요한 미네랄을 받는 것이 필수적이다.

어휘 **complex** 복잡한 **affect** 영향을 미치다 **beneficial** 유익한, 이로운 **vital** 필수적인 **glandular** (분비)선[샘]의 **digestive juice** 소화액 **supply** 공급[비축](량) **nerve** 신경 **tissue** 조직 **deficient** 부족한[결핍된] **hamper** 방해하다 **deficiency** 부족[결핍] **remedy** 개선하다, 고치다 **in turn** 결국[결과적으로]

구문 01~03행 Glands are **so** complex and are affected by so many different things **that** it would be very difficult to simply list~ .
→ <so ~ that ...> 구문으로 '너무 ~해서 …하다'의 뜻이다.

15~19행 Because the body obtains minerals through *the food* [that is eaten], **it is essential that** a variety of fresh, raw food **(should) be** eaten [so the body will receive the necessary minerals].
→ 첫 번째 [ ] 부분은 the food를 수식하는 관계절이다. <it is essential that ~> 구문에서 it은 가주어이고 뒤에 오는 that 이하가 진주어이며, that절이 당위성(~해야 한다)을 나타내고 있으므로 동사 앞에 should가 생략되었다. 두 번째 [ ] 부분은 '~하도록'의 의미를 나타낸다.

120 ⑤

해설 (A) 앞에 나온 명사 collective action을 대신하는 대명사로 that이 적절하다. one을 쓰면 '다른 사회적 운동 중의 하나'라는 말이 되어 문맥상 어색하다.
(B) 동사 focus on의 목적어로 동명사 correcting과 changing이 병렬구조를 이루어야 문맥에 맞는다.
(C) 이하 절이 주어와 동사와 목적어를 갖춘 완전한 문장이므로 관계부사 where가 나오는 것이 적절하다.

해석 컴퓨터 기술과 네트워크의 발전은 두서너 가지 예만 들면 환경 운동, 금연 운동, 음주 운전 반대 운동이나 여성 운동과 같은 다른 사회 운동들의 그것과 유사한 집단적 행동에 기인한다. 제각기 특정한 목표, 예를 들면 깨끗한 공기, 공공장소에서의 흡연 없애기, 음주 운전으로 인한 교통사고와 사망의 감소, 혹은 기회의 균등 등을 가지고 있지만, 그것들(= 사회 운동들)은 모두, 그것들이 반대하는 어떤 상황을 바로 잡거나 어떤 종류의 사회적 불이익으로 해를 당하는 집단을 위한 환경을 바꾸는 데 초점을 맞춘다. 마찬가지로, 컴퓨터화의 옹호자들은 사람들과 조직들이 최첨단의 컴퓨터 조작 장비를 사용하고 시공간의 물리적 제약이 극복되는 새로운 세계 질서를 개발하는 데 집중한다.

어휘 **rise** 상승, 발전 **collective** 집단의; 공동의 **anti-tobacco** 담배 금지, 금연 **to name a few** 두서너 가지 예만 들면 **specific** 특정한 **equality** 균등, 평등 **likewise** 똑같이, 마찬가지로(= **similarly**) **advocate** 지지[옹호]하다; 옹호자 **computerization** 컴퓨터화 **computing** 컴퓨터 조작[사용] **limitation** 한계, 제한 **conquer** 정복하다, 극복하다

구문 10~13행 they all focus ***on*** / **correcting** *some situation* [to which they object] / or **changing** the circumstances for *a group* [that is harmed by some kind of social disadvantage].
→ focus on의 목적어인 correcting과 changing이 or로 연결되어 동명사구를 이끌고 있다. 두 개의 [ ]는 각각 some situation, a group을 수식하는 관계절이다.

실전 모의고사 10회

121 ③ 122 ⑤ 123 ③ 124 ① 125 ④ 126 ⑤ | 본문 88p

121 ③ | are → is

해설 ③ 주어가 not putting이 이끄는 동명사구이므로 동사는 단수형이어야 한다.

① 원급 비교를 나타내는 두 개의 as를 떼고 보면, '빠르게 망가뜨리다(ruins swiftly)'라는 뜻. 동사를 수식하는 자리이므로 부사가 적절.
② 문맥상 친구에 의해 '숨 막힘을 느끼는' 것이므로 수동을 나타내는 과거분사 suffocated가 적절.
④ 문장의 주어 역할을 하는 동명사구를 이끄는 Having이 적절히 쓰였다.
⑤ Having diverse interests and friendships를 권한 뒤 이와 비교되고 있는 부분. those who have few에서 few는 few interests and friendships로 어법상 셀 수 있는 개념에 쓰이며 '거의 없는'이라는 의미를 가지는 few가 맞게 쓰였다.

해석 간절한 애정 갈구와 소유욕만큼 우정을 빠르게 망치는 것은 없다. 친구는 함께 많은 시간을 보낼 수 있는데 오직 서로 합의한 경우에 한해서다. 어느 한쪽이 상대방에게 너무 많이 요구하기 시작하자마자, 그 관계는 큰 어려움을 겪는다. 친구 때문에 질식할 것 같은 느낌은 도망가서 숨고 싶게 만든다. 이것이 바로 모든 달걀을 한 바구니에 담지 않는 것이 매우 중요한 이유이다. 다양한 관심사와 교우 관계를 갖는 것은 이를 적게 가진 사람들을 자주 괴롭히는 절망감을 줄이는 데 도움이 된다. 이렇게 생각해 보자. 당신의 삶은 케이크와 같다. 당신의 삶이 더욱 풍요로워질수록, 당신의 케이크는 더 훌륭해진다. 친구란 케이크에 입히는 설탕 옷은 될 수 있지만, 케이크 그 자체는 될 수 없다. 그것은 누구에게든 요구하기에 너무 과한 것이다.

어휘 **swiftly** 빨리, 즉시 **desperate** 간절히 원하는; 자포자기한 ***cf.* desperation** 절망, 자포자기 **possessiveness** 소유욕 **heaps of** 다량의 ~ **mutually** 서로 **arrangement** 합의; 준비 **suffocate** ~을 숨 막히게 하다 **diverse** 다양한

구문 09~11행 Having diverse interests and friendships (S) **helps** (V) **(to)** (O) **shrink** *the desperation* [**that** so often troubles (V′) *those* (O′) [**who** have few]].

→ 동명사구를 주어로 하는 SVO 구조. helps의 목적어는 to부정사와 원형부정사 둘 다 가능하다. those who는 '~한 사람들'이라는 의미.

122 ⑤ | do → are

해설 ❺ 비교되고 있는 것이 you're excited와 we're excited, 즉 be동사 are로 써야 할 자리이다.

① <spend+시간/돈+v-ing>: v하는 데 ~을 쓰다
② 앞의 명사 choice를 수식하는 형용사처럼 쓰인 to부정사.
③ <so ~ that ...(너무 ~해서 …하다)>의 결과를 나타내는 that.
④ 새로운 임무를 준 과거 사실에 대해 가정하고 있으므로 조동사 뒤에 완료형(have assigned)을 맞게 썼다.

해석 우리는 Silvia Killingsworth가 4월에 이곳에서 우리와 합류하게 될 것임을 발표하게 되어 매우 기쁩니다. Silvia는 현재 <뉴요커(The New Yorker)>의 편집장으로 그곳에서 잡지의 업무 흐름을 관장하며 지난 7년을 보냈습니다. Silvia의 경험의 폭과 풍부한 아이디어, 그리고 매사에 보이는 진정한 열의는 <머리핀(The Hairpin)>이 그다음 단계의 삶으로 진화하면서 그녀가 이를 이끌 분명하고 명백한 선택사항이 되도록 했습니다. 실은 우리는 사이트의 미래 모습에 대한 그녀의 청사진에 너무나 깊은 인상을 받아 <부엉이(The Awl)>도 지휘하도록 했습니다. 그것은 엄청난 일이기는 하나 그녀가 열렬히 원하고 해낼 능력이 있다는 확신이 전적으로 들지 않았다면 어떤 한 개인에게 그 일을 맡기지는 못했을 겁니다. 여러분도 우리만큼이나 이 새로운 단계가 펼쳐지는 것을 흥미롭게 지켜보시길 희망하며 Silvia가 새로 참가한 것을 환영하는 데 있어서 우리와 동참해 주시길 부탁드립니다.

어휘 **announce** 선언하다, 공표하다 **currently** 현재 **managing editor** 편집장, 편집 책임자 **workflow** 작업 흐름 **breadth** 폭, 너비 **genuine** 진정한, 진짜의 **enthusiasm** 열의, 열정 **head** ~의 선두에 서다, ~을 이끌다 **evolve** 서서히 발달[진화]하다 **take the reins** 통솔[지휘]하다, 고삐를 잡다 **undertaking** (중요한, 힘든) 일, 프로젝트 **assign** 맡기다, 배정하다 **eager** 열심인, 간절히 바라는 **phase** (변화, 발달 과정상의) 단계

구문 12~14행 ~ but we **would not have assigned** it to any one person unless we were completely convinced that she was eager(A) and able(B) to do it.

→ '과거 일에 대한 반대'를 가정해 보는 가정법 과거완료의 귀결절(would not have assigned(맡기지 않았을 것이다)) 형태를 보인다. 한편 if절은 가정법이 아닌, 실제 사실 그대로 조건절(과거시제)로 표현되어 있으며(실제로는 we were completely convinced that ~했다는 얘기) if we had not been completely convinced that ~의 가정법 조건절로도 쓸 수 있다.
→ be eager to-v와 be able to-v의 병렬구조.

123 ③ | happened → happening

해설 ❸ 문장의 동사는 are이므로 the huge changes를 수식하는 분사가 와야 한다. '큰 변화가 일어나다'란 뜻으로, the huge changes와 happen은 능동관계. 따라서 happening이 적절.

① 주어가 동명사구(Displaying ~ emotions)이므로 단수동사 affects가 알맞게 사용됨.
② 앞의 less와 함께 비교급 구문을 이루는 than이 적절히 쓰였다.
④ 타인을 통제하고 관심을 끌기 위해 난폭한 감정(violent emotions)을 사용하는 것이므로 '목적'을 나타내는 to부정사의 부사적 용법으로 적절히 쓰임.
⑤ 동사 feel의 보어 자리이므로 형용사 emotional이 적절.

해석 시기나 분노와 같이 강한 부정적인 감정을 드러내는 것은 당신 주위의 사람들에게 직접적으로 영향을 미쳐서, 그들 안에 당신에 대한 부정적인 감정을 일으킨다. 만약 당신이 종종 감정적인 폭발을 겪는다면, 그것은 아마도 자제심이 부족하기 때문이거나, 자신이 느끼는 바를 드러낼 당신의 '권리'에 대한 관심보다 당신이 일으키고 있는 문제에 대한 관심이 적기 때문이다. 십 대들의 감정은 그들의 신체와 호르몬에 일어나는 거대한 변화에 어느 정도 지배된다. 그러나 만약 십 대 청소년이 나쁜 감정들을 잘 다루는 법을 배우지 않는다면, 그 청소년은 타인을 통제하고 관심을 끌기 위해 난폭한 감정을 사용하는 지나치게 감정적인 성인이 되기 쉽다. 지나치게 감정적인 사람들을 도우려면, 그들이 자신과 타인에게 미치고 있는 영향을 보여주고, 감정적으로 느낄 때 지나치게 감정적으로 행동하지 않을 힘이 그들에게 있다는 것을 이해시켜라.

어휘 **display** (감정이나 자질을) 드러내다; ~을 진열하다 **jealousy** 시기 **rage** 격렬한 분노 **arouse** (감정이나 태도를) 유발하다 **outburst** (감정의) 폭발 **somewhat** 어느 정도, 다소 **at the mercy of** ~에 지배되는, 좌우되는 **violent** 난폭한

구문 04~07행 ~, it's probably **because** you have poor self-control or **because** you care ***less*** about *the trouble* [(*that*) you're causing ∨] ***than*** you care about your *"right"* (to show how you feel).

124 ① | be thrilled → thrill

해설 ❶ they(bottles)가 my sister를 thrill((기쁨, 전율 등으로) 떨리게 하다)시킬 것이므로 수동태가 아닌 능동태(they'd thrill ~)로 써야 한다.

② bottles가 복수이므로 지시대명사도 단수(that)가 아닌 복수(those)로 맞게 썼다.
③ 명사 a gift 대신 쓴 부정대명사 one.
④ <so ~ that ...(너무 ~해서 …하다)> 패턴의 일부.
⑤ 선물을 사는 일을 일로 여기게 된 (지금보다) '더 현명'했다는 의미.

해석 내가 여덟 살 때 난생처음으로 산 첫 번째 크리스마스 선물은 인형 크기만한 파스텔 색상의 다섯 개의 향수병이었다. 나는 그것들이 네 살짜리 내 동생 Joyce를 기뻐 어쩔 줄 모르게 할 거라는 걸 알았다. 그것들은 내 저금통을 싹 비울 만큼 비쌌다. 물론 Joyce는 금방 그 조그만 병들을 잊어버렸다. 하지만 나는 아직도 그 선물을, 주는 것의 즐거움을 내게 가르쳐 준 선물로 회고하곤 한다. 그녀의 선물을 사기 위해 내 잔돈을 세면서 누군가 딴 사람의 행복을 더 우선으로 하는 것이 어떤 의미인지 나는 깨달았다. 지금은 선물을 사는 일이 너무 복잡한 일이어서 주는 '일'로 느껴질 정도이다. 목걸이가 너무 유행에 앞서나? 스웨터가 너무 뻔한가? 내가 얼마나 (상대를) 신경 쓰고 있는가를 증명해낼 물건을 쉼 없이 찾아 헤매는 동안 나는 있는 힘을 쏙 다 빼버린다. 여덟 살 때 나는 더 지혜로웠다. 나는 내 동생을 행복하게 해주고 싶은 마음뿐이었다.

어휘 **perfume** 향수 **thrill** 전율(을 느끼게 하다) **piggy bank** 돼지 저금통 **look back on** ~을 회고하다 **joy** 기쁨 **change** 잔돈, 거스름돈 **put ~ front and center** ~을 가장 중요한 위치에 두다, ~을 중요하게 생각하다 **complex** 복잡한 **edgy** 최첨단의, 유행을 앞서가는 **predictable** 예측 가능한, 뻔한 **exhaust** (남김없이) 소모하다

구문 08~10행 When I counted out my change to buy her present, I(S) discovered(V) what **it**(O 가주어) meant ∨ ***to put*** someone else's happiness front and center(진주어).

→ 동사 discovered의 목적어절이 가주어, 진주어 패턴을 이루고 있다.

125 ④

해설 (A) 개작하는(adapt) 것은 문맥상 앞에 나온 characters' names이므로 이를 지칭하는 복수 대명사 them을 쓰는 것이 적절하다.
(B) If 다음에 leaving 또는 left를 써야 하는 것으로 보아 접속사가 있는 분사구문임을 알 수 있다. 이때 분사구문의 의미상 주어는 주절의 주어와 같은데, 주어인 names는 번역되지 않은 상태로 '남겨지는(left)' 수동의 의미이므로 과거분사를 써야 한다.
(C) putting young readers off가 avoid의 목적어이므로 능동 형태가 사용되어야 하므로 to avoid가 적절하다. 또한 is 다음의 보어 자리로 명사적 용법의 to부정사가 오는 것은 어법상 적절하다.

해석 캐릭터의 이름은 성인 소설의 번역에서 좀처럼 바뀌지 않는 반면, 어린이를 위한 글을 쓰는 번역가들은 예컨대 Hans/John/Jean, William/Guillermo/Guillaume, Alice/Alicia와 같은 표적 언어에서 상응하는 이름을 사용함으로써 그것들을 종종 개작한다. 그러나 이 문제는 많은 의견 불일치를 야기하는데, 이름이 사회적 그리고 문화적 맥락의 강력한 신호이기 때문이다. 번역되지 않은 채로 남아있으면, 이름은 어린 독자들에게 그들이 다른 나라 배경의 이야기를 읽고 있음을 끊임없이 상기시키는 반면 표적 언어에서 상응하는 이름 혹은 대체 이름을 사용하는 것은 이름과 배경 간의 어울리지 않는 관계로 이어질지 모른다. 그럼에도 불구하고, 편집자들과 번역가들은 어린이들이 외국 이름으로 고심하다가 Anthea Bell이 자신의 '번역가의 공책'에서 언급하는 딜레마를 초래할지 모른다고 두려워한다. '이 모든 것 이면의 생각은 어린 독자들에게 책을 여는 순간 이해할 수 없을 것처럼 보이는 일련의 외국 이름들을 제시함으로써 그들의 흥미를 잃게 하는 것을 피하겠다는 것이다. 그것은 아동 문학의 번역가들에게 끊임없이 도전을 가하는 종류의 문제이다.'

어휘 **translation** 번역(본) **adapt** 개작하다, (새로운 상황에) 맞추다[조정하다] **equivalent** 상응[대응]하는 것; 동등한 **context** 맥락; 배경; 문맥 **set** (연극·소설·영화의) 배경을 설정하다; 세트 **struggle with** ~로 고심하다; 씨름하다 **give rise to** 초래하다; 일으키다 **cite** 언급하다; 인용하다 **put A off** A로 하여금 흥미를 잃게 만들다

구문 08~14행 If left untranslated, names constantly ***remind*** young readers // **that** they are reading *a story* (set in another country), whereas the use of an equivalent name [or] an alternative in the target language / may lead to an incongruous relationship between names and setting.
→ 접속사 that이 이끄는 명사절은 동사 remind의 직접목적어이다. ( ) 부분은 a story를 수식하는 과거분사구이다. or는 밑줄 친 두 개의 명사구를 병렬 연결한다.

14~17행 Nonetheless, editors and translators *fear* **that** children might struggle with foreign names, thus **giving rise to** *a dilemma* [*that* Anthea Bell cites in her *Translator's notebook*]:
→ 굵게 표시한 that이 이끄는 명사절은 동사 fear의 목적어이다. giving rise to 이하는 결과를 나타내는 분사구문이며, [ ] 부분은 목적격 관계대명사 that이 이끄는 형용사절로 a dilemma를 수식한다.

126 ⑤ | complicatedly → complicated

해설 ⑤ 삽입 구문 where to eat ~ to buy의 수식을 받는 even the simplest decisions가 that으로 시작하는 관계절의 동사 make의 목적어이다. 목적격보어 자리에 부사는 올 수 없으므로 형용사 complicated로 써야 한다.
① 양보의 의미를 나타내고 뒤에 주어와 동사가 있는 절을 이끌어야 하므로 접속사 while은 적절하다.
② 비교급 faster를 강조하는 부사로 far가 적절히 쓰였으며 '훨씬'이라는 뜻이다.
③ <no matter how (아무리 ~하더라도)> 구문이며 '우리가 삶의 속도를 얼마나 많이 증가시키더라도(increase)'의 문맥이므로 how 뒤에 부사 much는 적절하다.
④ 보어 역할을 하는 that절의 주어인 our share of the world와 squeeze(쥐어짜다)는 수동의 관계이므로 감각동사 feels 다음의 주격보어 자리에 과거분사 squeezed는 적절하다.

해석 현대의 삶의 역설은 운송, 통신, 그리고 생산에서 기술적 가속이 '더 많은' 자유 시간을 제공하는데도, 그 똑같은 발명품들이 기하급수적인 속도로 우리가 선택할 수 있는 것을 늘린다는 것이다. 이메일이 보통 우편보다 훨씬 더 빨랐지만, 인터넷은 또한 트위터, 유튜브, 기타 등등을 가져왔다. 독일 사회학자인 Hartmut Rosa가 기술한 것처럼, "우리가 '삶의 속도'를 얼마나 많이 증가시키든지 간에", 우리는 정보의 홍수를 따라잡을 수 없다. 그 결과는 비록 우리가 더 효율적인 접근성을 얻게 될지라도 '세상에서 우리가 차지하는 부분'은 끊임없이 비좁아지는 것처럼 느껴진다는 것이다. 추정컨대 이 세상 자료의 90%가 지난 5년 동안 생겨났다. 우리는 모두 정보에 압도당하고 있는데, 즉 어디서 먹을지, 어떤 의료 보험에 가입할지, 어떤 커피메이커를 살지와 같은 가장 단순한 결정조차도 더 복잡하게 만드는 현실이다.

어휘 **paradox** 역설; 역설적인 사람[것/상황] **option** 선택(할 수 있는 것); 선택권 **snail mail** 보통 우편 **no matter how** 아무리 ~하더라도 **share** (여러 사람이 나눠 가지는 것의) 몫, 지분 **squeeze** (좁은 곳에) 밀어 넣다; 짜내다 **estimate** 추정(치), 추산 **drown in** ~에 압도당하다; ~에 덮이다 **health plan** 의료 보험 **sign up for** ~을 가입[신청]하다

구문 01~05행 The paradox of modern life is [that {while technological acceleration—in transportation, communication, and production—should provide *more* free time}, **those same inventions** / **increase** our options at an exponential rate].
→ [ ] 부분은 동사 is의 보어로 쓰였다. { } 부분은 뒤에 오는 절을 수식하는 부사절이고, that절의 주어는 those same inventions, 동사는 increase이다.

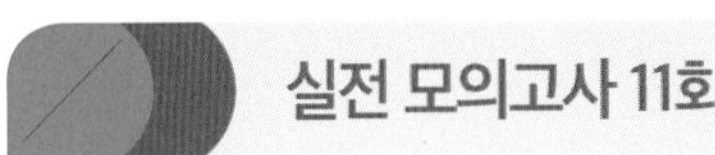

실전 모의고사 11회

127 ⑤ 128 ① 129 ⑤ 130 ④ 131 ③ 132 ④ | 본문 90p

127 ⑤ | was referred to → was referred to as

해설 ❺ <refer to A as B(A를 B라고 부르다[일컫다])>를 수동태로 쓴 곳. B에 해당하는 the surgeon general for ~ 앞에 as(~로, ~로서)가 빠져 있다.

① Some of 뒤에 복수명사 memories가 왔으므로 복수동사 are가 적절.
② 과거의 추측이므로 <might have p.p.>가 적절.
③ they(= spices)가 '사용되어 온' 것이므로 현재완료의 수동태(have been used)가 적절.
④ laborers를 수식하는 분사 수식어(building ~). 노동자들이 피라미드를 '짓는' 주체이므로 능동의 현재분사 building은 적절.

해석 내가 자라면서 가장 좋아하는 기억 중 몇 가지는 어머니가 만드신 맛있는 애플파이 한 조각을 몰래 먹기 위해 부엌에 살금살금 들어가는 것이다. 계피가 어디에서 왔는지 혹은 그것의 영양상 이점이 무엇인지는 나에게 미스터리였을지도 모르지만 그것의 특별한 맛 때문에 나는 계속 (부엌을) 다시 찾았다. 사람들은 음식에 특별한 향을 더하기 위해 수천 년 동안 향신료를 사용해 왔다. 그리고 향신료들은 그 약효 때문에도 사용되어 왔다. 예를 들어, 마늘은 질병을 피하기 위해 이집트 피라미드를 짓는 노동자들에게 먹여졌다. 그리고 생강은 배탈을 가라앉히는 것을 돕는 효능이 있다. 클라우디우스 1세와 네로 황제의 군의로 불렸던 디오스코리데스는 서기 77년에 유명한 <약물에 대하여>라는 책에서 생강이 '배를 따뜻하고 부드럽게 한다'고 썼다.

어휘 **fond** 좋아하는 **tiptoe** 발끝으로 걷다 **sneak** ~을 슬쩍하다; 살금살금 들어오다 **cinnamon** 계피 **nutritional** 영양의 **spice** 향신료 **flavor** 풍미, 맛 **medicinal** 약의, 약용의 **garlic** 마늘 **laborer** 노동자 **A be referred to as B** A가 B라고 불리다 **emperor** 황제

128 ①

해설 (A) 관계절 that have examined ~ self-efficacy and performance의 수식을 받는 the sport studies가 문장의 주어이므로 문장의 동사는 복수형 have yielded가 적절하다.
(B) when he developed ~ of their games는 앞의 내용을 수식하는 부사절이다. 부사절의 목적어로 쓰인 music videos와 show는 능동의 관계이므로 능동의 현재분사 showing을 써야 한다.
(C) 동사 found의 목적어가 필요한 자리이고, 뒤에 완전한 절이 온 것으로 보아 명사절을 이끄는 접속사 that을 써야 한다.

해석 과거의 행동은 현재의 자기 효능감 판단의 가장 강력한 예측 변수이다. 그래서 학습자는 자신이 성공적인 행동을 해내는 것을 관찰함으로써, 계속 발전하기 위해 기술을 가장 잘 수행하는 방법에 관한 정보에 더 큰 주의를 기울이고 이런 정보를 제공받는다. (연구가) 수적으로 제한되어 있긴 하지만, 자기 효능감과 경기력과 같은 심리사회적인 변수에 대한 자기 모델링의 효과를 조사해 온 운동 연구들은 고무적인 결과를 냈다. 예를 들어 Halliwell은 그가 (부상을 당하거나 혹은 슬럼프를 겪기 이전의) 프로 하키 선수들의 경기 중에서 성공적인 주요 부분들만 보여 주는 뮤직비디오를 개발했을 때, 부상이나 슬럼프를 겪은 이후에 돌아온 그들의 경기력과 자신감이 향상되는 것을 발견했다. 마찬가지로 Singleton과 Feltz는 대학 하키 선수들의 경기력에 대한 자기 모델링의 효과를 조사했고 자기 모델링을 접한 선수들이 대조 집단에 비해 슈팅 수행에 있어서 더 뛰어난 슈팅 정확도와 자기 효능감을 경험했다는 것을 발견했다.

어휘 **predictor** 예측 변수 **execute** 실행하다 **psychosocial** 심리 사회적인 **variable** 변수 **performance** 경기력 **yield** 내다, 생산하다 **confidence** 자신(감) **accuracy** 정확도 **control** 통제[대조] 집단, 대조 표준

구문 02~05행 So by [observing themselves executing successful moves], learners {pay greater attention to} and {are provided with} the information on how to best perform skills **to continue progressing**.
→ [ ] 부분은 전치사 by의 목적어 역할을 하는 동명사구로 주절의 주어인 learners가 의미상의 주어로 쓰였다. 두 개의 { } 부분은 and로 연결되어 the information on how to best perform skills를 전치사의 목적어로 공유한다. to continue progressing은 '~하기 위해'라는 의미의 부사적 용법으로 쓰인 to부정사구이다.

15~21행 Likewise, Singleton and Feltz [examined the effect of self-modeling on college hockey players' performance] and [found that *the players* {exposed to self-modeling} experienced greater shooting accuracy and self-efficacy for shooting performance **compared with controls**].
→ [ ]로 표시된 두 개의 동사구가 and로 연결되어 술부를 이룬다. 두 번째 [ ] 내에서 부분은 앞의 the players를 수식하는 분사구이고 compared with controls는 바로 앞 shooting performance에 대해 the players exposed to self-modeling과 비교하는 의미의 분사구문이다.

129 ⑤ | fulfilling → fulfilled

해설 ❺ fulfilling 뒤에는 fulfill(이루다, 성취하다)의 목적어가 와야 하는데, 이 문맥에서는 '마음이 채워지는'이라는 수동의 의미가 적절하다. 따라서 feel fulfilled로 고쳐 써야 한다.

① writer와 author 둘 간의 차이이므로 <between A and B(A와 B 둘 사이)>로 쓴 것이 맞다.
② think of의 주체가 특정인이 아닌 '일반적인 우리'를 가리키는 one이므로 of의 목적어로 재귀대명사 oneself를 쓴 것이 알맞다.
③ control completely의 <동사-부사> 호응 구조.
④ <ask+O+to-v>: O에게 v해달라고 부탁하다

해석 나는 늘 '글 쓰는 이'와 '작가'를 구분하려고 애썼다. 첫 번째 것은 어떤 행위를 추구하고자 하는 욕구를 내비친다. 두 번째 것은 다른 이들이 자기 작품을 소비함으로써 그 행위를 인정하게끔 하려는 욕구를 내비친다. 자신을 작가라고 여기는 것에 물론 잘못된 것은 아무것도 없다. 하지만 관점을 얻고 회의감을 극복하기 위해 이전의 마음가짐으로 돌아가는 것이 유용할 때가 많다. 자기 자신을 위해 글을 써라. 재미있기 때문에 글을 써라. 당신이 전적으로 통제할 수 있는 당신 인생의 한 부분이기 때문에 글을 써라. 당신이 쓴 작품을 평가하지 말고, 다른 사람들에게 당신을 위해 그걸 평가해 달라고 하지 마라. 당신 말고 다른 사람이 당신이 쓴 글을 보거나 할까 걱정하지 마라. 그냥 글 쓰는 사람이 되라. 그러고 나서 글 쓰는 게 당신의 매일 매일의 삶에서 소박하고도 즐거운 부분이 되면 작가가 되는 것에 대해 생각하기 시작해도 좋다. 혹은 안 그래도 되는데, 그건 당신의 선택이니까. 하지만 당신이 쓴 것에 대해 만족감을 느끼기만 한다면 타인의 의견은 결국 그다지 큰 의미가 없다.

어휘 **distinction** 구별, 차이 **author** 작가, 저자 **imply** 넌지시 나타내다, 은연중에 풍기다 **pursue** 추구하다, 좇다 **revert** 되돌아가다 **perspective** 관점, 시각 **joyful** 즐거운, 즐거움을 자아내는 **existence** 존재 **fulfilled** 성취감을 느끼는 **ultimately** 결국, 나중에 가서는

130 ④ | that's → it's

해설 ❹ 대명사 that이 쓰일 곳이 아니라 이어 나오는 진주어 to choose ~를 대신하는 가주어 it이 와야 할 자리이다.

① '~하기 위해서'의 뜻으로 쓰인 '목적'을 나타내는 to부정사.
② pay-how(어떻게 지불하느냐)로 연결되는 <동사-부사> 관계로 how를 쓴 것이 자연스럽다. how they pay you가 전치사 of의 목적어.
③ the chance(가능성, 공산)의 내용을 소개하는 동격의 that.
⑤ <so (that)+S+not[never] ~(S가 ~하지 않도록)>에서 that이 생략된 형태. <목적>을 나타냄.

해석 온라인 업체 소유주로서 (사이트를) 24시간 내내 고객에게 이용 가능하도록 하기 위해 압박을 느끼고 있을지 모른다. 그것은 믿을 만한 결제 시스템이 필요하다는 의미이다. 또한 고객에게 휴대폰 결제나 계좌 이체와 같은 지불 방식을 선택 가능하도록 하고 싶을 수도 있다. 장차 (결제 서비스) 제공자가 될 수도 있는 업체와 접촉할 때는 속도, 신뢰성, 보안의 세 요소를 고려해야 한다. 속도는 고객이 뜻대로 (결제가) 잘 안되어 거래를 포기하게 되고, 그리하여 판매 건을 못 올리는 결과를 가져올 가능성을 줄여주기 때문에 중요하다. 전자상거래 기반을 선택할 때 신뢰성도 중요한데, 결제를 받지 못하는[결제가 진행이 안 되는] 일 분 일 분이 돈을 벌지 못하는 일 분이기 때문이다. 그러나 고객 정보를 보호하고 업체의 평판을 지키는 것이 고객 충성도에 대한 핵심이다. 전자 상거래 편의 수단을 선택할 때는 사이버 범죄자들이 실제 카드 정보에 절대로 접근할 수 없도록 신용카드 번호를 암호화하는 서비스 제공업자를 선택하는 게 중요하다.

어휘 **available** 이용 가능한 **around the clock** 24시간 내내 **payment system** 결제 시스템 **rely on** ~을 신뢰하다, ~을 믿고 의지하다 **direct debit** 계좌 이체 **provider** 공급자 **reliability** 신뢰성 **security** 안전성 **take A into account** A를 고려하다 **abandon** 그만두다, 단념하다 **transaction** 거래 **platform** (어떤 일이 이루어지는) 작업대, 발판 **reputation** 평판 **loyalty** 충성도 **facility** 편의시설[수단] **access** 접근하다

구문 17~21행 When you're choosing an e-commerce facility, **it**(가주어)'s important **to choose**(진주어) *a provider* [**that** encrypts credit card numbers] [**so (that)** cyber criminals **will never** be able to access the real card data].

→ 주절이 <가주어-진주어> 구조를 이루고 있다. so ~ 이하는 <목적(~하지 않도록)>을 나타내는 부사절로 that이 생략되어 있는 형태.

131 ③

해설 (A) not your vision을 it is와 that 사이에 두어 강조한 구문이므로 that이 적절.
(B) 콤마 뒤의 절은 change blindness를 부연 설명하는 관계사절. 이어지는 절이 완전한 형태이므로 관계부사 where가 적절.
(C) A test subject에게 사진이 '보이는' 것이므로 수동태가 적절. 능동태로 바꾸면 <show+IO(a test subject)+DO(pictures of two faces)>이다.

해석 마술사가 당신을 속일 때 탓해야 하는 것은 당신의 시력이 아니다. 오히려 귀 뒤에 위치한, 집중을 돕는 뇌의 작은 부분인 두정피질을 탓해야 한다. 심리학자 닐리 레이비는 뇌의 이 부분이 변화 맹시라고 알려진 현상의 열쇠를 쥐고 있다는 것을 발견했는데, 이 변화 맹시는 주의가 흩뜨려질 때 사람들이 아주 분명한 것도 못 보고 지나치는 것을 말한다. 고전적인 예가 얼굴 실험이다. 피실험자에게 매우 빠른 속도로 잇달아 두 사람의 얼굴을 보여준다. 보통, 피실험자는 두 얼굴이 서로 다르다는 것을 인식하지만, 만약 숫자 세기 같은 과제로 피실험자의 주의가 전환되거나 화면의 깜빡임 등으로 산만해진 경우에는 두 얼굴의 차이를 대개 알아보지 못할 것이다.

어휘 **psychologist** 심리학자 **phenomenon** 현상 **overlook** ~을 못 보고 넘어가다, 간과하다 **divert** ~을 전환시키다 **distract** ~을 산만하게 하다 **flicker** 깜박임

132 ④ | what → that

해설 ❹ <take it for granted that ~>은 '당연히 (that절)이라고 믿다[생각하다]'라는 표현이므로 what을 that으로 고쳐야 한다.

① <one of+명사>가 주어일 때는 one에 수일치하여 단수동사가 뒤따르므로 is는 적절하다.
② 전치사 to 다음에 동명사 형태 acquiring이 온 것은 적절하다.
③ 앞에 있는 가주어 it에 대응되는 진주어 to-v가 적절하게 쓰였다.
⑤ <find+O+OC> SVOC 구조의 문장에서 목적어(O) 자리에 가목적어 it, 뒤에 진목적어 to-v가 뒤따르는 구문이 맞게 쓰였다.

해석 사회학 강의의 목표 중 하나는 학생들이 '사회학적 상상력', 즉 인간의 행동과 신념을 문화적 영향력의 측면에서 보는 능력을 기르도록 돕는 것이다. 문화가 인간의 삶을 어떻게 형성하는지를 이해하는 것은 사회학적 상상력을 얻는 데 필수적이다. 그러나 당신이 타국에 있을 때 문화의 널리 퍼져 있는 영향력을 감지하기는 꽤 쉽지만, 어떻게 '당신'의 문화가 '당신'을 형성하는지를 인식하는 것은 전혀 별개의 문제이다. 우리는 '우리'의 신념과 행동 방식이 지극히 자연스럽다는 것을 당연하게 여기면서도, 누군가가 우리에게 '왜' 그렇게 믿고 행동하는지를 묻는다면 대답하기가 매우 어렵다는 것을 깨달을 것이다. 혹자는 물고기가 절대 알아채지 못하는 것이 물이라고 말한 적이 있는데, 이것은 우리에게도 마찬가지이다. 우리는 우리를 지배하는 우리 자신의 문화의 힘을 거의 인지하지 못한다.

어휘 **sociology** 사회학 ***cf.*** **sociological** 사회학적인 **imagination** 상상력 **in terms of** ~면에서 **shape** ~을 형성하다 **essential** 필수적인 **acquire** ~을 얻다 **detect** ~을 감지하다 **pervasive** 퍼져 있는, 만연해 있는 **influence** 영향; ~에 영향을 미치다 **recognize** ~을 인식하다 **take it for granted (that)** 당연히 ~일 것이라고 믿다 **perceive** ~을 인지하다

133 ⑤ | give → be given

해설 ⑤ 주어인 The development ~ areas에 최우선순위가 '주어지는' 것이므로 수동태인 be given으로 바꿔야 한다.

① 수식받는 task가 '압박을 가하는'의 능동의 뜻이 문맥상 적절하므로 현재분사 pressing은 적절하다.
② 자동사인 occur가 Changes를 주어로 해서 현재완료의 형태로 알맞게 쓰였다. 자동사는 수동태로 쓰일 수 없으므로 have been occurred는 불가능하다.
③ 뒤에 보어로 쓰인 형용사 effective를 수식하는 부사 sufficiently가 올바르게 쓰였다.
④ 상관접속사 <either A or B> 구문으로 앞의 learn과 병렬구조를 이루어야 하므로 동사원형 develop이 알맞게 쓰였다.

해석 가장 긴급한 과제는 기후 변화 문제에 있을지도 모른다. 화석 연료가 고갈되기 훨씬 이전에, 우리는 이러한 연료 사용의 결과를 직시해야 할 것이다. 지구 온난화는 20년 후엔 현재보다 훨씬 더 큰 위협이 될 것이다. 대기 변화가 지금만큼 빠르게 일어난 적은 한 번도 없었다. 우리의 현재 장비와 사회 구조는 우리가 기후를 관리하거나 부적합한 환경에서 번영하기에 충분히 효과적이지는 않다. 우리는 기후를 우리에게 유리하도록 변화시킬 방법을 배우거나 우리가 다른 환경에서도 생존할 수 있도록 해 줄 기술을 개발해야 한다. 오늘날 이 두 가지 모두 분명히 부족하다. 그러므로 이러한 분야에서의 과학과 기술의 발전에 최우선순위를 줘야 한다. 만약 우리가 향후 수십 년 안에 이러한 문제들을 어떻게든 해결해 낸다면, 우리의 후손 또한 먼 훗날까지 살아남을 수 있을 것이라는 희망의 근거를 갖게 된다.

어휘 **pressing** 긴급한 **run out** 고갈되다 **face up to** ~을 직시하다; 받아들이다 **consequence** 결과 **hostile** (환경이) 적합하지 않은; 적대적인 **surroundings** 환경 **in one's favor** ~에 유리하게 **priority** 우선순위; 우선권 **manage** (어떻게든) ~해내다 **grounds for** ~의 근거 **descendant** 자손, 후손

구문 02~04행 Long before fossil fuels **run** out, we'll have to face up to the consequences of using these fuels.
→ 시간, 조건의 부사절에서는 반드시 미래시간을 현재시제로 써야 한다.

134 ④ | to give up → giving up

해설 ④ 엘비스가 그 역을 포기한 것을 후회했다는 의미이므로 '(과거에) ~한 것을 후회하다'라는 뜻의 <regret v-ing>가 적절. 따라서 부정사 목적어를 동명사 목적어로 고쳐야 한다. *cf.* <regret to-v>: v하게 되어 유감이다

① which의 선행사는 the Broadway musical of the same name. 동명의 브로드웨이 뮤지컬이 셰익스피어 작품에서 '각색되었다'는 내용이므로 수동태 적절.
② 문맥상 it이 가리키는 것이 the soundtrack album이므로 단수 대명사 적절.
③ 사역동사 make는 목적격보어로 원형부정사를 취하므로 decline은 알맞음.
⑤ 관계사절의 동사는 선행사에 수를 일치시킨다. 선행사는 many young stars이므로 복수동사 were가 알맞음.

해석 <웨스트사이드 스토리>는 로버트 와이즈와 제롬 로빈슨이 연출한 1961년도 영화이다. 그것은 동명의 브로드웨이 뮤지컬을 각색한 것인데, 이 뮤지컬은 윌리엄 셰익스피어의 <로미오와 줄리엣>에서 각색된 것이었다. 그 영화는 유나이티드 아티스트 사(社)를 통해 1961년 10월 18일 개봉되었다. 그 영화는 아카데미 11개 부문에서 (수상 후보로) 지명되어 10개의 상을 받았고, 영화음악 앨범은 그 이전에 만들어진 어느 앨범보다 높은 수익을 올렸다. 원래 엘비스 프레슬리가 그 영화의 토니 역으로 이야기가 되고 있었다. 그러나 그의 매니저가 그 역은 엘비스에게 맞지 않는다고 강하게 믿어서 그로 하여금 다른 뮤지컬 영화를 위해 거절하도록 했다. 그 영화가 크게 성공을 거두고 10개의 오스카상을 타자 엘비스는 그 역을 포기한 것을 무척 후회했다. 그는 토니 역할에 고려된 많은 젊은 스타들 중 한 사람이었을 뿐이었다.

어휘 **direct** ~을 연출하다; ~을 지도하다 **adaptation** 각색 ***cf.* adapt** ~을 각색하다; ~을 조정하다 **release** ~을 개봉하다, 출시하다 **nominate** ~을 지명하다, 임명하다 **soundtrack** 영화음악 **decline** 거절하다; 쇠퇴하다 **consideration** 고려

135 ② | anxious → anxiety

해설 ② <from A to B>는 mental health issues의 구체적인 예를 표현한 부분. A, B 둘 다 명사이어야 하므로 anxious가 아닌 anxiety가 되어야 한다.

① one of+복수명사: ~중의 하나
③ to부정사구가 주어(To tell ~ 'shake it off')이므로 단수동사(is)가 쓰인 경우.
④ '기운을 빠지게 하는'의 능동의 의미를 띠므로 depressed가 아닌 depressing이 맞게 쓰였다.
⑤ 논리적인 결론에 도달'할 때까지' 죽 '지속적으로' 생각을 펼쳐보는 것이 안 되는 특징에 대해 얘기하고 있는 부분. 접속사 until(~할 때까지)이 문맥에 맞게 잘 쓰였다.

해석 정신 질환이 마지막(까지 살아남은) 사회적 금기 중 하나이다. 우울증과 불안감에서 중독에 이르기까지 정신 건강상의 문제점들에 대해 언급하는 데 있어서 많이 나아진 게 사실이지만 정신병의 낙인은 남아 있다. 어떤 이들에게는 그것이 게으름의 결과로 생겨나며 관심을 구하는, (일종의) 약점으로 비칠 수 있다. 그러나 그것은 분명 신경생물학적 기원을 갖고 있다. 우울한 사람에게 단순히 '잊어버려'라든지 '떨쳐버려'라고 주문하는 것은 당뇨병을 가진 사람에게 이 말을 하는 것과 꼭 마찬가지다. 문제는 누군가가 돕고 싶어 해도 피해를 끼치는 진짜 증상이 나타나면 그들[도우려는 사람]이 피하게 되는 게 드문 일이 아니다. 우울증은 기운 빠지게 하는 것으로 도움을 주고 싶어 하는 사람에게도 그러하다. "나는 이런 대화를 더 이상 나눌 수 없어요. 그냥 돌고 돌기만 하거든요."라고 한 환자의 친구가 말한다. 그리고 그녀의 말이 옳다. 계속 맴돌기만 하는 생각들—논리적인 결론에 이를 때까지 생각을 머릿속에 죽 펼치는 걸 못하는 것—이 우울증의 전형적 특징이다.

어휘 **societal** 사회의, 사회 전체에 미치는 **taboo** 금기사항 **laziness** 게으름, 나태함 **neurobiological** 신경생물학적인 **snap out of** ~에서 재빨리 벗어나다, 기운을 차리다 **diabetes** 당뇨병 **back away** 뒷걸음질 치다, 피하다 **cycle** 주기; 순환되다 **sufferer** 고통받는 사람, 환자 **inability** 무능력, 할 수 없음 **logical** 논리적인

구문 10~12행 The problem is *(that)* **even if** someone wants to help, **it**'s not uncommon **for** them **to back away** [when the real, damaging symptoms appear].
(종속절: even if ~ help / 주절: it's ~ appear])
→ <The problem is that ~>에서 보어절인 that절이 다시 <종속절+주절>의 구조를 이루고 있고 다시 주절이 <주절 + 종속절(when ~)> 구조로 나뉘어 있다.

136 ④ | it → them

해설 ❹ 앞에 있는 many of the first musical instruments를 가리키므로 복수대명사 them이 되어야 한다. 가목적어 it을 써서 표현할 경우에는 make it hard to recognize them as ~와 같이 recognize 뒤에 them이 있어야 한다.

① look 다음에는 형용사나 <like+명사>가 오는데, 뒤에 like가 없으므로, 형용사가 의문사로 바뀐 how가 어법상 적절하다.
② 불특정한 수의 과학자들 중에서 몇몇은 앞 문장의 Some scientists로 다른 과학자들은 Others로 표현하는 것은 어법상 적절하다.
③ 주어인 many instruments는 '보존되어' 온 것으로 의미상 수동이 되어야 하므로 been preserved는 어법상 적절하다.
⑤ '~인지 아닌지'라는 의미를 나타내면서 figuring out의 목적어로 쓰이는 명사절을 이끌고 있으므로 어법상 적절하다.

해석 과학자들은 최초의 악기가 어떻게 생겼는지, 그리고 그것들이 언제 만들어졌는지에 대해 아직도 의견이 일치하지 않는다. 몇몇 과학자들은 최초의 진정한 악기는 꽤 최근에 만들어진 것으로, 대략 6만 년 전으로 거슬러 올라간다고 믿는다. 다른 과학자들은 초기 인간들이 간단한 도구를 사용해 왔던 것만큼이나 오랫동안 어떤 형태의 악기를 사용하고 있었다고 믿는다. 만약 이것이 사실이라면, 음악은 그 연대가 멀리 2백만 년 전까지 거슬러 올라갈 수 있다! 많은 악기들이 보존되지 않았을 수도 있기 때문에 시기를 정확히 찾아내기는 어렵다. 또한, 최초의 악기 중 많은 것들은 아마도 또한 다른 용도를 가지고 있었을 것이다. 이것이 그것들을 악기로 인지하는 것을 어렵게 만들 것이다. 오늘날 고대 유적지를 연구하는 과학자들은 어떤 물체가 소리를 위해 사용되었는지 혹은 단지 도구로 사용되었는지를 알아내는 데 어려움을 겪을 것이다.

어휘 **musical instrument** 악기 ***cf.*** **instrument** 악기; 기구; 수단; (비행기 등의) 계기 **fairly** 꽤, 상당히 **date back to A** (시기 등이) A까지 거슬러 올라가다 **preserve** 보존하다; 보호하다 **ancient** 고대[옛날]의; 아주 오래된 **archaeological site** 유적지 **have a difficult time v-ing** v하는 것에 어려움을 겪다 **figure out** 알아내다; 이해하다; 계산하다

구문 03~06행 Some scientists believe / that the first true musical instruments / were *a fairly recent development*, / **dating back to around 60,000 years ago.**
→ dating ~ ago는 분사구로 the first musical instruments 혹은 a fairly recent development를 보충 설명한다.

14~17행 *Scientists* **(working on an ancient archaeological site today)** / would have a difficult time figuring out / **if certain objects were used for their sound or were used only as tools.**
→ ( ) 부분은 Scientists를 수식하는 분사구이다.
→ if ~ tools는 figuring out의 목적어절로 이때 if는 '~인지 아닌지'의 의미이다.

137 ⑤ | likely to → likely

해설 ❺ you'll get ~에 more than likely(확실히)라는 부사어구가 더해진 구조이다. *cf.* <be likely to-v>: v할 것 같다

① their keeping multiple jobs가 주어 개념으로 동명사로 맞게 쓰였다. 동명사 keeping의 의미상의 주어가 their.
② 주어(concept)를 설명하는 보어절을 이끄는 접속사 that.
③ avoid는 동명사를 목적어로 취하는 동사. catch out하는 입장이 아니라 당하는 입장이므로 수동형 동명사(getting caught out)로 맞게 쓰였다.
④ 선행사 the employer는 from의 목적어(earn the highest income "from" the employer), 따라서 전치사 from이 필요한 자리이다.

해석 학생들이 학업을 진행하면서 수입 지출을 맞추기 위해[쓰는 만큼 벌려고] 아르바이트 일을 여러 개 하는 경우가 종종 있다. 세금 정산 시즌이 돌아오면 그들은 다수의 일을 하고 있는 것이 내야 하는 세금에 어떻게 영향을 미치는지 몰라 혼란스럽다. 알고 있어야 할 것은, 만약 호주에 거주하는 사람이라면 회계연도마다 당신이 버는 첫 1만 8천 2백 달러에 대해서는 세금을 내지 않는다는 점이다. 이는 세금 면제 한도로 불리며 여러 개의 직업을 유지하고 있는 경우 결정하기가 어렵다. 직업을 여러 개 가지고 있는 경우 이해해야 할 중요한 개념 한 가지가 이 과세 면제 한도가 당신이 버는 총액의 최초 1만 8천 2백 달러에 정확히 적용되는 것이지 고용주 1인당 적용되는 게 아니라는 것이다. 잘못이 적발되는 걸 피하려면 가장 높은 소득을 벌어들이는 고용주에게서만 과세 면제 한도를 요구하는 것이 좋겠다. 이것이 지금 당장은 당신이 유지하고 있는 다른 벌이에 대해서는 더 많은 세금을 내게 될 거라는 의미일 수 있지만, 세금 환급 시기가 오면 확실히 이 중 일부를 돌려받게 될 것이다.

어휘 **make ends meet** 수입과 지출의 균형을 맞추다 **be ignorant of** ~을 모르다, ~에 대해 무지하다 **affect** 영향을 미치다 **resident** 거주자, 주민 **financial year** 회계연도 **threshold** 문지방, 한계치 **tricky** 까다로운, 교묘한 **strictly** 엄밀히, 엄격히 **in total** 전체로서, 통틀어서 **recommend** 추천하다 **claim** ~을 돌려 달라고 요구하다

구문 13~16행 [To avoid *getting caught out*], **it**'s recommended
가주어
that you only claim the tax-free threshold from *the employer*
진주어
[(**whom**) you expect to earn the highest income from ∨].

→ <가주어(it)-진주어(that절)> 구문. 진주어절에 전치사의 목적어인 목적격 관계대명사 whom이 생략되어 있는 형태이다.

138 ④

해설 (A) 문장의 주어는 전명구 of these smaller all-adult households and single-person households의 수식을 받는 The increasing domination이므로 단수동사 has를 써야 한다.
(B) 문맥상 서로 다른 유형의 가구가 '관심이 있다'는 뜻이 되는 것이 자연스럽다. '~에 관심이 있다'는 수동태 be interested in~으로 나타내므로 to부정사의 수동태 'to be+p.p.' 형태가 알맞다.
(C) 문맥상 '~이든지 …이든지 간에'라는 의미의 접속사 whether를 써야 한다.

해석 1인 가구와 '둘만 사는 부부'는 생활양식과 선호하는 것이 규모가 더 큰 가정과 서로 다르다. 특히 독신자들은 편리함과 사람을 만나는 것 둘 다를 위해서 외식에 돈을 많이 쓴다. 이런 규모가 더 작은, 성인만 있는 가구와 1인 가구의 증가하는 우세는 식당 애용 방식에 영향을 미친다. 예를 들어, 포장해 가는 음식의 이용이 아이들이 있는 가구와 성인만 있는 가구(독신자와 부부) 모두에서 증가했다. 하지만 이런 서로 다른 유형의 가구는 서로 다른 유형의 포장해 가는 음식에 관심이 있는 경향이 있으며, 이유도 서로 다르다. 아이들이 있는 가정은 한 판의 커다란 피자나 한 통의 닭고기처럼 사람들을 기쁘게 하는 값싼 음식을 주문할 수 있지만, 독신 성인은 단지 한 사람을 위해 만들기에는 '너무 많이 번거로운' 고급 (주로 양상추를 넣은) 채소 샐러드를 퇴근 후 집에 가는 길에 사기 위해 들를 가능성이 더 클 것이다. 혼자 살거나 한 명의 다른 사람과 함께 사는 성인은, 나이가 더 많은 연령대에 속하든 더 젊은 연령대에 속하든 간에, 음식을 얻는 일상적인 방식으로 포장해 가는 음식에 의존할 가능성이 더 크다.

어휘 **household** 가구, 세대 **preference** 선호하는 것, 선호(도) **foodservice** 외식(산업) **occasion** 특별한 일, 행사 **domination** 우세, 우월 **implication** 영향; 함축, 암시 **sophisticated** 세련된, 고급의

구문 16~19행 ~, the single adult might be more likely to stop on the way home after work for *a sophisticated green salad* [that's "too much trouble" to make for just one person].
→[ ] 부분은 a sophisticated green salad를 수식한다.

19~22행 *Adults* [who live alone or with one other person] are more likely to rely on takeout as a routine pattern of sourcing food, **whether** they are in an older age group **or** a younger **one**.
→[ ] 부분은 Adults를 수식하는 관계절이다. 'whether A or B' 구문이 양보의 부사절로 쓰여 '~이든 …이든 간에'의 뜻이다. one은 앞에 나온 age group을 대신하는 대명사이다.

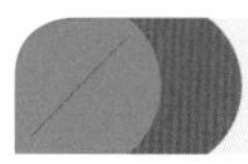

실전 모의고사 13회

139 ④ 140 ② 141 ④ 142 ④ 143 ① 144 ⑤ | 본문 94p

139 ④ | them → it

해설 ④ make의 진목적어는 to open them이므로 이를 대신하는 가목적어 it으로 바꿔야 한다.

① Making의 목적격보어 자리이므로 형용사 safe가 적절.
② every, each의 수식을 받는 명사는 단수 취급하므로 단수동사 contains는 적절.
③ 모든 의약품과 세제 용품이 '보관되어야' 하는 것이므로 수동태인 be stored가 적절.
⑤ 앞에 선행사 a mechanism이 있고 뒤에 주어가 빠진 불완전한 구조가 오므로 관계대명사 that이 적절.

해석 걸음마 하는 아기들을 위해 당신의 집을 안전하게 만드는 것은 신중한 계획을 필요로 한다. 모든 집에는 어린아이들에게 유혹적인 많은 물건이 있다. 전문가들은 저렴하고 손쉽게 아기들을 보호할 수 있는 유용한 아이디어를 많이 제안했다. 가장 중요한 것은 모든 의약품과 세제 용품은 자물쇠로 잠근 상자에 보관해야 한다는 것이다. 스토브와 같은 부엌 가전제품은 아이가 그것을 켤 수 없도록 안전장치를 장착해야 하며, 욕실과 부엌의 서랍도 아이들이 그것을 열 수 없게 하는 특별한 장치를 달아야 한다. 또한 전기 콘센트는 사용하지 않을 때는 자동으로 닫히는 장치로 덮어야 한다. 마지막으로 아이들이 부딪치더라도 부상을 피하기 위해 모서리가 둥근 테이블이나 가구를 사는 것도 좋은 생각이다.

어휘 **toddler** 걸음마를 배우는 아이 **tempting** 유혹하는 **appliance** 가전제품, 기구 **safety lock** 안전장치 **electrical** 전기의 **outlet** 콘센트; 배출구; 소매점 **mechanism** 기계장치, 기구 **injury** 부상

140 ② | could not → could

해설 ② barely, hardly 등은 단어 자체에 '부정'의 의미가 포함되어 있으므로 not을 쓰면 중복 부정이 되어 뜻이 달라진다. could로 바꿔야 적절.

① I가 기쁜 감정을 '느낀' 것이므로 과거분사 pleased는 적절.
③ After Leonard reached the top에서 접속사는 남기고, 문장 전체의 주어와 동일한 Leonard는 생략하고 만든 분사구문이다. 레너드가 정상에 '도달한' 것이므로 현재분사 reaching은 적절.
④ 문장 전체의 주어인 I가 자신감으로 가득 '채워진' 상태이므로 과거분사 Filled는 알맞음.

⑤ 부사 nearly의 수식을 받으며 명사 face를 수식할 수 있는 형용사 vertical이 적절하게 쓰였다.

해석 처음으로 절벽을 올랐을 때 얼마나 기뻤는지 나는 기억한다. 힘쓰느라 팔뚝에 얼마나 쥐가 났었는지 내 등반 파트너인 레너드 코인이 그 길을 뒤따라 올라올 때 나는 그 로프도 거의 잡아당겨 줄 수 없는 지경이었다. 정상에 오른 뒤, 레너드는 비록 이전의 등반가들은 가볍게 내려갔지만, 내려가는 길이 상당히 힘들다는 것을 안다고 말했다. 나는 지나친 자신감으로 가득 차, 로프를 땅 아래쪽으로 그냥 던졌다. 방금 험한 등반을 했으니 로프는 이제 필요하지 않을 것이었다. 그러고 나서 나는 거의 수직면을 타고 내려가기 시작했다. 갑자기 레너드가 외쳤다. "네가 붙잡은 곳이 헐거워! 내 다리를 잡아!" 발 디딘 곳이 부서져 내렸을 때, 나는 지상 150피트 상공에서 단단하지 않은 바위 조각 두 개를 붙잡고 로프에 매이지도 않은 채 거기에 있었다.

어휘 **forearm** 팔뚝, 아래팔 **cramped** 쥐가 난, 경련을 일으킨 **exertion** 매우 힘씀, 노력, 분발 **barely** 거의 ~않다; 간신히 **descent** 하강; 내리막(↔ **ascent** 올라감; 오르막) **overconfidence** 지나친 자신, 과신 **toss** ~을 던지다 **vertical** 수직의 **handhold** 손으로 잡을 수 있는 곳 **flake** 조각, 파편 **foothold** 발판, 디딤

141 ④ | to focus → focusing

해설 ④ 문맥상 늘 생존에 집중하던 것을 얼마든지 '그만둘' 수 있다고 하는 것이 어울리므로 <stop to-v(v하기 위해 (가던 길을) 멈춰 서다)>가 아닌 <stop v-ing(v하는 것을 중단하다)>로 쓰는 것이 알맞다.

① 사역동사 make의 목적격보어로 원형부정사 feel이 맞게 쓰였다.
② 전치사 upon의 목적어로 동명사가 맞게 쓰였다.
③ 준사역동사 help의 목적어로 원형부정사 protect, to부정사 to protect 둘 다 쓰일 수 있다.
⑤ 겁주는 것이 아니라 겁먹는 데서 느끼는 (기분의) 고조됨을 얘기하므로 동명사가 수동형으로 맞게 쓰였다.

해석 왜 우리는 롤러코스터를 그것 때문에 우리 뱃속이 우리 몸에서 완전히 떨어져 나가는 것 같은 기분이 드는데도 사랑하는 걸까? 왜 우리는 우리를 긴 소파 위에 이불을 덮어쓰고 그 아래 웅크려 있게 만드는 공포 영화를 보겠다고 우기는 걸까? 간단히 말해, 그게 재미있기 때문이다. "공포는 나쁜 평판을 갖고 있지만[공포와 가까이하기 다들 싫어하지만] 꼭 나쁜 것만은 아니다."라고 한 전문가는 말한다. 우리의 몸은 싸우느냐 도망치느냐의 기초적인 생리 반응으로 두려움에 반응하고, 에너지 수준을 올리고 고통을 느끼지 못 하도록 우리를 보호하고 귀찮게 하는 트집 잡는 생각 같은 비본질적인 시스템을 가동 중지시킴으로써 우리 자신을 보호하는 데 도움이 되는 화학물질을 분비한다. 진짜 위험에 처했을 때는 이런 생리적 반응들이 우리의 생존에 필요하다. 그러나 그냥 연속 다섯 번째로 롤러코스터를 탈 때와 같이 위험에 처한 게 아닐 때는 우리의 몸은 생존에 초점을 맞추던 것을 얼마든지 그만두고 '겁먹을 때 드는 자연적인 기분 고조'로밖에 묘사할 수 없는 소소한 것에 초점을 맞추기 시작한다.

어휘 **entirely** 완전히, 전적으로 **insist upon v-ing** v하겠다고 우기다[주장하다] **huddle** 웅크리다, 모이다 **reputation** 평판 **physiological** 생리적인 **flight** 도망, 도주 **boost** 신장시키다, 북돋우다 **pesky** 성가신, 귀찮은 **merely** 단순히, 그저 **in a row** 연속으로, 연달아

구문 07~12행 Our bodies **respond** to fear with the basic physiological reaction of fight or flight [and] (A) **release** (B) *chemicals* [that help protect us (by *boosting energy* (A′), *protecting* us from feeling pain (B′), [and] *shutting* down non-essential systems, (like pesky critical thought) (C′))].

142 ④ | weeks → week

해설 ④ 부활절 해당 주의 초콜릿 매출 증가 수치를 연간 기타 다른 주와 비교하는 상황이므로 weeks가 아닌 week가 되어야 한다.

① 12월 한 달 동안 소비가 얼마나 급증하는지 그 '차이, 정도'를 나타내는 부분에 by가 알맞게 쓰였다.
② cause(이유, 원인)가 to celebrate의 수식을 받고 있다.
③ spend (money)의 지출처로 명사(Valentine's Day shopping)가 오면 전치사 on을 쓴다.
⑤ events에 맞게 지시형용사도 복수(these)로 맞게 쓰였다.

해석 사람들은 공휴일과 계절적 이벤트 무렵에 쇼핑하기를 무척 좋아해서 실제로 12월에는 사람들이 축제 시즌을 준비하면서 소매 지출이 약 3분의 1 껑충 뛴다. 그건 선물 때문만이 아니고 크리스마스 때 칠면조 고기 소비도 두 배로 늘고 술도 60% 더 산다. 크리스마스가 분명 소매업자들에게 축하할 이유를 주긴 하지만 업체들에 주요 매출 신장을 가져다주는 데 도움이 되는 기타 계절별 이벤트와 행사들도 연중 많다. 예를 들어 2월에는 호주인들이 밸런타인데이 쇼핑에 거의 8억 달러의 지출을 하는데, 꽃장식 전문가가 딱 하루 동안 연간 매출의 10%를 올리는 양상이다. 3월 또는 4월의 부활절 토끼의 재림은 약 3십억 달러의 소비와 연중 어느 주보다 50% 더 많은 초콜릿 매출을 가져온다. 이를 염두에 두면 매출에 보탬이 되게 이 계절별 이벤트들을 이용할 기회가 있는 것이다.

어휘 **retail** 소매(의) **gear up for** ~을 위한 준비를 하다 **consumption** 소비 **occasion** (어떤 일이 일어나는 특정한) 경우, 행사 **florist** 플로리스트(꽃장식 전문가) **generate** 발생시키다, 만들어내다 **annual** 연간의, 해마다의 **take advantage of** ~을 이용하다

143 ①

해설 (A) 뒤에 완전한 절이 이어지며, '~라는 것'이라는 의미가 되어야 하므로, 명사절 접속사 that이 적절하다.
(B) 동사를 수식하며 '반드시 ~인 것은 아니다'라는 표현인 not necessarily가 되어야 하므로 부사 necessarily가 적절하다.
(C) need의 주어인 non-repetitive actions는 생각의 대상이므로, think about과는 수동의 관계이다. need 다음에 수동의 관계를 나타낼 때는 v-ing, 또는 to be p.p.를 쓰므로, thinking이 적절하다.

해석 농사를 지을 때의 노동을 조정하는 데 음악을 사용했던 것과 오늘날 상응하는 것은 공장에서 음악을 공급하는 것이다. 그 효과에 관해서는 의견이 나누어진다. 농사에서의 음악사용으로부터 판단해 보면, 음악은 공장 작업에서 흔한, 틀에 박힌 작업의 수행을 향상시킬 것이라고 예상할 수 있다. 음악의 리듬과 동시에 일어날 때 반복적인 동작은 덜 지루하다. 음악을 공급하는 것은 공장 노동자들 사이에서 분명히 인기가 높다. 하지만, 사기가 높아지는 것이 반드시 생산 증가를 수반하는 것은 아니다. 음악이 아마도 틀에 박힌 작업, 특히 반복적인 신체 동작이 팽배한 작업에서는 업무 수행을 향상시키지만, 생각을 요하는 비반복적인 행동을 수행하는 것은 방해하는 경향이 있다. 예를 들어, 음악이 타이핑을 할 때 오류의 수를 증가시킨다는 것을 나타내는 증거가 있다.

어휘 **equivalent** 상응[대응]하는 (것); 동등한, 같은 **coordinate** 조정하다 **provision** 공급, 제공; 준비; 식량; 규정, 조항 **routine** 틀에 박힌 (일); 일상적인; 일과 **repetitive** 반복적인, 반복되는 (↔ **non-repetitive** 비반복적인) **tedious** 지루한, 따분한 **heighten** 높아지다; 고조시키다 **morale** 사기, 의욕 **accompany** 수반하다; 동반 [동행]하다; 반주하다 **enhance** 향상시키다, 높이다 **prevail** 팽배하다, 만연하다; 승리하다, 이기다 **tend to-v** v하는 경향이 있다 **interfere with** ~을 방해하다 **evidence** 증거(물)

구문 12~16행 Whilst music probably enhances the performance of *routine tasks* , / especially those **[in which repetitive physical actions prevail]**, /

음악이 아마도 틀에 박힌 작업에서는 업무 수행을 향상시키지만, / 특히 작업(에서는) [반복적인 신체 동작이 팽배한],

it (=music) tends to interfere with the performance of *non-repetitive actions* **[which need thinking about]**.

/ 그것(음악)은 비반복적인 행동을 수행하는 것을 방해하는 경향이 있다 [생각을 요하는].

→ 첫 번째 [ ] 부분은 <전치사+관계대명사>가 이끄는 형용사절로서 those를 수식하며, 이때 those는 routine tasks를 의미한다.
→ 두 번째 [ ] 부분은 주격 관계대명사 which가 이끄는 관계사절로 non-repetitive actions를 수식한다.

144 ⑤ | how → what

해설 ⑤ no matter 이하가 의미상 '그 맥락이 무엇일지라도'가 되어야 적절하므로 how를 '무엇'에 해당하는 what으로 고쳐야 어법상 옳다. no matter how는 '아무리 ~할지라도'의 의미를 나타낸다.

① considered를 수식해서 '일반적으로 여겨지다'의 의미를 나타내므로 부사 universally는 어법상 적절하다.
② 관계사절(that were conducted after World War II)의 수식을 받는 주어 The Nuremberg trials에 대한 동사가 필요하므로 동사 supported는 어법상 적절하다.
③ 주어 many가 복수이므로 복수동사 were는 어법상 적절하고, 이 주어 many가 의미상 동사와 수동의 관계(유죄 판결을 받다)이므로 수동태 were found는 어법상 적절하다.
④ which의 선행사인 a higher moral order가 전치사 under의 목적어로 '그보다 높은 수준의 도덕적 질서 아래에서는'이라는 의미를 나타내고 있고, under which(전치사+관계대명사) 뒤에 완전한 절이 오므로 어법상 적절하다.

해석 특정 집단의 사람들을 계획적으로 살해하는 것인 집단 학살은, 제2차 세계 대전 기간 동안 나치 죽음의 수용소에서 발생한 것처럼, 비록 그것이 정부나 전체 사회에 의해 승인된 것이라도, 일반적으로 잘못되었다고 여겨진다. 제2차 세계 대전 후에 행해진 Nuremberg 재판이 이러한 점을 뒷받침해 주었다. 대부분의 피고인 개개인들은 자신들이 대단히 많은 유대인들과 다른 집단의 사람들을 살해하거나 살해를 계획했을 때에

자신들은 단지 명령을 따르고 있었을 뿐이라고 주장하려고 했음에도 불구하고, 다수가 유죄를 판결받았다. 그 논거는 보다 높은 수준의 도덕적 질서가 있고, 그 질서 아래에서는 인간의 특정한 행동들은 누가 그것들을 승인했든지 상관없이, 잘못되었다는 것이었다. 따라서 사건들을 문화적 상대주의 관점에서 보려는 대부분의 사회학자들의 욕구에도 불구하고, 그 (사건과 관련된) 맥락이 무엇일지라도, 그들은 어떤 특정한 행동들을 잘못된 것으로 생각한다.

어휘 **genocide** 집단 학살, 종족[대량] 학살 **willful** 계획적인, 고의의; 고집 센 **extermination camp** (특히 나치가 대량 살인을 위해 세운) 죽음의 수용소 **universally** 일반적으로, 보편적으로 **trial** 재판, 공판; 실험 **conduct** 수행[처리](하다); 행동(하다); 지휘하다; 전도하다 **the accused** ((형사)) 피고인 **claim** 주장(하다); 요구하다; (목숨을) 앗아가다 **order** 명령(하다); 질서; 순서; 주문(하다) **murder** 살해(하다) **arrange for** 계획을 짜다, 준비하다 **guilty** 유죄의; 죄책감이 드는 **reasoning** 논거; 추리; 이론 **moral** 도덕적인 **regardless of** ~에 상관없이 **desire** 욕구, 욕망; 바라다, 원하다 **relative** 상대적인, 비교상의; 친척 **standpoint** 관점, 견지 **find** 생각하다; 찾다 **context** 맥락, 환경; 문맥

구문 11~14행 The reasoning was that there is *a higher moral order* **[under which certain human actions are wrong regardless of who endorses them]**.
→ <전치사+관계대명사> 형태인 under which가 이끄는 절은 선행사 a higher moral order를 수식한다.
→ who endorses them은 전치사 of의 목적어로 쓰인 의문사절로, 의문사 who가 명사절의 주어 역할을 한다.

14~17행 Thus, despite **their desire to view events from a culturally relative standpoint**, most sociologists find certain actions wrong, no matter what the context (is).
→ their desire와 to view ~ standpoint는 동격 관계이다.
→ no matter what은 양보의 부사절을 이끌고, the context 뒤에는 is가 생략되었다.

실전 모의고사 14회

145 ④ 146 ② 147 ② 148 ⑤ 149 ④ 150 ⑤ | 본문 96p

145 ④

해설 (A) 주어는 관계사절 that permitted ~ forests의 수식을 받는 a controversial bill이므로 단수동사 was가 알맞음.
(B) 앞선 healthy trees를 수식하는 과거분사 considered가 적절.
(C) 과거보다 더 이전에 일어난 일을 나타내므로 과거완료가 적절. 현재와의 연관성을 알 수 없으므로 현재완료 시제는 쓸 수 없다.

해석 막강한 목재 업자들에 응하여, 국유림에서 폐기용 벌목을 허용하기로 한 논란이 많은 법안이 1995년에 법으로 제정되었다. 이 법은 벌목꾼들이 질병에 걸릴 위험이 있다고 생각되는 건강한 나무들뿐만 아니라 죽은 나무와, 곤충, 질병, 혹은 화재로 약해진 나무들도 벨 수 있도록 허용했다. 1996년 말에 만료가 된 그 법은 보통 때는 벌목이 허용되지 않는 다른 국유림 지역뿐만 아니라 북서부 산림계획에 의해 출입 금지 구역으로 공표되었던 숲의 몇 곳도 벌목꾼들이 출입하도록 허용했다. 그것은 또한 수질 오염 방지법과 멸종 위기종 보호법의 조항들을 따르는 것에서 목재 회사들을 면제시켜 주었다.

어휘 **timber** 목재 **interest** ((주로 복수형)) 이익단체; 흥미 **controversial** 논란이 많은 **bill** 법안; 청구서 **logging** 벌목 *cf.* **logger** 벌목꾼 **expire** 만기가 되다 **access to** ~로의 출입, 접근 **off-limits** 출입금지의 **excuse A from v-ing** A가 v하는 것을 면제해주다 **comply with** ~에 따르다, 응하다 **provision** 조항, 규정

구문 04~07행 The law(S) allowed(V) loggers(O) to cut down(OC) dead trees and *trees* (**weakened** by insects, disease, or fire), as well as *healthy trees* (**considered** to be in danger of catching a disease).
→ <allow+O+OC(to-v)> 구조. dead trees 이하는 to cut down의 목적어로 <A as well as B(B뿐만 아니라 A도)>가 쓰였다.

07~12행 The law,(S) / which expired at the end of 1996, / allowed(V) loggers access to *parts of the forest*(O) [**that** had been declared off-limits by the Northwest Forest Plan] ***as well as*** *other national forest areas* [not normally open to logging].

146 ② | disposed → disposed of

해설 ❷ dispose(처분하다)가 대상을 갖기 위해서는 전치사 of가 필요하다. items ~ will be disposed of[←will dispose of items]로 써야 맞다.

① A(move out), B(remove ~), and C(return ~)의 병렬구조에서 일관성 있게 동사가 쓰인 경우.
③ be동사 뒤에 형용사 present(있는)가 맞게 쓰였다.
④ '~하기 위하여'라는 뜻의 '목적'을 나타내는 to부정사.
⑤ 동사 neglect의 목적어로 쓰인 to부정사.

해석 학생들은 마지막 시험 24시간 후 또는 2016년 5월 15일 일요일 낮 12시까지 캠퍼스를 떠나야 함. 숙소를 비우는 데는 이사 나가고, 숙소 및 라운지에 있는 자기 물건을 모두 치우고, 열쇠를 반납할 것이 요구됨. 학생들은 다음에 대해 책임이 있음. 숙소에서 개인 물품을 일체 치울 것. (기숙사) 폐사 후 방에 남아 있는 물품은 기부 또는 처분될 예정. 대학은 남아 있는 물품에 대해 어떤 법적 책임도 없음. 입실 점검 시 숙소 내 있었던 가구 일체는 퇴실 점검 시 그대로 있어야 하고 양호한 상태여야 하며 안 그럴 시 교체물의 비용을 부담해야 함. 떠난 후 방에 손상 발생을 피하도록 퇴실 시 잊지 말고 문을 잠그고 창문을 닫을 것. 방문 및 창문 잠그는 것을 소홀히 하여 마지막 점검 시 방에 손상이 발견되거나 어떤 가구든 없어진 경우 본인이 책임져야 함.

어휘 **vacate** (장소 등을) 비우다 **belongings** 재산, 소유물 **residence** 거주지, 거처 **dispose of** ~을 처분하다, ~을 없애다 **assume** 떠맡다; 추정하다 **inspection** 사찰, 순시, 점검 **present** 있는, 존재하는 **charge** (요금을) 부과하다, 물리다 **replacement** 대체(물), 교체(물) **departure** 출발 **neglect** 소홀히 하다

147 ② | to listen → to listening

해설 ② ②번 밑줄이 있는 문장의 <change from A to B (A에서 B로 바꾸다)> 구절에서 A에 해당하는 자리에 동명사 reading이 쓰였다. B에 해당하는 자리에도 전치사 to 다음이므로 동명사를 써야 해서 to listening으로 바꿔 써야 한다.

① 뒤에 전명구(the rise ~ e-book)가 오므로 전치사 역할의 because of는 적절하다.
③ 뒤에 <주어(talking books)+동사(offer) ~> 형태의 절이 오므로 접속사 although는 적절하다.
④ 가정법 과거 if he or she were reading ~ 표현에서 if가 생략되고 주어와 동사가 도치되었다. 따라서 were는 맞게 쓰였다.
⑤ 접속사(when)가 생략되지 않은 분사구문으로 생략된 의미상 주어인 막연한 일반인이 '이용하는' 것이므로 현재분사는 맞게 쓰였다.

해석 활자 사이즈에 대한 고려는 몇몇 전자책에서 발견되는 음성 도서나 음성 텍스트 옵션의 이용 가능성이 높아져서 시대에 뒤떨어진 생각이 될 것이다. 예를 들어 Bouchard Ryan과 그녀의 동료들은 시력에 문제가 있는 나이 많은 성인들이 (일반적으로 작은 활자와 선명하지 못한 명암을 지닌) 신문과 잡지를 읽는 것에서 음성 도서를 듣는 것으로 바꿀 가능성이 더 높다는 것을 알았다. 그들은 또한 샘플 집단의 약 4분의 1이 활자를 확대하기 위해 컴퓨터 기술을 사용한다는 점에 주목했다. 그러나 비록 음성 도서가 시력 문제가 있는 사람들에게 해결책을 제공해준다 하더라도, 그것은 일반적으로 추정되는 것처럼 읽기에 대한 직접적인 대체물은 아니다. 두 가지 이유가 인용될 수 있다. 첫째, 화자는 청자가 자기 스스로 읽을 때 강조할 것과 일치하지 않을지도 모르는 것을 소리 내어 읽으면서 강조할 것이 거의 확실하다. 둘째, 독서에서는 방금 읽은 활자의 구절로 다시 돌아가거나 산문의 한 부분을 대충 읽어보는 것이 쉬운 일이다. 음성 도서를 이용할 때는 이를 행하기가 매우 어렵거나 불가능하다.

어휘 **print** 활자 **outmoded** 유행에 뒤떨어진 **observe** 말하다 **contrast** 명암 **substitute** 대체물 **cite** 인용하다 **place emphases upon** ~을 강조하다 **passage** 구절 **skim through** 대충 읽다

구문 14~18행 First, the narrator will almost certainly place emphases upon [*what is being read out*] {that may not match what the listener would emphasize / **were he or she reading** for themselves}.
→ [ ]은 upon의 목적어이다. { } 부분은 [ ]를 수식한다. were he or she reading은 if he or she were reading에서 if가 생략되고 주어와 동사가 도치된 구문인 가정법 과거 표현이다.

18~20행 Second, in reading **it** is easy to move back over *a passage of print* **just read**, or to skim through a section of prose.
→ it은 가주어이고 두 to-v구가 진주어로 병렬구조를 이룬다. just read는 과거분사로 수동의 의미이며 a passage of print를 수식한다.

20~22행 This is either very difficult or impossible to do ***when* using** a talking book.
→ using이 이끄는 분사구문의 뜻을 분명히 하기 위하여 분사 앞에 접속사 when을 그대로 둔 경우이다. 분사 using의 의미상 주어와 문장 주어(This)는 일치하지 않지만 의미상 주어가 막연한 일반인(we)을 나타내므로 이때는 생략할 수 있다. when we use a talking book으로 바꿔 쓸 수 있다.

148 ⑤ | have → has

해설 ⑤ 주어가 Being an actor로 추상적인 개념이므로 단수동사 has로 써야 한다.

① 멋진 역할에 '흥분되는' 것이므로 excited가 맞다.
② '비록 ~하더라도(even if)'가 문맥상(앞뒤 내용이 순조롭지 않은 점), 문장 구조상(문장이 이어지고 있는 점) 알맞다.
③ 조동사 must에 공동으로 걸리므로(must be in ~, belong to ~) 동사원형으로 쓰인 게 맞다.
④ an actress 대신 쓰인 부정대명사 one.

해석 "엄마, 난 배우가 될 거예요." "하지만 성공하지 못해서 네가 그토록 들떠 있는 그 멋진 역할들을 맡을 수 없으면 어떡할래?" "상관없어요. 그들이 내가 무대를 가로지르며 손수건 흔드는 것만 하게 해준대도 난 배우가 될래요." 몇 년이 지난 뒤, 수십 개의 중요한, 또 덜 중요한 배역을 맡은 뒤에, 극장 분야에서 수많은 실망과 불행한 일을 겪은 뒤에도 나는 동일한 진리 — 무대를 가로지르며 손수건만 흔든다 해도 나는 극장에 있어야 하며, 극장에 속하는 존재라는 —로 돌아왔다. 나는 배우란 배우로 태어나는 것이지 배워서 되는 게 아니라고 믿는다. 내 어린 시절 기억은 노래로든 연기로든 극 중 인물을 표현하고 싶다는 바람이었다. 나는 청중에 대해서는 생각하지 않았는데, 그것은 내겐 존재하지 않았다. 배우가 된다는 건 진정 성공과는 아무 관련 없는 것이다.

어휘 **part** 배역, 역할 **matter** 중요하다 **wave** 흔들다 **handkerchief** 손수건 **dozens of** 수십 개의 ~ **realm** 영역, 분야 **truism** 자명한 이치, 명명백백한 일 **belong to** ~에 속하다 **exist** 존재하다 **have nothing to do with** ~와 상관없다

149 ④

해설 (A) are full of people 뒤에 명사 people을 수식하는 분사구가 병렬구조로 이어진 것이므로 traveling이 적절.
Science fiction stories are full of *people* **disappearing** ~, **riding** in *starships* [that move ~ light], and traveling instantly to ~.
(수식 받는 명사)
(B) 문맥상 '알베르트 아인슈타인의 이론들'이라는 뜻으로, Albert Einstein's를 대신하는 소유격 관계대명사 whose가 적절.
(C) that절의 주어 serious physicists에 호응하는 동사가 없으므로 동사 comment가 와야 한다.

해석 공상과학소설의 이야기는 벽을 통과하여 사라지고, 빛보다 빨리 움직이는 우주선에 탑승하여 시공간 상으로 멀리 떨어진 곳까지 단숨에 이동하는 사람들로 가득하다. 이런 생각들이 창의력 있는 상상인 것처럼 보이지만 그것들은 사실 이론 물리학, 특히 눈에 보이지 않는 4차원의 시간과 더불어 3차원 공간에서 우주가 어떻게 커브를 그리며 되돌아오는지에 관한 이론들을 주장한 알베르트 아인슈타인의 업적으로부터 나온다. 만약 아인슈타인이 옳다면 (지난 백 년간 행해진 실험은 그가 옳다는 것을 시사한다) 그런 공상과학소설의 이야기들이 가능할지도 모른다. 이런 생각은 매우 호소력 있게 되어 신중한 물리학자들이 저명한 전문 잡지에서 이와 같은 기술들에 관해 정기적으로 언급하고 있다.

어휘 **starship** 우주선 **instantly** 단숨에, 즉시 **fantasy** 상상, 공상 **theoretical** 이론상의 **dimension** 차원; 넓이, 면적 **invisible** 눈에 안 보이는 **sci-fi** 공상과학소설 **appealing** 호소력 있는, 매력적인 **comment** 논평하다, 진술하다; 논평

150 ⑤ | worsening → worsen

해설 ⑤ 문장의 주어 The concerns에 호응하는 동사가 없으므로 문장의 동사 자리. worsening을 worsen으로 고쳐야 한다.

① that절의 주어 one byproduct가 단수이므로 단수동사 is가 적절.
② reanimate의 의미상 주어는 the microbes. 미생물이 '되살려지는' 것이므로 수동관계이며 전치사 of의 목적어 자리이므로 동명사의 수동태 being reanimated가 적절.
③ the entire biomass가 '갇혀 있는' 것이므로 hold와 수동관계. 따라서 과거분사 형태가 적절.
④ 이어지는 절이 동사의 목적어가 빠져 있는 불완전한 구조이므로 관계대명사 자리. 선행사 a major source of greenhouse gases를 수식하는 목적격 관계대명사로 알맞게 쓰였다.

해석 극지의 얼음이 녹는 것의 한 부산물이 75만 년도 넘게 얼어 있던 미생물의 방출이라는 것은 놀라운 사실일지 모른다. 하지만 진짜 놀라운 사실은 그 미생물들이 여전히 살아있으며 일단 녹으면 다시 살아날 수 있다는 것이다. <데일리 클라이밋>에 의해 보고되었듯이, 과학자들은 고대 질병의 갑작스러운 확산에 대해서가 아니라 오히려 분해하기 시작할 막대한 양의 유기물의 영향을 예측하기 어렵다는 점에 대해서 걱정하고 있다. 과학자들은 대륙 빙하에 갇혀 있는 전체 생물량이 지구상 인간 생물량의 1,000배 이상에 이를 수 있다고 추정한다. 방출되는 이산화탄소와 메탄의 양은 기후 과학자들이 생각지 못한 온실가스의 주요 원천이 될 것이다. 그러한 걱정은 과학자들이 이러한 고대의 미생물이 해양의 정교한 화학적 특성과 기존의 미생물군에 어떠한 영향을 줄 수 있는지 생각하기 시작할 때 더 심각해진다.

어휘 **byproduct** 부산물; 부작용 **microbe** 미생물 ***cf.*** **microbial** 미생물의, 세균의 **reanimate** ~을 되살리다, 소생시키다 **decompose** (화학작용에 의해) 분해[부패]하다 **biomass** (특정 지역 내의) 생물량 **ice sheet** 대륙 빙하, 대빙원 **constitute** ~을 구성하다; ~을 설립하다, 제정하다 **worsen** ~을 악화시키다, 악화되다 **chemistry** 화학; 화학적 특성

구문 01~03행 [It] might be surprising [that] one byproduct of polar ice melt (S') is (V') the release of *microbes* (C') [**that** have been frozen for more than 750,000 years].

→ it은 가주어, that절이 진주어이다.

03~06행 The real surprise (S), however, is (V) that the microbes are still alive (C1) [and] (*that* ***the microbes*** *are*) capable of being reanimated once (*they are*) thawed. (C2)

→ 전체 문장은 SVC 구조로 두 개의 that절이 and로 연결되어 문장의 보어 역할을 하고 있다. 반복되는 어구 that the microbes are가 생략되었으며, once 뒤에 생략된 they are에서 they는 the microbes를 가리킨다.

고난도 모의고사 2회

151 ③ 152 ② 153 ② 154 ① 155 ⑤ 156 ③ | 본문 98p

151 ③ | including → includes

해설 ③ 앞의 developed는 주어 Software를 수식하는 분사이므로 문장에 동사가 필요하다. 따라서 includes가 적절.

① a development method를 선행사로 하는 주격 관계대명사 that은 적절.
② 동사 permits는 to부정사를 목적격보어로 취하므로 to change는 적절.
④ 대명사가 지칭하는 것은 앞의 computer operating systems이므로 복수대명사 They가 알맞음.
⑤ Since가 이끄는 종속절에 주절이 이어진 구조. 주절의 주어로 동명사구(not having ~ your machine)가 적절히 쓰였다. 동명사의 부정형은 동명사 앞에 not을 쓴다.

해석 '오픈 소스'는 광범위한 사용자 평가의 힘과 (개발) 과정의 투명성을 이용하여 소프트웨어를 개발하는 한 방법이다. 이것은 사용자들이 그 소프트웨어를 변형하고 개선하며, 수정되거나 수정되지 않은 형태로 재배포할 수 있도록 한다. 오픈 소스의 장래성은 품질이 더 좋고, 신뢰도가 더 높으며, 좀 더 융통성이 있고 가격도 더 낮다는 것이다. 오픈 소스를 통해 개발된 소프트웨어에는 컴퓨터 운영 시스템도 포함된다. 그것들은 인터넷에서 다운로드할 수 있거나, 단 몇 달러의 지원 계약으로 이용 가능하다. 이러한 운영 시스템들은 새로운 컴퓨터 시스템 가격의 상당 부분을 차지하기 때문에, 당신의 컴퓨터와 함께 그것을 살 필요가 없다는 것은 당신이 큰돈을 절약하도록 해줄 수 있다.

어휘 **utilize** ~을 이용하다 **distributed** 광범위한, (널리) 분포된 ***cf.*** **redistribute** ~을 재분배하다 **transparency** 투명성 **permit A to-v** A가 v하도록 허락[허용]하다 **modify** ~을 수정하다, 변경하다 **promise** (성공할) 가능성, 장래성 **reliability** 신뢰도 **flexibility** 융통성; 유연성 **significant** 상당한, 중요한

152 ② | themselves → them

해설 ② 문맥상 사람들이 식용식물을 위한 새로운 환경을 창조한 것으로 앞 문장의 (these) food plants를 받는 대명사 them이 적절. 재귀대명사는 목적어와 주어가 일치하는 경우에 사용.

① 앞의 선행사 the evolutionary pressure를 수식하는 절을 이끄는 목적격 관계대명사로 that이 알맞게 쓰였다.
③ Seeds를 수식하는 분사 자리. Seeds와 recover(찾아내다)는 수동 관계이므로 과거분사인 recovered가 적절히 쓰였다.
④ 동사 remain 뒤의 보어 자리이므로 형용사 dormant는 알맞은 표현.
⑤ sown 앞에 they are가 생략된 형태이다. 시간, 조건을 뜻하는 접속사 뒤의 주어가 주절의 주어와 일치할 때 <주어+be동사>는 생략 가능하다.

해석 사람들이 저장된 씨앗 종자를 의도적으로 심기 시작했을 때 그들은 또한 자신의 식물을 보호하기 시작했다. 이는 이들 식용식물이 경험한 진화적 압박을 바꾸어버렸다. 왜냐하면 그것들은 더 이상 자연환경에서 살아남아야 할 필요가 없었기 때문이다. 대신에, 사람들은 그것들을 위한 새로운 환경을 창조했고, 자연이 이전에 가졌던 것과는 다른 특징들을 선택했다. 고고학적 현장에서 찾아낸 씨앗들은 옛날 농부들이 더 큰 씨앗과 더 얇은 씨앗 껍질을 선택했다는 것을 명백히 보여준다. 두껍고 강한 껍질은 흔히 씨앗이 자연환경에서 생존하기 위해 꼭 필요한데, 그 이유는 많은 야생 식물의 씨앗이 겨울이 가고 비가 오기 시작할 때까지 몇 달 동안을 휴면 상태로 있기 때문이다. 하지만 인간의 관리하에서 두꺼운 씨앗 껍질은 불필요한데, 농부들이 습기와 포식자를 피해서 씨앗을 저장하는 책임을 넘겨받기 때문이다. 사실, 더 얇은 껍질을 가진 씨앗은 먹거나 (가루로) 가공하기가 더 수월하고, 그것들은 파종되었을 때 묘목이 더 빠르게 발아하도록 하기 때문에 선호되었다.

어휘 **seed** 씨앗, 종자; 씨를 뿌리다 **intentionally** 의도적으로, 고의로 **evolutionary** 진화(론)적인; 진화의, 발달의 **archaeological** 고고학의 **hardy** 《생물》 내한성(耐寒性)의; 고난에 견딜 수 있는, 강건한 **dormant** 휴면기의, 활동[성장]을 중단한 **set in** ~이 시작되다 **take over** ~을 떠맡다, 인계받다 **predator** 약탈자; 포식자 **seedling** 묘목 **sprout** 싹이 나다; 자라기 시작하다 **sow(sowed-sown)** 씨를 뿌리다

153 ② | which → with which

해설 ❷ the hard cash는 보상의 '도구, 수단'이므로 with가 관계대명사 앞에 쓰여야 한다. (← reward her with the hard cash)

① 분사가 주격보어처럼 쓰이고 있는 경우. grow up accepting the house chores as part of ~.
③ 문장의 보어 부분에 선행사를 포함하는 관계대명사절, 즉 명사절이 왔으므로 자연스럽다.
④ 목적어(a job)가 do의 주체가 아니므로 <get+O+OC(p.p.)> 구조로 쓰였다.
⑤ 방법(집안일에 기여함으로써 보상을 받는) 얘기를 하고 있으므로 what이 아닌 how가 적절하다.

해석 아이들이 가끔 마지못해서이긴 하지만 가족생활의 중요한 부분으로 집안일을 받아들이면서 크는 것이 아이들을 정서적으로 정신적으로 더 강하게 해준다. 그리고 아이들을 그렇게 하도록 함에 있어서 아이들에게 자기가 들인 노력에 대해 보상을 해주는 것은 분명 잘 키우는 일이다. 가정이 돌아가는 데 기여하는 데서 우리 딸이 얻는 만족감, 그 결과 배우게 되는 삶의 기술, 그리고 보상으로 받게 되는 현금이 딸에게 책임감과 가치관, 그리고 목표 의식을 준다. 어떤 이는 이런 식으로 선행에 보상을 해주는 것은 잘못된 일이라고 할지 모르겠지만, 그게 어른의 일하는 삶 — 결국 그녀가 발 들여놓게 될 뭔가 — 의 전부 아닌가? 물론 어떤 일을 그 절반의 시간에, 아마도 그녀가 해낼 수 있는 것보다 더 높은 수준으로 해낼 수 있다는 생각이 들 때가 있다. 그러나 그녀가 모든 게 완전히 다 갖춰진 숙소에서 어린 시절을 보낸다면 이 밖에 어떤 방법으로 자기를 건사하는 법을 배우게 될 것인가?

어휘 **chore** 허드렛일, 일과 **accept A as B** A를 B로 받아들이다 **albeit** ~에도 불구하고 **unwillingly** 마지못해, 억지로 **part and parcel** 중요 부분, 본질 부분 **nurturing** 잘 보살피는 ***cf.*** **nurture** 양육하다, 보살피다 **reward A with B** A를 B로 보상하다 **eventually** 결국, 궁극적으로 **accommodation** 숙소, 시설, 거처

구문 05~09행 *The satisfaction* [(*that*) our daughter gains ∨ from contributing to the running of our home], *the life skills* [(that) she's learning ∨ as a result], and *the hard cash* [with which she's rewarded] give her **a sense of** responsibility, value and purpose.
(A: The satisfaction, B: the life skills, C: the hard cash; A′: responsibility, B′: value, C′: purpose)

→ SVOO 구조. 직접목적어 부분이 A′, B′ and C′ 모두 a sense of에 공통으로 걸리는 병렬구조를 이루고 있다.

13~15행 Naturally, there are times [**when** (I think) I could get(V′) a job(O′) done(OC′) [in half the time] and [perhaps to a higher standard than she might offer]].

→ 시간의 관계부사절 내의 I think는 삽입절. 소요 시간과 성취 수준을 얘기하는 두 개의 부사구가 나란히 오고 있다.

154 ① | effective → effectively

해설 ❶ they communicate more effectively의 문장구조에서 나온 것이므로 effective는 effectively로 고쳐야 한다.

② 완전한 문장을 이끌면서, '~할 때는 언제나'란 의미를 뜻하는 whenever가 적절히 쓰였다.
③ knows의 목적어가 되는 명사절을 이끄는 접속사로서 문맥이 자연스러운 where가 적절히 쓰였다.
④ requires의 목적어가 되는 명사절을 이끄는 접속사 that이 적절하다.
⑤ 문맥상 부모들 자신에 대한 불확신이므로, 주어인 the parents와 목적어가 일치한다. 그러므로 재귀대명사인 themselves가 적절하다.

해석 아이가 언젠가 부모의 통제로부터 자유로워지기 위해, 애정 어린 권위로 나타나는 부모의 영향력 안에서 안전해야 한다. 부모가 그 권위를 효과적으로 전달하면 할수록, 아이는 더욱 안심하며, 결국 자신의 삶을 더 잘 확립할 수 있을 것이다. 자립을 향한 이 여정 동안, 아이는 위협을 느낄 때마다 부모의 사랑과 권위라는 안전을 향해 되돌아온다. 다시 말해서, 아이가 말 그대로나 비유적으로나 부모가 정확히 어디에 있는지 알지 못한다면 그 아이가 자립하게 되는 것은 불가능하다. 물론 그것은 부모도 자신이 스스로 어디에 있는지 아는 것을 필요로 한다. 부모가 자신에 대한 확신이 없다면, 다시 말해서 자신의 권위에 자신이 없다면, 그들은 아이에게 안전함을 전달할 수 없고 아이는 그들로부터 성공적으로 떠나갈 수 없다. 그러한 경우에, 아이는 (부모에게) 매달리거나 반항하게 되거나, 혹은 두 가지 모두를 하게 된다.

어휘 **secure** 안심하는; 안전한, 확실한; 안정감 있는 (↔ **insecure** 자신이 없는; 불안정한) ***cf.*** **security** 안전; 안보; 안심 **represent** ~을 나타내다; ~을 대표하다; ~을 설명하다 **loving** 애정 어린, 다정한 **figuratively** 비유적으로, 상징적으로 **clinging** (옷이나 직물이) 몸에 달라붙는; (사람에게) 매달리는 **disobedient** 반항하는, 거역하는 (↔ **obedient** 말을 잘 듣는, 순종적인)

구문 01~03행 For a child to one day become free from his parents' control, the child must be secure in *his parents' power* [**as** (***it is***) represented by their loving authority].

→ it은 앞의 his parents' power를 대신한다. 이때의 as는 '~하는 바와 같은, ~한 경우의'의 의미로, 바로 앞의 명사를 수식하는 어구를 이끈다. 절이나 과거분사, 형용사가 이어지는 경우가 많다.
*e.g.*1. his way of life **as** *I know it* (내가 아는 그의 생활 방식)
*e.g.*2. the earth **as** *viewed* from a satellite (위성에서 본 지구)
*e.g.*3. the church **as** *separate* from the state (국가와 분리된 교회)

155 ⑤ | where → which[that]

해설 ❺ engaged in의 목적어가 될 수 있는 것은 명사 개념이므로 관계부사 where가 아닌 관계대명사 which 또는 that으로 고쳐야 한다.

① 아메리카 대륙이 발견된 것이 과거이고(discovered), 그전까지는 discovery라는 개념 자체가 유럽인에게 익숙하지 않았다고 하니, 그 시기는 과거 이전의 일을 표현하는 과거완료 시제로 표현되는 게 맞다.
② worldview의 내용이 이어져 나오는 동격의 절을 이끄는 접속사 that이다.
③ 문맥상 '결함이 있는'이라는 뜻의 과거분사형 형용사가 오는 것이 맞다.
④ 명사(secrets)를 꾸미는 형용사적 용법의 to부정사 앞에 discover의 주체, 즉 의미상의 주어가 for humankind의 형태로 맞게 쓰였다.

해석 콜럼버스가 미대륙을 발견했을 때 유럽 문화는 아직 발견이라는 개념을 제대로 파악하지 못하고 있었다. 여러 다양한 언어들에 '발견하다'로 번역될 수 있는 동사가 있긴 했으나 바위 밑에 있는 벌레 같은 것을 발견한다는 의미 정도의 동사만 있었다. 학자들은, 모든 지식이 지구 중심의 우주 하의 수학적 세부 사실들을 편찬한 천문학자인 프

톨레마이오스 같은 고대인들에 의해 이미 다 설명되었다고 보는 세계관의 틀 안에서 움직였다. 프톨레마이오스는 천문학자일 뿐만 아니라 고대 지리학자 중에서도 최고였다. 그래서 콜럼버스가 프톨레마이오스의 지리에 대한 이해가 결함이 있음을 보여줬을 때, 이는 코페르니쿠스가 프톨레마이오스의 우주관에 대해 그에게 이의를 제기할 길도 열어주었다. 사태를 지켜보고 있던 사고가 깊은 이들은 그때 자연은 인류가 '발견해낼' 비밀들을 보유하고 있다는 걸 깨달았다. "발견이라는 개념의 존재가 과학에는 필요하다."라고 역사가 David Wootton은 썼다. "1492년의 미대륙의 발견은 지성인들이 매진할 새로운 행위를 만들어 냈는데, 그것이 '새 지식의 발견'이었다."

어휘 **grasp** 파악(하다) **translate** 번역하다 **scholar** 학자 **worldview** 세계관 **astronomer** 천문학자 **compile** 편찬하다 **geographer** 지리학자 **flawed** 결함이 있는 **cosmos** 우주 **possess** 보유하다 **humankind** 인류 **existence** 존재

구문 11~14행 So when Columbus showed that Ptolemy's grasp on geography was flawed, it opened *the way* (**for** Copernicus) **to challenge** Ptolemy on his picture of the cosmos as well.

→ <명사 (+for+의미상 주어)+to-v>의 구조.

14~17행 *Deep thinkers* [**who** were paying attention] then realized that nature possessed *secrets* (**for** humankind) **to "discover."**

→ 마찬가지로 형용사적 용법의 to부정사 앞에 의미상의 주어가 쓰인 구조.

156 ③ | their → whose

해설 ③ 앞부분에 is라는 동사가 있고 뒷부분에 have라는 동사가 있다. 절과 절을 연결하는 기능을 가져야 하므로 대명사와 접속사 역할을 동시에 하는 관계대명사를 써야 한다. 그러므로 their를 whose로 바꿔 써야 한다.

① 동사 are를 수식하는 부사 자리이므로 essentially는 적절하다.
② 의문사 how가 이끄는 명사절에서 주어는 the knowledge ~ 이하이므로, 단수 동사 is는 맞게 쓰였다.
④ suited to는 '~에 어울리는'이라는 의미로 맞게 쓰였다.
⑤ 과학의 작동 '방식'이라는 문맥이므로 접속사 how는 맞게 쓰였다.

해석 모든 과학 분야, 혹은 심지어 모든 지적 분야가 본질적으로 같은 종류의 것, 즉 다른 주제에 관한 것일지라도 진리의 추구라는 게 일반적인 추정이다. 사실의 관점에서, 이것은 완전히 틀린 말이다. 각각의 지적 분야는 '진리'가 심지어 무엇을 뜻하는지에 대해, 무엇이 가치 있고 무엇이 사소한지에 대해, 얼마나 많은 혹은 적은 객관성이 가능한지에 대해, 획득될 수 있는 지식이 얼마나 확실한지에 대해, 그리고 훨씬 더 많은 것들에 대해 특유의 믿음을 수반한다. 학문적 분야를 문화로 간주하는 데는 합당한 이유가 있는데, 왜냐하면 그 구성원들이 공통의 지적 임무뿐만 아니라 많은 가치관과 많은 행동 특성을 공통으로 가지고 있기 때문이다. 각각의 학문 분야는 그 특정한 지적 임무에 들어맞는 뚜렷이 구별되는 문화를 발달시킨다. 순수 수학과 수리 물리학 간의 차이를 예로 들 수 있다. 한 가지 결과는 어떤 특정 질문들에 대해, 예컨대 과학의 작동 방식에 관하여, 다양한 학문 분야들에 의해 상이한 답변들이 제공될지도 모른다는 것이다. 각각의 학문 분야는 그 자체만의 방식으로 그 해답을 찾아 나서며, 각각은 자체적인 해답을 구한다.

어휘 **presumption** 추정 **discipline** 학문 분야 **essentially** 본질적으로 **pursuit** 추구 **albeit** 비록 ~일지라도 **in point of** ~의 점에서, ~에 관하여 **peculiar** 이상한, 특유의 **trivial** 사소한 **objectivity** 객관성 **distinct** 별개의, 구별되는 **mathematical physics** 수리 물리학 **given** 특정한 **as to** ~에 관하여 **manner** 방식

구문 01~04행 It is a common presumption **that** all fields of science ~ are essentially ***the same sort of thing***: *the pursuit of truth*, albeit about different topics.
→ It은 가주어이고 that 이하가 진주어이다. 콜론(:) 다음의 the pursuit of truth, ~ topics는 the same sort of thing에 대한 구체적인 진술이다.

14~18행 Each discipline develops *a distinct culture* (specifically **suited to** its particular intellectual task)—for example ***differences between*** pure mathematics ***and*** mathematical physics.
→ ( )은 수동의 의미로 a distinct culture를 수식한다. suited to는 '~에 어울리는, 적합한'의 뜻이다. <differences between A and B>는 'A와 B 사이의 차이들'의 뜻이다.

실전 모의고사 15회

157 ④ 158 ③ 159 ③ 160 ② 161 ⑤ 162 ④ | 본문 100p

157 ④ | saying → to say

해설 ④ 인사를 하려고 멈춰 섰다는 문맥이 자연스러우므로 '목적'을 나타내는 to부정사가 쓰여야 한다. 동명사를 쓰면 '인사하는 동작을 멈추다'라는 뜻이 된다.

① 앞의 an elderly lady를 꾸며 '앉아 있는' 부인이라는 의미를 나타내므로 능동의 현재분사 sitting이 알맞음.
② 동사 seemed의 주격보어 자리이므로 형용사 familiar가 적절.
③ 부인이 계속 배에 탑승한 것은 웨이터가 그것을 화자에게 말해주는 과거 시점보다 더 이전부터 계속된 일이므로 과거완료가 적절.
⑤ 부인이 배에 탄 것은 과거에서부터 화자와 이야기를 나누는 현재 시점까지 계속된 행위이므로 현재완료 시제는 적절.

해석 약 2년 전 친구와 나는 프린세스 호를 타고 서지중해를 통과하여 순항을 하고 있었다. 저녁 식사 때 우리는 중앙 식당에 혼자 앉아있는 연세가 지긋한 부인을 보았다. 또한 나는 모든 직원 즉, 고급 승무원들, 웨이터들 등 모두가 이 부인을 매우 잘 알고 있는 것처럼 보인다는 것을 알았다. 나는 그녀가 그 해운 회사를 소유하고 있다는 말을 듣게 되리라 예상하면서 담당 웨이터에게 그 부인이 누구인지 물었다. 그러나 그는 그녀가 지난 네 번의 유람선 여행에 잇달아 승선했었다는 것만 알고 있다고 말했다. 어느 날 저녁 그녀의 눈과 마주치자 나는 인사를 하려고 멈춰 섰다. 우리는 담소를 나누었고 나는 "당신이 지난 네 번의 유람선 여행에서 이 배를 타셨다는 것을 알고 있어요."라고 이야기를 했다. 그녀는 "네, 그것은 사실이에요."라고 대답했다. 내가 "저는 이해가 안 가요."라고 말하자, 그녀는 "그것이 양로원보다 더 싸기 때문이죠."라고 대답했다.

어휘 **cruise** 순항, 유람선 여행 **the Mediterranean** 지중해 **liner** 정기선(船) **line** 운송 회사 **back to back** 잇달아, 연속해서 **nursing home** 양로원

158 ③ | which → that

해설 ③ 뒤에 SVO의 완전한 구조가 오고, the fact의 내용을 설명하는 동격절을

이끌므로 접속사 that이 쓰여야 한다.

① 주어가 Rapid changes이므로 복수동사 are는 적절.
② 전치사의 목적어 자리이므로 동명사는 적절.
④ 선행사가 the same methods and materials이고 that 뒤의 절은 동사 have developed의 목적어가 없는 불완전한 형태이다. 그러므로 목적격 관계대명사 역할을 할 수 있는 that은 적절.
⑤ to부정사구(to keep up ~ learning)의 의미상 주어는 teachers이므로 <for+목적격>의 형태로 바르게 쓰였다.

해석 현대사회의 급속한 변화는 교육에 영향을 미치고 있다. 정보기술의 변화로 인해 교사도 학생도 오늘날의 학습에 대비할 수가 없다. 교사들은 그들이 모든 것을 알 수는 없다는 사실에 적응해야 하는 한편, 학습 지원도 해야 한다. 인터넷은 교사와 학생을 위한 새로운 학습 환경을 조성하는 하나의 방법이다. 오늘날의 교사들은 그들이 평생 수업하면서 발전시켜온 동일한 방법과 자료를 (그대로) 사용할 수 없다. 교사들이 변화에 뒤처지지 않고 평생 학습을 실천하는 것이 중요하다. 교사가 그 직업 안에서 성장할 수 있는 환경이 조성되지 않는다면 그들은 그들의 학생들에게 현대의 삶에서 성공하기 위해 필요한 모든 도구를 제공할 수 없을 것이다.

어휘 **affect** ~에 영향을 끼치다 **adjust to** ~에 적응하다, 맞추다 **material** 자료; 재료 **keep up with** ~에 뒤처지지 않다, 따라가다 **lifelong** 평생의 **profession** 직업

159 ③ | to purchase → to be purchased

해설 ③ what은 구매'되어야' 하는 식료품이므로 to부정사를 수동형(needs to be purchased)으로 써야 한다.

① 주의를 조금만 더 하면, 즉 '약간의' 추가된 주의로 가격의 지속적 파악이 가능하다는 얘기이므로 a little(약간의 ~)은 자연스럽다.
② our most-bought foods가 복수이므로 복수동사 cost가 적절.
④ <make+O+OC>의 구조에서 목적어 자리에 동명사구(creating a list)가 맞게 쓰였다.
⑤ 주어 자리에 동명사구(keeping track)가 맞게 쓰였다.

해석 장 보는 일이 가끔 어려운 일일 때가 있다. 재료는 비싸고 가격은 날씨나 식물 부족, 동물 질병을 원인으로 오락내리락한다. 그러나 우리 대부분은 늘 같은 재료들을 사는 경향이 있으므로, 약간의 신경만 더 쓰면 우리가 가장 많이 사는 식품들의 가격이 어떻게 되는지 주시할 수 있다. 주간 쇼핑목록을 이미 만들고 있지 않다면 지금 그렇게 하는 걸 시작하라. 나는 한 주의 초에 새 쇼핑목록 작성을 시작해 무엇을 구매해야 하는지와 다음 주 식사 아이디어를 메모하기 시작한다. 이렇게 하면 목록 만드는 일이 별거 아니게 된다. 나는 한 군데 이상에서 장을 보기 때문에 내가 정기적으로 구입하는 물건들의 가격을 내 쇼핑목록에 기록함으로써 예의 주시할 수 있다. 이 정보를 아는 것이 예산에 어마어마한 영향을 미친다. 분명히 계속 (가격을) 파악하는 것이 늘 필요로 하는 핵심 물품을 언제 어디서 사야 하는지 아는 데 도움이 된다.

어휘 **costly** 많은 돈이 드는, 값비싼 **fluctuate** 변동을 거듭하다, 오르내리다 **shortage** 결핍, 부족 **all the time** 내내, 항상 **make notes** 메모하다, 기록하다 **purchase** 구입하다 **keep track of** ~을 계속 파악하다 **budget** 예산, (지출 예상) 비용 **have an impact** 영향을 미치다 **core** 핵심, 중추 **require** 필요로 하다

160 ② | live → living[that live]

해설 ② 문장의 동사는 is로 앞에 나와 있고, 이 부분은 '어떤' 가정들에서 아동 학대가 흔한지 families를 수식해주는 수식어구가 올 자리이다. 능동의 의미의 현재분사 living이 알맞다. that live도 선행사를 수식하는 주격 관계대명사절로 가능하다.

① child abuse가 추상적인 개념으로 쓰였으므로 Most child abuse도 단수이다. 따라서 동사도 단수형.
③ thinking (that) they will ~ or that no one will ~로 이어지는 병렬구조. 생각하는 내용을 담은 두 개의 that절 중 두 번째 것이다.
④ 이어지는 부분이 문장이 아닌 단어이므로 because가 아닌 because of가 맞게 쓰였다.
⑤ a child continues ~ or is left ~로 연결되는 병렬구조. 아이가 '방치되는' 것이므로 수동태로 맞게 쓰였다.

해석 대부분의 아동 학대는 가정 내에서 일어난다. 위험 요인들에는 부모의 우울증, 부모가 어린 시절 학대를 경험한 것, 가정 폭력이 포함된다. 아이를 방치하고 학대하는 것은 빈곤 속에 사는 가정과 마약이나 알코올 중독자인 부모에게서 또한 흔히 보인다. 아동 학대는 모르는 사람이 아닌 (아이를) 돌보는 사람이나 아이가 아는 사람에 의해 이뤄지는 경우가 많다. 학대를 받고 있는 아이는 자기 탓이라고 비난받게 되거나 아무도 자기를 안 믿어줄까봐 누구한테도 얘기하기를 두려워하는 경우가 많다. 학대하는 사람이 자기가 아주 사랑하는 사람이어서 또는 두려움 때문에, 혹은 두 가지 이유 다로 얘기 않고 있는 경우도 더러 있다. 부모도 학대의 조짐이나 증상을 안 보고 넘어가려는 경향이 있는데, 이는 사실을 직면하길 원치 않아서이다. 이것은 심각한 잘못이다. 아이가 오랫동안 계속 학대받거나 그 상황을 자기 혼자 대처하게 방치될수록 완전히 회복될 가능성이 더 줄어든다.

어휘 **abuse** 학대, 유린; 악용, 남용 ***cf.* abuser** 학대자, 남용자 **parental** 부모의, 부모로서의 **depression** 우울, 의기소침 **domestic** 가정 내의 **neglect** 방치, 외면 **mistreatment** 학대, 잘못 다룸 ***cf.* mistreat** 학대하다 **caregiver** 돌보는 사람 **blame** 비난하다, ~의 탓으로 돌리다 **overlook** 간과하다, 넘어가다 **on one's own** 자기 힘으로, 자기 혼자 **recovery** 회복

구문 08~10행 *Children* [who have been mistreated] are often afraid to tell anyone, **thinking** *(that)* they will be blamed (A) [or] *that* no one will believe them. (B)

16~18행 **The longer** a child (S') continues to be abused (V'₁) [or] is left to deal with the situation on his own (V'₂), **the less likely** he (S) is ∨ to make a full recovery (V).

→ <the+비교급 ~, the+비교급 ...> 구문으로, 부사 long과 형용사 likely(be likely to: ~할 가능성이 있다, ~하기 쉽다)의 상관관계를 강조하고 있다.

161 ⑤

해설 (A) '무게를 지탱하며'의 뜻을 가져야 하므로 부대상황을 나타내는 분사구문이 와야 한다. 분사구문과 주절 사이에 콤마(,)가 반드시 오는 것은 아니다.
(B) 전치사 by에 carrying과 같이 병렬로 연결되는 것이므로 sleeping이 적절.
(C) 주어는 the disks이므로 복수동사인 lose가 적절.
~, because *the disks* (S') [**that** act ~ the neck] gradually lose (V') ~.

해석 우리의 목은 우리가 움직이고 있든 가만히 앉아 있든 머리의 무게를 지탱하며 매일 고되게 일한다. 어느 날 아침 통증 속에서 잠을 깰 때까지 우리는 이 중요한 신체 부위를 대개 무시한다. 이런 불편함은 무거운 가방을 어깨에 메거나 잘못된 자세로 잠을 잠으로써 더 심해질 수 있다. 그러나 아픈 목은 노화의 일부이기도 한데, 목의 각 뼈 사이에

서 완충작용을 하는 디스크의 두께가 점차 얇아지기 때문이다. 결국에는 뼈가 실제로 디스크를 찌그러뜨리게 된다. 이런 일이 생기면 당신의 몸은 목에서 관절로 머리의 무게를 옮김으로써 보완하는데 이는 어깨나 팔에 통증을 야기할 수 있다.

어휘 **vital** 중대한; 생명에 관한 **discomfort** 불편; 불쾌 **disk** 디스크 **cushion** 완충물; 쿠션 **gradually** 점차 **compensate** 보상하다, 보충하다 **shift** ~의 방향을 바꾸다, 이동시키다 **joint** 관절; 결합

162 ④

해설 (A) '과거의 어느 시점부터 현재까지'의 의미를 갖는 전치사 since가 쓰였으므로 현재완료 시제가 적절.
(B) 시간, 조건을 나타내는 부사절에서는 현재가 미래를 대신하므로 현재시제가 적절.
(C) 뒤에 구가 오는지 절이 오는지 구분해야 한다. 삽입된 such ~ states를 제외하고 보면 문장의 구조는 the continued existence [of conditions [that have helped to maintain nuclear peace]] cannot be guaranteed로서 절이므로 접속사 because가 알맞다.

해석 1945년 이후로 세계가 핵무기 휴전을 유지하고 있는 이유에 대한 한 가지 설명은 미국과 과거 소비에트 연방 간에 전쟁이 일어났더라면 지구 생명체의 거의 모두를 파괴했을 것이 분명했다는 점이다. 현재 핵확산이 계속된다면 더 작은 국가가 또 다른 국가를 상대로 사용하는 핵무기의 위험이 커질 것이다. 앞으로 이러한 일은 초강대국들 사이에서 발생한 핵전쟁보다 일어날 가능성이 더 큰데, 왜냐하면 핵 평화를 유지하는 데 도움을 주었던, 즉 반격할 수 있는 강력한 군대와 핵을 보유하고 있는 국가의 강력하고 안정된 정부와 같은, 조건들의 지속적인 존속이 보장될 수 없기 때문이다.

어휘 **cease-fire** 휴전 **destruction** 파괴 **proliferation** 확산, 급증 **superpower** 초강대국 **existence** 존재 **second-strike** 반격용의 **force** 군대; 힘 **stable** 안정된

구문 01~05행 **One explanation** for [why the world has maintained a nuclear cease-fire since 1945] **is** / **that *it was understood that*** war [between the United States and the former Soviet Union] **would have meant** almost total destruction of life on Earth.

→ 문장 전체의 주어는 One explanation ~ since 1945, 동사는 is, that 이하 전체가 보어 역할을 한다.

→ that절 내에 that절이 한 번 더 포함되어있는 형태. <be understood that>은 '~은 말할 필요도 없다, 당연하다'란 뜻.

→ 두 번째 that 이하의 절에는 <조동사 과거형+have p.p.>가 쓰여 과거의 일을 반대로 가정한다. if war between the United States and the former Soviet Union **had occurred**, it **would have meant** almost ~의 뜻으로 해석한다.

08~10행 In the future, such an event may be **more** *likely to occur* **than** nuclear war (between the superpowers) was (*likely to occur*), ~.

→ <비교급+than>의 구조로 such an event와 nuclear war를 비교하고 있다. was 뒤에는 앞에 나온 likely to occur가 생략되었다.

실전 모의고사 16회

163 ③ 164 ④ 165 ④ 166 ⑤ 167 ② 168 ① | 본문 102p

163 ③ | Confused → Confusing

해설 ❸ quantity를 success와 섞어 생각해서 혼동하는 것은 we이므로 능동형의 분사구문 Confusing ~이 되어야 한다. *cf.* confuse A with B: A를 B로 혼동[착각]하다

① 복수 대명사 us의 대부분이므로 복수 have experienced가 맞다.
② 전치사 뒤이므로 동명사형으로 쓰였다.
④ scoop up하는 모양새, 태도를 나타내는 부사가 맞게 쓰였다.
⑤ 비교급 문장으로 <more ~ than ...>이 잘 호응 된다. 비교급 이전의 원급 모양은 much 또는 a lot이다.

해석 우리들 대부분은 내용물을 '가볍게 스쳐 지나가고' '훑어보기' 위해 요리가 놓여진 2백 피트 되는 긴 탁자를 왔다 갔다 걸어 다닌 다음에 접시를 가득 채워야 한다는 걸 알만큼 충분히 뷔페 식사를 많이 해 봤다. 하지만 우리의 접시는 보통 처음 20피트를 못 가서 채워진다. 우리는 정보를 갖고도 같은 행동을 한다. 웹을 검색하고 2만 개의 결과가 나오면 기뻐서 얼굴이 환해진다. 양을 성공으로 착각하고 손에 닿는 것은 뭐든 게걸스럽게 퍼 올리고 나중을 위해 저장한다. 정보의 향연으로 다가갈 때 우리는 '뷔페 사고방식'을 경계해야 한다. 아마도 우리는 '더 많은 게 더 좋은 것'이라는 사고방식을 '더 적은 게 더 많은 것'의 사고방식으로 바꿔야 할 필요가 있을지 모른다. 지혜는 양보다 증류 및 축소와 더 관련이 있다. 검색은 광범위하게 하고 싶어 할 수 있겠으나 수확은 아껴서 현명하게 해야 한다.

어휘 **graze** 가볍게 스치며 지나가다; (풀을) 뜯어먹다 **browse** 가볍게 훑어보다 **load up** (짐 등을) 싣다 **hit** (검색으로 나온) 결과 **light up with** ~으로 빛나다, 기뻐하다 **quantity** 양 **greedily** 탐욕스럽게 **scoop up** 퍼 담다, 주워 담다 **beware of** ~을 조심하다, 경계하다 **mentality** 정신 구조, 의식 **feast** 향연, 연회 **replace A with B** A를 B로 바꾸다[교체하다] **mindset** 사고방식, 태도 **have a lot to do with** ~와 많은 관련이 있다 **reduction** 감소, 축소 **volume** 양, 부피 **harvest** 추수하다, 수확하다 **sparingly** 절약하며, 아끼며

구문 01~05행 Most of us have experienced **enough** buffet meals **to know** that we must walk up and down (A) ~ *before* loading up our plates (B).

→ <enough+명사+to-v>: v할 정도로 충분한 ~. '뷔페 경험이 많아서 that 이하를 잘 알고 있다'는 의미. 전치사 before 전후를 따져보면 'B 전에 A', 'A 이후에 B' 해야 한다는 점이 강조되고 있다.

164 ④ | stunned → stunning

해설 ❹ a piece가 나를 stun(깜짝 놀라게 하다)시키는 것이므로 능동의 stunning이 알맞다.

① hair가 '씻어지지 않은' 것이므로 수동의 과거분사 unwashed가 쓰인 경우.
② 명사절 whatever attracts you가 전치사 on의 목적어로 쓰였다. anything that attracts you의 의미.

③ look ∨ on you의 ∨ 자리에 쓰일 의문사로 how가 적절하다. good, great, amazing 등이 올 수 있는 자리이다.
⑤ so that(~할 수 있도록)에서 that이 생략된 형태로 문맥상 알맞다.

해석 당신은 땀복 차림으로 화장도 안 한 채 쇼핑을 가는가? 그건 좋은 생각이 아니다. 그걸 이런 식으로 생각해 보라. 머리는 안 감은 머리를 새집처럼 하고, 이마와 코는 번들거리는 채로 예쁜 옷을 입어볼 거라면 실패를 위한 준비를 얼마간 하고 있는 셈이다. 그 때가 바로 자기를 '어떤 것도 내게는 안 어울려' 식의 사고방식에 빠져들게 하는 때인데, 그건 우리 모두가 알듯이 재미있을 게 하나도 없다. 또 한 가지 중요한 조언은, 쇼핑하는 동안 눈길을 끄는 것은 무엇이든 다 입어봐야 한다는 것이다. 실제로 그것을 입어볼 때까지 어떤 것이 당신에게 얼마나 어울리는지 당신은 모른다. 옷이 옷걸이에 걸려 있을 때는 놀랄 만큼 멋진데 몸에는 잘 안 어울리는 때가 있고, 그 반대인 경우도 더러 있다. 어떤 스타일이 자기 몸에 가장 잘 어울리는 편인지 알려면 다양한 윤곽을 입어보는 것 또한 중요하다.

어휘 **makeup** 화장 **shiny** 반짝이는 **sort of** 얼마간, 다소 **look good on** ~에게 잘 어울리다 **tip** 조언, 팁 **try ~ on** ~을 입어보다 **attract** 눈길을 끌다, 끌어당기다 **stunning** 깜짝 놀랄, 굉장히 멋진 **hanger** 옷걸이 **frame** 골격, 뼈대, 체격 **the other way around** 반대로, 거꾸로 **a variety of** 다양한 ~

165 ④ | which → what

해설 ④ that's에 이어 주어인 that을 설명하는 보어절이 와야 할 자리이므로 선행사를 포함하는 관계대명사 what(~하는 것)이 와야 알맞다.

① '창피를 느끼게 하는' 상황이라는 의미이므로 현재분사 embarrassing은 맞게 쓰였다.
② 문맥상 '아무리 많이' 배우더라도 실전 경험 없이는 입을 뗄 수 없다고 하는 부분이다. 수가 아닌 양으로 표현될 부분이니 much로 쓴 것도 알맞다. (no matter how much you learn = however much you learn)
③ 정상 어순으로 보자면 you can be at ease in new situations(새로운 상황에서 편한 자세[상태]로 있다)로 be와 어울린다.
⑤ having a feel for his or her own language = what makes a native speaker = whether you can make the language your own의 관계로 native speaker와 native speaker가 아닌 사람을 구분하는 중요한 요소를 명사 개념으로 제시하고 있다.

해석 실수를 하겠다는 기꺼운 마음은 자신을 잠재적으로 창피를 느끼게 하는 상황에 처하게 할 준비가 되어 있음을 뜻한다. 이것은 두려울 수 있지만, 발전하고 나아질 수 있는 유일한 방법이다. 아무리 많이 배우더라도 스스로를 바깥세상에 놓아보지 — 낯선 사람에게 그 언어로 얘기하고 길을 묻고 음식을 주문하고 농담을 해보려 하지 — 않고서는 한마디도 할 수 없을 것이다. 이걸 더 자주 할수록 당신의 안전지대는 더 커지게 되고 새로운 상황에서도 더 편안할 수 있다. 처음에는 어려움 — 그게 발음의 어려움일 수도, 문법, 구문, 표현의 어려움일 수도 있다 — 에 처하게 될 것이다. 그러나 내 생각에는 가장 중요한 것은 그 언어에 대한 감을 개발하는 것이다. 원어민에게는 누구나 자기 언어에 대한 감각이 있고, 그것이 근본적으로 원어민을 (원어민으로) 만들어주는 것 — 그 언어를 모국어로 만드느냐 아니냐 — 이다."라고 한 전문가는 말한다.

어휘 **scary** 겁나는, 무서운 **comfort zone** 안전지대(편안하다고 느끼는 지대) **at ease** 마음이 편안한, 걱정 없이 **encounter** (어려움 등에) 맞닥뜨리다, 부딪히다 **basically** 기본적으로

구문 08~10행 **The more often** you(S) do(V) this(O) ∨(M), **the bigger** your comfort zone(S) becomes(V) ∨(C) [and] **the more at ease** you(S) can be(V) ∨ (in new situations)(M).

→ <The+비교급 ~, the+비교급 ...> 구문에서 ... 부분이 A와 B 두 가지로 소개되고 있다. ∨는 강조되어 나온 <the+비교급> 부분의 문장 내에서의 원래 위치를 표시한다.

166 ⑤ | Shopping → Shop

해설 ⑤ Shopping well이면 동사가 이어져야 하는데 접속사 and가 나와 문장으로 이어진다. <명령문, and ~(…하라, 그러면 ~)> 구조의 문장으로, 동사원형(Shop)으로 고쳐 써야 한다.

① '휴일 며칠 전에'라는 의미이므로 시간의 전치사 before가 맞게 쓰였다.
② 'if ~ not'의 의미를 갖고 있는 unless(~하지 않는다면)가 맞게 쓰였다. can't ~ unless의 <부정+부정> 구조로 우선 good food shopper가 될 것을 강조하고 있다.
③ most of the work and key decisions는 '되어야' 하는 일이므로 수동태로 맞게 쓰였다.
④ you'd think의 목적어절 속의 주어절이 what절이다. 선행사를 포함하는 관계대명사 what이 맞게 쓰였다.

해석 식료품 사는 것, 우리 대부분에게 그것은 귀찮은 일이다. 하지만 휴일을 하루 이틀 앞두고 Fairway의 west-side 가게에서 쇼핑을 해야 하는 때를 빼고는 실은 나는 그걸 좋아하는 편이다. 아무도 그걸 좋아하지 않는다. 보통 나는 나만의 장보기 강령을 실천하는데, 그것은 우선 먹을 것을 잘 쇼핑하지 못하고는 훌륭한 요리사가 될 수 없다는 것이다. 그건 우리가 집에서 하는 요리와 관련해 대부분의 일과 중요한 결정들이 우리가 부엌에 돌아왔을 때가 아니라 쇼핑할 때 이뤄지기 때문이다. 음식 네트워크나 음식 인스타그램에서 요리에 대한 이해에 이른 사람은 이를 절대로 이해하지 못할 것인데, 쇼핑에 관한 한 그곳에는 볼 것이 많이 없기 때문이다. 마찬가지로, 요리책이나 푸드 블로그를 참조하면 가장 중요한 것은 조리법이라는 생각이 들 것이다. 그렇지 않다. (중요한 것은) 장보기이다. 장을 잘 보면 잘 먹게 될 것이다. 그건 소소한 생각이지만 그 영향은 크다.

어휘 **chore** 귀찮은 일, 허드렛일 **when it comes to** ~에 관해서는 **refer to** ~을 참조하다 **matter** 중요하다 **recipe** 조리법 **impact** 영향, 충격

구문 13~14행 Similarly, if you refer to cookbooks and food blogs, you'd think *(that)* what matters the most(S′) is(V′) the recipe(C′).

167 ②

해설 (A) 뒤에 <주어(seeds)+동사(were planted)+부사구(in zero gravity)> 형태의 완전한 절이 나오므로 관계대명사는 불가. 선행사가 experiments이고 '그 실험에서'라는 문맥으로 보아 장소를 나타내는 관계부사 where가 적절.
(B) 이 문장에서 suggests가 '제안하다'의 의미로 쓰이지 않고 '암시하다, 시사하다'의 의미로 쓰였기 때문에 that절의 동사는 <(should+)동사원형>을 쓰지 않고 직설법을 써야 한다. 그러므로 responds가 적절.
(C) cause는 to부정사를 목적격보어로 취하는 동사이므로 to grow가 적절.

해석 씨앗은 어느 쪽이 위인지 어떻게 알까? 씨앗을 어떤 방향으로 심어도 줄기는 위로, 뿌리는 아래로 자란다. 무중력 상태에서 씨앗을 심은 실험에서 하나의 해답이 발견되었다. 무중력 상태에서는 씨앗이 모든 방향으로 자란다는 사실이 밝혀졌다. 이 결과는 씨앗이 중력에 반응함을 시사한다. 뿌리는 중력 쪽으로 자라고 줄기는 (중력 방향으로부터) 멀어지면서 자란다. 과학자들은 식물 세포에서 발견되는 무거운 녹말 입자들이 식물이 넘어지면 이동하게 되는 과정을 완전히 이해하지 못하고 있는데, 이 과정은 식물의 특정 부분에서 성장 호르몬을 생성한다. 이 호르몬은 줄기 맨 아래 부위의 세포가 더 빨리 성장하도록 하여 줄기를 위쪽으로 밀어 올리게 만든다.

어휘 **gravity** 중력 **cell** 세포

구문 09~12행 Scientists do not fully understand *the process* [**where** heavy starch grain (**found** in plant cells) shifts / if a plant falls over], // **which** produces growth hormones in certain areas in a plant.
→ which가 이끄는 계속적 용법의 관계대명사절은 the process를 부연 설명한다.

168 ①

해설 (A) 이 문장은 주어(new technologies)와 동사(have emerged)로 완전한 문장이어서, 만약 명사절, 즉 주어, 목적어 혹은 보어 구실을 해야 하는 what절이 생긴다면 그 what절은 문장 내에서 할 기능이 없다. 따라서 답은 관계대명사 that이며, that절은 주어 new technologies를 수식한다.
(B) they는 주어인 These technologies를 대신하는 것으로서, 가정의 활동과 패턴에 영향을 미치기 '시작하고 있는(beginning)' 것이며 '시작된(begun)' 것이 아니므로 능동형 beginning을 써야 한다.
(C) restrain의 목적어는 mobility를 지칭하므로 단수형인 it을 써야 한다.

해석 운송은 흥미롭고 빠르게 발전하는 분야이다. 변화의 주요 추진 요인은 기술적 진보와 사회의 진화이다. 최근 수년 동안 여객 정보 서비스와 기반시설 이용 가격 책정과 같은 응용프로그램에서의 주요한 혁신으로 이어지는 정보와 통신의 신기술이 모습을 드러냈다. 이러한 기술들은 또한 회사의 물류 업무를 완전히 바꾸어놓았으며, 그것들은 가정의 일상 활동과 이동 패턴에 두드러진 영향을 미치기 시작하고 있다. 여행의 양은 두 개의 반대되는 힘에 의해 영향을 받는다. 이동성을 증대시키는 경향이 있는 경제 성장과 그것을 억제하는 경향이 있는 환경과 에너지 공급에 관한 염려 말이다.

어휘 **transport** 운송 **evolving** 발전하는 **emerge** 모습을 드러내다, 나타나다 **innovation** 혁신 **application** 응용프로그램 **pricing** 가격 책정 **infrastructure** 사회 기반 시설 **usage** 사용, 용법 **profoundly** 완전히 **transform** 변형시키다 **firm** 회사 **noticeable** 뚜렷한, 현저한 **opposing** 서로 대립하는 **boost** 끌어올리다, 증대시키다 **mobility** 유동성, 이동성 **restrain** 저지하다, 억누르다

구문 13~15행 ~ *economic growth* [which tends to boost mobility] and *concerns about the environment and energy supply* [which tend to restrain it].
→ economic growth와 concerns about the environment and energy supply가 and로 연결되어 병렬구조를 이루고 있다. 두 개의 [ ] 부분은 각각 economic growth와 concerns를 수식한다.

실전 모의고사 17회

169 ④ 170 ③ 171 ① 172 ⑤ 173 ② 174 ③ | 본문 104p

169 ④ | is → are

해설 ④ 주어가 The different types of rock이므로 복수동사 are가 적절.

① a layer of topsoil을 선행사로 하는 관계사절. '겉흙층에서' 식물들이 자랄 수 있다는 문맥으로 보아 장소를 나타내는 전치사 in과 목적격 관계대명사 which는 적절. 원래의 두 문장은 Continental land masses are usually covered by a layer of topsoil + Plants can grow in the layer of topsoil.이다.
② 의미상 주어 tiny pieces of rock이 공기와 물과 '섞인' 것이므로 과거분사 mixed 적절.
③ <the+비교급 ~, the+비교급 ...> 구문으로 적절히 쓰임.
⑤ are made와 and로 연결된 병렬구조이므로 (are) formed가 적절.

해석 대륙의 땅덩어리는 대개 식물이 자랄 수 있는 겉흙층으로 덮여 있다. 이 겉흙은 몇 인치에서부터 몇 피트 깊이에까지 이를 수 있다. 그것은 작은 암석 조각들로 이루어져 있는데, 이는 공기와 물과 섞여 있다. 그러나 거름흙이라고 불리는, 겉흙의 가장 중요한 성분은 부패한 식물의 잔해로 구성되어 있다. 거름흙은 영양소를 함유하고 물을 흡수하기 때문에 흙이 더 많은 거름흙을 함유할수록 새로운 식물을 성장시키는 데 더 유리하다. 흙을 구성하는 암석의 여러 종류는 주로 지표 훨씬 아래에 있는 '모암(母巖)'의 잔해이다. 이 바위들은 광물로 이루어져 있으며, 화산에 의해서와 같은 다양한 방식으로 형성된다. 바람과 물에 의한 침식 작용이 그들을 미세한 입자로 바꾸었다.

어휘 **continental** 대륙의 **mass** 큰 덩어리; 다량, 다수 **layer** 층 **topsoil** 겉흙 **ingredient** 성분, 원료 **decompose** 분해[부패]되다 **remains** 잔해, 유해 **nutrient** 영양분 **absorb** ~을 흡수하다 **mineral** 광물; 무기물 **erosion** 침식, 부식 **fine** 미세한; 멋진; 벌금 **particle** 입자

170 ③ | shopping → to shop

해설 ③ <encourage+O+OC>의 패턴에서 목적격보어로 to부정사가 와야 한다.

① <whether A or B(A할지 B할지)>
② <worth v-ing(v할 만하다, v할 가치가 있다)>
④ 너의 눈에 들어온 '그' 새 옷을 가리키는 지시형용사.
⑤ 다른 사람이 아닌 '자기 자신'을 붙잡고 억제하는 것이므로 재귀대명사가 맞게 쓰였다.

해석 우리는 모두 어떤 새 옷을, 살 건지 그냥 지나쳐 버릴지 결정하려 애쓰며 이러지도 저러지도 못했던 경험이 다들 있다. 이런 일이 생기면 그 옷이 나의 옷장에 들어 있는 모습을 마음속에 그려보라. 어떤 사람들은 그걸 가질 만한 가치가 있으려면 같이 맞춰 입을 옷이 최소한 세 개는 떠올라야 한다고 얘기하지만 나는 한 개만 떠올릴 수 있으면 (살) 준비가 모두 끝난 거라고 생각한다. 이유(가 뭐냐고)? 네 맘에 쏙 들었고, 그것이 가장 중요한 것이다. 거기(맘에 쏙 들었다는 것)에서 출발하여 같이 입을 옷이 한 개만 있으면 되고 그러면 충분히 가도[사도] 되는 것이다. 이렇게 되면 당신의 안전지대 너머에서도 물건을 사보게 될 것이고, 그러면 그 새 옷과 어울릴 것들이 더 많이 눈에 들어오기 시작할 것이다. 스타일은 서서히 발전하는 것. 같은 것을 계속 선택함으로써 스스로를 억제하지 말라.

어휘 **be stuck** 꼼짝 못 하다 **wardrobe** 옷장 **pair A with B** A를 B와 짝을 맞추다 **as long as** ~하는 한 **comfort zone** 안전지대 **chances are (that)** ~의 가능성이 높다 **evolve** 진화하다, (점진적으로) 발달하다 **hold ~ back** ~을 억제하다, 누르다

171 ① | were occurred → occurred

해설 ❶ '발생하다'라는 뜻의 occur는 자동사이므로 수동태로 쓸 수 없다. occurred로 바꿔야 적절.

② 주어가 An aching back or neck and eye strain으로 복수이므로 복수동사 are는 적절.
③ Carpal Tunnel Syndrome을 대신하는 단수 대명사 it은 적절.
④ 이어지는 절이 전치사 in의 목적어가 빠져 불완전하므로 목적격 관계대명사절을 이끄는 that은 적절.
⑤ 조건의 부사절에서는 현재시제가 미래시제를 대신하므로 현재형 is는 적절. it은 the human arm을 가리킨다.

해석 과거에는, 소위 '반복적 동작으로 인한 장애'가 온종일 고기를 써는 육류 공장의 노동자들 사이에서 가장 많이 발생했다. 그러나 현재에는 컴퓨터가 늘 사용되면서 사무직 노동자들도 같은 증상으로 고통받고 있다. 허리나 목의 통증, 그리고 눈의 피로가 가장 흔한 통증들이다. 손목터널증후군은 손가락의 감각 상실과 손목 통증을 일으키며 고통을 덜기 위해서는 종종 수술이 필요하다. 통증은 키보드 위에 팔을 대고 있어서 생기는 불쾌한 결과로 의사들에 의하면 인간의 팔이 몇 시간이고 계속해서 취할 수 있는 자세는 아니라고 한다. 만약 그렇게 대고 있으면 통증이 생길 것이다.

어휘 **injury** 부상 **chop** ~을 썰다, 다지다 **eye strain** 눈의 피로(감) **complaint** 통증, 질환; 불평 **numb** 마비된 **on end** 계속해서

구문 10~13행 Pain is now the unpleasant result of holding our arms over the keyboard, a *position* [**that**, according to doctors, the human arm wasn't designed to be in ∨ for ~].
(동격) (삽입구)

→ a position을 수식하는 관계사절에 according to doctors가 삽입된 구조.

172 ⑤ | this → these

해설 ❺ periods가 복수이므로 this가 아닌 복수형 these로 써야 한다.

① 주어가 people로 복수이므로 동사도 복수형. An increasing number of는 a number of(많은 ~)의 변형.
② <with+명사+분사>의 구조에서 seven out of ten major retailers와 record가 능동의 관계이므로 현재분사 recording이 맞게 쓰였다.
③ '목적(~하기 위하여)'을 나타내는 to부정사가 주어에 앞서 온 경우.
④ <there is / are ~> 구문의 주어가 a number of things로 복수이므로 are가 맞게 쓰였다.

해석 점점 더 많은 수의 사람들이 집의 안락함 속에서 모든 쇼핑을 함으로써 시즌마다 (상점에 나오는) 군중들을 (그 수에서) 앞서는 것을 선호한다. 12월에, 주요 소매업자 열에 일곱이 자사의 웹사이트에 방문한 순 방문자 수가 엄청나게 증가하면서 온라인 판매에서의 급증이 있다. 사업체를 어떻게 보이게 전시할 것인가가 소비자의 (쇼핑) 경험 형성에 중요한 역할을 한다. 가게를 시즌에 맞는 테마로 꾸밈으로써 긍정적인 환경을 조성할 수 있다. 온라인 경쟁자들과는 달라 보이고 고객에게 보다 즐거운 쇼핑 경험을 조성하기 위해 할 수 있는 일로는 웹 사이트에 축제의 활기찬 분위기를 더하고, 블로그에 해당 시즌 주제의 내용을 더하고, 관련된 세일 상품과 선물 아이디어를 부각시키고, 막바지 배송 가능 선택사항을 넣고 배송 기간 선택을 보다 다양하게 하는 등 아주 많다. 올해 다가오는 축제와 행사들을 맞이하여 미리 계획하고 이 기간 동안에 매출을 끌어올릴 기회를 극대화하도록 영업 준비를 하라.

어휘 **beat** ~을 이기다, 때려눕히다 **comfort** 편함, 안락 **surge** 쇄도, 밀어닥침 **retailer** 소매업자 **unique visitor** 순 방문자(한 사람이 여러 번 같은 사이트를 방문했더라도 한 명으로 측정되는) **display** 전시, 진열 **theme** 주제, 테마 **stand out** 두드러지다, 눈에 띄다 **relevant** 관련된 **last-minute** 막바지의, 폐점 직전의 **ship** 배송하다 **upcoming** 다가오는 **maximize** 극대화하다 **boost** 신장시키다, 끌어올리다

구문 03~06행 In December, there is *a surge* (in online sales)—**with** seven out of ten major retailers **recording** major increases (in the number of unique visitors to their websites).
(O) (OC)

→ <with+명사+분사> 구조.

173 ②

해설 (A) 뒤에 <주어(a woman)+동사(was married)>의 완전한 절이 이어지므로 관계대명사 which는 올 수 없다. 접속사 that은 a sign의 내용을 설명하는 동격절을 이끌므로 적절하다.
(B) 붉은색이 빈디에 언제나 '사용되는' 것이므로 수동의 과거분사 used가 적절.
(C) the outfit을 선행사로 하는 목적격 관계대명사절을 이끌고 있으므로 that이 적절. what은 선행사를 포함한 관계대명사.

해석 인도에서 힌두 여성들은 주홍색 안료를 갈아서 만든 점을 전통적으로 그들의 이마에 붙여왔다. 그 장식점은 '빈디'라고 불린다. 빈디는 결혼반지를 끼는 것처럼 여성이 결혼했음을 알리는 표시였다. 힌두교에서 중요한 색깔인 붉은색은 언제나 빈디에 사용되었다. 그러나 현대의 인도에서 빈디는 패션의 표현이 되었다. 과거에는 결혼한 여자들이 오직 둥글고 붉은 빈디를 칠했던 반면, 이제는 결혼한 여자와 결혼하지 않은 여자들 모두 각기 다른 크기와 모양의 빈디를 그들의 이마에 붙이기 시작했다. 이제 그것들은 그들이 입는 의상의 색을 맞추기 위한 패션 스티커처럼 되어 다수는 구슬, 크리스털 혹은 반짝이로 장식되기도 한다.

어휘 **spot** 점; 장소 **ground** 가루로 빻은 **forehead** 이마 **decorative** 장식적인 ***cf.* decorate** ~을 장식하다 **statement** 표현, 전달; 진술 **outfit** 의상 **glitter** (장식용) 반짝이; 반짝반짝 빛나다

174 ③

해설 (A) while이 이끄는 절에서 주어 work that's safe to ignore에 호응하는 동사가 없으므로 tends가 적절.
(B) <spend+O+v-ing>: v하는 데 O를 쓰다
(C) <keep+O+OC> 구조에서 목적격보어 자리에는 형용사가 와야 한다. fairly는 형용사 messy를 수식하는 부사.

해석 어질러진 책상은 사실 효과적인 장치가 될 수 있다. 어질러진 책상에서, 일반적으로 가장 중요한 일은 손에서 가장 가까운 곳에 있기 쉽지만, 무시해도 될 만한 일은 책상 뒤편이나 맨 아래쪽으로 밀려나는 경향이 있다. 물론 어질러진 책상을 갖는다는 것은 당신의 시간 중 최소한 일부를 물건을 찾기 위해 뒤죽박죽 속을 뒤지는 데 보낸다는 것을 의미한다. 여기에서 당신의 소중한 시간을 일주일에 한 시간부터 하루에 한 시간까지 어느 정도 낭비할 수 있다. 그러나 당신이 적당한 정도로 어수선함을 유지하는 한, 당신은 일을 더 잘 처리하게 될지도 모른다. 설문 조사에 의하면, 매우 깔끔한 책상을 유지한다고 말하는 사람들이 책상을 꽤 엉망인 상태로 둔다고 말하는 사람들보다 일할 때 평균 36퍼센트의 더 많은 시간을 물건을 찾는 데 쓴다.

어휘 **messy** 어질러진, 엉망인 ***cf.* mess** 엉망인 상태 **effective** 효과적인 **tend to-v** v하는 경향이 있다 **root** (무엇을 찾으려고) 뒤지다; 뿌리 **anywhere** from A to B (수량, 시간, 가치 등이) A와 B 사이의 어딘가(에서) **disorder** 어수선함; 장애 **manage** ~을 처리하다, 관리하다 **survey** 설문 조사

구문 12~16행 ~, *people* [**who** say (that) they keep a very neat desk] **spend** an average 36 percent [more] time **looking** for things at work [than] *people* [**who** say (*that*) they keep their desks fairly messy].

→ 전체 문장은 <spend+O+v-ing(v하는 데 O를 쓰다)> 구조.

실전 모의고사 18회

175 ② 176 ② 177 ③ 178 ⑤ 179 ③ 180 ④ | 본문 106p

175 ② | Other → Another

해설 ❷ 뒤에 단수명사 thing이 오므로 복수명사를 수식하는 Other는 불가능. 문맥상으로도 '또 다른 하나'를 의미하므로 Another가 적절.

Another thing [which **causes** fatigue ~ of it] is the constant ~.

① 선행사 noise를 받는 목적격 관계대명사로서 계속적 용법으로 쓰일 수 있는 which는 적절.
③ '~인지 (아닌지)'의 의미로 명사절을 이끄는 접속사인 if가 적절히 쓰임.
④ 지시대명사 those는 people의 의미로서 관계대명사의 선행사가 될 수 있다. those who는 '~하는 사람들'이라는 뜻.
⑤ 선행사인 the crowd of strangers가 전치사 with의 목적어이므로 목적격 관계대명사 whom이 적절하게 쓰였다.
~ they are forced to have close contact **with** the crowd of strangers
= ~ **with** whom they are forced ~

해석 현대의 삶은 신경성 피로에서 벗어나는 것을 불가능하게 만든다. 근무시간 내내, 그리고 심지어 직장과 집을 오가는 시간에 훨씬 더 많이, 도시 노동자는 소음에 둘러싸여 있는데 그들은 그 소음의 대부분을 무시하는 것을 배운다. 우리가 의식하지 못하는 사이에 피로하게 하는 또 다른 요인은 낯선 이들이 항상 가까이 있다는 것이다. 사람을 포함한 모든 동물의 자연스러운 본능은 친구인지 적인지를 결정하기 위해 모든 낯선 것들을 조사하는 것이다. 이런 자연스러운 반응은 출퇴근 혼잡한 시간에 지하철에서 이동하는 사람들에 의해 억제될 수밖에 없다. 이런 끊임없는 억제의 결과는 그들이 가까이 접촉하도록 강요된 낯선 사람들의 무리에 대한 막연한 분노이다.

어휘 **nervous** 신경성의; 신경질의 **fatigue** 피로 **foe** 적 **inhibit** ~을 억제하다, 못하게 막다 ***cf.*** **inhibition** 억제

176 ② | to be influenced → to influence

해설 ❷ they가 the group에 능동적으로 영향을 미치는 것이므로 to be influenced가 아닌 to influence가 되어야 한다.

① 형용사(insurmountable)를 부사(seemingly)가 맞게 꾸미고 있다.
③ felt secure and (felt) protected의 병렬구조. they가 사회 속에서 protected 되는 입장이므로 수동의 과거분사 형용사를 쓴 것은 적절.
④ <some of+명사>에서 some의 수는 이어 나오는 명사가 결정한다. 수식해주는 of 이하의 명사가 structures로 복수(some of the structures ~)이므로 are가 맞게 쓰였다.
⑤ <allow+O+OC(to-v)>의 병렬구조이므로 (to) be employed가 적절. individuals가 고용하는 입장이 아니라 '되는' 입장이므로 to부정사의 수동형으로 쓰였다.

해석 테러가 약한 자가 강자에 대항하는 무기라는 점이 자주 주목받는다. 테러는 테러리스트가 대적해야 할 겉보기에 수행 불가능한 승산을 뛰어넘기 위해 이용된다. 테러리스트는 일반적으로 그들이 영향을 미치고 싶은 집단에 충격을 줄 타깃을 공격한다. 테러리즘 전문가는 "테러가 상대적으로 효과가 높은 것은 그것이 지니는 상징적인 성격에 기인한다. 테러리스트가 자신이 전시 효과를 노리고 있음을 충분히 이해하고 있다면 사람들에게 널리 알려지고 명분에 대한 지지를 끌어낼 수 있도록 최대의 상징적 가치를 지닌 타깃을 공격할 것이다."라고 말한다. 그 상징적인 타깃이 파괴되면 테러리스트는 예전에는 안전하고 보호받고 있다고 여긴 사회로부터 개개인을 고립시키는 데 성공을 거둔다. 정보화 시대에 사회를 '떠받치는 골격'을 이루는 그러한 구조 중 일부는 개개인 간의 통신과 자기 돈에의 접근, 고용을 가능하게 해주는 고도 기술 네트워크일 가능성이 있다. 따라서 그것들이 테러리스트의 주 타깃이 되는 것은 피할 수 없다.

어휘 **terrorism** 테러리즘, 테러 **utilize** 이용[활용]하다 **odds** (어떤 일이 일어날) 공산 [가능성] **strike out** 공격하다 **derive from** ~에서 유래하다 **comprehend** (충분히) 이해하다 **demonstration** 전시; 설명, 입증; 시위, 데모 **publicity** 세상에 알려짐; 언론의 주목 **elicit** 유도하다, 끌어내다 **cause** 대의명분 **isolate** 고립시키다 **formerly** 이전에, 예전에 **secure** 안심하는, 안정감을 느끼는 **constitute** 구성하다, 이루다 **framework** 뼈대, 근간 **access** 접근하다 **inevitable** 피할 수 없는, 필연적인 **primary** 주된, 제일 중요한

구문 13~15행 ~ then the terrorist has succeeded in isolating individuals from *the society* [**in which** they formerly felt secure [and] protected].

177 ③

해설 (A) 뒤에 <주어(he)+동사(helped)+목적어(destroy diseased birds)>의 완전한 절이 오므로 관계대명사 which는 올 수 없다. 문맥상 '때'를 나타내는 접속사 when(~할 때)이 적절.
(B) 형제들이 후에 감염된 사실과 병에 걸린 새와의 접촉이 없었던 사실은 인과관계를 나타내는 since(~이기 때문에)가 아닌 역접을 나타내는 접속사 although(~에도 불구하고)로 연결되는 것이 자연스럽다.
(C) 과거에 있었던 사례들을 언급하므로 앞선 시점을 나타내는 완료형의 to부정사 to have been이 적절.

해석 지난해 한 조류독감 발생 건에서 파키스탄의 한 가족이 인간 대 인간 감염의 높은

가능성을 보여주었다고 세계보건기구는 발표했다. 그 사례에서 한 수의사는 페샤와르에서 병든 새들을 도살 처분하는 일을 돕다가 조류독감 바이러스에 감염되었다. 그의 세 형제는 병든 새와 접촉한 적이 없었지만 나중에 감염되었다. 한 교수는 전문가들도 그 바이러스의 인간 대 인간 감염이 일어났다는 것을 백 퍼센트 확신할 수는 없다고 말한다. 그러나 그는 2007년 파키스탄과 중국에서의 경우를 포함해서 적어도 6번의 사례가 있었던 것으로 보인다고 말한다. 과학자들은 바이러스가 시간이 지나면서 사람들 사이에서 쉽게 퍼지는 형태로 바뀔 수 있다고 우려한다.

어휘 **probability** 확률, 있을 법함 **infection** 감염 ***cf.* infect** ~을 감염시키다

178 ⑤ | constant → constantly

해설 ⑤ 동사부 become on display(보이다, 전시되다)를 수식하는 수식어구로 부사(constantly)가 와야 자연스럽다. 부사 almost(거의)가 같은 부사를 수식하고 있다.

① be required to-v(~할 것이 요구되다)의 구조로 stars가 요구받는 입장이므로 수동태로 맞게 쓰였다.
② '스스로'를 창조하고 또 창조해내야 하는, 즉 (re)create의 대상이 곧 자기 자신이므로 재귀대명사가 맞게 쓰였다.
③ <전치사+동명사> 구조.
④ 동사 prove의 목적어 역할을 하는 명사절을 이끄는 접속사 that이 맞게 쓰였다.

해석 미디어에 올라온 가십이 점점 더 돌고 돌아 사람들에게 보다 널리 알려지면서 스타는 과거 어느 때보다 개인적인 삶에서 연기자가 될 것이 요구된다. 그들은 이제 스스로를 '자기가 주인공인 전기물의 등장인물'로 탄생, 또 재탄생할 것으로 기대된다. 연예인들의 가십을 다루는 전 세계적 시장과 연기자라는 직업 내에서의 한층 치열해진 경쟁 때문에 스타들은 자기 이미지가 갖고 있는 (대중을) 자극할 만한 점을 고조시킴으로써 스타로서의 자기 위상을 늘 재확인해야 한다. 한 사회학자는 스타들이 (대중에게) 끝없이 성공하고 있구나 하는 환상을 자아내기 위해서는 작품과 사적인 삶 (둘 다에서) 눈길을 끌 만한 점을 거듭 증명해 보여야 한다고 제안한다. 그러나 오늘날의 스타 이미지가 어디에나 널려 있다는 점이, 스타의 모습이 거의 늘 (대중에게) 보여지면서 소위 말하는 '스타의 모습의 약화'를 만들어내기도 한다.

어휘 **performer** 연기자 **biography** 전기(사람의 일생을 다룬 이야기) **profession** 직업 **status** 지위, 위치, 신분 **heighten** 고조시키다 **sensationalism** 선정주의, 흥미 본위 **sociologist** 사회학자 **contemporary** 동시대의, 현대의

179 ③ | furiously → furious

해설 ③ she rolled ~의 이유를 나타내는 분사구문으로 주어의 감정 상태를 설명하고 있다. (being) furious at ~에서 being이 생략된 형태. 부사가 아닌 형용사가 와야 할 곳이다.

① 동사(be pulled off)를 수식해주는 어구로 부사(gently(부드럽게, 조심스럽게))가 적절.
② 동사 뒤에 목적어(me)가 있고, her screams and wails가 나를 따라오는 것이므로 능동태 followed가 적절하게 쓰였다.
④ I would collect her in a couple of hours가 곧 assurance의 내용, 즉 동격이므로 동격의 that이 맞게 쓰였다.
⑤ <watch+O+OC> 구조. 지각동사의 목적격보어로 to 없는 원형부정사 take가 맞게 쓰였다.

해석 나는 내 딸 Julia를 유아원 첫 등교를 위해 데리고 갔던 그 날을 잊지 못할 것이다. 내가 딸아이를 두고 떠나려는데, 딸아이가 내 무릎에 너무 꽉 매달린 나머지 젊은 선생님 두 분이 딸을 부드럽게 떼어 놓아야 했다. 내가 도망을 나와 정거장으로 허둥지둥 가는데, 부모가 자기를 버리는 이 행위에 격노하여, 두어 시간 있다가 (아빠가) 데리러 올 거라는 온갖 안심의 말들은 귀에 들어오지도 않은 채 마룻바닥 위를 미쳐 데굴데굴 구르며 딸아이가 내는 비명과 통곡이 거리를 걸어 내려가는 내내 나를 쫓아왔다. 18년의 시간이 훅하고 흘러 딸의 Newcastle 대학 졸업식이 되었고 이번에는 그 눈물이, 아내와 내가 성장한 딸이 위대하고 넓은 성인의 일의 세계에 첫발을 디디는 것을 지켜보는 가운데 부모의 얼굴을 타고 흘러내리고 있다.

어휘 **nursery school** 유아원, 어린이집 **cling (clung-clung)** 매달리다 **scurry off** 허둥지둥 가다 **wail** 통곡, 울부짖음 **frenzy** 광분, 광란 **furious** 격노한 **abandonment** 버림, 유기 **assurance** 확언

구문 05~09행 **As** I made my escape ~ (종속절), her screams and wails followed ~ (주절), [as she rolled ~, *(being)* furious at ~, *(being)* deaf to *all assurances* [*that I would* ~]] (종속절; [that I would ~]: 동격의 that절).
→ <As ~, ...> 구조에서 주절 부분이 다시 주절과 종속절로 나뉜 구조이다. 한편 주절 속 as절은 being이 생략된 두 개의 분사구문을 포함하고 있다.

180 ④

해설 (A) 문장 전체의 주어는 Identity thieves, 동사는 gain과 pass이다. information과 you 뒤에 각각 콤마로 분리되어 나오는 구는 앞의 동사구를 수식하는 부사구. 따라서 (A)는 부사구를 이끌 수 있는 to make가 되어야 한다. 문맥상 '~하기 위해'란 뜻으로 목적을 나타내는 to부정사구.
(B) 주어 Signs와 호응하는 동사 자리. 주어가 복수명사이므로 복수동사 include가 정답. that ~ stolen은 주어의 구체적인 내용을 설명하고 있는 동격절.
(C) 뒤에 오는 명사구를 이끌 수 있는 전치사 concerning이 정답. 문맥상으로도 '~에 관하여'란 뜻의 concerning이 알맞다. concerned는 '걱정[염려]하는, 관계가 있는'이란 뜻의 형용사.

해석 '신분 도용'은 미래에 대한 공상 문학 작품에나 나올법한 일처럼 들릴 수도 있지만, 그것은 엄연히 실재하고 전 세계에서 일어나고 있다. 신분 도용자들은 대개 인터넷이나 이메일을 통해 당신의 개인 정보에 접근하고 자신을 당신인 것처럼 위장하는데 이는 어김없이 물건 구매나 은행 거래를 하기 위해서이다. 당신의 신분이 도용되었음을 나타내는 징후로는 당신이 하지도 않은 신용 거래 신청을 승인하거나 거절하는 편지 또는 전화, 신용카드 명세서에 실린 당신이 구매하지 않은 물건에 대한 청구액, 우편으로 신용카드 명세서를 받지 못하는 것, 당신이 개설하지도 않은 예금 계좌와 관련해 채무 회수 대행사로부터 전화나 방문을 받는 것 등이 있다.

어휘 **identity theft** 신분 도용 **futuristic** 미래의; 초현대적인 **gain access to+명사** ~에 접근하다 **pass A off as B** A가 B인 체하다 **invariably** 변함없이, 반드시 **transaction** 거래, 업무; 매매 **approve** ~을 승인하다 **reject** ~을 거절하다 **application** 신청; 적용, 응용 **credit** 외상 (판매); 신뢰 **charge** 청구 금액, 요금; (요금 등을) 청구하다 **credit card statement** 신용카드 명세서 **agency** 대행 회사, 대리점 **open a bank account** 예금 계좌를 개설하다

구문 07~15행 Signs ~ include *letters or phone calls* (approving or rejecting an application for ***credit*** [that you didn't make]); charges on your credit card statement for things you didn't buy; failing to ~ the mail; and receiving calls ~ didn't open.
→ letters or phone calls를 후치 수식하는 분사구 내에 credit을 한정하는 목적격 관계대명사절이 삽입된 형태. 신분이 도용되었음을 나타내는 여러 가지 징표(Signs)들이 세미콜론(;)에 의해 연결되고 있다. 세미콜론은 앞에서 언급한 내용을 부연 설명하거나 등위절을 연결할 때 사용한다.

181 ④ | giving → give

해설 ④ 앞에 있는 동사 stand와 and로 묶여 병렬구조를 이루는 형태이므로 동사원형 give가 와야 한다.

① 동사 notice의 목적어로 쓰이는 명사절을 이끌면서 '~라는 것'의 의미가 되어야 하므로 접속사 that은 적절하다.
② 앞에 있는 명사 the water and nourishment와 require는 수동의 관계이므로 과거분사인 required는 어법상 적절하다. <be required of (~에게 요구되다)> 표현으로 주로 쓰인다.
③ 부정어 nor가 문장 앞에 쓰이면 도치 구문 <부정어+do[does, did]+주어+동사원형 ~>의 형태가 된다. 그러므로 do we criticize는 어법상 적절하다.
⑤ 앞에 있는 동사 be는 보어를 가지는 '~이다'의 의미가 아니라, 뒤에 부사구 in the process of change가 이어지면서, '있다, 존재하다'의 의미로 쓰였다. 따라서 ⑤는 동사를 수식하는 자리이므로 부사 constantly는 어법상 적절하다.

해석 땅속에 장미 씨앗을 심을 때, 우리는 그것이 작다는 것을 알지만 '뿌리가 없고 줄기가 없다'고 비난하지는 않는다. 우리는 씨앗에게 요구되는 물과 영양분을 제공하면서 그것을 씨앗으로 대한다. 처음 땅에서 솟아오를 때, 우리는 그것을 미숙하고 발달이 덜 되었다고 비난하지 않는다. 또한 꽃봉오리가 나올 때, 피지 않는다고 그 꽃봉오리를 비난하지도 않는다. 우리는 그 과정이 일어나는 것에 감탄하며 그 식물의 발달 단계마다 그것이 필요로 하는 돌봄을 제공한다. 장미는 씨앗일 때부터 죽을 때까지 장미이다. 그것은 자신 안에 언제나 자신의 온 잠재력을 포함하고 있다. 그것은 계속 변화의 과정에 있는 것처럼 보이지만, 매 상태, 매 순간, 그것은 있는 그대로 완벽하게 괜찮다.

어휘 **rootless** 뿌리가 없는 **stemless** 줄기가 없는 **shoot up** 솟아오르다 **condemn** 비난하다 **immature** 미숙한 **underdeveloped** 저개발의 **bud** 꽃봉오리 **potential** 잠재력

구문 03~04행 We treat it as a seed, **giving** it *the water and nourishment* (required of a seed).
→ giving ~ seed는 주어인 We를 의미상의 주어로 하는 분사구문으로 부수적으로 일어나는 상황을 나타낸다. ( ) 부분은 the water and nourishment를 수식하는데, 요구되는 대상이므로 required를 사용했다.

182 ⑤ | that → which

해설 ⑤ 선행사 its unique filing system을 보충 설명하는 관계대명사 자리. that은 계속적 용법으로 사용할 수 없으므로 which가 적절하다.

① 1930년대에 '건립된' 사진 도서관이므로 과거시제 수동태가 적절.
② a picture library를 대신하는 소유격이어야 하므로 its는 적절.
③ contains의 주어는 바로 앞의 the archive이므로 단수형은 적절.
④ 그녀의 치마를 '바람에 날리게 하는' 도로 통풍구라는 문맥으로, her skirt를 목적어로 취하는 현재분사 ventilating이 적절.

해석 베트만 아카이브는 독일인 이민자인 오토 베트만에 의해 1930년대에 건립된 사진 도서관이다. 그는 뉴욕에 두 개의 사진 가방을 가지고 도착해서 사진 도서관을 개관했는데, 그는 이 도서관을 그런 종류 중 세계에서 가장 큰 영리 기관으로 만들었다. 그 자료 보관소가 보유한 수백만 장의 사진 중에는, 도로 통풍구 위에서 치마를 날리며 서 있는 메릴린 먼로와 혀를 내밀고 있는 아인슈타인처럼 20세기에 가장 기억할 만한 사진들 중 몇몇이 있다. 베트만에 의하면, 그 보관소의 성공은 독특한 자료 정리 시스템 덕분이었는데, 그 시스템은 신문 잡지의 요구에 맞게 그가 고안한 것이었다. 예를 들어, 모나리자는 '회화'나 '레오나르도 다 빈치' 항목 밑에 정리된 것이 아니었다. 그것은 '미소' 항목 밑으로 정리되었다.

어휘 **archive** 아카이브, 보관(소), 보존 **immigrant** 이민자 **commercial** 영리적인; 상업상의 **memorable** 기억할 만한, 인상적인 **grate** 쇠로 만든 문살이나 창살 **ventilate** ~에 바람을 통하게 하다, 환기시키다 **stick out** ~을 내밀다 **due to** ~ 덕택으로, ~ 때문인 **file** ~을 (항목별로) 정리하다 **journalistic** 신문[잡지]의, 기자의

구문 06~09행 Among ~ *photographs* [(**that**) the archive contains ∨] are some of ~ century: ~.
(are: V, some of ~ century: S)
→ 부사구가 앞으로 나오면서 <주어-동사>가 도치된 구조.

183 ② | cook → cooking

해설 ② <devote+시간/노력+to(~을 …에 쏟아 붓다)>에서 to는 전치사이므로 그 뒤에 명사 개념이 온다. to부정사가 아닌 동명사 cooking으로 써야 한다.

① advance가 명사 orders를 꾸며주는 형용사로 쓰인 경우.
③ to부정사가 <목적(~하기 위하여, ~하도록)>으로 쓰인 경우. ensure 뒤에 접속사 that이 생략된 구조.
④ seated(좌석이 찬, 착석된)를 수식할 수 있는 말은 부사.
(= the tables (which are) currently seated)
⑤ 식당 주인이 식당에 들어서는 손님의 수를 통제하는 <목적(~하기 위하여)>을 나타내고 있다. 부사적 용법으로 쓰인 to부정사.

해석 요리사들은 예약을 사랑한다. 미리 하는 주문은 훨씬 더 사랑한다. 그것은 점칠 필요가 없이 주문량을 예측하고 야단법석을 떨지 않고서도 식사 공간을 준비하며 요리를 잘 해내는 데 전념할 수 있게 될 거라는 걸 뜻한다. 그러니 유쾌한 식사 경험을 하고 싶거든 음식을 미리 주문하라. 훌륭한 주인은 주방이 (주문으로) 넘쳐나지 않도록 예약 건이나 매장에 들어오는 손님을 띄엄띄엄 배치할 것이다. 어떤 식당 여주인들이 여기저기 비어 있는 테이블이 분명 눈에 띄는데도 왜 꽉 찼다고 하는지 그 이유가 궁금해 본 적이 없는가? 현재 손님이 앉아 있는 테이블을 한번 잘 보라. 많은 사람이 음식을 기다리고 있는 게 보이면 그건 주방이 일로 압도되어 있기 때문이다. 상황이 더 나빠지지 않도록 하려면 여주인은 상황이 다시 통제할 수준이 될 때까지 예약 없이 방문한 손님들의 입장을 중지시킬 것이다.

어휘 **chef** 요리사, 주방장 **reservation** 예약 **advance** 미리 하는, 사전의 **volume** 양, 부피 **dine** 식사하다 **fuss** 법석, 소동 **devote** 바치다, 헌신하다 **get swamped** (처리가 힘들 정도로 일이) 넘쳐나다[쇄도하다] **seat** ~을 앉히다 **overwhelm** 압도하다 **put a halt on** ~을 중단시키다, ~에 제동을 걸다 **walk-in** 예약이 안 된; 예약하지 않고 가는 사람

184 ④ | used → using

해설 ④ 앞의 clearly까지는 완전한 문장을 이루고 있으며 used의 의미상 주어는 writers이다. 의미상 주어와 능동 관계이고 문맥상 부대상황을 뜻하므로 using으로 고쳐야 한다.

① ample evidence와 동격을 이루는 명사절을 이끄는 접속사 that이 알맞게 쓰였다.

② 주어는 One difference이므로 단수동사 lies가 적절. 이때의 lie는 자동사로서 '(생각·문제 등이 ~에) 있다, 발견되다'란 의미이다.

③ 문맥상 for the listener를 의미상 주어로 하는 to ask와 and로 연결된 병렬구조로 보는 것이 적절.

⑤ 앞에 나온 many second language writers를 가리키므로 복수형 their가 적절.

해석 초기 발달 단계의 읽고 쓰는 능력에 대한 관점은 아동이 자신들의 음성 언어를 초기의 읽고 쓰는 언어 능력 발달을 위한 밑거름으로 사용한다는 충분한 증거를 제공하였다. 비록 문자 언어가 음성 언어의 확장이긴 하지만, 두 언어 사이에는 많은 중요한 차이점들이 있다. 음성 언어와 문자 언어의 한 가지 차이점은 관습에 있다. 일부 언어 학습자들에게는 예상되는 독자 또는 실제 독자를 위한 글쓰기에서, 문장과 단락이 서로 연결되도록 하고, 단어의 철자를 적고, 생각을 구성하게 하는 명시적 교수법이 필요하다. 글쓰기와는 달리, 음성 언어는 청자가 (의미를) 명확히 하기 위해 질문을 하고 언어적, 비언어적 맥락 단서를 모두 적용할 더 많은 기회를 제공한다. 그러나 글쓴이는 예상 독자에게 주는 부연 설명의 도움 없이도, 정밀하고 정확한 언어를 사용하여 자기 생각을 분명하게 표현하는 것을 배워야 한다. 이것이 많은 제2언어 글쓴이들이 영어로 글을 쓰는 초기 단계에 겪는 주요한 난관이다.

어휘 **emergent** 초기 발달 단계의, 신생의 ***cf.* emergence** 출현, 발생 **emerge** 모습을 드러내다, 나타나다 **literacy** 글을 읽고 쓸 줄 아는 능력 **perspective** 관점; 전망; 원근법 **ample** 충분한, 풍부한 **oral** 구두[구어]의 **extension** 확장; (기간의) 연장; 구내전화 **convention** 관습, 관례; (대규모) 대회 **explicit** 명시적인, 명백한 (↔ **implicit** 암시된, 내포된) **clarification** (액체 등을) 깨끗하게 함; 명확한 설명 **verbal** 언어적 (↔ **nonverbal** 비언어적) **elaboration** 자세한 설명; 공들임 **prospective** 잠재적인; 장래의, 유망한

구문 07~11행 Some language learners require explicit instruction **to make** sentences and paragraphs connect to each other, **to spell** words, **and** **to organize** ideas in writing for an imagined or a real audience.
→ to make ~, to spell ~, to organize ~는 and로 연결되어 병렬구조를 이룬다.

185 ⑤

해설 (A) <find+O+OC>의 구조라면 보어인 형용사가 와야 하지만 O인 prey를 보충 설명하는 것이 아니라 동사 find를 수식하고 있으므로 부사 more easily가 와야 한다.
(B) 문장의 주어는 Evidence로 단수이므로 단수동사 was가 와야 한다. 동사 바로 앞에 쓰인 복수명사 chicks는 주어 Evidence를 수식하는 전명구 for the development ~ in chicks에 속한 명사이다.
(C) 동사 suggests 뒤의 that절이 '~해야 한다'라는 당위성을 담고 있는 게 아니라 사실을 전달하는 내용이므로 시제에 맞는 동사 형태가 와야 한다. 여기서는 병아리들이 먹이를 빨리 찾아내어 먹기 전에 적합한 탐색 이미지를 형성한 것이므로 대과거(had p.p.)를 쓰는 것이 적절하다.

해석 Krebs와 Davies는 포식동물들이 먹이를 잡을 가능성을 높일 수 있는 방법들을 발견했다. 포식동물들은 향상된 시력을 통해 (먹이를) 찾는 더 효과적인 방법을 발달시킬 수 있다. 아니면 그 대신에 그들은 탐색 이미지를 형성하여 더 쉽게 먹이를 찾을지도 모르는데, 이는 먹이의 시각적 특징에 대해 알게 되는 것을 포함한다. 탐색 이미지를 형성하는 것은 또한 향상된 주의집중 과정과도 연관될 수도 있다. 병아리에게 있어서 탐색 이미지 발달에 대한 증거가 Dawkins에 의해 보고되었다. 먹이는 색깔이 있는 쌀 알갱이들이 그와 같은 색깔의 배경 또는 매우 다른 색깔 중 하나의 배경 위에 있는 것으로 구성되었다. 병아리들은 처음에 먹이가 배경과 같은 색깔이었을 때 그것을 찾아내는 것을 어려워했다. 그러나 몇 분 후, 그것들은 먹이를 보다 빨리 찾아내기 시작했는데, 이는 병아리들이 적합한 탐색 이미지를 형성했음을 시사한다.

어휘 **identify** 발견하다, ~을 찾다; ~을 확인하다 **predator** 포식자, 포식동물 **odds** ((복수형)) 가능성 **alternatively** 그 대신에, 그렇지 않으면 **attentional process** 주의집중 과정 **evidence** 증거, 흔적 **chick** 병아리; 새끼 새 **consist of** ~으로 이루어지다, 구성되다 **initially** 처음에 **detect** ~을 발견하다, 탐지하다

구문 13~15행 The chicks initially found **it** hard **to detect the prey** when it(=the prey) was **the same** color **as** the background.
→ 주절의 it은 가목적어이고 to detect the prey가 진목적어이다. when절의 it은 the prey를 지칭한다. <the same A as B>는 'B와 같은 A'라는 뜻이다.

186 ①

해설 (A) 문장의 동사가 없으므로 동사 move로 시작하는 명령문이 되는 것이 적절.
(B) '…와 같은 수[양]의 ~'라는 의미의 <as many[much]+명사+as ...> 구문이 약간 변형된 형태이다. 복수명사인 sheets의 '수'를 말하는 것이므로 many가 적절.
(C) '페인트가 빗나가 튀는 것을 막기 위해'라는 문맥. not to trip over it과 and로 병렬 연결되는 to keep out이 적절하다.

해석 방에 페인트를 칠하는 것은 특히 날씨가 바뀔 때 종종 상쾌한 경험이 된다. 당신의 방에 가구가 있다면, (페인트를 칠하기 위해) 준비하기 위한 예비 단계는 가구를 보호하는 것이다. 먼저 모든 가구를 벽에서 방의 중앙부로 옮기고 가능한 한 적은 바닥 공간을 쓰기 위해 가능한 곳 어디에든 쌓아 올린다. 만약 카펫이 고정되어 있지 않다면, 각각의 모서리에서 방 중앙으로 그것을 둘둘 말아라. 다음 단계는 가구를 덮개로 덮는 것이다. 값싸고 가벼우며 한 번 쓰고 버릴 수 있는 비닐이 제일 좋다. 가구와 카펫을 보호하기 위해 9×12피트짜리 시트를 당신이 필요한 만큼 사용하라. (비닐에) 걸려 넘어지지 않고 페인트가 튀는 것을 막기 위해 보호 테이프를 이용하여 헐렁한 비닐을 단단히 고정하라.

어휘 **furnishings** 가구, 비품 **preliminary** 예비의, 준비의 **stack** ~을 쌓아 올리다 **disposable** 사용 후 버릴 수 있는, 일회용의 **trip over** ~에 걸려 넘어지다 **keep out** ~을 막다 **stray** 빗나간; 길 잃은 **spatter** (액체 등이) 튄 것

187 ⑤ | hinder → hinders

해설 ❺ 단수주어(Poor blood flow)이므로 단수동사 hinders가 되어야 적절. to the feet and hands는 주어를 수식하는 어구.

① <It takes+A(시간이나 돈)+to부정사>는 '~하는 데 A가 들다'란 뜻. to부정사의 의미상 주어로 <for+목적격>이 알맞게 쓰였다.
② those를 수식하는 분사 자리. 능동관계이므로 현재분사 imagining이 적절.
③ 비교급 longer를 꾸며주는 부사.
④ 앞의 the body를 받는 대명사로 단수 형태가 적절.

해석 양의 숫자를 세는 것이 잠이 드는 데 도움이 되지 않는다는 것을 과학자들이 알아내는 데에는 오랜 시간이 걸렸다. 이를 증명해보기 위해, 옥스퍼드 대학의 연구원들은 50명의 불면증 환자들에게 며칠 밤에 걸쳐 여러 다른 집중 방법을 시도해 보게 하였다. 평균적으로, 휴가를 보내는 것 같이 편안한 장면을 상상하는 사람들은 20분 더 일찍 잠이 들었고, 양의 숫자를 세거나 자기가 하고 싶은 대로 하도록 내버려 두었던 사람들은 정상적인 경우보다 조금 더 오래 걸렸다. 이후, 수면용 양말을 신거나 뜨거운 물병을 끌어안는 것이 수면제보다 더 도움이 될 수 있다고 제안하는 스위스의 연구 결과가 나왔다. 짐작건대, 잠이 들기 시작하면 (우리) 몸은 몸의 중심부에서 손과 발로 열을 재분배한다. 이와 동시에, 몸은 멜라토닌과 같은 호르몬을 분비한다. 발과 손으로 가는 혈액의 흐름이 약해지게 되면 이런 과정은 방해를 받는다. 손가락과 발가락을 따뜻하게 하는 것은 그 과정이 잘 진행되도록 도와줄 것이다.

어휘 **figure out** ~을 알아내다, 이해하다 **insomniac** 불면증 환자 **a series of** 연속의, 일련의 **on average** 평균적으로, 대체로 **leave A to A's own devices** A를 자기 생각대로 하도록 내버려 두다 **sleeping pill** 수면제 **apparently** 보기에, ~같은; 명백히 **drift off** 잠이 들기 시작하다, 차츰 잠이 들다 **redistribute** ~을 재분배하다 **core** 중심부; 핵심 **release** ~을 배출하다, 방출하다 **hinder** ~을 방해하다 **mechanism** (정해진) 과정, 방법(= **process**); 메커니즘, 기계론

188 ①

해설 (A) 분사구문을 이끄는 분사 자리인데 주어 Early containers와 leave의 관계는 능동이므로 현재분사 leaving이 알맞다.
(B) made 이하는 <make+목적어+목적격보어>의 구조로, 이때 긴 목적어 the great ~ and Mesoamerica와 목적격보어가 도치되었다. 따라서 목적격보어 자리에는 형용사 possible이 와야 적절하다.
(C) 전치사 of의 목적어 역할을 하는 명사절을 이끌며 뒤에 불완전한 절이 이어지는 의문사 what이 적절하다. whether는 접속사로서 뒤에 완전한 절을 이끈다.

해석 항아리, 가방, 바구니는, 그리고 결국에는 병까지 초기 보존 기술의 핵심이었다. 이 영역에서의 혁신은 수천 년에 걸친 길고도 시간이 오래 걸리는 과정이었고 쉽게 그것의 단서 전부를 드러내지 않는 과정이었다. 초기의 용기들은 의심의 여지 없이 잎사귀나 풀잎이나 가죽과 같은 썩기 쉬운 재료로 만들어져 고고학적 기록에 거의 또는 전혀 흔적을 남기지 않았다. 이후의 도자기와 유리 기술은 자연의 산물을 보존하는 인간의 능력을 급격하게 확장했고 중국, 인도, 수메르 그리고 중앙아메리카의 위대한 고대 문명을 가능하게 했다. 이런 일들이 일어나는 동안의 변화는 산업 혁명 이후에, 특히 1900년 무렵의 세대에서 가속화되었다. 산업화된 컨테이너에 의한 화물 수송은 세계 전역에 음식을 유통시키는 것을 가능하게 했는데, 깡통, 판지 상자, 그리고 병에 든 음료가 없는 세상에서 산다는 것이 어떤 것일지 생각만 해보라.

어휘 **preservation** 보존, 보호 **realm** 영역, 범위 **drawn-out** 시간이 오래 걸리는 **extend** 지속되다 **millennium** 천 년 (***pl.*** **millennia**) **give up** (정보 등을) 드러내다; 포기하다 **perishable** 잘 썩는[상하는] **archaeological** 고고학의 **ceramic** 도자기 **radically** 급진적으로 **accelerate** 가속하다, 속도를 높이다 **distribute** (상품을) 유통시키다 **tin can** 깡통 **cardboard carton** 판지 상자

구문 15~19행 Industrial containerization made **it** possible **to distribute** foods throughout the globe; think only of what it would be like **to live** in a world without tin cans, cardboard cartons, and bottled drinks.
→ 앞에 나온 it은 made의 가목적어이고 to distribute ~ the globe가 진목적어이다. 뒤에 나온 it은 가주어이고 to live 이하가 진주어이다.

189 ③ | close → closely

해설 ❸ 아주 세세한 것까지 '면밀히' 짝을 맞췄다는 얘기이므로 closely로 써야 한다. *cf.* close: (거리상으로) 가깝게; 가까운

① 과거(Several years ago)의 사실을 말하고 있으므로 과거시제가 적절.
compare A to[with] B: A와 B를 비교하다
② 대조되는 부분(nine poets who committed suicide)의 시제(일반동사의 과거시제)에 맞게 대동사 did not을 쓴 것이 적절.
④ '자살한 시인들이 1인칭 단수형을 더 많이 사용한 것'이 연구 결과를 나타내는 시점(showed, were)보다 더 이전의 일이므로 완료형 부정사가 적절.
⑤ 동사(increased)를 꾸며주는 수식어로 부사(commonly)가 쓰인 경우.

해석 수년 전, 문자 데이터 분석 소프트웨어를 이용하여 연구자들은 자살한 9명의 시인이 쓴 156개의 시와 자살하지 않은 9명의 시인이 쓴 135개의 시를 비교했다. 두 그룹의 시인들은 국적, 교육 수준, 활동 시기, 성별에서 가능한 한 가깝게 맞춰졌다. 2001년 <the Journal of Psychosomatic Medicine>에 발표된 그 연구는 자살한 시인이 자살하지 않은 시인보다 시에서 I, me, my 같은 1인칭 단수 대명사를 더 사용하는 경향이 있었고 we, us, our 같은 1인칭 복수 대명사를 덜 사용했다는 것을 보여주었다. 그들은 또한 시간이 흐름에 따라, 자살한 시인은 '말하다, 나누다, 듣다' 같은 용어를 덜 사용한 반면 자살하지 않은 시인은 이런 단어를 점점 더 많이 사용했다는 것도 알아냈다.

어휘 **commit suicide** 자살하다 ***cf.*** **suicidal** 자살하고 싶어 하는; 자살의 **match** ~와 맞추다; ~와 어울리다 **nationality** 국적 **era** 시기, 시대 **singular** 단수의 **plural** 복수의

190 ③ | that → what

해설 ❸ 동명사 identifying의 목적어 역할을 하는 명사절을 이끄는 자리로, 명사절 내에 do의 목적어가 빠져있는 불완전한 구조이므로 선행사를 포함한 관계대명사 what으로 써야 한다. 앞의 so를 보고 <so ~ that ...> 구문으로 생각하면 문맥상 말이 되지 않고 문법적으로도 옳지 않다.

① 동명사 helping의 목적격보어 자리로 원형부정사 improve가 적절히 쓰였고, to improve도 가능하다.
② '~하는 것을 의미하다'는 뜻의 동사 means의 목적어구를 이끄는 동명사가 적절하

게 쓰였다.
④ 주어는 관계절 who ~ warranted의 수식을 받는 Coaches이며 문장의 동사 자리이므로 assume이 적절히 쓰였다.
⑤ 주절 뒤에 이어지는 분사구문으로, 주절의 주어와 동일한 의미상 주어 this가 선수들(them)에게 의문을 품게 한다는 문맥이므로 능동 관계. 따라서 현재분사가 적절하게 쓰였다.

해석 때때로 코치들은 선수들의 향상을 돕는 데 너무 주력해서 좋은 성과를 위한 노력을 당연하게 여긴다. 강화 반응을 하지 않는 것은 선수의 노력, 기량의 발휘, 그리고 성과 향상을 인정하는 데 실패한 것을 의미한다. 향상시키기 위해 선수들이 해야 할 필요가 있는 것을 파악하는 데 너무 주력해서 긍정적인 것들을 언급하는 데 실패한 적이 있는가? 그것은 빠지기 쉬운 함정이다. 정당할 때 강화 반응을 제공하는 데 실패한 코치들은 선수들이 자신의 노력이 주목받고 인정받는 것을 알고 있다고 추정한다. 실제로는 엄청난 노력과 경기력을 인정하는 데 실패할 때, 이것은 선수들에게 부정적인 메시지를 전달해서 그들이 자신의 노력과 향상이 인정받고 소중히 여겨지는지에 의문을 품게 한다.

어휘 **take A for granted** A를 당연시하다 **reinforcement** 강화 **acknowledge** 인정하다 **execution** 발휘, 실행 **communicate** 전달하다 **value** 소중하게 여기다

구문 14~15행 ~, **leaving** them **to question** whether their effort and improvement are recognized and valued.
→ to question 이하가 leaving의 목적보어로 쓰였다.

191 ⑤

해설 (A) convince는 '~을 납득시키다'라는 뜻의 타동사이다. 이 문장의 주어인 perspective가 다른 사람들을 납득시키는 것이므로 convincing이 되어야 한다.
(B) giving이 되면 becoming과 병렬구조를 이루어 from의 목적어가 되는데 '당신이 느끼는 방식을 더 통제하는 것을 못 하게 한다'는 뜻이 되어 문맥에 맞지 않게 된다. prevents와 병렬구조를 이루는 gives가 되어야 적절하다.
(C) whether 이하 절이 문장 요소를 갖춘 완전한 절이므로 what은 들어갈 수가 없다.

해석 사물을 바라보는 방식이 언제나 다양하다는 것이 사실이라면 어려운 점은 선택할 다른 관점을 찾는 것이다. 특히 흥분한 상태에서는, 자신의 관점이 반드시 가장 납득이 가게 느껴지게 될 것이다. 당신의 관점에서 한 걸음 물러나 생각하고, 사실을 객관적으로 보고 스스로에게 관점의 선택권을 주도록 노력하라. 자신의 관점을 바꿀 때, 당신은 자기 기분 역시 바뀐다는 것을 알게 될 것이다. 새롭고 더 포괄적인 관점을 찾는 것은 당신이 한쪽으로 치우친 관점에 갇히는 것을 막고 당신이 느끼는 방식을 더 통제하게 해준다. 당신이 그것을 통해 세상을 보는 안경은 너무나 익숙하여 그것을 쓰고 있다는 것을 거의 알아채지 못한다. 그것을 벗고 다른 것을 시도해 봄으로써 당신은 어떤 것들이 초점이 맞지 않았는지와 왜곡되거나 채색된 렌즈를 통해서 보고 있던 것은 아닌지 깨달을 수 있다.

어휘 **perspective** 관점, 시각(= **point of view**, **view point**) **be bound to-v** 반드시 ~하다, ~하게 되다 **convince** ~을 납득시키다, 깨닫게 하다 **step back** 한 걸음 물러나 생각하다 **trap** ~을 가두다 **one-sided** 한쪽으로 치우친, 편파적인 **spectacle** 구경거리, 광경; ((복수형)) 안경 **be out of focus** 초점이 맞지 않다 **distort** ~을 왜곡하다

구문 12~14행 *The spectacles* [**through which** you view life] are so familiar that you hardly notice that you are wearing them.
→ 주어는 The spectacles이고 동사는 are이다. which 앞에 through는 you view life through the spectacles의 through를 나타낸다.

192 ③ | Striving → Strive

해설 ③ 문장에서 to make 이하는 <사역동사(make)+목적어(the contents of your recall)+원형부정사(include)>의 구조이다. 문장 전체에 동사가 없으므로 준동사 Striving은 동사 Strive로 써야 한다.

① 접속사 that 다음의 what has been recalled가 주어인데 단수 취급하므로 동사 is를 잘 사용했다.
② that 이하는 the likelihood의 동격절이다.
④ 동사 express를 수식하는 자리이므로 부사 prudently가 맞게 쓰였다.
⑤ what you have recalled는 전치사 in의 목적어가 되는 명사절이다.

해석 수업 중에 질문에 대답을 하거나 구술시험을 볼 때, 신뢰할 수 있는 방식으로 자신을 표현하라. 어떤 사람이 어떤 사회적인 상황에서 어떤 것을 성공적으로 기억해 내었을 때조차도, 그 사람은 기억해 낸 것이 옳다고 다른 사람들을 확신시켜야 하는 문제를 여전히 가지고 있을지도 모른다. 다른 사람들이 여러분이 기억한 것을 믿을 가능성을 높일 수 있는 다섯 가지 방법이 있다. 적절한 정도의 자신감을 가지고 여러분이 기억한 것을 표현하라. 여러분이 기억한 것의 내용이 가장 필수적인 세부 사항들을 포함하도록 노력하라. 알고 있다고 말하는 것의 정확성에 대해 여러분이 가진 자신감의 수준을 솔직하게 말하라. 여러분의 확신이나 의심을 신중하게 표현하라. 여러분이 기억한 것에 대한 자신감을 과장하는 말이나 축소하는 말을 피하라. 그 대신에, 수줍어하지는 말라. 여러분이 알고 있는 것을 확신한다면 자세를 바로 하고 자신감 있게 말하라.

어휘 **oral** 구두의 **credible** 믿을 수 있는 **convince** 확신시키다 **likelihood** 가능성 **recall** 기억하다 **appropriate** 적절한 **strive** 노력하다 **prudently** 신중하게 **overstatement** 과장한 말, 허풍 **understatement** 절제된 표현 **alternatively** 그 대신에 **sit up** 자세를 바로 하다

구문 11~12행 Claim an honest level of confidence in the accuracy *of* **what (you say) you know**.
→ what you say you know 부분은 of의 목적어이며, you say는 삽입구문이다.

193 ⑤ | whom → whose

해설 ❺ 선행사 a century-old steam locomotive와 engineers가 소유의 관계이므로 소유격 관계대명사 whose가 적절.

① no desire를 수식하는 to do와 to take가 anything but으로 연결된 구조. 반복되는 to는 생략할 수 있다. <anything but+동사원형>은 '~ 이외에는 무엇이든'이란 뜻.
② that은 early를 수식하는 지시부사로 '그렇게'란 뜻.
③ the time ~ Dandenong Ranges를 강조하는 <it was ~ that> 강조구문.
④ 앞의 명사구 densely forested hills를 수식하는 자리로 locate(~을 위치시키다)가 과거분사로 알맞게 쓰였다.

해석 새벽에 눈을 뜨자마자, 편히 쉬는 것 외에는 어떤 것도 할 마음이 들지 않던 날이었다. 호주, 멜버른에서의 세 번째 날이었다. 그날의 일정이었던 Dandenong Ranges 국립공원으로의 여행은 그렇게 이른 시간에는 그다지 매력적이지 않았다. 하지만, 아주 흥미롭게도 비행기를 타고 집으로 돌아오는 날, 내 기억 속에 계속 맴돌던 것이 바로 Dandenong Ranges에서 보냈던 시간이었다. Dandenong Ranges는 멜버른 동쪽에 위치한 빽빽하게 숲이 우거진 언덕으로, 하늘 높이 자란 유칼립투스 나무가 장엄한 분위기를 만들어내는 곳이다. 이 지역은 또한 길고 하얀 턱수염이 난 기관사들이 전 세계에서 온 관광객들을 실어 나르는 100년 된 증기 기관차 Puffing Billy의 고향이기도 하다.

어휘 **anything but** ~ 이외에는 무엇이든 **appeal** 매력; 마음에 들다 **hover** 공중을 맴돌다 **densely** 빽빽하게 **forested** 숲이 우거진, 나무로 뒤덮인 **eucalyptus** 유칼립투스, 유칼리나무 **majestic** 장엄한 **atmosphere** 분위기 **steam** (수)증기 **locomotive** 기관차 **transport** ~을 수송[운송]하다

구문 01~02행 It was *a day* [**when**, ***upon opening*** my eyes at dawn, I had *no desire* (**to do** anything but (*to*) take a good rest).
→ when이 이끄는 관계부사절이 a day를 수식하고 있다. <upon[on]+-ing>는 '~하자마자'란 뜻. to부정사구는 앞의 no desire를 수식하는 형용사적 용법.

09~11행 The Dandenong Ranges are *densely forested* ***hills*** (**located** to the east of Melbourne), **where** sky-high eucalyptus trees create a majestic atmosphere.
→ 과거분사구는 앞의 densely forested hills를 수식하며 where가 이끄는 계속적 용법의 관계부사절은 hills를 부연 설명하고 있다.

194 ③ | to pose → posing

해설 ❸ 전치사 by의 목적어 referring ~ their speeches와 or로 병렬 구조로 연결된 문장이므로 동명사 posing이 적절하다.

They(S) try(V) to show that they are 'plain folks'(O) / by **referring** to hard times ~ or **posing** for photographs // while (*they are*) **wearing** ~ and **mingling** with ~.

① 생략된 주어가 these candidates이고 이들이 '당선되는' 것이므로 과거분사 elected가 적절.
② presenting의 의미상 주어 some candidates와 목적어가 같으므로 재귀대명사가 적절.
④ '목적'을 나타내는 so that(~하기 위하여, ~하도록)이 적절히 쓰였음.
⑤ 명사 a family business를 수식하고 있으며, 가족 기업이 '운영되는' 대상이므로 과거분사는 적절.

해석 많은 유권자가 부자이거나 교육을 잘 받은 정치 후보자를 신뢰하지 않는다. 그들은 만약 이런 후보들이 당선되면 자신들과 같은 평범한 노동자들의 문제를 이해할 수 없을 거라고 생각한다. 따라서 몇몇 후보들은 '보통 사람' 기법을 사용하여 자신들을 평범한 일반 시민으로 소개한다. 그들은 연설에서 그들의 삶의 어려웠던 시절을 언급하거나 안전모를 쓰고 일반인들과 어울려 사진을 찍기 위해 자세를 취함으로써 자신이 '보통 사람'임을 보여주려고 한다. 그들은 심지어 너무 교양 있는 것처럼 들리지 않으려고 연설을 바꾸기도 한다. 이와 비슷하게, 마치 평범한 사람들에 의해 운영되는 가족 기업인 것처럼, 거대 기업의 회장이 회사 광고에 출연할 수도 있다.

어휘 **distrust** ~을 믿지 않다 **well-educated** 잘 교육된, 교양 있는 **plain** 평범한; 명백한 **folk** 사람들 **mingle with** ~와 어울리다; ~와 섞이다

195 ③

해설 (A) '~하게 되다'의 의미일 때 grow는 뒤에 형용사 보어가 필요하므로 curious가 어법상 적절하다.
(B) enable은 목적어를 설명해주는 목적격보어로 to부정사를 취하는 동사이므로 to raise가 어법상 적절하다.
(C) 앞 문장에 있는 일반동사 collected와 added를 대신하고 있으므로 did가 어법상 적절하다.

해석 1990년에 연구원들이 가난한 시골 마을의 아동 영양실조와 맞서 싸우기 위한 프로그램을 실시하기 위해 베트남으로 이동했다. 그 문제의 범위를 이해하기 위해 조사를 하는 동안, 그들은 다른 모든 가정만큼 가난한 가정 출신임에도 불구하고 완벽하게 건강한 소수의 아동, 즉 긍정적 일탈자에 관해 호기심이 생겼다. 이 가정들은 무엇을 다르게 하고 있었는가? 만약 그들이 물질적으로 가장 궁핍한 부모조차도 건강한 아이들을 기를 수 있도록 하는 행동을 발견할 수 있다면, 그 영향은 엄청날 것이었다. 그들은 모든 긍정적 일탈자의 부모가 어떤 이유 때문인지 논에 있는 게 껍데기와 새우 껍질의 작은 조각을 모아서 고구마 윗부분의 녹색 잎과 함께 그것들을 아이들의 식단에 첨가했다는 것을 발견했다. 다른 가정 중 어느 곳도 그렇게 하지 않았다. 비록 원한다면 누구에게나 무료이고 누구나 이용 가능했지만, 이 두 가지 재료들은 아이들에게 위험하지는 않지만 대개 부적절한 것으로 간주되었고, 그래서 일반적으로 그들의 식단에서 제외되었던 것이다.

어휘 **set up** ~을 실시하다 **malnutrition** 영양실조 **conduct** (업무 따위를) 실시하다 **scope** 범위, 영역 **deprived** 궁핍한 **tremendous** 엄청난, 굉장한, 대단한 **inappropriate** 부적절한, 부적합한 **exclude** 제외[배제]하다

구문 18~20행 Both these ingredients, though (*they were*) free and available to anyone for the taking, / **were** commonly considered ~.
→ 주어는 Both these ingredients이고 동사는 were이며, 중간에 though free ~ taking이 삽입되어 있다. though절은 원래 though they were free and available ~이지만 they were가 생략되어 있다.

196 ① | yourself → you

해설 ❶ pretend하는 주체는 them이지 you가 아니므로 재귀대명사를 쓸 자리가 아니다. 목적어와 목적격보어는 의미상 <주어-동사> 관계.

② Using ~은 분사구문으로, Family Profile이 무엇인지 부연 설명하는 부분(a pilot ~ by Uber,) 뒤에 본 문장으로 이어지고 있다.
③ 동사 pay를 수식하는 수식어로 부사가 맞게 쓰였다.
④ if절이 invite ~, give ~, and then delete ~로 이어지는 병렬구조로, 현재시제의 동사가 맞게 쓰였다.
⑤ that절의 주어부이므로 동명사 allowing이 맞게 쓰였다.

해석 만약 당신이 우버로 다른 사람의 승차에 대해 돈을 지불하고 싶으면 친구의 위치를 넣고 친구가 당신인 체하는 것과 같이 교묘한 수를 써야 하는데, 그건 뭔가 불편하다. 곧 더 나은 방법이 생길 것이다. 우버가 만든 시범 프로그램인 '가족 프로필'을 이용하여 당신이 아는 다른 우버 이용자 누구든 당신의 '가족'에 가입하라는 이메일 초대를 받아들이면 돈을 안 내고 승차하게 할 수 있다. 이 특징은 다른 이용자를 위해 정기적으로 돈을 지불하고자 하는 사람을 위해 만들어진 것이긴 하지만, 누군가를 '가족 프로필'에 초대하고 승차하게 한 뒤 그 이름을 제거하면 이 새로 추가된 특징을 일회용 선물로 사용할 수 있다. 하지만 누군가를 '가족'에 들게 허용한다는 것은 당신이 요금을 내고 어디 어디를 타고 다니는지를 그들이 볼 수 있다는 것 또한 의미한다는 것을 명심하라.

어휘 **ride** 승차 **clever** 영리한, 교묘한 **trick** 속임수, 요령 **location** 위치 **pretend to** ~인 척하다 **pilot program** 견본 프로그램(개편에 앞서 새로운 아이디어를 갖고 만든 시험용 프로그램) **via** ~을 통해서, ~을 경유하여 **feature** 특징, 특색 **profile** (얼굴의) 옆모습, (개인의) 약력 **keep in mind** 명심하다

구문 05~09행 Using "Family Profile," [*a pilot program* (created by Uber)], you can give *any other Uber user* [(*whom*) you know] a free ride, **as long as** they accept *your invitation* (via email) **to join** your "Family."
(동격: "Family Profile" = a pilot program / IO: any other Uber user [(whom) you know] / DO: a free ride / to join → your invitation)

→ as long as는 '~하는 한'으로 일종의 조건을 나타낸다. to join이 앞의 명사구 your invitation을 수식하고 있는 구조.

197 ②

해설 (A) know의 목적어로 '얼마나 힘든지'라는 의미의 명사절을 이끄는 접속사가 필요하므로 how가 적절. however는 '아무리 ~일지라도'라는 의미로 부사절을 이끎.
(B) 명사 only companies를 선행사로 하면서 뒤에 오는 절의 주어가 되는 주격 관계대명사 which가 적절.
(C) inform의 직접목적어가 되는 명사절을 이끌면서, 뒤에 완전한 형태의 절이 오는 접속사 that이 적절.

해석 여러분은 현재의 시장 상황이 얼마나 힘든지와 우리가 최근 어려운 상황을 겪었음을 알고 있을 것입니다. 이제 적자생존의 문제가 되었으니 우리는 우리 자신을 적응시켜야 합니다. 우리의 유일한 선택은 비용을 삭감하는 것이며, 그것은 곧 인력을 감축하는 것을 의미합니다. 이 같은 일시 해고로 우리 노동자 대부분을 지킬 수 있길 희망합니다. 오늘날의 기업 경영 풍토에서는 고용 비용을 줄이기 위해 신속한 조치를 취할 준비가 되어 있는 기업만이 살아남을 것입니다. 도산이나 파산만이 유일한 다른 선택입니다. 우리는 제안된 일자리 축소가 경영진, 사무직원, 그리고 공장 노동자를 포함한 모두에게 똑같이 적용될 것임을 알려 드립니다.

어휘 **slim down** (직원을) 줄이다 **lay-off** 일시 해고 **bankruptcy** 파산

198 ① | because → because of

해설 ❶ 뒤에 명사구 some combination ~ expectations를 이끌므로 because of 형태가 되어야 한다. 문장 전체의 구조는 '가정하다, 가령[만약] …이라고 하다'를 의미하는 suppose (that)이 두 개의 절(one devotes ~ and one ends up ~)을 이끌고 있으며, 그 두 개의 절 사이에 because of가 이끄는 부사구가 위치하고 있다.

Suppose ┌ **one devotes** ~,
  [and] then, ***because of*** ┌ some combination ~,
    missed opportunities,
    [and]
    └ high expectations,
  └ **one ends up** ~.

② 주어가 The questions로서 복수형이므로 복수동사인 are가 적절하다.
③ <It seems ~>에서 It이 가주어이고 to blame 이하는 진주어이다.
④ 문장의 주어가 되면서 뒤에 나오는 the world를 목적어로 취할 수 있는 동명사 blaming이 적절히 쓰였다.
⑤ 주어(the choice set), 동사(grows)가 포함된 절을 이끌 수 있는 접속사이면서 '~함에 따라'라는 의미를 나타낼 수 있는 as가 잘 쓰였다.

해석 어떤 사람이 어떤 결정을 하는 데 많은 시간과 에너지를 쏟아붓고 나서, 후회, 놓친 기회, 그리고 높은 기대 등이 결합되어 결국 그 결과에 실망한다고 하자. 이 사람이 할 가능성이 있는 질문은, "왜지?" 또는 "뭐가 잘못된 걸까?" 또는 "누구의 잘못일까?" 등이다. 그러면 이 질문들에 대한 그럴듯한 답은 무엇일까? 선택 집합이 작을 때는 실망스러운 결과에 대해서 세상을 탓하는 것이 자연스럽고 간단해 보인다. "세 가지 스타일의 청바지밖에 없었어. 내가 뭘 할 수 있었겠어? 내가 할 수 있는 최선을 다했어." 하지만, 선택 집합이 클 때는, 세상을 탓하는 것이 훨씬 덜 그럴싸한 선택이다. "이용 가능한 선택 사항이 아주 많아서 이룰 수 있는 성공도 거기 존재했었지. 실망스러운 결과에 대해 내가 탓해야 하는 사람은 나 자신뿐이야." 다시 말해, 선택 집합이 커짐에 따라 실망스러운 결과에 대해 자기 비난을 할 가능성이 더 커진다.

어휘 **devote ~ to v-ing** ~을 v하는 데 바치다[쏟다] **combination** 조합 **end up** ~로 끝나다 **likely** 그럴듯한 **straightforward** 간단한 **blame** 비난하다 **self-blame** 자기 비난

구문 01~05행 *Suppose* (*that*) [one **devotes** a great deal of time and energy **to making** a decision], [and] then, because of some combination of regret, missed opportunities, and high expectations, [one **ends up** (*being*) ***disappointed*** with the results].
→ Suppose 다음에는 접속사 that이 생략되어 있고, 두 [ ] 부분은 suppose의 목적어로서 병렬구조를 이룬다. <devote ~ to v-ing>는 '~을 v하는 데 바치다[쏟다]'의 뜻이며, to 뒤에 v-ing형을 써야 한다는 것도 같이 알아두자.
→ <end up v-ing>는 '결국 ~하게 되다'의 뜻인데, 형용사 disappointed 앞에 being이 생략된 것으로 볼 수 있다.

199 ③ | were → was

해설 ❸ 문장의 주어는 관계사절(that ~ concerts)의 수식을 받는 어구 Much of the music이고 동사 자리이므로 주어에 맞게 단수동사 was로 고쳐야 한다.

① 고전 음악이라는 개념(the idea of classical music)이 '받아들여지는' 상황이므로 수동의 과거분사 accepted를 적절히 사용했다.
② 청중이 돈을 내는 상황이므로, 능동의 현재분사 paying은 적절하다.
④ The cantatas ~ Bach가 to부정사의 의미상의 주어로, '불리는' 것이므로 to부정사의 수동태(to be sung)로 적절하게 사용되었다.
⑤ 절에 동사가 없으므로 주어가 생략된 채 동사로 시작하는 명령문 구조. <명령문+and>는 '~해라. 그러면 ~할 것이다'의 의미이다.

해석 오늘날 널리 받아들여지는 고전 음악이라는 개념이 대략 300년 전까지는 존재하지 않았다는 것은 기억할 만한 가치가 있다. 본질적으로 즐겁고 의미 있는 것으로, 콘서트홀에서 돈을 지급한 청중에게 음악을 연주한다는 것은 18세기까지는 들어보지 못했고 19세기 전까지는 널리 자리 잡히지 않았다. 콘서트홀, 청중, 그리고 고전 음악의 '걸작'이라는 개념은 모두 사실상 18세기 중에 유럽의 도시에서 만들어졌다. 지금 대중 콘서트에서 연주되는 음악의 대부분은 그 목적을 위해 작곡되지 않았다. 예를 들어, J. S. Bach의 칸타타는 Bach가 성가대 합창 지휘자였던 라이프치히의 성 토마스 성당에서 예배 중에 부르기 위해 작곡되었다. 이 곡들은 주간 예배의 일부였으며, 신도들이 노래를 부르며 참여할 수 있도록 합창곡(찬송가)을 포함했다. 오늘날 이 작품들 중 하나를 현대의 콘서트홀에서 연주하는 동안 따라 부르면, 조용히 하라는 말을 듣게 될 것이다.

어휘 **be worth v-ing** v할 가치가 있다 **inherently** 본질적으로; 선천적으로 **masterpiece** 걸작, 명작 **effectively** 사실상; 효과적으로 **compose** 작곡하다 **religious service** 예배 **worship** 숭배, 예배

구문 01~03행 **It is worth remembering that** the idea of classical music widely accepted today did not exist until about 300 years ago.
→ It은 가주어이고 that 이하가 진주어이며, <be worth+v-ing>는 '~할 가치가 있다'의 의미이다.

03~07행 **Performing** music in concert halls to a paying audience, (as something inherently pleasurable and significant), was pretty much unheard of until the eighteenth century and not widely established until the nineteenth.
→ Performing이 이끄는 동명사구가 문장의 주어 역할을 하고 있고, ( ) 부분은 전명구로 앞에 있는 Performing ~ audience를 수식하고 있다.

200 ③ | links → linking

해설 ❸ 동사는 이미 나와 있고(offers), link 이하는 (the only simple) route를 꾸며주는 수식어구 자리이므로 형용사로 쓰이는 현재분사(linking)로 시작하는 것이 자연스럽다.

① your industry가 어려움에 face(직면하다, 맞부닥뜨리다)하는 것이므로 능동형으로 쓴 is facing은 자연스럽다.
② 선행사 a venture의 사업 상황을 설명하는 관계사절에서 명사 services와 함께 주어 역할을 할 수 있으면서 명사를 수식할 수 있는 소유격 관계대명사 whose가 맞게 쓰였다.
④ 앞 문장에서 언급된 경우가 두 가지이므로(if transoceanic shipping was to cease or if a new canal were built) Both로 받는 것이 자연스럽다.
⑤ all을 꾸며주는 부사로 이때 almost는 '거의'의 뜻이다.

해석 몇 해 전에 컨설턴트가 경영인들에게 "당신의 산업 분야가 생산 과잉 상태와 격한 가격 경쟁에 직면해 있나요?"라고 질문을 제기했다. 한 사람을 제외한 전원이 "그렇다."라고 말했다. 유일한 "아니요."는 유일무이한 조직인 파나마 운하의 관리자에게서 나왔다! 이 관리자는 그 제공하는 서비스가 선박회사에서 몹시 원하는, 그리고 대서양과 태평양을 간단히 연결하는 유일한 노선을 제공하는 업체를 책임지고 있는 운 좋은 사람이었다. 그 운하의 성공은 대양 횡단 운송이 중단되거나 새 운하가 건설되는 경우에만 위협받을 수 있을 것이다. 이 두 가능성 모두 극히 희박하다. 한 조직이 처한 환경이 안정적이고 예측 가능할 때 경영자는 그저 계획하고 실행할 수 있으며 그들의 계획이 시간이 지나면서 나타나는 변화에 의해 위태로워지지 않을 것임을 확신할 수 있다. 그러나 그 컨설턴트의 경험이 보여주듯이 변화가 거의 모든 조직의 전략에 영향을 미치기 때문에 오직 소수의 경영자만이 안정적이고 예측 가능한 상황을 누릴 수 있다.

어휘 **pose a question** 질문을 제기하다 **executive** 경영 간부 *cf.* **execute** 실행하다, 집행하다 **overcapacity** 과잉 생산 능력, 설비 과잉 **fierce** 사나운; (경쟁 등이) 격렬한 **venture** 벤처 사업, (사업상의) 모험 **desperately** 필사적으로 **route** (지나는) 길, 경로 **transoceanic** 대양 횡단의 **cease** 중지하다, 그만두다 **remote** (거리가) 먼; (가능성이) 희박한 **stable** 안정적인 **undermine** 훼손하다, 약화시키다

구문 05~09행 This manager was fortunate to be in charge of *a venture* [**whose** services(S) are desperately needed(V) by shipping companies] and [**that**(S′) offers(V′) the only simple *route* (**linking** the Atlantic **and** Pacific Oceans)].
→ 선행사 a venture 뒤에 관계대명사절이 두 개 나란히 온 구조.
<link A and B>: A와 B를 연결시키다

201 ③ | aware → aware of

해설 ❸ aware는 형용사로 be aware of A(A를 알고 있다, A를 의식하고 있다)의 형태로 쓰인다. The main thing이 A로, 전치사 The main thing to be aware of가 되어야 한다.

① 비교급(more timely) 앞에 강조하는 말 even(훨씬)이 맞게 쓰였다.
② 동사 (have affected)를 수식하는 어구로 부사가 맞게 쓰였다.
④ 강조하는 말 the very(바로 그)가 명사 앞에 맞게 쓰였다.
⑤ 종속절(no matter how great the shoe)에 이어 주절이 시작되는 부분으로, 주어가 동명사구(occasionally going barefoot)로 맞게 쓰였다.

해석 2천 년 전에 히포크라테스가 말한 것으로 전해지는 "걷는 것이 인간의 가장 좋은 약이다."라는 어구는 오늘날 훨씬 더 적절하다. 이 사실은 새 과학기술이 우리가 일하는 방식을 바꿔 놓았을 뿐만 아니라 그보다 더 심오하게는, 우리의 일상적인 활동 대부분에 드는 육체적인 노력을 줄임으로써 우리의 생활방식에 또한 영향을 끼친 산업화된 사회에서 특히 그러하다. 걷기가 필요하다는 것이 이제 납득이 되었다면 이제 걷기용 신발 좋은 것을 하나 살 때이다. 유념해야 할 중요한 한 가지는 딱딱한 아치 모양의 보강물이 있는 신발이나 부츠를 선택하지 않는 것이다. 그것들은 시간이 지나면서 발의 타고난 유연성을 저하시킬 수 있다. 이는 (발의) 아치형 부분을 복원력 있게 해주는 바로 그 근육이 신발의 전혀 굽혀지지 않는 성질 때문에 결국은 약화될 수 있기 때문이다. 또 한 가지

는, 신발이 아무리 좋은 것이더라도 가끔씩 맨발로 다니는 게 좋은데, 이유는 맨발인 채로 있는 것이 발의 원래의 유연성을 일부 복원시킬 수 있기 때문이다.

어휘 **allegedly** 전해진 바에 의하면 **millennia** 천 년 **timely** 적절한, 때맞춘 **profoundly** 깊이, 심오하게 **rigid** 신축성 없는, 딱딱한 ***cf.* rigidity** 경직 **arch** 아치, 아치형의 **support** 버팀대, 보강물 **degrade** 질을 저하시키다 **flexibility** 유연성 **resilient** 복원력이 있는, 탄력 있는 **owing to** ~ 때문에 **unyielding** 굽히지 않는, 단단한 **footwear** 신발류 **barefoot** 맨발(로, 의) **restore** 복원하다, 재건하다

구문 03~07행 This fact is particularly true in *industrialized societies* [**where** new technologies have **not only** changed the way [we work] **but**, (even more profoundly), have **also** affected our lifestyles (by reducing ~)].
→ 긴 관계부사구가 선행사 industrialized societies를 수식하고 있는 구조. 관계부사절에서는 new technologies가 어떤 변화를 가져왔는지 <not only A but also B>의 구조로 보여주고 있다. B가 더 강조된 형태.

202 ③ | attach → attaching

해설 ❸ By A and B(A하고 B함으로써)의 구조에서 A가 동명사구이므로 B도 같은 형태(attaching)를 취해야 한다.

① 공룡 Dreadnoughtus schrani가 존재했던 것은 추정해 보는 오늘날보다 이전이므로 to부정사가 완료형 to have been으로 쓰였다.
② 전치사 of 뒤이므로 be를 동명사 being으로 맞게 썼다.
④ 동명사 주어(Using a physical model like this)는 추상적인 개념이므로 단수 취급한다. 따라서 동사도 enables로 쓰였다.
⑤ 전치사 of의 목적어로 의문사 what으로 시작하는 명사절이 왔다.

해석 일군의 과학자들이 공룡 Dreadnoughtus schrani를 재탄생시키는 데 성공했는데, 이는 크기와 무게가 보잉 737편과 같았던 것으로 추정된다. 그것이 어떻게 걸었는지 알아내기 위해 과학자들은 다리뼈를 3D 스캔하였다. 그러나 먼저 그들은 7천 7백만 년 동안 바위의 일부로 있으면서 가해진 손상을 고치고, 그런 다음 그 뼈들을 다룰 수 있는 크기로 줄일 필요가 있었다. 연골을 3D 프린트한 후 이 모든 것을 한 데 붙여 모터를 닮으로써 그 물리적 모델을 소생시킨 다음, 컴퓨터 시뮬레이션을 이용했을 때 가능할 것보다 더 정확하게 (모델을) 분석했다. 이와 같은 물리적 모델을 사용하는 것이 (작업을) 빨리 진척시키는 걸 가능하게 한다. 인대와 근육, 힘줄을 다양하게 배치해 볼 수 있고, 작동이 안 되면 로봇을 다시 조립하고, 그러면 아마도 다음번에는 더 잘 작동하게 된다. 충분한 단계를 밟고 나면 결국 실제 공룡 다리의 모습으로 정말 그럴듯한 모형의 로봇 다리를 얻게 될 수도 있다.

어휘 **estimate** 추정하다 **manageable** 다루기 쉬운, 조작 가능한 **attach** 붙이다, 첨부하다 **bring A to life** A에 기운을 불어넣다, A를 소생시키다 **simulation** 모의실험, 시뮬레이션 **advance** 진척시키다 **arrangement** 배열, 배치

203 ⑤ | do → be

해설 ❺ 앞의 was forceful을 대신해야 하므로 do가 아닌 be로 고쳐야 한다.

① 동사 was talented and driven을 수식하는 부사 extremely가 적절하게 쓰였다.
② '너무 ~해서 …하다'라는 뜻의 <so ~ that ...> 구문이므로 that은 적절하다.
③ 주어 Bauer가 '(말을) 들었다'라는 문맥이므로 tell의 수동태 be told는 적절하다.
④ <be committed to (~에 헌신하다)> 표현에서 to는 전치사이므로 뒤에 동명사 형태의 helping이 쓰였다.

해석 Lillian Bauer는 극히 재능 있고 의욕이 넘쳤지만, 베풂이 지나쳐서 그로 인해 자신의 평판과 생산성을 빼앗겼다. "그녀는 어떤 것에도 결코 안 된다고 하지 않았어요." 그녀의 컨설팅 동료 하나가 설명했다. "그녀는 자신의 시간에 너무나 관대하고 너그러워서 만만한 사람이 되는 덫에 빠졌죠. 그것은 정말로 그녀의 파트너에 비해 그녀의 승진을 늦추었어요." 인사 고과에서, Bauer는 기대에 부합하지 못하고 있다는 말을 들었다. 그녀에게는 컨설팅 파트너에게 요구되는 확신에 찬 날카로움이 부족했다. 그녀는 자기 주변 사람들을 발전시키는 데 너무나 많은 시간을 썼고 고객들을 돕는 데 너무나 헌신적이어서 그들의 요청을 들어주느라 비상한 노력을 했다. Bauer는 "고객들이 가혹한 진실을 들을 필요가 있는, 혹은 고객들이 잘못된 방향으로 안건을 밀어붙여 왔던 중대한 상황에서 고객들을 밀어붙이는 데 그녀는 그럴 필요가 있다고 사람들이 느끼는 만큼 단호하지 못했다"고 알려졌다. Bauer에게, 베푸는 사람이 된다는 것은 경력을 제한하는 행동인 것으로 드러났다.

어휘 **driven** 의욕이 넘치는 **take ~ far** ~을 도를 지나치게 하다 **productivity** 생산성 **fall into the trap of v-ing** v하는 덫에 빠지다, v하는 오류를 범하다 **performance review** 인사 고과 **assertive** 단정적인, 확신에 찬 **edge** 날카로움, 격렬함 **be committed to v-ing** v에 헌신[전념]하다 **bend over backward** 비상한 노력을 하다 **forceful** 단호한, 강력한 **crucial** 중요한 **harsh** 거친, 가혹한 **agenda** 안건

구문 10~13행 She **spent** too much time **developing** those around her, and she was ***so*** committed to helping clients ***that*** she bent over backward to meet their requests.
→ <spend (시간) v-ing>는 '(시간)을 v하는 데 쓰다'의 뜻이다. <so … that ~> 구문은 '너무 …해서 ~하다'의 뜻이다.

15~17행 ~ in *those crucial situations* [**where** *clients needed to hear a harsh truth*, or *clients had been pushing an agenda in the wrong direction*].
→ [ ] 부분은 those crucial situations를 수식한다. clients needed ~ truth와 clients had been ~ direction이 or로 연결되어 병렬구조를 이룬다.

204 ③ | take → taking

해설 ❸ take를 쓸 경우 동사 are와 병렬을 이루어 '이러한 행동들이 세상의 사건과 사물에 관심을 둔다'라는 의미로 문맥상 어색한 문장이 되는데, 앞에 나온 전치사 by의 목적어인 동명사 moving과 병렬을 이루어 taking이 되면 '세상의 사건이나 사물에 관심을 두는 것'으로 These behaviors의 특징을 이루는 것을 나타내어 자연스러운 해석이 되므로 take를 taking으로 고쳐 쓰는 것이 적절하다.

① 관계대명사 that이 이끄는 관계사절 내에 동사 signal의 목적어절을 이끄는 접속사로 that의 쓰임이 알맞다.
② 사역동사 letting의 목적격보어로 원형부정사 know의 쓰임이 적절하다.
④ Beginning early in life 이후에 완전한 문장이 나오고, 접속사는 따로 없으므로 분사구문임을 알 수 있다. 분사구문의 의미상 주어가 문장의 주어와 같으므로 children과 능동 관계인 현재분사 beginning의 쓰임은 알맞다. begin은 자동사이므로 여기에서 수동 분사로 쓰일 수 없다.
⑤ <의문사+to부정사> 형태인 what to expect는 명사구로 동사 learn의 목적어 역할을 한다.

해석 아이들은 편안함이 필요하다고 부모에게 신호를 보내는 다양한 애착 행동을 보이는데, 예를 들어 아이는 울 수도 있고, 부모를 쫓아가거나 부모에게 매달릴 수 있다. 아이는 이 순간에 자신에게 관심과 보살핌이 필요하다는 사실을 부모에게 알리고 있는 것이다. 비슷하게, 아이는 자신이 주변의 세상을 탐색할 준비가 되었다는 신호를 보내는 다양한 탐구적 행동을 한다. 이런 행동은 부모에게서 떨어져서 세상의 사건과 사물에 관

심을 둔다는 특징이 있다. 민감한 보호자는 이런 신호를 읽고 매 순간 아이를 지원할 수 있다. 안정적인 애착이 그들 사이에 형성된다. 생애 초기부터 시작하여, 아이들은 관계가 어떻게 작용하는지 이해하기 위해 이런 경험을 활용한다. 관계의 원형 또는 기억이라는 내재적인 작동 모델이 형성되는데, 이것이 현재, 그리고 미래의 관계 둘 다에서 아이들에게 지침이 될 것이다. 아이들은 이 초기 경험의 결과로 다른 사람들로부터 무엇을 기대할 수 있는지를 알게 된다.

어휘 **a range of** 다양한 **attachment** 애착; 부착 **signal** 신호(를 보내다) **comfort** 편안함, 위안 **cling to** ~에 매달리다 **attention** 관심, 주목 **nurture** 보살핌, 양육 **exploratory** 탐구적인, 탐구하는 **investigate** 탐색하다, 조사하다 **caregiver** 보호자, 양육자 **on a moment-to-moment basis** 매 순간 **internal** 내재적인

구문 01~04행 Children have *a range of attachment behaviors* [that *signal* (to the parents) that they need comfort]—for example, a child might cry, follow or cling to the parent.

→ [ ] 부분은 관계사절로 선행사 a range of attachment behaviors를 수식한다. 밑줄 친 that절은 [ ] 내 동사 signal의 목적어 역할을 한다. 밑줄 친 that절 앞에 to the parents는 삽입구이다.

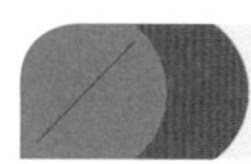

실전 모의고사 22회

205 ④ 206 ④ 207 ⑤ 208 ③ 209 ② 210 ② | 본문 116p

205 ④ | strangers → like strangers

해설 ④ '~하게[처럼] 느끼다'라는 의미의 feel은 뒤에 주로 형용사를 보어로 취하며, 명사가 올 때는 반드시 <feel like+명사> 형태가 되어야 한다.

① 주어가 One of ~ environments로 단수이므로 동사도 단수동사인 lies가 적절.
② 구동사 object to의 목적어로 명사 상당어구가 와야 하므로 명사절을 이끄는 관계대명사 what은 적절.
③ <부분 표현(percent)+of+명사>가 주어. 단수명사 the city's population이 쓰였으므로 단수동사 is는 적절.
⑤ 형용사 incensed 뒤에 두 개의 that절이 and로 병렬 연결된 구조. 감정을 나타내는 형용사 뒤에 that절이 오면 감정의 원인, 이유를 나타낸다.

해석 문화 제국주의를 자세히 살펴볼 수 있는 가장 좋은 환경 중의 하나는 서부 유럽이나 개발도상국들에 있는 것이 아니라 플로리다 주의 마이애미에 있다. 그 도시의 백인들과 흑인들은 소위 라틴 문화 제국주의라는 것에 자주 반기를 들고 있다. 그 도시는 인구의 40퍼센트 이상이 라틴계(스페인어를 사용하며, 주로 멕시코, 쿠바, 푸에르토리코, 중앙아메리카 또는 남아메리카 출신)이기 때문에 비 라틴계 사람들은 자신의 나라에서도 이방인 같은 느낌을 받는다. 그들은 마이애미의 스페인어 신문, TV 방송국, 라디오 방송국과 라틴계의 정치적인 우위를 지적한다. 몇몇 백인들과 흑인들은 그들이 두 언어를 배울 필요가 점점 더 많아지며 만약 그들이 배우지 않는다면 고용 기회가 심각하게 제한된다는 사실에 특히 분개한다고 말하고 있다.

어휘 **imperialism** 제국주의 **what they call** 소위, 이른바 **station** 방송국; 정거장 **predominance** 우위, 우세 **incensed** 격노한 **hamper** ~을 제한하다; ~을 방해하다

206 ④ | which → who

해설 ④ many smart people을 선행사로 하는 주격 관계대명사 자리이므로 who가 적절.

① 주절에 recommend와 같이 '제안, 주장' 등을 나타내는 동사가 있고 that절에 '~해야 한다'라는 당위성의 내용이 오면, that절에 '(should+)동사원형'을 쓴다. 이때 종속절을 이끄는 접속사 that은 생략할 수 있다.
② 선행사인 Erasmus라는 인물을 부가 설명하는 계속적 용법의 관계대명사 who가 적절.
③ <not because A but because B> 구문으로 'A 때문이 아니라 B 때문이다'의 의미.
⑤ 뒤에 SVO의 완전한 구조가 이어지므로 접속사 that이 적절. 여기서 that절은 동사 fear의 목적어이다.

해석 삶에서 의미심장한 변화를 만들 준비가 되어 있는 사람에게 읽어야 한다고 추천해 줄 만한 것으로 대니얼 골먼이 쓴 <감성 지능>이라는 제목의 책이 있다. 책 속에서 골먼은 16세기 인도주의자인, 로테르담의 에라스무스의 말을 인용하고 있는데, 그는 감정에 바탕을 둔 사고가 이성적인 사고보다 24배나 더 강력할 수 있다고 말하고 있다. 흔히 사람들은 지식이 부족해서가 아니라 실패하는 것이 두려워서 뭔가를 하는 데 성공적이지 못하다. 이를테면, 나는 학점이 우수한 많은 똑똑한 사람들을 알고 있는데 그들은 단지 실수를 하거나 실패하는 것이 두려워서 그들이 (사실) 할 수 있는 것보다 덜 성공한다. 많은 사람이 돈을 잃는 것을 두려워하기 때문에 돈을 벌지 못한다.

어휘 **entitle** ~에 (~라고) 제목을 붙이다 **quote** ~을 인용하다 **rational** 이성적인, 합리적인

구문 01~03행 There is (V) *a book* (S) (**written** by Daniel Goleman) (**entitled** *Emotional Intelligence*) [**that** I recommend (*that*) people (*should*) read ∨ // if they are ready to make ~].

→ 주어 a book을 written, entitled가 각각 이끄는 과거분사구, 그리고 that이 이끄는 관계대명사절이 수식하고 있다.

207 ⑤ | smiling → to smile

해설 ⑤ 문맥상 '미소 지을 것을 잊지 마라'라는 뜻의 미래의 일을 나타내므로 to부정사가 적절.

① 이미 웃고 있는 나에게 친구들이 '웃지 마!'라며 외친다는 뜻이므로 smiling은 알맞음.
② 문맥상 '과거 사실'에 대하여 확신에 찬 추측(기분이 좋아졌음이 틀림없다)을 나타내고 있으므로 must have felt는 적절.
③ '다른 사람들, 타인'을 뜻하는 others가 문맥상 적절.
④ '~을 생각하라'라는 뜻의 명령문이므로 절의 맨 앞에 동사원형 think가 오는 것이 적절.

해석 내가 미소를 지을 때 친구들은 장난삼아 나에게 소리친다. 나는 "그만 웃어!" 또는 "너는 너무 잘 웃어."라는 말을 자주 듣는다. 그러나 이 친구들은 내가 웃는 것을 막지 못한다. 나는 이 냉담한 세계에서 나와 잘 웃는 다른 사람들이 정말로 변화를 가져온다

고 생각한다. 만일 사람들에게 미소를 짓는다면, 그들은 대개 미소로 답한다. 그들은 누군가가 자신들을 보고 웃었다는 것에 대해 기분 좋게 느꼈음이 틀림없다. 그들은 기분이 더 좋아졌기 때문에 다른 사람에 대한 행동도 더 친절해질 것이다. 당신의 미소 짓는 얼굴을 단 한 사람에게만 비추더라도, 그것이 그 사람의 하루를 얼마나 밝게 할지 생각하라! 그리고 당신의 미소는 또한 '당신'에게도 좋다. 예를 들어, 당신의 얼굴에 진심 어린 미소가 있을 때 당신은 슬프다고 느끼거나 나쁜 생각을 하는 것이 거의 불가능하다. 그러므로 다음에 당신이 집을 나설 때, 미소 짓는 것을 잊지 마라. "미소 없이는 옷을 다 차려입은 것이 결코 아니에요"라는 노래처럼.

어휘 **playfully** 장난삼아 **make a difference** 변화를 가져오다, 차이를 낳다

208 ③ | to be surprised → to surprise

해설 ③ he가 '놀라게 하는(surprise)' 주체이므로 능동형 to surprise로 써야 한다.

① ingredients를 꾸미는 수식어 부분으로 ingredients가 exotic하다고 '여겨지는' 것이므로 수동을 나타내는 과거분사로 쓴 것이 맞다.
② one of ~에 이어지는 명사는 복수명사(chefs)로 쓴다. *cf.* <one of+복수명사>: ~ 중 하나
④ blood가 a single wildflower를 surround(둘러싸다)하고 있으므로 능동의 의미의 현재분사(-ing)를 쓴 것이 자연스럽다.
⑤ 뒤에 이어지는 동사 means의 목적어에 해당하는 what. <가주어-진주어> 구조(it means what to fine-dine)

해석 요리사 Rene Redzepi의 얘기를 다루고 서구에서는 이국적으로 여겨지는 음식 재료—곤충, 나무껍질, 동물 피 등 —를 탐구하는 다큐멘터리 <Noma: 내 완벽한 폭풍(Noma My Perfect Storm)>은 오늘날 가장 흥미로운 요리사 중 하나의 마음속과 그의 엉뚱한 작품들을 들여다보는 통찰력을 제공한다. 그의 요리들은 음식 같아 보이기보다는 일련의 설치 미술품 같아 보인다. 그는 (세상을) 놀라게 하려고 애쓰며 예술가처럼 온 세계가 그가 생각하는 식사 — 아이스크림을 소용돌이 모양으로 낸 것 위에 개미를 끼얹은 것을 통해서든 곰삭은 피(Redzepi가 가장 즐겨 쓰는 소스 중 하나)로 야생화 한 송이를 두른 것을 통해서든 — 의 진가를 알아보기를 원한다. 음식이란 것에 대한 우리의 인식 면에서, 또 '잘 차려진 식사를 한다'는 게 무엇을 의미하는지란 점에서 그가 새 영역으로 들어가고 있음은 의심의 여지가 없다. 또한 많은 레스토랑 운영자들이 Redzepi가 당대의 가장 영향력 있는 요리사라는데 동의하고 있다는 건 놀랄 일이 아니다.

어휘 **profile** 인물평을 쓰다 **chef** 요리사, 주방장 **exotic** 이국적인 **bark** 나무껍질 **insight** 통찰력 **outrageous** 양식에 어긋난, 터무니없는, 엉뚱한 **a series of** 일련의 ~ **installation** 설치(물) **strive** 애쓰다, 노력하다 **come around to** ~의 가치를 알다, ~에 동조하다 **vision** (마음속에 떠오르는) 상 **dine** (잘 차린) 식사를 하다 **swirl** 소용돌이 **topped with** ~을 얹은 **ferment** 발효시키다 **territory** 지역, 영토 **perception** 지각, 인지 **restaurateur** 식당 경영자 **influential** 영향력 있는

209 ②

해설 (A) 명사구가 이어지므로 전치사구 Because of가 적절. forced는 바로 뒤 명사 isolation을 수식하는 과거분사.
(B) 주격 관계대명사 which의 선행사는 복수명사 Areas이므로 복수동사 were가 적절.
(C) '야생동물을 보호하는 데 이용될 수 있을지'라는 의미가 되어야 하므로 preserve가 적절. *cf.* <be used to v-ing>: v하는 데 익숙하다

해석 남한과 북한 사이의 비무장지대는 길이 약 150마일, 폭 약 2.5마일의 사람이 살지 않는 좁은 땅이다. 그곳에는 어떠한 정착지나 영구 구조물도 허용되지 않고 지난 50년 동안 오직 몇몇 군인들, 관찰자들, 그리고 남쪽 경계선에 있는 대성동이라는 작은 마을의 주민 225명만이 출입이 허용되었다. 이런 강제적 격리 때문에 정치적으로 긴장된 그 지역은 우연히도 야생생물의 보호구역이 되었다. 이곳처럼 한때 전쟁 구역이었던 지역들은 때때로 동식물이 인간의 방해 없이 번성하는 장소가 될 수 있다. 최근에 분쟁이 없었던 나라에서조차, 자연 보호론자들은 사람이 살지 않는 국경지대가 야생생물을 보호하는 데 어떻게 이용될 수 있을지 탐구하고 있다.

어휘 **demilitarized zone** 비무장지대 **settlement** 정착지; 정착 **isolation** 격리, 고립 **tense** 긴장된 **sanctuary** 보호지역; 신성한 장소 **flourish** 번성하다, 번창하다 **interference** 간섭, 방해 **conservationist** 자연 보호론자

210 ②

해설 (A) a great many dandelion weeds came up에서 came up을 대신 할 수 있는 did가 적절하다.
(B) '가까운 곳에 있는'을 의미하므로 nearby. *cf.*nearly: 거의
(C) 여기서 recommended는 의미상, a few methods eradicate ~로 이어지는 절을 이끄는 것이 아니라 '제거하기 위한' 방법을 의미하는 구를 이끄는 것이므로 정답은 for eradicating.

해석 이슬람교의 신비로운 수피교에서 전해지는 전래 이야기에서, Nasreddin이라는 이름의 한 소년이 아름다운 화원을 갖고 싶었다. 그 소년은 씨를 심었지만, 꽃이 자라나자 꽃들 사이에 너무나 많은 민들레 잡초도 자라났다. Nasreddin은 가까운 곳의 몇몇 정원사들에게 어떻게 하면 그 잡초를 없앨 수 있는지 물어보았다. 그들의 제안들 중 하나도 성공하지 못했다. 마침내, Nasreddin은 직접 왕실 정원사의 충고를 구하러 궁궐로 갔다. 그 친절한 노인은 잡초를 제거하는 몇 가지 방법을 제안했지만, 슬프게도, Nasreddin은 그것들을 이미 시도했었다. 그 둘은 오랫동안 말없이 앉아 있었다. 드디어 그 노인이 Nasreddin을 바라보며 말했다. "얘야, 네가 할 수 있는 일이 딱 한 가지 남았구나. 너는 그것들을 사랑하는 법을 알아야겠다."

어휘 **dandelion** 민들레 **weed** 잡초 **eradicate** ~을 박멸하다, 뿌리째 뽑다

211 ③ | believing → believed

해설 ③ players를 수식하는 분사가 believing이 될 경우 '선수들이 믿는' 것이 되어서 문맥에 맞지 않다. 본문의 내용으로 보면 선수들이 믿는 것이 아니라 '~하다고 믿어지는 선수들'이라는 뜻이 되어야 하므로 believing이 아닌 과거 분사 believed가 어법상 적절하다.

① purely는 형용사 random을 꾸며주는 부사로 쓰임이 적절하다.
② that은 접속사로 쓰임이 적절하다. <to the extent that ~>은 '~할 정도까지'의 뜻 이다.
④ how는 접속사로, 이하 절이 완전한 문장 요소를 갖추고 있고, 동사 changes의 목적어절을 이끌어 적절하다.
⑤ if절의 주어는 those increased opportunities로서 여기서 increased는 주어를 those로 하는 동사의 과거형이 아니라 과거분사로 명사 opportunities를 수식하고 있다. 그러므로 동사로 translate가 나오는 것이 적절하다.

해석 핫 핸드에 대한 믿음은 만약 한 선수가 연속적인 호조를 보인다면, 그 선수가 '계속해서' 득점할 가능성이 그 사람 개인의 평균치보다 높다는 것이다. 그리고 이것은 그 경기가 전적으로 무작위일지라도 사실이라는 것이다. 그것은 과거의 성공이라는 단순한 사실이 미래의 성공 확률을 바꾼다는 것을 말한다. 이 현상에 대한 매우 강한 믿음이 있는데, 심지어는 그것이 경기에 영향을 미칠 정도다. 농구에서, 팀 동료들은 종종 연속적인 호조 상태에 있다고 믿어지는 선수들에게, 그들의 잇따른 슛의 성공이 다음번에 그들로 하여금 좀 더 득점할 가능성이 많게 해줄 것이라고 믿으며 공을 패스하곤 한다. 그것은 핫 핸드 현상에 대한 믿음이 선수들이 행동하는 방식을 변화시킨다는 것과 바로 그 변화가 득점의 가능성을 바꿀 수 있다는 것을 보여준다. 그것은 설령 각각의 시도에서의 득점 가능성을 바꾸는 것이 아니라 할지라도 공을 받는 선수에게 틀림없이 더 많은 득점 기회를 줄 것이다. 그리고 그렇게 증가된 득점 기회가 더 많은 점수로 바뀐다면 그것은 연속적인 호조에 대한 느낌을 강화할 수 있다.

어휘 **streak** (성공·실패의) 연속; 줄(무늬), 선 **score** 득점하다 **average** 평균치, 승률 **purely** 아주, 순전히 **random** 무작위의, 임의의 **alter** 바꾸다, 고치다 **probability** 확률, 개연성 **phenomenon** 현상 **to the extent that** ~할 정도까지 **sequence** 연속, 잇따라 일어남 **translate** 바꾸다, 변형하다 **could well** (어쩌면) ~일 수 있다 **reinforce** 강화하다

구문 01~03행 The hot hand belief is **that** if a player is in a hot streak, the chance **that that** player will continue to score is higher than his or her personal average, ~.
→ 첫 번째 that은 접속사로 문장의 보어 역할을 하는 명사절을 이끈다. 두 번째 that은 동격절을 이끄는 접속사로 the chance와 that 이하는 동격 관계이다. 세 번째 that은 player를 수식하는 지시 형용사이다.

212 ② | it → them

해설 ② neuronal connections를 가리키기 때문에 복수 대명사 them이 적절.

① 명사 our ability를 수식하는 형용사적 용법으로 to부정사구가 적절히 쓰임.
③ <not A but rather B> 구문에서 A와 B는 같은 문법적 성격이어야 하므로 developing과 병렬을 이루는 relaxing은 적절.
④ 동사 tell이 목적격보어로 to부정사 구문을 수반하는 경우이므로 적절.
⑤ 잠에서 깼을 때 이미 사라져 버리고 '지금 없는 상태'를 나타내기 위해 현재완료 시제가 적절히 쓰임. 또한 some이 복수 명사인 synapses의 일부를 의미하므로 복수형 have도 적절.

해석 수면은 우리의 기억하는 능력과 다소 관련되어 있다. 지배적인 이론은 수면 중 뇌의 활동이 낮 동안 활발했던 뉴런을 다시 활성화해 뉴런의 연결을 강화하고 그것이 기억으로 굳어지게 만든다는 것이었다. 그러나 신경과학자인 길리오 토노니는 수면 과학자들이 잘못 생각하고 있다고 말한다. 즉, 우리는 기억하기 위해 잠을 자는 것이 아니라 잊어버리기 위해 잠을 잔다는 것이다. 그는 우리가 잠을 자는 동안 뇌는 발달하는 것이 아니라 오히려 휴식한다고 한다. "위아래로 왔다 갔다 하면서 기본적으로 모든 뉴런이 발화한 다음 모든 것이 조용해집니다. 그것은 뇌가 시냅스(신경세포의 연결 부위)에게 약해지라고 명령하는 정말 놀라운 방식이죠." 토노니는 이렇게 설명한다. 그래서 우리가 잠에서 깨면 시냅스는 강하지 않고 어떤 것들은 사라져버린다. 그것들과 함께 우리의 가장 희미한 기억들이 영원히 사라질 수도 있다.

어휘 **reign** 지배하다, 군림하다 **reactivate** ~을 재활성화하다 **neuron** 뉴런, 신경세포 *cf.* **neuronal** 뉴런의, 신경단위의 **neuroscientist** 신경과학자 **cement** ~을 굳히다; ~에 시멘트를 바르다 **vanish** 사라지다

구문 02~05행 The reigning theory (S) has been (V) that brain activity (S′) (during sleep) reactivates (V′) *neurons* (O′) [**that** were active during the day], **strengthening** neuronal connections and **cementing** them (= neuronal connections) into memories.

→ strengthening 이하의 분사구문은 앞 동작의 '결과'를 나타낸다.

213 ②

해설 (A) 주어가 단수인 our exploitation이므로 동사는 is가 되어야 한다.
(B) 목적격 관계대명사 that은 tricks를 수식하고 (B)에 들어갈 것은 tricks를 설명해주는 목적격보어이므로, amuse((남을) 즐겁게 하다)의 능동형인 amusing이 어법상 적절하다.
(C) 앞의 be동사(is) 다음에 나오는 보어가 아니라 to be condemned를 수식하는 말이므로 부사인 morally가 어법상 적절하다.

해석 만약에 고래가 권리를 가지고 있다면, 그렇다면 그것들은 존중하는 마음으로 다루어져야 한다. 그것들의 가치와 존엄성은 우리의 계획, 목적, 프로젝트에 있어서 그것들의 위치에 근거하지 않는다. 이런 관점에서 우리가 오락 목적으로 고래를 이용하는 것은 도덕적으로 받아들일 수 없다. 그것들은 자기 자신의 삶과 그 삶을 자기 방식대로 이끌 수 있는 능력을 가지고 있는, 내재적 가치를 지닌 생물이다. 그것들을 수중 공원에 가두어 놓고 사람들이 재미있다고 생각하는 재주를 공연하게 하는 것은 그것들을 우리 자신의 창조물로 다시 만들려고 하는 것이다. 그런 하찮은 목적 때문에, 그런 놀랍고 아름다운 생물을 부당하게 이용하려는 이러한 시도는, 게다가 이는 그것들에게 자유를 허락하지 않는데, 도덕적으로 비난을 받아야 한다.

어휘 **dignity** 존엄성; 위엄, 품위 **rest on** ~에 근거하다, 기초하다 **place** 위치; 장소; 놓다, 두다 **perspective** 관점, 시각 **exploitation** (부당한) 이용, 착취 **inherent** 내재적인, 내재하는 **capacity** 능력; 용량, 최대 수용량 **aquatic** 수생의, 물의 **trick** 재주; 속임수; 장난 **attempt** 시도(하다) **marvelous** 놀라운, 믿기 어려운, 신기한 **magnificent** 아름다운, 훌륭한 **trivial** 하찮은, 시시한 **deny** 허락하지 않다; 부인[부정]하다 **liberty** 자유, 해방 **in the bargain** 게다가, 그 위에 **condemn** 비난하다

구문 06~08행 They are creatures of inherent value / with lives of their own / and *the capacity* (**to lead them in their own ways**).

그것들은 내재적 가치를 지닌 생물이다 / 자기 자신의 삶 / 그리고 능력을 가지고 있는 (그 삶을 자기 방식대로 이끌 수 있는).

→ ( ) 부분은 the capacity를 수식하는 to-v의 형용사적 용법이다.

11~15행 **This attempt** / **to** appropriate such marvelous and magnificent creatures / for such trivial purposes,

이러한 시도는 / 그런 놀랍고 아름다운 생물을 부당하게 이용하려는 / 그런 하찮은 목적 때문에,

/ **which denies them their liberty in the bargain,** / is morally to be condemned.

/ 게다가 이는 그것들에게 자유를 허락하지 않는데, / 도덕적으로 비난을 받아야 한다.

→ This attempt와 to appropriate ~ purposes는 동격 관계이다.

→ 콤마(,) 뒤의 관계대명사 which는 앞부분 전체를 가리킨다.

214 ⑤ | are → being

해설 ⑤ 전치사 plus(~뿐만 아니라, ~도 또한) 뒤에 목적어가 the benefits이며 이어지는 that은 the benefits를 선행사로 하는 관계대명사이다. 이 that이 이끄는 절에는 이미 동사 come이 있으므로 그 외는 준동사 형태여야 한다. 전치사 from의 목적어가 되도록 are가 아니라 동명사 being을 써야 하며, 이때 everyone around them은 being의 의미상 주어이다.

① when은 시간을 나타내는 관계부사로 앞의 an age of expertise에 대한 추가적인 설명을 제시한다.

② 동사 leads를 수식하므로 부사 typically가 적절하다.

③ 주어가 an extra year이므로 단수형 동사 is가 적절하다.

④ that people ~ skilled people 절은 the idea와 동격이다.

해석 우리는 전문 지식의 시대에 살고 있는데, 이 시대는 수입과 지식이 밀접하게 연관된다. 각각의 근로자에게 있어, 학교 교육을 추가로 1년 더 받는 것은 일반적으로 약 8퍼센트 더 높은 수입으로 이어진다. 평균적으로, 한 나라의 전체 인구가 학교 교육을 추가로 1년 더 받는 것은 1인당 국내총생산에서 30퍼센트 이상의 증가와 결부된다. 교육과 한 나라의 국내총생산 사이의 두드러진 상관관계는, 다른 숙련된 사람들 주변에서 일할 때 사람들이 더 생산적이게 된다는 개념을 뜻하는 용어인, 이른바 경제학자들이 말하는 인적자본의 외부 효과를 반영할지도 모른다. 한 나라가 더 많이 배우게 될 때, 사람들은 그들 자신의 추가적 교육의 직접적 효과뿐만 아니라 그들 주변의 모든 사람이 더 숙련되는 데서 오는 이익도 경험한다.

어휘 **expertise** 전문적 지식[기술] **earnings** 수입, 소득 **link** 관련짓다, 연결되다 **extra** 추가의, 가외의 **schooling** 학교 교육 **associated with** ~와 결부된 **gross domestic product per person** 1인당 국내총생산 **striking** 두드러진, 현저한 **correlation** 상관관계 **human capital** 인적 자본 **externality** 외적 영향, 외형 **productive** 생산적인

구문 07~10행 **The** striking **correlation between** education **and** a country's GDP / may reflect / what economists call human capital externalities, a term for the idea that ~.

→ <the correlation between A and B>는 'A와 B 간의 상관관계'라는 뜻이다. 주어는 The striking correlation이며 동사는 may reflect이고 what은 reflect의 목적어절을 이끄는 관계대명사이다. human capital externalities와 a term~은 동격 관계이다.

215 ③

해설 (A) 식민지에 죄수가 이송된 적이 없는 것은 뒤의 '식민지가 죄수를 요청했다'는 과거 시점보다 더 이전의 이야기이므로 과거완료를 이루는 had가 적절.

(B) help가 '~하는 데 도움을 주다'라는 의미로 쓰일 때는 목적어로 to부정사나 원형부정사를 사용하므로 build가 적절.

(C) 호주가 국가를 세운 것은 '과거'의 일인데 이를 반대로 가정하는 것이므로 가정법 과거완료형인 <wouldn't have p.p.>의 have been이 적절.

해석 죄수들이 웨스턴 오스트레일리아로 이송된 적은 한 번도 없었지만 19세기 중반에 그 식민지에서 갑자기 그들을 요청했다. 그 지역은 노동력이 부족했고 죄수 노동력 없이 그 식민지는 발전할 수 없었다. 영국은 1850년에서 1868년까지 그 식민지에 죄수들을 보냈고, 그 죄수들은 도로, 교량, 교도소 그리고 다른 공공건물들을 건설함으로써 식민지를 건설하는 것을 도왔다. 총 162,000명의 남녀가 죄수의 신분으로 호주에 왔다. 영국의 죄수 이송 정책이 끝날 즈음 호주의 인구는 1백만 이상으로 증가했다. 처음에는 종으로서 그리고 나중에는 정착민으로서의 죄수들의 고된 노동이 없었더라면, 정부와 자유 정착민들이 국가를 세우는 것은 불가능했을 것이다.

어휘 **convict** 죄수; ~에게 유죄를 선고하다 **colony** 식민지 **shortage** 부족 **region** 지역 **progress** 발달하다, 전진하다; 전진 **construct** ~을 건설하다 **transportation** 이송, 수송 **settler** 정착민

216 ④ | lies → lie

해설 ④ At the heart of the mystery ***lies*** **cells**는 <장소부사구+V+S> 어순의 도치구문이다. 주어가 복수형(cells)이므로 동사도 복수형 lie로 일치시켜야 한다.

① how astonishing it is에서 주어인 it은 life를 지칭하고, life가 놀라움이란 감정을 느끼는(astonished) 것이 아니라 불러일으키는 것(astonishing)이므로 능동 형태로 잘 사용하였다.

② 재귀대명사는 주어와 같은 대상을 지칭하는 목적어 자리에 쓰는 대명사이다. Living things draw matter and energy to themselves에서 주어는 Living things이고 전치사 to의 목적어 역시 의미상으로 living things를 지칭하기 때문에, 대명사로 바꿔 쓰면 them이 아니라 themselves가 된다.

③ everything they do에서 they do는 everything을 수식하는 관계대명사절이다. they는 Living things이고, do는 일반동사로 '~하다'의 뜻으로 쓰였으며 현재 시제와 복수형, 능동형이 올바르게 사용되었다.

⑤ highly는 '대단히'라는 뜻의 부사로서 형용사인 integrated를 수식하기에 적절하다.

해석 생물은 매우 친숙하고 어디에나 있어서 생물이 얼마나 놀랄 만한지, 그리고 살아있지 않은 것들과 생명체들이 얼마나 뚜렷하게 다른지 잊어버리기가 쉽다. 생명체들은 물질과 에너지를 자기들에게 끌어오고, 자기들의 고유성을 유지하고, 그들 자신의 종을 번식시키고, 시간이 흐르면서 진화한다. 알려진 우주에서 다른 어떤 것도 이러한 능력을 갖고 있지 않다. 생명체들은 생명이 없는 화학물질들로 이뤄져 있는데, 그것들(생명체들)의 구성과 하는 모든 일은 물리와 화학의 법칙들과 일치한다. 그렇다 하더라도 그런 법칙들에는 생물의 거처가 되는 우주를 예상하게 할 아무것도 존재하지 않는다. 그 신비의 중심에는 생물의 기본 단위이자 생물의 모든 특성들을 보여주는 가장 작은 독립체인 세포가 있다. 모든 생물체는 단세포이든 다수의 세포이든 세포로 구성되어 있고, 모든 세포는 그 자체로 우주에서 구조화된 수백만 분자들이 고도로 통합된 총체이다.

어휘 **ubiquitous** 어디에나 있는 **astonishing** 놀랄 만한, 놀라운 **sharply**

뚜렷이, 날카롭게 **identity** 고유성, 개성 **reproduce** 번식시키다, 재생하다 **evolve** 진화하다 **capacity** 능력; 용량; 수용력 **composition** 구성, 기질; 구성 요소들; 작곡; 작문 **be consistent with** ~와 일관되다, 일치하다 **harbor** 거처가 되다; (생각 등을) 품다; 항구; 피난처 **entity** 실재, 존재, 독립체 **integrated** 통합된; 완전한 **molecule** 분자 **structure** 구조화하다, 체계화하다 **in space** 우주에서

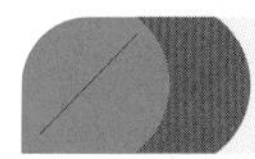

실전 모의고사 24회

217 ④ 218 ③ 219 ③ 220 ① 221 ⑤ 222 ⑤ | 본문 120p

217 ④ | heavily → heavy

해설 ④ 동사 feel은 보어로 형용사를 취하므로 heavy가 적절.

① to find out의 목적어절을 이끌면서 문맥에 어울리는 '어떻게'라는 의미를 가진 how가 적절.
② This plane을 가리키므로 단수형 its가 적절.
③ 함께 비행기를 탄 '다른 사람들'을 의미하는 others는 적절.
⑤ 의미상 주어인 We가 여기저기로 '튀는' 것이므로 능동관계를 나타내는 현재분사 bouncing이 적절.

해석 나는 날아다니는 실험실로 더 잘 알려진 러시아의 IL-76 MDK 항공기인, 무중력 상태 모의 훈련 장치에서 실제로 어떤 느낌이 드는지를 알아낼 기회가 있었다. 이 비행기는 탑승자들에게 무중력 상태를 모의 실험하기 위해 하늘로 날아올라 기동 연습을 몇 차례 한다. 나는 11명의 다른 사람들과 함께 날아오른다. 확성기의 목소리가 "준비하세요."라고 말하면 갑자기 눈에 보이지 않는 힘이 우리 모두를 바닥으로 내리누른다. 잠시 동안 우리는 보통 때의 두 배로 무겁게 느껴지고 그런 다음 모두 완전히 무중력 상태로 바닥에서 장엄하게 떠오른다. 우리는 서로에게, 벽이나 천장에 부딪히면서 비행기 여기저기를 둥둥 떠다닌다. "시간이 다 됐습니다. 내려오세요!" 갑자기 무중력 상태가 끝나고 우리는 모두 바닥으로 떨어진다.

어휘 **simulator** 모의 훈련 장치 ***cf.* simulate** ~을 모의 실험하다; ~을 가장하다 **maneuver** 기동 작전; ((복수형)) 기동 연습 **occupant** 탑승자; 점유자 **majestically** 장엄하게, 당당하게 **weightless** 무중력 상태의 **bounce** 튀다, 튀기다 **abruptly** 갑자기, 불쑥 **tumble** 굴러떨어지다

218 ③ | to gasp → gasping

해설 ③ lying down과 and로 연결되는 병렬구조이므로 gasping이 적절. lying down과 gasping은 <see+O+OC> 구조가 수동태가 되면서 동사 뒤에 남은 목적격보어.

① 부사 always를 수식하고 있으므로 부사 nearly는 알맞게 쓰임.
② 문맥상 '~와는 달리'라는 뜻의 전치사 unlike가 적절히 쓰임.
④ 동사 get은 목적격보어로 to부정사를 취하여 '~가 …하게 하다'라는 의미를 가지므로 to sweat은 알맞음.
⑤ 진주어 to concentrate를 대신하는 가주어 it과 동사가 필요하므로 it's는 알맞음.

해석 뉴잉글랜드 주의 여름은 짧아서, 6월 1일에 시작해서 8월 마지막 날에 끝난다. 그러나 그 석 달 내내 날씨는 기분 좋게 따뜻하고 거의 항상 해가 난다. 가장 좋은 점은, 내가 자란 곳이자 여름에는 하루가 지날 때마다 온도와 습도가 꾸준히 올라가는 아이오와 주와는 달리 기온이 대체로 알맞은 정도로 유지된다는 것이다. 8월 중순까지 아이오와 주는 너무도 덥고 바람이 없어서 파리들조차 등을 대고 누워서 조용히 숨만 헐떡거리는 것을 볼 수 있을 지경이다. 심지어 백화점에 있는 마네킹도 땀을 흘리게 한다. 어떤 중요한 일을 마치려고 해도, 집중하기가 거의 불가능하다.

어휘 **agreeably** 기분 좋게 **humidity** 습기 **airless** 바람이 안 부는, 공기가 안 통하는 **gasp** 헐떡거리다 **mannequin** 마네킹 **concentrate** 집중하다

219 ③

해설 (A) 접속사 than 다음에 주어와 동사가 도치되어 있다. 주어가 an inn이 아니라 the case이기 때문에 '여관의 경우가 그런 것보다'의 뜻이 되려면 동사는 does가 아닌 is가 되어야 한다.
(B) which절의 동사인 means의 목적어절을 이끄는 that이 있다. the meals는 그 목적어절의 주어, (B)는 동사 자리이므로 have를 써야 적절하다.
(C) 바로 뒤의 명사 job은 앞에 나온 a waiter의 job이고, 두 문장 the restaurant has offered meals served by a waiter와 job is limited to this를 연결하려면 소유격 관계대명사 whose가 적절하다.

해석 식당은 본질적으로 음식도 제공하는 (여관 같은) 지역 회합 장소나 여행자 쉼터가 아니라 식사하는 장소로서 찾는 곳이다. 시설의 제한된 영업시간 내에서, 식당은 다양한 요리를 제공하는데 여관의 경우보다 더 많이 그렇게 한다. 따라서 대부분의 식당은 아침 식사를 위해 문을 열지 않으며, 아침 식사를 제공하는 식당들은 (호텔이나 현대의 여관을 제외하고는) 어느 정도 그것(아침 식사 제공)을 전문으로 하는데, 이는 이러한 아침 식사 식당들이 제공하는 식사가 전통적인 여관이 제공할 수 있는 것보다 더 많은 선택권을 제공함을 의미한다. 식당에서 사람들은 종종 광범위한 메뉴 중에서 원하는 것을 먹는다. 식당 역사의 대부분 동안 식당은 음식을 시중드는 것에 한정된 일만 하는 웨이터가 시중드는 식사를 제공해 왔다. 여관이나 게스트하우스에 있는 다른 손님과 함께 모이기보다 식당의 손님은 친구들과 오고, 다른 사람들과는 떨어져 앉으며, 식사를 마치면 특정 식사에 대해 값을 지불한다.

어휘 **destination** 목적지, 행선지 **in itself** 본질적으로 **inn** 여관, 여인숙 **gathering** 회합, 모임 **shelter** 숙소, 피난 장소 **restricted** 한정된, 제한된 **establishment** 점포, 시설 **outside of** ~을 제외하고 **modern-day** 현대의, 현재의 **specialize in** ~을 전문으로 하다 **to some extent** 얼마간, 어느 정도까지 **extensive** 광범위한 **lodger** 숙박인, 하숙인 **guesthouse** 여관, 고급 하숙

구문 06~12행 Thus most restaurants do not open for breakfast, // and ***those*** (S′) [that do serve breakfast (outside of hotels or modern-day inns)] / **specialize** (V′) to some extent in it, / which means / *that* ***the meals*** (S″) [these breakfast restaurants serve] ***have*** (V″) more options than a traditional inn could provide.

→ 절의 주어가 모두 [ ] 부분의 수식을 받아 동사와 멀어진 경우이다. 즉 those의 동사는 specialize, the meals의 동사는 have이다.

220 ① | because → because of

해설 ❶ the advantages (that it brings)는 관계대명사절의 수식을 받는 명사구에 불과하므로 절을 이끄는 접속사 because는 쓸 수 없다. 전치사구 because of로 써야 한다.

② 동사 become의 보어 자리이므로 형용사 enthusiastic이 적절.
③ desire가 현재 '불타고 있는', 즉 진행 중이므로 진행을 나타내는 현재분사가 적절.
④ as절의 주어(they)와 동사(present)의 목적어가 동일(opportunities)하므로 재귀대명사 themselves가 적절.
⑤ <drive+O+OC>의 SVOC 구조에서 목적격보어로 to부정사가 온 경우.

해석 많은 사람들이 뚜렷한 목표 없이 많은 것들과 싸우며 삶에서 표류하고 있다. 목표를 결정하기는 쉽지 않을지도 모른다. 그러나 목표를 결정하는 것이 가져오는 이득 때문에 노력할 가치가 있다. 당신이 무엇을 원하는지 안다면 그것은 당신이 올바른 방향으로 움직이게 할 것이다. 당신이 목표에 관해 더 많이 생각할수록 당신은 더 열정적이게 된다. 열정은 타오르는 욕망이 될 수 있다. 그것은 당신의 일상생활에서 기회가 나타날 때 당신이 그것을 재빠르게 알아챌 수 있도록 도움을 줄 것이다. 그것은 경험이나 재능의 부족을 보완해 줄 수도 있다. 그러므로 마침내 꿈을 결정했을 때, 그것을 쉽게 포기하지 말라. 대신 열정을 지켜라. 왜냐하면 그것이 당신을 성공하도록 이끌 힘이 될 것이기 때문이다.

어휘 **drift** 표류하다 **aimlessly** 목표 없이 **clear-cut** 뚜렷한, 명쾌한 **enthusiastic** 열정적인 ***cf.*** **enthusiasm** 열정 **alert** 재빠른, 기민한; 경계하는 **settle on** ~을 결정하다 **hold on to** ~을 지키다, 고수하다

221 ⑤

해설 (A) 문맥상 '너무 ~해서 …하다'라는 의미의 <so ~ that ...> 구문이 적절하므로 that이 알맞다.
(B) they가 가리키는 농작물(Crops)은 '수송되는' 것이므로 수동태 be transported가 적절하다.
(C) 관계절 내의 동사는 선행사와 수일치 해야 하는데 선행사가 전명구 in the ~ Ocean의 수식을 받는 high ocean temperatures이므로 복수동사 are가 알맞다.

해석 대략 한 세기 전에 기록관리가 시작된 이래 최악의 아마존의 가뭄이 2005년에 시작되어 아마존 강 유역에 많은 문제를 가져왔다. 서부 브라질에서 2005년 9월에 2004년 9월 동안보다 세 배 많은 화재가 있었다. 어떤 지역에서는 수면이 너무 낮아져서 수송을 강에 의지하는 몇몇 지역사회는 완전히 고립된다. 농작물은 시장으로 수송될 수 없어서 썩고, 아이들은 학교에 갈 수 없다. 어류는 얕은 물에서 죽어서, 사람들은 정부가 제공하는 음식 꾸러미에 의존할 수밖에 없다. 강은 분뇨를 제거하기에 충분할 정도로 흐르지 않고 오물의 축적은 콜레라와 다른 수인성 질병의 확산에 대한 두려움을 증가시킨다. 고여 있는 웅덩이는 모기가 번식하게 하는데, 그것은 말라리아 환자의 수를 증가시킬 가능성이 있다. 아마존의 가뭄은 카리브 해와 대서양의 높은 바닷물의 온도 때문이고, 그것은 지구 온난화의 결과인 것 같다.

어휘 **drought** 가뭄 **stream** 강, 시내, 개울 **isolated** 고립된 **rot** 썩다, 부패하다 **shallow** 얕은 **backup** 축적 **sewage** 하수, 오물 **waterborne** 물에 의해 운반되는 **case** (질병이나 부상) 환자, 사례 **blame A on B** A를 B의 탓으로 돌리다

구문 01~03행 *The worst Amazon drought* [since record keeping began about a century ago] / **began** in 2005, **bringing** many problems to the Amazon basin.
→ 주어 The worst Amazon drought가 since ~ ago의 수식을 받고 있으며, 동사는 그 뒤에 이어지는 began이다. 현재분사 bringing은 분사구문을 이끌고 있다.

05~08행 In some areas water levels have dropped so low that *some communities* [**that** depend on streams for transportation] are completely isolated.
→ [ ] 부분은 some communities를 수식하는 관계절이며, that은 주격 관계대명사이다.

222 ⑤ | coming → comes

해설 ❺ 문장의 주어는 The outstanding flavor이고 found in superior preserved foods는 주어를 수식하는 후치수식 분사이다. 문장에 동사가 없으므로 coming은 동사인 comes로 고쳐 써야 한다.

① be stressed를 수식하는 부사 자리이므로 strongly가 적절하다.
② what you put in은 동사구 get back out의 목적어가 된다.
③ to serve 이하는 proud라는 감정의 '이유'를 제시해주는 to부정사구이다.
④ known 이하는 수동의 뜻으로 every technique을 수식한다.

해석 집에서 만드는 통조림에 쓸 재료를 선택하는 것의 중요성은 아무리 강하게 강조해도 지나치지 않다. 넣은 것을 다시 꺼낼 뿐이라는 옛 속담은 집에서 만드는 통조림 음식에 관해서라면 절대적으로 사실이다. 질 좋은 재료는 여러분이 가족과 친구들에게 자랑스럽게 대접할 저장 식품을 만드는 데 가장 중요한 요소이다. 여러분은 통조림을 만드는 모든 절차를 정확히 그대로 따르고, 아마도 여러분이 할 수 있는, 최고의 저장 음식을 만드는 것으로 알려진 모든 방법을 이용할 수 있지만, 질이 떨어지는 재료를 이용한다면 결과물은 실망스러운 것이 될 것이다. 질적으로 우수한 저장 음식에서 발견되는 뛰어난 맛은, 구할 수 있는 그야말로 최상의 과일과 채소에서, 그리고 어떤 재료의 질도 줄이지 않는 데서 직접적으로 생긴다.

어휘 **ingredient** (요리) 재료 **canning** 통조림 제조 **stress** 강조하다 **saying** 속담 **when it comes to** ~에 관해서는 **preserve** 보존하다 **serve** (음식을) 제공하다 **procedure** 절차 **to the letter** 정확히[글자] 그대로 **inferior** 질 낮은, 열등한 **outstanding** 두드러진, 뛰어난 **superior** (질적으로) 우수한 **cut down on** ~을 줄이다

구문 01~02행 The importance of selecting ingredients for use in home canning **cannot** be stressed **too** strongly.
→ <cannot ~ too>는 '아무리 ~해도 지나치지 않다'의 뜻이다.

03~04행 **The old saying** [that you only get back out what you put in] / ***is*** absolutely true ~
→ [ ] 부분은 주어 The old saying의 동격절이며, 동사는 is이다.

223 ③ | to be seated → to seat

해설 ❸ 문맥상 아이들을 앉혔다는 내용인데, seat은 '~을 앉히다'라는 의미의 타동사이고 뒤에 목적어 the kids를 취하고 있으므로 능동형이 되어야 함. <manage to-v>는 '간신히 v해내다'라는 뜻.

① '인솔하기 위해' 고용되었다는 내용이므로 '목적'의 의미를 갖는 부사적 용법의 to부정사 to lead는 적절.
② 과거의 일을 나타내고 있으므로 과거동사 attempted는 적절.
④ enter는 '~에 들어가다'라는 의미의 타동사로, 전치사 없이 바로 목적어를 취할 수 있다.
⑤ 분사의 의미상 주어이면서 문장의 주어인 She(= the principal)가 능동적으로 '지켜보는' 것이므로 현재분사 observing은 알맞음.

해석 그것은 내가 처음으로 가르치는 것이었고, 나는 멋진 첫인상을 만들기를 간절히 원했다. 나는 활기 넘치는 4세 그룹을 인솔하기 위하여 고용되었다. 부모들이 아이들과 동행해 방으로 들어오자, 나는 우는 아이, 눈물 맺힌 엄마와 긴장한 아빠들을 응대하려고 애썼다. 마침내, 나는 간신히 아이들을 카펫에 앉혔으며 우리는 '모닝 서클 타임(둥글게 앉아서 단체 활동을 하는 것)'을 시작할 준비가 되었다. 우리가 'Old MacDonald'라는 열정적인 공연을 하던 도중에, 문이 열리면서 유치원 원장 선생님이 방으로 들어오셨다. 원장 선생님은 문 옆에 서서 조용히 아이들과 나를 관찰하셨다. 내 목소리와 미소는 절대 흔들리지 않았지만 솔직히 나는 매우 긴장했다.

어휘 **vibrant** 활기 넘치는 **escort** ~와 동행하다; ~을 호위하다 **attempt to-v** v하려고 시도하다 **teary-eyed** 눈물이 글썽거리는 **tense** 긴장한; 팽팽한 **rousing** 열렬한 **stumble** 더듬거리다, 실수하다; 비틀[휘청]거리다

224 ④ | open up → to open up

해설 ❹ 문맥상 '그들이 터놓고 말하게 하다'라는 내용이 되어야 한다. <get+O+to-v (~로 하여금 v하게 하다)> 구문을 이루는 to open up이 적절.

① aggression을 선행사로 하는 목적격 관계대명사 자리이므로 that이 적절.
② resent는 목적어로 동명사를 취하는 동사이다.
③ if는 '~인지 (아닌지)'를 의미하는 접속사로서 ask의 직접목적어가 되는 명사절을 이끌고 있다.
⑤ writing down ~ these questions가 뒤에 나오는 동사 might help에 호응하는 동명사구 주어로 적절히 쓰였다.

해석 이를 가는 것은 종종 긴장에 대처하는 하나의 방식이다. 그것은 직접적으로 드러낼 수 없었던 공격성을 간접적으로 표출하려는 시도일지도 모른다. 예를 들어, 직장에서 혹은 인간관계에서 누군가에게 굴복해야 했던 것을 분하게 여기고 있는지도 모른다. 우선 인간관계가 긴장의 원인은 아닌지 자신에게 물어보라. 삶에서 해결되지 않은 어떤 문제점들이 스트레스를 일으키고 있는가? 우리는 심리치료에서 사람들이 그들의 문제에 관해 터놓고 말하도록 이러한 질문들을 던진다. 이런 질문들에 대한 답을 적어 보는 것만으로도 치료사의 도움 없이 자신의 감정을 이해하는 데 도움을 받을 수 있다. 어떤 스트레스나 긴장을 없애는 것을 돕기 위해서, 요가나 호흡 연습, 명상과 같은 활동이 도움이 될 수 있다.

어휘 **grind** ~을 갈다, 빻다 **release** ~을 방출하다; (부정적인 감정을) 없애다 **aggression** 공격성 **resent v-ing** v하는 것에 분개하다 **submit** 복종하다, 굴복하다 **unresolved** 미해결의, 결정되지 않은 **psychotherapy** 심리치료, 정신치료 **therapist** 치료 전문가 **meditation** 명상

225 ③

해설 (A) high(높은; 높이)는 형용사와 부사의 형태가 같으며, highly는 '매우, 아주'라는 뜻이다. 따라서 '높은 수행 능력을 가진'이라는 뜻을 나타내기 위해서는 high를 써야 한다.
(B) 동사 should not be taken을 수식하는 부사 seriously를 써야 한다.
(C) that절의 주어 the work environment에 대한 동사는 뒤의 shapes이므로 (C)는 준동사 자리. 따라서 includes가 아니라 including을 써야 한다.

해석 리더십 능력이 유전된다면, 잠재적인 지도자로서 관리자들을 선발하고 채용하는 것은 오직 지원자의 부모와 선조에만 중점을 둘 것이며, 업무 경력 증거는 평가되지 않을 것이다. 게다가 지도자가 태어나는 것이고 키워지는 것이 아니라면, 높은 업무 능력을 지닌 사람들은 사업 환경이나 그들의 관리 능력 혹은 직원을 잘 고용하고 선발하거나, 또는 지도하고 멘토가 되고 훈련하고 발전시키고 평가하려는 회사의 의지와 상관없이 항상 나타날 것이다. 게다가 업무 수행을 향상시키려는 시도는 비효율적인 일이 될 것이다. 이런 생각은 너무 심각하게 받아들여져서는 안 되는데, 그러면 왜 내가 그것을 언급했을까? 내 경험에 의하면, 순전히 몇몇 관리자들은 이런 생각에 근거하여 그들의 사람(직원)을 관리하고, 그것은 그들이 향상된 업무 수행으로 이끄는 사원 관리 기술과 기법을 적용하는 것을 못 하게 하기 때문이다. 관리 활동을 포함하는 업무 환경이 사람들의 행동과 능력을 형성하며, 모든 관리자는 선천적인 특성과 상관없이 사람들을 관리하는 법을 향상시킬 수 있다는 점을 받아들이는 게 훨씬 더 낫다고 생각한다.

어휘 **inherit** (유전적으로) 물려받다 **recruitment** 채용; 신병 모집 **potential** 가능성이 있는, 잠재적인 **candidate** 지원자 **value** (가치·가격을) 평가하다 **emerge** 나타나다 **regardless of** ~와 관계없이 **wasteful** 비효율적인, 낭비적인 **innate** 타고난, 선천적인

구문 14~18행 Simply because, in my experience, some managers manage their people based on this idea, and it **prevents** *them* **from** applying the person-management skills and techniques [that lead to improved performance].
→ '~가 …하지 못하게 하다'라는 뜻의 <prevent ~ from+v-ing> 구문이 쓰였고 이때 applying의 목적어 두 개가 and로 연결되어 병렬구조를 이루고 있다. [ ] 부분은 techniques를 수식하는 관계절이다.

226 ⑤ | tending → tend

해설 ❺ while이 이끄는 절의 동사 자리이므로 이에 맞게 tend가 되어야 한다.

① '나중의', '늦게 온'의 의미로, later가 명사 앞에서 형용사로 쓰인 경우.
② 비교 대상(than ~)이 생략됐지만 문맥상 첫째 아이와 나머지 아이들을 비교하고 있으므로 비교급이 적절하게 쓰인 경우.
③ 이유를 나타내는 관계부사 why로 앞에 선행사 reason이 생략된 형태.
④ are (less) anxious ~ and are (more) relaxed ~로 이어지는 병렬구조. relaxed(편안한, 긴장하지 않은)가 형용사처럼 쓰이고 있다.

해석 첫째 아이는 종종 동생들보다 부모로부터 더 많은 훈육을 받지만, 부모는 또한 그들에게 더 많은 관심을 쏟는다. 연구자들은 이것이 첫째들에게 성공에 대한 더 강력한 욕구를 주는데, 이 욕구가 그들이 동생들보다 더 높은 성적을 받고, 대학에 진학하며, 대학에서도 계속 잘할 가능성이 많은 이유라고 생각한다. 당신은 잡지의 표지에서 혹은 대기업의 CEO로서 첫째를 보게 될 가능성이 더 많다. 그에 반해서, 동생들은 성공하는 것에 대해 덜 걱정하고 인간관계에서 더욱 느긋하다. 첫째는 변화를 좋아하지 않으며 보수

적인 사상을 지지하는 경향이 있고, 반면 나중에 태어난 형제, 자매는 더 반항적이며 자유로운 사상을 지지하는 경향이 있다.

어휘 **discipline** 훈육, 훈련; ~을 훈육하다 **sibling** 형제, 자매 **corporation** 회사, 법인 **be inclined to-v** v하는 경향이 있다 **conservative** 보수적인 **rebellious** 반항적인 **liberal** 자유주의의

227 ⑤

해설 (A) 문맥상 '방식, 방법'의 의미가 되어야 하므로 how가 적절.
(B) 달의 한쪽 반구가 지구를 '향하고 있는' 것이므로 능동을 나타내는 현재분사 facing이 적절.
(C) 전체 문장의 동사 역할을 하는 것이 없으므로, 동사 show가 와야 한다.

해석 만약 당신이 당신 집의 전면만 볼 수 있고 후면은 언제나 숨겨져 있다고 상상해보라. 그것이 천문학자들이 많은 시간 동안 느끼는 방식인데, 우리는 우주의 가장 흥미로운 장소들 중 일부의 오직 한 면만을 관찰할 수 있기 때문이다. 가장 친숙한 예가 달이다. 달은 언제나 한쪽 반구를 지구 쪽으로 향하고 있기 때문에 우리는 매달 똑같은 '달 표면의 사람' 무늬를 본다. 천문학자들은 (달의) 반대쪽도 보이는 쪽과 똑같으리라고 오랫동안 추정해왔다. 그러나 틀렸다. 1959년 소련의 우주선 루나 3호에 의해 찍힌 사진은 매우 다른 풍경을 보여준다. 이제 우리는 달이 균일하지 않게 둥글다는 것을 아는데, 지구의 중력이 달의 질량을 우리 쪽으로, 중심에서 약간 벗어나게 끌어당기기 때문이다.

어휘 **astronomer** 천문학자 **assume** ~라고 추정하다 **unevenly** 고르지 않게; 평평하지 않게 **gravity** 중력

228 ⑤ | test → be tested

해설 ⑤ '그의 가설(his hypothesis)'은 검증하는 것이 아닌 검증'되는' 것이므로 test를 be tested로 바꾸는 것이 적절하다.

① 과거분사 known이 observation을 '알려진'이라는 수동의 의미로 수식하므로 적절하다.
② 주어는 This이고 동사 is와 appears가 and로 연결되어 병렬 구조를 이룬다.
③ 주격 관계대명사 which가 뒤에 불완전한 절을 이끌면서 선행사 the facts를 수식하므로 적절하다.
④ whether a given ~ already known은 ascertain의 목적어 역할을 하는 명사절이다. 불확실한 상황이므로 접속사 that이 아닌 whether가 적절하다.

해석 가설을 만들었을 당시 가설을 만든 사람에게 알려진 동등한 양의 관찰에 대한 설명보다 성공적인 예측이 가설을 더욱 강하게 뒷받침해 준다고들 대개 생각한다. 이것은 오로지 논리적인 근거로 옳음을 증명하기 어렵지 않으며 경험의 결과로 타당한 것처럼 보인다. 아마 추가적인 설명은 다음과 같을 것이다. 가설은 그것의 창조를 가져온 사실에 들어맞아야 할 뿐만 아니라 나머지 과학계와 양립할 수 있어야 한다. 이것은 현대 과학의 범위와 복잡성으로 인해 충족시키기에 굉장히 어려운 조건이다. 특정 가설이 기존에 알려진 모든 것과 사실 양립할 수 있는지를 확인하는 것은 고된 일이다. 그러나 연구자가 자신의 가설이 가까운 미래에 그것의 예상되는 결과에 기반을 둔 실험으로 검증될 것임을 안다면, 그는 아마 가설이 알려진 사실에 정말로 부합하는지 알아보기 위해 이러한 종류의 즉각적인 검증을 예상하지 못하는 경우보다 훨씬 더 세심할 것이다.

어휘 **observation** 관찰 **hypothesis** 가설 **justify** 옳음을 증명하다; 정당화하다 **purely** 오로지, 순전히 **ground** 이유, 근거 **valid** 타당한; 유효한 **bring about** ~을 일으키다[초래하다] **compatible** 양립할 수 있는, 조화되는 **scope** 범위 **laborious** 고된, 힘든; 부지런한 **investigator** 연구자, 조사자

구문 07~10행 A hypothesis **not only** should fit *the facts* [which brought about its creation] **but** should **also** be compatible with the rest of the body of science.
→ <not only A but also B>는 'A뿐만 아니라 B도'의 의미이다. [ ]은 관계사절로 the facts를 수식한다.

18~20행 ~, he will probably be **much more careful** to see if it does fit the known facts **than** will be the case if he does not expect an immediate test of this sort.
→ <비교급+than> 구문이 쓰였고, much는 비교급을 강조하는 부사이다. 두 개의 밑줄 친 부분은 모두 if가 이끄는 명사절로 '~인지 아닌지'의 의미이다.

실전 모의고사 26회

229 ④ 230 ① 231 ③ 232 ① 233 ② 234 ① | 본문 124p

229 ④ | to find → finding

해설 ④ <have difficulty+(in)+v-ing>의 구조로 'v하는 데 어려움을 겪다'란 뜻. 따라서 to find는 finding이 되어야 한다.

① 문맥상 과거의 습관이나 반복적인 행동을 나타내므로 '~하곤 했다'란 뜻의 <used to+동사원형>은 적절.
② 문맥상 '~라면, …할 텐데'의 의미로 가정법 과거 구문. 주절에는 <주어+would+동사원형>이, 종속절에는 <if+주어+동사의 과거형>이 사용되었다. 가정법 과거 구문에서는 인칭에 상관없이 were를 쓰기도 한다.
③ finishing과 and로 병렬 연결되므로 earning은 적절.
⑤<regret+v-ing>는 과거에 한 행동에 대해 후회를 한다는 의미이다. 참고로 <regret+to-v>의 경우는 'v하게 되어 유감이다'란 뜻.

해석 내 친구 Martin은 Los Angeles라는 도시에 대해 항상 불평을 하곤 했는데, 그는 박사학위를 받는 3년 동안 그곳에 살았다. 그는 스모그와 교통, 그리고 돈이 많이 드는 생활에 대해 끊임없이 불평을 해댔다. Martin은 만일 다른 도시로 옮길 수만 있다면 삶은 훨씬 더 장밋빛일 거라고 확신하고 있었다. 학습 과정을 마치고 학위를 취득하고 난 몇 주 내로, 그는 소지품들을 꾸려 Boulder로 갔다. 거기에 도착한 지 몇 달도 채 되지 않아 그는 추운 날씨와 느리게 흘러가는 생활, 그리고 자신의 수준에 맞는 집을 구하는 것이 얼마나 어려웠는지에 대해 불평을 하기 시작했다. 그는 갑자기 Los Angeles의 화창한 날씨와 재미있었던 생활에 고마워하지 않았던 것을 후회했다.

어휘 **doctorate** 박사학위 **incessantly** 끊임없이 **convince** ~을 확신시키다; ~을 설득하다 **rosy** 장밋빛의, 유망한, 밝은 **degree** 학위; 정도 **belongings** 소지품 **have difficulty (in)+-ing** ~하는 데 어려움을 겪다 **appreciate** ~을 고맙게 생각하다; 진가를 인정하다

230 ① | chooses → choose

해설 ① 선행사가 those이므로 관계사절의 동사는 복수동사 choose로 바꿔야 한다. those who는 '~한 사람들'이라는 뜻.
② 사역동사 makes는 목적격보어로 동사원형을 취하므로 laugh는 적절.
③ help는 목적격보어 자리에 원형부정사나 to부정사 모두 취할 수 있으므로 적절.
④ 뒤에 주어가 없는 불완전한 구조가 이어지며 선행사가 사람(people)이므로 주격 관계대명사 who는 적절.
⑤ can build와 and로 연결된 병렬구조이므로 동사원형 practice는 적절.

해석 대부분의 사람은 텔레비전을 보는 것이 아주 좋지는 않다고 믿는다. 그래서 자신이 보는 프로그램을 신중하게 선택하는 사람들은 사실 텔레비전이 꽤 유익할 수 있다는 것을 알면 놀랄지도 모른다. 당신을 웃게 하는 것은 무엇이든지 유익하므로, 텔레비전의 코미디 프로그램이나 재미있는 드라마를 보는 것은 좋다. 그리고 당신이 과학, 의학, 역사, 예술과 같은 중요한 분야들을 이해하는 것을 돕는 훌륭한 교육 프로그램과 다큐멘터리가 많이 있다. 텔레비전은 고령이거나 질병 때문에 집밖에 자주 나갈 수 없는 사람들, 그리고 특히 병원의 환자들에게 매우 도움이 된다. 영어를 배우는 학생들에게 TV는 매일의 언어 연습 기회를 제공하는데, 학생들은 외국어로 된 프로그램을 보면서 어휘를 늘리고 듣기를 연습할 수 있다.

어휘 **beneficial** 유익한, 이로운 **field** 분야; 들판

구문 03~05행 ~ television(S) can actually be(V) quite beneficial(C) for *those* [who choose(V′) carefully *the programs*(O′) [(*that*) they watch ∨]].

231 ③

해설 (A) 이하 절의 문장이 주어, 동사, 목적어를 갖춘 완전한 문장이므로 관계대명사 what이 나올 수 없다. <in that ~>은 '~라는 점에서'의 뜻이다.
(B) 주어가 participation으로 단수명사이기 때문에 단수동사 is가 적절하다. in acts ~ consumption이 주어를 수식하고 있음에 주의한다.
(C) 문맥상 동명사 consuming과 and로 연결되어 병렬구조를 이루는 동명사 producing이 적절하다. consuming과 producing은 둘 다 뒤의 명사 media를 목적어로 취하고 있다.

해석 신조어를 만들어내는 데에는 종종 좋은 이유가 있다. 예를 들어 prosumption (production+consumption)과 produsage (production+usage)는 우리를 생산과 소비가 수반하는 것에 대해 다시 생각해 보게 한다. 그러나 우리의 입장에서 이 두 개념은 문제가 있는데, 그 개념들이 생산과 소비라는 두 개별 관행의 점점 더 연관되는 속성과 이 두 관행의 결합을 혼동되게 한다는 점에서 그렇다. Beer와 Burrows는 "생산과 소비의 경계를 희미하게 하는 행동에의 참여는 이제 수백만 사람들의 일상생활의 정착된 일부가 되었다"라고 썼다. 이러한 구별 흐리기가 바로 우리가 의문을 제기하고자 하는 것이다. 사람들이 이전의 어느 때보다 매체를 소비하고 생산하는 데 더 많은 여가 시간을 쓰고 있다는 것은 틀림없이 사실이지만 그것이 그 관행들이 흐릿해진다는 것을 의미하지는 않는다. 그 대신 그들은 두 개의 구별되는 관행으로서 존속한다.

어휘 **coin** 동전; (새로운 낱말·어구를) 만들다 **anew** 다시, 새로 **entail** ~을 수반하다, 일으키다 **in that** ~라는 점에서 **blur** ~을 흐리게 하다 **definitely** 분명히, 틀림없이

구문 05~09행 However, in our view **these two concepts** are problematic **in that they confuse** the increasingly connected nature of two separate practices—**production and consumption—with** the conflation of **these two practices**.
→ 주어 these two concepts와 in that절의 주어 they는 앞 문장의 "Prosumption (production+consumption)" and "produsage (production+usage)"를 지칭한다.
→ <confuse A with B>는 'A와 B를 혼동하다'의 뜻인데, the increasingly ~ and consumption이 A에 해당하고 the conflation ~ practices가 B에 해당한다. the conflation of these two practices에서 these two practices는 production and consumption을 가리킨다.

232 ① | judged → judging

해설 ① most of us가 판단 받는 대상이 아니라 다른 사람들의 성격을 판단하는 주체이므로 능동의 현재분사 judging이 되어야 한다. when (we(= most of us) are) judging character in others에서 we are가 생략된 구조.
② '~이든 아니든'의 의미로 부사절을 이끄는 <whether ~ or not>으로 적절하다.
③ 타인을 판단할 때 stereotype에 근거해 판단하는 경향을 지적하고 있는 글. muscular people → strong → good leaders로 추론하는 일례에서 추측을 나타내는 must(~임이 틀림없다)가 적절하게 쓰였다.
④ just as ~ (as the rest of us)에서 비교 대상이 생략된 형태.
⑤ the way 뒤에 양태(~하는 식)를 나타내는 관계부사절 that ~이 이어지고 있는 구조. the way how라고는 하지 않는다.

해석 우리 중 많은 이들은 사람들을 단지 관찰함으로써 성격을 알 수 있다고 생각한다. 그러나 연구자들은 우리 대부분이 다른 사람들의 성격을 판단할 때 고정관념을 이용한다고 믿는다. 즉, 우리는 특정 유형의 사람이 어떤 특정한 성격을 가질 것이라고 예상하고, 그래서 그것들이 (그 사람에게) 있든 없든 그 특징들을 보게 된다. 예를 들어, 근육질의 사람은 강하기 때문에 그들은 훌륭한 리더임에 틀림없다(라고 생각한다). 그러나 종종 그들은 실제로는 수줍고 소심하다. 뚱뚱한 사람들은 명랑하고 낙천적이며 따뜻한 마음을 가졌다고 생각되지만 그들도 못지않게 우울해질 가능성이 있다. 많은 경우 사람들은 그들이 생각하기에 타인이 그들에게 행동하기를 기대하는 방식으로 행동하기도 할 것이다. 그들은 (타인들이 자신에게 기대하는) 그 유형이 되기 위해 노력할 것이다.

어휘 **personality** 성격; 인물 **stereotype** 고정관념 **trait** 특성 **muscular** 근육질의; 근육의 **timid** 소심한, 겁 많은 **jolly** 명랑한, 즐거운 **optimistic** 낙천적인, 낙관적인 **warmhearted** 마음씨가 따뜻한 **depressed** 우울한, 슬픈

233 ②

해설 (A) 양보의 부사절을 이끄는 no matter what[which]은 명사를 바로 앞에서 수식할 수 있다. 같은 뜻을 가지는 복합관계대명사인 whatever나 whichever도 마찬가지이다. *e.g.* No matter which side wins, I shall be satisfied. = Whichever side wins, ~.
(B) appear가 '~인 듯하다'의 의미로 SVC 구조를 취할 때 보어 자리에 형용사, to부정사, 또는 that절이 올 수 있다. 따라서 보어로 쓰일 수 있는 형용사 committed가 적절. committed는 '헌신적인'이라는 뜻.
(C) 문장의 주어가 동명사구인 Using words ~ these이므로 단수동사로 받아야 한다.

해석 훌륭한 작가의 일차적 목표는 독자가 이해할 수 있도록 자기 생각을 명료하게 제시하는 것이다. 그렇게 하지 못한다면 어떠한 종류의 창의성 혹은 통찰력을 보여준다 하더라도 그들은 실패하는 것이다. 오해를 피하기 위해서는 정확한 단어를 선택하는 것이 중요하다. 그러나 많은 사람이 특정한 관점에 너무 얽매인 것처럼 보이는 것을 두려워하며 가능한 한 합리적이고 공정하게 보이기를 원한다. 그들은 '다소', '꽤', '얼마간' 같은 한정사를 사용한다. 이와 같은 단어들을 사용하는 것은 주장이나 견해를 확신이 없어 보이게 만들어 그 영향력을 약화시킨다. 그러니 만약 당신의 생각을 더 강하게 표현하려면 불필요한 한정사를 제거하고 당신의 의견에 자신감을 가지고 글을 써라.

어휘 **primary** 제1의, 주요한; 최초의 **creativity** 창의력, 독창성 **insight** 통찰력 **misunderstanding** 오해 **fair-minded** 공정한 **qualifier** 한정사, 수식어구 **weaken** ~을 약화시키다 **argument** 주장; 논의, 토론 **position** 견해, 의견; 위치 **eliminate** ~을 제거하다

234 ① | where → which[that]

해설 ❶ 뒤에 주어가 없는 불완전한 문장이 나오므로 관계부사 where는 쓸 수 없다. developed의 주어 역할을 할 수 있는 주격 관계대명사 which 또는 that이 적절.

② before는 전치사와 접속사로 모두 쓰이므로 구와 절 모두 취할 수 있다. 뒤에 주어, 동사를 갖춘 절이 나오므로 적절.
③ <permit A to-v (A가 v하게 허락하다)>의 구조.
④ 이 문장의 주어는 The rivers로 두 개의 동사 divided와 created가 연결된 병렬구조로 알맞게 쓰였다.
⑤ what은 선행사를 포함하는 관계대명사로 앞에 선행사가 없고 what이 이끄는 명사절이 전치사 beyond의 목적어 역할을 하므로 적절.

해석 미국에서 가장 큰 열 개 도시 중 여덟 곳에 19세기에 개발된 내부 도심 구역이 있다. 이러한 도시들은 자동차와 버스가 널리 보급되기 전에 모두 정착되었고, 따라서 사람들이 직장과 집 사이를 걸어 다닐 수 있도록 둘 사이가 서로 가까워야 했다. 이 구역이 위치한 곳의 강은 보통 도시를 나누고 육상 교통에 대한 장벽이 되었다. 댈러스, 로스앤젤레스, 피닉스 같은 신생 도시들은 비록 도로 시스템이 설계되었을 때 예상되었던 것 이상으로 인구가 증가함에 따라 여전히 교통 정체를 겪고 있지만, 차량 수송을 최우선에 두고 설계되었고 수로 경계가 더 적다.

어휘 **automobile** 자동차 **widespread** 널리 보급된, 널리 퍼진 **permit A to-v** A가 v하게 허락하다 **barrier** 장벽, 장애물 **transportation** 수송, 운송 **uppermost in mind** 최우선으로

구문 07~09행 *The rivers* [**on which** they are located] often divided the cities and created barriers to land transportation.
→ <전치사+관계대명사>는 관계부사로 바꿔 쓸 수 있으며 선행사가 장소이므로 where로 바꿔 쓸 수 있다.

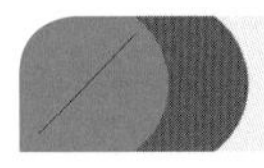

실전 모의고사 27회

235 ④ 236 ③ 237 ⑤ 238 ① 239 ④ 240 ⑤ | 본문 126p

235 ④ | which → where[in which]

해설 ❹ 뒤에 <주어(a beneficial mutation)+동사(is carried)+부사구(by everyone ~ population)> 형태의 완전한 절이 나오므로 관계대명사 which는 올 수 없다. 문맥상 '게놈의 영역'이라는 뜻이므로, 장소를 나타내는 관계부사 where나 관계부사 역할을 하는 in which가 와야 한다.

① 의미상 주어인 evolution이 변화를 '만드는' 것이므로 현재분사 making이 적절. 부대상황을 나타내는 분사구문을 이끈다.
② 10 percent of the human genome이 최근의 돌연변이와 '관련되는' 것이므로 수동태 be linked가 적절.
③ including은 '~을 포함하여'란 의미의 전치사이므로 명사구가 이어진다.
⑤ 동명사는 전치사 by의 목적어가 될 수 있으므로 looking은 적절.

해석 새로운 유전적 증거에 의하면, 진화는 과거 10만 년 이내에도 변화를 만들어내며 계속해서 인류를 형성해왔다. 연구자들은 인간 게놈의 10퍼센트 정도가 최근의 돌연변이 혹은 적응성의 유전적 변화와 연관 있을지 모른다는 사실을 발견했다. 집단 유전학자들은 아프리카계 미국인, 유럽계 미국인, 그리고 중국인을 포함한 24명의 DNA 표본에서 백만 개가 넘는 유전자 변종을 분석했다. 그들은 유익한 돌연변이가 집단의 모든 사람에 의해 옮겨지는 게놈의 영역들을 찾고 있었다. 그들은 돌연변이를 둘러싼 DNA의 변이성을 살펴봄으로써 돌연변이가 집단에 퍼져 나가기 시작한 지 얼마나 되었는지 알아낼 수 있었다.

어휘 **genetic** 유전의 ***cf.* geneticist** 유전학자 **evolution** 진화 **species** 종(種) **be linked to** ~와 관련되다 **adaptive** 적응성의, 적응할 수 있는 **variation** 변종 ***cf.* variability** 변이성 **beneficial** 유익한

236 ③ | amusing → amused

해설 ❸ 주어인 some(일부 고양이들)이 '즐거움을 느끼는' 것이므로 과거분사가 적절하다.

① 뒤에 how가 이끄는 명사절이 오므로 명사 상당어구를 목적어로 취하는 전치사 because of는 적절.
② 동사 get은 'O가 v하게 만들다'라는 의미로 쓰일 때 <get+O+to-v> 구조를 취하므로 목적격보어 자리에 to hate가 적절히 쓰였다.
④ 뒤에 <주어(cats)+동사(are attracted)+부사구(to the motion ~)> 형태의 완전한 절이 오며 동사 is의 보어절을 이끄는 자리이므로 명사절 접속사 that은 적절.
⑤ 문맥상 '애완동물의 반려인'이라는 뜻으로, one's(= a pet's)를 대신하는 소유격 관계대명사 whose가 적절.

해석 어떤 고양이들은 우리가 그들 주위에서 물을 다루는 방식 때문에 물을 무서워할지도 모른다. 많은 시끄러운 수고양이가 길에서 물이 든 양동이를 뒤집어써 왔고, 장난꾸러기 아이들은 종종 정원용 호스로 새끼 고양이들을 괴롭힌다. 고양이를 강제로 목욕시키는 것은 고양이가 물을 싫어하게 하는 확실한 방법이다. 이러한 예시들을 제외하고는, 사실 고양이가 물을 좋아한다는 증거는 많다. 많은 고양이가 물이 가득 차 있는 개수대나 물이 흐르는 샤워기로 뛰어드는 것을 망설이지 않으며, 몇몇은 실제로 물이 수도꼭지에서 머리 위로 똑똑 떨어질 때 즐거워하는 것처럼 보인다. 그런 긍정적인 반응들의 한 가지 이유는 고양이들이 물의 움직임과 소리에 끌린다는 것이다. 고양이는 습관의 동물이므로, 어렸을 때부터 물에 많이 노출된 애완동물은 그 반려인이 안전을 염려해 물로부터 지켜줬던 애완동물보다 목욕을 훨씬 더 잘 참을 것이다.

어휘 **tomcat** 수고양이 **bucket** 양동이 **naughty** 버릇없는, 말을 안 듣는 **tease** ~을 괴롭히다, 놀리다 **aside from** ~ 외에는 **amuse** ~을 즐겁게 하다 **faucet** 수도꼭지 **drip** (액체가) 똑똑 떨어지다 **companion** 동반자 **shield** ~을 보호하다; 방패

구문 02~03행 **Many a** noisy tomcat ***has*** had a bucket of water thrown its way, ~.
→ <many a + 단수명사>는 <many + 복수명사>와 같은 표현이다. 내용상 복수이지만 단수 취급한다.

13~16행 ~, so *a pet* [**that** has been exposed to water // since it was young] will tolerate a bath much better than *one* [**whose** human companion shielded it from water / out of fear for its safety].

→ 비교 대상이 되는 a pet과 one(= a pet)이 각각 관계사절의 수식을 받고 있다.

237 ⑤

해설 (A) were never asked 다음에 쓰인 간접의문문 what you were seeking과 what you could afford to spend의 뒤를 이어 간접의문문이 위치해야 하므로 접속사 that이 아닌 if[whether]가 맞다.
(B) ~ *the salesperson* [who was indifferent to a potential customer's needs] was soon out of a job에서 볼 수 있듯이 [ ] 부분에 의해 수식을 받는 the salesperson의 동사 자리이므로 was가 되어야 한다.
(C) one [whose business or approval / we need to earn]에서 볼 수 있듯이 [ ]부분이 one(= a reader)을 수식하는 구조이다. [ ] 부분에서 밑줄 부분은 earn의 목적어가 된다. 즉 one을 수식하는 어구를 이끄는 것과 동시에 earn의 목적어를 이루는 business or approval 앞에 쓰일 수 있는 것은 소유격 관계대명사인 whose이다.

해석 당신이 새 컴퓨터를 찾아 가게에 들어가는데 당신이 만난 첫 번째 판매사원이 즉시 일렬로 늘어선 컴퓨터들을 가리키며 "저것들 중 어떤 것도 괜찮아요."라고 말한 후 떠난다면, 당신 역시 합당한 이유로 떠나게 될 가능성이 높다. 왜 그럴까? 당신은 당신이 무엇을 찾고 있는지, 얼마를 쓸 여유가 있는지, 혹은 그 컴퓨터가 일을 하기 위해 쓰일 것인지 즐거움을 위해 쓰일 것인지 혹은 자녀의 숙제 과제를 위해 쓰일 것인지와 같은 질문을 결코 받지 않았기 때문이다. 간단히 말해서, 그 판매사원은 당신의 요구와 선호에 대하여 결코 고려도 질문도 하지 않았다. 잠재 고객의 요구에 무관심한 판매사원이 곧 일자리를 잃는 것을 알게 되는 것이 충격이 아니듯이, 독자를 무시하는 작가들에게도 마찬가지의 것이 적용된다. 독자는 작가의 '고객'이고 그의 일이나 승인을 얻을 필요가 있는 사람이다. 독자에 대하여 더 많이 알면 알수록, 그의 필요와 기대를 충족시킬 가능성은 더 커진다.

어휘 **row** 줄, 열 **chance** 가능성 **assignment** 과제 **in brief** 간단히 말해서 **preference** 선호 **indifferent** 무관심한 **out of a job** 실직해서 **hold true** 진실이다, 유효하다 **approval** 승인, 찬성

구문 11~13행 **Just as *it*** wouldn't be a shock *to learn* (*that*) the salesperson ~ was soon out of a job, ~
→ Just as는 '~한 것과 꼭 마찬가지로'의 뜻이다. it은 가주어이고 to learn ~ a job이 진주어이며, learn 뒤에는 접속사 that이 생략되어 있다.

238 ① | calmly → calm

해설 ❶ be동사의 보어로 형용사들(smart, witty, and polished)이 이어지고 있는 구조에서 부사 calmly는 적절치 않다. that은 형용사를 공통으로 강조하는 부사로 쓰였다. 앞 문장에서 목격한 public speakers만큼 '그렇게' 똑똑하고 평온하며 위트 있고 말주변 좋을 수는 없을 거라고 부러워한다는 얘기.

② <what A is about>: A가 무엇인가 하는 본질
③ audience는 집합명사로 단수 취급하므로 doesn't가 적절.
④ used to는 '~하곤 했다'라는 과거의 습관을 나타내는 조동사이므로 뒤에 동사원형 put이 온 것이 적절.
⑤ 사역동사 make는 목적격보어로 원형부정사를 취하므로 feel이 적절.

해석 우리 중 많은 이들은 대중 연설가들을 지켜보며 속으로 생각해 왔다. "와, 나는 절대로 저렇게 똑똑하고, 침착하고, 재치 있고, 세련될 수 없을 거야." 그러나 대중 연설을 성공적으로 하기 위해서 완벽할 필요는 없다. 대중연설이란 그런 것이 아니다. 그것은 당신과 당신의 청중이 당신의 연설에서 무엇을 기대하느냐에 전적으로 달려 있다. 당신의 청중은 완벽을 기대하지 않는다. 이것을 알기 전에, 나는 완벽한 연설을 하기 위해 나 자신에게 믿을 수 없는 정도의 압박을 가하곤 했다. 대중 연설의 핵심은 이것이다. 당신의 청중에게 가치 있는 어떤 것을 제공하여라. 가치 있는 어떤 것을 얻는다면 그들은 감사해 할 것이다. 만일 당신이 사람들을 비판하거나, 궁극적으로는 그들에게 혜택을 주고자 그들을 자극한다면 비록 그 당시에는 당신이 그들의 마음을 언짢게 할지라도 그들은 여전히 당신에게 감사할 것이다.

어휘 **polished** 세련된, 우아한; 광이 나는 **perfection** 완벽 **incredible** 놀라운, 믿기 어려운 **essence** 핵심, 본질 **criticize** ~을 비판하다; ~을 비난하다 **stir up** ~을 자극하다, 흥분시키다 **ultimately** 궁극적으로

239 ④

해설 (A) 앞에 완전한 구조가 나오므로 whatever는 올 수 없다. whatever는 문장에서 주어, 목적어, 보어 역할을 하는 명사절을 이끌기 때문이다. 따라서 부사절을 이끄는 however가 정답. 문맥상으로도 '아무리 ~해도'라는 뜻의 <however+형용사+주어+동사> 구문이 적절하다.
(B) 절과 절을 연결해주는 말이 필요하므로 접속사 When이 정답. Then은 부사이므로 두 절을 직접 연결해 하나의 문장을 만들 수 없다.
(C) 선행사 anything은 단수 취급하므로 주격 관계대명사절의 동사도 단수동사 preserves가 적절. -thing, -body, -one으로 끝나는 대명사는 단수 취급한다.

해석 일기를 쓰는 것은 당신의 영혼에 매우 좋은 영향을 끼칠 수 있다. 그것은 당신에게 위안을 주며 당신이 얼마나 화가 나는지, 행복한지, 또는 무서워하는지에 관계없이 당신 자신에 대해 표현하게 한다. 당신은 마음을 터놓을 수 있다. 일기장은 불평하거나 불필요한 조언을 주지 않고, 당신이 그것을 잘 숨겨놓기만 하면 다른 누구도 당신의 비밀에 대해 듣지 못하리라고 확신할 수 있다. 마음에 있는 것을 수정하지 않고 모두 글로 적어놓으면, 당신의 생각들은 더 명확해지고 당신은 자신을 발견할 수 있다. 그리고 일기들은 개인적인 일대기의 훌륭한 기록이 된다. 예를 들어, 당신이 한때 얼마나 어린애 같았는지, 성숙해졌는지, 또는 얼마나 많이 달라졌는지를 알 수 있다. 또한 당신은 (일기를) 글로 제한할 필요가 없다. 친구들에게 받은 쪽지, 사진, 영화 입장권, 기억을 간직하는 어떤 것이든 일기에 풀이나 테이프로 붙일 수 있다.

어휘 **keep a journal** 일기를 쓰다 **do wonders** 매우 좋은 영향을 미치다, 기적을 행하다 **edit** ~을 수정하다; (책 등을) 편집하다 **childish** 어린애 같은, 유치한 **paste** ~을 풀로 붙이다

240 ⑤ | them → it

해설 ❺ 문맥상 '차에 타자마자 안전벨트 매는 것을 습관으로 만들다'라는 뜻. 진목적어인 to부정사구를 대신할 수 있는 가목적어로 대명사 it이 쓰여야 맞다.

① 문맥상 '~한다면'의 의미이므로 if는 적절.
② 동명사 부정은 <not+v-ing>.
③ the proper use에 수일치하므로 단수동사 has는 적절.
④ 안전벨트를 매는 '사람들'의 의미로 불특정 다수를 의미하는 those는 알맞다.

해석 당신은 운전할 때 안전벨트를 하시나요? 물론, 하시겠죠, 대부분의 시간 동안은요. 하지만 하지 않는다면 그 이유가 무엇인가요? 싱가포르, 쿠알라룸푸르, 마닐라에서 3,000명을 조사해보니, 응답자의 3분의 2가 가끔, 보통 짧은 거리를 이동할 때 안전벨트를 매지 않는다고 인정했습니다. 조사에 따르면 안전벨트의 적절한 사용이 수십만 명

의 생명을 구했습니다. 안전벨트를 매지 않는 사람들은 안전벨트를 매는 사람보다 중상을 입을 위험이 훨씬 더 크다는 것은 분명합니다. 어떤 사람들은 고속도로에서는 안전벨트를 매지만 근처를 갈 때는 매지 않습니다. 그것은 심각한 실수입니다. 통계에 따르면 대부분의 차 사고는 집에서 5km 이내에서 일어납니다. 차에 타자마자 안전벨트를 매는 것을 습관으로 하세요.

어휘 **buckle up** 안전벨트를 매다 **survey** 조사 **respondent** 응답자 **admit to+명사(상당어구)** ~을 인정하다 **proper** 적당한, 알맞은 **freeway** 고속도로 **statistic** 통계(자료); 통계학

고난도 모의고사 4회

241 ③ **242** ④ **243** ④ **244** ④ **245** ② **246** ④ | 본문 128p

241 ③ | **When exploding → When these stars[the stars/they] explode**

해설 ③ 분사구문의 의미상 주어는 앞 문장에서 언급된 massive stars like Antares로서 문장 전체의 주어(their oxygen)와 일치하지 않으므로 의미상 주어를 생략한 채로 두는 것은 적절치 못하다.

① <there+V+S> 구문에서 주어는 동사 뒤에 오는 the three lightest elements이므로 복수동사 were가 적절.
② '결과'를 나타내는 to부정사가 적절히 쓰였다.
④ 앞의 the iron을 가리키므로 단수 형태의 it이 적절.
⑤ a cloud of gas and dust를 선행사로 하는 주격 관계대명사 자리이므로 that은 적절.

해석 우주의 시초에는 오직 세 개의 가장 가벼운 원소들, 즉 수소, 헬륨, 그리고 약간의 리튬만이 있었다. 그러나 생명체는 우리가 들이마시는 산소와 우리 혈액 속에 있는 철과 같이 더 무거운 원소들을 필요로 한다. 안타레스처럼 거대한 별들은 그들의 수명 동안 헬륨 핵을 결합해 산소를 만들어 낸다. 이 별들이 폭발하면 산소가 우주로 방출되고 폭발 그 자체는 철을 만든다. 천문학자들은 초신성 폭발이 대부분의 철을 만들었고 그것과 산소를 우주로 방출했다고 생각한다. 이런 원소들은 다른 원소들도 포함한 가스와 먼지 구름의 일부를 이루었고 우리 태양계를 생성시켰다.

어휘 **element** 원소; 요소 **iron** 철분; 철 **massive** 거대한 **nuclei** nucleus ((원자)핵)의 복수형 **explode** 폭발하다 ***cf.* explosion** 폭발 **cast** ~을 던지다 **solar system** 태양계

242 ④ | **they were → it was**

해설 ④ 문맥상 'that 이하(that ~ contamination)가 생각되었다'라는 의미가 자연스러우므로 진주어 that절을 대신하는 가주어 자리로 보는 것이 적절. 따라서 it was로 고쳐야 한다.

~, **it** was thought **that** *this bacterial DNA* (**found** during genome mapping) was ~.
(S′: this bacterial DNA, V′: was)

① 주어가 복수명사 Areas이므로 복수동사 have가 적절히 쓰였다.
② DNA가 '침략받는' 대상이 되므로 수동 형태가 적절.
③ 뒤에 완전한 형태의 절이 왔고 문맥상 의문사 where의 뜻도 없으므로 밑줄 친 곳은 관계부사 자리이다. 계속적 용법의 where는 and there로 바꿔 쓸 수 있고 이때 there는 on its(= the fruit fly's) DNA를 의미한다.
⑤ 진주어를 이끄는 접속사 that으로 적절.

해석 과학자들이 유전자 암호를 더 많이 연구할수록, 그들은 놀라운 것들을 더 많이 발견한다. 종종 '정크 DNA'라고 불리는 DNA의 영역은 쓸모없는 것이 아니라 강력한 조절 역할을 하고 있다. 또한, 새로운 연구는 DNA가 다른 종에서 온 유전자의 침략을 받을 수 있다는 사실을 발견했다. 초파리는 DNA에 박테리아의 게놈을 전부 가지고 있다는 것이 발견되었는데, 그 DNA에서 박테리아의 게놈은 계속해서 (후대에) 전해질 것이다. 초파리 유충은 이 DNA를 가지고 태어날 것이다. 게놈 지도를 작성하는 과정에서 발견된 이 박테리아 DNA는 우연한 오염에 의한 것으로 수십 년 동안 생각되었다. 우리 인간에게도 같은 일을 하는 침입자가 있을까? 지금까지 발견된 것은 없지만 박테리아가 그들의 DNA를 전승하기 위해 우리의 DNA를 이용하는 일도 가능하다.

어휘 **genetic** 유전학의 ***cf.* gene** 유전자 **regulatory** 규제하는 **invade** ~을 침범하다, 침략하다 ***cf.* invader** 침입자 **species** ((생물)) 종 **fruit fly** 초파리 **pass on** ~을 전달하다 **accidental** 우연한, 임시의 **contamination** 오염 **transfer** ~을 전하다, 옮기다

243 ④ | **made it possible → made possible**

해설 ④ 동사 made의 긴 목적어(what is called "horizontal reading" ~)가 목적격보어 possible 뒤에 이어 나오므로 가목적어 it이 올 자리가 아니다. 목적어가 길어 보어 뒤에 놓인 경우.

① the times (before the printing press)가 선행사로 시간을 나타내고 있으므로 when이 적절하다. 그 시절은 사정이 어땠는지를 설명하는 관계부사절.
② 전치사 with 뒤에 동명사가 쓰인 구조. 의미상의 주어가 certain passages로, 동명사의 수동형 being revisited가 맞게 쓰였다.
③ 전달되는 언어의 성격에 따라 return visits가 어떠한지 설명하는 부분. 만족'시키는', 즉 '만족스러운' 일이 되므로 능동의 의미를 띠는 분사 satisfying이 보어로 맞게 쓰였다. and로 이어지는 challenging의 -ing도 같은 성격.
⑤ 동사 자리에 fuel이 쓰였다. 수식 부분을 뺀 나머지 주어가 the information으로 단수이므로 단수형 fuels로 맞게 쓰였다.

해석 '깊이 읽기(사변적 독서)'는 극소수의 사람들에 의해 극소수의 책이 소유되었던 인쇄기 이전의 시대에 그 역사적인 뿌리를 두고 있다. 책은 대개 어떤 글귀는 이해를 위해 거듭거듭 '재방문'되면서 읽히고 또 읽히는 성경과 같은 어떤 것이었다. 언어가 더 비유적이고 시적일수록 재방문은 더 만족스럽고 도전할 만하였다. 그러나 인쇄기의 도래는 많은 주제에 대한, 훨씬 더 많은 사람을 위한, 훨씬 더 많은 책의 생산이라는 결과를 가져왔는데, 이는 소위 '수평적 읽기' — 깊이 읽기의 전통을 전반적으로 대체한 보다 광범위한 정보 수집의 형태 — 를 가능하게 한 변화였다. 적절한 균형을 유지한다면 수평적 읽기로 수집된 정보가 깊이 읽기에서 이뤄지는 사고에 불을 지필 것이다. 그러나 문제는 두 가지 읽기 형태 사이에 건강한 균형을 찾기가 쉽지 않다는 것이다.

어휘 **printing press** 인쇄기 **own** 소유하다 **Bible** 성경, 성서 **repeatedly** 반복적으로 **metaphorical** 은유적인, 비유적인 **poetic** 시적인, 시의 **satisfying** 만족스러운 **horizontal** 수평선의, 횡적 **replace** 대체하다, 대신하다 **fuel** 연료를 대다, 촉진하다

구문 09~13행 The arrival of the printing press, however, resulted in the production of *far more books* (**on** many topics) (**for** far more people), *a change* [which made possible what is called "horizontal reading" ~].

동격의 콤마(,) V′ OC′ O′

→ far more books를 수식하는 전명구 두 개가 이어 나온 구조. 훨씬 더 많은 책이 만들어지게 된 것을 다음 수순으로 일어날 현상의 원인에 해당하는 a change로 보고 있다.

→ 사역동사 <make + O + OC> 구조에서 긴 목적어를 목적어 자리에 쓰지 않고 목적격보어 뒤에 썼다.

244 ④ | it → which

해설 ④ 두 문장이 접속사 없이 연결되고 있으므로 대명사 it(= a steep set of stairs)이 아니라 관계대명사 which로 연결되어야 한다.

① 계속(for most of their adult lives)을 나타내는 현재완료가 맞게 쓰였다.
② we know (stories) to be fiction의 목적격보어 자리에 해당하는 to be로 맞게 쓰였다. (we know ∨ to be fiction)
③ <S+V+O(first draft)+OC(difficult)>의 구조에서 형용사(difficult)를 부사 painfully가 맞게 수식하고 있다.
⑤ 앞에 나온 말(you will get where you are going)을 받는 so이다.

해석 성인으로서의 삶의 대부분을 글을 쓰며 지내 온 나와 같은 사람들에게는 글쓰기란 꿈꾸기와 같은 무의식적인 행위가 의식적인 것으로 변형된 것인 것 같다. 왜 우리는 꿈꾸는가? 진정으로 아는 이는 없는 것 같다. 마치 왜 우리가 이야기를, 특히 허구로 알고 있는 이야기를 갈망하는지 진짜 아는 사람이 없는 것 같이 말이다. 나의 글쓰기 경험은 늘 처음에 영감을 받고 그보다 더 힘들고 한 발 한 발 나아가야 하는, 영감을 실행에 옮기는 일이 뒤섞인 어떤 것이다. 대부분의 작가는 초고 내기가 가파른 계단을 그 끝이 눈에 보이지 않는데 힘들게 오르는 것처럼 고통스러울 정도로 힘들다고 느낀다. 우리는 그저 인내하며 나아갈 수밖에 없다! 결국엔 네가 가고 있는 곳에 닿게 될 것이다. 혹은 그러기를 희망한다. 그리고 그곳에 도달했을 때 당신은 '왜 (그랬지)?' 하고 묻지 않을 것이다. 당신이 느끼게 될 안도감은 잠깐 내쉬는 마법에 불과할 뿐 곧 또 다른 영감과 또 다른 초고, 또 다른 가파른 오름으로 다시 시작하게 된다.

어휘 **conscious** 의식적인 ***cf.*** **unconscious** 무의식적인 **variant** 변형, 이형 **crave** 갈망하다 **fiction** 허구, 꾸며낸 이야기 **invariably** 변함없이, 항상 **blend** 섞다; 섞은 것, 혼합물 **initial** 최초의, 시초의 **inspiration** 영감 **plod** 무거운 걸음으로 걷다, 천천히 나아가다 **execution** 실행, 실천 **draft** 초안, 초고 **painfully** 고통스럽게, 힘들게 **steep** 가파른 **in sight** 시야 안에, 눈에 보이는 곳에 **persevere** 인내하며 계속하다 **relief** (고통 등의) 제거, 경감 **brief** 잠시 동안의 **spell** 주술, 마력

구문 09~11행 Most writers find first drafts painfully difficult, like climbing *a steep set of stairs*, the end of **which** isn't in sight.

V O OC = a steep set of stairs

→ <콤마(,)+which>의 변형으로, 계속적 용법의 관계대명사는 <접속사+대명사>의 역할을 한다.(= ~ like climbing a steep set of stairs, and the end of it isn't in sight)

245 ② | to sleep → sleep

해설 ② 사역동사 let의 목적격보어 자리이므로 원형부정사 sleep으로 바꿔야 적절.

① 전치사 without의 목적어로 동명사 drowning이 왔으므로 적절.
③ 문맥상 뇌의 절반(half)을 먼저 언급한 후 나머지 절반을 언급하고 있으므로 the other (half)는 적절.
④ '숨을 쉬기 위해'라는 의미의 '목적'을 나타내는 to부정사가 적절. 앞의 (to) surface는 to swim과 병렬구조를 이루어 the ability를 수식한다.
⑤ swimming 이하는 logging을 부연 설명하는 동격 어구. logging과 문법적 성질이 대등한 동명사 swimming이 적절히 쓰였다.

해석 사람은 몇 초마다 한 번씩 자동적으로 숨을 쉬지만, 돌고래는 자기 임의대로 숨을 쉬고 30분 이상 숨을 참을 수도 있다. 돌고래는 어떻게 익사하지 않고 잠을 잘까? 잠자는 동안 호흡을 조절하기 위해, 돌고래는 한 번에 한쪽 뇌만 잠을 자도록 한다. 돌고래의 뇌 활동을 측정하는 뇌전도는 수면 주기에서 돌고래의 한쪽 뇌가 정말로 '멈추는' 반면, 다른 쪽 뇌는 기초 생명 기능을 유지한다는 것을 보여 준다. 연구자들은 돌고래가 하루에 약 8시간 동안 이러한 상태에 있는 것을 관찰했다. 돌고래는 헤엄치는 능력과 숨쉬기 위해 수면으로 올라오는 능력을 유지하면서도 8시간 동안 잠을 잔다. 이런 이상한 수면 습관은 '로깅'이라고 알려진 행동을 설명할 수 있는데, 이는 돌고래가 움직임이 거의 없이 수면을 따라 천천히 헤엄치는 것이다.

어휘 **automatically** 자동적으로 **voluntarily** 임의로, 자발적으로 **shut down** 멈추다; 문을 닫다 **approximately** 대략 **surface** 수면으로 올라오다; 표면

246 ④ | require → are required

해설 ④ 바로 앞에 위치한 관계대명사 which의 선행사는 certain trace elements (in our body)이므로 certain trace elements는 require의 주체가 아니라 대상이 된다. 그러므로 require는 수동태로 바뀌어서 are required가 되어야 적절하다.

① such는 셀 수 있는 단수 명사와 같이 쓰일 때 <such+a(n)+명사>의 어순이 되므로 어법상 적절하다.
② 관계대명사 which는 앞에 나온 명사 vegetables를 받는 것이므로 그 쓰임이 적절하다.
③ 관계부사 where가 이끄는 절이 앞에 나온 선행사 other examples를 수식하고, where 이하절이 문장 요소를 갖춘 절이므로 쓰임이 적절하다.
⑤ 동명사 lowering이 주어 역할을 하는 것이므로 어법상으로 적절하다.

해석 식품은 (우리 혀의) 미뢰와 눈에 더 즐겁게 될지라도 그것의 가치를 잃을 정도로 정제된다. 식품을 준비하는 과정에서 우리는 상당수의 비타민을 잃는 경향이 있다. 한 가지 예가 채소를 삶는 것인데, 채소의 대부분은 너무 삶게 되면 그것들의 가치를 잃어버리는 경향이 있다. 쌀을 정미하고 설탕을 정제하는 것도 더 좋은 모습에 대한 선호가 식품으로서의 그것들의 필수적인 가치의 파괴로 이어지는 다른 사례들이다. 모두에게 알려진 것처럼 우리 몸속에는 우리를 건강하게 유지해 주는 데 필요한 어떤 미량 원소가 있다. 신체 체계 속에 그것들의 적은 양이 줄어드는 것도 많은 질환을 초래할 수 있는데, 예를 들어 혈액 속의 철분 부족은 빈혈과 허약함을 초래할 것이다. 나트륨 결핍도 마찬가지로 많은 질환을 초래한다.

어휘 **refine** 정제하다 **extent** 정도, 범위 **taste bud** 미뢰, 맛봉오리 **polish** 정미하다 **preference** 선호(도) **essential** 필수적인 **trace element** 미량 원소 **give rise to** ~을 초래하다 **disorder** 질환, 질병 **weakness** 허약함, 쇠약함 **deficiency** 결핍, 부족

구문 09~11행 **As** is known to everybody, there are *certain trace elements* in our body [**which** are required to keep us in good health].

→ As는 '~한 것처럼'의 뜻이다. 관계대명사 which의 선행사는 certain trace elements이다.

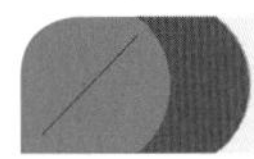

실전 모의고사 28회

247 ④ 248 ⑤ 249 ③ 250 ④ 251 ② 252 ② | 본문 130p

247 ④ | what → that

해설 ④ 이어지는 절이 SVO의 완전한 구조이므로 불완전한 구조가 이어지는 관계대명사 what은 올 수 없다. be동사의 보어절을 이끄는 명사절 접속사 that이 적절.

① 명사구 the Spanish Civil War ~ 1930s를 이끌므로 '~ 동안'이라는 뜻의 전치사 During은 적절.
② 주어가 동명사구(Deciding ~ aid)이므로 단수동사 was는 적절.
③ 색다른 단체가 '알려진' 것이므로 과거분사 known이 적절. known as는 '~로 알려진'이라는 뜻.
⑤ 주어가 단수명사 the organization이므로 단수동사 gives는 적절. 앞의 동사 buys, gives와 and로 연결되어 병렬구조를 이룬다.

해석 1930년대 후반 스페인 내전 시기에 농부 댄 웨스트는 자원봉사 구호 요원으로 일하고 있었다. 한정된 식량 원조물을 어떻게 배분하는가를 결정하는 것은 그에게 매우 좌절감을 느끼게 하는 일이었다. 고국에 돌아오자 그는 지금은 '하이퍼 인터내셔널'이라고 알려진 색다른 단체를 설립했는데, 이 단체의 목적은 가정에 그들의 소유가 되는 소를 주어서 영원히 기아를 구제하는 것이었다. 이 프로그램의 특이한 점은 각 가정이 자신들의 동물의 암컷 새끼 중 적어도 한 마리씩을 이웃에 줘야 한다는 것인데, 그것을 받은 이웃도 차례로 그것의 새끼 중 한 마리를 전달하는 식이다. 처음 이 프로그램은 해외로 소를 수송했지만, 이제 이 단체는 닭, 염소, 오리, 낙타, 꿀벌 같은 많은 동물을 그 지역에서 사서 나눠주며 나무도 준다.

어휘 **volunteer** 자원봉사자, 지원자 **relief** 구호(품); 안심 **distribute** ~을 분배하다 **aid** 원조, 도움 **frustrating** 좌절감을 주는 **offspring** 새끼, 자손 **originally** 처음에, 원래

248 ⑤ | saving → to save[save]

해설 ⑤ help는 목적어로 to부정사나 원형부정사를 취하므로 to save 또는 save가 적절하다.

① '목적'을 나타내는 <so (that) S+can ~(S가 ~할 수 있도록)>에서 that이 생략된 형태.
② animals는 둘이 아닌 그 이상이므로 each other가 아닌 one another로 쓴 것이 알맞다.
③ 문장의 동사 talked와 병렬구조를 이루므로 동사의 과거형 wrote가 적절.
④ '동시동작'을 나타내는 분사구문. '설명하면서' 다녔다는 얘기.

해석 에번 그린은 숲이 개간될 때 동물들이 사는 곳이 파괴되는 것을 항상 우려했다. 그가 어렸을 적에 어머니에게 말했다. "저는 아무도 그 위에 건물을 짓지 못하게 세상의 모든 땅을 사고 싶어요." 그는 동물들이 서로에게 어떻게 의지하고 있는지에 대해, 그리고 우림의 나무들이 모두를 위해 공기를 정화하도록 돕는다는 것을 배웠다. 에번은 모든 사람에게 땅을 보호하는 것에 관해 이야기했고 기업체와 학교에 편지를 썼다. 그는 야생지를 구하기 위한 기금을 모으고 있는 이유를 설명하며 집집이 돌아다녔다. 마침내 그는 레드 드래건 보호 팀을 만들어 그들이 모은 돈으로 코스타리카에 있는 링콘 우림의 16에이커 이상을 구하는 데 도움을 주었다.

어휘 **clear** ~을 개간하다; ~을 제거하다 **conservation** 보호

249 ③

해설 (A) a (significant) majority of처럼 부분을 나타내는 표현은 뒤따르는 명사가 단수면 단수로, 복수면 복수로 취급한다. 여기서는 A significant majority of 뒤에 the most celebrated highlights라는 복수 표현이 나왔으므로 복수형 동사 come을 선택한다.
(B) <have+O+p.p.>는 'O가 ~되게 하다', 'O가 ~받다' 등의 의미이다. their names와 engrave의 관계가 수동이므로 과거분사형인 engraved로 쓴다.
(C) 주어는 the reason, 동사는 has이다. they use 앞에는 목적격 관계대명사가 생략되었으며, 앞의 the excuses를 수식하는 관계대명사절이다. 문장에 동사가 있고 관계대명사절 안에도 use라는 동사가 있어 동사를 또 쓰면 안 되므로 to justify를 고른다.

해석 운동선수로서 강한 사고방식을 가지는 것은 많은 큰 경기가 결국 몇 인치와 몇 분의 일 초로 귀결되기 때문에 필수적이다. 대부분의 스포츠 역사상 가장 유명한 하이라이트의 상당수는 결국 아주 작은 부분의 문제가 된다. 시계상에서 4분의 1초가 추가되거나 왼쪽으로 2인치만 더 가면 완전히 다른 선수 집단의 이름이 저 상징적인 트로피에 새겨지게 되고 스포츠에서 가장 탐이 나는 보석을 얻는 것으로 끝이 난다. 그러면 무엇이 숨막힐 정도로 대단한 선수들과 보통 선수들을 구별 짓는가? 많은 팬들은 경기에서의 분기점을 잘못 튄 공이나 심판의 잘못된 판정 탓으로 돌린다. 그들의 생각에, 어떤 선수들은 다른 선수들보다 운이 더 많은 것 같다. 그들의 태도는 약하며 그들이 만족하지 못하는 이유는 그들이 자신들의 단점을 정당화하기 위하여 사용하는 변명과 매우 깊은 관계가 있다.

어휘 **mindset** 사고방식 **indispensable** 없어서는 안 될, 필수적인 **come down to** 결국 ~이 되다; (한마디로) 요약되다 **fraction** 파편, 단편, 소부분 **engrave** (문자·도안 등을) 새기다 **iconic** 우상의, 상징적인 **breathtaking** 숨이 막히는 **attribute A to B** A를 B의 탓으로 돌리다 **turning point** 전환점; 위기, 고비 **call** (심판의) 판정 **referee** 심판 **shortcoming** 결점, 단점

구문 11~13행 Many fans **attribute** turning points in games **to** a bad bounce or poor call by a referee.
→ <attribute A to B>는 'A를 B의 탓으로 돌리다'의 뜻으로, A 부분이 결과이며 B 부분이 이에 대한 원인이다.

250 ④ | being exposed → exposing

해설 ④ 형식상으로는 <전치사+동명사>로 문제없어 보이지만 뒤이어 동사 expose의 목적어(larger amounts of water)가 오므로 능동형으로 써야 맞다. <expose A to B>: A를 B에 노출시키다

① 주어(only ~ Arctic sea ice)가 목적어(the summer of 2007)를 survive(살아남다)한 것이므로 능동태로 쓴 것이 적절. 2007년 여름이 지나도 녹지 않고 얼음의 형태로 그대로 남아 있었다는 의미.
② 현재(is)의 양과 특정 과거시점(in the 1950s)의 양을 비교하는 비교급 틀에서 과거의 양을 나타내는 부분이므로 과거시제가 적절.
③ than과도 호응이 되고, far(훨씬 더 ~한)의 수식도 받을 수 있는 비교급 earlier(더 일찍)가 맞게 왔다.
⑤ 관계대명사 what은 단수 개념이므로 이어지는 동사로 happens가 맞게 쓰였다.

해석 국립빙설자료센터(NSIDC)에 따르면 4백 3십만 제곱킬로미터의 북극해 얼음만이 2007년의 여름을 견뎌냈다고 한다. 그것은 기록상 역대 9월 말 중에서 가장 적게 남

겨진 것이다. 국립빙설자료센터는 또한 전체 북극 빙하의 양이 현재 1950년대 (빙하의) 양의 반이라고 추정한다. 더 나쁜 소식은 북극 빙하의 녹는 속도가 가속화되고 있다는 것이다. 북극의 모든 빙하가 2030년경이면 사라질지도 모르는데, 이는 이전에 예측한 것보다 훨씬 이른 것이다. 해빙이 해수면 상승을 일으키지는 않지만 그것은 더 많은 양의 물을 태양에 노출함으로써 지구 온난화를 가중시킨다. 북극의 기후가 어떻게 변하고 있는지는 완전히 파악되지 않았지만 우리는 이것만큼은 알고 있다. 그곳에서 벌어지는 일이 결국 우리 모두에게 영향을 미치리라는 것이다.

어휘 **Arctic** 북극의 **survive** ~을 견디다, 살아남다 **least** 최소량; 가장 적은 **on record** 기록된 **estimate** ~을 추정하다 **accelerate** 빨라지다, 가속하다 **prediction** 예측 **expose** ~을 노출시키다 **eventually** 결국

251 ②

해설 (A) '장점과 약점이 무엇인지'라는 의미가 되어야 하므로 what이 적절.
(B) 주어 You가 놀라움을 '느끼는' 것이기 때문에 과거분사 amazed가 적절.
(C) '(앞으로) 스스로 한계를 짓지 말 것을 기억하라'는 의미이므로 미래성을 나타내는 to부정사가 적절.

해석 교육은 관점과 사고방식을 바꾸기 때문에 삶에 근본적인 변화를 일으킬 수 있다. 고등학교 졸업 후 최고의 교육적 선택을 하기 위해서, 친구들이나 가족 구성원들에게 당신의 강점과 약점이 무엇이라고 생각하는지 물어보라. 당신에게 이상적인 학습 과정에 관한 그들의 제안을 받아들여라. 당신이 미처 깨닫지 못했던 당신에 관한 것들을 그들이 어떻게 알고 있는지에 당신은 깜짝 놀랄 것이다. 스스로에 한계를 두지 말 것을 기억해라. 요즘에는 정말 많은 기회가 있고 당신이 변호사나 간호사가 되어야 할 필요는 없다. 아마 그것이 당신이 되고 싶은 것일 수도 있지만 다른 가능성에 당신의 마음을 활짝 열어두라. 목표는 당신이 해야만 하는 것이 아니라 하고 싶은 것을 찾는 것이다.

어휘 **fundamental** 근본적인 **outlook** 관점; 전망 **suggestion** 제안 **possibility** 가능성

252 ② | increases → increase

해설 ② increases는 관계절 내의 동사로 선행사 other changes에 수가 일치되어야 한다. 따라서 복수동사 increase가 적절하다.

① was made의 보어 자리에 형용사 possible이 적절하게 쓰였다.
③ 원래 문장 New data is not only stored ~.에서 not only가 강조를 위해 앞으로 나가 주어와 동사가 도치된 구문. 주어가 new data이므로 동사 is는 적절하다. 뒤에 수동의 p.p.를 이끌어야 하기 때문에 does로 쓸 수 없다.
④ collectors를 받는 3인칭 복수 목적격 대명사 them이 적절하게 쓰였다.
⑤ 목적을 나타내는 to부정사의 부사적 용법이 문맥과 어법에 적절하다.

해석 당신에 대한 방대한 데이터 라이브러리는 항상 보충되고 있다. 이러한 진보는 이런 모든 데이터를 포착하고 저장할 수 있는 컴퓨터와 특히 2000년대 초반 동안 데이터 저장 용량 비용의 갑작스러운 하락에 의해 가능해졌다. 그러나 컴퓨터는 또한 당신의 취약성과 당신에 대한 정보의 가치를 증가시키는 다른 변화들도 가능하게 했다. 이 새로운 데이터는 전자적으로 저장될 뿐 아니라 검색이 가능한 데이터베이스 안에 존재하기도 한다. 그것들은 정보를 수집하는 사람들이 자신들의 흥미를 끄는 데이터의 유형의 유용한 목록을 만드는 것을 가능하게 해준다. 다음 토요일에 있을 콘서트의 모든 예매권 구매자들의 명단이나, 누가 토요일에 체육관에 등록했는지를 보는 것과, 그러고 나서 당신이 찾는 사람의 부류를 정확하게 알아내기 위해 성별, 나이, 소득 수준, 또는 우편 번호로 이 목록을 추가로 더 처리하는 것은 쉽다.

어휘 **supplement** 보충하다 **advance** 진보 **capture** 포착하다 **capacity** 수용 능력 **electronically** 전자적으로 **reside in** ~안에 존재하다 **advance ticket** 예매권 **zip code** 우편 번호

구문 02~05행 This advance was made **possible** **[by computers** that can capture and store all of this data], and especially **[by the sudden drop** / in the price of data storage capacity / through the early 2000s].
→ 두 개의 [ ] 부분은 수동태의 행위자를 나타내는 by ~ 표현이며 and로 묶여 병렬 구조를 이루고 있다. possible은 능동태에서 목적격보어의 자리이기 때문에 수동태에서도 그대로 형용사 보어로 사용되었다.

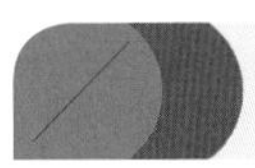

실전 모의고사 29회

253 ③ 254 ① 255 ③ 256 ④ 257 ④ 258 ④ | 본문 132p

253 ③ | is → are

해설 ③ 부사구인 Especially at risk가 문두에 옴에 따라 주어와 동사를 도치시킨 구문. 주어가 our youngest citizens이므로 복수동사인 are가 적절.

① 진목적어인 to부정사구(to smoke ~ old)를 대신한 가목적어 it으로 적절히 쓰였음.
② 뒤에 <주어(harmful secondhand smoke)+동사(is)+보어(more concentrated)> 형태의 완전한 절이 이어지므로 접속사 that은 적절. 여기서 that절은 say의 목적어 역할을 하는 명사절이다.
④ 지금까지 다른 주들도 비슷한 법을 '통과시켰다는' 의미이므로 능동의 현재완료가 적절.
⑤ 문맥상 앞 문장의 similar laws를 지칭하므로 복수 대명사 them이 알맞음.

해석 메인 주(州)의 운전자들은 길을 나설 때 새로운 규칙을 따라야만 한다. 새로운 법은 4월 10일 주 전역에서 시행되었는데, 16세보다 어린 승객을 태우고 있는 차에서 흡연하는 것을 불법으로 규정하고 있다. 건강 전문가들은 해로운 간접흡연이 차와 같이 밀폐된 환경에서 보다 집중되어 있다고 말한다. "특히 어린 시민이 위험한데, 그들은 위험한 간접흡연에 노출될지 말지에 대한 선택권도 없습니다."라고 메인 주의 주지사 존 발다치는 말한다. "이 법안은 어린이들의 건강을 지켜줄 것이기 때문에 중요합니다." 아칸소 주, 캘리포니아 주 그리고 루이지애나 주는 비슷한 법률들을 통과시켰다. 지지자들은 그것들이 중요한 조치라고 보고 있다. 이전에 대부분의 흡연 반대 법안들은 공공장소에서의 흡연만을 금지했다.

어휘 **hit the road** 출발하다, 여행하다 **take effect** 시행[발효]되다, 효력을 나타내다 **statewide** 주 전체에 **illegal** 불법의 **secondhand** 간접의; 중고의 **concentrate** ~을 집중하다; ~을 농축하다 **governor** 주지사, 통치자 **bill** 법안; 청구서 **ban** ~을 금지하다

구문 07~09행 Especially at risk are(V) our youngest citizens,(S) **who** don't have the choice **of** whether or not to be exposed to dangerous secondhand smoke. (the choice = whether ~ : 동격)

→ 부사구(Especially at risk)가 앞으로 나오면서 <동사-주어>로 도치되었다. who 이하는 our youngest citizens를 부가 설명한다. whether 이하는 the choice를 구체적으로 설명하는 동격 어구. 전치사 of는 동격 관계를 나타내기도 한다.

254 ① | puzzled → puzzling

해설 ❶ 새로운 범주가 '어리둥절하게 하는' 주체이므로 현재분사 puzzling이 적절.

② 문장 전체의 주어 A real planet을 가리키므로 its가 적절히 쓰임.
③ <leave+O+OC (~을 …한 상태가 되게 하다)> 구조. 천문학자들이 혼란스러움을 '느낀' 것이므로 목적어와 목적격보어는 수동관계이다. 따라서 목적격보어 자리에 과거분사 형태가 적절.
④ 전치사 By의 목적어 자리에 동명사가 온 것으로 적절.
⑤ allow는 목적격보어로 to부정사를 취하므로 to continue는 적절.

해석 국제천문학협회가 새로운 규칙을 채택하여 태양계는 이제 왜소(矮小)행성이라고 불리는 애매한 새로운 범주의 행성들까지도 포함한다. 진짜 행성은 태양계 내의 그 주변에서 중력이 가장 세지만, 왜소행성은 태양 둘레를 도는 물체로서 위성이 아니며 거의 원형에 가깝다. 이런 불명확한 정의는 천문학자들을 혼란스럽게 만들었다. '거의 원형'이라는 것은 얼마나 둥근 것을 말하는가? 이로써 새로운 물체가 왜 소행성인지 아니면 단지 '작은 태양계 천체'에 불과한지를 두고 장차 과학자들 사이에 논쟁이 있으리란 것은 거의 확실하다. '왜소행성'이라는 새로운 용어를 만듦으로써 국제천문학협회는 명왕성이 다른 범주에 속한다는 것을 인정하지만 수백만 명의 학생들은 명왕성을 계속 행성이라고 부른다.

어휘 **astronomical** 천문학의 *cf.* **astronomer** 천문학자 **adopt** ~을 채택하다; ~을 양자로 삼다 **gravitationally** 중력으로 **dominate** (어떤 장소에서) 가장 크다, 두드러지다; 지배하다 **definition** 정의(定義) **confused** 혼란스러운, 당황한 **all but** 거의(= almost) **coin** (새로운 용어를) 만들어내다 **acknowledge** ~을 인정하다 **Pluto** 명왕성

255 ③

해설 (A) '너무 ~해서 …하다'의 의미인 <such (a)+명사+that ...> 구문을 만드는 that을 써야 한다.
(B) 문장에 동사가 없으므로 동사 set을 써야 한다. 주어가 생략된 명령문의 형태.
(C) 문맥상 '~했지만 결국 v하다'라는 의미가 적절하므로 <only+to-v> 형태로 쓴다.

해석 당신은 어딘가에 도착하기 위해 너무 서둘러서 그 여정에 대한 기억이 희미한 적이 있는가? 당신의 경력을 발전시켜 주거나 그 완벽한 인맥을 제공해 줄 바로 그 특정한 사람을 찾고 있다면 역시 같은 상황이 적용될 수 있는데, 당신은 인생에서 매우 영향력이 있을지도 모를 몇몇 사람들을 놓칠 수 있다. 만약 그것이 당신의 포부를 발전시켜 줄 것이라고 결론을 내린 것이라면, 어떻게 해서든지 특정 범주나 직책에 속하는 집단 전체의 사람들과 접촉하는 목표를 스스로 설정하되, 그 여정도 또한 반드시 즐겨라. 당신은 어떤 사람들이 시간이 지나면서 당신의 인생에 어떻게 영향을 미칠지 전혀 알지 못한다. 당신은 상점 주인이 라디오의 디제이가 되고자 하는 당신의 열망에 아무런 도움이 안 될 거라고 단정할지도 모르지만, 결국 그의 누이가 지역 방송국의 유명 진행자라는 것을 알게 될 수도 있다. 당신은 사과에 있는 씨앗의 개수를 셀 수는 있으나, 씨앗에 있는 사과의 개수는 셀 수 없다.

어휘 **faint** 희미한 **specific** 특정한 **connection** (인간적·사회적) 관계 **by all means** 어떻게 해서든지, 당연히 **further** 발전[성공]시키다 **ambition** 야망, 포부 **make sure** 반드시 (…하도록) 하다 **aspiration** 열망 **presenter** 진행자, 사회자 **seed** 씨앗

구문 07~11행 By all means **set** yourself a goal of contacting *a whole group of people* [**that** fall into a specific category or job title] / if **that** is [what **you have decided** will further your ambitions], // but **make sure** you enjoy the journey, too.
→ 전체적으로 보면 동사 set과 make sure이 but으로 연결된 병렬구조의 명령문이다. 첫 번째 [ ] 부분은 a whole group of people을 수식하는 관계절이다. if 다음의 that은 contacting ~ job title을 가리키는 대명사이다. 두 번째 [ ] 부분은 주격보어 역할을 하며, you have decided는 삽입되었다.

13~16행 You may determine / **that** the shop owner will be of no benefit to your aspirations of being a DJ on the radio, **only to find** that his sister is the star presenter on the local station.
→ that은 determine의 목적어가 되는 명사절을 이끈다. <only to-v>는 '결국 …하다'라는 결과의 의미를 나타낸다.

256 ④ | its → their

해설 ❹ 문맥상 animals or people을 받으므로 단수형 소유격 its가 아닌 복수형 their로 써야 한다.

① When절의 생략된 주어 most people이 '요청을 받는' 입장이므로 수동형 asked가 적절. When (they are) asked ~.
② <have difficulty v-ing>: v하는데 어려움이 있다
③ <find+O+OC>의 구조에서 목적어인 명사를 묘사하는 말로 형용사 adorable이 쓰인 게 적절.
⑤ 신체적 특징이 귀여움을 자아내는 한 요소라는 얘기가 끝나고 또 하나의 요소인 행동 방식에 관한 얘기가 시작되는 곳이다. 분사구문으로 또 다른 화제를 유연하게 꺼내고 있다. If[When] we look at actions의 의미.

해석 대부분 사람들은 강아지와 새끼 고양이가 귀엽다고 생각한다. 그러나 새끼 고양이와 강아지가 왜 귀엽다고 생각하는지를 설명해달라고 하면, 대부분의 사람들이 명쾌한 설명을 하는 데 아마 애를 먹을 것이다. 그러나 왜 우리가 이 동물들이 사랑스럽다고 생각하는지에 대한 명백한 과학적 이유가 있는 것으로 밝혀졌다. 귀여움은 분명히 몇 가지 요소에 달려있는데 그들 중 몇 가지는 신체적인 것이고 또 다른 몇 가지는 이 동물들이 행동하는 방식과 관련이 있다. 첫째, 아기와 많은 다른 새끼 동물들이 그렇듯이, 귀여움은 대부분 그들의 머리와 눈의 크기에 비해 작은 몸을 가진 동물들이나 사람들과 주로 관련이 있다. 행동하는 걸 보면 장난기가 귀여운 것으로 간주된다. 이것은 또한 아기들의 또 다른 특징이다.

어휘 **adorable** 사랑스러운 **apparently** 분명히; 보기에 **be associated with** ~와 관련이 있다 **playfulness** 장난기 **characteristic** 특징

구문 09~13행 First, cuteness(S) is most often associated with(V) *animals or people* [**that** have small bodies when (*they are*) compared to the size of their head and eyes, as is(~처럼) ~ animals].

257 ④

해설 (A) that children consume ~ to save와 동격을 이루는 the fact가 주어이므로 단수동사 ignores를 써야 한다.
(B) countries를 수식하는 관계절이 완전한 문장이므로 관계부사 where를 써야 한다.
(C) 동사 has stated의 목적어 역할을 하는 that절 안에서 주어가 전명구 above ~

a year의 수식을 받는 population growth rates이고 동사가 없으므로 that절의 동사 자리이다. 따라서 복수동사 act를 써야 한다.

해석 많은 나라에서 인구 증가가 발전에 부정적인 영향을 끼쳤을지도 모르지만, 이 영향의 크기는 가늠하기 어렵다. 그리고 몇몇 경우에는 아마도 인구 증가가 발전을 촉진했을 것이다. 예를 들어 아이들이 재화와 서비스를 소비하므로 국가의 저축 능력을 떨어뜨린다는 사실은 그 아이들이 성장해서 생산력을 가진 성인이 된다는 사실을 무시하는 것이다. 게다가 기반 시설에서 교육과 의료 서비스로의 투자 전환이 반드시 손실은 아닌데, 교육과 의료는 노동력의 생산성을 증대시킬 것이기 때문이다. 인구 증가의 해로운 영향은 이용할 수 있는 땅과 물이 상대적으로 부족한 나라에서 가장 두드러질 것이다. 인구 증가를 용인할 수 있는 정도에 대한 일반화가 모든 상황에 다 들어맞는 것은 아니지만, 세계은행은 한 해에 2%를 초과하는 인구 증가율은 경제 발전에 제동 장치 역할을 한다고 말했다.

어휘 **magnitude** 규모, 중대(성) **assess** 평가[사정]하다 **stimulate** 자극하다, 활발하게 하다 **diversion** 전환 **pronounced** 현저한, 두드러진 **relatively** 상대적으로 **scarce** 부족한 **state** 말하다, 진술하다

구문 05~09행 For instance, **the fact** [that children consume goods and services and thus lower the ability of a nation to save] ignores **the fact** [that the children grow up and become productive adults].

→ 각각의 [ ] 부분은 앞에 있는 the fact와 동격 관계의 명사절이다.

13~16행 The harmful effect of population growth / should be most pronounced in *countries* [**where** usable land and water are relatively scarce].

→ [ ] 부분은 관계절로 countries를 수식한다.

258 ④ | them → it

해설 ❹ 뒤에 진목적어 역할을 하는 that절이 있는 것으로 보아 가목적어가 와야 할 자리이다. 따라서 it으로 바뀌어야 한다. <make, think, believe, find, consider 등의 동사+it+보어+to-v/that절> 구문이다.

① 문장의 동사는 should have received이므로 준동사 자리이며 about ~ Plan의 수식을 받는 a copy of information과 send는 수동의 관계이므로 과거분사 sent는 적절하다.
② ~ if we should face a wildfire 절에서 if가 생략되고 주어와 조동사가 도치된 구문이다.
③ 문장의 주어는 전명구 for the start of this year의 수식을 받는 The weather conditions이므로 복수동사 have는 적절하다.
⑤ '특정 기간(the first week of school) 동안'을 나타내는 전치사 during이 적절하게 쓰였다. 수치적 기간이 아닐 때는 for가 아니라 during을 쓴다.

해석 모든 학부모님은 연초에 학생 편에 가정으로 보내 드린 Bakersfield 고등학교 산불 대처 방안에 관한 안내문을 한 부씩 받으셨을 것입니다. 학생과 교직원 모두가 산불에 직면할 경우 무엇을 해야 하는지 아는 것은 필수적입니다. 이 (대처) 방안의 중대함은 모든 학생에게 면밀히 설명되었습니다. 올해 초의 기상 상태는 꽤 온화했지만, 화재의 위험성은 여전히 심각하여, 모든 학생과 교직원이 무엇을 해야 하는지 아는 것을 중대하게 만들었습니다. 학교 전체가 개학 첫 주 동안에 산불 발생 시 지정된 '산불 대피 장소'인 Yontville 스포츠 센터로 대피하는 것과 비상 상황 통제 절차를 연습했습니다. 학생들은 그 훈련에 성숙하고 진지하게 임하여 매우 인상적이었으며 이에 대해 칭찬받아야 할 것입니다.

어휘 **wildfire** 산불 **vital** 필수적인 **face** 직면하다 **critical** 중대한 **rehearse** (예행) 연습하다 **evacuation** 대피 **designate** 지정하다 **refuge** 피난처 **emergency** 비상 (상황) **procedure** 절차 **impressive** 인상적인 **mature** 성숙한 **drill** (반복) 훈련

구문 01행 All parents **should have received** a copy of information ~.

→ <should have+p.p.>는 '~했어야 했는데 (안 해서 유감이다)'라는 뜻으로 주로 쓰인다. 하지만 여기서는 should 자체에 '추측'의 의미가 있기 때문에 '~했을 것이다'라는 과거 사실에 대한 추측의 의미로 쓰였다.

04~05행 It is vital that all students and staff know what to do [**should we** face a wildfire].

→ [ ] 부분은 '~가 혹시라도 … 한다면'의 의미로 <If+주어+should+동사, ~> 구문에서 If가 생략되고 도치되어 <should+주어+동사 ~>의 형태로 쓰였다.

실전 모의고사 30회

259 ① 260 ⑤ 261 ④ 262 ③ 263 ① 264 ⑤ | 본문 134p

259 ① | recovering → recovered

해설 ❶ 문장에 동사가 없고 문장의 주어인 Men이 '회복했다'라는 의미가 자연스러우므로 recovered가 되어야 적절. Men은 관계사절 whose ~ surgery의 수식을 받는다.

② that절의 주어인 동명사구 being married or partnered의 동사 자리이므로 단수동사가 적절.
③ <from A to B>로 이어지는 구문. 전치사 to 뒤의 목적어로 쓰였으므로 동명사가 맞다.
④ 요소(factor)가 '동기를 부여하는' 것이므로 능동의 현재분사 motivating은 적절.
⑤ 앞의 to smoke와 or로 연결된 병렬관계이므로 engage는 맞게 쓰였다. to부정사가 등위접속사로 병렬 연결될 때 뒤의 to는 생략하는 경우가 더 많다.

해석 연구에 의하면 독신 남성에 비하여 결혼한 남성이 더 건강하다. 수술 후 아내가 자주 찾아왔던 남자들이 더 빨리 회복했다. 의학박사인 존 고어는 말한다. "우리도 그 원인을 명확하게 말할 수는 없습니다. 그러나 한 가지 학설은 결혼했거나 짝이 있다는 것은 당신이 궁지에 몰렸을 때 당신의 안녕을 보살피고 삶의 많은 압박을 덜게 도와줄 누군가가 있다는 것을 의미한다는 것입니다." 청구서를 지불하는 것에서부터 사교 행사에 참여하는 것에 이르는 모든 것들에 대해 스트레스가 덜 느껴지는 것은 우리가 그 모든 것들을 혼자 하지 않아도 된다고 느낄 때이다. 배우자는 건강한 생활양식을 선택하는 데 있어 종종 동기 요소가 된다. 결혼한 남성들은 담배를 피우거나 위험한 활동에 관여하는 확률이 더 낮다.

어휘 **surgery** 수술 **recover** 회복하다; ~을 되찾다 **definitively** 명확하게 **welfare** 안녕, 행복 **spouse** 배우자 **when it comes to** ~에 관한 한 **engage in** ~에 관여[참여]하다 **risky** 위험한

260 ⑤ | which → where[in which]

해설 ⑤ 뒤에 <주어(the now purified water)+동사(is collected)> 형태의 완전한 절이 나오므로 관계대명사 which는 불가. 선행사가 another flask이고 '그 플라스크 안에' 정화된 물이 모인다는 문맥이므로, 장소를 나타내는 관계부사 where 나 관계부사 역할을 하는 in which가 적절.

① the components of liquid mixtures를 받으므로 복수형 their가 적절.
② foreign matter(이물질)가 '용해되어' 있는 것이므로 수동을 나타내는 과거분사가 적절.
③ '~에 이르다'라는 뜻의 reach는 타동사이므로 전치사 없이 바로 목적어를 취한다.
④ 분사구문의 의미상 주어인 the steam이 원래의 액체 형태로 '돌아가는' 주체이므로 현재분사 returning은 적절.

해석 서로 다른 끓는점에 근거해서 액체 혼합물의 구성성분을 분리하는 과정을 증류라 한다. 증류는 또한 그 안에 용해된 다른 이물질로부터 순수한 물을 분리함으로써 물을 정화하는 데 사용될 수도 있다. 그 과정은 비교적 간단하다. 이물질이 섞인 물은 버너 위의 유리 플라스크 안에서 끓는점에 도달할 때까지 가열된다. 끓는점에서 물은 증기로 증발되는데, 이 증기는 상승하여 응축기라고 불리는 관으로 향하게 된다. 응축기에서 증기는 식어서 원래의 액체 형태로 되돌아간다. 응축관은 아래로 기울여져 다른 플라스크에 연결되는데, 거기에는 이제 정화된 물이 모인다. 모든 입자나 이물질은 끓여진 플라스크에 남겨진다.

어휘 **component** 구성 요소, 성분 **liquid** 액체의 **mixture** 혼합물 **purify** ~을 정화하다 **foreign** 이질적인; 외국의 **dissolve** ~을 용해하다 **relatively** 상대적으로 **impure** 불순물이 섞인, 순수하지 못한(↔ **pure**) **vaporize** 증발[기화]하다 ***cf.*** **vapor** 수증기 **condenser** 액화[농축] 장치 ***cf.*** **condense** ~을 응축하다; ~을 압축하다 **angle** ~을 비스듬하게 하다; 각도 **particle** 입자

261 ④

해설 (A) 앞뒤의 두 절을 연결하면서 문장의 주어 역할을 할 수 있는 것은 계속적 용법의 관계대명사 which. 여기서 which가 가리키는 것은 stress.
(B) 문장 전체의 동사 자리이므로 동사 역할을 할 수 있는 report가 와야 한다. have suffered는 주어 people을 수식하는 관계대명사절의 동사.
(C) 문맥상 people을 의미하므로 them이 알맞다.

해석 연구에 의하면 용서는 스트레스 수준을 낮춰주는데, 스트레스는 심장질환 및 다른 질병에 대한 주요 위험 요인이다. 자신에게 잘못을 저지른 사람을 용서하는 것을 상상해보라고 요청받았을 때 사람들은 혈압, 근육 긴장, 그리고 면역 반응이 즉각적으로 개선되는 것을 보여주었다. 지독한 피해를 입었던 사람들조차 자신을 공격한 사람을 용서한 후 기분이 나아졌다고 말한다. 반면, 용서하기를 거부하는 것은 심장질환과 암 같은 질병을 발전시킬 위험을 높이는 것처럼 보인다. 사람들은 자신에게 잘못을 저지른 누군가를 용서하지 않는 상상을 하라고 요청받았을 때, 혈압과 근육긴장, 면역 반응 모두 악화되었다.

어휘 **factor** 요인, 요소 **wrong** 잘못된; 부당한 행위, 잘못; ~에게 나쁜 짓을 하다 **immediate** 곧 일어나는, 즉시의 **blood pressure** 혈압 **tension** (정신적, 신체적인) 긴장 **immune** 면역의 **devastating** 지독한, 충격적인; 파괴적인

구문 03~05행 When (***people were***) **asked** to imagine forgiving *a person* [**who** has done them wrong], / ***people*** showed immediate improvements ~.
→ 주절의 주어와 같은 부사절의 주어 people과 be동사 were를 생략하고 과거분사만 남긴 구조. who ~ wrong은 a person을 수식하는 주격 관계대명사절.

262 ③ | because of → because

해설 ③ because of 다음에는 구가 나와야 하는데 being in a group이 주어이고 makes가 동사인 절이 나오기 때문에 절을 이끄는 접속사 because를 쓰는 것이 옳다.

① 주어 Animals와 protect의 목적어가 동일한 대상을 가리키므로 복수형의 재귀대명사 themselves가 적절하다.
② 주어가 단수형 scanning이고, 문맥상, 살피는(scan) 것이 구성원 사이에 '공유되는' 것이므로 수동태 is shared가 적절하다.
④ any food를 선행사로 하는 주격 관계대명사 that이 적절히 쓰였다.
⑤ 주어가 animals가 아니고 The ideal size이므로 단수명사를 받는 동사 is가 적절하다.

해석 동물들은 보통 포식자를 피하거나, 적당한 양의 먹이를 얻기 위해, 또는 자기 종의 다른 구성원에 맞서서 스스로를 지키기 위해서 집단에 합류한다. 포식자를 유심히 살피는 것이 집단의 구성원들 사이에서 함께 이루어지기 때문에 집단은 포식자들에 맞서 (스스로를) 지킨다. 집단 안에 있는 동물들은 더 많은 음식을 얻을 수도 있는데, 왜냐하면 집단 안에 있다는 것이 먹이를 찾거나 잡거나 또는 잡아 놓은 먹이를 지키는 것을 더 쉽게 만들어주기 때문이다. 그럼에도, 집단에 속해 있다는 것에는 확보된 어떤 음식에 대한 집단 구성원 간의 경쟁과 같이 치러야 할 대가가 있을 수 있고, 기생충과 질병으로부터의 위험이 증가한다는 점도 있다. 집단의 이상적 규모는 보통 작지도(포식자를 면밀히 살피는데 너무 많은 시간이 소모되기 때문에) 크지도(싸우는 데 너무 많은 시간이 쓰이는) 않은 것이다.

어휘 **predator** 포식자, 포식 동물; 약탈자 **obtain** ~을 얻다, 획득하다 **adequate** 적당한, 충분한 **scan** ~을 자세히 조사하다, 세밀히 살피다 **prey** 먹이, 사냥감 **parasite** 기생충; 기생 동물

263 ①

해설 (A) 주어가 Oxygen and carbon dioxide이므로 복수동사 travel이 적절. Oxygen과 carbon dioxide 뒤에는 각각 이를 보충 설명하는 명사구가 삽입되어 있다.
(B) a message를 뒤에서 수식하는 분사 자리. 메시지가 '말해주는' 것이므로 현재분사 telling이 적절.
(C) 문맥상 '왜 하품이 전염성이 있는지를 알지 못한다'가 되어야 하므로 why가 적절.

해석 우리는 왜 하품을 하는가? 하품은 충분히 깊게 숨 쉬지 않아서 생기는 자연스러운 신체 작용이다. 신체가 기능하는 데 필요한 기체인 산소와 우리의 신체 작용에 의해 생산된 배출 가스인 이산화탄소는 폐를 통해 당신의 몸에 출입하면서 혈류를 타고 이동한다. 당신이 충분히 깊게 숨을 쉬지 않으면 이산화탄소가 체내에 축적된다. 당신의 뇌는 그것을 제거하기 위해 깊이 숨을 쉬라고 당신에게 말하는 메시지를 받는다. 당신은 종종 연달아 하품할 필요가 있다. 더 큰 미스터리는 만약 당신이 다른 사람이 하품하는 것을 보면 당신도 종종 하품하기 시작한다는 것이다. 과학자들조차 왜 하품이 전염성이 있는 것처럼 보이는지 이해하지 못하고 있다.

어휘 **yawn** 하품하다; 하품 **bloodstream** 혈류 **contagious** 전염성의

구문 03~06행 **Oxygen**, (*the gas* [that ~ to function]), **and carbon dioxide**, (*the waste gas* (produced by our body processes)), /
S
travel in your bloodstream, ~.
V

264 ⑤ | them → those

해설 ⑤ 비교급 more anxiety than으로 비교되는 두 대상은 동일한 형태와 격을 이루어야 한다. 앞에 나온 those competing for~과 비교되고 있으므로 those로 써야 알맞다. 또한, 대명사 them 뒤에는 수식어구가 올 수 없다.

① <the+비교급, the+비교급> 구문에서 두 번째 the more 다음은 find의 목적어 it을 설명해주는 목적격보어에 해당하므로 형용사 stressful은 적절하다.
② 앞에 있는 it is와 함께 <it ~ that> 강조구문을 이루고 있다.
③ 주어 they는 talent scouts나 their family에 의해서 '지켜봐지는' 대상이므로 수동형인 being watched가 적절히 쓰였다.
④ 선행사 an experiment는 뒤에 오는 관계사절 event importance was artificially set up in에서 전치사 in의 목적어 역할을 하므로 in which는 어법상 적절하다.

해석 스포츠 경기가 더 중요할수록 우리는 그것이 더 스트레스를 많이 준다고 생각할 가능성이 있다. 예를 들어 대부분의 축구 선수들은 친선 게임에서보다 월드컵에서 경기하면서 더 많이 긴장하게 될 것이라고 말하는 것이 아마 옳을 것이다. 그러나 중요한 것은 그 경기가 개인에게 주는 중요성이라는 것을 우리는 기억해야 한다. 이것은 반드시 그 경기의 중요도에 달린 것은 아니다. 예를 들면 재능 있는 신인을 발굴하러 다니는 사람이나 혹은 처음으로 자신의 가족이 지켜본다는 것을 아는 운동선수들은 특히 긴장감을 느낄 수 있다. Marchant와 그의 동료들은 경기의 중요성이 인위적으로 만들어진 실험을 이행하였다. 두 명으로 짝을 이룬 골퍼들이 3개의 새 공(낮은 중요도) 또는 새 골프 신발 한 켤레(높은 중요도)를 두고 경합을 했다. 예상한 대로 새 신발을 두고 경합을 하던 사람들이 골프공을 두고 경합한 사람들보다 더 많은 불안감을 느꼈다.

어휘 **friendly** 친선의 **count** 중요하다 **necessarily** 반드시, 필연적으로 **status** 중요도; 지위 **talent scout** 재능 있는 신인을 발굴하러 다니는 사람 **colleague** 동료 **carry out** ~을 이행하다, 수행하다

구문 07~09행 This does **not necessarily** depend on the status of the competition.
→ not necessarily는 '반드시 ~인 것은 아니다'라는 의미의 부분 부정을 나타낸다.

09~12행 For example, *athletes* [**who** know they are being watched by talent scouts, or perhaps by their family for the first time], may feel particularly anxious.
→ [ ] 부분은 주어인 athletes를 수식하는 관계절로 이후에 동사 may feel이 온다.

12~14행 Marchant and his colleagues carried out *an experiment* [in which event importance was artificially set up].
→ [ ] 부분은 an experiment를 수식하는 관계절이다. 절 안의 주어는 event importance, 동사는 was이다.

실전 모의고사 31회

265 ⑤ 266 ② 267 ④ 268 ② 269 ① 270 ④ | 본문 136p

265 ⑤ | are → is

해설 ⑤ that절의 주어가 the increase이므로 단수동사인 is가 적절. in the number ~ food allergies는 the increase를 수식하는 전명구이다.

① <have trouble[difficulty] v-ing>: v하는 데 어려움을 겪다
② 선행사로 tree nuts를 취하고 계속적 용법으로 쓰일 수 있는 관계사는 which이다.
③ 알레르기를 가진 아이들이 점점 늘어서 그들이 더는 혼자가 아니라는 문맥이므로 부정의 의미를 갖는 hardly가 적절.
④ 앞 문장의 Kids를 지칭하므로 복수형 대명사가 와야 하며, to부정사의 의미상 주어인 <for+목적격>의 형태로 바르게 쓰였다.

해석 엘리자 레이더가 17개월이 되었을 때, 그녀는 땅콩버터를 맛보았다. 그 후 바로 그녀는 두드러기가 났고 숨쉬기가 힘들었다. 나중에, 검사를 통해 엘리자가 심각한 땅콩 알레르기가 있고 참깨뿐만 아니라 아몬드, 개암, 호두와 같은 견과류에도 알레르기가 있다는 것이 확인되었다. 지금 엘리자는 12살이다. 그녀는 "나는 아이들이 좀 더 편안하고 안전하게 느끼도록 하고 싶어요."라고 말한다. 그러나 엘리자가 알아냈듯이, 그녀처럼 음식 알레르기가 있는 아이들은 더는 혼자가 아니다. 한 연구에서 땅콩 알레르기가 있는 어린이들이 지난 5년 사이에 두 배가 되었다는 것이 밝혀졌다. 아이들은 일반적으로 자라면서 우유와 계란 알레르기에서 벗어난다. 그러나 전문가들은 오늘날 그들이 그렇게 되는 것(알레르기에서 벗어나는 것)에 더 오랜 시간이 걸리고 있다고 말한다. 어떤 의사들은 음식 알레르기가 있는 아이들의 수가 증가하는 것이 가볍게 볼 일이 아니라고 말한다.

어휘 **break out in** (피부에) ~이 잔뜩 나다 **confirm** ~을 확인하다 **allergy** 알레르기 ***cf.* allergic** 알레르기의 **sesame** 참깨 **nut** 견과 **hazelnut** 개암 **walnut** 호두 **outgrow** (성장하여) ~에서 벗어나다; ~보다 커지다 **nothing to sneeze at** 가볍게 볼 수 없는, 만만치 않은

266 ② | themselves → them

해설 ② 문맥상 people을 의미하는 목적어 자리인데, 문장의 주어는 The way이므로 목적어로는 재귀대명사가 아니라 them을 써야 한다.

① 선행사를 포함하면서 문장의 주어가 되는 관계대명사절을 이끄는 what이 적절.
③ <부분 표현(the majority, most, some 등)+of+명사>에서 동사의 수는 of 뒤의 명사의 수(people)에 일치시킨다. 따라서 복수동사 regard는 적절.
④ is의 보어 역할을 하는 명사절을 이끄는 that이 적절.
⑤ 앞의 to부정사인 to follow와 병렬관계이므로 (to) extend는 적절.

해석 보너스와 인센티브는 잊어라. 근로자의 생산성 박동을 정말로 높일 것은 오후의 기분 좋은 낮잠이다. 사람들이 자는 방식은 9시부터 5시까지의 전통적인 근무 시간이 요구하는 바에 그들을 제대로 준비시키지 못한다. 사람들 대다수가 자신들이 저녁 또는 아침에 근무를 최고로 잘하는 것으로 생각한다. 아침이나 저녁 근무에 대한 선호도를 보여줌으로써, 대다수가 한낮에는 정신이 충분히 맑지 않다는 것을 암시하는데, 이 시간은 더운 나라들에서 전통적으로 낮잠을 자는 시간이다. 다시 말해서, 전통적인 9시부터 5시까지의 근무시간은 다수에게 적합하지 않다. 근로자들에게 그들의 자연적인 수면 습관을 따르고 자신들의 일하는 시간을 늘리도록 하면 더욱 생산적일 것이다.

어휘 **pump up** ~을 많이 증가시키다; ~에 (펌프로) 공기를 채우다 **regard A as B** A를 B로 여기다[간주하다] **preference** 선호 **implication** 암시; 영향, 결과 **alert** 정신이 맑은; 경계하는 **extend** ~을 연장하다, 늘이다

267 ④ | which → that

해설 ④ 뒤에 <주어(the great Biblical flood)+동사(happened)> 구조의 완전한 절이 이어지므로, 불완전한 절을 이끄는 관계대명사 which는 올 수 없다. 문맥상 '~이라는 증거'가 자연스러우므로 동격절을 이끄는 접속사 that이 적절.

① 의문사 what이 전치사 for의 목적어 역할을 하는 명사절을 이끌고 있으므로 적절.
② 과거의 일을 말하고 있으므로 과거형 fit은 적절. 동사 fit의 과거형으로 fit, fitted 둘 다 쓰인다.
③ '가루로 만들어 그것을 삼켰다'는 내용이므로 powder를 받는 단수 대명사 it은 적절.
⑤ 과거 시점을 나타내는 부사구 millions of years ago가 있으므로 과거시제 lived는 적절.

해석 증거에 기초한 과학적 방법이 확립되기 훨씬 이전에, 사람들은 화석이 무엇인지 그리고 어떻게 그 화석들이 발견된 자리까지 오게 되었는지에 대한 해석을 내놓고 있었다. 놀랄 것도 없이, 이 해석 중 많은 것이 신화와 전설 또는 기존의 믿음에 화석들을 끼워 맞췄다. 고대 중국에서 농부들은 가끔 거대한 도마뱀의 뼈로 보이는 것을 파내곤 했는데, 어떤 사람들은 그 '용의 뼈'를 빻아서 가루로 만든 다음, 그것이 좋은 약이 될 것이라 생각하며 삼켰다. 유럽에서는 산에서 발견된 조개껍데기와 물고기의 화석이 성서에 나오는 대홍수가 실제 일어났다는 증거로 많은 사람에게 받아들여졌다. 18세기 무렵부터 계속해서, 현대의 과학 운동은 우리가 오늘날 믿고 있는 설명을 만들어내기 시작했다. 즉, 화석은 무려 수백만 년 전에 살았던 식물과 동물들의 유해라는 것이다.

어휘 **establishment** 확립, 설립 **come up with** (해답 등을) 내놓다 **explanation** 설명 **fossil** 화석 **existing** 기존의, 현존하는 **occasionally** 가끔 **lizard** 도마뱀 **grind** (ground – ground) ~을 빻다, 갈다 **swallow** ~을 삼키다 **biblical** 성서의, 성서 속의 **onwards** (특정 시간부터) 계속; 앞으로 **formulate** ~을 (세심히) 만들어내다 **remains** 유해, 유적 **as many as + 숫자** 무려 ~나 되는

268 ②

해설 (A) 관계부사 how 뒤에는 완전한 문장이, 관계대명사 what 뒤에는 불완전한 문장이 온다. 네모 뒤에 완전한 문장이 왔으므로 how가 어법상 적절하다. 이 문장에서 learn은 자동사이다.
(B) 문맥상 앞에 나온 일반동사인 fit을 대신하는 대동사가 필요하므로 do가 어법상 적절하다.
(C) 관계대명사절(that coheres ~ beliefs)의 수식을 받는 주어 the first explanation이 단수이므로 단수동사 invokes가 어법상 적절하다.

해석 우리는 우리가 이미 알고 있는 것에 빠르게 그리고 쉽게 들어맞는 것들을 믿는다. 이것은 놀랍지 않은데, 일관성이란 정확히 우리가 학습하고 세계에 대한 이해를 확장하는 방식이기 때문이다. 놀라운 것은 우리가 들어맞는 신념은 환영하고, 동시에 들어맞지 않는 신념은 거부하는 격렬함이다. 그것은 우리가 기존의 지식에 들어맞는 정도에 대해 가능한 설명들을 시험하기 때문만이 아니라, 또한 (기존의 지식에) 들어맞는 개념들을 경솔히 그리고 무비판적으로 받아들이기 때문이다. 우리가 확신을 향해 돌진할 때, 우리의 이전에 받아들인 신념의 망에 들어맞는 첫 번째 설명은 안다는 느낌을 불러일으키면서, 인지적 확신을 만들어 낸다.

어휘 **fit** 들어맞다; 적절하다; 적합한; 건강한 **coherence** 일관성 ***cf.* cohere (with)** (~와) 들어맞다[일치하다] **precisely** 정확히; 바로, 꼭 **expand** 확장시키다, 확장하다 **interpretation** 설명, 해석, 이해 **degree** 정도; (각도, 온도 등의) 도; 학위 **unthinkingly** 경솔히, 생각 없이 **uncritically** 무비판적으로, 비판력 없이 **rush** 돌진(하다); 서두르다; 분주함 **certainty** 확신; 확실(성) **generate** 만들어 내다; 발생시키다 **cognitive** 인지의, 인식의 **confidence** 확신; 신뢰; 자신감

구문 05~07행 **What is surprising** is *the ferocity* [**with which** we **both** **welcome** *beliefs* [that fit] **and** **reject** *beliefs* [that do not]].
→ 선행사를 포함하는 관계대명사 What이 이끄는 명사절이 문장에서 주어의 역할을 한다.
→ [with ~ not]에서 관계대명사가 전치사의 목적어일 경우에, <전치사+관계대명사>의 어순으로 쓸 수 있다. both A and B의 상관접속사가 동사 welcome과 reject를 연결한다.
→ 주격 관계대명사 that이 이끄는 두 개의 [ ] 부분들은 각각 앞에 있는 beliefs를 수식한다.

11~14행 ~, *the first explanation* [**that** coheres with our web of (previously accepted) *beliefs* / invokes the feeling of knowing, **generating cognitive confidence**.
→ [that ~ beliefs]는 주격 관계대명사 that이 이끄는 관계사절로 the first explanation을 수식하고, previously accepted가 beliefs를 앞에서 수식한다.
→ generating cognitive confidence는 분사구문으로 동시동작을 나타낸다.

269 ①

해설 (A) 새가 '이주하는' 주체이기 때문에 현재분사 migrating 적절.
(B) 철새가 길을 찾기 위해 별들이나 달을 이용할지도 모른다는 현재의 추측이므로 might use가 적절. <might have p.p.>는 '과거'의 일을 가리킨다.
(C) made by ocean waves의 수식을 받을 수 있는 대명사 those가 적절. 관계대명사의 선행사와 같은 역할을 한다. (= those (which are) made ~)

해석 일 년에 두 번, 수백만 마리의 새들이 집을 떠나 수백, 수천 마일을 여행한다. 이 이동하는 새들은 같은 지역들을 매년 왔다 갔다 한다. 그들은 어떻게 그들의 길을 찾는 것일까? 과학자들이 많은 이론을 가지고 있지만 우리는 아직 확신하지 못하고 있다. 그들이 길을 안내해주는 별들이나 달을 이용할지도 모르지만, 구름이 낀 밤에는 그들이 길을 잃지 않을까? 아마도 그들은 어느 방향이 북쪽인지 그들에게 알려주는 일종의 체내 나침반을 가지고 있는지도 모른다. 그들은 또한 파도가 만들어내는 소리와 같이, 방향에 관한 단서를 제공하는 낮은 소리를 감지할 수 있는지도 모른다. 많은 새가 하나 이상의 비행 기술을 조합하여 사용하고 있는 것 같다.

어휘 **migrate** 이동하다; 이주하다 **back and forth** 앞뒤로 **internal** 체내의; 내부의 **detect** ~을 감지하다 **combination** 조합 **navigational** 비행의, 항해의

270 ④ | asking → asked

해설 ④ when 다음에 they(= Most parents and friends) are가 생략된 분사 자리라고 보았을 때, asking이 되면 대부분의 부모와 친구들이 도움을 요청하는 것이 되고, asked가 되면 도움을 요청받는 것이 되므로 문맥상 asked가 나와야 적절.

① enough는 부사로 동사 rely on을 수식하고 있어 쓰임이 적절.
② that이하 절이 문장 요소가 모두 갖추어진 형태로서 worry의 목적어가 되어야 하므로 접속사 that의 쓰임이 적절.
③ 대명사 it은 앞에 나온 명사구 their anxiety를 가리키기 때문에 쓰임이 적절.
⑤ doing은 rather than 다음에 나온 동명사 providing과 병렬 관계이므로 적절.

해석 일부 불안해하는 10대들은 자기들이 불안감에 대처하는 것을 도와주는 친구들과 가족에게 너무 많이 의존하는 것처럼 느낀다. 그러나 이러한 10대들은 친구들과 가족에게 충분히 의지하지 않고 있다! 그 10대들은 자기들이 그들의 도움을 요청하면 그들을 싫어하게 만들거나 속상하게 할 것을 걱정하기 때문에 도움을 구하기를 꺼린다. 다른 사람들을 성가시게 하고 싶지 않은 십 대들은 부모와 친구에게 도움을 요청하는 것이 자신

들의 문제로 그들에게 부담을 주거나, 자신들의 불안감이 너무 심해서 그것이 그들을 어쩔 줄 모르게 만들 것이라고 생각할지도 모른다. 하지만 이보다 더 진실에서 먼 것은 없을 것이다. 대부분의 부모와 친구들은 어떤 10대를 불안감을 관리하는 수단을 배워 적용하는 데 도움을 주라는 요청을 받으면 흔히 영광으로 여긴다. 부모와 친구는, 불안한 10대 아이를 진정시키기 위해 많이 안심시켜 주거나 불안감 때문에 그가 할 수 없는 모든 일을 해 주는 것보다, 이런 방식으로 돕기를 훨씬 더 좋아한다.

어휘 **anxious** 불안한 **cope with** ~에 대처하다 **anxiety** 불안, 걱정 **be unwilling to-v** v하기를 꺼리다 **put ~ off** ~을 불쾌하게 하다 **upset** 걱정시키다, 당황케 하다 **burden A with B** A에게 B로 부담을 주다 **overwhelm** 당혹스럽게 하다, 압도하다 **feel honored** 명예스럽게[영광으로] 여기다 **reassurance** 안심시키기; 안심시키는 말[행동]

구문 06~10행 Teens who do not want to bother other people may think **that** asking parents or friends for help will burden them with their problems [or] **that** their anxiety is ***so*** extreme **that** it will overwhelm them.

→ 세 개의 that이 나오는데, 첫 번째와 두 번째 that은 or로 연결되어 think의 목적어절을 이끄는 접속사 that이다. 세 번째 that은 '너무 ~해서 …하다'는 뜻의 <so ~that …> 구문의 접속사 that이다.

실전 모의고사 32회

271 ③ 272 ② 273 ④ 274 ④ 275 ⑤, 276 ④ | 본문 138p

271 ③ | take → takes

해설 ③ 주어인 A photographer에 호응하는 동사 projects와 and로 연결된 병렬구조이므로 takes가 되어야 한다.

① to부정사의 의미상 주어인 a child가 '진단받는' 것이므로 to부정사 수동형이 적절.
② a computer program을 수식해 주는 to부정사가 적절히 쓰였다.
④ face 'maps'를 뒤에서 수식하는 분사. face 'maps'가 다양한 유전병과 '관련된' 것이므로 과거분사형이 적절.
⑤ children을 선행사로 취하고 뒤의 명사구 genetic disorder와 함께 관계사절의 주어 역할을 하므로 소유격 관계대명사 whose가 맞다.

해석 몇몇 유전병의 증상은 원인이 너무도 다양해서 아동이 (그 병을) 진단받는 데 수년이 걸릴 수도 있다. 유니버시티 칼리지 런던은 다양한 유전병에서 나타나는 얼굴의 특징들을 발견해내는 컴퓨터 프로그램을 개발 중이다. 사진을 찍는 사람이 환자의 얼굴에 수천 개의 점을 일정한 패턴으로 쏜 다음 디지털카메라로 다양한 각도에서 사진을 찍는다. 소프트웨어는 데이터를 받아 그것을 다양한 유전병과 관련된 각종 얼굴 '지도들'과 비교할 수 있는 3차원 얼굴 '지도'로 변환한다. 그 기술은 얼굴 형태 모델들에 유전병의 자료가 수집된 아동들 중에서 90% 이상의 정확성을 보인 진단을 내놓았다.

어휘 **nonspecific** ((병리)) 원인이 다양한; 불특정한 **diagnose** ~을 진단하다 ***cf.*** **diagnosis** 진단(법) (***pl.*** **diagnoses**) **project** ~을 비추다, 투사하다 **convert** ~을 변환하다, 전환하다 **three-dimensional** 3차원의 **accuracy** 정확성 **compile** (자료 등을) 수집하다

구문 09~12행 The software(S) takes(V_1) the data [and] converts(V_2) it into *a three-dimensional 'map' of the face* [**which** can be compared to *the different face 'maps'* (**linked** to various genetic diseases)].

272 ②

해설 (A) 주격 관계대명사 that절(that ~ animals)은 문맥상 '다른 동물과 구별되게 하는 몇 가지 점'이란 뜻이 되어야 하므로 the few things를 선행사로 취한다. 따라서 복수동사인 set이 적절. one을 선행사로 착각하지 않도록 주의한다.
(B) by speech 바로 뒤에 문장의 동사인 is가 나온 구조이다. 따라서 바로 앞의 명사구 the amount of information을 수식하는 과거분사 exchanged가 적절.
(C) <so[neither]+V+S (S도 역시 그러하다)>의 구조이다. so는 긍정문, neither는 부정문의 동의 표현이며, 앞 절이 긍정문이므로 so가 적절.

해석 말은 우리를 다른 동물과 구별되게 하는 몇 가지 점 중 하나이며 추상적으로 생각할 수 있는 우리의 능력과 밀접하게 관련되어 있다. 그럼에도 불구하고 글이 말보다 더 중요한 의사소통 수단이라고 생각하는 것은 당연하다. 이것은 문자와 인쇄물이 정보를 전달하는 데 더 효율적이고 오래 지속되는 방법인 것처럼 보이기 때문이다. 하지만, 아무리 많은 양의 책과 신문이 인쇄되고, 아무리 많은 양의 기록물이 온라인상에 만들어지더라도, 말로 주고받는 정보의 양은 여전히 더 많다. 인터넷, 책, 다른 인쇄 매체를 통한 정보의 교환이 크게 늘고 있지만, 그만큼 전화, 라디오, 텔레비전을 통한 구두 의사소통 또한 크게 늘고 있다.

어휘 **set A apart from B** A를 B와 구별하다 **be connected with** ~와 관계가 있다 **abstractly** 추상적으로 **it is fair to-v** v하는 것이 당연하다 **means** 수단, 방법 **output** 결과 **printing press** 인쇄기 **durable** 오래 견디는, 내구성 있는 **transmit** ~을 전달하다, 전송하다 **via** ~을 통하여, 경유하여 **media** (대중) 매체 **expand** 늘어나다, 확장하다

구문 08~12행 Yet, **no matter how *many*** books and newspapers are printed, *and* **(*no matter*) how *much*** written matter is produced online, the amount of information (exchanged by speech) ***is*** still greater.

→ no matter how가 이끄는 복합 관계 부사절이 and로 연결된 형태. '아무리~하더라도'란 뜻으로 how 뒤에는 일반적으로 형용사나 부사가 온다. no matter how는 however로도 바꿔 쓸 수 있다. 주절의 주어는 the amount ~ by speech, 동사는 is.

273 ④ | was filled → filled

해설 ④ a young boy가 곧 I를 가리키며 I를 좀 더 묘사하고 있는 부분이다. 접속사가 없으므로 주어와 동사를 갖춘 절이 올 곳이 아니다. 명사를 수식하는 분사구 filled로 고쳐 써야 한다.

① 동사 were chirping을 부사(excitedly)가 적절히 꾸미고 있다.
② disaster(파국, 재난)에 '가까이' 다가갔다는 의미로 물리적인 '거리'를 나타내는 close(가까이)를 수사적으로 쓴 경우.
③ puff adder라는 뱀에 대한 정보를 더 소개하는 계속적 용법의 관계대명사절(which is the snake ~)에서 보어(the snake) 뒤에 이어지는 that은 '어떤' 뱀인지를 말해주는 관계대명사절을 이끄는 that이다.
⑤ 동사 lift를 수식하는 부사 자리. 뱀이 머리를 '높이' 치켜들었다는 의미가 자연스러우므로 high는 적절. *cf.* highly 매우

해석 내가 길을 걸어 내려가고 있을 때 새 한 쌍이 근처 덤불에서 흥분하여 짹짹거리고 있었다. 나는 그들의 경고에 주의를 기울이지 않았기 때문에 재앙에 가까이 다가갔다. 갑자기 나는 아프리카 산(産) 큰 독사 바로 앞에 서 있었는데, 그 독사는 아프리카에서 다른 어떤 것보다 더 많은 죽음의 원인이 되는 뱀이다. 공포에 질린 어린 소년인 나는 그곳에 맨발로 서 있었다. 나는 가까스로 뛰어올라 길 가장자리에 올라섰다. 나는 뱀이 다이아몬드 모양의 머리를 높게 치켜들고 내 쪽으로 무턱대고 공격하는 것을 보았다. 뱀의 공격은 거리에 미치지 못했지만 나는 도망갈 틈을 찾을 수 없었다. 나는 그 자리에서 꼼짝을 못했다.

어휘 **chirp** 짹짹 지저귀다 **pay attention to** ~에 주의를 기울이다 **responsible for** ~의 원인이 되는; ~에 책임이 있는 **barefoot** 맨발의; 맨발로 **blindly** 무턱대고 **fall short** 미달하다, 미치지 못하다

274 ④ | what → that

해설 ④ 뒤에 SVC 구조의 완전한 절이 나오므로 what은 불가. 동사 have shown의 목적어절을 이끄는 접속사 that이 적절하다.

① have는 사역동사로서 목적격보어로 원형부정사를 취한다.
② 동명사구 주어. <continue to-v>: 계속해서 v하다
③ 분사구문의 의미상 주어인 It(=Exercise)이 혈소판이 달라붙는 것을 '막는' 것이므로 능동의 현재분사 preventing이 적절하게 사용되었다. '결과'를 나타내는 분사구문.
⑤ 동사 showed의 목적어절에서 who ~ fit의 수식을 받는 주어 women의 동사 자리이므로 복수동사 were는 적절.

해석 의사가 당신이 건강하고 혈압과 콜레스테롤 수치도 좋다고 말하도록 하는 것이 아무런 노력도 없이 편안히 쉬면서 스스로 만족할 이유는 아니다. 이런 희소식이 계속되는 것은 당신이 건강에 좋은 습관을 택할 것이냐, 나쁜 습관을 택할 것이냐에 달려 있을 것이다. 운동은 심장에 매우 중요하다. 그것은 혈압을 낮추는 것을 돕고 동맥과 정맥의 염증을 경감시킴으로써 혈소판이 혈관 벽에 달라붙는 것을 방지한다. "나는 언제나 운동을 최우선에 둡니다."라고 메메트 오즈 박사는 말한다. 여러 연구는 운동이 식이요법보다 더 중요하다는 것을 보여준다. 한 연구는 뚱뚱하지만 건강한 여성이 날씬하지만 건강이 좋지 않은 또래들보다 뇌졸중이나 심장마비가 일어날 가능성이 더 낮다는 것을 보여주었다.

어휘 **be in good shape** 건강이 좋다(↔ **be out of shape** 건강이 나쁘다) **sit back** (일에서) 손을 떼다, 방관하다, 편안히 있다 **adopt** ~을 채택하다; ~을 입양하다 **inflammation** 염증 **artery** 동맥 **vein** 정맥 **vessel** (혈)관 **stroke** 뇌졸중 **peer** 또래, 동료

275 ⑤

해설 (A) 앞에 있는 두 개의 동명사구(promoting ~, encouraging ~)와 and로 연결되어 병렬구조를 이루므로 동명사가 적절하다.
(B) 문두에 부정어구(Not only)가 오는 경우 도치가 발생하는데, <there+(조)동사> 구문인 경우 <(조)동사+there ~>의 어순이 된다. 따라서 there have been fatal incidents ~에서 there와 have가 도치되어야 한다.
(C) 네모 뒤에 이어지는 절은 완전한 문장 구조를 이루며 앞의 the suggestion과 동격을 이루고 있으므로 동격절을 이끄는 접속사 that이 와야 한다.

해석 올림픽 경기에 대한 몇몇 비평가들은 올림픽 경기가 공격성을 조장하고 상업주의를 예찬하며 국가는 우월하거나 열등하고 결코 서로 동등하지 않다는 위험한 견해를 지지하고 있다고 주장한다. 다른 한편에서는 전 세계적으로 탁월함을 증진하고 이해를 북돋우며 친선을 도모한다는 이유로 올림픽 경기를 예찬하는 이들이 있다. 두 진영 모두 지지자들이 있으나 히틀러가 1936년 베를린 올림픽을 주최한 이래 전자의 주장을 의심하게 할 일들은 별로 없었다(즉, 올림픽 경기의 부정적 측면을 예증하는 사건들이 많이 있었다는 뜻). 테러리즘과 폭력으로 말미암은 치명적 사건들이 올림픽에서 있었을 뿐 아니라 그 사건들은 또한 무수히 많은 외교적 충돌을 일으켰다. 문제에 대한 해결책을 모색하는 과정에서, 운동선수들이 개별 국가의 시민으로서가 아니라 각 개인으로서 경쟁해야 한다는 제안이 어느 정도 희망을 준다.

어휘 **critic** 비평가 **foster** ~을 조성하다; ~을 양육하다 **aggression** 공격, 호전성 **glorify** ~을 찬양하다 **commercialism** 상업주의 **superior** 우월한(↔ **inferior** 열등한) **one another** 서로 **goodwill** 친선, 호의 **discredit** ~의 평판을 나쁘게 하다, 믿지 않다 **former** (둘 중에서) 전자의 **fatal** 치명적인, 파멸적인 **diplomatic** 외교적인 **conflict** 갈등, 충돌 **compete** 경쟁하다

구문 01~03행 Some critics (of ~ Games) argue **that** the events foster aggression, glorify commercialism, and support the dangerous view **that** nations are ~.
→ 첫 번째 that은 동사 argue의 목적어절을 이끄는 접속사 that이며 두 번째 that은 dangerous view의 내용을 설명하는 동격절을 이끄는 that이다.

276 ④ | although → despite

해설 ④ Huge numbers of one-time bus riders / still believe it to be like this / although *the investment* [(*that*) bus companies have made in *new vehicles* [which are cleaner, faster, quieter, and more comfortable]].
the investment 뒤에 that이 생략된 관계대명사절이 the investment를 수식하는 구조이므로 절과 함께 쓰이는 although는 올 수 없으며 despite로 바꿔야 한다.

① 앞에 나온 bus users 중의 많은 사람들이 다른 교통수단으로 이동한 것이므로 이를 관계대명사로 받으면 many of whom이 적절하다.
② <so ~ that ...>의 형태로 '너무나 ~하여 …하다'라는 뜻을 나타내므로 that이 적절히 쓰였다.
③ sitting과 having이 be tired of 뒤에 목적어로 나오며 병렬구조를 이루고 있다.
⑤ <it takes … to-v> 형태로 'v하는 데 …가 필요하다[걸리다, 들다]'의 뜻이 되어야 하므로 알맞게 쓰였다.

해석 제품 품질과 마찬가지로, 일단 어떤 조직이 형편없는 서비스로 평판을 만들어가게 되면, 그것을 떨치기 힘들다. 이것은 확실히 버스 이용자들에게도 사실인데, 그들 중 많은 사람들이 지난 10년에서 15년에 걸쳐 다른 교통수단으로, 특히 승용차로 옮겨갔다. 비싼 유지비, 혼잡한 도로, 그리고 도시에서 차를 주차시키는 것의 어려움에도 불구하고, 고객들은 결코 오지 않는, 혹은 너무 늦게 와서 두 대가 함께 오는 버스를 버스 정류장에서 기다리는 데 진저리가 났다. 그들은 더러운 좌석에 앉아서 창밖을 보기 위해 응결된 곳에 구멍을 내려 닦아내야 하는 것이 지긋지긋해졌다. 그들은 불친절한 기사와 소음, 냄새, 그리고 은퇴 날짜를 넘긴 지 오래인 차량으로부터의 진동을 좋다고 생각하지 않는다. 대단히 많은 수의 일회성 버스 탑승객들은 버스 회사들이 더 깨끗하고 더 빠르고 더 조용하며 더 편안한 새 차량에 해놓은 투자에도 불구하고 그것이 이와 같을 거라고 여전히 믿는다. 오래된 의견은 쉽게 사라지지 않으며, 사람들을 버스로 다시 데려오는 데에는 의견(혹은 법률 제정)에서의 큰 전환이 필요할 것이다.

어휘 **reputation** 명성, 평판 **the case** 사실, 실상 **defect to** ~로 전향하다 **means** 수단 **transport** 운송, 수송 **operating cost** 운영비 **be fed up with** ~에 진저리가 나다 **unimpressed** ~이 좋다고 생각하지 않는 **vibration** 진동 **vehicle** 차량, 탈것 **die hard** 쉽게 사라지지 않다 **legislation** 법률 제정, 입법

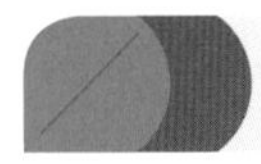

실전 모의고사 33회

277 ③ 278 ① 279 ③ 280 ③ 281 ④ 282 ④ | 본문 140p

277 ③ | what → why

해설 ❸ explains의 목적어절이면서 she will suddenly bite or scratch you라는 완전한 형태의 절을 이끄는 접속사 자리이므로, 관계대명사인 what은 오지 못한다. 문맥상 이유를 나타내는 why가 적절.

① given은 전치사로 쓰이면 '~을 고려하면(= considering)'을 의미한다.
② 동사 will make에 호응하는 주어로 동명사구(petting ~ time)는 적절.
④ 고양이가 갑자기 물거나 할퀴는 이유는 같은 곳을 계속 어루만져 '방금 막 고양이를 과도하게 자극한' 탓이라는 내용. 현재완료의 '완료' 용법이 적절히 쓰였다.
⑤ to부정사의 부정은 not을 to 앞에 둔다.

해석 개와 고양이의 진화 역사를 고려해 볼 때, 그들이 거의 모든 점에서 정반대라는 것은 놀랄 일이 아니다. 예를 들어, 개는 반복을 좋아하여 똑같은 방식으로 오랫동안 어루만져 주는 것은 그들을 매우 행복하게 만든다. 반면 고양이는 반복에 쉽게 과잉 자극을 받는데, 이것은 당신이 고양이를 아주 잘 쓰다듬고 있다고 생각하는 와중에 고양이가 갑자기 당신을 물거나 할퀴는 이유를 설명해준다. 당신의 고양이는 당신을 미워하지 않는다. 단지 당신이 고양이를 과도하게 자극한 것이다. 고양이를 기분 좋게 만드는 방법은 한 부분을 오랫동안 만져주는 것이 아니다. 머리로 귀로 턱으로 등으로 애정을 이리저리 옮기고 나서 이를 반복하며 고양이가 가장 좋아하는 부분으로 계속 움직여라.

어휘 **evolutionary** 진화의 **stimulate** ~을 자극하다 **session** 기간

278 ① | are → is

해설 ❶ 주어가 The number 즉, '수' 자체이므로 단수동사 is가 적절. The number of people [who became ~ first ventures] is small.

② <such+명사+that ...> 구문으로서 '너무 ~여서 …하다'를 의미한다.
cf. <so+형용사+that ...>: 너무 ~해서 …하다
③ 분사의 의미상 주어인 he와 try는 능동관계이므로 현재분사를 쓴 것은 적절.
④ 전치사인 to의 목적어 자리이므로 동명사는 적절.
⑤ 명사구가 이어지고 있으므로 전치사 During은 적절.

해석 '성공'하기 위해 고전(苦戰)하고 있는 사람들에게는, 마침내 성공하기 전까지는 실패자였던 사람들의 목록을 보는 것이 용기를 준다. 그들의 첫 번째 일에서 성공한 사람의 수는 적다. 험프리 보가트는 대학에서 상당한 부적응자여서 교수를 분수대에 내던진 일로 쫓겨났다. 그는 월스트리트의 주식 중개인으로서, 그리고 심지어 예인선 조사관으로서도 실패했다. 그는 무대감독으로서 연예 공연업도 시도했지만 해고당했다. 그는 연기로 방향을 돌려 자신의 첫 무대 출연에서 잡일꾼을 연기했다. 첫날밤 공연에서, 그는 뜻하지 않게 접시들을 올려놓은 쟁반을 떨어뜨리기도 했다. 그러나 그는 결국 배우로서 성공했고, 영화계의 전설이 되었다.

어휘 **inspiring** 용기를 주는, 영감을 주는 **venture** (새로운) 일, 사업 **expel** ~을 내쫓다, 추방하다 **stockbroker** 주식 중개인 **tugboat** 예인선 **inspector** 조사관, 검사관 **houseboy** 잡일꾼 **accidentally** 뜻하지 않게, 우연히 **score** 성공하다; 득점하다

279 ③ | to fly → flying

해설 ❸ '~하는 것을 멈추다'라는 의미가 되어야 하므로 동명사가 되어야 한다.
cf. stop to fly 비행하기 위해 멈추다

① <see+O+OC> 구조로 the white trails가 '뒤따르는' 것이므로 능동을 나타내는 현재분사는 적절. 지각동사의 목적격보어 자리에 현재분사가 쓰이면 '진행'의 의미를 강조한다.
② 앞에 나온 명사 the effect의 반복을 피하기 위한 대명사 자리이므로 단수형 that은 적절.
④ 뒤에 <주어(condensation trails)+동사(reduce)+목적어(the temperature range)>의 완전한 절이 이어지므로 접속사 that이 적절. that 이하는 the hypothesis의 내용을 설명하는 동격절.
⑤ contribute to는 '~에 기여하다, ~에 공헌하다'라는 의미의 표현.

해석 당신은 하늘에서 하얀 흔적이 비행기 뒤를 따르는 것을 본 적이 있는가? 그것은 비행운(雲)이라고 불리는데 뜨거운 배기가스에 의해 형성된다. 그것은 햇빛을 반사할 뿐 아니라 열이 우주로 나가는 것도 막는다. 낮 동안에는 들어오는 복사열을 차단한 효과가 (대기에) 갇힌 열의 효과보다 더 커서 대기를 식힌다. 9/11 테러 공격 이후 미국에서 사흘 동안 모든 비행기가 운항을 멈추었을 때, 전국의 주간 온도는 약간 올랐지만 야간 온도는 떨어졌다. 이 증거는 비행운이 낮 동안에는 대기를 식히고 밤에는 대기를 데워 온도의 범위를 줄인다는 가설을 뒷받침했다. 그러므로 밤샘 비행이 대기 온난화에 더 기여를 한다.

어휘 **exhaust** 배기가스; ~을 기진맥진하게 하다 **radiation** 복사열; 방사선 **outweigh** ~을 능가하다 **trap** ~을 가두다; ~을 덫으로 잡다 **hypothesis** 가설

280 ③ | by → until

해설 ❸ 문맥상 어떤 시점(a later date)까지 지속됨을 말하므로 until로 고쳐야 한다. 전치사 by는 '완료'를 나타내고, until은 '계속'을 나타낸다.

① 뒤에 주어(the tenure committee)와 동사(considered)가 있는 완전한 절을 이끌므로 '~하는 동안'의 의미로 접속사 while이 적절하다.
② 문맥상 and 뒤에 이어지는 절의 목적어인 you가 투표된 것이므로 전치사 on의 목적어로 동명사의 수동형 <being+p.p.> 형태가 적절하다.
④ 뒤에 오는 명사구 research projects in progress를 수식하는 자리로 '유망한'이라는 의미의 현재분사 promising이 알맞게 쓰였다. promised로 쓰면 '약속된'이란 의미로 전체 문맥에 맞지 않는다.

⑤ 동사 wish 뒤에 간접목적어(you), 직접목적어(continued success ~ career)가 오는 구조.

해석 종신 교수 재직권 심의위원회가 귀하의 부교수로의 승진 가능성을 검토하는 동안 참고 기다려 주셔서 감사드립니다. 귀하께서 가르침으로 생물학과에 상당한 기여를 했다는 점에 저희 모두는 동의하며, '올해의 우수 교수'로 선정된 것을 축하드립니다. 하지만 귀하의 출판물 목록을 검토한 후 부교수로의 승진을 나중으로 보류하기로 했습니다. 귀하께서 유망한 연구 과제를 여러 개 진행 중이지만, 위원회는 부교수 지위를 부여하기 전에 더 많은 출판물을 보고 싶습니다. 귀하의 출판물 수가 많아지고 질이 향상된다면 귀하의 승진 요청을 내년에 기꺼이 재고하겠습니다. 다시 한 번 귀하께서 저희 학과에 기여하신 점에 경의를 표하며 직업과 학문 경력에서의 지속적인 성공을 기원합니다.

어휘 **promotion** 승진 **associate professor** 부교수 **significant** 중요한; 상당한 **contribution** 기여 **biology** 생물학 **publication** 출판물 **withhold** 보류하다 **promising** 유망한 **in progress** 진행 중인 **grant** 주다, 부여하다 **status** 지위 **advancement** 승진 **salute** 경의를 표하다 **professional** 직업의

281 ④

해설 (A) 분사구문의 의미상 주어인 she와 redefine이 능동 관계이므로 현재분사 redefining을 써야 한다.
(B) 뒤에 <주어(the public reaction)+be동사(is)> 형태의 불완전한 절이 오므로, 주격보어가 될 수 있는 의문대명사 what이 와야 한다. 의문부사 how는 뒤에 완전한 형태의 절을 이끈다.
(C) 문맥상 many artists united ~ music and movies in a major campaign이므로, a major campaign을 선행사로 받는 관계대명사 which 앞에 전치사 in이 필요하다. unite는 자동사, 타동사로 둘 다 쓰일 수 있으나 여기서는 '합동하다, 결합하다'란 뜻의 자동사로 쓰였다.

해석 Madonna Louise Veronica Ciccone Ritchie는 20살 때 명성을 얻으려는 꿈을 좇으려고 미시간 대학교를 떠나 주머니에 겨우 35달러만 가지고 뉴욕으로 갔다. 그녀의 첫 앨범은 매우 성공했고 그녀는 곧 세계적으로 유명한 스타가 되어 새 앨범마다 그녀 자신과 자신의 음악을 재정의했다. 늘 솔직하고 종종 충격을 주는 그녀는, 대중의 반응이 어떻든지 간에 자신이 원하는 것은 무엇이든 하는 여자로 알려져 있다. 몇 년 전 그녀는 음악 저작권 침해와 P2P 파일 공유 사이트에서의 불법 다운로드에 반대한다고 거리낌 없이 말했다. 이것은 많은 예술인들이 음악과 영화의 불법 다운로드와 저작권 침해를 비난하기 위해 뭉친 주요 캠페인으로 이어졌다.

어휘 **pursue** ~을 추구하다; ~을 뒤쫓다 **redefine** ~을 재정의하다 **outspoken** 거리낌 없는, 솔직한 **speak out** 거리낌 없이 이야기하다; 큰 소리로 말하다 **piracy** 저작권 침해, 해적 행위 **peer-to-peer** 동등 계층 통신(인터넷에서 개인과 개인이 직접 연결되어 파일을 공유하는 형태)의 **unite** 일체가 되다, 합동하다; ~을 결합하다 **condemn** ~을 비난하다, 옳지 않다고 보다

구문 07~10행 Always (*being*) **outspoken**, often (*being*) **shocking**, / she is known as *a woman* [**who** does whatever she wants, / ***no matter what*** the public reaction is].
→ <(being)+형용사>형태의 분사구문은 being을 생략한 채로 자주 쓰인다. who 이하는 a woman을 수식하는 관계대명사절. no matter what은 복합관계대명사 whatever로 대체할 수 있다.

282 ④

해설 (A) 의미적으로 과거분사인 held를 수식하므로 부사 commonly가 적절.
(B) 주어가 Dampness and high humidity이므로 복수동사인 are가 적절. 각각 뒤에 meaning이 이끄는 분사구가 삽입되었다.
(C) the workings를 대신하므로 복수형인 those가 적절. 앞에 나온 명사의 반복을 피하기 위해 that이나 those를 사용한다.

해석 습기가 관절 통증을 더 악화시킨다고 일반적으로 받아들여지는 의견에도 불구하고, 의학 연구는 관절염 통증과 날씨 사이에 아무런 관련성도 찾지 못했다. 사물 표면의 물기를 의미하는 습기(dampness)와 공기 중 많은 양의 수분을 뜻하는 높은 습도(high humidity)가 관절염을 더 악화시키는 특징들이라고 많은 사람은 생각한다. 그러나 이 동일한 환자들은 목욕이나 수영을 할 때는 그들의 증상이 심해지는 경험을 하지 않는데, 이것들은 비슷한 환경 상태라고 생각될 수 있다. 고기압 또한 원인이 아닐지 모른다. 환자들은 비행기 여행 시에, 폭풍이 부는 동안 일어나는 것과 동일한 기압의 증가를 쉽게 견뎌낸다. 일반화된 믿음은 몸의 작용보다 마음의 작용에 관해서 더 많은 것을 보여준다.

어휘 **dampness** (사물 표면의) 습기, 축축함 **joint** 관절 **humidity** (대기 중) 습도

구문 04~08행 **Dampness**, (meaning ~ things), and **high humidity**,(S) (meaning ~ the air), / are(V) *characteristics*(C) [**that** (many people think) cause(V′) their arthritis(O′) to worsen(OC′)].
→ Dampness와 high humidity를 보충 설명하는 분사구가 삽입되어 주어 부분이 길어졌다. that절에는 <cause A to-v> 구조가 쓰였다. many people think는 삽입절.

283 ⑤ | what → that

해설 ❺ 앞의 that the inferences ~ about themselves와 and로 연결된 병렬구조이고, 뒤에는 완전한 절이 왔으므로 접속사 that이 적절.

① 셀 수 있는 명사의 복수형 ways를 수식하는 a few는 적절.
② 뒤에 나오는 or와 <either A or B> 구조를 이루어 'A나 B 둘 중 하나'라는 의미를 나타내므로 적절.
③ 명사 way를 꾸미는 수식어 자리이므로 형용사적 용법의 to부정사 to find out이 올바름.
④ 앞에서 언급된 명사 the inferences의 반복을 피하기 위해 대명사 those가 적절히 쓰임.

해석 우리가 다른 사람들의 경험에 대해 알 수 있는 분명한 몇 가지 방법이 있다. 경험은 몸짓, 눈물, 웃음 등의 형태로 자연적인 신호를 통해서, 혹은 언어 사용에 의해서 우리에게 전달된다. 다른 사람이 생각하고 있거나 느끼고 있는 것을 알아내는 아주 좋은 방법은 물어보는 것이다. 사람들은 대답하지 않을지도 모르고, 대답한다 하더라도 솔직하게 대답하지 않을 수도 있지만, 대개는 솔직하게 대답할 것이다. 그러나 우리는 말에만 의존하지는 않는다. 즉 실제로, 우리가 사람들의 비언어적 행동에서 끌어낸 추론이 그들이 그들 자신에 대해 말한 것에 바탕을 둔 추론보다 더 믿을 수 있고, 행동이 말보다 더 솔직하게 이야기할지도 모른다.

어휘 **inference** 추론 **nonverbal** 비언어적인, 말을 사용하지 않는 **dependable** 의존할[믿을] 수 있는

구문 09~14행 ~; it may be, indeed, **that** *the inferences* (S'₁) [which we draw ∨ from people's nonverbal behavior] are (V'₁) more dependable (C'₁) than *those* [**that** we base ∨ upon what they say about themselves], and **that** actions (S'₂) speak (V'₂) more honestly than words.

284 ③ | is called → called

해설 ❸ a piece of software가 주어이고 문장의 동사는 decides이다. '프린터 드라이버라고 불리는 소프트웨어'라는 의미이므로 is called는 called로 후치수식 분사가 되어야 한다.

① 주격 관계대명사인 that의 선행사는 dots(이미지의 각 파트를 구성하는 점들)이므로 복수동사인 make up은 적절.
② 명령문을 이끄는 동사 자리이므로 동사원형인 consider가 적절. 동사 shows와 are는 각각 how와 which가 이끄는 절 내의 동사이다.
④ each는 형용사, 부사, 대명사로 다 쓰일 수 있다. 여기서는 create를 수식하는 부사로 쓰인 것이다. create의 주어는 앞의 복수명사인 These ~ textures이며 each가 주어가 아니므로 단수동사가 되면 안 된다.
⑤ <the+비교급 ~, the+비교급 ...>의 구조이므로 the less가 알맞게 쓰였다.

해석 컴퓨터 프린터로 나오는 그래픽 출력물의 품질은 dpi(1인치당 점들)로 측정된다. 이미지의 각 부분을 이루는 점들의 밀도를 변화시키는 것만으로, 프린터는 거의 사진처럼 보이는 이미지를 나오게 할 수 있다. 이것이 어떻게 작용하는지를 이해하려면, 흑백 사진이 실제 생활에서는 색채들인 음영을 어떻게 보여주는지를 생각해보라. 각각의 색은 각기 다른 회색 음영이다. 컴퓨터 프린터로 그래픽이 나오도록 하기 위해, 프린터 드라이버라고 하는 소프트웨어 프로그램이 각각의 색 음영을 나타낼 점의 패턴을 결정한다. 이런 다른 패턴과 조직들은 각각, 우리 눈이 회색 음영들로 해석하는 개개의 효과를 만든다. 그러나 그 이미지를 가까이에서 볼수록 실물처럼 보이는 느낌이 덜하다.

어휘 **output** 출력, 산출 **measure** ~을 측정하다, 재다 **density** 밀도, 농도 **make up** ~을 구성하다 **photographic** 사진(술)의 **shade** (그림의) 음영; 그늘 **represent** ~을 나타내다, 표현하다 **translate** ~을 해석하다; ~을 번역하다 **lifelike** 실물 그대로인

구문 09~12행 ~, *a piece of software* (S) (**called** a printer driver) decides upon (V) *a dot pattern* (O) [**which** will represent each color shade].

285 ③ | their → its

해설 ❸ 문맥상 Chi를 가리키는 것이므로 단수인 its로 바꿔야 적절.

① the body, ~ spirit이 '간주되는' 대상이 되므로 수동태 are viewed가 적절.
② 여러 개 중 하나는 one, 그 나머지 모두는 the others. 여기서는 문맥상 하나의 구성요소(one component)가 나머지 구성요소 전부에 영향을 준다는 내용이므로 the others가 적절.
④ that절의 주어가 the best cure로 단수이므로 was는 적절.
⑤ 질주하는 마음을 안정시키는 '방법'을 배우라는 문맥이므로 how는 적절.

해석 명상은 인간을 전체론적 관점에서 다룬다. 즉 신체, 감정, 마음, 그리고 정신은 기(氣, 생명 에너지)가 연결하고 있는 통합체로 간주된다. 어떤 하나의 구성요소에서의 상처나 스트레스는 다른 모든 부분에도 영향을 준다. 걱정, 긴장, 과도한 생각은 기의 균형을 깨뜨리고 흐름을 막는다. 이는 시간이 지나면서 신체적, 정서적 문제를 일으킬 수 있다. 고대인들은 과로한 마음에 대한 가장 좋은 치료는 명상이라는 것을 발견했다. 이것은 신체, 감정, 기, 정신이 다시 균형을 찾을 수 있는 기회를 얻을 만큼 충분히 마음을 안정시키는 것을 목표로 한다. 질주하는 마음을 안정시키고 당신의 몸을 건강한 방식으로 이완시키는 방법을 배워라.

어휘 **meditation** 명상 **holistic** 전체론의 **perspective** 관점 **injury** 부상 **component** 구성요소, 성분 **affect** ~에 영향을 끼치다 **tension** 긴장 **excessive** 과도한 **upset** (계획, 상황 등을) 어긋나게 하다; ~을 속상하게 만들다 **inhibit** ~을 막다, 억제하다

286 ④ | despite → while[although]

해설 ❹ 앞의 내용과 반대되는 내용이 이어지고 있고 뒤에 <주어(the pleasantness of uneaten foods)+동사(remains)>가 있는 절을 이끌고 있으므로, 전치사 despite가 아니라 접속사 while[although]이 와야 한다.

① 수식받는 선행사 variety seeking이 이어지는 관계절 the priority is to vary one's product experiences in에서 전치사 in의 목적어 역할을 하는 구조이다. 이때 전치사 in이 관계대명사 앞으로 이동한 형태로 in which는 어법상 적절하다.
② <be likely+to-v (v할 것 같다)> 구문에 쓰인 to부정사이므로 적절하다.
③ a phenomenon과 know는 수동의 관계이므로 과거분사 known은 어법상 적절하다.

⑤ 다른 음식들 중 일부를 가리키고 뒤에 복수명사(possibilities)가 이어지므로 other는 어법상 적절하다.

해석 가끔, 사람들은 단순히 새로운 것을 해 보고 싶어 하는 것 같다. 즉 그들은 다양성 추구에 관심이 있는데, 그 경우의 우선 사항은, 어쩌면 일종의 자극으로서 혹은 지루해지는 것을 피하기 위하여, 상품에 대한 자신의 경험에 변화를 주는 것이다. 다양성 추구는 특히 사람들이 기분이 좋을 때나 그들의 환경 안의 어딘가 다른 곳에 비교적 자극이 거의 없을 때 일어나기 쉽다. 식품과 음료의 경우, 다양성 추구는 '감각 특정적 포만'으로 알려진 현상 때문에 일어날 수 있다. 간단히 말해, 이것은 방금 먹은 식품에 대한 즐거움은 줄어들고, 반면에 먹지 않은 식품에 대한 즐거움은 변하지 않은 채로 있다는 것을 의미한다. 그러므로 우리가 좋아하는 음식을 먹긴 하지만, 우리는 여전히 다른 가능성(음식들)을 맛보고 싶어 한다. 아이러니하게도, 소비자들은 더 친숙한 선택 사항을 더 즐기기는 하지만, 다양성을 위해 덜 선호하는 선택 사항으로 실제로 바꿀 수도 있는 것이다.

어휘 **seek** 추구하다 **priority** 우선 사항 **vary** 변화를 주다, 바꾸다 **relatively** 비교적 **stimulation** 자극 **beverage** 음료 **phenomenon** 현상 **sensory** 감각의 **sample** (음식을) 맛보다, 시식하다 **sake** 목적; 이익

구문 01~05행 Sometimes, **it** seems **that** people simply like to try new things—they are interested in *variety seeking*, [in which the priority is to vary one's product experiences, perhaps as a form of stimulation or to avoid being bored].

→ it은 가주어이고 that ~ new things가 진주어이다. [ ]로 표시된 부분은 관계절로 variety seeking을 보충 설명한다.

15~18행 Ironically, consumers may actually switch to less preferred options for variety's sake / **even though** they *enjoy* the **more** *familiar* option **more**.

→ even though 이하는 양보를 나타내는 부사절이다. 여기서 첫 번째 more는 뒤의 비교급 familiar를 수식하고 두 번째 more는 동사 enjoy를 수식한다.

287 ④ | however → whatever

해설 ④ 명사(means)를 수식할 수 있는 것은 whatever. however는 형용사나 부사를 수식한다.(e.g. however difficult ~, however hard ~)

① 형용사(low)를 수식하는 부사(unsustainably)가 맞게 쓰였다.

② 문맥상 선택의 여지가 '거의 없는' 경우이므로 a little이 아닌 little이 왔다.

cf. have no[little] option[choice] but to-v: v하는 것 말고는 아무[거의] 선택의 여지가 없다

③ to earn ~의 의미상의 주어(for workers)가 그 앞에 맞게 쓰였다.

⑤ environment가 둘러싸는(surround) 주체이므로 능동을 나타내는 현재분사를 써서 surrounding environment로 표현하였다.

해석 슈퍼마켓들은 열대 과일 공급망 전체에서 가장 강력한 힘을 발휘하는 역할자이다. 그것들이 지니는 구매력으로 공급자들을 짜내고, 유지할 수 없을 정도로 낮은 가격을 과일값으로 치름으로써 막대한 이윤을 거둘 수 있다. 기타 악용되는 관행들에는 특별 할인 요구, 지불 지연, 공급자 협박이 있다. 식품 시장 분야가 소수 소매업자의 손에 집중되면서 공급자들은 그런 조건을 받아들이는 것 외에 선택의 여지가 별로 없다. 이런 행태는 노동자들에 대한 계속적인 착취와 수출을 하는 지역사회의 자연환경 파괴를 가져온다. 연구 결과 많은 사례에서 공급망의 아래로 전달되는 돈 자체가, 노동자들이 가정에 기본적으로 필요한 것들을 감당할 '생계' 임금을 벌기에 충분할 만큼이 되지 않는다는 것이 입증된다. 돈을 덜 벌게 되니 공급자들은 농약을 어떻게 저장하고 쓸 것인가에 대해, 주변 환경의 대기와 물을 오염시키는 것에 대해 책임을 덜 지는 등, 비용을 줄이는 데 필요한 어떤 수단이든 다 쓰게 되는 것이다.

어휘 **tropical** 열대지방의 **supply chain** 공급망((상품의) 연쇄적인 생산 및 공급 과정) **substantial** 상당한, 엄청난 **squeeze** 쥐어짜다 **unsustainably** 지속할 수 없게 **abusive** 학대하는, 폭력적인 **in the hands of** ~의 손에 들어가 있는[지배하에 있는] **retailer** 소매업자 **exploitation** 착취, (부당한) 이용 **household needs** 가정에 필요한 것들 **means** 수단, 방법 **agrochemical** 농약 **store** 저장하다

구문 13~16행 Research demonstrates that (in many instances) there(S) is simply not enough(V) *money* (passing down the supply chain) (**for** workers **to earn** a *'living' wage* [**that** covers basic household needs]).

→ money를 분사구와 to부정사구 두 개의 수식어구가 수식하고 있는 구조.

288 ③ | what → that

해설 ③ 동사 confirm의 목적어 역할을 하는 완전한 구조의 명사절을 이끌므로 접속사 that으로 고쳐 써야 한다.

① '~하기 위해'라는 의미의 부사적 용법으로 쓰인 to부정사 형태가 잘 사용되었다.

② 앞에 나온 to take ~ appearance를 받는 대명사 자리인데, to부정사구는 단수 취급하므로 it이 적절하다.

④ 형용사 similar를 수식하는 부사 extraordinarily는 적절하다.

⑤ which ~ specimens는 Molecular studies를 보충 설명하는 관계절이고, 분사구문의 의미상의 주어 Molecular studies와 use는 능동 관계이므로 현재분사 using이 적절하다.

해석 아주 최근에 과학자들은 생물체의 분류에 한 단계의 복잡함을 보탤 수 있게 되었다(한 단계 더 복잡한 생물 분류도 가능해졌다). 연구자들은 이제 분류학적 기법을 보완하기 위해 유전학적 기법 또는 분자 기법을 사용한다. 구체적으로 말하면, 그들은 생물체를 관련성의 정도에 따라 분류하기 위해 생물체의 DNA를 본다. 이 능력은 중요한데, 왜냐하면 실사 먼 친척들이 어떤 이유로 이득이 되기 때문에 비슷한 외양을 띠게 되었는데도, 비슷한 외양을 근거로 동물들이 자주 동일한 범주에 속하는 것처럼 보이기 때문이다. 이러한 혼동케 하는 외양의 유사점의 한 예로서, 많은 파리들은 호박벌처럼 보인다. 비록 파리가 표면적으로 호박벌처럼 보일지라도 유전학적 기법과 분류학적 기법은 그것들이 개가 고양이에게 연관된 만큼 (아주 멀리) 연관돼 있다는 것을 확인해 준다. 유전학적 연구는 또한 죽은 연구 표본만을 가지고 있는 문제에 도움을 줄 수 있는데, 말벌과 꿀벌은 행동이 관찰될 수 없을 때는 서로 몹시 유사해 보일 수 있다. 분자 연구는, 죽은 표본을 사용하여 수행될 수 있는데, 그것들이 정말로 먼 사촌이라는 것을 확인해 줄 수 있다.

어휘 **complexity** 복잡(성) **organism** 유기체, 생물(체) **genetic** 유전의; 유전학의 **molecular** 분자의 **relatedness** 관련(성) **come to-v** v하게 되다 **take on** (양상 등을) 띠다 **misleading** 오해의 소지가 있는 **bumblebee** 호박벌 **extraordinarily** 유별나게, 이례적으로

구문 07~12행 This capability is important because animals frequently seem to belong in the same category based on a similar appearance [**when**, in fact, these distant relatives have come to take on a similar appearance {because it became advantageous for one reason or another}].

→ 부사절 [ ] 안에 접속사 when은 양보를 의미하여 '~하는데도'라는 뜻이다.

Memo

쎄듀 초등 커리큘럼

영역	예비초	초1	초2	초3	초4	초5	초6

영역	교재	설명
구문	초등코치 천일문 SENTENCE	1001개 통문장 암기로 완성하는 초등 영어의 기초
문법	초등코치 천일문 GRAMMAR	1001개 예문으로 배우는 초등 영문법
	신간 왓츠 Grammar Start 시리즈	초등 기초 영문법 입문
	신간 왓츠 Grammar Plus 시리즈	초등 필수 영문법 마무리
독해	신간 왓츠 리딩 70 / 80 / 90 / 100 A / B	쉽고 재미있게 완성되는 영어 독해력
어휘	초등코치 천일문 VOCA & STORY	1001개의 초등 필수 어휘와 짧은 스토리
	패턴으로 말하는 초등 필수 영단어 1 / 2	문장 패턴으로 완성하는 초등 필수 영단어
ELT	Oh! My PHONICS 1 / 2 / 3 / 4	유·초등학생을 위한 첫 영어 파닉스
	Oh! My SPEAKING 1 / 2 / 3 / 4 / 5 / 6	핵심 문장 패턴으로 더욱 쉬운 영어 말하기
	Oh! My GRAMMAR 1 / 2 / 3	쓰기로 완성하는 첫 초등 영문법

쎄듀 중등 커리큘럼

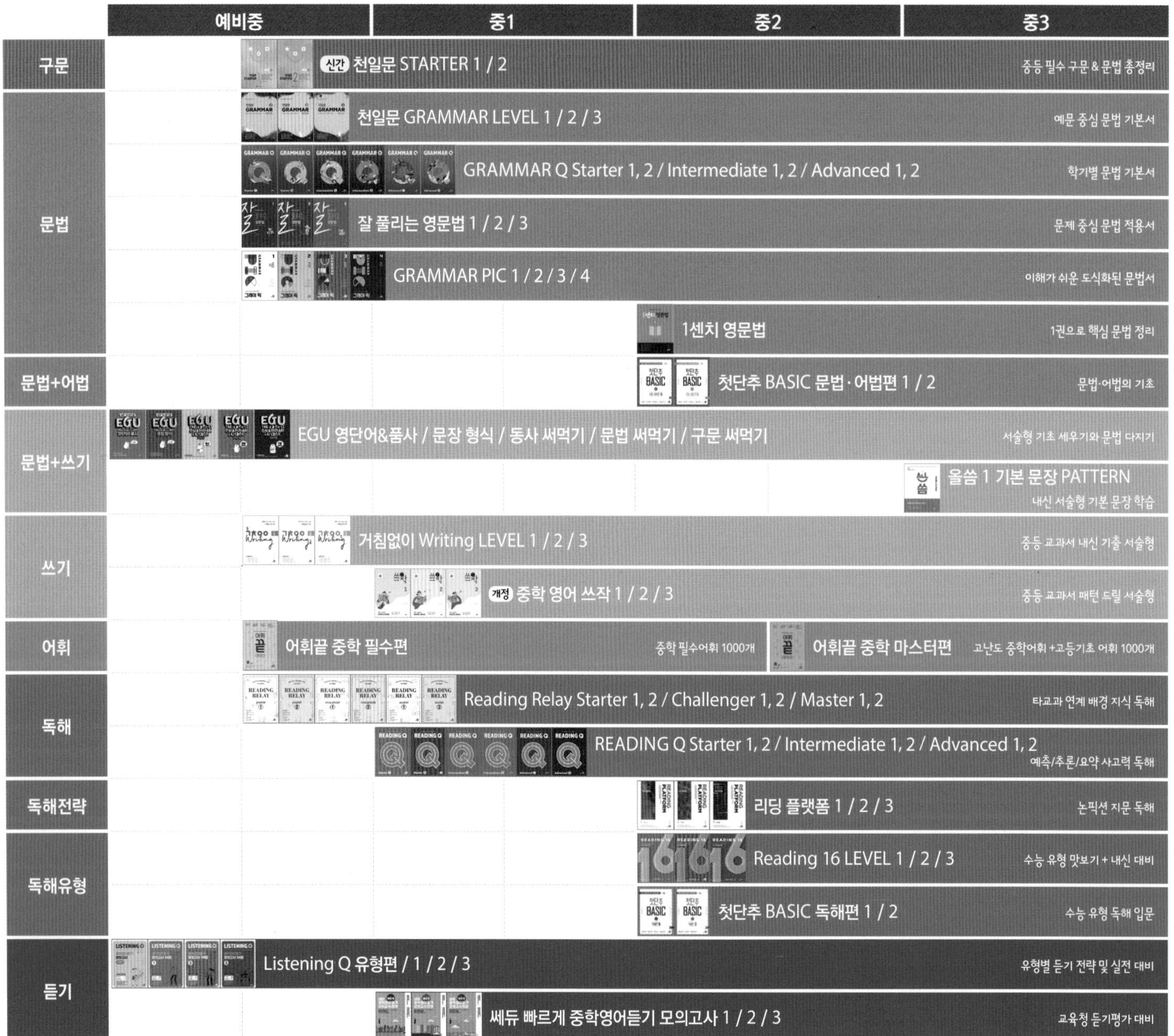

영역	예비중	중1	중2	중3

영역	교재	설명
구문	신간 천일문 STARTER 1 / 2	중등 필수 구문 & 문법 총정리
문법	천일문 GRAMMAR LEVEL 1 / 2 / 3	예문 중심 문법 기본서
	GRAMMAR Q Starter 1, 2 / Intermediate 1, 2 / Advanced 1, 2	학기별 문법 기본서
	잘 풀리는 영문법 1 / 2 / 3	문제 중심 문법 적용서
	GRAMMAR PIC 1 / 2 / 3 / 4	이해가 쉬운 도식화된 문법서
	1센치 영문법	1권으로 핵심 문법 정리
문법+어법	첫단추 BASIC 문법·어법편 1 / 2	문법·어법의 기초
문법+쓰기	EGU 영단어&품사 / 문장 형식 / 동사 써먹기 / 문법 써먹기 / 구문 써먹기	서술형 기초 세우기와 문법 다지기
	올씀 1 기본 문장 PATTERN	내신 서술형 기본 문장 학습
쓰기	거침없이 Writing LEVEL 1 / 2 / 3	중등 교과서 내신 기출 서술형
	개정 중학 영어 쓰작 1 / 2 / 3	중등 교과서 패턴 드릴 서술형
어휘	어휘끝 중학 필수편	중학 필수어휘 1000개
	어휘끝 중학 마스터편	고난도 중학어휘 +고등기초 어휘 1000개
독해	Reading Relay Starter 1, 2 / Challenger 1, 2 / Master 1, 2	타교과 연계 배경 지식 독해
	READING Q Starter 1, 2 / Intermediate 1, 2 / Advanced 1, 2	예측/추론/요약 사고력 독해
독해전략	리딩 플랫폼 1 / 2 / 3	논픽션 지문 독해
독해유형	Reading 16 LEVEL 1 / 2 / 3	수능 유형 맛보기 + 내신 대비
	첫단추 BASIC 독해편 1 / 2	수능 유형 독해 입문
듣기	Listening Q 유형편 / 1 / 2 / 3	유형별 듣기 전략 및 실전 대비
	쎄듀 빠르게 중학영어듣기 모의고사 1 / 2 / 3	교육청 듣기평가 대비